# VIETNAM AIR WARFARE

THE STORY OF THE AIRCRAFT, THE BATTLES, AND THE PILOTS WHO FOUGHT

EDITORS

ROBERT F. DORR & CHRIS BISHOP

CHARTWELL
BOOKS, INC.

Published by
**CHARTWELL BOOKS, INC.**
A Division of **BOOK SALES, INC.**
114 Northfield Avenue
Edison, New Jersey 08837

ISBN 0-7858-1530-9

Jacket design by
Amber Books Ltd.
Bradley's Close
74–77 White Lion Street
London N1 9PF
UK

Portions of the text of this book have appeared in different form
in *Air War South Vietnam* and *Air War Hanoi*, © Robert F. Dorr

Printed in Italy

# CONTENTS

# STRUGGLE FOR VIETNAM

**It was America's longest war. The military might of the world's greatest power was thrown against a wily and elusive enemy. In spite of using the latest technology, with air power being the main difference between the sides, the American military never really got to grips with the foe. Heroism there was in plenty, but there were few pitched battles.**

"It took us eight years of bitter fighting to defeat you French... the Americans are much stronger than the French, though they know us less well. It may perhaps take 10 years to do it, but our heroic compatriots in the South will defeat them in the end."

That was Ho Chi Minh, Vietnamese revolutionary, Communist, and venerated 'Uncle' to his people, explaining to writer Bernard Fall how he evaluated the coming conflict. He was speaking with considerable prescience in late-1962.

Vietnam was a quicksand for America; the more she struggled, the more deeply engulfed she became. It is a quarter of a century since the last B-52 dropped its earth-shattering load of iron bombs through the jungle tree canopy, since the last Phantom flew

*Vietnam was a media war, more than any previous conflict. Cameramen recorded every aspect of the struggle, for broadcast in the USA and around the world. Constant exposure meant that weapons like the Bell UH-1 'Huey' became icons of the war, instantly recognizable to anyone who watched television or read newspapers.*

MiGCAP, and the last 'Wild Weasel' went downtown trolling for SAMs. Some of the scars have healed; some of the lessons have been learned, while others have been forgotten already.

America started in that war by forgetting – or choosing to ignore – all the lessons the French learned so very painfully along the Street without Joy, or in the hell that was Dien Bien Phu.

## No reason to fight

"Indochina is devoid of decisive military objectives and the allocation of more than token US armed forces in Indochina would be a serious diversion of limited US capabilities. The principal sources of Viet Minh military supply lie outside Indochina."

Those two sentences, part of a 1954 study by the Joint Chiefs of Staff, accurately summarized the war in Vietnam between the French and the Viet Minh. As it was true in 1954, so was it true later. In fact, the truth was so basic, and the implications of ignoring that truth so serious that one wonders even now how and why the United States' involvement in the war ever came about.

It is glib to say that President John F. Kennedy's Camelot and Premier Nikita Khrushchev's Communism couldn't coexist, but there is truth in that statement. Under Kennedy, the first escalation of effort occurred, and the basic policies of his administration were inherited and expanded upon by the succession of later Presidents.

In later years Vietnam would be a word denoting a trauma to the American psyche, but in 1963 it was still the not very well-known name of a divided country in Southeast Asia. Don Harris, a young soldier heading to Qui Nhon to join a US Army helicopter

company, tried something most Americans had not tried: he looked up Vietnam in an encyclopedia.

Harris read of a long thin slice of geography which ran 1,200 miles (1931 km) from north to south, varying in width from 25 to 200 miles (40 to 360 km), divided at the 17th Parallel between Communist North Vietnam; capital Hanoi, population 17 million, and South Vietnam; population 14 million plus. Ninety per cent of Vietnamese, read Harris, derived their livelihood from agriculture.

## Theater of battle

The beautiful land had been a battlefield for more than 1,000 years. Ethnic and cultural wars, wars of enslavement and aggrandizement, colonial and imperial wars have washed over the river deltas and jungles, through the rice paddies and over rugged mountains.

North and South Vietnam were similar in area, each about 64,000 square miles. Both were created in July 1954 as the result of a conference at Geneva, ending the war between French and native Viet Minh forces, which had begun just after World War II. North Vietnam, with Hanoi its capital, was headed by Communist Ho Chi Minh, perceived by many as a longtime fighter for independence from outside forces. South Vietnam, the gem of Saigon its capital, boasted Emperor Bao Dai until a referendum in 1955 deposed him and established a republic with authoritarian Ngo Dinh Diem as president.

The trappings of a republic, including a legislature, did little to hide the fact that South Vietnam was rigidly controlled by Diem and his ruthless brother, Ngo Dinh Nhu. Authoritarian was the accepted word for the regime; corrupt was the word used by many. Middle-grade army officers, many of them trained in the United States, privately told their American contacts that no progress could be made against the Viet Cong until Diem was booted from office. Domestic plotting against Diem rose and fell in cycles. 1960 had been a big year for it. 1963 was to be another. Some of those officers friendly to the West felt that if they did not get Diem out, the Viet Cong would.

When he arrived at Qui Nhon, Harris discovered that most of his Army buddies had no interest in even these rudimentary facts.

"I spent a year doing admin work which supported our helicopter operations. The South Vietnamese troops, the ARVN, got carted around the country by our choppers. When they were in a combat situation, they froze up. They refused to take advantage

*For much of the war, American air power was used to support the counter-insurgency battle against the Viet Cong. Finding an elusive enemy under the canopy of jungle was hard, and it was soon found that obsolete propeller-driven aircraft like the A-1 Skyraider were more effective than the latest high-tech jet-powered fighters.*

of air mobility. They didn't want to fight. And we just sat there and counted the number of days we had left..."

For the professional soldiers, sailors and airmen called upon to manage the war, it was to be a continuing frustration. There was no defined objective for the US involvement. There were rules of engagement that severely restricted operations. There were directives, orders, teletypes and visitors from Washington, all taking precedence over the usual prerogatives of a field commander to run the war from the scene of the action.

With no goal, and with no way of measuring the progress toward a goal, it is hardly any wonder that the war degenerated into a conflict whose purpose seemed to be the production of favorable, cost-effective statistics: so many dead Viet Cong in the South, so many bridges destroyed in the North, so many trucks left burning on the Ho Chi Minh Trail, so many pounds of rice and rounds of ammunition captured in bivouac areas over-run by so many US troops.

There was another basic truth about the war in Vietnam that was never broadly recognized or understood, and it needs to be stated here: ideology cannot be destroyed by killing its adherents.

More than 6.3 million tons of bombs fell on Vietnam, Laos and Cambodia during the war years from 1964 to early-1973. A little more than one-third of that amount helped defeat both the Third Reich and the Japanese Empire during World War II.

And yet, for all the outward appearance of massive strikes and continued bomber offensives, the air war was never run the way the airmen wanted it to be handled. One senior air officer said later, "The way the strikes were flown, they were of no importance. They accomplished virtually nothing. It was not worth the effort."

It was seen as a war of attrition, but the US achieved only a stalemate. By any measurable terms, the United States came out of that war in far worse shape than when it had entered it, and that is one of the definitions of a defeat. The costs of that conflict, in lives, careers, broken homes, inflation and taxes, were incalculable. The effect of the war was seen daily, in almost every home in America, and felt daily by everyone.

It has been a cruel lesson in fighting the wrong war in the wrong place at the wrong time.

# THE FRENCH WAR

**World War II left the old order of European empires dotted around the world in a shambles. Colonial administration had largely broken down, independence movements had flowered, and re-imposition of pre-war order was to be difficult and bloody. Nowhere was that more true than in the beautiful old French colonies in Southeast Asia.**

The defeat of Japan left a power vacuum in the French colonial possessions in Indochina, and the Vietnamese Communists under the charismatic political leadership of Ho Chi Minh stepped in to take power. France, smarting from its defeat by Germany and the need to be liberated by the allies, moved to restore the pre-war empire.

On 24 March 1945, while Japan was still in control of the region, de Gaulle's new French Government was announcing a vague plan for the incorporation of Annam, Cambodia, Cochin China, Laos and Tonkin, the five nations of Indochina, into a French-styled commonwealth (L'Union Francaise).

On 2 September, 10 days before the arrival of the first French forces, the independence of Vietnam was unilaterally proclaimed.

*Spitfire Mk IX fighters of G.C. 1/3 'Navarre' and G.C. 2/3 'Champagne' on the line at Nha Trang in 1950. The Spitfire met with only limited success in the Indochina conflict, mainly because of its limited range. The corrosive climate in Vietnam was always a problem for aircraft operations, and the Spitfire was one type which did not adapt well.*

Soon Viet Minh bands began murdering or incarcerating French settlers and officials and, accordingly, France decided to send more troops and aircraft. Thirty years of warfare was about to start.

Hostilities did not begin fully until December 1946, when the Viet Minh tried and failed to wrest control of Hanoi and other cities from French troops. This first phase of the undeclared war ended in March 1947, with the French in control of the major cities and

*A glass-nosed B-26C Invader of G.B. 1/25 'Tunisie' is seen bombing Viet Minh positions over Tonkin on 24 May 1952. The Invader represented the most potent weapon the French could throw into the air in their battle against a determined enemy who had no aircraft at all. Invaders were a vital part of the French effort – and later of the Americans'.*

*P-63 Kingcobras of Groupe de Marche (G.M.) 1/9 'Limousin' at an air strip in Tonkin in February 1951. All three Kingcobras are carrying belly and wing ferry tanks. Like the Americans to follow in the early-1960s, the French fought the war with a mix of veteran World War II warplanes.*

lowland areas, notably the Red River delta.

Later in 1947 the French moved over to the offensive with operations against the Viet Minh base area in northern Tonkin, but were unable to crush the Vietnamese partisan forces which simply melted into the jungles and mountains where they could wage a protracted guerrilla war. Over the next three years the Viet Minh consolidated their position in the rural areas of northern Indochina, and made considerable strides in the central region of the country. In the South the Communists had less of a following, and the French were able to reach an accommodation with the Cao-Dai and HoaHao nationalist factions.

The nature of the conflict caused the Armée de l'Air to adopt a command structure which contrasted drastically with previous French practice. It involved the creation of two tactical *groupes*, each suited to the particular terrain characteristics of its theater: the Northern Tactical Group (TFIN) seeking to control Tonkin and northern Annam, and the Southern Tactical Group, (TFIS) which operated in Cochin China and southern Annam. This organization was improved in June 1950 with the creation of three tactical air *groupes* (GATAC) adapted to cover Tonkin (GATAC North), Annam (GATAC Central) and Cochin China (GATAC South). Each *groupe* comprised fighter, bomber, reconnaissance and transport elements. Each was autonomous and of equal status with the ground command structure, thereby allowing the most effective use of the air power available.

From the beginning the French air staff wanted to deploy the Republic P-47 Thunderbolt, an aircraft which equipped a number of escadrilles of the metropolitan air force. However, the USA was in a particularly anti-colonial mood, and warned France that it would not continue to provide spares for its aircraft in such a case, and prevented the despatch of these aircraft.

The French therefore decided to acquire, under the terms of the Hartemann-Dickson Agreement signed with the UK in September 1945, some Supermarine Spitfire Mk IXs, and these arrived at Saigon in February 1946. In spite of a number of serious shortcomings; notably their short range, unsuitable radio equipment, and tricky handling in cross-wind landings, the Spitfires were retained for lack of anything better until the early 1950s.

## Unsuitable equipment

In the meantime, immediately after the outbreak of active operations the previous October, the French had borrowed some Spitfire Mk VIIIs from RAF units in Southeast Asia, and, at the same time, attempted to employ some Nakajima Ki-43 'Oscars' left behind by the defeated Japanese. Age and a total lack of spares meant that the Ki-43's saw little use.

Unsuitable though their mounts might have been, the four Spitfire escadrilles (the 1e, 2e, 3e and 4e ) achieved remarkable results. Such was not the case with the de Havilland Mosquito which, flown by G.C. 1/3 'Corse' served in Indochina between January and May 1947, but whose wooden construction was wholly unsuitable for conditions in the tropics. Nevertheless, thanks to its considerable range (1,500 miles/2400 km), this twin-engine aircraft was able to reach areas otherwise inaccessible to the single-engine fighters.

During 1948-49 the demonstrated inability of the French aircraft industry to come up with an aircraft suitable for service in-theater, coupled with the growing need to cover the distant borders with neighboring China, prompted a renewed appeal to the USA. This proved to be an apt moment to make overtures to America, now

*An SBD-5 Dauntless of Flottille 4F is catapulted from the deck of the Arromanches with its perforated trailing-edge flaps extended. The Dauntless dive-bomber was used by the French in Indochina from 1947 through into 1949 before being replaced by the SB2C Helldiver.*

worried by the Communist victory in China, and therefore more than willing to help the French to secure the borders near Tonkin.

During the second half of 1949 the USA authorized the despatch of war material to the Far East under the terms of the Mutual Aid Program (the North Atlantic Treaty having been signed in April 1949). Of the 300 Bell F-63 Kingcobra fighters which were received from the USA, France sent about 50 to Indochina to equip the 5e Escadre de Chasse (EC 5). Despite some criticisms of the vulnerability of its engine and long take-off and landing runs, the Kingcobra was an important weapon since it had the range to cover the Tonkin area, a mission that could not be achieved by the Spitfire.

## Communist guerrilla successes

By 1950 Chinese assistance had given the Viet Minh, directed by guerrilla genius Vo Nguyen Giap the military strength to step up their pressure on the French, who suffered the first of many setbacks with their enforced evacuations of Cao Bang and Lang Son in October. French fortunes were partially restored in 1950 and 1951 under the brilliant leadership of General de Lattre de Tassigny, when the Viet Minh were defeated at Vinh Yen and Mao Khe. It

*A PBY-5A Catalina identical to this one became the first aircraft of the French Navy to arrive in Vietnam following the end of World War II, reaching Vietnam on 27 October 1945 and attracting curious glances from Japanese prisoners of war then being held by the French.*

*PB4Y-2 Privateer patrol bombers and reconnaissance aircraft served with the French Navy's Flotille 8F, flying from Tan Son Nhut airfield near Saigon. These single-tailed off-spring of the famous Liberator wore the distinctive 'hooked' roundel of the French maritime service.*

was a temporary setback for the Communists: by the end of 1951 the Viet Minh had recovered, and French morale and capabilities received a major blow early in 1952 with the death of de Lattre de Tassigny.

It was in 1950 that the Grumman F6F Hellcat first made its appearance, replacing both Spitfire and Kingcobra. It remained in service until January 1953 when G.C. 2/21 'Auvergne' finished re-equipping with the Grumman F8F Bearcat. Of all the fighters employed in Indochina between 1945 and 1954 the Bearcat was unquestionably the best. Its high speed, agility and load-carrying ability allowed it to use a wide range of ground-attack weapons, including 5-in (127-mm) rockets, napalm and HE bombs of up to 1,000 lb (454 kg). It wasn't perfect – the F8F's radius of action was only 190 miles (300 km), and it was not an easy aircraft to fly in conditions of poor visibility. Its restricted downwards view also led to a number of accidents and hindered pilots in their principal combat tasks.

## Bombers reintroduced

Between 1945 and 1951 the Armée de l'Air deployed no bomber forces in Indochina. Until the beginning of the 1950s the idea of employing bombers in Southeast Asia had not been possible, firstly while the dispersed nature of enemy forces in Indochina rendered them invulnerable to setpiece bombing, and secondly because the Armée de l'Air had disbanded all its bomber units immediately after World War II.

In June 1950 the military authorities discussed the prevailing situation with an American military mission and gained the promise of the supply of sufficient Douglas B-26s to equip two bomber *groupes*. Despite the onset of the Korean War, the United States honored their promise and on 7 November 1950 the first B-26s arrived at Saigon, where they were taken on charge by G.T. 2/62 and G.T. 2/64. Meanwhile, in France the first bomber unit was established as I/19 'Gascogne' with 17 B-26Bs and eight B-26Cs, before going on active service in the Far East in February 1951. During the next two years two more B-26 *groupes* were formed and a fourth planned.

The Armée de l'Air used its B-26s for a wide range of tasks, completing 33,000 flying hours in the course of 15,000 sorties between 1951 and 1954, dropping 19,000 tons of bombs. The bomber's ruggedness was reflected in the success it achieved in Indochina, while its handling and maneuverability, though obviously less than those of a fighter, were superb. Despite lacking the armor protection normally associated with a close-support bomber, its vulnerability to ground fire did not give cause for concern.

## Aerial firepower

The B-26's major asset was undoubtedly in the power of its 0.5-in (12.7-mm) guns, up to 16 being carried underwing, and gun pods were added to the eight fixed guns in the nose. Moreover the internal and wing-mounted bomb racks could accommodate all manner of American weapons, including up to 5-in (127-mm) HVAR rockets and napalm bombs.

Until 1954, when a subordinate bomber command was created, the B-26s operated under the control of the GATACs, playing an essential part in operations against the Viet Minh and on many occasions saving the hard-pressed French army units from annihilation. They also flew reconnaissance missions, a capability that had been lacking since 1946.

During 1952 and 1953 the fighting was concentrated in western Tonkin and north-eastern Laos. The new French commander General Henri Navarre, devised a tactical concept to defeat the Viet Minh: a 'honeypot' garrison in Viet Minh territory would be supplied from the air and entice the enemy forward to a decisive

*The Morane-Saulnier M.S.500 Criquet, a French derivative of the Fieseler Storch, was ideally suited to the rigors of combat operations in Indochina with its extraordinary short-field landing and take-off ability. Criquets were used by the French air force and by French army units.*

*Lifting off from an improvised helipad in Hanoi some time in 1954, this Westland S-55 of the Armée de l'Air's EHM 2/65 is providing humanitarian service in a downtown medevac mission. The US equivalent, the H-19, was later to serve the Vietnamese air force.*

*Moving supplies and men*

Air transport operations restarted in July 1945 when three Douglas C-47s were sent out from Europe. From then on the process of expansion continued, and the following year a subordinate air transport unit was expanded into two *groupes*. These units embarked on a regular service between Paris and Saigon, taking in most of the larger towns in the region and sustaining Hanoi which suffered a famine at the beginning of 1947. The formation of transport *groupe* 'Tonkin' was followed in 1949 by transport *groupe* 'Franche-Comte' and *groupe* 'le Senegal' at Tourane in January 1954.

### Faithful old Junkers

During the nine years of the war, air transport largely depended upon the Junkers Ju 52/3m or its French-built AAC.1 version known as the Toucan and the Douglas C-47 Dakota. Both were easy to operate and maintain, and were ideally suited to a country where support facilities were never more than modest. Nevertheless, at the end of 1950

the Armée de l'Air was forced to admit that the low speed of the sturdy old Junkers rendered it particularly vulnerable to improving enemy weapons. The Toucan accordingly gradually gave place to the C-47, its junior partner since 1946, and the last examples were retired in 1953.

The classic Douglas transport was the workhorse of French air transport in Indochina, as it had been for the allies in World War II, although its war load was not

outstanding. Around 100 were involved in support of Dien Bien Phu during the bloody siege.

By then, larger transport aircraft including the Bristol Type 170 Freighter and Fairchild C-119 Packet (or Flying Boxcar) were being introduced. As the ceasefire was being negotiated, Groupe de Transport 'Anjou' was re-equipping with the Nord 2501 Noratlas, which only undertook trials in Asia but was beginning to equip units in Algeria.

*Black-bellied C-47s of G.T. 2/62, 2/63 and 2/64 transported French soldiers, helped during the Dien Bien Phu siege, and evacuated Vietnamese Christians from Nam Dinh (Tonkin) at war's end. Many went on to serve the nascent Cambodian, Lao and Vietnamese air forces.*

*The AAC.1 Toucan, or French-built Junkers Ju 52 tri-motor, was a transport, paratroop ship, and bomber with G.T. 1/64 'Bearn' and G.T. 2/62 'Franche-Comte'. The tri-motor served until 1954.*

battle in which superior French equipment and firepower would prevail. Some early successes encouraged the French, who sited such a honeypot at Dien Bien Phu, near the border between Tonkin and Laos. After a long and bloody siege, Dien Bien Phu fell to the Viet Minh in May 1954. The psychological blow to France was enormous, and this lent impetus to the peace negotiations about to begin in Geneva. A ceasefire, or more properly an agreement of the Viet Minh's victory, was signed on 20 July 1954. Further, less formal agreements amounted to a temporary partition of Vietnam along the 17th parallel, with the intention to hold Vietnam-wide elections to decide the fate of the country.

After the ceasefire, hundreds of thousands of people streamed North or South according to their political or religious beliefs.

North Vietnam fell in behind Ho Chi Minh's Communists. In the South, Ngo Dinh Diem, a powerful politician and prominent member of the Roman Catholic elite became premier. In 1955, in the face of coup attempts and opposition from Buddhists, nationalists, and even members of his own family, Diem defeated Bao Dai in a rigged election. In 1956 the French evacuated the last of their troops from the South, and by 1957 Ho Chi Minh was ready to launch the struggle which he believed would unite the whole country under his leadership. Key to his plans were the 6,000 or so Communists who had stayed behind in the South, who were to be the cadre for the programme of assasination and guerrilla war which would achieve the northern aim. They were to become known around the world as the Viet Cong.

# Aéronavale in Action

Naval aviation was involved in the war almost from the start. In October 1945 Flottille 8F arrived in the region with the Consolidated PBY Catalina, being joined soon afterwards by four Japanese Aichi E13A1s of Escadrille 8S. Placed at the disposal of the overall air command in Indochina, the naval air components took part in numerous operations, of which one involved the return of French forces to Tonkin in March 1946. The E13A1s of Escadrille 8S were joined in August 1947 by Supermarine Sea Otters, and shortly after by Flottille 3F with Douglas SBD Dauntless aircraft, and later still by Flottille 4F, also with Dauntless.

The escalation of the war at the start of the 1950s prompted the Aéronavale to acquire Grumman F6F Hellcats, which were also being introduced by the Armée de l'Air, and Curtiss SB2C Helldivers. Flottille 3F took on charge its first

Consolidated PB4Y-2 Privateer, an aircraft which eventually played a major role in the battle of Dien Bien Phu. In March 1952 Escadrille 8S re-equipped with the Grumman JRF-5 Goose while Flottille 9F, flying Helldivers, was transferred to Indochina where it fought alongside Flottille 12F with Hellcats from September 1952.

In July 1953, as a result of a rearrangement of Aéronavale unit numbering, Flottille 8F became 28F. About 10 weeks later the aircraft carrier *Arromanches* arrived to reinforce the naval force with Flottilles 11F (F6Fs) and 3F (SB2Cs); in addition Flottille 14F, equipped with Vought AU-1 (F4U-6) Corsairs, took part in the battle of Dien Bien Phu.

*Left: Flown by both the Armée de l'Air and Aéronavale during the war in Indochina, the Grumman F6F-5 Hellcat was the first fighter supplied by the United States to French forces in that conflict. Carrier operations were mounted from the carrier Dixmude (formerly HMS Biter) during 1950.*

*Below: France acquired the British light fleet carrier Colossus in 1946. As the Arromanches she made four deployments to Far Eastern waters between 1949 and 1954. Seen here arriving in Indochina in 1953, the carrier's air wing consisted of 24 American-supplied F6F and SB2Cs.*

## Aéronavale Bearcat

Grumman F8F-1 Bearcats arrived in Indochina in January 1951 and became the premier fighters used by the French air arm in the Indochina conflict.

### F8F-1 Bearcat missions

Bearcats flew air-to-ground missions where their speed and maneuverability enhanced pilots' prospects of surviving under enemy fire. This example, complete with wing bomb shackles, is from G.C. 2/21 'Auvergne'.

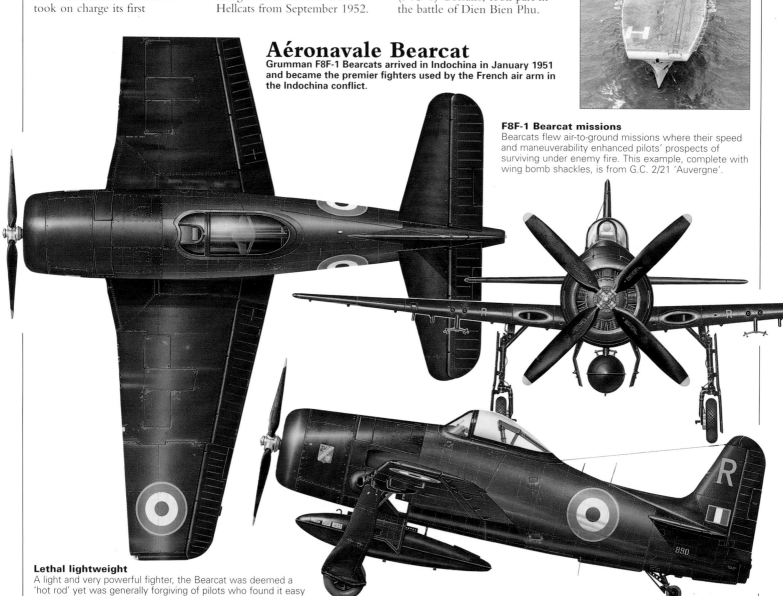

### Lethal lightweight

A light and very powerful fighter, the Bearcat was deemed a 'hot rod' yet was generally forgiving of pilots who found it easy to handle. It performed well during the Dien Bien Phu siege.

# Last Stand at Dien Bien Phu

*France's final catastrophe*

The decision to take the village of Dien Bien Phu on the Vietnam/Laos border and to occupy it as an 'airhead' was taken by General Henri Navarre, commander-in-chief of French forces in Indochina since May 1953, against the strong advice of the man he appointed to control the operation, General de Division Rene Cogny.

Five parachute battalions were dropped into the valley from Douglas C-47s over four days from 20 November 1953. The tasks of lengthening and reinforcing the existing airstrip and digging field defenses began, and it looked as though Operation 'Castor' could be successful.

## Seeds of disaster

The elegant cavalry Colonel Christian de la Croix de Castries, was dropped in with orders both to turn Dien Bien Phu into a fortress to be held "without thought of withdrawal", and at the same time to employ at least half his strength in offensive forays. This would not only dominate the valley in which the village lay, but also drive the enemy off at least the lower foothills around and make possible a link up with other French forces in Laos.

During the weeks that followed, de Castries' strength increased to 10,814 men, the combat units consisting of native T'ai infantry, Algerian and Moroccan *tirailleurs* and four Foreign Legion battalions.

But already the garrison was suffering casualties. To the astonishment of both Navarre and de Castries, the landing-strip came quickly under fire from Viet Minh 4.13-in (105-mm) guns, the weight of fire increasing as the weeks passed.

General Vo Nguyen Giap was already assembling a force more numerous and far better armed and supplied than the French

dreamed possible. By the beginning of March three Viet Minh infantry divisions comprising 28 battalions were in position.

They were supported by 105-mm artillery, heavy mortars and recoilless rifles – none of which the French had known the Viet Minh to have at Dien Bien Phu.

Anti-aircraft weapons of every caliber were arriving with each day that passed, and by mid-April the civilian C-119 pilots supporting the base were refusing to fly over what had become known as 'the chamber-pot'.

The first, stunning blow fell on the French during the evening and night of 13 March 1954. Heavy and accurate fire deluged the entire area, blowing in shelters, smashing trenches and gun positions, setting alight every aircraft except three fortunate Bearcats which scrambled during the first minute of the attack and were then forced by the almost total destruction of the airstrip to fly back to Hanoi. Then came a 'human wave' infantry assault delivered with supreme disregard for casualties.

By the morning a French outpost known as Beatrice had fallen. There were seven more – Dominique, Eliane, Claudine,

*Legion paratroopers are dropped from C-47s, almost immediately finding themselves in action against a well-equipped enemy entrenched in the hills around the fortress of Dien Bien Phu.*

Francoise, Huguette, Anne-Marie and Gabrielle, all it was said named after de Castries' mistresses – and the elimination of each outpost was Giap's first objective. As they were located beyond the range of any support except from the central position, and as the heavy artillery there had already been pounded almost into annihilation, this threw their defence entirely upon the individual outpost garrisons, varying between 500 and 2,000 men, each of which would face attacks by whole brigades.

## Siege tightens

During the next weeks the Viet Minh grip on Dien Bien Phu tightened implacably. The only way to reach and support the outpost was by air – and with the runway unusable and combat aircraft lacking range, French air power was not enough.

The garrison was also under new command as the 'parachute Mafia' of battalion commanders had decided between them that de Castries was not the man for

the job, and had themselves taken over in a polite, bloodless but uncompromising coup.

The end came on 7 May. Giap had brought up some Soviet-made Katyusha rocket-launchers and these added devastating weight to the bombardment which crashed down on the evening of 6 May, continued through the night and by morning had reduced the French position to a few hundred square meters around the southern end of the airstrip. At noon, de Castries (still nominal commander) spoke to Cogny by radio and informed him that there were now barely 1,000 men still on their feet; and that afternoon Giap was informed that French firing would cease at 17.30.

So ended the battle of Dien Bien Phu. Giap allowed 900 of the worst wounded to be flown out, but the rest made up part of the 9,000 men who started out on what became known as the 'Death March'. None of the wounded who had suffered head, chest or stomach wounds ever came back, and not a very high proportion of even the unwounded. But most of the casualties of the battle lie still where they fell. As Bernard Fall, one of the best historians of the episode has written:

"Most of the French dead are, like royalty, swathed in silk shrouds. Parachute nylon, like courage, was one of the commonest items at Dien Bien Phu, and on both sides."

*Viet Minh troops over-run the remnants of Dien Bien Phu in a triumph which signalled the beginning of the end of French colonial interest in Indochina.*

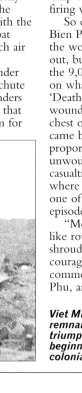

# ELECTION YEAR

**1960 was a watershed year. Vice-President Richard M. Nixon and Senator John F. Kennedy locked horns in an incredibly close campaign for the American presidency. A few cautious voices were uttering a warning that Americans might have to go to war in the Belgian Congo or Cuba, but few people had even heard of Vietnam.**

As there had been for two decades in the USA and would be for nearly two more, there was universal conscription – the draft. Every able-bodied young American was expected to serve in the Army, Navy, Air Force, Marine Corps or Coast Guard. It was taken for granted. Military service was honorable. Using force of arms in defense of freedom was not merely an acceptable course of action but, in this new era, an inevitable one.

If people thought about the prospects of being hurled into conflict – and they thought about anti-Communism a great deal, as each candidate tried to be more anti-Communist than the other – people worried mostly about the increasing size and number of atomic bombs being built by the Americans and Russians, and about Premier Nikita Khrushchev's militancy. There was an excellent chance that Nixon might win the election and become President solely because he had once been photographed poking a finger into Khrushchev's face.

And in a distant corner of Asia, brushfire wars spluttered and flared in the recently created nation, if it could be called a nation, of South Vietnam.

### An unknown country and an unknown war

In 1960 people generally knew little about Vietnam and thought about it even less. In stateside garrisons the US Army and Marine Corps were making increasing use of helicopters in support of ground operations, but if anyone thought that the helicopter was going to revolutionize warfare, most people simply did not know it then. Aboard US Navy carriers, naval aviators practised their always-risky trade in a combination of propeller and jet aircraft, a few of them aware that the newly-developed McDonnell F4H-1 Phantom was a kind of revolution in itself, but rarely did their 'area specific' exercises focus on Southeast Asia. In the US Air Force, dominated in that era's obsession with the atomic bomb by Strategic Air Command generals, they wanted more B-52s, capable of bombing the Soviet Union. In another two or three years, of course, it was understood that a new bomber would come along to replace the ageing Boeing design, but the nuclear confrontation with the Soviet Union would continue.

The USAF's Pacific component, PACAF, started the year with 61,876 people, 567 aircraft, six major subordinate commands, 27 tactical squadrons and 11 bases. USAF officers were nervous in a number of places in Asia. Vietnam was not one of them. In Korea Syngman Rhee, at the advanced age of 85, was re-elected, then thrown out of office by a student uprising on 19 April 1960.

Indeed, PACAF's official history contains only two entries about

*Lt Ken Moranville poses with the commander of the Vietnamese fighter squadron he helped create. Moranville was picked when US Pacific Fleet commander Admiral Harry D. Felt, Jr decided to send 25 AD Skyraiders to Bien Hoa with a lone US naval aviator as advisor and instructor. Six enlisted sailors helped launch the US role in Vietnam.*

Vietnam. The first says that in September Communist North Vietnam announced the formation of the National Liberation Front (NLF) in South Vietnam. The second reported that, also in September, the US supplied South Vietnam with the first of 25 Douglas AD-6 Skyraider attack aircraft, taken from US Navy inventory, to replace ageing Grumman F8F Bearcats.

America also delivered 11 Sikorsky H-34 helicopters to the South Vietnamese forces. That year the US Army convened the Rogers Board to look at various aspects of aviation, and members of the board began to speak of a new concept called 'air mobility', in which helicopters would be used to transport infantry troops to and from the battlefield. Some officers doubted that this would ever happen. The helicopter was fast proving itself a valuable servant in many ways, but many had still to be convinced that the helicopter had a major role in warfare. There was much to learn.

Not the least of which was that the Communist guerrilla movement in South Vietnam was very real and not merely a device created by Hanoi. The NLF, which quickly became known as the Viet Cong, was in every way a genuine uprising by natives of South Vietnam, some of whom were Communists, some not. The opposition to a corrupt dictatorship in Saigon was neither entirely Communist nor controlled from Moscow or Peking, although US policy was based on the notion that it was. Half-truths and untruths did not matter much to the American people as long as they were uttered about a place where not much was happening, but those same distortions – above all, the failure to understand that the uprising in South Vietnam was genuine – was to be crucial long after the Asian nation emerged at the forefront of American consciousness.

# Enter the Skyraider

If PACAF's history for 1960 says nothing about the USAF in Vietnam, the reason is that the American war in the air was begun by a young naval officer. And above all, by a naval warplane – a unique machine for a unique conflict.

With its huge, four-bladed propeller hanging out front and a tailwheel at the back, the Douglas Skyraider seemed less an aircraft than a collection of heavy iron, a relic of an earlier age of warfare. The Skyraider's big Wright R-3350 Cyclone engine smoked, belched and wheezed, dripped oil, and dripped more oil. This was not a leak exactly, more like a programmed drip (pilots always had dirty flight suits). The joke

*Viet Cong guerrillas in their jungle redoubts were hard to find, hard to identify, and hard to bomb. But the World War II technology A-1E Skyraider flying low and slow was just the weapon to succeed.*

was, "If 'Charlie' don't get you, you'll die by slipping on one of the oil slicks on any Skyraider flightline."

But the big old carrier bird had a lot of plus points when it came to fighting an insurgency war. It could loiter over a Viet Cong force for an hour or more, while jets gulped their fuel and had to leave after a few minutes. Jet aircraft had become so complex that they depended on everything from trouble-prone transistors to a steady flow of costly parts. The Skyraider, in contrast, could be, and was, put in the air with what one pilot described as spit, prayer and baling wire. When one jet pilot signed up for the job, they looked at him and wondered why a qualified jet jockey would want to fly the prop-driven 'Spad'. His answer: "I want to fly low enough so I can see people on the ground."

*This A-1E Skyraider (designated AD-5 until late-1962) has Vietnamese insignia and a Vietnamese observer on board. But the flight controls and the bombload are the business of an American pilot in US uniform.*

The first six Skyraiders for the VNAF (Vietnamese Air Force) were shipped aboard a former US Navy 'jeep' (escort) carrier now employed as a merchantman, and arrived in Vietnam in September 1960. The old carrier came steaming up the Saigon River in full view of the Viet Cong on the city's outskirts, half the population of the capital, and the jet-set crowd who watched the war from the rooftop terrace restaurant at the Caravelle Hotel.

## Paris of the east

The ship docked at the foot of Rue Vatinat, the road of revelry known in later years as Tu Do Street. For foreigners who could afford to travel a little out of the way, Saigon was the 'Paris of the Orient', offering a special ambience. The arrival of the warplanes doubtlessly seemed gauche. After all, it was only a small war, a little romantic, and it had little impact on the open-air cafés or the night life.

Navy Lieutenant Ken Moranville arrived that month, the first US naval officer in action in Vietnam. Moranville began training Vietnamese Skyraider

pilots of the 1st Fighter Squadron (later redesignated the 514th). Soon he and fellow Americans were, in effect, flying 'on call' missions against the Viet Cong.

During Moranville's time there were constant coup attempts. On 11 November 1960 he was at Bien Hoa when paratroopers rebelled against President Diem. The squadron's Vietnamese Skyraider pilots went aloft to bomb the coup leaders. The armed planes circled over the rebels' heads and intimidated them into surrendering. Diem was assassinated a couple of years later, but the palace intrigue continued and VNAF Skyraider pilots were involved in several intended coups.

*The pyrotechnics may mean that this A-1E Skyraider has hit a Viet Cong ammunition dump. The 'Spad' had the durability, bomb capacity, and versatility to acquit itself well in air-to-ground action. But the VC had an advantage, too. As one said: "We live here."*

# THE ADVISORS

**As a new decade began, Soviet Premier Khrushchev announced that the Soviet Union would "whole-heartedly" support "wars of national liberation" such as "the armed struggle waged by the people of Vietnam". Despite the rhetoric, Soviet aid to the North was restrained and North Vietnam did not yet control the Viet Cong insurgency in the South.**

On 20 January 1961, in a Washington blizzard, Americans inaugurated John F. Kennedy, 43, the youngest man ever elected President and a US Navy hero of World War II. Kennedy's inaugural speech boomed with Cold War sentiment about halting Communism around the globe. It soon became apparent that Kennedy was intrigued by unconventional warfare and fond of the US Army's Special Forces, the Green Berets.

In private, Kennedy acknowledged that Saigon's Ngo Dinh Diem was not exactly the world's leading champion of democracy. The Kennedy administration's view of Diem was characterized by an American diplomat who said, "He's a son of a bitch but he's our son of a bitch." Critics argued that the Viet Cong insurgency in South Vietnam – at that time, still an uprising of people who lived in the South – gained support as long as Diem stayed in office.

Kennedy's choice as Defense Secretary was Robert S. McNamara, a former 'whizkid' of industry and an ideas man who believed that the US could assure survival of its South Vietnamese ally. McNamara insisted that the Viet Cong were infiltrators from the North, which they were not, and that the people of South Vietnam supported Diem, which they did not. Diem's failure to

*Clasping an M1A1 carbine, this American personifies a commitment made by John F. Kennedy to "pay any price, bear any burden" to defend allies like those in Saigon. In 1961, the war was small and – to some – romantic, and it attracted men of adventure. Few could have foreseen what the real price of this seemingly unimportant conflict would be over the next 13 years.*

# First USAF Airmen

**"S**aigon in 1961 was wonderful. It was a little bit of Paris in the Orient. The food was wonderful, the girls beautiful, and the pace relaxed."

The first USAF unit to arrive in South Vietnam on permanent duty status began its work on 26 September 1961. The detachment from the 507th Tactical Control Group at Shaw AFB, South Carolina, set up a command reporting post of 67 men plus MPS-11 search and MPS-16 height-finder radars at Saigon's Tan Son Nhut Airport.

The first American combat aircraft in Vietnam were McDonnell RF-101C Voodoos of the 15th Tactical Reconnaissance Squadron (the 'Cotton Pickers') at Kadena, Okinawa, commanded by Lieutenant Colonel Earl A. Butts. A detachment of four Voodoos, codenamed 'Pipe Stem', with six pilots and an intelligence officer and headed by Major Russell F. Crutchlow, arrived at Tan Son Nhut on 18 October 1961.

It happened to be the day the Mekong River overflowed its banks and flooded hundreds of square miles of the countryside. The four RF-101Cs began photographing both the floods and the Viet Cong on 20 October. Another RF-101C detachment, known as 'Able Mable', positioned itself at Don Muang, Thailand, and performed photo-reconnaissance over Laos.

Captain A. Robert Gould was one of 'Pipe Stem's' RF-101C Voodoo pilots. In later years he remembered: "It really came as a surprise when we got the order to go to Saigon for a Vietnamese Armed Forces Day. The general order indicated that there were [American] planes of all types going to be on display. We (the 15th TRS) were just part of the crowd. Then, all of a sudden, there was an announcement, in the newspapers yet, that the whole deal had been cancelled. Except we did not get orders to cancel."

## Saigon by night

"We lived in the Caravelle Hotel, drove our Jeeps to Tan Son Nhut for our 08.00 take-off, usually four flights per day, and were back at the hotel by 15.00-16.00 hours. We found we had to modify our sleeping schedule somewhat, however. Trying to find something to eat at 7 p.m. was nearly impossible. Nightlife started at 10 p.m. But we had an 05.00 wake-up. The solution was to come home in the afternoon, take a two- or three-hour nap, and then go out to eat at 10 or 11.

"We promptly started flying missions for the American Embassy [in adjacent Laos]. Our primary targets were airfields, bridges, and all the other normal military-type targets. A lot of area covers were flown using the Voodoo's 36-inch focal length split vertical cameras. We used French maps. There were no US maps of sufficient detail."

Captain Dophus E. Guillotte, Jr, the intelligence officer accompanying the RF-101C detachment, found that there was little intelligence to be had. The Voodoos were tasked with reporting on what the Russians were doing in Laos. "We knew the Russians were para-dropping supplies. We had pictures of the 'chutes on the ground. We even saw Russian transports flying over the area. But catching them in the act was tough."

*Air commando hat ajaunt, Capt. Richard Head slides into an A-1E Skyraider at Bien Hoa. The A-1E was likely to shudder and to make plenty of noise. It was also quite accurate and came to be respected as a foe by the VC.*

*The 45th TRS based at Misawa in Japan alternated with the 15th TRS to provide the four-ship 'Pipe Stem' and 'Able Mable' RF-101 detachments to Vietnam and Thailand. "Kill 'em with film," exorted Major Alexander Butterfield, commander of the first Voodoo squadron in theater. His 'recce' pilots did exactly that.*

hold elections, his iron grip on the country through its police and military forces, and his tendency to line his own pockets were conveniently overlooked.

Critics of US escalation in Vietnam were to have no paucity of public figures to attack, among them White House aide McGeorge Bundy, military advisor General Maxwell Taylor, and Secretary of State Dean Rusk. But for some reason, especially after the Bay of Pigs fiasco in April 1961 when a planned invasion of Cuba went awry, the critics focused on the fact that Robert McNamara's middle name was Strange. Like it or not, McNamara was to be seen by many as the architect of a US build-up in South Vietnam.

The USAF was controlled in that era by bomber generals and its Chief of Staff, General Curtis E. LeMay, felt that strategic readiness was more important than some backwater of Asia. Still,

*In 1961, a small number of highly-motivated American troops went to Vietnam to advise the Army of the Republic of Vietnam, quickly dubbed 'Arvin' in GI slang. Soon, Americans were in actual combat.*

**Above: The Piasecki CH-21 Workhorse was the US Army's first principal helicopter in Vietnam. Here, pilots and co-pilots of the 57th Transportation Company do what soldiers since the beginning of time have done – hurry up and wait – before hauling South Vietnamese troops into action.**

**Left: The 57th was a transport unit, but often found itself receiving VC fire. As a result, the unit's lumbering CH-21 helicopters were provided with defensive armament. This gunner mans a pre-World War II vintage Browning .30-caliber machine-gun, mounted in the door of the twin rotor machine's troop compartment.**

LeMay picked up on President Kennedy's infatuation with unconventional warfare.

On 14 April 1961 the General established the 4,400th Combat Crew Training Squadron, codenamed 'Jungle Jim', at Eglin AFB, Florida. Airmen began training for a guerrilla conflict in old prop-driven C-47, B-26 and T-28 aircraft. Called Air Commandos (a name not officially adopted until the following January), they quickly garnered a reputation for their unkempt appearance, lack of attention to military detail – and for great courage.

In May 1961 25 AD-6 Skyraiders arrived to join the six already serving with the VNAF's 1st Fighter Squadron at Bien Hoa. This effort was being handled by the US Navy although the Air Force, which had never operated the Skyraider, began looking at the plane for its Air Commando force. Ironically, the Skyraiders for Saigon's air arm were in better condition than AD-4s being flown by the US Navy. They had been through a stateside re-work facility and were as good as new.

## Vice-President visits

The first member of the new administration to visit Vietnam was Vice-President Lyndon Johnson, on 11-13 May 1961. The Texas politician, a respected figure but hardly a Kennedy intimate, reported that Diem was in control and that the US military advisory group, its strength now approaching 1,000, was doing well. As a result of the Johnson-Diem discussions, the US agreed to support an ARVN force increased in size from 170,000 to 200,000 men, to provide the VNAF with a second fighter squadron made up of North American T-28s, and to supply additional L-19 Bird Dogs to the VNAF's three liaison squadrons.

Plans were made to equip the VNAF's 2nd Fighter Squadron at Nha Trang with 44 T-28s and the liaison squadrons with 15 L-19s. But the T-28s were first to be flown by American pilots – the Air Commandos from Eglin and other US personnel who, on arrival, would be identified by the codename 'Farm Gate'.

At President Kennedy's request, General Maxwell Taylor went to Vietnam in October 1961. Taylor met Diem, reviewed the situation, and made note of the lack of mobility of the Army of the Republic of Vietnam (ARVN) troops.

The US Army's Rogers Board had been succeeded by the Howze Board which was studying air mobility and was contemplating the formation of an entirely new kind of mobile unit, the air cavalry division. Board chief Lieutenant General Hamilton Howze also proposed a solution to mobility problems in backwaters like Vietnam by equipping the Army with de Havilland Canada AC-1 Caribou cargo planes. For more than a dozen years the USAF had had sole jurisdiction over all fixed-wing aircraft except those used for administrative work, so Army officers liked Howze's idea and Air Force officers were enraged by it. Meanwhile, ARVN troops remained paralyzed by Vietnam's poor road network, non-existent river transport, and clinging, clawing jungles.

Taylor recommended advisors and helicopters. He did not, perhaps would not, point out that many of the ARVN simply did not want to fight. At his suggestion, the US Army's 8th and 57th Transportation Companies (Light Helicopter), equipped with the Piasecki H-21 Shawnee, embarked for Southeast Asia. Like Skyraiders before them, the H-21s were brought up the Saigon River by a former jeep carrier – but unlike the Skyraiders, the H-21s retained their US insignia.

## Wider war

Throughout the first year of the Kennedy administration, plans unfolded gradually to bring the US military presence in South Vietnam up to as many as 4,000 men. With hindsight, many close to Kennedy have argued that he never intended the presence to grow any larger, that he was comfortable with a few thousand and had no notion that the figure would one day exceed half a million.

Certainly, the kind of equipment reaching Vietnam was not yet new or modern and the US continued to focus its foreign policy interests elsewhere. But some say that Kennedy pushed a snowball from the top of a hill and that, as it gathered speed, it grew larger – until, in the period just ahead, it would grow out of control. If ever there existed an opportunity to restrain the escalation of the war, it was now. The opportunity was not seized.

### USAF Air Commandos in action

On 11 October 1961 deployment began of the USAF's 'Jungle Jim' detachment. The unit, designated the 1st Air Commando Group and using the name 'Farm Gate' once in-country, included 151 officers and men with eight T-28, four SC-47 and four RB-26 aircraft. Both the command reporting post and the RF-101C Voodoos had preceded them, but 'Farm Gate's' airmen were really the first Americans in combat.

The 'R' for reconnaissance prefix on the B-26 was the first of many deceits, intended to bely their combat role. The second came when Vietnamese markings were painted on the T-28s, which went into action on 26 December.

The markings on their T-28s were a fiction. They went through the pretense of carrying Vietnamese 'crew members' in their B-26 Invaders and T-28 Trojans, but they were doing the work and the fighting – beginning the long and painful US presence in a seemingly endless conflict. Their equipment, like their term for themselves, Air Commandos, came from World War II but their spirit reflected the youthful optimism of the Kennedy era. They wore ANZAC campaign hats, walked around toting tiny sub-machine-guns and bandoliers of ammunition, and spoke of completing their 'advisory' task within a few months.

The Douglas B-26 Invader, powered by two 2,400-hp Pratt & Whitney R-2800-103W radial engines with three-bladed reversible propellers, had begun life as the A-26 during World War II and the original designation was at times resurrected in Vietnam. The B-26 could carry eight forward-firing 0.5-in (12.7-mm) machine-guns plus various combinations of bombs and rockets exceeding 10,000 lb (4500 kg). At a time when the US insisted that the problem in Vietnam was 'Aggression from the North' (which was the title of the State Department's White Paper pointing the finger at Hanoi), the B-26 was ideal for dealing with the real problem – Viet Cong guerrillas, themselves part of the population of the South, who operated in the bush and, being highly mobile, presented only a fleeting target.

### B-26 problems

Unfortunately, the Air Commandos found that the B-26 was not without its problems. B-26B and RB-26B Invaders were flown by American crews and with South Vietnamese markings. They were initially quite effective against 'Mister Charles', as the

Cong came to be nicknamed, but their war was to be shortlived.

Although 'Farm Gate's' Americans were now flying around in T-28s with Vietnamese markings, aircraft intended for the South Vietnamese themselves began to arrive only in December 1961 when 15 T-28B trainers were transferred to the VNAF from the US Navy. These aircraft were to be replaced later by T-28D fighter-bombers.

*Above: T-28 trainers serving as fighter-bombers were effective weapons during Operation 'Farm Gate'. To bolster the Saigon's air arm, the VNAF 2nd Fighter Squadron was formed at Nha Trang in 1961.*

*Below: The A-26/B-26 Invader was one of the few veterans of both World War II and Korea to be used in combat in Vietnam. The first B-26s to reach Vietnam in 1961 had a short service life, curtailed by structural problems.*

*T-28 fighter-bombers of the VNAF's 2nd Fighter Squadron search for targets of opportunity in the northern portion of South Vietnam in the early-1960s. Numerous T-28s were delivered to Saigon aboard the transport ship Breton in February 1962 and went to the 2nd squadron at Nha Trang, the only VNAF squadron equipped with these aircraft.*

*Below: The L-19 Bird Dog (redesignated O-1 in 1962) was the ideal aerial spotter and was widely used. This rocket-armed O-1 (51-12236) belongs to the VNAF's 112th Observation Squadron at Bien Hoa. Together with the military version of the Cessna 185E which became the U-17, the Bird Dog performed yeoman service in the observation role for the Vietnamese army and air force.*

# COUNTER INSURGENCY

**President Kennedy, addressing the West Point class of '62 – which would be decimated in Southeast Asia – talked presciently of the growing war in Southeast Asia. It was a conflict "new in its intensity, ancient in its origin – war by guerrillas, subversives, insurgents, assassins. If freedom is to be saved, we need a new kind of strategy, a wholly different kind of force."**

When in January 1962 eight T-28s and three B-26s bombed, rocketed and napalmed the VC-held village of Ba Thu in the Parrot's Beak, a region of Cambodia poking deep into Vietnam, everyone involved was certain that the Communists had been taught that the border was to be respected. But a Cambodian complaint a few days later led to the US State Department pressuring the South Vietnamese to 'apologise' for the incident. It was exactly the kind of decision which was bad for the morale of both American and South Vietnamese pilots.

On 2 February 1962 a UC-123B Provider belonging to the 'Ranch Hand' defoliation people crashed on a low-level training flight. Enemy ground fire or sabotage was suspected, although it could not be certain. The three crew members became the first USAF fatalities in Southeast Asia.

In February 1962 the US created MACV (Military Assistance Command Vietnam), a curiously named headquarters which amounted to a combat field command in every way except name. Lieutenant General Paul D. Harkins was named chief of MACV, which was roughly modeled after US-Taiwan Defense Command. After conferring with President Kennedy in Florida in January, Harkins was promoted to full General and took the helm in Saigon – supposedly equal to US Ambassador Frederick E. Nolting.

Frederick Nolting, nicknamed 'Fritz', was expected to be nice to President Diem rather than honest with him. He did report to Washington that Diem's brother Nhu and his wife, the notorious Madame Nhu, were widely hated for their authoritarian role in Diem's regime. A proper Virginia gentleman, Nolting was also a solid, able man. Had he been given the authority to do so, he might have prodded Diem to liberalize his rule.

## Attack from the air

On 26 February 1962 two mutinous South Vietnamese pilots in AD-6 Skyraiders attacked President Diem's palace. Although it was the sort of thing that was to happen again and again, Americans were instructed to avoid Vietnamese politics at all costs.

There was a real fear of air attack. Fearing that Peking would introduce modern aircraft, perhaps Ilyushin Il-28 bombers, to the conflict, 405th Tactical Fighter Wing despatched a part of its 509th Fighter-Interceptor Squadron from the Philippines to Tan Son Nhut. The three Convair F-102As (and one TF-102A two-seater) ran practice GCI missions (ground control intercept) but

*A CH-21 Workhorse (also called Shawnee) silhouetted by the sun in South Vietnam, 1962. At first, helicopters carried platoon- or company-sized units of soldiers into action, generally to augment the bulk of the troops who traveled to battle by land. But as the war progressed, entire battalions – even divisions – would be taken into combat by newer helicopters.*

# 'Mule Train' and 'Ranch Hand'

When Fairchild C-123B Provider twin-engined transports began landing at Tan Son Nhut airfield on 2 January 1962, no carpet was rolled out, no fanfare laid on. Lieutenant Colonel Floyd D. Shofner, the HMFIC (Air Force slang which translates loosely – and politely – as 'Head Man in Charge') made no speeches, shook no hands. A simple one-liner for the press noted that the squat, high-winged C-123Bs belonged to 'Mule Train' – a "temporary duty detachment designed to give logistic support to Vietnamese and American forces".

The C-123Bs came from the 346th Troop Carrier Squadron at Pope AFB, North Carolina. Sixteen C-123B Providers made up the detachment, although only four arrived on the first day. In the period ahead the reliable but unglamorous C-123Bs were to be among the hardest-working machines in South Vietnam.

## Defoliation

They were not, however, the only Providers in the country. Three UC-123B Providers, each fitted with an internal 1,000-gallon chemical tank and removable spray bars attached under the wings, arrived at Tan Son Nhut a few days later on 7 January 1962.

President Diem was an ardent advocate of the use of herbicides to destroy crops and to strip away foliage concealing enemy activities. President Kennedy's approval, however, came with severe limitations and called for carefully controlled clearing of key road and rail routes before attempting food denial.

The cargo planes began spraying 200-meter wide swathes with chemical defoliant. Known as 'Ranch Hand' this operation was to become one of the most controversial programs of the war.

Defoliation, to use the new word which entered the vocabulary, satisfied almost nobody. In nine years of

*'Ranch Hand' UC-123B Providers carried 12,000 lb (5443 kg) of chemical defoliant, intended to remove jungle canopy and lay bare the movements of the Viet Cong. A typical spray mission took two hours, all at low-level.*

operations over South Vietnam and Laos, 'Ranch Hand' aircraft were to spray an incredible 2.5-million hectares (6.2-million acres) with herbicides including the notorious Agent Orange. What should have been foreseen, but was not, was that there would be devastating effects on the health of people who came in contact with chemical Orange, Vietnamese natives and American servicemen alike.

*This Farm Gate B-26 Invader is flown by American Air Commandos. The Vietnamese national insignia maintained an appearance of sovereignty, as did the Vietnamese airman who was invariably aboard. He had few actual duties to perform, other than simply being there.*

# Advisors in Action

The record seems clear that President Kennedy and Secretary McNamara wanted USAF airmen to train the South Vietnamese, with the goal of being able to withdraw at some future time.

By contrast, many officers in Vietnam wanted to increase the size of 'Farm Gate'. To help in the pretense that US fliers were only 'training', the VNAF supplied 15 enlisted men to fly with the Americans, whose sole job was to provide a Vietnamese presence in the air.

On 26 March 1962 the *San Francisco Chronicle* told readers that the two US Army Helicopter Companies in Vietnam were doing a little more than just 'advising' the South Vietnamese. "How US Copters Face Red Gunfire" the story was titled. Their low-level flying to get ARVN troops in and out of battle areas "would frighten an instructor back in the States", one H-21C

pilot was quoted as saying.

The paper did not publish what Army H-21C pilots called 'The Air Force Prayer' which read, "God, grant me the eyes of an eagle, the stealth of a stalking tiger, and the balls of an Army helicopter pilot."

Army fliers felt that they were on the cutting edge of this war: dangerous and with a real possibility of death, but which was still on a small scale and somewhat romantic in nature. One Army H-21C pilot told with pride his story of setting down in a landing zone only to see Viet Cong combatants pouring out of the trees and coming at him, rifles blazing. As the story is told, 'Charlie's' squad leader had instructed his troops that they could shoot down an American aircraft only by leading it with their fire. The H-21C pilot watched bullets thunking into the ground in front of his craft, took off without being hit, and escaped.

The L-19 Bird Dog (the O-1, after 1 October 1962) was the perfect aircraft for American pilots to give 'advice' in. Often, while the US Army or US Air Force pilot in the front seat was 'training' a Vietnamese, he just happened to find Viet Cong and call in artillery or fighter-bomber strikes.

encountered no opposition in the air. The reality was that China and Vietnam had been enemies for at least a thousand years. The Chinese Government was ignoring the war to its south, while North Vietnam had not yet begun to build an air force of its own.

On 9 April 1962 Marine aviation arrived with Colonel John F. Carey and 'a few good men' who came into Soc Trang, in the Mekong Delta, in an R4D-8, the Corps' workhorse 'Super DC-3'. They were followed by three Marine OE-1 Bird Dogs from squadron VMO-2 and 24 HUS-1 Seahorse choppers of HMM-362. Situated 85-miles (137-km) south-west of Saigon, the field had a remarkably good paved runway but almost no amenities.

## A Vietnam classic arrives

On 2 May five helicopters of the US Army's 57th Medical Detachment (Helicopter Ambulance) arrived. Their mission, soon to be nicknamed 'Dust Off', introduced one of the great icons of the war – the Huey helicopter. Indeed, with *Newsweek* taking the lead, in 1962 it seemed certain that the conflict would become formally known as 'The Helicopter War'.

Three weeks later, on 23 May, the US Army's 73rd Aviation Company arrived with 32 L-19D Bird Dogs, two-seat observation machines which were quickly scattered all around the country. These were used for artillery adjustment, target acquisition, command and control, message pick-up and radio relay.

On 25 July 15 more HU-1A Iroquois helicopters reached South

Vietnam with the US Army's Utility Tactical Transport Helicopter Company (UTTHCO). These Hueys, equipped in the field with gun and rocket armament, began flying from Tan Son Nhut, which was becoming more and more crowded.

By mid-August the number of Americans in South Vietnam had risen to 11,412. In every area things were slowly expanding. The Air Force decided to send four Helio L-28 Couriers to 'Farm Gate' for forward air controller (FAC) duty. In addition 'Mule Train' acquired a second C-123B Provider squadron.

A new type of Army aircraft arrived in the war zone in September 1962 when six Grumman AO-1 Mohawks of the 23rd Special Warfare Aviation Detachment were sent to Nha Trang to support ARVN forces in the area. Like their Air Force brethren, Army pilots of the two-seat Mohawk were required to carry a Vietnamese observer. They were supposed to conduct their surveillance of the Viet Cong without shooting at anyone unless fired upon. In fact, the AO-1 had been designed from the outset to carry guns and rockets, and they were soon being used.

On 6 October 1962 the co-pilot and crew chief of a crashed UH-34D from squadron HMM-162 were the first naval or Marine aviators killed in action in Vietnam.

In October 1962, not long after the creation of MACV under General Harkins, the USAF command in Saigon became the 2nd Air Division, under Major General Rollen H. Anthis. Still a two-star slot, command of Air Force personnel in South Vietnam in later

*It took guts – or something – to sit in the greenhouse front seat of a CH-21 going into an LZ (landing zone) and to know that the enemy used models to train riflemen how to kill helicopter pilots. There was some armor around the CH-21 jock, but not enough.*

The Marines always seemed to get into the small, dirty wars at the beginning, and the swampy forests of the Mekong Delta were the ideal setting for the Corps' expertise in unconventional warfare. Not that the men were enthusiastic about operating their ageing Sikorsky HUS-1 helicopters from the old Japanese base at Soc Trang in the southern extremity of the country. They were miles from the bars and bistros of Saigon, and the Delta was where 'Charlie' was strongest. But the HUS-1s were needed near the river's mouth precisely because ARVN troops were faced with a real challenge from highly mobile, dedicated Viet Cong units, and helicopter mobility was supposed to turn things around.

HMM-362 was one of the first Marine units in-country,

arriving on 15 April 1962 as part of Operation 'Shu Fly' which was tasked with assisting local forces. Staff Sergeant Dave Remington wrote that the living conditions were abominable, maintenance was atrocious, and the HUS-1 just did not want to perform in the wet heat. "We drop the ARVN. We pick them up. Sometimes they engage the VC. Sometimes they don't."

## Working under fire

As if coping with cantankerous helicopters was not enough, the officially non-combatant Marines frequently came under fire.

Second Lieutenant Steven Harding felt that they were accomplishing something. The advantage of helicopter mobility seemed to increase ARVN fighting spirits. "The Viet Cong still control vast areas here, and

*These Marine HUS-1s (called UH-34Ds after 1 October 1962) are original 'Shu Fly' aircraft of squadron HMM-362, and are seen here ferrying South Vietnamese infantrymen on 26 July 1962.*

we can't touch 'em at night. But we are beginning to deny them freedom of movement."

In fact, 'Shu Fly's' helicopters gave the relatively ill-equipped South Vietnamese Army an important boost in mobility and logistic support.

The Marines came to have a sense of belonging. When the decision was made to shift the 'Shu Fly' operation to Da Nang where the HUS-1 offered better performance at higher altitude, some expressed disappointment.

"We'll be living better. But the Army guys who replace us in the Delta will be fighting the real battle with the VC."

years was to become a four-star posting and the headquarters was eventually to be renamed Seventh Air Force.

But that month, the Cuban missile crisis brought the world to the brink of nuclear war, and even the few people who had begun to think about Vietnam had their attention turned elsewhere.

Figures showed that at the end of 1962, the US Army had 199 aircraft in Vietnam, the Air Force 61. The number of Army helicopter companies increased from two to five. To many, the US seemed to be achieving its goal of propping up the shaky Vietnamese Government which had been threatened by coups early in the year.

The Viet Cong, or National Liberation Front as they wanted to be known, were not getting noticeably stronger, were not yet 100 per cent controlled by Hanoi, and in 1962 were still willing to

accept a partial victory in the form of a neutral state in the South. In 1959 Ho Chi Minh had predicted victory within a year. In 1962 he was saying with remarkable prescience that victory might take 15 to 20 years. Foreign observers in Hanoi conjectured that Ho was in fear of a development few Americans were thinking about – a US bombing campaign against North Vietnam.

*The F-102A Delta Dagger deployed to the war zone several times after its first arrival early in 1962, guarding against an air attack from North Vietnam that never came. Called the 'Deuce' by pilots, the F-102A was the wrong candidate for a conventional war in a tropical setting. It had been designed to intercept Russian bombers attacking North America over polar regions. Not a dogfighter, the F-102A came out second-best on 3 February 1968 when two of them battled two North Vietnamese MiG-21s: one of the American jets was shot down and its pilot killed.*

# END OF A SMALL WAR

**The war in Southeast Asia remained a relatively small affair, although the numbers of American servicemen and planes advising and supporting the Republic of Vietnam was growing quite fast. Also growing fast was the sophistication of the opposition, and large numbers of Viet Cong were now being trained in anti-helicopter tactics.**

As the new year began, the war in Vietnam was still not receiving much attention from the American public. The question of what was being accomplished in that distant Asian land was not receiving much scrutiny either. While an authoritarian regime in Saigon attempted to control a countryside which seemed to belong to 'Victor Charlie' at night and, perhaps, to the ARVN by day, the number of US advisors slowly increased.

Elsewhere in the region other Asian cities were becoming holiday spots for American servicemen on R & R (rest and recuperation) leave, which was jokingly referred to as I & I (intoxication and intercourse). Americans on leave were being seen on the sidewalks from Sydney to Seoul – and not a few were traveling all the way home to be with wives and girlfriends.

In Hong Kong the local expatriates gathered at a Kowloon Bar where civil aviator Wally Gayda liked to drink with the men and try for the women. Gayda had flown C-46s and C-47s in the 'Big War', the one everybody remembered from just 18 years ago, and had even shot down a Japanese fighter with a Browning automatic

rifle stuck out of his 'Gooney Bird's' window. "They say this thing down in Vietnam is a small war," he intoned. "It ain't going to be that way much longer."

"How do you know?" probed Dutch Hemmel, an Air America pilot who was flying C-46s and C-47s in this war. Dutch was ferrying a C-46 down to Vientiane where it would join the CIA/Air America war in Laos.

"I'll tell you how I know." Gayda later made this sentiment in a letter to the editor in a local journal. "It's because of the girls in the bars, is how I know. The girls in the bars say the war is going to get a lot bigger."

"And I'll tell you what else," Gayda insisted. "You talk to these American Special Forces guys who come up here. These Green Berets. They say the ARVN won't fight. They say the ARVN can't fight. That's how the hell I know."

A sign of how things were going to be was the 2 January 1963 battle at Ap Bac where ARVN troops and their American advisors were soundly defeated. A UH-1B Huey was shot down, an H-21C damaged. Friendly troops lifted into battle by helicopter were overwhelmed and over-run. In an about-face from their earlier performance, the Viet Cong showed themselves unafraid of helicopters, especially 'slick' (transport) helicopters when they were not properly escorted by gunships.

*The ageing piston-driven H-21 (foreground) was not to be around much longer, replaced by the turbine-powered UH-1. As the war widened – and questions about South Vietnam's staying power persisted – the 'Huey' was to become one of the most enduring symbols of the war.*

# Army – Air Force Friction

*The US Army CV-2 Caribou (to be redesignated C-7 in 1967) met soldiers' needs as a tactical transport but it also violated a rule giving the US Air Force a monopoly on heavy, fixed-wing aircraft. The Air Force fought the VC bravely but fought the Army with just as much tenacity.*

The debate about close air support had raged for years – in 1960-61 the Army had tested the Italian-built Fiat G.91 in the close air support role, in defiance of the rules – and Air Force leaders really fumed when calls for close support from formations on the ground went to the men in green in preference to USAF (or VNAF) support.

US Army aviation was beginning to focus principally on rotary-wing aircraft, either as part of a ground unit or for general utility duties. However, and it was much on men's minds in those days, the 'rules' stated that the Army could operate fixed-wing aircraft for 'administrative' purposes only. In fact, fixed-wing aircraft were being employed for reconnaissance and logistics duties in addition to straightforward liaison and communications.

The Grumman OV-1 Mohawk was becoming an increasingly familiar sight from one end of Vietnam to the other. This twin-engined aircraft, which had originally been developed as an Army-Marine Corps joint venture (although in the end the Marines purchased none) was a handy machine when only short, rough runways were available and ground units needed almost instantaneous photo coverage.

Although supposedly unarmed, it carried machine-gun pods under the wings for defense and support missions. Air Force officers took due note of the Mohawk's ability to carry not merely self-protection but offensive armament. This caused Air Force commanders to complain that the Army was violating the 'rules'.

## Who flies fixed-wing?

They argued that if the Army needed gun or rocket support, the USAF could supply it. The Army knew perfectly well that the Air Force had no assets with which to provide Mohawk-style support to the dogface on the ground and, furthermore, with its own aircraft the Army would be able to respond almost instantaneously rather than go through an increasingly cumbersome chain of command.

In due course the dispute was resolved in typical fashion. The Army could keep its Mohawks but went on record as assuring that henceforth they would be unarmed. The Mohawks continued to fly with gun and rocket loads. The Air Force took comfort from the agreement, while the Army was encouraged by the reality of the situation.

There were those in the Air Force who did not even want the Army to have large helicopters. One of their targets was the Sikorsky H-37; not a new craft by any means but in 1963 the Army's largest load-hauling rotary-wing aircraft. Once it was pointed out that there was no reasonable alternative, not in Army khaki and not in Air Force blue, this portion of the ongoing inter-Service dispute evaporated.

A heavy-lift helicopter was one thing, a large transport quite another. While experts searched for clear direction in Vietnam, the USAF became increasingly vocal about an irritant to which it kept returning – the Army's CV-2 Caribou. This exceptional cargo plane had been procured by the Army to bridge the size gap between its largest helicopters and the Air Force's C-130 Hercules four-engined transports. Capable of lifting almost 3 tons of supplies or 32 passengers, the Canadian-built CV-2 Caribou was able to get large loads into and out of small unimproved airstrips – including some which even the C-123B Provider could not reach. In 1963 the USAF continued to argue – not as yet successfully – that if anybody was going to operate Caribous, it should be the Air Force.

*Left: the JOV-1A Mohawk was equipped to carry a variety of 2.75-in and 5-in air-to-ground rocket projectiles. Though the US Air Force opposed the Army's use of fixed-wing aircraft, in 1963 the armed Mohawk was the ideal reconnaissance, observation, and light-attack ship to support Vietnamese troops and their American advisors.*

*Right: A Mohawk fires a rocket during a mission in the Mekong Delta. The JOV-1A designation was assigned to several standard OV-1As configured for ground-attack duty in Vietnam and sent to the combat zone in 1963-5.*

The Viet Cong were becoming much better informed about aviation. Helicopter LZs (landing zones) were covered by fire, or booby-trapped by means of spears planted in the ground to puncture the bellies of helicopters. A captured document showed how the VC informed their personnel:

"The helicopter type used to carry troops [H-21C] is very large and looks like a worm. It has two rotors and usually flies at an altitude of 200 to 300 meters. To hit its head, lead by either one length or two-thirds of a length when it flies horizontally. The type used by commanders and casualties [UH-1] looks like a ladle. Lead this type one length when it is in flight..."

At Ap Bac many other things went wrong – effective communication between US and ARVN personnel was the first casualty – but helicopter people in particular felt that their performance and their tactics had to be reviewed. A gunship escort was to become routine with helicopter insertions.

### Viet Cong strength

Viet Cong attacks on villages and government outposts were on the increase. The Communist guerrillas in the South were poorly equipped for a prolonged war – most of their infantry weapons in 1963 were captured from ARVN troops, not supplied by Hanoi or Moscow – but the insurgents were receiving more and more arms from the North. And the Viet Cong clearly had the will to fight, which the ARVN lacked. Most American decision-makers charged that Hanoi was controlling the VC – this was to become a self-fulfilling prophecy in years to come – but none wanted to say that the VC were winning the war.

On 24 March 1963 USAF C-123s and VNAF C-47s dropped 1,150 ARVN paratroopers on to drop zones in Tay Ninh province in Operation 'Phi Hon 11'. It was not clear whether this airborne assault surprised or outwitted the Viet Cong. Most US Army leaders acknowledged that the helicopter was replacing the parachute as a means of inserting troops into the combat zone.

In April 1963 the 777th Troop Carrier Squadron arrived at Da Nang with 16 C-123Bs to augment the 29 at Tan Son Nhut. Other increases in US aircraft strength in Vietnam consisted of Army aircraft, eight U-1A Otters, 16 O-1A Bird Dog observation planes, 10 UH-1B Iroquois (Huey) helicopters, and four additional CV-2 Caribous.

It was a strange time for Diem's regime to make arrangements for legions of disaffected enemy to come over to Saigon's side in the war. April 1963 saw the inception of the Chieu Hoi ('Open Arms') amnesty program aimed at rallying Viet Cong defectors to the government's side. Air Commando U-10Bs were to drop leaflets urging the VC to come over. Army UH-1B Hueys with loudspeakers were to broadcast the same message. The Chieu Hoi program was to continue throughout the war, but in 1963 many rural Vietnamese – and South Vietnam was 90 per cent rural – were

# O-1 Reconnaissance
### *Spotting from the Bird Dog*

The Army's Bird Dog became perhaps the most ubiquitous fixed-wing aircraft in the war zone. The tandem, two-seat high-wing liaison craft could land almost anywhere. Being very small it was no easy target to hit from the ground, and its simple construction meant that there was less danger of damaging something vital if it was hit. These qualities made the O-1 a good candidate for observation duties over Viet Cong-dominated territory. As the US Army shifted toward an airmobile concept making increased use of helicopters, and training of fixed-wing pilots declined, the Army decided that its O-1 Bird Dogs were needed more in Vietnam than at training bases.

### Combat spotters
A significant number of TO-1D Bird Dog trainers (formerly TL-19Ds) were sent back to Cessna

going in the opposite direction.

There were actually plans to remove some American units by the end of 1963. Still, more and more Americans were arriving and many of them were exponents of the 'new' unconventional warfare of which President Kennedy was so enamored. The Army's Special Forces, or Green Berets, sometimes seemed to have carte blanche in their efforts to support Saigon's army in the hinterlands. Air America, the airline carrier which was essentially owned by the CIA, was flying plain and unmarked aircraft in Laos and South Vietnam.

### Escort from the air

As 1963 drew on, Vietnamese and American pilots discovered that the mere presence of an aircraft overhead was often sufficient to keep 'Victor Charlie' away. Vietnamese O-1 Bird Dogs escorted truck convoys and trains, occasionally accompanied by an A-1H Skyraider or T-28 fighter-bomber. Experience showed that the Viet Cong usually would not launch one of their typical ambushes if an aircraft was on the scene, even an unarmed O-1.

On 11 June 1963 an aged Buddhist monk burned himself to death in public. Encounters between Saigon police and demonstrating Buddhist leaders constituted only one aspect of growing discontent against President Diem, his brother Ngo Dinh Nhu and the latter's 'Dragon Lady' wife, the diminutive but spiteful Madame Nhu. The Diem government was harsh, authoritarian and corrupt. Congressman Otto Passman reflected the views of many when he said that Americans did not want to prop up an unpopular

**South Vietnam's corrupt and dictatorial President Ngo Dinh Diem was touted by President Kennedy as a champion of democracy in Asia, worthy of US support. Neither leader was to survive to the end of 1963.**

to be modified for combat duties. In addition to other improvements, underwing racks were installed, enabling the machine to carry smoke/marker rockets. Most of the aircraft were returned to the Army as O-1Ds but 22 were loaned to the Air Force for forward air controller (FAC) duties as the O-1F.

The first Army O-1Ds to reach the battle zone belonged to the 73rd Aviation Company commanded by Major John S. Kark. This unit became the latest of many tenants at Saigon's Tan Son Nhut airfield, beginning in May 1963. As reported by historian Al Adcock, Kark's unit logged some 30,000 combat hours in its first year, performing resupply of forward troops, medical evacuation, flare drops, spotting and forward air control.

*An O-1 Bird Dog descends over South Vietnam. Note the fixed landing gear, whip-style HF (high frequency) radio antenna, and the high-wing, all-metal structure of this remarkable aircraft. At the height of the Vietnam conflict, the Bird Dog was one of the ubiquitous sights of the war as hundreds of aircraft scurried about from the Mekong Delta to the Demilitarized Zone.*

*Right: Sneaking through the trees was not unusual for the O-1, and pilots could fly up to five perilous observation sorties in a single day. The Bird Dog was simple, inexpensive, and straightforward, but despite a disagreeable climate and a hostile adversary, it kept going with minimal maintenance.*

*Left: Capt. Gilbert Ysais, one of the first O-1 forward air controllers, said, "I took the job because my mother wanted me to fly down low where I could see lots of people." Flying a Bird Dog this low invited a reaction if those people were Viet Cong guerrillas.*

regime which was lukewarm about its struggle against Communism. President Kennedy reiterated that some Americans would be withdrawn from Vietnam by the end of the year.

In July 1963 the USAF's 19th Tactical Air Support Squadron, or 19th TASS, began arriving with O-1 Bird Dogs. The Air Force Bird Dog pilots were to train Vietnamese in forward air control, visual reconnaissance and observer procedures.

Opposition to President Diem was mounting from several quarters. American leaders were apparently unaware that a major

plot against Diem was being mounted by Generals Duong Van Minh, Tran Van Don, and others. In a kind of general response to unrest at the end of October, a US naval task force was positioned off Vietnam and three F-102s were flown in to Tan Son Nhut. There was no role for either when the coup began on the morning of 1 November 1963.

Troops took over key installations and surrounded Diem and Nhu in the palace. Four A-1H Skyraiders and two T-28s flew overhead, joining in the uprising. An occasional splutter of rifle fire

# Busy Tan Son Nhut

Tan Son Nhut was Saigon's main airfield, and as American involvement in Southeast Asia continued to rise it became one of the busiest airports in the world.

In addition to commercial flights, there was an ever-increasing stream of transports flying to and from American bases all over the Pacific. Flights came in from Guam, from Japan, and from the Philippines, and the airport was also an important terminus for the trans-Pacific air bridge crossing from continental USA. Chartered jets brought a

rising number of troops to Vietnam, while large quantities of supplies and equipment were also coming in by air.

But Tan Son Nhut was also an important military operating base. Indeed, the number of front-line aircraft operating from the airport's runways was getting out of hand. The figure reached 233, including Convair F-102s and Douglas EA-1F Skyraiders brought in to guard against an imagined enemy air offensive. In due course the interceptors were deemed unnecessary and were withdrawn.

*A C-124C Globemaster II (51-0172) of the USAF's Military Air Transport Service (to be re-named Military Airlift Command on 1 January 1966) dominates a scene at Tan Son Nhut which also includes Pan American Boeing 707s, C-130 Hercules and C-123 Providers.*

# 1963: End of a Small War

*Right: 'Farm Gate' pilots were trained in special operations warfare at Hurlburt Field, Florida, but most needed little training to be adept with stick and rudder in a T-28. The aircraft (nicknamed 'Trojan' in its US Navy version only) was the standard advanced trainer for a generation of US Air Force, Navy, Marine, and Coast Guard fliers. Its qualities and shortcomings were very familiar to all.*

*Below: The B-57 Canberra, settled as the US Air Force's standard light bomber for a decade before it reached Vietnam, routinely used explosive gas-generating cartridges to get its turbojet engines going – hence the rising clouds of smoke at any B-57 flight line.*

was heard in that area of Saigon but resistance to the coup was scattered and weak. Fighting continued into the next day when Diem and Nhu – after attempting to escape via an underground tunnel from the palace – were captured. Placed inside a vehicle near the palace, the pair were murdered – although some versions of the event say that Nhu was given an opportunity to commit suicide. The rebels established a Military Revolutionary Council headed by General Minh.

The war did not slow down for the coup. Viet Cong attacks on government installations increased. At one point, 'Farm Gate' pilots had to fly close support for a beleaguered outpost without having the requisite Vietnamese crew member aboard. The Vietnamese fliers were too busy with the coup.

The US supported the new rulers in Saigon and continued its activities throughout South Vietnam. A small number of Americans were withdrawn before year's end, reflecting President Kennedy's wish to bolster Saigon's forces and reduce the US presence. Some of Kennedy's supporters claim that he wanted to have a larger and more visible withdrawal of US troops from Vietnam in time for his re-election campaign in 1964. It can never be proven, however.

The President was assassinated in Dallas on 22 November 1963 in one of those wrenching historical moments which affect everyone, everywhere, and the question of what to do in Vietnam passed into the hands of Lyndon B. Johnson.

While the world reacted with shock, a battle unfolded that showed that the Viet Cong were increasingly ready for larger-scale actions. Before dawn on 24 November 1963, the Viet Cong launched a well-planned ambush at an outpost named Chu La and a strategic hamlet on the Ca Mau peninsula, both in An Xuyen Province. Defending South Vietnamese troops were over-run while the VC shot down a US Army H-21C Shawnee.

As the battle continued with US and South Vietnamese aircraft overhead, VC gunfire damaged 10 H-21CS and UH-1 Hueys. American and VNAF A-1Hs, B-26s and T-28s attacked at low altitude, returning again and again to hit the VC within a short distance of friendly troops.

In another of the rare airborne assaults of the war, C-47s and C-123Bs dropped a battalion to cut off the VC line of withdrawal. The 'Mule Train' C-123Bs put most of the paratroops on the wrong side of the Cai Nuoc River, enabling most of the VC to escape. At the same time, the VC seriously damaged a B-26 which later went down with the loss of its crew.

## VNAF progress

Progress by Saigon's own air force was an important sign of hope as 1963 neared its end. So fast was the VNAF growing that it had to redesignate all its units – the 1st Fighter Squadron became the 514th, the 2nd the 516th, and so on. Now, the VNAF had five wings located at Da Nang, Nha Trang, Pleiku, Bien Hoa and Tan Son Nhut. Included in this force were two squadrons of A-1 Skyraiders, two of T-28 Trojans, two of H-34 helicopters, three of O-1 Bird Dogs and two of C-47 Skytrains. The VNAF was not only bigger, it was better: training received strong emphasis. In later years the quality of VNAF pilots was to deteriorate, but in 1963 most were very good.

Earlier in the year Defense Secretary McNamara had announced that the Vietnamese would soon be able to fight their own war and that it would become possible to withdraw the remaining 15,640 US military personnel. The US role in Vietnam would end during 1965, said McNamara. Some of what McNamara said was taken seriously by the people involved, who thought they would be going home soon.

President Johnson sent McNamara to Vietnam for a 19-20 December visit. Although publicly he exuded optimism, McNamara found the Minh government shaky and indecisive, and

*UH-1B/C Huey helicopters in tight formation. The US Army had been exploring airmobile operations before getting involved in Vietnam, and as the concept was refined and expanded, Hueys were divided into unarmed 'Slick' troop carriers with smooth fuselage sides, heavily-armed 'Hogs' carrying machine-guns and rocket pods, and 'Dustoff' medical evacuation helicopters. These last ensured the survival of a much higher proportion of combat casualties in Vietnam than in any previous conflict.*

# First Combat Jets

In May the 6091st Reconnaissance Squadron, USAF, flew two RB-57E Canberra reconnaissance aircraft to a temporary site at Tan Son Nhut. Part of a program called 'Patricia Lynn', the Canberras were the first jets to be based in Vietnam, rather than a temporary detachment from elsewhere. 'Patricia Lynn' was billed as a temporary program; it was to be one of the longest deployments of the war, its aircraft remaining until August 1971.

These particular Canberras, originally built as target-towing aircraft, were fitted with reconnaissance systems by General Dynamics at Fort Worth. Initially the forward nose housed a KA-1 36-in forward oblique and a low panoramic KA-56 camera. Mounted in the inside of the bomb bay door was a KA-1 vertical camera, K-477 split-vertical day-night camera, and a KA-1 left oblique camera. The RB-57E Canberras were so badly needed that ferry pilot Captain Bill Scott and navigator Lieutenant Bill Sung were pressed into service – combat service, it might be added – to fly the first mission on 7 May 1963, using aircraft 55-4243.

Soon afterwards, new crews arrived from the States and the 'Patricia Lynn' RB-57Es became permanent residents. They used the callsign 'Moonglow'. Their photography of Viet Cong installations proved invaluable.

There were problems, however. When equipment worked properly, which it often did not, the US intelligence apparatus was frequently unable to exploit the information gained. No courier aircraft were available to deliver reconnaissance film rapidly throughout Vietnam until the arrival of two Cessna U-3 aircraft (militarized versions of the Cessna 310) later in May. Intelligence information from Air Force RB-57Es was seldom compared with information from Army OV-1 Mohawks, so there was a duplication of effort.

*RB-57E Canberras modified for the 'Patricia Lynn' program – a hi-tech reconnaissance effort – were long-term residents of Saigon's Tan Son Nhut airport, along with UC-123B/K Providers like the camouflaged transport in the background. The RB-57E used reconofax VI infra-red sensors to provide night-time intelligence images of Viet Cong and North Vietnamese infiltration.*

that infiltration from North Vietnam was increasing. He authorized flights by Lockheed U-2 reconnaissance aircraft to cover infiltration routes. U-2s were quickly moved to Bien Hoa for this purpose.

The end of 1963 was, to US Navy Captain Deke Thatcher, the last juncture at which Vietnam could be called a small war. The number of Americans committed was still small enough for the citizenry at large to be little affected, and even some of the men in the combat zone could continue viewing the war as small and romantic. Thatcher, part of a Fleet evaluation group examining the size and structure of carrier air wings, sat through a three-hour meeting at the Pentagon, recalling later that Vietnam had not been mentioned once.

## Ever-increasing air traffic

At Tan Son Nhut on New Year's Eve, USAF Airman Walter Todd took a smoke break by propping himself in a seating position on loading docks that were under construction. He drew in on a Marlboro, savoring the odd hues created under the sodium-vapor lamps which lit up the tropical night.

Like most airmen at the base, Todd had noticed men and material being brought into South Vietnam by the marvel of long-range airlift. The Douglas C-124 Globemaster was a frequent sight and people at Tan Son Nhut were beginning to see larger numbers of the Lockheed C-130A Hercules. "You know," Todd told a pal, "they're bringing an awful lot of stuff in here. They say we'll be finished here in the near future. You know what? I don't believe it."

Wally Gayda, Deke Thatcher and Walt Todd did not survive the decade of the 1960s, but back there at the dark beginning the few who saw what was coming might as well have been clairvoyant. At Alameda, on the American west coast, the USS *Bon Homme Richard*

(CVA-31) was preparing to put to sea in January. As Thatcher knew, even if no-one else did, the war which included the US Army and Air Force was about to have an increasing role for the carrier Navy as well.

*UC-123K Providers, fitted with auxiliary jet engines for extra power, lay 200-yard-wide swathe of defoliants onto the Vietnamese countryside.*

# WIDENING WAR

**Men walked around bare-chested, wearing bush hats, carrying sub-machine-guns and draped in bandoliers of ammo. The wheeze of a propeller turning over, the cough and roar of a reciprocating engine coming to life were characteristic sounds. But all was about to change, and the World War II veterans were about to lose their place in what was rapidly becoming a jet-powered conflict.**

Operating their ageing fleet of B-26 and T-28 aircraft at Bien Hoa, 200 USAF Commandos made up the 'Farm Gate' detachment which, by 1964, was rapidly swelling in size. The 34th Tactical Group was established to give Air Force people in Vietnam a unit which sounded more appropriate for their growing size reporting, of course, to 2nd Air Division in Saigon. At first there was a clandestine aura to the presence of the airmen. They wore civilian clothes and kept in the background. They used a term that had become fashionable – COIN, meaning counter-insurgency. Some of them scarfed up blackmarket weapons, of which the most popular was the Swedish K sub-machine-gun.

## Counter-insurgency

Up through November 1964 – which meant through the Diem regime and for the year that followed – it was still a counter-insurgency air operation. Men and aircraft, working in small numbers, were effective against the Viet Cong insurgents. Throughout this period, combined VNAF and USAF efforts mounted up to 35 sorties per day. The intent was to enable Saigon's

*A visitor to 'Farm Gate' took in the scent of high-octane fuel, heard the growl of piston engines, and sighed, "This is World War II all over again." The B-26 Invader evoked a spirit of adventure in the hands of swaggering Air Commandos. But B-26s proved troublesome to maintain and suffered structural failures. Temporarily, they had to be withdrawn.*

forces to function more effectively in the bush, and it worked.

Apparently in the belief that the war was being won, the 19th Tactical Air Support Squadron, equipped with Cessna O-1F Bird Dogs, was deactivated in August 1964. It was one of many signals to the airmen that the war was almost over. Indeed, if they did not know the war was almost over, Secretary of Defense Robert S. McNamara told them it was over with each new public utterance.

That same month, the North Vietnamese attacked US ships and retaliatory air strikes were flown, but for participants of the 'in-country war', it felt as if things were winding down. When the 19th TASS was reactivated a few months later, everyone assumed that this was just another of the many changes that kept occurring. Everyone said the VC were being licked and the guys would soon be able to go home.

## Coup d'etat

On 30 January 1964 Major General Nguyen Khanh led a coup against the indecisive Minh regime and installed yet another new, military government in Saigon. Khanh had power but not popularity. Americans quickly indicated their support.

On 11 February 1964 all B-26 Invader bombers in South Vietnam were grounded after a wing had failed on an aircraft in the US. It became clear that the B-26 could not handle the 750-lb (227-kg) bombs it had been carrying without suffering structural damage. Colonel Benjamin S. Preston, Jr, head of the 34th Tactical Group at Bien Hoa, struggled to keep his B-26s in the air but every aircraft had cracked stress plates and loose rivets throughout its wings.

On 1 April the last B-26 was flown out of South Vietnam. Plans to bring in the On Mark B-26K variant were shelved. To provide an interim strike capability, the 1st Air Commando Squadron borrowed nine T-28s from the VNAF.

Then disaster struck the T-28s. On 24 March one aircraft had lost its wing on a bomb run. This was followed by another T-28 wing

# Door Gunners

By 1964 the Bell UH-1 Iroquois helicopter had all but replaced the twin-rotor Piasecki H-21C in US Army units. Up at Qui Nhon, on the coast where beautiful beaches faced aquamarine sea, the 117th Aviation Company painted its Hueys in an unusual blotched camouflage scheme. Carl Vogel, a young private first class in the 117th, noticed that nobody was referring to the Iroquois by its official name. First called the XH-40, then the HU-1, and now the UH-1, the helicopter was now, and always would be, the Huey. The name Huey was used so widely that most people never knew it had any other name.

## Enter the door gunner

In the US Army a new species was being bred to go with the helicopter – the door gunner. Army aviation was serious about the role this gunner played in protecting the other members of his crew and issued some advice which seemed to make sense. With hindsight, this instruction tells us much about how helicopter crewmen were regarded at the time. To quote:

"Learn the way of the tiger.

"That's the theme of the program for training 'Shotgunners' – or officially Aerial Door Gunners – those tough, skilled soldiers who, in the tradition of their counterparts on the stage coaches of the old West, are protecting their UH-1 'Skycoaches' while flying over South Vietnam.

"Because demands on the men serving as shotgunner are severe, each candidate must pass a class 111 flight physical examination in which vision, color blindness, hearing and other physical conditions are closely checked.

"Training is primarily with the M60 machine-gun, but the soldier also must be an expert with the .50-caliber machine-gun, M-79 grenade-launcher, .45-caliber pistol, M-3 sub-machine-gun, .30-caliber M-2 carbine and the new M-16 rifle. Always present is the basic infantry weapon, the M-14 complete with bayonet.

"Recently it was decided that because of an increased number of night missions being reported from Vietnam, added emphasis would be placed on night weapons-firing training. Additional emphasis also has been placed on familiarization with the various types of helicopters, and on offensive and defensive flying tactics in Southeast Asia.

"The training platoons are first introduced to helicopter flight from a mock-up. They are orientated in the various gun mounts and also in free firing with the 'Bungee cord', a resilient strap slung in the door of the craft to support the weapon.

"As training progresses, the men learn techniques of aerial observation and firing at various altitudes and how to respond with instantaneous but planned reactions. Accuracy is constantly emphasized, especially in the descent-to-a-landing-zone phase. While supplying suppressive fire, the shotgunners must keep an eye on accompanying support helicopters as they continue to assist troops from the craft – all in split seconds.

"In addition to training in weaponry and tactics, the already jungle-trained 25th Division men receive a thorough reorientation in jungle survival. They are also taught to swim fully clothed and to maneuver in treacherous waters against the chance of being forced into such a situation. Intensive training is also given by the Division surgeon's office to prepare men to meet and overcome the health hazards of disease-infested jungle regions.

## The way of the tiger

"As did their counterparts of old who fought off robbers and Indians in the wild and wooly West, they have learned the ways of a tiger in order to kill a tiger; and they prove every day that they can meet the guerrilla forces of what has become a wild and wooly East."

At this point, the document from this period concludes with a plug for one of the best-known US Army divisions: "(Door gunners) prove every day that men of the 25th Division are 'Ready to Fight, Anywhere! Any time!'" This final note reflected the kind of innocent confidence that still possessed Americans at that time. It would take more time to teach the lesson that Lyndon Johnson's America was not nearly as ready as everyone believed to fight and win a prolonged and brutal land war in Southeast Asia.

Whether firing a .30-caliber machine-gun left over from previous wars as seen here, or using the US Army's newer M60, the door gunner rarely achieved more than to add confusion to the battle. The helicopter's speed, angle and altitude challenged any effort to be accurate.

loss on 9 April. Major General J. H. Moore, 2nd Air Division chief in Saigon, lamented that, "[We are] practically out of business." American T-28s were replaced in May 1964 by the A-1E Skyraider, the 'widebody' version of the versatile attack aircraft which had side-by-side seating up front.

At times the requirement for the Americans to carry a Vietnamese passenger – who was ostensibly being trained – became ludicrous.

During yet another visit to Saigon in May, Secretary McNamara reiterated the administration's policy that all US airmen should be out of combat within a matter of months. American fliers were told to limit their activities to providing genuine training only, and apparently McNamara meant it this time.

To make up for the loss of USAF strike aircraft, four VNAF squadrons would receive A-1H Skyraiders and another two squadrons would be added, the aircraft coming from US squadrons slated for withdrawal. McNamara touted this as a continuation of withdrawals which had begun the previous year with the 'Dirty Thirty' transport personnel.

Also in May the 1st Air Commando Squadron which had been operating the T-28 received its initial increment of six A-1E Skyraiders. Nine more came the following month. The eventual plan was to have 60 Skyraiders in-country.

## War in Laos

The press and public were focusing not on Vietnam but on Laos. A detachment of the 1st Air Commando Squadron had moved to Udorn, Thailand, in March with a force of four T-28s, its mission to train the Royal Laotian Air Force in operations and maintenance. Few Americans knew who was who in Laos – or for that matter in Vietnam, enabling the *San Francisco Chronicle*'s Arthur Hoppe to write hilarious columns about the dreaded Vietnarians, the Loyal Royal Army, and a princely leader named Ngo Manh Ngo. In fact, the T-28s, known now by the program name 'Water Pump', were helping the royal Lao regime against the Pathet Lao guerrillas. By June, F-100 Super Sabres located at Da Nang were also striking Pathet positions in Laos.

A major change of command took place on 20 June 1964 when the lackluster General Harkins was replaced by General William D. Westmoreland. The new senior American officer had served in the 9th Infantry Division during World War II and had distinguished himself as a paratroop leader with the 187th Airborne Regimental

Secretary of Defense Robert S. McNamara (center) was the architect of US policy in Vietnam under Presidents Kennedy and Johnson. McNamara hand-picked General William D. Westmoreland (right) as the American field commander. Officially the head of MAC-V (Military Assistance Command-Vietnam), Westmoreland was the de facto boss in Saigon.

Combat Team in Korea. He was also a former superintendent of the United States Military Academy, West Point, which produced so many of the nation's heroes and leaders; 'Westy', those who were friendly called him. In due course, those who were not would nickname him General 'Waste More Men' because of his repeated calls for increased troop strength.

Shortly afterwards, on 2 July, Henry Cabot Lodge was replaced as American Ambassador by General Maxwell D. Taylor, another paratrooper and war hero. Taylor had been Kennedy's man and had survived the transition to become Johnson's man. He was distinguished by a total lack of experience in diplomatic affairs.

Some in South Vietnam continued to feel that they should be prepared to cope with an air threat from up north, whether North Vietnamese or Chinese. On 26 June 1964 three F-102 interceptors were deployed to Da Nang for 10 days under the program name 'Candy Machine'.

The ostensible cause of the air war against North Vietnam was the 'Gulf of Tonkin incident', an attack by North Vietnamese P-4

Left: Silvery F-100 Super Sabres – a two-seat F-100F is seen in the foreground – began operations with temporary-duty stints at Don Muang and Takhli in Thailand and Da Nang in South Vietnam. Four wings of F-100s were eventually to fight in Vietnam.

Below: Carrying a non-standard strike camera on the centerline behind its extended dive brake on a combat mission in the Mekong Delta, this F-100D (56-3097) also displays a stateside Tactical Air Command badge. F-100s arrived in large numbers in 1964-65.

# Skyraider Pilots

*Into action with the 'Spad'*

The A-1 Skyraider was perhaps the most numerous warplane in South Vietnam at the time, being operated by the VNAF's 514th, 516th and 518th Fighter Squadrons and by the USAF's First Air Commando Squadron. Armorers at Bien Hoa realized that the A-1 or 'Maytag Washing Machine', as someone christened the aircraft, had carried numerous varieties of underwing ordnance over the years. Each time a new bomb or rocket was introduced, the Skyraider was rewired to carry it. One crew chief remembered finding some of the aircraft with up to 500-lb (227-kg) of wire inside the wings. "Nobody could remember which wires were connected to what. So we had no way to remove the excess, and our pilots paid a penalty in extra flying weight."

Communications were poor. Faulty bomb fuses caused a premature mid-air detonation of 500-pounders which killed a

*By 1964, the inside of Skyraider wings had been rewired so many times, no accurate record existed to cover every item of ordnance they could carry. Here, USAF Air Commandos 'bomb up' an A-1 Skyraider at Bien Hoa.*

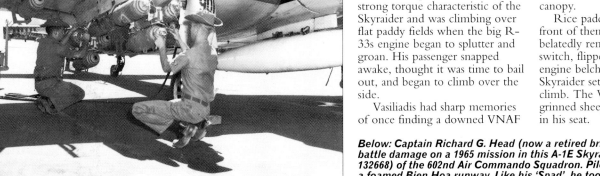

squadron pilot near Rach-Gia in the Mekong Delta. The old 20-mm cannon on the Skyraider were so worn out that they sometimes exploded and threw shrapnel in all directions, on one occasion narrowly missing a pilot's head.

## Wide-body 'Spad'

Major Charles Vasiliadis, known as 'Vas' for short, arrived at Bien Hoa in November 1964 to join the First Air Commando Squadron, and racked up the first of no fewer than 493 combat missions in the A-1E, the 'wide-body' version of the Skyraider, or 'Spad' as it was now being called. One day, leading a flight while using the callsign 'Norm 61', Vas bombed a Viet Cong tunnel complex in a densely wooded area 8 miles (13 km) west of the Ben Cat US Special Forces camp.

*Above: A-1E Skyraiders loaded with cluster-bomb munitions prepare for take-off from Saigon's Tan Son Nhut airfield in 1965. US Air Force pilots abruptly found themselves using and praising an obsolete warplane that had served first in the Navy.*

*Right: The Skyraider might have been a leaky old bucket of bolts, but pilots like this could use its flexible weapons load and long endurance to loiter for long periods over a battlefield, delivering ordnance with pinpoint accuracy repeatedly.*

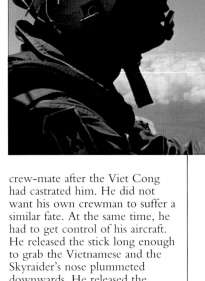

A few days later he was carrying 500-pounders (227-kg bombs) against a VC-occupied village a mere 20 miles (32 km) north-west of Bien Hoa.

## Engine out

On this mission, Vas forgot to throw a switch to change from the Skyraider's external fuel tank to internal fuel. Pulling away from a bomb run, his requisite Vietnamese passenger sound asleep beside him, Vas applied full rudder to cope with the very strong torque characteristic of the Skyraider and was climbing over flat paddy fields when the big R-33s engine began to splutter and groan. His passenger snapped awake, thought it was time to bail out, and began to climb over the side.

Vasiliadis had sharp memories of once finding a downed VNAF

crew-mate after the Viet Cong had castrated him. He did not want his own crewman to suffer a similar fate. At the same time, he had to get control of his aircraft. He released the stick long enough to grab the Vietnamese and the Skyraider's nose plummeted downwards. He released the Vietnamese long enough to grab the stick and the man tried to bail out again. "No, no, no!" Vas shrieked above the spluttering of the engine and the roar of the airstream blasting into the open canopy.

Rice paddies spun crazily in front of them as Vasiliadis belatedly remembered the fuel switch, flipped it, and felt the engine belch back to life. The Skyraider settled into a gentle climb. The Vietnamese nodded, grinned sheepishly, and sat back in his seat.

*Below: Captain Richard G. Head (now a retired brigadier general) took battle damage on a 1965 mission in this A-1E Skyraider (bureau no. 132668) of the 602nd Air Commando Squadron. Pilot Head bellied-in on a foamed Bien Hoa runway. Like his 'Spad', he took little damage.*

torpedo boats against the destroyer USS *Maddox* (DD-731) on 2 August 1964. Overlooked at the time was the fact that *Maddox*, although in international waters, was carrying out a 'Desoto Patrol' gathering communications intelligence from Hanoi's military radio nets. The torpedo boats are widely understood to have returned on the night of 4 August when *Maddox* was accompanied by USS *Turner Joy* (DD-951) and a furious sea battle raged for hours.

Commander James B. Stockdale, skipper of the 'Screaming Eagles' of fighter squadron VF-51 aboard the carrier USS *Ticonderoga* (CVA-14) was overhead in an F-8E Crusader during the second incident. Stockdale's efforts to acquire a radar vector on the torpedo boats were in vain. The messages he received from the destroyers were frantic and confusing.

Stockdale is certain that, on the second occasion, the North Vietnamese boats were a figment of the Americans' imagination. He followed voice instructions from the destroyers, only to find the sea empty where the boats were supposed to be. Nor was there any damage to the destroyers to confirm their attackers' existence. Still, *Ticonderoga* Crusaders plus one A-4 Skyhawk remained overhead until relieved by more Skyhawks from USS *Constellation* (CVA-64) near midnight. At the time, two torpedo boats, the same boats found non-existent by Stockdale, were reported sunk.

## Tonkin Gulf retaliation

It was scarcely noticed that the American destroyers had been on an intelligence gathering mission perceived by Hanoi as provocative. It mattered very little that only the first of the two torpedo boat attacks was real. The North Vietnamese attack on the destroyers enabled President Johnson to secure Congress's 7 August passage of the Gulf of Tonkin resolution – a rubber stamp of his decision to carry the war to the North. In the short run, the attack on US vessels on the high seas led Johnson to retaliate. *Ticonderoga* and *Constellation* were ordered to mount strikes against torpedo boat bases, POL facilities and other targets.

Johnson announced the strikes before the carriers had all of their aircraft aloft. Secretary of Defense Robert S. McNamara identified the targets while the strikes were *en route*. The carriers were about 400 miles (643 km) from their targets and, whether or not McNamara inadvertently helped them, the North Vietnamese defenses were ready.

Carrier air wing CVW-5 on *Ticonderoga* launched 34 aircraft including 16 F-8E Crusaders of VF-51 and VF-53 led by Stockdale. Six of the Crusaders attacked torpedo boats at Quang Khe, 60-miles

*P-4 torpedo boats of the North Vietnamese navy challenged patrolling US destroyers on the night of 2 August 1964, but a second attack claimed by the Pentagon two days later probably never occurred. President Johnson cited the provocation as his reason for widening the conflict.*

(96-km) north of the 17th Parallel, using Zuni rockets and 20-mm cannon fire to destroy eight P-4 boats and damage 21. Stockdale's force, which included A-4C Skyhawks of VA-55 and VA-56 accompanied by A-1 Skyraiders, assaulted the POL facilities at Vinh. The *Constellation* strike force included F-4B Phantoms of fighter squadrons VF-142 and VF-143 flying top cover.

The strikes left plumes of smoke rising thousands of feet into the sky. Clearly, they inflicted damage. But there was a price. AAA (anti-aircraft artillery) damage forced one Crusader to divert to Da Nang, the airfield in South Vietnam closest to the demarcation line which would, in time, become the customary refuge for aircraft suffering battle damage over the North. One A-1 Skyraider (139760) from VA-145 on *Constellation* was shot down and its pilot killed. One Connie A-4C Skyhawk (149578) belonging to VA-144

*The Gulf of Tonkin air strikes occurred just as the carrier USS Constellation (CVA-64) came on station. Connie's air wing included two squadrons equipped with a new fighter, the F-4B Phantom.*

# RF-101Cs in Combat

## RF-101C

The long-nosed, stub-winged RF-101C Voodoo was the first combat aircraft to see duty in Southeast Asia as part of an operational unit. Beginning with a 1961 temporary-duty stint, the Voodoo did a superb job of photographing the Pathet Lao and Viet Cong, giving US officers a priceless look at their adversary.

**Swept-wing superstar**
With its 69-ft 3-in (21.1-m) fuselage mated to a short 39-ft 8-in (12.09-m) wing, the Voodoo moved through the sky faster than a bullet. In fact, over Hanoi, Voodoos logged the fastest combat missions ever flown.

**'Hard to handle' aloft**
The Voodoo's wide-track landing gear made it easy to taxi, but the forgiving ground-handling of the RF-101C was its only blessing. In the air, the Voodoo was difficult to handle and prone to pitch-up problems. Pilots who mastered it were at ease with other aircraft.

**'Polka Dots'**
RF-101C Voodoo 56-0166 wears standard T.O. 1-1-4 camouflage and the white AH tail code assigned to the 45th TRS, part of the 460th TRW, at Tan Son Nhut. The squadron flew RF-51D Mustangs in the Korean War, adorning them with the same white dots against a blue field which now appear on the fin of this Voodoo and which gave the squadron its nickname.

**'Big jet' power**
The RF-101C was heavy at 48,720 lb (22 099 kg) gross weight. A pair of Pratt & Whitney J57-P-13 turbojets gave it more than enough muscle – 14,880-lb (6750-kg) thrust with afterburner.

Though no US aircraft were yet officially flying in combat, the 'Able Mabel' commitment to carry out reconnaissance missions over South Vietnam and Laos had resulted in six McDonnell RF-101C Voodoos being detached to Saigon's Tan Son Nhut Airport.

The Voodoos were maintaining a rigorous flight schedule of up to 35 hours a month, a heavy strain for the men of the 45th Tactical Reconnaissance Squadron, placed temporarily under the USAF's headquarters in Saigon, the 2nd Air Division. On 30 April 1964, this hard-pressed reconnaissance force was increased to 10 RF-101Cs. Though North Vietnam was 'off limits' for the Voodoos, part of their mission was to acquire photography of infiltration routes from North Vietnam. They shared this job with US Navy RF-8A Crusaders, one of which was shot down over Laos on 6 June. The subsequent loss of another Crusader acting as armed escort for a Laotian reconnaissance flight led on 8 June to a retaliatory strike by eight USAF F-100 Super Sabres against anti-aircraft sites at Xien Khouang, Laos. Reconnaissance pilots were now seeing large numbers of truck convoys moving down the Ho Chi Minh Trail – evidence of a massive increase in North Vietnamese support for the Viet Cong.

*Left: No-one ever claimed it was pretty but the RF-101C was a triumph of function over fashion. The elongated nose offered a voluminous repository for a wide variety of aerial cameras, film and instruments.*

*An F-105D Thunderchief (62-4370) replete with nose 'buzz number' and natural metal finish, leaves Yokota en route to Thailand in 1964. The 67th TFS 'Fighting Cocks' and other Thunderchief squadrons began to arrive in Southeast Asia at the end of the year as a wider war loomed.*

was also downed and its pilot, Lieutenant Everett J. Alvarez, captured. Alvarez, the first POW (prisoner of war) held in North Vietnam, would be a prisoner for eight years and seven months.

The Gulf of Tonkin raids were soundly condemned by Hanoi and its allies. Hanoi took the position that it was merely giving fraternal support to an uprising in South Vietnam which was, in fact, a local uprising. Washington insisted that the war in the South was caused by infiltration from the North. The truth lay somewhere in between and at this juncture the Communist forces in the South, who called themselves the National Liberation Front (NLF) but were called Viet Cong by everyone else, really were to a large extent controlled by leaders with local ties. Over time, Hanoi would expand its control over the Viet Cong so that in effect, by attacking North Vietnam, the US created the very aggression from the North which it cited as a reason for attacking North Vietnam. Furthermore, it took on a new enemy. North Vietnam had its own regular forces, formidable and distinct from the insurgents in the South, and immediately after the Gulf of Tonkin raids, a small number of MiG-17 fighters were brought into North Vietnam from the Soviet Union – the beginning of what would become a powerful air force.

In the South, on 5 August 1964, B-57 Canberra light bombers

*The 31 October 1964 Viet Cong attack on Bien Hoa killed four Americans and left shattered, burned-out B-57 Canberra bombers from one end of the airfield to the other. Remarkably, Washington did not use this particular event for a pretext for immediate retaliation – although later, similar VC attacks provoked the sustained bombing of North Vietnam.*

were brought in to Bien Hoa and F-100 Super Sabres deployed to Da Nang. In addition, F-105 Thunderchiefs were sent to neighboring Thailand.

Although the US Air Force did not participate in the Gulf of Tonkin raids, the incident reversed a long trend towards reduction of the men and aircraft equipping the USAF's Pacific Air Forces (PACAF). Project 'Clear Water', a long-term program to trim PACAF's fighting strength throughout the region from Hawaii to Southeast Asia, was reversed when the Gulf of Tonkin incident resulted in an accelerated build-up of men and aircraft.

On 5 August, B-57s from Clark Field, Philippines, deployed to Bien Hoa AB, South Vietnam. The first combat employment of the Republic F-105D Thunderchief – the 'Thud' – took place on 14 August after 18 F-105Ds of the 36th TFS from Yokota AB, Japan deployed to Korat RTAFB, Thailand. Accompanying this build-up from stateside Tactical Air Command (TAC) assets were three further tactical fighter squadrons, two troop-carrier squadrons and six reconnaissance aircraft.

About 70 USAF aircraft were rushed to Southeast Asia in the first phase of this build-up. Composite Strike Force 'One Buck', including six RF-101C Voodoos from Shaw AFB, SC, was sent to reinforce the 'Able Mabel' reconnaissance force at Tan Son Nhut. By now, some 15 RF-101Cs were operating over Laos and South Vietnam – but had not yet been sent North.

## Carriers on station

The US now began to maintain a fleet presence off the Vietnamese coast. *Ticonderoga* and *Constellation* had been on station during the Gulf of Tonkin incident and had been able to carry out the *ad hoc* air strikes independently, making it unnecessary to rely upon additional forces or upon the permission of another country for airbase or overflight rights. To be certain that naval forces remained ready if further strikes were needed, the carriers *Ranger* (CVA-61) and *Kearsarge* (CVS-33) were assigned to steam toward the Gulf of Tonkin, *Ranger* to provide additional capability and the ASW (anti-submarine warfare), *Kearsarge* to guard against possible Chinese submarine activity. It was not the last time the US would think of the Chinese as an enemy in this struggle, although the truth was that Hanoi was far more closely allied with Moscow than with Peking.

This coincided with the movement of several Air Force units into South Vietnam. In the event there was no immediate call for naval forces. Many believed that the Viet Cong threat remained a less serious matter than the internal struggle and bickering within the government of the South.

In another of the seemingly endless changes in the Saigon regime, on 26 October the former mayor of the capital, Tran Van Huong, was installed as premier of a provisional civil government. Huong was to prove unable to bring order to his administration or to be right about significant victories over the Viet Cong.

The growing US presence now included no fewer than 47 B-57 Canberra light bombers of the 13th Bomb Squadron under Lt Col Billy A. McLeod and the 8th TBS under Lt Col Frederick W. Grindle, Jr, moved from Clark Field in the Philippines to Bien Hoa airfield about 10 miles (16 km) north of Saigon. The B-57 commitment at Bien Hoa, more formally called 405th ADVON 1, was an unpopular TDY (temporary duty) posting for airmen who'd been deployed to 'show the flag' but who were still constrained from participating in actual combat. As it turned out, their presence posed a tempting target for the Viet Cong.

On the bloody Hallowe'en night of 31 October/1 November 1964, the Viet Cong staged a mortar attack on Bien Hoa. In a hellish scene of fiery explosions and carnage, four Americans were killed and 30 wounded. No fewer than five B-57Bs (53-3892, 53-3924,

52-1555, 53-3914 and 53-3894) were destroyed along with an HH-43B helicopter, and 13 more bombers were badly damaged.

## Johnson wins election

On the first Tuesday in November, Lyndon Johnson defeated Barry Goldwater at the polls and was elected for a four-year term of office. Johnson would be eligible to run for a second four-year term in 1968 and it was widely assumed that he would do so. He had promised Americans a 'Great Society', built with government aid to broad sectors of the economy. He had also convinced many that Goldwater – a Reserve general in the USAF and a military pilot – would have solved the Vietnam problem by launching a bombing campaign against North Vietnam. While there were few direct quotes on the question, most voters believed Johnson would not do such a thing.

December saw the first overseas deployment of the USAF's F-4C Phantom fighter – the Navy F-4B had reached the Gulf of Tonkin aboard the USS *Constellation* earlier in the year – when the 'Triple Nickel' 555th Tactical Fighter Squadron arrived at Okinawa and prepared for a temporary deployment to Thailand. Within weeks F-4s were in South Vietnam at Da Nang and Cam Ranh Bay.

Nobody ever claimed that the Brink Hotel in Saigon was any great shakes. Even so, the old colonial-style building had been taken

*The F-105D in the foreground wears the camouflage which was soon to become standard for the US Air Force in Southeast Asia. The F-4C Phantom in the background (a future MiG killer) wears the two-tone, gull-gray and white scheme in which it was originally delivered.*

# The Stratotanker Arrives

**W**ith American airpower becoming more deeply involved in Southeast Asia and the possibility of bombing North Vietnam being actively debated, it was apparent that a combat air refueling capability would be needed. A few, little-publicized refuelings had occurred during the 1950-3 Korean War but against North Vietnam, the KC-135 Stratotanker, fuel-carrying cousin of the Boeing 707, would become an ubiquitous and routine sight. On 7 June 1964, the Pentagon's Joint Chiefs of Staff (JCS) ordered the Strategic Air Command (SAC) to move six KC-135s from Andersen AB, Guam, to Clark AB, Philippines, to refuel F-100D strike aircraft operating in Laos. SAC retained control over its tankers throughout the conflict, never surrendering jurisdiction to the 2nd Air Division (later Seventh Air Force) in Saigon.

The KC-135s flew their first combat refueling mission over southern Laos on 9 June 1964 as part of the 'Yankee Team Tanker Task Force', the name being derived from reconnaissance operations then being conducted over Laos. Later, the KC-135 force would be known as 'Young Tiger' and SAC's 4,252nd Strategic Wing under Brigadier General Morgan S. Tyler, Jr, would despatch 15 tankers to operate from Thailand's Don Muang airfield, which was also the Bangkok international airport. General Tyler was a hard-driving taskmaster who believed that in-flight refueling could be effective in actual combat operations and who seemed to have clairvoyant knowledge that just such operations would be mounted from Thailand against the North Vietnamese homeland. What he could not know was that between 1964 and 1973, SAC KC-135s would be called on to fly 194,687 combat sorties and achieve no fewer than 813,878 individual mid-air refuelings.

*A KC-135 Stratotanker hangs out its 'flying boom' on a 1964 sortie in Southeast Asia. Although most tanking sorties were in support of tactical aircraft, Strategic Air Command retained 'opcon' (operational control) of all Air Force tankers in the combat zone.*

*The sight of a refueling boom extended from a KC-135 tanker was to become one of the most ubiquitous images of the war. Tankers became a vital resource when the war moved North. This F-100 Super Sabre, a mature veteran of the 'Century series' of fighters, is hooking up.*

On the afternoon of 24 December 1964, tinsel hung from the ceiling in the dining area and a plastic Christmas tree was alight in a corner. As Army advisors prepared to celebrate Christmas Eve, a Viet Cong sapper on a bicycle hurled a 250-lb (113-kg) plastique (explosive charge) into the place and the Brink Hotel exploded, throwing flames and debris out into the street and collapsing upon itself. Two Americans and 51 South Vietnamese were killed.

Unknown then, of course, was the fact that Ambassador Maxwell Taylor had urged that there be swift and powerful retaliation against North Vietnam for any such VC provocation. Taylor had been consulting in Washington during the week of 27 November 1964, and found himself caught between policymakers who wanted to withdraw and those who wanted to retaliate. He had suggested a compromise under which the US would strike back for specific VC provocations, but only with South Vietnamese participation to preserve the 'native' character of the war. That did not happen this time, however. The latest South Vietnamese government under General Nguyen Khanh was in turmoil, seeking to cope with protests by Buddhist agitators, and was in no condition to participate in a credible joint response. The Brink Hotel bombing came and went.

A week later, in a furious action at Binh Gia, VC troops overwhelmed an ARVN force and killed 177 South Vietnamese soldiers and six Americans. Unlike the Saigon hotel bombing, it scarcely made the newspapers. At Binh Gia a Special Forces advisor sat in the grass looking at burned out huts and destruction. He inserted a blade of grass between his teeth, turned to a buddy, and shrugged. "When the hell are we going to be able to hit these bastards back, anyway?"

On 31 December 1964 the number of American troops in South Vietnam was 23,000.

over as a US Army officers' billet and was replete with all the little pleasures Americans always needed to fight a war, including a shoeshine stand, a small PX selling nylons, make-up and cosmetics to our all-male force, and a dining area nicknamed 'the Pit'. Prices being low everywhere, most of the men preferred to eat up the street where several joints offered hamburgers and other amenities.

# Enter the F-4C Phantom II

The US Navy's F-4B Phantom had been introduced to battle during the Gulf of Tonkin raids, although it had only a peripheral role. The US Air Force's F-4C Phantom was introduced to the western Pacific, and moved closer to the combat zone, when a Tactical Air Command rotational squadron, the 555th TFS, arrived at Naha AB, Okinawa in December 1964 to replace an F-102A Delta Dagger unit. The 'Triple Nickel' squadron would be heard from again. So would the Phantom and within a few months, a second F-4C squadron, the 45th TFS, had taken up temporary station at Ubon, Thailand. This would become the first unit to claim North Vietnamese MiGs.

The Phantom had first flown as the F4H-1 on 27 May 1958. Following lengthy delays in its own TFX (tactical fighter, experimental) program, the USAF reluctantly adopted the Navy design. For years, the Phantom would be seen as the best multi-

role fighter and strike aircraft in service, the standard against which all others would be measured. Powered by twin 16,150-lb (7324-kg) thrust General Electric J79 engines (which emitted telltale smoke, making the Phantom an easy target), the F-4C would eventually join and one day replace the F-105s in carrying the war to Hanoi.

For the moment, however, airmen discovered that the world's best fighter was far from perfect. The Phantom's AIM-7 Sparrow radar-homing missiles had a high rate of malfunction. Some F-4Cs sprang wing tank leaks that had to be resealed after each flight and 85 of them developed cracked ribs on outer wing panels. The Phantom's UHF (ultra-high frequency) radio was located under the rear ejection seat, which had to be removed at the cost of two hours' time even for minor repair.

No-one ever said the Phantom was easy to fly, and in the Air Force, the F-4C was crewed by two full-fledged pilots. Notwithstanding all of the

problems, the F4C Phantom was the finest fighter in USAF inventory and would remain so for many years. The men of the 45th TFS at Ubon were soon to be blooded in it.

*Carrying a strike camera beneath the two M117 bombs on its left inboard pylon, this F-4C Phantom (63-7656) is gassing up from a tanker on an early mission into North Vietnam. Note the open fuel receptacle behind the crew.*

For some time the USAF had been experimenting with the notion that a large fixed-wing aeroplane flying in a pylon turn could bring side-mounted guns to bear on a ground target with great intensity. Although there were doubters, among them Tactical Air Command's General Walter C. Sweeney, Jr, who felt that a gunship could not survive the gunfire expected in Vietnam and fulfill its mission, Air Force General John P. McConnell was impressed by stateside test results with a Convair C-131 and Douglas C-47. McConnell noted in particular that a gunship might be effective in defending hamlets and outposts under night attack. He was determined to test the idea under live fire.

On 2 December 1964 a test team headed by Captain Ronald W. Terry arrived at Bien Hoa airfield not far from Saigon and were quickly followed by gun kits, gunsights, and ammunition to convert two C-47s. Terry

began a series of test flights, some of them over water, to teach C-47 pilots how to acquire a target, roll in on it, and commence the turn.

The ancient 'Gooney Bird' now had a 'fighter' version, as the aircraft was originally designated FC-47. The aircraft flew the first of several day combat missions on 15 December 1964. Captain Terry and crew worked with a forward air controller (FAC), firing successfully on Viet Cong sampans, buildings, trails and suspected jungle staging areas.

From the beginning the FC-47 had been seen as a night weapon – one of a number of ways the US sought to take command of the night from 'Victor Charlie', or the Viet Cong – and was capable of dropping flares while

*An AC-47 of the 4th Special Operations Squadron sets off on a mission. Gunship developments gave the normally unthreatening Douglas veteran a new and highly lethal combat role, ideal for a counter-insurgency warfare.*

orbiting overhead to relieve a besieged encampment.

The FC-47's first night mission on 23-24 December 1964 seemed to prove that this new role for the 'Gooney Bird' could blunt the ever-increasing night attacks on South Vietnamese outposts. Once again, the gunship 'Gooney Bird' showed itself to be very effective

*A gunship's view of a night engagement reveals streams of tracer being pumped out by the AC-47's side-firing guns curling down through the night.*

in hosing down formations of enemy troops. In due course the aircraft was to be redesignated AC-47 and known to many as 'Puff the Magic Dragon'.

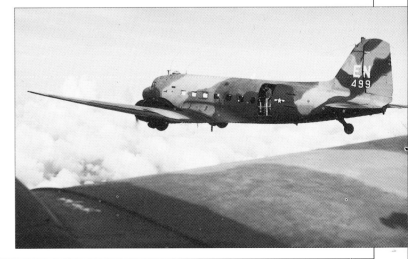

# YEAR OF BUILD-UP

**It was the single event that most altered the perceptions of Americans – those on the scene, and those at home – about what was happening in Vietnam. On 10 April 1965 two battalions of United States Marines landed, the first American combat troops in the war zone.**

Before the Marine landing, those first weeks of 1965 were unique. It was the last time Vietnam was far down on the list of topics which concerned most Americans. Other events at the time captured more attention. Congressmen Jerry Ford launched a successful attempt to replace Charles A. Halleck as the House Minority Leader. Egypt's fiery Gamal Abdul Nasser spouted off against the US and one of his MiGs shot down an unarmed cargo plane belonging to a US oil company.

When Robert F. Kennedy was sworn in on 4 January to serve in the same chamber as Edward M. Kennedy, it marked the first time brothers had served in the United States Senate in 162 years. In London the absence of Vice-President Hubert H. Humphrey from the 31 March funeral of Sir Winston Churchill was viewed by many Britons as an affront. In New York city Mayor Robert F. Wagner was being sorely criticized because his city was said to have reached an intolerable state with its strikes, slums, crime, traffic snarls and racial tensions. Vietnam? At the outset of 1965 a black person was still called a Negro, and sometimes worse, and the struggle for racial integration received more headlines than the storming ashore at Da Nang of United States Marines.

## The Marines arrive

In March, during the feverish post-monsoon weather, 3,500 Marines had put to sea aboard the vessels *Mount McKinley*, *Henrico*, *Union* and *Vancouver*. These four ships of Amphibious Task Force 76 took six weeks to reach the Vietnam coast and spent the last few days pitching up and down in vile seas.

The Marines could have arrived by stepping off a commercial

*The A-4 Skyhawk was the US Navy's standard, carrier-based light-attack aircraft as the situation heated up in Vietnam in 1965. The lightweight single-seater had been designed for a nuclear mission. It proved versatile and highly survivable, but its range was inadequate.*

# Marines Land

If a single event altered American perceptions of what was happening in Vietnam, it was the landing of two battalions of US Marines at Da Nang on 10 April 1965. Marine fighter squadron VMFA-531, the 'Gray Ghosts', under Lt Col William C. McGraw, Jr, arrived with its F-4B Phantoms at Da Nang on the same date. The squadron's exec, Major Orie E. Cory, stepped out into the parched tropical heat and promptly labelled the place a 'shithole'. The build-up of airpower was continuing and Marine squadrons VMFA-115 and VMFA-323 were soon to follow. Though the Marine Corps Phantoms and Skyhawks were used primarily for close support missions in the South, they would also perform many thankless combat missions in the Route Package One area just above the DMZ.

That same day, the first EF-10B Skyknight arrived to join Marine composite squadron VMCJ-1 at Da Nang. Pilot

*'Drut' – another word spelled backward – was the feisty nickname for the EF-10B Skyknight, which went to Vietnam to gather intelligence for Marine squadron VMCJ-1.*

Lieutenant Frank Littlebury reported that he felt extremely safe inside the EF-10B, which was sturdy and tough. More than 20 years old, with high airframe hours and limited life, the EF-10B initially provided the sole electronic warfare capability for Air Force and Navy missions over the North. Variously nicknamed the 'Whale' or the 'Drut' (the latter term being best appreciated if spelled backwards), the EF-10B escorted the first anti-SAM attacks, which came to be known as 'Iron Hand' missions.

*The 'Gray Ghosts' of VMFA-531 came to Da Nang with F-4B Phantoms in February 1965. The USAF's 531st TFS with F-100s ended a temporary stint days earlier, averting a situation where two squadrons served at the same base with the same number.*

jetliner, as other US servicemen did. Instead, they waded out of the sea, M-14 rifles at the ready, field packs and pit shovels clanking – the same way that they had landed on Tarawa, Saipan and Iwo Jima. Exhausted, muggy, seasick, Major General Frederick J. Karch's Marines made a full-fledged landing, assaulting an empty beach. There were Viet Cong in the area – an entire regiment were to confront the Marines soon – but at the time of landing there was no enemy ready to fight.

To PFC James L. Waple, the worst thing about it was being seasick and retching all over the inside of the LST [landing ship, tank] that took them from Okinawa to Da Nang. "They decided to put us ashore Hollywood-style, on the beach near Da Nang. Unfortunately, there was no enemy entrenched on the beach so we got wet for nothing. We came ashore drenched with salt water and were greeted by a few Marines, who were mostly curious, and a couple of children with flowers."

Other Marines grumbled about getting wet while carrying the 100 pounds (44 kg) of gear a Marine needed to live. The Da Nang

area and the Chu Lai peninsula were hot and dry in April, but the Marines stepped on to solid ground soaking wet.

It was the end of a small and distant guerrilla war which had seemed romantic and a little dangerous but not very important. The sight of regular Marines storming ashore was played across TV screens in America and no-one believed – nor should they have – the official explanation. The official story was that Marines were in Vietnam solely to protect American airfields. In fact, they were going into combat. Although the fiction of an air base defense role was to be maintained stalwartly, the truth was that Americans were advisors no longer.

Looking back at 1965 (and at events which preceded the Marines' arrival), it hardly seems possible that the year began with US troop strength in South Vietnam at a mere 23,000.

## Opposition to war

There remained an innocence, and a vulnerability, about Americans, who had not been involved in a large-scale shooting war since the end of the Korean struggle 12 years earlier. In 1964, few noticed a student upheaval called the Free Speech Movement at the University of California at Berkeley, but it was the first major campus demonstration in the United States and the first of hundreds of protests that would follow when it became clear that once again Americans were going to fight and die in a remote corner of Asia.

Lyndon Johnson, inaugurated for a new term on 20 January 1965, followed up his election victory by appointing an inter-agency working group to examine all alternatives available to him in Vietnam. Such groups rarely arrived at unpopular conclusions but Johnson's lieutenants did report that the latest Saigon regime headed by Major General Nguyen Khanh was tottering, that the Communists were pouring men and materiel into South Vietnam, and that the very survival of a valued American ally was in danger.

Dissatisfaction with General Khanh's regime in Saigon led to street demonstrations and violence throughout South Vietnam,

*The build-up gathers steam. A citizen army of young soldiers, about two-thirds of them drafted, began funneling its best and brightest into Saigon in growing numbers in 1965. Gen. Westmoreland is on hand to greet this G.I. For the next three years, the MAC-V commander was to repeatedly ask for larger numbers of troops.*

# 'Flaming Dart'

*The F-8 Crusader was a key player in the 'Flaming Dart' effort and in subsequent 'Rolling Thunder' combat missions against North Vietnam. The Crusader routinely operated from modernized World War II-vintage Essex-class carriers which were too small to handle the F-4 Phantom.*

*The catapult officer on **USS Ranger (CVA-61)** is making the final signal while the carrier's powerful steam catapult is ramming its way home to send this A-4E Skyhawk toward North Vietnam on 27 March 1965.*

some of it caused by the Viet Cong. The United States sent a team of officials headed by presidential security advisor McGeorge Bundy to observe the situation and make recommendations.

Returning from his visit on 6 February 1965, Bundy drafted a memo for President Johnson urging a policy of 'sustained reprisal' against the North. Bundy put forth a widely-held view that the war in South Vietnam was being lost and could be turned around only through aerial retaliation against Hanoi. "The situation in South Vietnam is deteriorating and without new US action, defeat appears inevitable...."

Bundy's memo was written hours before a Viet Cong attack on US military advisors at Pleiku which killed nine and wounded 76 – an attack which led US officials in Saigon to seek Acting Prime Minister Nguyen Xuan Oanh's concurrence in a bombing campaign against the North. Bundy recommended "the development and execution of a policy of sustained reprisal against North Vietnam – a policy in which air and naval action against the North is justified by and related to the whole Viet Cong campaign of violence and terror in the South."

## Reprisal strikes

He was still not seeking a sustained aerial campaign against the North but, rather, a policy of conducting air strikes specifically in reprisal against Viet Cong actions. "We might retaliate against a grenade thrown into a crowded café in Saigon but not necessarily to a shot fired into a small shop in the countryside." Bundy added, however, that "an 'air war' may, in fact be necessary...".

How necessary would remain debatable, but on 7 February, President Johnson ordered all dependents of US personnel out of Saigon. Many departed on Pan American flights for San Francisco.

At this worst possible juncture, *US News & World Report* revealed that the new US Ambassador, Maxwell Taylor, had gotten off on the wrong foot with Khanh and even worse with Khanh's powerful wife. *Life* magazine said that Johnson's first priority was "to come to grips with the badly deteriorating situation in South Vietnam". Critics warned Johnson against a bigger investment of blood and treasure, pointing out that the South Vietnamese often lacked the will to fight and that no number of Americans, not even 10 times those now in country, could prop up a corrupt regime and faltering

army. Johnson's decision, it seemed, was clear: he should withdraw US forces and waste no men or weaponry in a faraway land that few Americans could find on the map.

Ironically, 10 times 23,000 was less than half of the eventual American commitment. Even in early 1965, Saigon-based General Westmoreland was saying that he needed more US troops. It was the beginning of a prolonged period in which the general would repeatedly increase his estimate of the number of men he required.

To be fair, Westmoreland was repeatedly provoked by a determined and relentless enemy. For years Pentagon officers had told anyone willing to listen that the US could fight effectively only by carrying the war to North Vietnam.

Johnson authorized the first sustained air strikes against North Vietnam, known initially as 'Flaming Dart'. By 7 March 1965 this had evolved into the ongoing campaign of air strikes against North Vietnam known as 'Rolling Thunder', destined to last more than three years with intermittent breaks aimed unsuccessfully at prompting negotiations.

*The early bombing campaign against the North involved aircraft like the F-100 Super Sabre and the B-57 Canberra. These were not really suitable for long-range operations over high-threat areas, and were soon replaced by faster, more powerful aircraft like the F-105 Thunderchief.*

In response to the killing of Americans at Pleiku, President Johnson authorized a retaliatory air strike against the military barracks and staging area at Dong Hoi, just above the 17th Parallel in North Vietnam. The mission was given the evocative name 'Flaming Dart I'. A very unusual twist, with virtually no military effectiveness but much policy import, was the participation of the South Vietnamese Air Force, its A-1H Skyraiders led by the flamboyant chief of staff, General Nguyen Cao Ky.

The brunt of the strike was borne by 49 aircraft from USS *Coral Sea* (CVA-43) and USS *Hancock* (CVA-19), attacking Dong Hoi, plus 34 aircraft from USS *Ranger* (CVA-61) which ranged inland to the barracks at Vit Thu Lu. Ranger's aircraft, confronting inclement weather, were ineffective but the Dong Hoi strike drew enormous secondary explosions and razed buildings. One A-4E Skyhawk

(150075) of attack squadron VA-156 from *Coral Sea* was hit by ground fire. Lieutenant E. A. Dickson limped out to sea in the burning Skyhawk and ejected but was not rescued. The loss of a pilot marred the mood of his squadron mates who wondered now if they had merely escalated into another round of enemy provocation followed by retaliation.

## Reprisal raid

On 10 February, the Viet Cong blew up a hotel being used as a billet for American soldiers at Qui Nhon, killing 23 men. It was still not generally acknowledged that American GIs were in combat but the incident made inevitable another retaliatory strike against North Vietnam. On 11 February, *Coral Sea*, *Hancock* and *Ranger* mounted strikes at a military logistics complex north of the DMZ. This was the mission known as 'Flaming Dart II'. Operating in foul weather, the strike force of 99 aircraft had

limited success bombing the Chanh Hoa installation.

An A-4C Skyhawk (49572) of squadron VA-153 on *Coral Sea* was hit by Triple-A (anti-aircraft artillery, or AAA) but the pilot coaxed his aircraft out to sea, ejected and was rescued. Less lucky was the pilot of an F-8D Crusader (148633) of VF-32 on the same ship, who was shot down and became a POW. At a very early juncture, US naval aviators now knew of the difficulties posed by the north-east monsoon and of the potency of

*A-4E Skyhawk (bureau no. 152017) of VA-144 'Roadrunners' releases a Mark 84 2,000-lb (907-kg) bomb on 11 March 1968. In 1965, Skyhawks were spearheading 'Alpha' strikes by carrier-based warplanes in the area around Haiphong.*

Hanoi's AAA defenses. Ironically, North Vietnam may not at this juncture have had any control over Viet Cong provocations, but Hanoi was determined to defend itself and was quietly asking for Soviet help, including advanced radar systems and surface-to-air missiles (SAMs).

The South Vietnamese Air Force had been growing slowly and, for a brief time, participated in air strikes up North, flying A-1 Skyraiders. In fact, on the first raid above the 17th Parallel, USAF Captain Al Bache, advising the VNAF's 514th Fighter Squadron, watched in awe as Air Marshal Nguyen Cao Ky led his Skyraiders to Vinh only to attack the wrong target. Ky was a popular and charismatic figure on the Saigon scene, not only in the Air Force but also in the volatile world of South Vietnamese politics. Originally a transport pilot who transitioned to the Skyraider, Ky has been described by men who flew with him as personally

extremely courageous, a superb leader but, at best, an average pilot.

On 5 April, an RF-8A Crusader reconnaissance aircraft returned to its carrier with the first photographic evidence that North Vietnam was constructing a surface-to-air missile network. As if being inadequately prepared for MiGs and for combat rescue were not discouraging enough, it would now be necessary to cope with

*Reports of Viet Cong activity near Bac Lieu resulted in this attack as an F-100 blast a suspect site alongside a canal with Napalm. The 'Hu' flew more in-country missions than any other aircraft, and was probably the most important 'mud mover' in the first six years of USAF operations.*

an entirely new kind of weapon – the SAM. The air war over North Vietnam was now under way in earnest.

In South Vietnam there was much debate about what to do next. It had long been evident that this war would never have traditional front lines or rear areas. One could get killed at Tan Son Nhut airport as easily as on combat patrol. Westmoreland and other commanders no longer liked British expert Robert Thompson's idea of establishing 'strategic hamlets' – this notion seemed to relinquish rural areas and nocturnal hours to the Viet Cong without a fight – but were hard put to come up with a better idea. American and ARVN troops had long been carrying out 'search and destroy' missions, but these seemed increasingly irrelevant as the size of ground battles grew. While Americans poured into the country and experts searched for a coherent strategy, airpower was used to hit the enemy in the North and South.

### Air-to-air kills

If the fluke encounter with Chinese MiGs is not counted, the first air-to-air kill of the war occurred on 17 June 1965 as the old carrier USS *Midway* (CVA-41) launched strikes against targets in North Vietnam. Barrier combat air patrol (BARCAP) cover was provided by F-4B Phantoms of the 'Freelancers' of VF-21. In an encounter with MiG-17s, the Phantom at the head of a division (151488), flown by Commander Louis Page and his backseat radar intercept officer (RIO) Lt John C. Smith, Jr, succeeded in downing a MiG with the Sparrow radar-guided missile. A second F-4B Phantom (152219) crewed Lt Jack E. D. Batson, Jr and his RIO, Lt Cdr Robert B. Doremus soon despatched a second MiG-17, evening the overall score in the air war at two kills for each side.

Naval aviators had long believed, as did their Air Force colleagues, that the Phantom was superior to the MiG-17 in almost every performance regime where a realistic fight could take place, although the absence of a gun on the American aircraft would continue to be frustrating, especially in the Navy which evaluated under-wing gun pods but never adopted them. Commander Page had enthusiastic remarks about the Sparrow missile, however, as it had enabled him to defeat the MiG in a head-on attack, where the latter could fight only when it closed to within gun range.

On 20 June 1965, a downright bizarre air engagement occurred in which ageing A-1H Skyraider propeller-driven aircraft from *Midway* were covering a rescue mission when two MiG-17s pounced on them. The bulky but slow Skyraiders kept turning inside the faster jets. After five minutes of sweat-drenching maneuver, Lt Clinton B. Johnson and Lt Charles Hartman closed in behind a MiG-17 and shot it down with 20-mm cannon fire, each receiving half credit for the kill. The surviving MiG went scurrying

*VF-21 'Freelancers' was the third US Navy squadron to fly the F-4B Phantom in the Vietnam conflict. Part of Air Wing 2, VF-21 began a combat cruise aboard USS Midway (CVA-41) on 6 March 1965, taking station in the war zone on the 22nd of that month.*

**W**ith the sole exception of the State Department's George Ball who favored negotiations, virtually everyone in the Johnson administration felt that the 'Flaming Dart' raids were a step in the right direction and many felt that they were not enough. Most supported McGeorge Bundy's recommendations and agreed with the views of State Department counsellor Walt Rostow, who advocated a gradual escalation of pressures on North Vietnam until the North Vietnamese decided that a Viet Cong victory was not worth the price. Thus, the policy of attacking North Vietnam only on a retaliatory basis was abandoned and 'Flaming Dart' operations gave way to the sustained air campaign known as 'Rolling Thunder'.

### Protracted campaign

It may be useful for the reader to think of the air war against North Vietnam as consisting of four distinct phases – the 'Rolling Thunder' campaign (1965-68), the 'bombing halt' (1968-72), the 'Linebacker' campaign (May-October 1972) and the final 'eleven-day war' known as 'Linebacker II' (17-29 December 1972).

'Rolling Thunder', as conceived and begun, had three objectives: to reduce infiltration, to boost South Vietnamese morale and to make it clear to Hanoi that continuation of the insurgency in the South would become increasingly expensive.

In Hanoi, however, 'Rolling Thunder' was seen as one more obstacle to overcome in a long struggle to remove foreign influence and unify a divided Vietnam under Vietnamese rule. Ho Chi Minh's followers had removed the Japanese and the French. Now, they would search for a way to withstand the American air assault. They would seek to make the war too expensive, not to Hanoi but to Washington.

### North determined

North Vietnam did not yet fully control the Viet Cong insurgency in the South – it was simplistic to believe that every attack viewed as a provocation, such as the killing of Americans at Pleiku, was ordered directly by Hanoi – but it was going to achieve such control. No official in the North Vietnamese leadership ever saw the American air strikes as evidence that it was time to succumb.

The first USAF participation

*The first American jet bomber to drop live ordnance in any conflict was a B-57B Canberra of the 13th Bomb Squadron flying from Bien Hoa on 19 February 1965. The last light bomber in USAF service, the Canberra won scant recognition but performed well.*

in 'Rolling Thunder' was on 2 March 1965, with B-57s, F-100Ds, and F-105Ds. Of the 150 aircraft available at Thai bases, 25 F-105Ds from the 12th TFS and 67th TFS (both part of the 18th TFW) accompanied B-57s to an ammunition depot at Xom Bong, about 35-miles (56-km) above the DMZ (demilitarized zone) and inflicted heavy damage.

### USAF losses

On this first raid, no fewer than five aircraft were lost to ground fire – two F-100D Super Sabres (55-2857, 56-3150) and three F-105Ds (61-214, 62-4260, 62-4325) and the first USAF pilot, Captain Hayden J. Lockhart, was taken prisoner. Already, illusions that bombing would quickly subdue North Vietnam required further examination.

From the beginning, critics of the sustained campaign against North Vietnam would argue that it didn't really roll and wasn't particularly thunderous. The planning of air strikes was a complex and unwieldy business that began in the Situation Room at the White House where President Johnson retained firm control over what could and could not be attacked. Decisions as routine as the choice of ordnance for a particular sortie were made at this level, thousands of miles from the fighting.

Johnson's decisions were relayed to McNamara, who in turn informed the Pentagon. Directives were then passed to CINCPAC (commander-in-chief, Pacific forces, in Hawaii) which then fragmented or 'fragged' the

*The triangle on the tail of this F-100D was the earmark of the 481st Tactical Fighter Squadron, 'Crusaders' which began a TDY (temporary duty) deployment to Vietnam on 29 June 1965, flying from Tan Son Nhut airfield.*

various targets among USAF, USN and – on rare occasions – South Vietnamese aircraft. The USAF headquarters in Saigon, the 2nd Air Division, made recommendations but could not choose targets. Lt Gen. Joseph Moore, who commanded 2nd Air Division, was an accomplished old fighter hand who kept making suggestions for an effective campaign against the North Vietnamese road and rail transportation network, only to

find targets approved on what seemed a random basis.

A complicating factor was the expansion of the North Vietnamese air force. Radar-directed AAA guns were a serious enough challenge to the US strike aircraft but they would soon be joined by MiGs and by guided SAMs. The first electronic countermeasures (ECM) capability to be mounted in the conflict was employed on 29 March 1965, when three RF-101C Voodoos, each carrying QRC-160 pods, flew ECM support missions

accompanying a 'Rolling Thunder' strike force to target. The QRC-160 proved unsatisfactory and was quickly withdrawn from the combat theater, but steps were under way to develop some means of jamming or deceiving the enemy's radar defenses.

*The 1965 transition from natural metal to protective camouflage is at the mid-way point while these F-105D Thunderchiefs refuel from a KC-135 Stratotanker. The F-105 was to bear the brunt of the 'Rolling Thunder' campaign against North Vietnam.*

away to escape from an American plane with a paddle-blade propeller up front and a maximum speed of around 390 mph (627 km/h).

With Thailand-based F-105Ds and US Navy aircraft in the Gulf carrying the bulk of the bombing campaign against the North, on 12 May 1965 a new term entered the lexicon of warfare, or, perhaps, of diplomacy – the 'bombing halt'. Eventually, the history of the war would involve so many bombing halts that, years later, even a serious effort by US government historians would leave open the question of precisely how many there had been.

## Bombing halts begin

The idea was simple enough. Show Hanoi how it feels not to be bombed for a few days (or weeks, or years). In return, Hanoi will become reasonable and aquiesce to an end to the war. The idea was simple, and it was tried repeatedly, and from beginning to end it suffered from one fatal flaw: the North Vietnamese believed that not being bombed was a natural state of affairs, that they had a sovereign right not to be bombed and that they need not be expected to make concessions in exchange. There exists no evidence that Ho Chi Minh, his followers, his successors or the Politburo in Hanoi ever gave any consideration to doing something because the US had ordered a cessation of bombing.

In CINCPAC's official report on the war, the first of its many bombing halts was dealt with in a few words: "During the bombing suspension initiated in May 1965, information was collected to permit an evaluation of the results of 'Rolling Thunder'. On 16 May, CINCPAC suggested to the Joint Chiefs of Staff that further respite for North Vietnam would serve to make future problems more difficult in South Vietnam and Laos. On this basis CINCPAC

*A Martin B-57 Canberra makes an attack on a Viet Cong position in South Vietnam. One of the first jet bombers, the British-designed Canberra had superb high-altitude performance, but found itself getting 'down and dirty' in a very different low-level war in Southeast Asia.*

recommended resumption of 'Rolling Thunder' and received authorization to resume operations on 18 May 1965."

Under the resumption, armed reconnaissance and bombing missions were severely limited in size, scope and geographical area, with but one strike being authorized further than 20° North – against Quang Suoi Barracks.

## Complex rules of engagement

A captain flying F-105D fighter-bombers from Takhli recalls arriving just as the brief bombing-halt ended.

"Those of us who flew the missions were in a bit of confusion. We had trained hard, worked hard, to become the best in the world at flying the Thud against enemy defenses and carrying our bombs to the target. Suddenly, we had to memorize ROE [rules of engagement]. We had to learn a set of restrictions so complex, so bewildering, that it was almost humanly impossible to avoid making a mistake. You couldn't fly here. You couldn't shoot at this. You couldn't fly there. You couldn't shoot at that. Worse, we were warned, and we believed it, that serious discipline would follow if we broke any of the rules."

With the widening of the war, the US Navy temporarily had four aircraft-carriers on station in Vietnamese waters. 'Yankee Station' was the dot on the map in the Gulf of Tonkin where carriers launched missions against North Vietnam. Increasingly, however, 'Dixie Station' in the South China Sea – springboard for air strikes on South Vietnam – gained importance.

# Enter the Sidewinder

**A**merican air-to-air missiles were of two types, the heat-seeking or infra-red (IR) missiles typified by the AIM-9 Sidewinder and the semi-active radar homing (SARH) missiles like the AIM-7 Sparrow.

Developed on a shoestring budget by a small US Navy team at China Lake, the Sidewinder had seen combat with Chinese F-86F Sabres as early as the 1958 Taiwan Straits crisis. The missile was 113-in (2.87-m) long and had a range of 11 miles (17.7 km). Its infra-red seeker head had to be cooled before it could lock onto a target and be fired, but this was a

fairly straightforward process.

The Sidewinder was rapidly becoming standard armament for most USAF and USN fighters, and although rarely carried by Super Sabres, was first used in Vietnam, to little effect, by F-100Ds early in April 1965. In spite of its inauspicious start, the

AIM-9 was to become not only the most successful air-to-air missile of the Vietnam conflict but also one of the most influential missiles in all history. It scored more aerial victories in the conflict than any other weapon, and provided the majority of the US Navy's air-to-air kills.

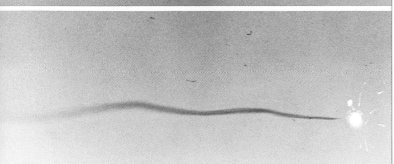

*Left: An early AIM-9 is fired from an F-100 Super Sabre. Moderate combat success before Vietnam gave no indication that it was to become the most successful air-to-air weapon of the war in the skies over Hanoi.*

*Below: Ordnancemen load an AIM-9 Sidewinder infra-red missile on the shoulder pylon of an F-8 Crusader aboard the USS Bon Homme Richard. Most Crusader kills were scored with this missile rather than guns.*

# Sparrow in Action

The Hainan Island incident saw the first American combat use of the long-range Sparrow air-to-air missile. The AIM-7D was 144-in (3.66-m) long, introduced a Thiokol pre-packaged liquid rocket motor and had been adopted in 1960 for the F-4 Phantom. The radar-guided Sparrow had a range of up to 28 miles (44 km) and could be employed well in advance of an eye-to-eye sighting of an enemy fighter. This capability, which was not possessed by the enemy, should have given the Phantom (the only principal US fighter to carry this missile) an enormous advantage – if only the rules permitted engaging from beyond visual range (BVR).

All fighter Phantoms could carry four Sparrows semi-recessed beneath the fuselage with target illumination by the fighter's own radar (the inboard wing pylons, where a fifth and sixth Sparrow could be fitted, proved more useful as stations for Sidewinders, bombs and ECM pods).

Radar failures and Sparrow malfunctions occurred more often than pilots wanted, but the controversial Sparrow remained a key part of the US arsenal. Eventually, Sparrows would account for the bulk of Air Force

MiG kills in the conflict, and the missile must be considered, overall, a success.

*Below: When combined with the far-reaching radar on the F-4 Phantom, the AIM-7 missile was supposed to offer a capability to shoot down an enemy beyond visual range. Actual combat rarely occurred at such distance.*

*On the F-4 Phantom, Sparrows could be carried on inboard wing pylons – though these were more often used for tanks or air-to-ground weaponry – and in four recessed bays in the lower fuselage. The backseater – a second pilot in the early days, but later to become a full-time Weapons Systems Officer or WSO – handled the radar engagement with an enemy but the shooting was done by the pilot.*

# First Air Force MiG

With the USS *Hancock* (CVA-19), *Coral Sea* (CVA-43), *Ranger* (CVA-6X) and *Midway* (CVA-41) operating in the combat zone, the Navy was very busy, North and South.

Flying a pre-planned air strike or an impromptu close support mission in South Vietnam was no picnic, and one frustrating aspect was not being able to see ground fire when the enemy was shooting from jungle cover in broad daylight. Studies showed, however, that carrier pilots were more nervous about making a hook-arrested landing on the pitching deck of the flat-top than about being shot at.

## Fliers at sea

An aircraft-carrier had a crew of between 3,000 and 5,000 men, of whom perhaps 300 were pilots or aircrew members. Life aboard ship was no picnic either, especially for the ship's company and the men in the Carrier Air Wing who routinely clocked 14- or 16-hour days simply to 'keep 'em flying'. Men worked when exhausted. They worked at night in the eerie glare of sodium lamps. They worked amid wrenching claustrophobia. By virtue of its very purpose, the aircraft-carrier had everything stuffed into the minimum space needed to contain it – bunks and bombs, food and fighters, refrigerators and rockets. Back home, self-appointed experts in economics might scold Lyndon Johnson for seeking guns and butter at the same time; the aircraft-carrier had both, but in the most cramped space possible.

Although there were differences based on size and age of the ship, a typical Carrier Air Wing had two fighter squadrons (Vought F-8 Crusaders or McDonnell F-4 Phantoms), two or sometimes three light-attack squadrons (Douglas A-4 Skyhawks), and a medium-attack squadron (Douglas A-1 Skyraiders). At this juncture some carriers had a detachment of a heavy attack squadron (Douglas A-3 Skywarriors). Most had reconnaissance detachments (Vought RF-8 Crusaders), airborne early-warning craft (Grumman E-1B Tracers or EA-1E/EA-1F Skyraiders) and helicopters (Kaman UH-2 Seasprites).

Operating with a mixture of jet and propeller-driven aircraft, which needed different fuels, was a tough proposition and some

*Duels between fast jets often lasted for split-seconds only, so it was rare when adversaries were caught on film. This dramatic shot of an F-105 Thunderchief and a MiG-17 mixing it up near Hanoi was made through the gun camera reticle of a third F-105 while the fight was on.*

With the 45th TFS on station at Ubon with the F-4C Phantom – a big banner claiming 'First to Fight' dangling in the parched heat at the Thai airbase – it was only a matter of time before the USAF would avenge the air-to-air loss of two 'Thuds' and catch up with the Navy in the MiG-killing business. It happened on 10 July 1965.

"In the summer of 1965," Colonel Robert Titus recalls, "as USAF pilots began to strike targets in the northern industrial regions of North Vietnam, a regular pattern in the MiG activity was detected. The MiGs would become airborne as the first strike flight entered the area but delay their attacks until the last flights, low on fuel, departed."

## Ambush planned

In order to exploit this observed trend, a mission was planned for 10 July 1965 which was to give AF Phantoms their first kills. A flight of F-4s would follow the last F-105 flight into the target area flying the same speeds, altitudes and flight paths as the strike flights, thereby giving the impression to the North Vietnamese radar that they were the last strike formation.

"The flight reached its orbit point without incident. Their altitude was 22,000 ft (6705 m), somewhat lower than the usual CAP altitude of 30-38,000 feet (9144-11 582 m) used at that time. They had almost reached Bingo fuel, a predetermined

minimum level on which a normal return is based, when the lead aircraft picked up a radar contact at 33 miles. He immediately called for a 'loose deuce' formation, a pre-arranged tactic calculated to provide a seven-to-10 mile (11-to-16 km) separation between elements so that the lead element could make positive identification, break away, and permit the second element to attack head-on with Sparrows.

"Things didn't quite work out that way. Due to their low fuel level the lead element was unable to accelerate in afterburner, so only about 3 miles (5 km) separation had been achieved prior to visual acquisition. Two MiG-17s passed slightly high and to the left, and dropped their tanks as they turned tightly in behind #3 and #4 and opened up with cannon fire. The F-4s went into burner and turned into the MiGs while punching off their drop tanks. The first element went high and out of the engagement.

"The second element of F-4s which we'll call Blue 3 and 4 (Colonel Titus could not remember the real callsigns, nor were they recorded elsewhere) found the MiGs out-turning them but their rapid acceleration in afterburner enabled them to gain separation. Blue 4, initially flying a fighting-wing position on 3, opted into a right turn to 'sandwich or split' the MiGs. The MiGs did split, one following Blue 3 and the other Blue 4. Blue

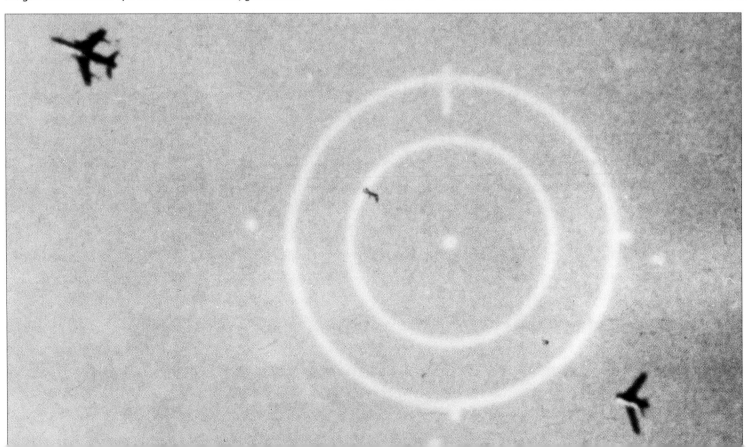

*The pair of two-man crews who shot down MiG-17s on 10 July 1965, together with a few wing men, whoop it up at Ubon following their success. The 45th TFS members may have thought the rest of the war would be this easy. It was not to be.*

3 executed several reverses and forced the MiG to overshoot. He then rolled off into a 30° dive, gained about five miles separation, and bent back around in a hard turn for a head-on pass.

## Radar out

"He called for 'boresight' unaware that the radar was out just after his GIB [guy in back, or backseater] said, 'Go heat,' meaning prepare to fire a heatseeker Sidewinder missile. The MiG passed very close, head-on, firing but scoring no hits. Blue 3 in a slight left turn to keep the MiG in sight went into a steep (60°) dive to 10,000 feet (3000 m) and ran his speed up to Mach 1.3. With the MiG about one mile (1.6 km) back, Blue 3 pulled into a high-G barrel roll. The MiG closed and opened fire at about one-half mile (800 meters) but overshot as the F-4 dished out.

## Fireball

"Blue 3 pumped off four Sidewinders within 10 seconds and the MiG, erupting into a large fireball, entered a cloud. Blue 3 didn't observe his first and last missiles, but the second detonated at or just to the right of the tailpipe, producing the fireball. The third went off to the

MiG's right.

"In the meantime, Blue 4 was in a Mach 1.4 dive to 12,000 feet (3657 m) followed by a high-G climb to 33,000 feet, or 11 000 m, from which he came back over the top in a 'sort of Immelmann'. He saw his MiG some 4,000 feet (1219 m) below, falling off on the left wing in a 90° bank. His radar completely out, Blue 4 attacked with Sidewinders. The first, fired without tone, detonated 4-6 feet (less than 1.5 meters) from the MiG's left wing tip. He hastily fired a second, also without tone. The third, with a good growl

(tone) tracked well and exploded just short of the tailpipe. The MiG emitted dense white smoke, continued down until at 6,000 feet (1828 m) it was inverted and in a 60° dive. Blue 4, closing rapidly and about to overshoot, rolled inverted, pulled his nose through the MiG, and fired his last Sidewinder. By this time he was aware of heavy flak and began to jink his way out of the area. As the flight proceeded outbound they were trailed at 10-15 miles (16-24 km) by a large flight of MiGs. Happily, those jokers failed to attack."

The two crews, consisting of

Captains Kenneth E. Holcombe and Arthur C. Clark and Captains Thomas S. Roberts and Ronald C. Anderson, each were down to a perilously tight fuel situation which would imperil Phantom crews throughout the war. They landed at Udorn, which was closer than their home base at Ubon, with a mere 1,800 lb (820 kg) of fuel left in one F-4C and an absolutely frightening 275 lb (120 kg) in the other, the latter amount being insufficient even for a 'go-around' whilst on landing approach. The Phantom crews taxied to their temporary parking spots while operating on fumes!

# The MiG 17

U ntil the advent of 'Rolling Thunder', the North Vietnamese had kept their MiG-17s in safety in China while despatching additional pilots to the Soviet Union for training. The MiG-17 was dated, scarcely more than an upgrade of the Korean War vintage MiG-15, but it was agile and, unlike the Phantom, armed with guns. Capable of 710 mph (1145 km/h) at 10,000 ft (3048 m), the MiG-17 was armed with three NR-23 cannons.

When it became clear to North Vietnam's tacticians that the arcane American rules of engagement would not permit strikes on airfields, the MiG-17s were brought in to their bases and put on alert. With the Americans not yet successful in downing a MiG in air-to-air

*The MiG-17 was a "bat out of hell", one American fighter jock proclaimed. Although neither new nor fast, it was remarkably maneuverable and its trio of 23-mm and 37-mm cannons packed a truly lethal punch.*

combat, the MiG-17 was going to give a good account of itself in air-to-air action. It had downed two 'Thuds' with no losses.

America's first probable air-to-air kill of the war, surprisingly,

seems not to have involved the North Vietnamese at all. On 9 April, F-4B Phantoms from *Ranger* battled Chinese MiG-17s near Hainan Island. The Phantom flown by Lt (JG) Terence M.

Murphy and Ensign Ronald J. Fegan, members of the 'Black Falcons' of squadron VF-96, was credited with a probable MiG-17 shootdown but did not return from the mission. The Chinese promptly reminded everyone that it was not their war. They also claimed, and other evidence seems to confirm, that Murphy and Fegan were shot down by an AIM-7 Sparrow missile fired by one of their own wingmen!

*The hi-tech A-6A Intruder's baptism of fire was marred by glitches with its sophisticated navigation and bombing system. Once the Navy cured some technical troubles, the A-6A took command of the night, flying when others could not. Intruders bombed with devastating accuracy, leaving Air Force officers to lament that they had no comparable warplane which could hit targets day and night, whatever the weather.*

Navy planners were already looking into the possibilities of an all-jet Carrier Air Wing in the future.

Because of budgetary constraints prior to the big build-up, as soon as the war expanded in 1965 the Navy began suffering from serious shortages of aircrew, aircraft, ordnance and carriers. Intake and preparation of new personnel was increased at Naval Air Training Command bases back home, but some things just could not be done quickly.

Design, development, purchase and construction of a new aircraft-carrier was a major political, fiscal and physical effort and very time-consuming. Throughout the entire war in fact, only two carriers were commissioned, the USS *America* (CVA-66) in January 1965 and the USS *John F. Kennedy* (CVA-67) in September 1968 – and the latter vessel never reached the war zone.

Several other carriers were of World War II vintage and were near the end of their useful lives or due for major refit. This was true of the USS *Midway* (CVA-41), which is usually remembered as the vessel which got the first and last Navy MiG kills of the war. *Midway* departed the combat zone in 1965, went back to Alameda, California, for a major refit, and was not in service again until five years later.

Weather over the South China Sea and the Indochinese land mass infuriated every man who flew, but particularly angered the carrier-based naval aviator who faced the full range of nasty conditions over sea and land. During a 'good' day in 'clear' weather, every nook and cranny beneath the Vietnamese ridgelines was shrouded beneath patches of cloud.

The winter north-east monsoon season between December and May brought violent storms with cloud cover which often extended from 2,000 or 3,000 feet (600 or 800 meters) to 40,000 feet (over 12 000 meters). Long periods of dismal visibility and the almost complete absence of all-weather strike aircraft (save only the Grumman A-6 Intruder) meant that pilots were almost always flying in the worst conditions. Meanwhile the wet murk formed a protective cloak over the massive influx of men and materiel being sent to the Viet Cong from North Vietnam.

## All-weather bomber

The Grumman A-6A Intruder arrived in Southeast Asia with the 'Sunday Punchers' of attack squadron VA-75 aboard the USS *Independence* (CVA-62), flying its first combat mission on 1 July 1965 against targets 'up North'. The twin-engined Grumman product was decidedly subsonic, with a maximum speed of perhaps 684 mph (1102 km/h) at sea-level and a combat radius of around 600 miles (960 km). If it worked right – the 'Sunday Punchers' had been sent to war to find out – the Intruder would almost certainly be the Navy's antidote to the scummy weather.

The key to all-weather operations in the Intruder was the computerized internal system known as DIANE (digital integrated attack and navigational equipment). The acronym had been created because Diane was the name of Grumman engineer Bob Nafis' daughter. But DIANE was no lady in 1965. There were maintenance and reliability problems. 'Down' time was unconscionable. At first there was real doubt that the A-6 Intruder would be successful.

A two-man, side-by-side cockpit straddled the nose of the

# EC-121 Deployment

It was clear that an airborne early warning (AEW) capability would be needed if US aircraft were to challenge MiGs and still deliver ordnance to their targets. The EC-121D Warning Star, an AEW development of the Lockheed Super Constellation with bulbous radar antennas protruding from its sleek fuselage, was given the job.

Orbiting off the enemy coast, it used radar and other sensors to detect MiGs taking off.

Air Defense Command 'Big Eye' EC-121Ds deployed to Southeast Asia in April 1965, flying in support of 'Rolling Thunder' operations. Based at Tainan, Taiwan, the EC-121Ds flew their missions out of Tan Son Nhut AB near Saigon. This

was the first use of the EC-121D in combat. Working with Navy radar picket ships, using the callsign Red Crown, the EC-121D gave strike force commanders a 'real time' picture of what the enemy's air defenses were doing.

The initial deployment was not without problems. Crew of the aircraft could range from 16 to 30 men, depending upon the mission being flown and its intended duration. Tan Son Nhut airbase was chock-a-block and its facilities were stretched to the limit, making it difficult to accommodate the EC-121D crews in any degree of comfort.

All units on the base, as at many bases in South Vietnam (unlike those in Thailand), shared the problems caused by periodic mortar and sapper attacks, but for the Warning Star crews more mundane comforts like food, lodging and air conditioning were usually inadequate. Because a typical mission could extend up to ten hours in duration, commanders regarded morale as important but, in the early stages, were unable to provide the creature comforts that go with high spirits.

Following a 1967 move from Tan Son Nhut to Ubon then to Udorn, the program would be codenamed 'College Eye' and the EC-121Ds of the 552nd Airborne Warning and Control Wing would use the radio callsign Disco. Fighter pilots credited Disco with preventing numerous MiG ambushes.

*Graceful and elegant were words readily applied to the 'Super Connie' when it plied the world's commercial airways. As a flying radar station prowling the coast of Vietnam, the EC-121D kept its good looks in wartime service.*

# 'Route Packages'

One F-105D pilot looked at a map of North Vietnam and likened the shape of it to a Colonel Sanders fried chicken drumstick. Names like Xom Bong and Vinh Linh did not roll easily from American tongues, especially in the hyped radio chatter of combat, so to simplify navigation and planning, the country was divided into sections known as 'Route Packages', or RPs. Pilots talked about RP One or Pak Six. Roman numerals were supposed to be used (Route Package VI) but rarely were.

## Target areas

Moving north from the DMZ at the 17th Parallel, the country was partitioned into Route Packages One, Two, Three and Four, each consisting of a horizontal slice. The wider region farther north was divided into Route Package Five to the west and Six to the east. It was RP Six which contained the most important targets, the heaviest defenses and the cities of Hanoi and Haiphong.

For the F-105D pilots bearing the brunt of the campaign against the North, Route Package One was a training area. Newly arrived pilots flew 10 missions against that area's relatively less intense defenses before earning the right to go into RP Six and, later in the war, to go 'downtown' – to Hanoi.

Originally, there was some

*North Vietnam was divided into six target areas, or 'Route Packages'. The most heavily defended areas were those around Hanoi and Haiphong, which was known as Route Package Six, itself divided into two areas of responsibility. Although there was no hard and fast division, the Air Force generally dealt with targets inland and the Navy usually attacked coastal sites.*

thought of dividing the route packages between Air Force and Navy. The US Navy now kept carriers at Dixie Station in the South China Sea for operations in the South and at Yankee Station for strikes against the North. Aircraft from *Hancock* and *Coral Sea* had begun the Navy's participation in 'Rolling Thunder', on 18 March, and carrier-based warplanes began ranging up and down the coast, striking at transportation and supply targets. The first air-to-air engagement was fought on 3 April, when MiG-17s briefly appeared to challenge aircraft from both carriers near Thanh Hoa.

## Air-to-air losses

On 4 April 1965, the day Lt Col Risner's 'Thud' pilots mounted their second strike against the Dragon's Jaw, North Vietnam's air force achieved its first air-to-air kills when two F-105Ds (59-1754, 59-1764) belonging to Zinc flight of the 355th TFW at Takhli were shot down by MiG-17s.

The MiG fighters appeared behind the 'Thuds', which were laden with ordnance, and blew them out of the sky. It was a sad beginning to an air-to-air war for

the Americans, a two-to-nothing score in favor of the enemy.

That same day, Risner narrowly missed being shot down when AAA fire hailed around his 'Thud'. (Later, Risner would be shot down twice, would be captured the second time, and would become a key leader of the POWs' resistance campaign against their captors.)

## Ground fire

One of Risner's aircraft was claimed by ground fire, its pilot, Captain Carlyle S. (Smitty) Harris becoming a POW. Harris would introduce the 'tap code' which enabled POWs to communicate with each other while in solitary confinement.

But Harris would probably not have been shot down at all had it not been for his need to make that perilous second pass over the target. And the chances were that he would not have been captured either, had a more effective SAR (search-and-rescue) capability existed in the combat zone. But that was something for the future.

*Bomb spill toward the clouds as a brace of F-105D Thunderchiefs take their cue from an EB-66 Destroyer pathfinder. Radar bombing was widely used in North Vietnam's Route Packages, though its effectiveness was debated.*

**Map labels:**

CHINA

NORTH VIETNAM

VIA

VIB

Phuc Yen
Gia Lam
Kep
Cat Bi
Paul Doumer Bridge
Hanoi
Haiphong
Kien An
Restricted zone

V

IV

III

II

I

Thanh Hoa Bridge

LAOS

Vinh

GULF OF TONKIN

Vientiane

THAILAND

Dong Hoi

SOUTH VIETNAM

Route pack boundary

● Major Airfield

Prohibited area

Miles
0   25   50   75   100

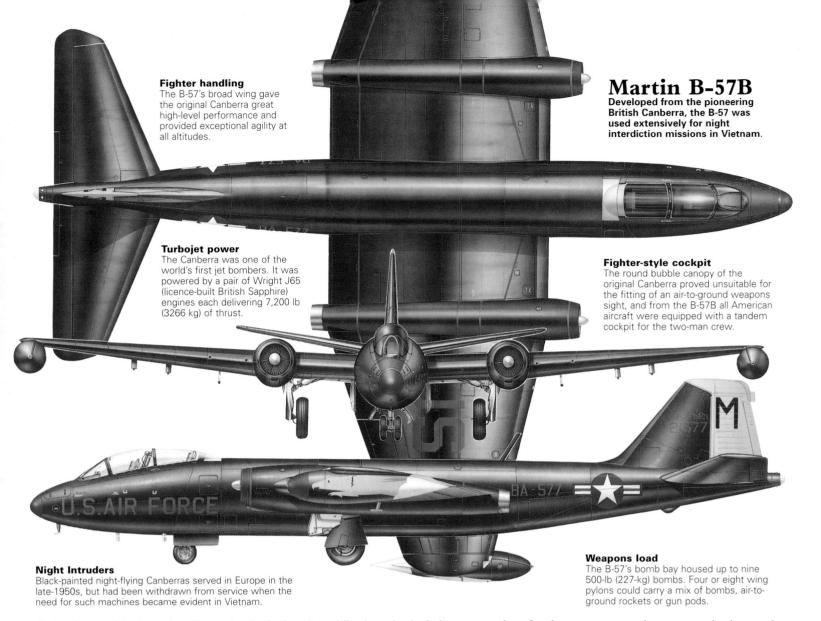

**Fighter handling**
The B-57's broad wing gave the original Canberra great high-level performance and provided exceptional agility at all altitudes.

## Martin B-57B
Developed from the pioneering British Canberra, the B-57 was used extensively for night interdiction missions in Vietnam.

**Turbojet power**
The Canberra was one of the world's first jet bombers. It was powered by a pair of Wright J65 (licence-built British Sapphire) engines each delivering 7,200 lb (3266 kg) of thrust.

**Fighter-style cockpit**
The round bubble canopy of the original Canberra proved unsuitable for the fitting of an air-to-ground weapons sight, and from the B-57B all American aircraft were equipped with a tandem cockpit for the two-man crew.

**Night Intruders**
Black-painted night-flying Canberras served in Europe in the late-1950s, but had been withdrawn from service when the need for such machines became evident in Vietnam.

**Weapons load**
The B-57's bomb bay housed up to nine 500-lb (227-kg) bombs. Four or eight wing pylons could carry a mix of bombs, air-to-ground rockets or gun pods.

distinctly ungainly Intruder. Humorists looked at the oddly shaped aircraft and insisted that the pointed end was supposed to be at the front. Elegant or not, the Intruder was soon flying missions over South Vietnam where, increasingly, American troops directly engaged the Viet Cong.

Aboard the USS *Kitty Hawk* (CVA-63) the 'Black Falcons' of VA-45, the second medium-attack squadron to fly the Intruder in the war zone, saw action from 'Dixie Station', beginning in November 1965. After a vicious land battle and the virtual slaughter of the ARVN 7th Regiment, *Kitty Hawk*'s Carrier Air Wing 11 bombed, rocketed and strafed VC positions in the Michelin plantation, a scant 45-miles (70-km) north of Saigon, inflicting heavy casualties and providing relief to beleaguered ground forces.

### Marine air power

The April 1965 arrival of US Marine ground forces was accompanied by an impressive show of Marine airpower. Captain John D. Cummings, a back-seat F-4B Phantom RIO (radar intercept officer) with the 'Gray Ghosts' of Squadron VMFA-531, found conditions at Da Nang incredibly crude when the Marine Phantom crews arrived:

"I remember choking clouds of dust, everywhere. The only other guys at Da Nang were the Marine UH-34 helicopter guys from the 'Shu Fly' operation which dated to 1963, and we harbored a little resentment because they lorded their combat experience over us and were living in old, cool French colonial buildings while we had tents or slept beneath the wings of our Phantoms. We'd arrived in Vietnam with our toilet bags, our flight gear, and our socks. We were dusty and gritty, waiting for portable showers to arrive. I found the only flush toilet on our side of the base and I kept the location secret from most of the guys.

"In those days nobody knew much about flying air-to-ground missions at night. It was true that 'Charlie' ruled the night. The VC

had almost complete freedom to run patrols, set up ambushes, and reposition their units. We did fly some night missions, including one with a C-123 orbiting over some VC, dropping million-plus candlepower flares which just about burned our eyes out.

"We flew all sorts of missions in the Phantom. I flew one all the way down by the suburbs of Saigon. We had the newer, low-drag bombs rather than the box-finned World War II stuff the stateside Marine units were equipped with, but we never had enough of the bombs, not ever. Our guys would go out with a six-bomb MER [multiple ejector rack] with only three bombs. This was during the 'non-bomb', as McNamara called it."

Throughout the conflict, there would be instances when the number of bombs available was insufficient for the aircraft committed to battle.

While Marine Phantoms operated from Da Nang, across the airfield from Air Force F-100s and F-104s, more Marines moved into Chu Lai to build an airfield where none had existed before. The air base resulted from the expanding Marine presence; by July 1965 ground combat Marines were pitted against the Viet Cong in Operation 'Starlite' and it was publicly acknowledged that they were taking offensive action. Initially Chu Lai was home to two squadrons of A-4 Skyhawks, the same lightweight, single-seat attack craft serving aboard Navy carriers off-shore.

At Bien Hoa, where a VC mortar attack had destroyed five B-57 Canberras and damaged 13 the previous Hallowe'en, it was time for a debacle which would forever evoke unpleasant overtones to men in the B-57 community – and this time, the Communist guerrillas had nothing to do with it.

On Sunday morning, 16 May 1965, Captain Charles Fox was about to start engines to lead 'Jade' Flight, a formation of four B-57s, on a strike mission. Fox was carrying a typical bombload – nine 500-lb (227-kg) bombs in his Canberra's internal bay and four 750-pounders (340-kg) under the wings.

A key challenge, one for which US tacticians were not fully prepared, was to deny the enemy the night. This was especially important in the campaign to interdict supplies flowing from North to South. Almost everything being carried down the Ho Chi Minh Trail by foot, pedicab, bicycle, truck and convoy was moving during the hours of darkness. Eventually, C-130 Hercules transports, already flying leaflet missions, operated as forward air control (FAC) flare ships, illuminating night targets in Laos while using the callsign Blind Bat and operating over North Vietnam with the callsign Lamplighter. At first, however, strike aircraft like the B-57 Canberra had to carry their own flares.

## Canberra at night

The first B-57 night interdiction mission took place a few days before a brief bombing halt, on 21 April 1965. Captain Howard Greene and Captain Fred Huber took two B-57 bombers up to what Robert C. Mikesh called "a vast spiderweb of supply routes leading south from the city of Vinh," midway between the 17th

*Infiltration into South Vietnam was carried out mostly under the cloak of darkness, and mostly with impunity to air action. The A-26K Invader set forth to work under flarelight to find infiltrators and attack them.*

Parallel and Hanoi. The B-57s carried eight pods containing seven 2.75-in folding fin aircraft rockets, six 500-lb (227-kg) bombs and their own Mark 24 flares.

The Bien Hoa-based B-57s went in to attack two bridges near Vinh and were subjected to heavy anti-aircraft fire. Night strikes of this kind were especially risky: vertigo frequently resulted from the pilot's lack of visual reference to the horizon, the flares themselves disrupted men's night vision, and maps and terrain-following tools were

inadequate or nonexistent. An added problem was that B-57 pilots and navigators began these missions fatigued since they had to sleep in 90°F heat during the day, without air conditioning. Only a few of these missions were flown before an accidental explosion at Bien Hoa on 16 May 1965, not caused by enemy action, destroyed 10 B-57s and killed 28 men.

The US Navy's answer to the night interdiction challenge was a new aircraft, the Grumman A-6A Intruder. By 16 May, the 'Sunday Punchers' of attack

*The B-57 Canberra did not have the fancy technology of the Navy's A-6 Intruder, but under the right circumstances it could be very effective against the Viet Cong during the nocturnal hours. The USAF ran several programs to give the B-57 enhanced night capability.*

squadron VA-75 had finished working up and were *en route* to the battle zone aboard USS *Independence* (CVA-62), the first of several Atlantic Fleet carriers which would share the burden of the Pacific Fleet's fighting in Asia.

One moment, there was no hint that anything was wrong. The next, Fox's aircraft exploded with a brilliant flash and a concussion that sent shrapnel and debris raining along the Bien Hoa flight line. Captain Howard Greene, pilot of the nearby B-57 using the callsign 'Jade 4', led his backseater in abandoning their aircraft. Greene, his seat parachute flapping against his hind side, sprinted past fuel storage bladders, leapt over concertina barbed wire, and took cover in a ditch – just as new explosions reverberated. For more than a minute new explosions shook the Bien Hoa ramp as B-57s went up, bombs exploded, and 20-mm cannon shells cooked off.

Fox and six other members of 'Jade' Flight were among those who died in the gaseous, flaming carnage. The reverberations sent an entire J65 engine flying for half a mile. In all, 28 men were killed, 105 wounded. Among aircraft totally destroyed were 10 B-57s, 11 VNAF A-1H Skyraiders and a Navy F-8 Crusader which had landed only moments earlier.

## Army aviation

On 7 May 1965 the first full-scale combat unit of the US Army, the 173rd Airborne Brigade, arrived from its peacetime garrison on Okinawa and took up positions around Bien Hoa and Vung Tau. Again, the Johnson administration flogged the fiction that the troopers' purpose was to provide airfield security. This final attempt publicly to deny an American combat role evaporated on 27 June when the 173rd spearheaded the largest airlift of the war, with 144 Army helicopters carrying men into War Zone D in an area where allied forces had not operated for a year.

Strategic Air Command's giant B-52 Stratofortress bombers, built to carry hydrogen bombs, flew the first of countless conventional bombing missions under the program name 'Arc Light' on 17 June 1965, with 28 B-52Fs striking Viet Cong concentrations in Binh Duong Province. A stupid tactical mistake caused two of the B-52Fs to collide while marshaling off the coast, killing both crews.

## Change of regime – again

On 18 June 1965 yet another change in the Saigon leadership occurred. Major General Nguyen Van Thieu was installed as president and Nguyen Cao Ky, the VNAF commander, as premier. Ky, it will be recalled, had started his flying career in transports and moved to the A-1H Skyraider. He and his beautiful wife liked to

An especially difficult F-105 mission, illustrating the difficulty of maintaining the 'Rolling Thunder' campaign, was mounted on 5 October 1965. Six flights of 'Thuds', consisting of four aircraft each, from the 23rd TFW at Takhli, refueled from KC-135 tankers and moved towards the Lang Met Bridge, 50-miles (80-km) north-east of Hanoi. Crucial to the flow of supplies from China to North Vietnam (many of which actually originated in the Soviet Union), the bridge spanned the Rong River and was protected by small arms, AAA guns and SAMs. MiGs, too, were an obvious threat.

### Run-in to target

At Bao Ha on the Red River, the formation dropped down to about 2,000 feet (609 m) and began its run-in on the target. The flights were spaced five minutes apart to assure that only one four-ship flight would be exposed to the target's air defenses at a time. Each 'Thud' was carrying two 3,000-lb (1377-kg)

*UH-1 Huey helicopters of the 173rd Airborne Brigade, the first air-mobile infantry unit deployed to Southeast Asia, employ the miracle of vertical flight to set up a firebase, probably in a sector of Vietnam that would prove difficult to reach by road.*

tour military installations in matching flight coveralls. Some American critics, already torpid from the seeming endlessness of the conflict, questioned whether Thieu and Ky would provide any more leadership or stability than their hapless predecessors.

In July 1965 Secretary of Defense Robert S. McNamara made one of his periodic visits to Saigon, but now McNamara was no longer uttering the previous year's language about American withdrawals. Now McNamara spoke of a 'phased build-up' of US forces in Vietnam, as if there existed a master plan and everybody in Washington was of one mind.

Phase I, said McNamara, was defined as the period when the US would "stop losing the war". Phase II would be the period "in which we intend to start winning".

In fact, the American foot soldier was going to begin winning on the battlefield almost immediately. Winning the war was another proposition. As if to confirm that Americans really were being killed and wounded, the Internal Revenue Service, for purposes of establishing an income tax exemption, reached a finding that Vietnam had been a combat zone since the beginning of the previous year.

In a move just as fitting, Pacific Air Forces (PACAF), the Hawaii-based headquarters for the USAF in the region, proposed that aircraft in the combat zone be dressed in war paint. A three-color camouflage scheme was created, and is usually known as the T.O. 14 paint scheme after the technical order which created it. Forward air controller (FAC) Cessna O-1 Bird Dogs retained their uncamouflaged finish to enhance visibility against the jungle

*Right: A revealing glimpse of a busy airfield in action. In 1965 at Takhli, where Thai officials were delighted to serve as hosts for an American bombing campaign, these F-105 Thunderchiefs were flying daily sorties into the war zone. It was at about this time that all American combat aircraft in-theater began to be repainted in camouflage colors.*

*F-105D Thunderchiefs, possibly posing for the camera, line up like lemmings to take on fuel from a KC-135. 'Thuds' were all based in Thailand during the war, and on the long combat missions deep into North Vietnam they needed to gulp up gas in mid-air on nearly all flights.*

bombs and carried a 650-US-gallon centerline fuel tank.

Captain Richard McKinney, not satisfied that they were low enough, took his four-ship down to a height no greater than 300 feet (91 m). McKinney's earphones were clogged with radio reports of the action as the first flight arrived over the bridge. Yet to arrive, McKinney ordered his wingmen to pickle their fuel tanks and to advance their throttles to full military power. At 600 mph (1016 km/h) and seven miles (11.2 km) out, they could see the target area, marked by a huge pall of smoke caused by the bomb explosions and AAA fire.

Three miles (4.8 km) out, the flight 'popped up' to gain altitude and begin its dive-bombing run on the bridge. At 7,000 feet (2133 m), Captain McKinney rolled in and lined up his pipper on the bridge. Noticing that the center span was already down in the river, he aimed for one of the bridge approaches.

## Bombs gone

As puffs of smoke appeared around the 'Thuds' and red and orange tracers filled the air, McKinney flicked the bomb release and felt the aircraft lurch upward as the 6,000-lb (2718-kg) bombload left its wings. He turned south and rejoined his wingman whose aircraft had been badly riddled by shrapnel. As they started a slow climb for home they heard the beeper signals from survival radios on the ground. Some of their wingmen had been hit and were forced to eject.

The mission took three hours and covered 1,350 miles (2172 km). Of the initial strike force of 24 'Thuds', only eight actually returned to Takhli. Three were shot down and the rest had to make diversions to closer airfields because of battle damage. One was so badly damaged that its pilot was awarded the Silver Star for bringing it back in more or less one piece to Da Nang. Once again, as had already happened so often – this time to men of McKinney's 562nd TFS/23rd TFW – it was demonstrated that going North in the F-105D aircraft was not an easy task and not for the faint-hearted.

*Below: Two of three F-105 Thunderchiefs are carrying AGM-12A/B Bullpup air-to-surface missiles. As the war became more intense and more grim, the luxury of a mediocre missile could no longer be afforded. 750-lb (340-kg) bombs became standard.*

background. The first aircraft in-theater to receive camouflage paint was a C-130 Hercules transport.

On 6 August 1965, after more than two years of combat flying in South Vietnam, the 'Patricia Lynn' RB-57E Canberra detachment suffered its first casualty. On a night infra-red reconnaissance mission in aircraft 55-4243, pilot Captain Dick Damon and navigator Lieutenant Dick Crist were hit by small-arms fire. The aircraft was set afire. The crew ejected and the aircraft crashed a short distance from Tan Son Nhut.

Landing by parachute in the darkness, Crist came face-to-face with a Vietnamese. Drilled to cope with the enemy, Crist grabbed the man by the collar and pressed his cocked .38 service pistol into the man's stomach. Seeing others gathered around, he belatedly realized that he was in a group of friendly South Vietnamese. Embarrassed, Crist put his pistol away. His story was later widely told among flight crews to make the point that a quick trigger finger could cause a friendly group to become suddenly very unfriendly. The 'Patricia Lynn' detachment, which had grown from two Canberras to five, now had four aircraft left.

## More troops

Now the build-up of American forces gathered momentum. Secretary McNamara revealed what everyone already knew, that the number of American troops fighting in South Vietnam – the *raison d'etre* for the campaign against the North – had now risen to 50,000. American innocence may have been fading, but in mid-1965 it remained possible for many Americans to believe that their superior know-how and fighting prowess would quickly bring the conflict to a halt. Protest against the US role in the war was beginning to spread, but had not yet reached the scale or intensity that would come later.

On those occasions where American infantrymen faced Viet Cong guerrillas, or even the vaunted and very professional North Vietnamese regulars, they acquitted themselves well and almost always won the battle, but this seemed to have no influence on increasing popularity of the Viet Cong. Drug problems and racial conflict within the US forces were also beginning to be seen but had not yet reached the size and severity that would come later. Many still believed, despite a body of evidence to the contrary, that 'Rolling Thunder' was choking off the flow of supplies to the Communist fighters in the South's rain forests.

On 27 June 1965, the US Army's 173rd Airborne Brigade launched a major offensive north-east of Saigon which was widely considered to be successful.

Ho Chi Minh himself said, and other Hanoi officials repeated, that even if the Americans sent 10 times their 50,000 troops into South Vietnam – which, in fact, they eventually did – it would make no difference. While insisting that the Viet Cong were natives of the South rising up against a harsh Saigon regime and that the North's support for them was largely moral support – an assertion which was increasingly inaccurate as Hanoi tightened its hold on the VC leadership and increased its infiltration – the North Vietnamese leaders also said that if the Americans bombed them forever, they would not succumb. Their own claims for American

# Arc Light

*Another busy airfield – Kep, in North Vietnam. Activity is less visible here than at American bases in Thailand and South Vietnam. Unlike the Americans who are constitutionally incapable of routine caution, Hanoi's airmen have bunkered their MiG-17s in shielded revetments.*

aircraft shot down were often several dozen times the number actually located in the combat zone. Still, their message was clear. 'Rolling Thunder' saw 'Thuds', Phantoms, Crusaders, Skyhawks and brave men flying into battle at almost unprecedented peril. They were dropping a good many bombs but failing to influence the course of the war. The 'progressive squeeze' of 'Rolling Thunder' was not working.

## North Vietnam's airfields

As the air war intensified, the North Vietnamese air force grew. MiG-17s (mistakenly reported by US intelligence as MiG-21s) from Phuc Yen were making limited sweeps south of Thanh Hoa and were now being regarded at the 2nd Air Division in Saigon as a growing threat to control of the air. A further concern was the threat to friendly forces in the South posed by the handful of Phuc Yen-based Ilyushin Il-28 bombers. Indeed, had the North Vietnamese known how much the Americans fretted about a batch of ancient Il-28s which never numbered more than eight airframes, they might have hurled all of them against the South! The JCS proposed, as it had done earlier, that the taboo on bombing airfields be lifted and that sustained attacks be mounted to neutralize Phuc Yen and render it unusable.

The increasing strength of the North Vietnamese air force was demonstrated on 24 and 25 August 1965 when seven US aircraft and a reconnaissance drone were shot down. General Earl Wheeler, Chairman of the JCS, vigorously sought permission from his boss, McNamara, to attack Phuc Yen. McNamara again refused the request, citing the highly dubious proposition that strikes on North Vietnamese airfields might cause the Chinese to take over the air defense mission in North Vietnam. Again, the Secretary of Defense was overlooking the fact that serious differences existed between Hanoi and Peking. Some leeway was left for a change of this decision at some future time.

On 27 August 1965 the 1st Cavalry Division (Airmobile), the renamed 11th Air Assault Division which had pioneered large-scale helicopter operations in the US, began to arrive at Anh Khe. A shoulder patch with a silhouette of a stallion's head was the mark of the historic First Cav. Now the Cavalry rode helicopters instead of horses. The First Cav had 15,787 men, 1,600 vehicles and 428 helicopters, plus six Grumman OV-1 Mohawk spotter aircraft.

The Cavalry spirit is potent, and was typified by the new division's first commander, Brigadier General John Wright, Jr. He bounded out of a Huey with machete in hand and ordered the scrub to be cleared until it was as close-cut as a 'Golf Course', the

Although not yet a part of the campaign against the North, the entry of the giant B-52 Stratofortress into the conflict was an important milestone. The use of the B-52 had been seriously considered from the beginning of 'Rolling Thunder' although, from the beginning, doubts were expressed as to whether the big, slow aircraft could survive 'up North' against MiGs, missiles and AAA. It was decided that B-52 missions would be carried out at first only in the more permissive environment of South Vietnam.

Arc Light bombing operations began on 18 June 1965 with a mission which was heralded at the time as a considerable success, although it was marred by the loss of two B-52s, victims of a mid-air collision in the refueling area.

There were five refueling tracks, but all at the same altitude; there was a 20 nautical mile (37 km) separation between tracks, but this proved inadequate under the circumstances. As yet there was no provision for the B-52s flying triangular patterns just prior to entering the refueling area to correct timing discrepancies. Thus it was that one bomber cell or formation of three aircraft arrived at the refueling area well ahead of schedule and, on making a turn to use up time flew into another cell which was just approaching the area. Two of the massive Boeing bombers collided, and both crews were lost.

Corrective measures taken as a result of this accident included:

establishing multiple refueling tracks at different altitudes, separating neighboring tracks more widely, instituting timing triangles on the approach and (later) establishing an *en route* refueling procedure. Also, the Philippine government consented to the relocation of the refueling tracks somewhat closer to the Philippine Islands. To some extent, however, Arc Light refueling areas had to compete for space with commercial airline routes for the duration of the conflict, and Manila Air Traffic authorities naturally tended to give preference to the profitable commercial business.

## Tall-tail B-52s

The first Stratofortress introduced into the South was the B-52F, which had a tall tailfin. The two machines lost in the collision belonged to the 7th Bomb Wing based at Andersen AB, Guam. Among the 27 bombers in that first mission, some also came from the 320th Bomb Wing at Andersen.

General William C. Westmoreland, commander of US forces in South Vietnam, was convinced of the effectiveness of using B-52s for saturation bombings of Viet Cong base areas but, if an Army general and SAC people (the latter being outside the Saigon chain of command) liked the B-52F, other officers lamented the independence given to SAC.

"The inability of the USAF air commander in Vietnam to

integrate Arc Light operations into the overall air campaign is a contradiction difficult to accept, impossible to reconcile with USAF doctrine and worst of all results in far less than effective

While B-52F bombers were being flown over the South (and, said some critics, merely destroying a good many trees), SAC decided it needed more load carrying ability than the 'F' model's of 27 750-lb (340-kg) bombs carried internally and 24 bombs externally. The entire fleet of B-52D bombers, also distinguished externally by a tall tailfin, was being prepared for the conflict, almost certainly with the notion that the big machines would eventually fight in North Vietnam.

A 'Big Belly' modification program was begun in December 1965 to increase the capacity of the B-52D to carry 500-lb (227-kg) bombs from 27 to no fewer than 84, or its capacity to carry 750-lb (340-kg) bombs from 27 to 42 internally. In addition, the B-52D could still carry 24 500-lb (227-kg) or 750-lb (340-kg) bombs externally. The maximum bombload rose to about 60,000 lb

*Left: Depending on whether the Viet Cong were there or not, a string of bombs from a B-52 could inflict heinous damage to the enemy or dig out rows of useless potholes. The sound and vibrations were felt for miles.*

employment of this useful instrument of airpower."

(27 215 kg).

In a seemingly contradictory move, Secretary of Defense McNamara announced that all older Stratofortress variants including the B-52D, would be retired by June 1971. McNamara, also quoted during this period as seeing "the light at the end of the tunnel" which signified an imminent end to the hostilities in Southeast Asia, could hardly have been more wrong. It would be more than a year after its announced retirement when the B-52D finally appeared not merely over North Vietnam, but over downtown Hanoi.

*Above: Bombs tumble earthward from a B-52F Stratofortress high over South Vietnam. Introduction of the 'Buff' – Big Ugly Fat F***er – in 1965 began with a fatal mid-air collision, but no further B-52s were to be lost in action for seven years. To the guerrilla in the jungle, the B-52 was so far out of reach of defensive weapons that it might as well have been in orbit.*

*Below: Just before the B-52 was committed to battle, the US Air Force released this shot (below) of a 'Buff' heading aloft from the American soil of Andersen AFB, Guam – the base from which Arc Light missions were carried out from 1965 to 1973.*

*At Ia Drang in 1965, American soldiers fought their first full-scale action against North Vietnamese regulars. They won, and were never defeated on the battlefield thereafter. Here, Air Cavalrymen call in flare missions after a night ambush at a landing zone in the Ia Drang Valley.*

nickname quickly applied to the Anh Khe base.

In October 1965 the air cavalry was called into action when the largest unit of North Vietnamese regulars yet seen laid siege to the Special Forces camp at Plei Mei. There followed a series of fire fights and maneuvering engagements with numbers of American soldiers inserted on the battlefield by air for the first time. The expanding battle between Cavalrymen and NVA regulars lasted 31 days. It marked the first time a division had fought a continuing action using helicopters for virtually all troop movements.

## Helicopter battles

The Battle of Ia Drang Valley, it was called. Ia Drang was the first test of the helicopter in a division-scale battle. It was also the first challenge to a citizen army, the first ever maintained by the US in peacetime through universal conscription. Most important, at Ia Drang for the first time the American soldier came face-to-face not merely with Viet Cong guerrillas but with the NVA (North Vietnamese Army), Hanoi's seasoned regulars, the same fiercely motivated troops who had booted the French out of Southeast Asia. In 1965 the NVA regular was among the best-trained and most experienced fighting soldiers in the world. But at Ia Drang, over the length of two fortnights, he was defeated by the American Air Cavalryman in a battle so decisive that there should never again have arisen any question about who would prevail on the battlefield.

The Battle of Ia Drang Valley saw the use of all helicopters then in inventory. The Bell UH-1B Huey was used as a gunship or medical evacuation ('Dust-off') ambulance, while the longer, more powerful Bell UH-1D Huey was the usual 'Slick', or troop transport. The bubble-topped Bell OH-13G Sioux ('Possum') and the Hiller OH-23 Raven were standard LOH, or light observation helicopters. The Sikorsky CH-54 Tarhe or Flying Crane carried freight, artillery pieces and supplies in a detachable cab beneath its fuselage. The twin-rotor Boeing CH-47 Chinook – which Americans unavoidably named the 'Shithook' – became another carrier of freight, artillery, or men.

At Ia Drang 434 aircraft flew 54,000 sorties carrying 73,700 personnel, delivered 5,048 tons of cargo to the troops and brought an additional 8,216 tons into Pleiku from port cities like Qui Nhon. Artillery batteries were re-located 67 times by Chinooks.

## Air Force operations

The USAF had begun the year with four principal bases in South Vietnam. These were Saigon's Tan Son Nhut airfield (used since October 1961); Bien Hoa air base (since November 1961), Da Nang (January 1962) and Pleiku (July 1962). Binh Thuy air base was opened in May 1965 and Cam Ranh Bay in November 1965. The latter, built in tidal marsh and mudflats on the coast, was an engineering miracle, a marvel of the excesses of American technology. F-4 Phantoms flew from Cam Ranh Bay in operations

# Enter the HH-3E

A development of the Sikorsky S-61 which had first flown on 11 March 1959, and was widely used by the US Navy as the SH-3A Sea King, the slender, 54-ft 9-in (16.69-m) CH-3E was powered by two 1,500-shp (1119-kW) General Electric T58-GE-5 turboshaft engines.

Because of the opening of the bombing campaign against North Vietnam, there was an urgent need for an improved rescue helicopter in Southeast Asia. The Kaman HH-43 Huskie was being used in a role for which it was never really suited, and the longer range and greater speed of the big Sikorsky helicopter made it a natural candidate for

development as a combat rescue machine.

The CH-3E transport derivative of the S-61 had a high-set tailboom and rear loading ramp. A number of aircraft were quickly converted for the rescue role as the HH-3E. Principal improvements included the addition of crew armor, self-sealing fuel tanks, rectractable inflight refueling probe, rescue hoist with jungle penetrator and 0.5-in (12.7-mm) machine-guns.

None of these features was found on the HH-43B/F, so the Jolly Green Giant was expected to be a significant improvement. With a maximum speed of 166 mph (267 km/h) and a combat

# Combat Rescue

*The HH-43B/F Huskie with its distinctive intermeshing rotors had been designed for local air-base rescue and firefighting duty. In 1965, before longer-ranged helicopters were on hand, Huskies sometimes traveled a considerable distance to attempt rescues far behind enemy lines.*

As 'Rolling Thunder' air strikes continued, the need for better ways to rescue downed aircrews in North Vietnam became urgent. Plans were afoot to supplant the limited Kaman HH-43B/F Huskie with a larger and longer-range helicopter, the Sikorsky HH-3E. Two examples of the transport variant of the latter machine, the CH-3E, had been borrowed from Tactical Air Command and were being rushed to Nakhon Phanom, or 'Naked Fanny', as Americans called the Thai airbase. A few HC-130 Hercules transports, called King Birds, were becoming available to replace HU-16B Albatross and HC-54 Skymaster flying command posts. Greater loitering capacity by the rescue command ship, coupled with larger and longer-legged rescue helicopters would mean for the first time that a downed pilot had a genuine chance of rescue.

## Shot down

On 23 June 1965, Major Robert Wilson of the Takhli-based 357th TFS/355th TFW was on a combat mission in an F-105D (62-4319) when he was hit by ground fire over south-western North Vietnam. Wilson strained and coaxed, but his crippled 'Thud' refused to gain enough altitude to get over a ridge ahead of him. Wilson ejected towards a green jungle canopy and soon found himself hanging upside down in a tree 150-feet (46-m) above a shadowy jungle floor, gasping for breath and swinging from side to side. Wilson managed to use the inertia of his body to swing into the crotch of a tree, cut himself out of his parachute harness and retrieve the seat pack containing his AN/URC-II survival radio. This item itself was one of the drawbacks in combat rescue, a more durable and powerful combination voice/beeper radio being badly needed, but, in Wilson's case, the radio was adequate. His signal reached an HC-54 Skymaster command ship which vectored a flight of four A-1H Skyraiders from 'Naked Fanny'. The Skyraider pilots, whose aircraft were better known by their callsign Sandy, obtained visual sighting of Major Wilson's parachute canopy and saw no enemy troops in the area.

Should enemy troops try to intervene, the Sandy pilots were prepared to cover Wilson with 20-mm cannon fire and 500-lb (227-kg) bombs. Theirs was an especially hazardous task, since they might have to fight at treetop level where even a single bullet from an infantryman's rifle was a danger.

## Helicopter rescue

For once, the short-legged HH-43B/F helicopter was able to effect a rescue in the enemy's back yard. More than an hour after Major Wilson's bailout, an HH-43 from a forward operating location (FOL) in Laos – guided by radio traffic from HC-54, A-1Hs and Wilson himself – swooped down and, with a major effort by its para-rescueman, or PJ, plucked the major from the foliage. With Wilson present, no member of the chopper crew was able to pay for a drink that night at the Naked Fanny officers' club.

*The classic rescue team of HH-3 and A-1 Skyraider soon proved its worth in rescuing downed US aviators from enemy territory.*

radius of 625 miles (over 1000 km), the HH-3E was fast enough and had a long enough range that it could be accompanied by HC-130 command craft and A-1 Skyraider escorts.

Soon thereafter, the HH-3E proved its mettle. Its job, after all, was to prevent downed airmen from becoming POWs, where they faced torture, interrogation and propaganda exploitation by their North Vietnamese captors. Its US Navy cousin, the SH-3A, although designed originally for the anti-submarine warfare role, was soon carrying out the same kind of rescue missions from carriers and destroyers based in the Gulf of Tonkin.

# F-100F 'Wild Weasels'

The first four 'Wild Weasel' aircraft arrived at Korat on 26 November 1965. These were two-seat F-100F Super Sabres from the 33rd TFW at Eglin AFB, Florida, modified so that the back-seat operator had newly-installed RHAWS (radar homing and warning systems) to determine the location of active SAM sites. What had begun as a 90-day evaluation was to become a permanent part of the war – 'Wild Weasel' flights, codenamed Iron Hand, carrying out the very demanding and hazardous job of attacking any SAM site which threatened the strike force.

The mission was complex and perilous but highly effective. An Iron Hand formation consisted of four aircraft: two 'Wild Weasels' carrying air-to-ground missiles and two more loaded with conventional bombs or cluster bomb units.

## Anti-radar missiles

The 'Weasels' would eventually carry four AGM-45A Shrike anti-radiation missiles although it would be several months before the F-100Fs used a Shrike in combat. Later, Shrikes were replaced by AGM-78A Standard Arm missiles, having a longer

A backseater's view of an F-100F attack. The Super Sabre had not been designed to take out enemy missiles, but it did the job well. Employed at first only with bombs, the F-100F also used the AGM-45 Shrike missile after the wiring and the backseater's position were modified.

range and a larger warhead. These missiles homed-in on the emissions from the Fan Song radars found at SAM sites (although they lacked the 'memory' to continue homing if the enemy shut his radar down).

Iron Hand missions and tactics were little-changed through the course of the war and their effectiveness was often debated. While it was never clear how many SAM sites they actually destroyed, it was evident that they suppressed SAM defenses to the extent that the missiles could not be fired with nearly as much effectiveness against US aircraft. Another new term was coined, the backseater of the 'Wild Weasel' being officially an EWO (electronic warfare officer) but, more often, called a 'Bear'.

The men in strike aircraft like Phantoms and 'Thuds' depended on 'Wild Weasels', particularly in attacks on heavily-defended areas such as Hanoi and Haiphong. The very high risk associated with the 'Wild Weasel' mission was proven in short order on 20 December 1965 when Captains John

Pitchford and Robert Trier achieved the dubious distinction of being the first 'Wild Weasel' crew shot down. The pair are listed as having been lost in an F-100F (58-1231) of the 6,234th TFW, the provisional designation for the unit at Korat. Pitchford was escorting four 'Thuds' when he detected the Fan Song radar emissions associated with a SAM site. As he rolled in to make a run on the missile installation, a 37-mm cannon shell exploded in the aft section of his aircraft.

## AAA damage

Captain Pitchford found time to fire marking rockets at the SAM installation before turning towards the Gulf of Tonkin some 60 miles (97 km) away. The 'Thuds' expended their own ordnance on the SAM site, then escorted Pitchford in the hope he could go 'feet wet' (get over water) where a rescue would be more likely. It

over South Vietnam. Most missions against the North were mounted from airfields in Thailand.

On 18 February 1965 Americans were at last relieved of the requirement to carry a Vietnamese crew member while flying combat missions. This removed the fiction that USAF pilots were advisors. At Bien Hoa, where the 1st Air Commando Squadron was flying the A-1 Skyraider, Major Charles C. Vasiliadis threw up his hands with joy. On a recent mission the sleeping Vietnamese beside him had been having nightmares and began talking to himself.

Public attention throughout 1965 was focused on the air war up North where Phantoms and Thunderchiefs were attacking heavily-defended targets and fighting MiGs. There was plenty of action in the South, however, with the same Phantoms and 'Thuds', as well as many other types. On 23 October the 4,503rd Tactical Fighter

An F-5 Freedom Fighter trundles out on the 12,000-ft (3715-m) parallel taxiway at Bien Hoa. Tailored for small air forces in a sector of the globe described by a term that was new in 1965 – the Third World – the F-5 was brought to Vietnam by USAF pilots who tested it in action.

Squadron (Provisional), with its 12 Northrop F-5A Freedom Fighters, arrived and set up shop at Bien Hoa air base. These were the only F-5s in US inventory, having been diverted from production for foreign F-5 purchasers. As part of Operation 'Skoshi Tiger', to test the suitability of the F-5 as a potential first jet for the VNAF, the American squadron flew its first combat mission five hours after arriving from the States.

## 'Freedom fighter'

The F-5A had been designed as an inexpensive lightweight tactical fighter. At the very time the F-5A was being blooded, Northrop was beginning worldwide sales to Third World air forces, which were to continue for nearly two more decades and result in over 3,000 sales of the F-5A and subsequent versions. The twin-engined configuration offered extra insurance against hits from low-level VC ground fire. The first supersonic fighter to reach many of the air forces which used it, the F-5A could fly at 818 mph (1315 km/h) and could be dived at Mach 1.4.

Near the end of 1965, bad weather and indecision on both sides brought a period of low activity to the stalemate between American airpower and the North Vietnamese nation. It was probably true, as one airman at Korat wrote to his parents, that an irresistible force had met an immovable object. It was often pointed out that Hanoi was not going to budge, that the resolve of its people would endure relentless bombing, and that the 'Rolling Thunder' campaign had failed to cow Ho Chi Minh and his leadership.

Even Secretary McNamara acknowledged that the bombing of targets in North Vietnam had failed to produce clear-cut results. Far less often, far less loudly, it was also said – though not as many listened – that American airmen possessed a resolve of their own,

was not to be. His F-100F was disintegrating and sending back ugly black clouds of smoke even as Pitchford managed to gain a few feet of altitude. Pitchford's was one of those classic struggles which should have ended in success but didn't. He actually succeeded in extinguishing his engine fire warning light by reducing power and was on the radio to the 'Thud' flight leader, talking with optimism about how

he hoped to coax the Super Sabre to the water. Abruptly, he discovered that he had no hydraulic fluid! This was tantamount to having no aircraft and meant there was no choice but to eject while still feet dry.

Captain Trier ejected first. Pitchford followed. The F-100F blew itself to pieces in mid-air seconds later. Trier was to be listed as MIA (missing in action), while Pitchford became the first

'Wild Weasel' POW. His incredible challenge was to prevent the North Vietnamese from torturing him into revealing details of the new anti-SAM operations. As if to avenge the loss of a comrade, 18 more sorties were mounted in the area where Pitchford had been hit.

Although it would soldier on as a 'fast FAC' (forward air controller) north of the 17th Parallel, the F-100F Super Sabre

*Originally built as a dual-control trainer with reduced weapons capability, the F-100F was suitable for conversion to specialist combat roles calling for a two-man crew. These included 'Fast FAC' forward air control and 'Wild Weasel' suppression of enemy air defense radar and missile sites.*

was considered too vulnerable for the 'Wild Weasel' role in high-threat areas and was replaced by F-105Fs, F-105Gs and F-4Cs.

# Camouflage

Throughout 1965 and into 1966, aboard *Kitty Hawk* and other carriers, the Navy experimented with a camouflage scheme called vomit green by deck crews. This paintwork appeared at various times on A-4C Skyhawks, F-4G Phantoms, A-6A Intruders and other types. It was part of an experiment to see whether masking the appearance of an aircraft as seen against the jungle mattered.

Because there was no enemy air opposition in the South, and because the dark paint scheme made aircraft hard to see and caused accidents on carrier decks at night, the experiment was soon abandoned. Navy aircraft returned to their traditional gray tops and white undersides.

## Air Force change
An official history lists 24 November 1965 as the date the first Air Force aircraft in Southeast Asia, a C-130, was camouflaged. Aircraft began to appear in the two-tone brown and tan design, with light undersides, often called T.O.114

*Below: This experimental paint scheme on an F-4G Phantom of VF-213 'Fighting Blacklions' was tried in the combat zone but not adopted. It worked, but it posed problems of visibility for deck personnel during night-time carrier operations.*

camouflage in reference to the technical order which prescribed it. Ever since the Korean conflict, it had been conventional wisdom that camouflage was valueless because no paint had been

developed which would not impede the performance of the aircraft and which would be able to endure the wear and friction of jet-speed flight.

Camouflage on early RF-

*To purists who admired the subtle finish and bright unit colors on USAF aircraft prior to 1965, few sights seemed more obscene than an F-102A Delta Dagger in warpaint. According to conventional wisdom, an interceptor was supposed to be gray – but times were changing.*

101C Voodoos, among the first types to be so painted, added as much as 500 lb (226 kg) to the weight of the aircraft. Worse, the paint frequently peeled after only a single sortie.

Gradually the quality of paint was improved and its weight reduced, and camouflage was to become the order of the day for the Air Force, not merely in Southeast Asia but for a generation to come.

*The F-104 Starfighter, once dubbed the "missile with a man in it," flew escort missions and prowled for MiGs, but the confident fighter jocks who flew this jet never found the air-to-air duel they kept looking for. Deployed twice, F-104s accomplished almost nothing in the war zone.*

that they continued to fly into the face of heavy air defenses day after day with no sign of relenting, and that not even protests against the war by their own countrymen detracted from the sheer, stubborn courage which caused them to continue the fight. If North Vietnam was solid as concrete in the face of the American attacks, those attacks came on nevertheless with the power and force of a pile driver.

No MiGs were shot down in the second half of the year and no important new targets were opened up to the Skyhawks, 'Thuds' and Phantoms that kept flying north each day. Pilots of the Convair F-102A Delta Dagger interceptor, poised to cope with the enemy's Il-28 bomber, never saw an Il-28 at all. Some of them went aloft on night missions, using the infra-red seeker devices on their aircraft to detect hot pinpricks in the jungle, and unleashed 2.75-in rockets at Viet Cong campfires.

In a larger sense, the whole arsenal of American airpower was being misused in the same manner as the IR seeker on the F-102A. Even before he arrived in the battle zone to become one of the war's better-known 'Thud' drivers, Colonel Jack Broughton thought it peculiar that F-105s were being used to attack strategic targets in the North while B-52 Stratofortresses were being employed to dump bombs on tactical targets in the South. In 1965, as would remain true decades later, men like Major General Gordon M. Graham considered it unconscionable that no reliable air-to-air missile had been developed for fighter-versus-fighter combat. Almost nobody could figure out why men were sent to fly and fight without an organization well equipped to assure their rescue if shot down behind enemy lines.

## Bombing limitations

Above all, there were the frustrating rules of engagement which made it possible to bomb a truck on a highway but not the factory where the trucks were built; to decorate men for valor in combat one day and court-martial them for inadvertently striking forbidden targets the next; to engage a MiG in mid-air but not to attack that MiG on the ground. The problem with the rules of engagement, so often cited in every narrative about the war and so essential to its understanding, lay not merely with a civilian leadership which insisted on making targeting decisions as far from the war as Washington; even within the military ranks, men were far from able to agree on which targets should be attacked and why. It was almost as if men behind 'Rolling Thunder' needed the bad weather, to allow them to pause and reflect.

As the year drew to an end, a number of aircraft types saw combat for the first time. The RF-4C Phantom began flying reconnaissance missions from Tan Son Nhut in October. The F-100 Super Sabre and F-104 Starfighter flew from Da Nang from early in

the year. The introduction of the B-52 Stratofortress in May, with the first of many 'Arc Light' missions, was, of course, an event of major significance.

Approaching year's end, the policymakers authorized a strike on the thermal power plant at Uong Bi, one of the first instances when a hard industrial target was 'allowed' under the rules of engagement. Accompanied by *Ticonderoga* and *Kitty Hawk*, the *Enterprise* launched what was to become known as an 'Alpha Strike', sending more than 120 aircraft to pulverize the facility 15 miles (23 km) from Haiphong. It was the closest, so far, that airpower had come to the urban centers of Hanoi and Haiphong. The fighter cover flew the mission unopposed and unscathed but *Enterprise* lost two A-4C Skyhawks (148305, 149521) from squadron VA-76.

## Second bombing halt

On Christmas Eve 1965, in what seemed a puzzling contradiction to the Uong Bi air strike, the US suspended operations against North Vietnam in the latest of what was to become an almost endless succession of bombing halts intended to encourage Hanoi's leadership towards negotiations. As would happen frequently when the US attempted to send a signal in this manner, the message became completely lost, achieving no apparent purpose and persuading no-one of anything. This time, the halt lasted for 37 days. The North Vietnamese simply denounced the halt as a US trick when they finally got around to mentioning it at all. And, of course, Hanoi's General Giap directed that the respite be exploited to rebuild North Vietnam's strength and to speed the infiltration of men and supplies southward.

A new ally joined in the war when the first South Korean combat troops began taking up positions in South Vietnam near the end of 1965. In November 1965, protests against the US role in the war reached a national scale. In some locations, demonstrations became riots. By year's end, the number of US troops in South Vietnam had risen in a year's time from 23,000 to 181,000. It was the making of a quagmire.

# Enterprise

In December 1965 the first nuclear-powered aircraft-carrier, the mighty USS *Enterprise* (CVAN-65), brought the newest in combat technology to the Gulf of Tonkin. Carrying the most powerful air wing ever deployed aboard a fighting ship up to that time, the *Enterprise* had made a highly unusual Indian Ocean crossing, being supplied by air from Tananarive, Madagascar.

Arriving in the combat zone, *Enterprise* conducted combat operations very briefly from 'Dixie Station', sending its F-4B Phantoms and A-4C Skyhawks against Viet Cong guerrillas in South Vietnam. Before long, however, the world's biggest warship had moved north to join *Kitty Hawk* and *Ticonderoga* on 'Yankee Station' flying missions into North Vietnam.

Two aircraft from the massive carrier were downed over the South, an F-4B Phantom (151409) on 2 December 1965 and an RA-5C Vigilante (151633) on the 15th. All crew members were rescued. After moving to the North, *Enterprise* suffered four more aircraft losses in the final days of December — an unusually high toll.

# Fixed-Wing Gunships

Above: Fixed, sideways-firing guns in an AC-47 gunship. Three SUU-11A gun pods containing 7.62-mm rotary miniguns, shown here, replaced a quartet of less effective air-cooled .50-caliber (12.7-mm) machine-guns carried by the very first AC-47s.

Left: Time-lapse photography proves a point that should have been obvious long before Pentagon officers took note of it: a sideways-firing fixed-wing aircraft in a stable pylon turn could direct a veritable firestorm at a chosen location on the ground, wreaking enormous destruction.

An experiment the year before, the fixed-wing gunship lost its novelty and became a guardian angel to besieged combatants at isolated outposts. On 8 February 1965 the FC-47 gunship with its array of side-firing 7.62-mm machine-guns was sent to the Bong Son area in the face of the Viet Cong offensive in the central highlands. In under five hours, the gunship poured 20,500 rounds of ammunition into a hilltop where the Viet Cong had dug in. The strike killed about 300 VC.

General Joseph H. Moore, Jr, was the top Air Force officer in Vietnam, heading what was known at the beginning of the year as Second Air Division, although it was soon to be renamed Seventh Air Force. Moore was impressed with 'Puff the Magic Dragon', as the FC-47 version of the military DC-3 was called, especially with its ability to bring gunfire to bear on the enemy with withering accuracy. Moore requested a squadron of 16 gunships and noted that, because of the FC-47's small size,

it would be more effective to use the Convair C-131 or T-29, militarized versions of the twin-engined Convair 240/340 as the gunship airframe.

As it turned out, the Douglas aircraft was the only transport then available and by year's end it had been re-christened AC-47 to mark its 'attack' role. In rather hurried fashion, the Air Force put together the 4th Air Commando Squadron with 20 AC-47s (16 plus four for command support and attrition). The 4th arrived at Tan Son Nhut air base near

Saigon on 14 November 1965. Because of delays in receiving miniguns, the squadron was only beginning to ready itself for operations at year's end.

*Known initially as the FC-47 ('F' for 'fighter'), the gun-equipped version of the world-famous Gooney Bird was quickly redesignated AC-47 ('A' for 'attack'). The USAF wanted GAU-2/A 7.62-mm gun pods for the AC-47 but had to fit SUU-11A pods, designed to be carried under aircraft wings, as an interim measure.*

A floating city, USS Enterprise (CVAN-65) was the world's largest warship when it arrived in the combat zone in 1965. It was the first nuclear-powered aircraft carrier to go into battle. Heading for Vietnamese waters via the Indian Ocean, it picked up supplies in Madagascar before arriving in the South China Sea to unleash its air wing.

# LYNDON JOHNSON'S WAR

**After a 37-day Christmas and New Year halt, 'Rolling Thunder' bombing resumed on 31 January 1966. It was an unusual campaign. Tactical decisions – what time of day to launch a mission, what ordnance to carry – were being made not by commanders on the scene but thousands of miles away in the White House situation room.**

Stopping and starting an aerial campaign in this fashion was supposed to send signals, aimed at persuading the enemy to engage in peace talks. Instead, the US appeared to broadcast its own confusion and crossed purposes. Bombing alone was unlikely to win the war, but a halt to the bombing would never bring peace.

"The lack of a comprehensive plan for Southeast Asia which clearly stated US objectives and outlined the steps to reach those objectives was a major obstacle to sound planning and achievement," said an Air Force report. This was a polite way of saying that nobody knew what the hell they were doing. In Vietnam and Laos, where the situation was dire, absence of clearly stated goals contributed to failure to stabilize the military and political situations. Comprehensive inter-agency planning for overall US objectives and policy in the region was long overdue.

*An A-4 Skyhawk is slammed into the air by a carrier's steam catapult. At 16,216 lb (7355 kg) loaded, the 'Scooter' was a bantam by US standards. But as the tempo of fighting quickened and the US build-up grew, the Skyhawk became a heavy-duty performer in a widening war.*

When it became clear that the bombing halt was not going to sway Hanoi's support for the insurgency in South Vietnam, a meeting was arranged in the middle of the Pacific. President Johnson and South Vietnamese President Thieu and Premier Ky met in Honolulu for a two-day conference beginning on 7 February 1966. Their talks covered political, economic and social aspects of the war and included general agreement that the 'Rolling Thunder' campaign against North Vietnam should be continued.

As North Vietnam's SAM network grew, so too did the size and scope of air operations committed against it. The Douglas EB-66C Destroyer EW (electronic warfare) aircraft could provide effective blocking of acquisition radars. Two pairs of EB-66s, flying in anchor orbit 30 miles (48 km) from a target at its north-east and south-west extremities could provide, in effect, a jamming beam into and out of Hanoi for the Phantom or 'Thud' strike aircraft.

## Increasing threat

At first, it was feasible to position the EB-66s at optimum altitude of 25,000 ft (7616 m) with F-4 Phantom fighter cover, but the SAM and MiG threat eventually rendered the EB-66 too vulnerable and required its withdrawal to much greater distances, blunting its effectiveness. The type's vulnerability was demonstrated on 25 February 1966 when an EB-66C (54-0457) of the 41st TRS/460 TRW was shot down by an SA-2. It was the second loss of the very expensive EB-66 airframe in the conflict, one which could hardly be afforded. At a later juncture, on 14 January 1968, an EB-66C (55-0388) of the 41st TEWS/355th TFW was shot down by a flight of two MiGs and the type had to be withdrawn to jamming duties in more permissive areas.

# Helo Gunships

While some US Army officers were questioning the continuing build-up of US troops in South Vietnam and whether it had a clear purpose, most of these men believed in early-1966 that the war was being won. They felt that it was only a matter of time before American firepower would prevail. In battlefield terms, they were almost certainly right – the Viet Cong and NVA were no match for an airmobile assault force – but they had forgotten whose country it was. Vietnam was to demonstrate that winning the battle did not necessarily mean winning the war.

One of Army aviation's most effective tools was the helicopter gunship. The most potent example in 1966 was the UH-1C version of the familiar Huey. Standard armament systems for the UH-1C included the M21 package with one forward-firing 7.62-mm XM134 minigun and an XM158 seven-tube 2.75-in FFAR (folding-fin aircraft rocket) launcher mounted externally on each side of the fuselage. The XM16 was another package in which four 7.62-mm M60 machine-guns replaced the minigun. The all-rocket XM3 package consisted of two 24-tube FFAR launchers. In addition, the UH-1C was fitted – often as a result of field modifications – with all manner of extra armament, including a chin-mounted 40-mm grenade-launcher and M24A1 20-mm cannon pods.

Unfortunately the burden of a heavy armament load degraded performance, so that UH-1C gunships had difficulty keeping up with the 'slick' UH-1B troop transport helicopters. It was clear that in due course a dedicated gunship would be needed.

## The Cobra arrives

In March 1966 the US Army ordered the Bell AH-1G Cobra into production and Cobras began arriving in Vietnam later in the year. Lightweight two-seaters, Cobras could carry an impressive load without any sacrifice in performance, and were generally armed with a 7.62-mm minigun in the nose turret, a grenade-launcher and up to 52 FFAR rockets in four pods. The AH-1G Cobra built up an impressive combat record and helped reduce transport helicopter losses by providing fire suppression during troop insertions.

Starting on 13 May 1966, the 53rd Aviation Detachment (Field Evaluation) began operating four ACH-47A Chinook armed helicopter gunships at Vung Tau. The 228th Aviation Battalion and the 147th Aviation Company had successfully operated the CH-47A Chinook cargo-hauler from here for a year. The ACH-47A was something else, however. Nicknamed 'Guns A Go-go', it was armed with machine-guns, cannon, rockets and grenade-launchers.

Making an extra-heavily-armed gunship out of such a big helicopter seemed, on the surface, a good idea. It was not. Three of the four ACH-47As were lost, with loss of life, one in a bizarre and tragic accident when a mounting pin on a 20-mm cannon separated during a firing run, causing the gun to elevate and obliterate the forward rotors. All the crew were killed.

*A crew chief – always a flight crew member in US Army practice – checks out the situation around an early UH-1B Huey gunship. The Huey is armed with flexibly-mounted forward-firing machine-guns and rocket pods.*

*Above: An early UH-1B gunship, or 'Hog' displays its primary armament rocket pods and guns. UH-1s were not ideal for the gunship mission, so the Army developed the AH-1 HueyCobra.*

*Right: Operation 'Game Warden' was the Navy's attempt to cut the Viet Cong's river supply routes with helicopters, aircraft and riverine craft. Here, a Navy UH-1B gunship of squadron HAL-3 is working with PBR patrol boats in the Mekong Delta.*

# Marine Skyhawks

*A very personal kind of war*

Marine A-4 Skyhawk pilot Dorsie Page insists that a forward air controller who called in Skyhawks to bomb Viet Cong as they attacked American positions, found himself in trouble because the A-4s had to roll into their 'break' over the Bob Hope show, the roar of their jet engines upsetting the entertainer's program. Snake and Nape (Snakeye fin-retarded bombs and napalm) were the standard Marine medicine for the Viet Cong, but the conditions under which the men worked were a challenge 24 hours a day.

There was one Marine air

*Marines do not expect the Ritz when they set up shop in a war zone, but Chu Lai disappointed even the most modest of expectations. Maintenance of these Marine Skyhawks (at right, background) was performed out-of-doors by men living in tents.*

group (MAG-11) at Da Nang but no fewer than three (MAG-12, -13 and -36) at Chu Lai, the rough Marine airfield on the peninsula of the same name, where Marines were packed together in what Page called "sandy, scary tents, all metal with sand underpinning". In addition to three squadrons of A-4 Skyhawks (24 aircraft per squadron,

of which 18 or 19 were operational at a time), Chu Lai was home to Marine F-8 Crusaders and, after Christmas 1966, the A-6A Intruders of the 'Hawks' of VMA(AW)-533.

## Roughing it

Chu Lai had a runway like a piano board, as pilot Con Silard described it. The airfield was on an area of sand and laterite and was paved with metal stripping known as SATS (short airfield for tactical support). Its first runway, 70-ft wide and 8,000-ft long, was adequate for the Skyhawk but offered no margin for luxury. The

*Marine aviation expanded greatly during the Vietnam years, the Corps adding the hi-tech A-6 Intruder to an inventory which boasted several hundred A-4s. The Skyhawk always performed the bulk of Marine Corps sorties in the early years of the war.*

second, crosswind runway, 4,000-ft in length, required Skyhawks to use JATO (jet assisted take-off) and hurl themselves aloft amid billowing clouds gushing back from the JATO bottles. A likeness to an aircraft-carrier deck, complete with wire-arrested landing apparatus and an LSO (landing signal officer) on 24-hour duty, helped to compensate for the airfield's inadequacies. "But landing there was hairy," Page remembered. "There were usually no runway lights because there wasn't enough electricity."

It was also difficult keeping track of who was doing what to whom in this war. Over Laos at a time when the administration said Americans were not fighting in Laos, Page was hit by a small-caliber bullet which passed horizontally through his cockpit and through both his legs just above the knees. Bleeding

---

The Marine Corps introduced a new aircraft type on 8 March 1966 when 27 Boeing-Vertol CH-46A Sea Knight helicopters of squadron HMM-16 flew ashore and landed at the growing Marine helicopter field at Marble Mountain near Da Nang. With a crew of three, the tandem-rotor transport helicopter could carry 24 troops or 4,600 lb (2087 kg) of cargo.

The CH-46A was generally a tough, capable machine but it soon demonstrated a serious allergy to the powdery white sand of the Vietnamese lowlands. Its engines gobbled sand, then went on the blink – sand was getting into the fuel system, clogging the works. It was not the last time Americans were to have difficulty with helicopters that did not operate well in sandy conditions.

## Army aviation consolidates

With its huge fleet of helicopter and fixed-wing aircraft scattered everywhere in South Vietnam, the US Army had difficulty finding a way to standardize training, operational methods and combat procedures. An attempted 'fix' was the formation of the 1st Aviation Brigade on 1 March 1966. Although units in the field retained operational control over their aircraft and helicopters, the brigade offered a centralized focus and helped assure that 'lessons learned' were learned everywhere.

To the American television viewer back home, who rarely went an evening without observing and hearing the distinctive beat of UH-1 Huey rotors, it was almost impossible to understand what progress was being made in the war. After the Battle of the Ia Drang Valley late in 1965 the American soldier never again had to fear losing on the battlefield. But such pitched battles were the exception.

The public affairs experts in Saigon came up with the idea of naming military operations with American terms. The TV audience could hear about Operations 'Attleboro', 'Irving', 'Thayer', 'Paul Revere' (and later 'Cedar Falls', 'Junction City', 'Pershing', 'Pegasus' and 'Delaware') without learning a thing about Vietnamese geography. Spokesmen at the evening press briefing in Saigon – the famous 'Five O'Clock Follies', in the jargon of correspondents – used the arithmetic of body counts to make the point that the war was being won without ever describing the size or shape of the Viet Cong and NVA enemy.

These operations, most of them helicopter insertions of large numbers of troops over periods of days or weeks or even months, were in fact wearing down the Viet Cong and NVA. In Operation 'Paul Revere IV' in late-1966 the newly arrived 4th Infantry Division, supported by elements of the 25th Infantry Division and First Cavalry, was lifted into mountainous, jungle-covered terrain near the Cambodian border of Pleiku Province to search out regular NVA units and their base camps. Six weeks of campaigning netted almost a thousand enemy dead along with tons of captured weapons, equipment and supplies. Had the operation been given a name based on geography, TV watchers and correspondents alike might have had a better feel for what was going on.

As 1966 drew on, the Douglas AC-47 fixed-wing gunship proved to be one of the most potent aerial weapons available to friendly forces. In a war without sharply defined front lines and rear areas, defeat or victory – however temporary – was often determined by how US and ARVN troops handled an enemy assault on one of their outposts. If the Viet Cong or North Vietnamese reached the point where they were 'coming through

profusely, he managed to land at Chu Lai to be told that tomorrow's Skyhawk operations would take place over South Vietnam. "I had five different ROE cards," said Page, referring to the white flash-cards which told pilots the rules of engagement, "one for each situation we might get into. There were so many rules and restrictions, no pilot could remember them all."

Page recalls that squadron mate Pete Kruger displayed his view of military authority by naming his dog Major. A captain himself, Kruger, where appropriate, would put off a caller with the news that he was 'busy with Major right now'. Kruger went on to fly more than 500 combat missions in A-4 Skyhawks and O-1C Bird Dog observation aircraft.

## Ground support

The Marine Corps has always taken pride in its aviation arm, which exists primarily to provide direct support to the combat Marine on the ground. Aviators with the Corps are Marines before they become pilots – they go through the same basic infantry training as their fellow Marines and as a result have a real affinity for the 'grunt' slogging through the mud below.

Men like Page, Kruger and Bill Egen, the skipper of the 'Green Knights' of VMA-121, took pride in bringing their A-4s down to treetop level in a hail of enemy fire to deliver Snake and Nape within a few hundred yards of Marines in contact with the enemy. Marine pilots were considered especially good at this difficult job, often delivering their ordnance with great precision right in front of friendly troops. The Skyhawk in particular was regarded as highly effective – a light, agile yet very heavily-armed and very survivable aircraft, ideal for the close-support mission.

*Using old-fashioned muscle and sweat, Marines load Mark 80 series bombs on an A-4C Skyhawk at Chu Lai in 1966. The Skyhawk carried up to 9,155 lb (4153 kg) of bombs and rockets and was armed with 20-mm guns.*

the wire', things were really serious. But even then, a massed assault could often be beaten back if an AC-47 could position itself in a pylon, turn above the enemy and begin hosing down the area with its side-mounted machine-guns. Known as 'Spooky' or 'Puff the Magic Dragon', the AC-47 fought effectively during the nocturnal hours, when 'Charlie' was at his best. No outpost was ever over-run, by night or day, when an AC-47 was on the scene.

On 8 March 1966 the 14th Air Commando Wing was organized at Nha Trang to manage and control the diverse Air Commando squadrons and detachments located in Southeast Asia.

## Medal of Honor

The next day, 9 March, the battle at A Shau demonstrated how air support could and could not help the fighting man on the ground. The Special Forces camp at A Shau in South Vietnam was attacked by an estimated 4,000 North Vietnamese regulars. At first A-1E Skyraiders and other fighter-bombers were able to help the besieged friendlies to hold off the onslaught, but bad weather closed in and reduced available air support. A few Skyraider pilots were able to get in and out, but with overwhelming numbers the enemy was able to force evacuation of the camp on the evening of the second day.

During the day Major Bernard F. Fisher of the 1st Air Commando Squadron saw another Skyraider belly-in on the camp's

*A-1E Skyraider pilot Major Bernie Fisher rescued downed airman Captain Datford 'Jump' Myers with a daring landing under fire at A Shau. Fisher became the Air Force's first living recipient of the Medal of Honor since World War II. His 'Spad', later displayed at the Air Force Museum in Dayton, Ohio, became the first Medal of Honor aircraft to be preserved.*

wreckage-strewn airstrip. A Shau was under heavy fire at that moment and the airstrip itself appeared virtually unusable. Fisher believed a rescue was possible. He landed his A-1E Skyraider on the airstrip. The downed pilot came running and dived into the cockpit head first while Fisher poured on the coals and made a daring take-off. Major Fisher was later awarded the Medal of Honor, the first Air Force recipient of this war.

The Skyraider was ideal for the 'Sandy' role, directing rescue forces to pick up airmen downed by enemy fire. On a typical rescue flight, two to four A-1E Skyraiders worked under controllers in an airborne command post – a Grumman HU-16B Albatross in 1964-65, an HC-130P Hercules from 1966. A two-plane Skyraider flight escorted rescue helicopters to the crash site. A second Skyraider flight at the rescue area determined the condition of the downed aircrew, its location, and the disposition of enemy defenses with relation to terrain. This A-1E flight leader decided whether conditions would enable him to engage enemy guns and bring in rescue forces.

At times the rescue mission involved exotic armaments. The A-1E Sandy aircraft could carry an encyclopedic assortment of ordnance anyway, but by 1966 riot control munitions were approved for use during rescues. The controversial weapons included CBU-19A/B (cluster bomb unit) and CBU-30A anti-personnel area denial bombs, which were essentially tear gas bombs, as well as the BLU-52A/B (bomb live unit) weapon concocted by mixing bulk tear gas with the ingredients of the BLU-1C fire bomb.

## F-100 Super Sabre

**F-100D 56-3184 of the 416th TFS 'Silver Knights', 37th TFW at Phu Cat. The 'Hun' eventually racked up 360,000 sorties in the Southeast Asia conflict, more than any other aircraft. This ship has four 750-lb (340-kg) bombs, plus two fuel tanks and four 20-mm M39E cannons.**

On 14 March 1966 the latest of a number of new airfields opened at Phan Rang. Like Tuy Hoa to be opened later in the year, Phan Rang is best remembered for F-100 Super Sabre operations. The two squadrons of B-57 Canberras in the country, the 8th and 13th, were also assigned to the Super Sabre wing and made the move to Phan Rang later in the year.

The F-100 Super Sabre had been transformed, in effect, into airborne artillery for the support of friendly ground troops. F-100s hauled bombs from home bases to locations on the map where there were 'troops in contact' – that is, a battle going on – and followed guidance from FACs, who marked the enemy with smoke rockets. The missions were predictable and unglamorous: brief, take-off, cruise to target area, find the FAC, drop on his smoke, strafe, climb out, cruise home, land, debrief. The next day, more of the same. But once in a while there was an empty billet when an F-100 pilot lost a disagreement with enemy guns on the ground.

An unrelenting demand for close air support resulted in the deployment to Vietnam of additional F-100 squadrons and to the formation in-country of new tactical fighter wings. Two of the earliest

# Airlift

In addition to the USAF C-123s, Army CV-2s and VNAF C-47s, the airlift mission inside South Vietnam was being increasingly taken on by the Lockheed C-130 Hercules. Although assigned on a rotating basis rather than bedded down permanently in South Vietnam, the Hercules force had risen to 44 C-130A, C-130B and C-130E aircraft by 1 November 1966.

Hercules aircrews felt that operating conditions in Vietnam were unsafe. Professionals, accustomed to regimented methods, they sometimes viewed C-47 and C-123 pilots as 'cowboys' who took undue risk. Hazardous taxiing conditions were everywhere, not only at the over-crowded larger airfields but at forward sites where taxi strips were used by vehicles, helicopters, and sometimes water buffalo. Ramp delays were endemic, communications were poor, and cargo offloading facilities ranged from poor to non-existent.

In time things improved. Nevertheless, Defense Secretary McNamara supported recommendations that the C-130s continue to 'shuttle' in and out of South Vietnam for 15- or 30-day stays rather than be based permanently in the country.

By late 1966 the Hercules had hauled more tonnage in Vietnam than C-123s, CV-2s and C-47s combined. With the growing role of the C-130, up to 12 squadrons were providing aircrews and aircraft to the combat zone at a time. Maintenance on the older C-130A models continued to be a nagging problem, but eventually dramatic efficiencies were achieved in Hercules operations. As 'people-movers' the C-130s complemented Army helicopters in giving the infantryman a high degree of mobility – usually an advantage over the Viet Cong.

The job never got easier and more than one C-130 pilot sucked in his breath and stiffened with apprehension while setting down a cargo-laden aircraft at a tiny outpost where Viet Cong rocket attacks or mortar shells could fall at any time.

## Tuy Hoa opens

On 15 November 1966 Tuy Hoa opened. It was the first and only air base in Vietnam designed and constructed under USAF supervision. The base was built by a contractor under the 'turnkey' concept, under which PACAF moved in to a complete, ready-to-use facility.

As another of the seemingly endless years of American involvement in South Vietnam drew to a close, more and more Americans were wondering if it would ever be over. At Tan Son Nhut where he was a loadmaster on an Air Force cargo aircraft, Staff Sergeant Vernon L. Sewell was talking about his experiences

*The C-123B Provider was one of the first US Air Force aircraft to be sent to Vietnam. It was not always big enough or fast enough, but it pioneered assault landings and short-field take-offs in remote hinterland outposts.*

to one of the newer men.

"You know," Sewell said, "I came in here in 1962 when I was on a C-124 Globemaster. In those days every once in a while we would carry out a coffin with an American flag draped around it.

"I started coming back in 1964 when I was on a C-133. One day, the crew made a big deal out of the fact that we were taking out two coffins wrapped with American flags. Then on one of our flights it was three.

"Now I'm stationed in-country and we're getting this new cargo plane, the C-141, coming in here from outside. Now we fill an entire airplane with coffins covered by American flags. An entire airplane! You want to know something?" He asked with a growing sense of anger. "I'd like to know if this war is ever going to end."

Above: The Hercules, represented here by a comparatively late C-130E model, seemed capable of flying from any surface, even aluminium matting gouged out by Viet Cong mortar fire. The 'Herc' handled the bulk of intra-theater transport duties, popping in and out of airfields large and small.

Right: The C-141A StarLifter combined the interior dimensions of the Hercules with jet speed and long range. Most troops came to Vietnam on chartered airliners, but much equipment and weaponry crossed the Pacific in the fuselage of a StarLifter.

# 'Hot' War in the Intruder

*Lt Gen. Joseph Moore was quick to congratulate two F-4C Phantom crews who shot down MiGs in July 1966. Moore's 2nd Air Division became Seventh Air Force soon afterward, one measure of the growing magnitude of the American commitment.*

F-100 wings were the 3rd and 35th, at Bien Hoa and Phan Rang respectively. Home-based at England AFB, Louisiana, the 3rd TFW moved to Bien Hoa at the end of 1965 and eventually had four squadrons, one of which, the 416th TFS, was shuffled around, moving from Tan Son Nhut to Bien Hoa to Phu Cat in 1966. Pilots of the 3rd TFW completed more than 13,000 sorties in their first six months in the combat zone. The 35th TFW was activated in April 1966 at Da Nang and moved in October to Phan Rang.

On 1 April 1966, a major change in US Air Force command structure reflected the growing scale of US involvement in the war. The 2nd Air Division, which had been responsible for USAF operations in Vietnam, was discontinued and replaced by the Seventh Air Force (which should have been referred to correctly with its number designation spelled out, but which was often abbreviated as 7th Air Force or 7AF), headquartered at Tan Son Nhut airbase near Saigon. By becoming a numbered air force in its own right, the new command was no longer subordinate to Thirteenth Air Force in the Philippines but, rather, reported directly to PACAF headquarters in Hawaii.

Command relationships were to remain cumbersome throughout the war. Seventh Air Force commander Lt Gen. Joseph H. Moore reported to MACV (Military Assistance Command Vietnam) chief, General William Westmoreland, for some purposes and for others to PACAF chief, General Hunter Harris. Moore had control of all USAF aircraft 'in country' but not over Navy aircraft which flew similar missions against the same targets. He had fighter wings at his disposal but never commanded the in-theater KC-135 and B-52 assets which remained under the purview of SAC.

## Caribou dispute resolved

On 6 April agreement was belatedly reached on an issue that had provoked strong sentiment on both sides, the dispute between the Army and Air Force over control of the CV-2 Caribou aircraft. There were now no fewer than 88 Caribous in the country and the Army had stated its intention to acquire 120 CV-7 Buffalo aircraft from the same manufacturer, de Havilland of Canada.

The chiefs of staff inked in an agreement which turned the entire Caribou fleet over to the USAF. The Army received virtually nothing in exchange, other than a meaningless concession on the right to operate helicopters in the supply role. Effective at year's end, the Caribou, now designated C-7A, continued flying throughout the country but with Air Force pilots at the controls.

In April 1966, American warplanes still had not attacked Hanoi or Haiphong. There had been extensive discussion about

In the spring of 1966, the fighting in the North was heating up. There was a gradual but relentless improvement in the size and effectiveness of a defense system which now employed elaborate radar and visual warning networks to co-ordinate the guns, fighters and missiles which were extracting an increasing toll from the attackers. MiG-17 fighters challenged US strike aircraft more frequently and more tenaciously, and the Soviet Union began supplying newer MiG-21s.

MiG tactics still entailed low-risk commitment to battle, making single passes at strike aircraft and scurrying away from contact with escorting fighters. It was precisely this caution which dampened the hopes of fighter pilots itching for a fair contest with the MiG and which limited further air-to-air victories. While fighter pilots ached to get a shot at a MiG, strike pilots could evade them only to be driven into a position of greater vulnerability to another, such as the surface-to-air missile. MiGs were not particularly successful in shooting down the attackers but did harry and harass, forcing them to abandon run-ins against targets or to jettison bombs prematurely.

But there was one aircraft which under certain conditions could be sure of avoiding MiGs. The Grumman A-6A Intruder with its complex electronic suite, had been viewed with some scepticism by naval aviation traditionalists, but the heavy-jowled aircraft with its odd bulbous shape was pressing home attacks in driving rain and blackest murk, when no other warplane on ship or land could get aloft.

## Early losses

Intruders had proven an especially potent addition to the carrier-borne arsenal, but not without cost. The first squadron to employ the Intruder, the 'Sunday

*Right: With two 250-gal tanks and 18 Mark 82 500-lb (227-kg) Snakeye bombs, an A-6A Intruder of VA-85 'Black Falcons' rushes aloft from USS Kittyhawk (CVA-63) on a 1966 sortie. The huge black radome was later replaced by one with a white neoprene coating.*

Punchers' of VA-75 aboard *Independence* lost four aircraft and crews before the big carrier completed her cruise and retired from the war zone.

The second Intruder squadron, the 'Black Falcons' of VA-85 on *Kitty Hawk*, fared little better, suffering the loss of two A-6As in combat and one more in an operational accident early in their own cruise. The men were paying a steep price for introducing the first fully-integrated, computerized, all-weather attack and navigation system, an array of black boxes that reduced standard flight instruments and procedures to back-up status.

## Non-stop action

The A-6A Intruder was in continuous action against North Vietnamese road and rail targets, industrial plants, airfields and ports. This went on day and night, week after week, often in the foulest of weather. Later, it was learned that no other aircraft so impressed the North Vietnamese as a symbol of American persistence, although the North Vietnamese mistakenly believed during some Intruder strikes that they were being bombed by B-52 Stratofortresses!

*Kitty Hawk* Intruders concentrated on nocturnal interdiction when the weather, which was never really good, became marginal enough to enable

*An A-6A Intruder of VA-85 shows off the camouflage tried on an experimental basis in 1966. It was thought that the color would make US Navy warplanes less likely to be spotted and attacked from above by MiGs.*

other naval aircraft to find the designated targets during the day.

## Poor weather

This was one area of the world where marginal conditions were, by any comparison, favorable. North Vietnam is consistent with its continuously poor weather during the late winter and early spring, with a surfeit of low cloud, fog and driving rain, and VA-85 often had to be employed in daylight as a pathfinder for Alpha Strikes by Phantoms and Skyhawks.

To minimize their exposure to the increasingly numerous SAM batteries, Intruder crews used a high-speed, low-altitude approach to the target, and then a steep climb to altitude before commencing the bombing run. To further reduce the chance of being detected and tracked by the SA-2's Fan Song radar, the Intruders flew singly or in pairs in 'lone wolf' fashion.

The third US Navy A-6A Intruder squadron to enter the

*A pair of bomb-laden A-6As of VA-196 'Main Battery' on a mission from **USS** Constellation (CVA-64). The debut of the A-6 Intruder was grim and unhappy, but this medium-attack aircraft overcame its early troubles and compiled a superb war record.*

battle area was the 'Tigers' of VA-65, heading into harm's way aboard USS *Constellation* (CVA-64). The 'Batmen' of US Marine Corps squadron VMA-242 also used Intruder from land,

including some operations over North Vietnam.

The Marines also introduced a much-needed augmentation for their EF-10B Skyknight in the shape of an electronic warfare

variant of the Intruder, the EA-6A, first operated in the combat zone by the 'Playboys' of squadron VMCJ-2. The Marine squadrons operated from Chu Lai and Da Nang.

*The US Navy experimented with green camouflage on this RA-5C Vigilante, among others. Flying daily into harm's way, the RA-5C was an ideal candidate to test the new colors in action. However, the dark shade was hard to see on deck at night, and the experiment was dropped.*

carpet-bombing the two major population centers, and even some discussion about how quickly the use of a couple of tactical nuclear weapons might bring the war to a quick end. There had also been discussion about bombing the network of dams and dikes which covered North Vietnam's flooded paddy fields during the growing season. The latter action would have caused major flooding throughout extensive rural areas of the country and would have seriously damaged North Vietnam's road and rail network.

Another debate about targeting revolved around North Vietnam's supply of petroleum. The rules of engagement would not permit attacking tankers unloading fuel at Haiphong, and this was not likely to change, but it was thought that strikes against POL (petroleum, oil, lubricant) storage facilities were both justified and directly related to North Vietnam's infiltration of the South. Debate about attacking the POL would continue until it actually happened a couple of months later. Meanwhile, protest against the war intensified and debates on other aspects of the fighting continued.

Other problems in the late spring of 1966 included serious shortages of everything from personal survival equipment to pilots themselves. The famous 'bomb shortage', which would recur two years later, left both Air Force and Navy strike groups without sufficient bombs to load their aircraft. A fighter capable of carrying six to eight 750-lb (340-kg) bombs would now fly into North Vietnam with as few as one or two – the risk to its crew being, of course, the same.

## Camouflage experiment

While USS *Kitty Hawk* (CVA-63) drew near the end of her spring 1966 combat cruise and was running out of numerous items which could not be resupplied, including bombs, the carrier's experiment of painting half of its aircraft in dark-green camouflage was found to be less than successful; indeed, the green was dangerous on a crowded flight deck during the hours of darkness, while gray/white aircraft could be more easily seen. The Navy decided to employ the camouflage scheme no further. Dark-green A-4C Skyhawks, F-4B/G Phantoms, RA-5C Vigilantes and A-6A Intruders were thus a brief and passing sidelight to the war at a time when fighting was intense and losses of aircraft were heavy.

Only 12 F-4G Phantoms were built and the 'Black Lions' of *Kitty Hawk*'s squadron VF-213 operated 10 of them, a few of which

later ended up in the hands of sister squadron the 'Aardvarks' of VF-114. From the outside, the F-4G appeared little different than the widely-used F-4B. It had come off the St Louis production line, however, with a two-way datalink system installed behind the rear cockpit, which could relay information from the carrier concerning mission requirements. The AN/ASW-21 datalink system also allowed the pilot to make a 'hands off' approach to his carrier. Studies were already under way at McDonnell to introduce a simplified, one-way version of the system in a newer model of the Phantom which was not yet ready to arrive in the battle zone, the F-4J. Curiously, the Navy never installed guns on F-4B, F-4G or F-4J at any time during the entire conflict.

The Phantom was proving itself in other ways. Three more MiG-17s fell to Air Force Phantoms in air-to-air combat at the end of April 1966, but so far not a single Phantom had been lost to a MiG. More importantly, Marine Corps aviation was expanding and Marine pilots were taking their Phantoms into Route Package One,

# Enter the MiG-21

The origins of the next fighter to be acquired by the North Vietnamese lay in the Korean War. Reports from the losing side led Soviet pilots to demand an air superiority fighter from which all unnecessary equipment would be eliminated, leaving a simple, nimble, lightweight craft designed for the air-to-air role.

Limited in range and payload, and not easy to learn to fly, the new fighter – the MiG-21 – was far from perfect, but it had a twin-barrel 23-mm GSh-23 cannon at a time when most Phantoms had no guns; it could also carry up to four KA-13 (AA-2) Atoll air-to-air missiles, the enemy's closest equivalent to the Sidewinder. Powered by a 16,500-lb (7500-kg) thrust Tumansky R-25 turbojet with

afterburner, the MiG-21 could fly at 1,320 mph (2125 km/h) or Mach 2 at 36,000 ft (11 000 m).

Air-to-air combat in North Vietnam had already proven that speed was not an important attribute when you were trying to outfight a Phantom, but the Atoll missiles provided a capability not usually found on the earlier MiG-17 (although neither MiG ever operated with radar-guided missiles like the Sparrow).

## Advanced threat

The MiG-21 was advanced enough to worry US airmen considerably, even though North Vietnam's best pilots continued to prefer the MiG-17. Usually armed only with guns, the older jet could out-turn almost anything in the sky and at close range, the American Phantoms

# 11 April 1966: B-52s Strike North

As part of the continuing effort to choke the network of supply routes known collectively as the Ho Chi Minh Trail, B-52 Stratofortresses entered North Vietnamese airspace for the first time on 11 April 1966. Their target was Route 15 at the Mu Gia Pass between North Vietnam and Laos, about 65-miles (104-km) south of Vinh. B-52 strikes, known as Arc Light missions, were already under way in the south.

The first SAC bombers committed to the conflict were B-52F models, with a maximum payload of 51 750-lb (340-kg) bombs, 27 carried internally and 24 externally. Meanwhile, the entire B-52D fleet was being rebuilt for the conflict.

The 'Big Belly' modification program would increase the B-52D's capacity to carry 500-lb (227-kg) bombs from 27 to 42 internally. In addition, the B-52D could still carry 24 500-lb (227-kg) or 750-lb (340-kg) bombs externally. The 'Big Belly' B-52D maximum load of 60,000 lb (25154 kg) was about a 50 per cent improvement over the B-52F.

At any one time, two B-52 wings plus augmentee aircraft and crews were maintained at Andersen AB, Guam, for combat operations in Southeast Asia. While committed to the conflict,

*A B-52 over Vietnam. Meant from the start as a nuclear weapon, the B-52 performed well in the conventional bombing role.*

*Some of the bombs carried by B-52 Stratofortress crews had literally been in the US Pacific stockpile since the end of World War II. This still-life on Guam shows row after row of conventional gravity bombs stretched out beside B-52s.*

these B-52 wings were assigned to the 3rd Air Division's 4133rd Bomb Wing, Provisional, which had been organized on 1 February 1966.

The first strikes into North Vietnam coincided with the April arrival at Andersen of the 28th and 484th Bomb Wings with the 'Big Belly' B-52D to replace the B-52F as the SAC bomber in the Vietnam conflict. So far, Stratofortresses were going north only into Route Package One, in the relatively permissive environment at the southern extremity of North Vietnam. For propaganda reasons, Hanoi wanted very much to shoot down a B-52 and claimed, untruthfully, to have done so several times. For the moment the big bombers would be kept clear of heavily defended areas where this could actually happen.

had no weapon with which to counter a gun.

Examined close-up, the MiG-21 is a remarkably crude-looking aircraft and gives the impression of having been put together under lax Third World working conditions by people who do not care if the wings match exactly. Older MiG-21s are held together by relatively crude rivets. A simple device in a nose pitot probe tells the pilot when he is at a dangerous angle of attack. The cockpit is narrow and cramped.

It would be easy indeed to view the MiG-21 with a kind of snobbish disdain, but this would be a mistake. American fighters had the drawback of being too expensive, too complex, and equipped with too many secondary systems which added to weight and reduced performance. The MiG-21 was relatively simple to maintain, and gave great performance at much less cost.

*One North Vietnamese MiG-21 pilot eventually received considerable attention in Hanoi when he was credited with downing 13 American warplanes. Americans scoffed at the simple construction technique which created the MiG-21, but in combat the 'Fishbed' was no joke.*

# A Voodoo Pilot's View of Combat

"I have been so scared under fire that I once forgot to turn on my cameras, perhaps because of the fascination of seeing muzzle flashes for the first time. I have tossed and turned in the night, and gagged in the morning when I brushed my teeth. At times I have slept like a child. I have worried about myself and worried about the mission of others. I have seen men go to God and men go to booze. I have not seen a hero. I have seen a man for what he is, and a war for what it brings."

The first air-to-air victories in more than nine months came when two MiG-17s were shot down by F-4C Phantoms of the Ubon-based 'Triple Nickel' squadron, the 555th TFS/8th TFW, on 23 April 1966. At about this time, a young pilot sat down and penned his thoughts for those who would follow him into the high risk area where men now faced MiGs, flak and SAMs.

## Combat revealed

Classified 'Secret' until well after the end of the war, the impressions of Captain Edward W. O'Neil, Jr, pilot of an RF-101C Voodoo reconnaissance craft, use some jargon in creating guidelines for others to follow. He also describes how it feels in the cockpit. He flew 59 combat missions with the 20th TFS/460th TRW and was left to reflect upon why some men lived and some died.

*A reconnaissance aircraft catches the shadow of an attacking aircraft as it passes over the burning wreckage of a North Vietnamese patrol boat. Post-attack damage assessment was a key and highly dangerous task for all reconnaissance platforms.*

"I do not believe the people who came back were lucky, but I cannot help thinking some of the people who did not return were unlucky. The atmosphere was hostile but we were not always threatened by MiGs. We lost three crews, very competent crews, each with over 60 missions. We lost them to something – if only we knew what.

"The missions I flew involved flights over all areas of Route Packages Five and Six north of Hanoi. I have never been to the area within 10 miles of Hanoi, or immediately south of that city. I have never executed a sea entry or escape. I have never seen a MiG.

"I have done and have seen and have experienced the following. I have been to Kep airfield, the Bac Ninh POL installation, the Thai Nguyen steel works, Yen Bai airfield, Thud Ridge, and throughout and around the valley around these areas many times. I have tried it 'high' and I have tried it 'in the weeds'. I have been hit and have watched them fire at me. I have seen a SAM launched at a flight of Thuds.

## On your own

"The single ship concept for reconnaissance in both highly defended and undefended targets is the most profitable employment of aircrews and aircraft and offers the following advantages:

1 Maneuverability, without wingman consideration.
2 High-speed low-level terrain masking.
3 Weather penetration at any time.
4 Minimum radio transmissions.
5 Maximum speed employment.

*Routinely, the RF-101C Voodoo flew day reconnaissance missions at speeds of Mach 1.8 or higher. The Voodoo toted over 9,000 lb (4082 kg) of oblique and forward-aimed cameras to a radius of 1,400 miles (2253 km).*

6 Minimum enemy target development.
7 Optimum use of fuel – in a two-ship flight, the wingman will normally use more fuel than leader.
8 A chance to be alone in a decision and a plan.

"The high-threat SAM will always, except in the most unique situation (i.e. movement of a SAM site to previously undefended area in order to surprise launch into known used flight paths) be located in highly defended areas. Therefore, consideration must also be given to automatic weapons, 37, 57, 85 and 100 mm, as well as the SAM. High-altitude flying in a SAM area is out of the question. Although the probability of the enemy launching against a single ship is much less than their launching against a flight, you can expect a launch of up to three SAMs (minimum separation 6 seconds) at any time you fly above treetop level.

## Jinking and weaving

"How can you effectively acquire a target in a highly-defended, high-threat SAM area? Flying at 4,600 to 8,000 feet (1491 to 2432

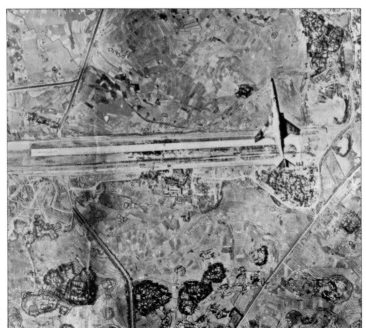

*Lt Col John Bull Stirling of the 20th Tactical Reconnaissance Squadron whips across the main runway at North Vietnam's Kep Airfield. RF-101C Voodoo pilots went right into the path of enemy guns at enormous risk to bring back accurate intelligence.*

Some of RF-101C Voodoo pilot O'Neil's comments at the start of a combat mission apply only to his own, highly specialized aircraft. Many others are just as applicable to the general situation faced by all airmen penetrating North Vietnamese skies in the spring of 1966. O'Neil's 'nitty gritty' details are the sort of minutia frequently left out of combat narratives.

"The proper time to get your target folder and start the plan, I believe, is three hours before take-off, not before and not later. I find that laying out the map, and just looking at it, is the best way to start. Have a cup of coffee and just look. Look at the target. Look at the high-threat SAM sites. Just look. I sometimes just look for one-half hour. I digest the map. I go to the relief map and digest the terrain. I watch others planning. Where are they going, and how are they going in? What escape routes are they using? I watch and ask questions.

**Camouflaged RF-101C Voodoos ready for action in 1966. Those who flew and maintained these big, fast jets took perverse pride that their aircraft was hard to maintain, hard to fly, and prone to mechanical problems. They had good cause, for when used to good advantage the RF-101C was the most capable tactical reconnaissance ship of its era.**

"We in recce are individuals, flying single-seat, individual aircraft. We all have ideas, based on self confidence, training, our experience, and the experience of others. When we plan a route, we are all trying to accomplish the same end result.

### It's your plan

"When a recce pilot plans a mission, he alone is responsible for that plan, his life depends on the success of the plan, so never, never volunteer suggestions on how he should plan his flight. If he asks your opinion of his flight plan, tell him it is the best route you have ever seen. If you are asked for information, give it gladly, but do not be critical of anyone else's plan. Confidence in the mission is necessary, and the reasoning behind his plan is not known to you, so look and ask questions but do not volunteer information. The only exception would be something that happened to you over an area in his proposed flight."

Many of O'Neil's comments reflect the pride felt by Voodoo pilots in flying a very large and very sophisticated aircraft alone. By this stage in the war, the RF-4C Phantom was becoming almost as numerous as the RF-101C and some pilots were already making the transition, but few Voodoo pilots ever felt the same love for the two-man Phantom that they held towards the single-place Voodoo. That pride in being 'alone, unarmed and unafraid,' is reflected in the final paragraph of O'Neil's report.

"If you have to go in one or two hours after the strike for post-strike reconnaissance, they'll be waiting for you. They're shooting at you, fellow, and all the training and skill that you have acquired is directed towards this moment. So good luck!"

m), jinking, jinking heavily until you're almost sick, works if you don't have to stay up too long. If you have to be up [moving at high altitude over the target area] longer than two minutes, this method is not satisfactory, and the only way I think you can do it is 'in the weeds'. By that I don't mean so low that flying becomes more dangerous than the enemy. I mean below the peaks in the mountains and about 50 feet (17 m) in the flatlands. You fly 'in the weeds' except over major roads, railroads and rivers. At these points you 'pop', jinking, up to at least 4,600 feet (1491 m), then descend, jinking, back to low level. About two minutes before getting into the defenses surrounding your target – always expect defenses around the targets we are presently flying – you hit afterburners, pull the trigger for cameras, and 'pop up', jinking and looking. You keep all cameras going, and continue to jink up to altitude for your target.

"During the 'pop' you've got to think about missiles, so when you get a launch indication or see a SAM coming at you your best maneuver is down. Unfortunately, down means into a high concentration of guns, but the higher you are, the longer the SAM can track you, the less your chances are of ducking it and ending up 'in the weeds' or behind a knoll to avoid others.

### Dodging SAMs

"You have to go down, and this does not mean performing a split-S. (A split-S is just long enough in the 'roll over' phase to get a hit in your back.) It means push the stick forward and keep your eye on the missile. You have to keep seeing it to avoid it. You have to force the SAM into a turn it can't make. Remember, Gs are relative to airspeed and the SAM is going so fast it cannot out-turn you, even in the RF-101C. SAMs can pull about eight Gs, but that is not much of a turn radius when you're going Mach 2.

"Once you have acquired the target it is time to get out and get home, keeping out of the hostile areas and on the deck. Don't go after bonus targets. If you have had your cameras on all the way, and you are in a heavily-defended area you'll have a lot of bonus targets without knowing it. You'll also be able to see most of the AAA positions that fired at you – their muzzle flashes and smoke are evident on the film. Even the Fan Song radar pointing at you will be noticeable on your film. The mission is fragged (ordered), so fly the frag – follow orders. That is what you are there for."

**The trail of an SA-2 'Guideline' missile blasts safely clear of a reconnaissance aircraft. According to Captain O'Neil, any time a Voodoo flew at anything above treetop height in high threat areas its pilot could expect at least three missiles to be fired at him.**

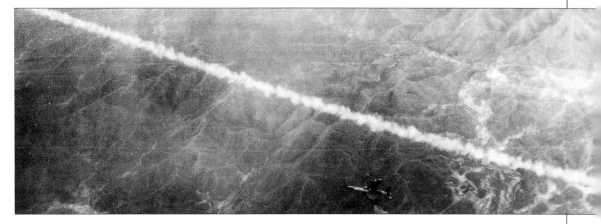

# Wins and Losses

An F-8E Crusader of Marine squadron VMF(AW)-235 'Death Angels' on the ramp at Da Nang. The four 20-mm cannons have been fired. This Crusader has almost certainly dropped a lot of bombs lately, as well.

At the end of the previous month, on 28 August 1966, Major Kenneth T. Blank of the 34th TFS/388th TFW at Korat had employed 20-mm gunfire from his F-105D to shoot down a MiG-17 deep in North Vietnamese airspace.

On the day of the USAF's first Phantom shootdown, 21 September 1966, more 'Thud' victories were scored. 1Lt Fred A. Wilson, Jr of the 333rd TFS/355th TFW at Takhli, flying another F-105D, also scored a cannon-kill against a MiG-17. The same day, 1Lt Karl W. Richter of the 421st TFS/388th TFW at Korat also claimed a MiG-17. These victories took place amid fast and furious actions

*A 388th TFW F-105D pilot briefs with a ground crewman. At Korat, airmen wore the Anzac campaign hat introduced by Australian and New Zealand soldiers. 'Thud' pilot Karl Richter wore a US Air Force Academy ring, one of the first heroes from a school which began in 1959.*

which included heavy bomb strikes by Air Force and Navy aircraft.

Richter, although very junior, was one of the most respected of 'Thud' pilots. He was a graduate of the Air Force Academy at Colorado Springs, was universally respected as a tough and very aggressive fighter pilot and seemed to have a bright future – the kind of man who would kill MiGs in his twenties, command a fighter wing in his thirties and be Chief of Staff in his forties.

### Killed in action

But the fortunes of war were not to allow Karl Richter to fulfil his promise. He was to ignore the opportunity to go home after 100 combat missions over North Vietnam, going on to complete nearly 200 before dying in a rescue helicopter from injuries sustained while ejecting over the North.

Men like Blank, Wilson and Richter were uncommon heroes in an unusual war. In September

the southernmost part of North Vietnam, where they were cleaning out transportation and logistics targets. The 'Bengals' of squadron VMFA-542 arrived at Da Nang in their brightly-painted F-4B Phantoms, increasing Marine strength which now consisted primarily of Skyhawks at Chu Lai and Phantoms at Da Nang.

The Marines frequently got less credit than they deserved. Because the duration of their missions into Route Package One was often as little as an hour or less, some Marine airmen racked up three or four missions in a day. Unlike their Air Force counterparts, they were given no promise of a trip home after completing 100 missions. They did, however, contribute significantly to denying the enemy the use of daylight hours during the spring of 1966. Increasingly, North Vietnam's General Giap and other leaders had to ignore the fact that their nation bordered on South Vietnam and shift the infiltration away from a straight north-south axis, away from the Marines, away from the impact of repeated US air strikes, and to the more circuitous route followed by the Ho Chi Minh Trail which went through the Mu Gia Pass and through Laos before reaching South Vietnam.

### Chinese incident

On 12 May 1966, China protested that a Chinese military aircraft was shot down over Yunnan Province by five US fighters. An official US history claims that an F-105D had pursued and shot down a North Vietnamese MiG-17 and inadvertently crossed the border. However, no F-105D kill of any MiG-17 was credited on this date. The only air-to-air kill on 12 May was a MiG-17 shot down by an AIM-9 Sidewinder from an F-4C Phantom (64-660) crewed by Major Wilbur R. Dudley and 1Lt Imants Kringelis of the 390th TFS/35th TFW. Dudley's Phantom, incidentally, would eventually claim three MiGs and survive to remain in service 20 years later.

Still, there were problems with the Phantom's missiles. Missile activity had remained low up to this juncture in the war, although in eight engagements in the previous month, 15 Sparrows and 21 Sidewinders had been fired for five recorded kills. As one pilot recalled: "In the summer of 1966 targets in Route Package Six

came under daily attack, and air combat activity increased accordingly. The missiles were a disappointment. That should come as no surprise when we consider that not one of our missiles was designed to do the job they were asked to do in Vietnam. Every one of those weapons was designed as an air defense weapon to be employed against a large, non-maneuvering target."

On 1 July 1966, Lieutenant General William W. (Spike) Momyer replaced Moore as commander of Seventh Air Force in Saigon. Momyer was a veteran fighter man who had been an ace in World War II, was regarded as an expert tactician, and could not have failed to experience frustration over the way airpower was being used willy-nilly against North Vietnam, without proper planning and with too many restrictions.

Momyer also had a sense for history. "He was one of the few senior officers who kept a personal, hand-written diary," a subordinate recalls. "Every day after the work was finished he would have a 15-30 minute review with his deputy while he wrote notes in his horrible handwriting in his old-fashioned, ledger-type diary. He had been doing this for his entire service career and had a two-drawer safe full of these books. He always had a male secretary, a sergeant who had been, or was, a court reporter. The sergeant was just about the only person who could decipher his handwriting."

*Hard-pressed F-105 pilots did not always see the muzzle flashes of the North Vietnamese guns that stalked them. But the clang of metal flying around and the crunch of explosions from larger-caliber shells could be heard even inside the 'Thud's' cockpit.*

1966, there was no line of employment on this planet more dangerous than flying the F-105 Thunderchief into North Vietnam.

One method of assembling numbers proved, beyond doubt, that it was statistically unlikely for any pilot to complete 100 missions. Despite its toughness and survivability, the 'Thud' was to suffer proportionately the greatest losses of any American aircraft type ever flown in any war, at any time, anywhere.

*Taking a respite from oxygen, possibly not a good idea at medium to high altitude, this Thunderchief pilot watches other F-105s 'gas up' from a KC-135 tanker.*

*North Vietnamese civilians examine the wreckage of an American fighter. 'Thuds' bore the brunt of the campaign over the North, and accounted for one in five USAF fixed-wing losses between 1965 and 1967.*

# ECM Pods
## *High-tech electronic protection*

A late-year assessment in 1966 failed to yield any proof that the original purpose of the war against North Vietnam was any closer to attainment, but it was abundantly clear that the war was becoming more sophisticated. Although early ECM pods (introduced briefly with the RF-101C Voodoo almost two years earlier) had been a resounding failure, improved ECM pods became available in September 1966. F-105Ds of the 355th TFW at Takhli, now commanded by Colonel Robert R. Scott, tested these new tools of electronic warfare in action against SAMs and radar-controlled gun defenses.

Heading into battle, it was customary for an F-105D flight leader to order his wingmen to, "clean 'em up, green 'em up, and turn on your music". In other words, clear your cockpit of any loose objects to prepare for action, turn on your armament switches (from red to green) and switch on your ECM pod. The 'music' was barrage jamming, intended to foul the enemy's radar reception. The pod introduced at this time, designated ALQ-71, was not yet the final word in this very new field of electronic warfare, but it was reported by 'Thud' pilots to be a significant improvement over the unsuccessful pods tried earlier.

*In Saigon, Seventh Air Force top brass put together statistics which demonstrated that the crew of this F-4 Phantom had a 33 per cent greater chance of survival over North Vietnam with an early ECM pod hanging under their aircraft. Electronic warfare was still a primitive art when the fighting in Southeast Asia began. It matured quickly.*

# Fighter Leader

### Robin Olds and the 8th TFW 'Wolfpack'

On 30 September 1966, command of the 'Wolfpack' – the 8th TFW flying F-4C Phantoms from Ubon – passed from Colonel Joseph G. Wilson to Colonel Robin Olds. Wearing a handlebar mustache throughout much of his tour, exuding a particular image of roughness and ruggedness, Olds was quite simply the best-loved and most able fighter wing commander of the war, a leader whose men would follow him into the pits of hell if it meant a crack at North Vietnam's MiG pilots. Olds had been an all-American tackle at West Point, had achieved 24 1/2 aerial victories in Europe during World War II and had married a film actress. He had missed out on the Korean conflict despite repeated requests for combat duty there, and he was not going to miss out again.

## Veteran commanders

Also on Robin Olds' team was Colonel Vermont Garrison, an old fighter hand who had been an ace in Korea with eight MiG kills, and Colonel Daniel (Chappie) James, a dedicated and aggressive fighter man who was one of the Air Force's early black aviators.

In a word-play on the names of comic-book characters, the deputy commander for operations and the wing commander, when they flew together, were known as Blackman and Robin. When he was a young second lieutenant, eager to fly his P-51 Mustang against the Luftwaffe, Chappie James was assigned to an all-black squadron, standard practice before President Truman integrated the armed forces in 1948. Chappie James fought for civil rights and he fought his country's enemies from fighter cockpits. With Robin Olds, Vermont Garrison and Chappie James directing the 'Wolfpack' against North Vietnam, dramatic events were about to take place.

But it was a junior officer, Captain John B. Stone, who put into motion the events that would make the 'Wolfpack' the prime

*Col Robin Olds, West Point class of July 1943, took ideas developed by Capt. J. B. Stone and others, and plotted the Operation 'Bolo' ambush of North Vietnamese MiG-21s near Hanoi. World War II ace Olds led the 8th TFW in F-4C and F-4D Phantoms.*

---

Two weeks after Momyer settled in at his Saigon headquarters, his deputy arrived in the person of Major General Gordon M. Graham. Another fighter man, Graham had just about done it all: he had been an ace in World War II; he had commanded a wing of F-84F Thunderstreak aircraft; he had delivered the first operational F-4C Phantom to Tactical Air Command; and he had done the test-flying on a new aircraft which would soon be taken into combat not by the Air Force, not yet at least, but by the Navy – the Vought A-7 Corsair II. Major General Graham was another accomplished fighter man in a war that seemed to be run by bomber men. He was especially well known for his interest in 'people problems' – he cared about the young fighter pilots who were being sent into North Vietnam and he wanted them to succeed.

Graham was incapable of fighting the war from behind a desk. At Tan Son Nhut, he would fly combat missions in RF-4C Phantom recce aircraft of the 16th TRS/460th TRW with Captain Jerry West as his 'guy in back' or backseater. The 460th TRW, commanded by Colonel Bob Williams, operated both the RF-101C and RF-4C, and General Graham proved so effective in the

latter aircraft that he received a 'recce pilot of the month' award.

The targeting situation remained an abomination, to say the least. The Seventh Air Force commander could only 'nominate' targets, the actual approval of any target requiring separate endorsements from PACAF, the Pentagon, Secretary of Defense McNamara, and not infrequently from President Johnson himself. Quite apart from political restraints, which prevented attacks on North Vietnamese airfields and other tempting targets, numerous opportunities for effective use of airpower were lost simply because, even when a target was approved, by the time the decision was made the military advantage was lost.

## Command problems

General Momyer felt that a single commander should have been responsible for all air operations. "Our command structure is more complex than any arrangement we had in World War II. In my judgment, we have gone backwards in our command arrangements. The mere fact that the organization works is a tribute to the intelligence and skill of the people in it."

It was at about this time that the *New York Times* pointed out that the United States, with less than three million men under arms, now had more generals and admirals than it had had at the height of World War II with 13 million. Admiral Sharp (CINCPAC) and General Harris (PACAF) in Hawaii, General Westmoreland (COMUSMACV) and General Momyer in Saigon (Seventh Air Force) and their numerous subordinates added up to a situation where there were simply too many people in charge.

In a major move which widened the war and brought it home to the enemy's urban centers for the first time, North Vietnam's POL facilities near Hanoi and Haiphong were removed from the restricted target list and were struck by air on 29 June 1966 – almost

*In 1966, the flight crew of a US Air Force F-4 Phantom consisted of two full-fledged pilots, although the backseater did not always have vast experience in fighters. Later, the service took navigators and trained them as weapons systems officers (WSOs, or 'wizzos') to sit in the rear cockpit of the Phantom and operate the radar and ordnance.*

MiG killers of the period. Stone remembered a ruse which had worked once before – disguising F-4C Phantoms on their ingress into North Vietnam so that they resembled bomb-laden and vulnerable F-105 Thunderchiefs. Stone wanted to try this again on a larger scale. With Secretary McNamara's rules of engagement making an assault on enemy airfields impossible, this seemed the only way to score an effective blow against Hanoi's MiG force. Reportedly, Stone suggested the idea directly to Colonel Olds.

Young captains do not usually tell senior colonels what to do. In this instance, Olds is reported to have replied, "I was thinking of that myself. We'll try to talk them into letting us do it."

The 'Wolfpack' was about to go a hunting.

*An F-4C Phantom (63-7544) of the 497th TFS/8th TFW 'Wolfpack' seen on a ground-attack mission in November 1966. This Phantom carries external fuel and canisters each holding 19 2.75-in rocket projectiles. The 497th became adept at risky high-speed, low-level night operations.*

# The 'Wolfpack' goes Truck Hunting

One of Olds' early tasks was to commit his resources to night operations against the Ho Chi Minh Trail. The Phantoms of the 497th TFS, part of the 8th TFW, drew this task. As recalled by Lieutenant Myron L. Donald, who was later shot down and became a POW; "the 497th was primarily a night truck-hunting squadron that flew over Laos and Route Package One in the southern part of North Vietnam.

"Usually, we had no assigned targets at the time of take-off. We checked with the C-130 Hercules Airborne Combat Control Center (ABCCC) that would assign us an area. The lead aircraft carried flares, CBUs (cluster bomb units), and bombs. Lead would usually attack in the dark if he saw truck lights, or would drop flares in a likely area. Two would be in trail far enough back so that he could be over the area as the flares lit. The number two aircraft usually had CBUs, rockets and bombs. Both had guns (centerline pods, introduced a few months after Olds' arrival). Once we were on a target, we would fly a racetrack pattern over the target until we were out of ordnance or fuel.

"We flew out and back in radar trail and rarely saw each other during a mission, which usually lasted from one hour to one and a half hours. At that time, the F-4 was crewed by two pilots. The command pilot would turn off all his cockpit lights so that he could see outside better. The night missions were flown at between 50 and 100 feet (15-20 m). On all but the blackest of nights, flares were unnecessary. With a little experience, it was possible to work under a 500-foot (161-m) overcast at night without flares.

"The back-seat pilot did not watch the attack. Without instruments, the front-seat pilot would occasionally become disoriented. Therefore, once in an attack pattern, the back-seat pilot couldn't take his eyes off the instruments, and instantly took control of the aircraft if anything didn't look just right. At those low altitudes and high speeds, the F-4 could hit the ground in less than a second. About 50 night missions were necessary to become really proficient at truck-hunting, and to have the same crew flying both day and night missions does not work."

## Moving down the Trail

Infiltration down the network known as the Ho Chi Minh Trail had, at the beginning, amounted to nothing more than thousands of men carrying small items, like mortar shells, on their backs or on bicycles. But that had changed.

"Prior to my arrival at Ubon, the North Vietnamese had been moving in large convoys. But once the first and last vehicles were stopped the convoy could be destroyed at will. Eventually the Vietnamese were moving supplies in single trucks or groups of two and three. Truck hunting became very difficult and, I must say, quite ineffective."

This last observation seems to be one sign that the aerial campaign at night was, in fact, having an impact on the supply of Viet Cong forces in the South.

*Lieutenants Victor C. Seavers and Tom Noonan take their black-bellied Phantom into battle at night. The 497th TFS wreaked havoc among Hanoi's truck convoys during nocturnal hours. while companion squadrons in the 8th TFW wing fought MiGs over the North by day.*

# Crusader Versus MiG-21

An F-8E Crusader of VF-111 'Sundowners' gets the cat officer's launch signal and is about to be hurtled aloft from no. 2 catapult on the wooden deck of USS Oriskany (CVA-34). The old carrier was soon to suffer a catastrophic fire.

On 9 October 1966, the US Navy scored its first victory over the MiG-21 and racked up another kill for the prop-driven Skyraider, these being the 24th and 25th aerial victories of the war.

Commander Richard (Dick) Bellinger was skipper of the 'Superheats' of VF-162 aboard USS *Oriskany* (CVA-34), an aircraft carrier soon to become victim of a fatal fire. Bellinger had been shot down himself five months earlier, on 17 July, when a MiG-17 hit him with cannon fire and sent him limping out to sea where his F-8E Crusader (150300) was too badly damaged to take on fuel from a tanker and he had to eject.

Bellinger's chance to get even came as he went aloft in another F-8E Crusader (149159) leading the air cover for an Alpha Strike from USS *Intrepid* (CVS-11). Bellinger and his division of Crusaders were directed towards approaching MiGs by a Grumman E-1 Tracer, the Navy's carrier-borne airborne warning and control (AWACS) aircraft.

Beginning at wavecap level, Bellinger led his flight over the beach and up to meet the MiGs at 3,000 feet (900 m). He chose a MiG-21, engaged it in a close maneuvering contest, and unleashed two AIM-9D Sidewinder missiles. Bellinger levelled off to see his MiG-21 splattered across a rice paddy below him.

On the same day, LtJG William T. Patton of VA-176 from *Intrepid* shot down a

MiG-17 with 20-mm fire while flying an A-1H Skyraider (137543). The big prop plane had prevailed again.

Carrier operations in the Gulf of Tonkin were essentially so routine that they received far less attention than they deserved, at least until something went wrong. On 26 October 1966, something

simultaneously with a major press conference by Secretary McNamara announcing the event. The technique of 'war by announcement' would have its critics from beginning to end. The attacks only four miles from Hanoi were carried out mostly by F-105Ds, with one 'Thud' being lost to AAA.

Excellent results were claimed, but lessons were only being learned and General Momyer observed that the absence of ECM pods on some aircraft and RHAWS gear on others was simply intolerable in a high-threat region.

Three more MiG-17s and two MiG-21s were shot down by Air Force and Navy aircrews in June and July. It was abundantly clear that the North Vietnamese expected their opponents to return to Hanoi and were girding-up for a long struggle.

Although the F-8E Crusader had been in the fight from the start, its first chance to prevail over a MiG came on 12 June 1966. Commander Harold L. Marr, a veteran Crusader airman and skipper of the 'Checkmates' of squadron VF-211 from Hancock found himself in trouble while escorting an A-4 Skyhawk force.

# Tailcodes

By 2 December 1966, most Air Force fighters in Southeast Asia were beginning to wear tailcodes, the two-letter 'tactical unit identifiers' which were supposed to help tell the observer what squadron the aircraft came from. Lieutenant Kenneth Cordier, back in Southeast Asia for his second tour, unaware that he would soon be a POW, remembers seeing the letters XC painted on the tail of a Phantom and thinking, "Gee, I thought that stood for cross-country."

In fact, XC happened to be the tailcode assigned arbitrarily to the 557th TFS/12th TFW at Cam Ranh Bay, the Phantom outfit from which Ken Cordier was about to make a one-way journey to the Hanoi Hilton.

The intention at the time was

for all aircraft in a single squadron to have the same two-letter code, the first letter of which would apply to all aircraft in the wing. Thus, the 'Thuds' at Takhli belonging to the 355th TFW wore codes like RE (44th TFS/355th TFW), RK (333th TFS/355th TFW), RM (354th TFS/355th TFW) and so on. The tailcodes were supposed to be

45.7-cm wide for each letter and 60.9-cm high. Years later, in 1972, a major change would see all aircraft in the same wing wearing the same two-letter code.

## Unique tailcodes

At Da Nang, the 'Gunfighters' of the 366th TFW under Colonel Allan P. Rankin regarded the purpose of the whole thing very

This F-4C Phantom (64-0829) was Robin Olds' in the 8th TFW. But earlier, when it wore an XC tail code, the Phantom was with the 557th TFS/12th TFW at Cam Ranh Bay. All aircraft in this wing had 'X' as the first letter on the tail.

differently. Although most of the Air Force did not fly with 'hard' crews, Rankin's F-4C people frequently did, and wanted to use

did. The inadvertent explosion of a magnesium flare ignited a fire aboard the ageing USS *Oriskany* (CVA-34), killing 44 sailors and injuring 38. One A-4E Skyhawk was destroyed and had to be dumped over the side. The disaster at sea sent *Oriskany* limping back towards the US West Coast for repairs.

**Right: These Crusaders are neatly holding formation. But once inside a 'furball' (dogfight), Vought's nimble jet fighter could literally fling itself all over the sky.**

**Below: In a camouflage flight suit horse-traded from an Army man in Saigon, Dick Bellinger waves to describe his aerial victory over a MiG-21 while flying a VF-162 F-8.**

the tailcodes to be able to identify individual crews visually while in combat – a purpose for which they had never been intended.

As General Robert F. Titus, a lieutenant colonel at the time, describes it: "F-4C s/n 820 [64-820] was my airplane, which carried AT on the tail. I convinced the wing CO that we needed individual tail markings and that was because of an experience I had had shortly prior.

## Instantly identifiable

"The idea was so that you could identify who was up there without getting in too close to check the small black tail numbers and compromise your electronic jamming pattern in the process (all this after becoming separated in the combat area).

"I suggested that the 389th TFS be the A squadron, the 390th the B and the 480th the C. On my bird, the T was for Titus,

hence AT. Bob Janca was AJ. Sandy Vandenberg, the 390th CO was BV, etc."

Frederick C. (Boots) Blesse, a Korean War ace and another well-known fighter pilot among the Da Nang crowd, was in the 390th TFS and flew an F-4C Phantom nicknamed 'The Blue Max', with tailcode BB. "Today each wing has two tail letters and every plane has the same letters. What this accomplishes eludes me."

**No, the RE did not stand for REpublic, which built the F-105. Arbitrarily, the RE tailcode was the symbol of the 44th TFS 'Vampires', a squadron of the 355th TFW at Takhli.**

**The 366th TFW at Da Nang, unlike other wings, had tailcodes with a different second letter for each individual plane. Only one Phantom wore BF (left) and only one wore CJ. The F-105 uses the common squadron-code method.**

*'No shakes, no cakes' is the policy of the Tailhook Association's publication – a journal for carrier aviators – but this June 1966 handclasp by Phil Vampatella (left) and Hal Marr broke the rule and got into the Hook anyway, because both Crusader pilots shot down MiGs.*

Four MiG-17s engaged Marr's Crusader formation. Commander Marr turned into the MiGs, fired a Sidewinder which missed and unleashed a second missile which blew apart a MiG-17. The persistent Marr then kept after the North Vietnamese with 20-mm fire and a second pair of Sidewinders. He was credited with bagging one certain MiG and one probable, both with AIM-9D Sidewinders. These were the first US Navy air-to-air victories in a full year. LtJG Phillip V. Vampatella, who had been in the air with Marr that day, repeated the feat on 21 June when he used an AIM-9D Sidewinder to dispose of a MiG-17 that challenged his Crusader.

On 5 August 1966, two years after the Gulf of Tonkin incident, Seventh Air Force people in Saigon put together their estimate of the tremendous increases in North Vietnam's defenses. The number of radars had increased from 24 to 271; the number of AAA guns of all calibers from 500 to 4,400; the number of SAMs from zero to 20-25 battalions, and the number of MiGs from a half-dozen to 65. Further deliveries were under way of the Fire Can radar unit associated with radar-directed AAA guns, of SAM equipment including its Fan Song radar and of the Soviet-built MiGs. The numbers all pointed to an obvious conclusion – that two years of warfare north of the 17th Parallel had only strengthened the Communists' resolve.

## McNamara begins to have doubts

On 10-14 October 1966, the Secretary of Defense visited South Vietnam for a firsthand look at US bases and installations. Because men were being asked to fly dangerous missions without being given the authority to bomb important targets, because of the kind of reasoning which permitted destroying a MiG in the air but not on the ground, some airmen had begun to remark upon Robert Strange McNamara's middle name. In fact, the architect of 'Rolling Thunder' and the most influential decision maker on targeting, was now beginning to experience doubt for the first time.

Soon after McNamara's fact-finding expedition, President Johnson made a 17-day, seven-nation Asian tour which included a stopover at Cam Ranh Bay airbase. At Cam Ranh Bay, Johnson asserted that "the most important weapons in Vietnam are patience

# Black Friday

It was not for nothing that Rankin's men at Da Nang, Robin Olds' men at Ubon and a host of naval aviators aboard carriers at sea were scheming and plotting to take on the North Vietnamese air force. The triple-threat defense system of SAMs, MiGs and Triple-A had caused too many losses and confounded the 'Rolling Thunder' campaign more than anyone was prepared to accept.

Some men were talking about a North Vietnamese fighter-wing commander, Colonel Tomb, who was supposed to be as good a pilot as Robin Olds. That was probably a muddled version of some intelligence report. The North Vietnamese had been flying fighters since 1964, while Olds had been flying them since 1944. Tomb is not even a name in the Vietnamese language.

The fact remained, the North Vietnamese were getting better, and their defenses were taking a heavier toll. It was not uncommon for two or three Air Force and Navy aircraft to be lost on a single day. This situation was simply unacceptable. And it was going to get worse.

## Black Friday

Black Friday, 2 December 1966, was perhaps the worst day in the war up to that point.

Ken Cordier woke up that morning at Da Nang in the full knowledge that he was at the height of his profession. To be an Air Force officer flying the F-4C Phantom in combat against targets in Route Package Six was just about the highest achievement a man could attain. Walking out to his aircraft on an earlier mission, he had remarked to his GIB, "We're on top, the very top." Ken did not know that he was to become a guest of the North Vietnamese for seven years.

It was a day when there was heavy activity up North and the risks were high. The campaign against POL facilities, begun a few months earlier, was

continuing. Early in the morning, F-105D Thunderchiefs from Brigadier General William S. Chairsell's 388th TFW at Korat and F-4C Phantoms of Rankin's 366th TFW at Da Nang were charged with attacking POL facilities near Phuc Yen, which was also the enemy's best-known MiG base. F-4C Phantoms from Ken Cordier's 12th TFW out of Cam Ranh Bay were tasked with flying cover to keep a sharp eye out for MiGs. These air strikes, as had so many before them, inflicted severe damage on the chosen targets at a time when prohibited targets remained unscathed and the North Vietnamese leadership showed no sign of bending. The cost, on Black Friday, was eight American aircraft and crews lost in combat.

### First of eight losses

The first was an F-4C Phantom (64-663) of the 389th TFS/366th TFW which suffered a fatal near-miss detonation from a SAM. With the aircraft on fire, both crew members ejected and became prisoners. One survived the ordeal. The other died in captivity.

Victim number two was also one of Rankin's Da Nang-based birds with the individualistic tailcodes, an F-4C Phantom (64-653) of the 480th TFS/366th TFW which was flying fighter cover when it, too, was hit by a SAM. The crew ejected. Both became POWs, illustrating again the difficulty of any hope of rescue in a high-density area. Both survived captivity to be released at war's end.

In the late morning, a 'Thud' striking Phuc Yen was also claimed by one of the dozens of SAMs racing through the air. The

*When the US began its build-up in 1965, Hanoi had only a few dozen modern warplanes and pilots. North Vietnamese fliers went through training in the Soviet Union and came home to fly the hundreds of Soviet-supplied aircraft – in service by late 1966.*

F-105D went in and its pilot was killed.

Victim number four was an RF-4C Phantom, apparently from the 460th TRW at Tan Son Nhut, which was hit by gunfire at about the same time. It was trying to gain photo coverage of the Phuc Yen strikes (without the benefit of SLAR side-looking airborne radar, which still had not been used successfully in combat but soon would be). The RF-4C Phantom (65-829) almost made it to the coast and the crew ejected, but only one of the pair survived captivity.

A Navy F-4B Phantom (151014) from the 'Black Knights' of VF-154 from USS *Coral Sea* (CVA-43) was also shot down that day. Victims six and seven were both A-4C Skyhawks from the same carrier. Then it was Ken Cordier's turn. Being at the height of his profession was about to have less reward for Ken than he had hoped.

## A veteran goes down

Ken was at the controls of an F-4C Phantom (63-7608) of the 559th TFS/12th TFW with the newly-adorned XC tailcode (later changed to XT), which had caused him so much initial puzzlement. His is an excellent source for pinpointing the time by which these codes had appeared, because Ken knows he was using them, and he could not have seen them a day, a week or a year later.

Cordier was last into the battle area, escorting an EB-66C electronic warfare aircraft on a jamming mission, when more SAMs began to heave violently through the air around him. The Americans' electronic systems were beginning to damage the enemy's effectiveness with the surface-to-air weapon, but Hanoi's response was simply to fire larger numbers of the SAMs with less accuracy and to prove that numbers did make a difference. Soviet Premier Kosygin had said openly that the USSR would supply Hanoi with all the SAMs it wanted. While orbiting near Phuc Yen in support of the EB-66C mission, Ken's Phantom was struck by yet another SAM. The blast from the missile caused a fire in the cockpit and burned both crew members severely. Ken ordered an ejection and, as usual in Phantoms, his backseater Captain Bob Lane went out of the aircraft first. Both men were captured immediately.

SAMs, MiGs and Triple-A were causing too many problems for the strike forces and the rules of engagement prevented the logical reaction – bombing them into oblivion. Some other solution had to be found and the man to find it was in command of Ubon's 'Wolfpack', Colonel Robin Olds.

Major General Gordon Graham said that "Robin Olds is the most courageous fighter pilot I know. He took on some chores in Southeast Asia which no-one else would have done and he personally headed some missions which were almost suicidal."

Olds was to get his chance at Colonel Tomb's MiG force, but it was not to come until the arrival of the new year. At the end of 1966, the old year looked very bleak for American airpower in many respects.

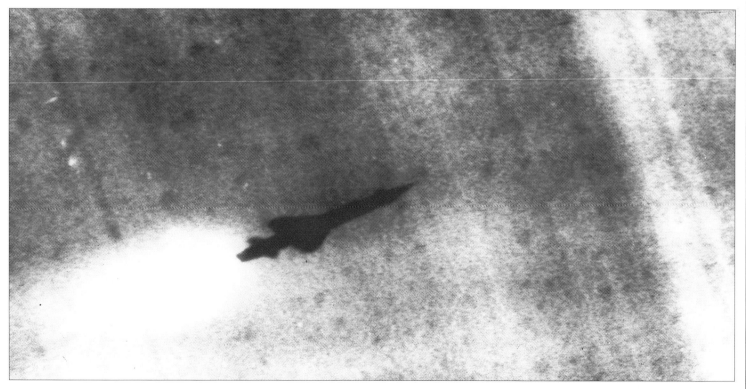

*A crew-chief's view of the action, as a Navy UH-1B of HAL-3, the 'Sea Wolves' engages a suspected Viet Cong position in the Mekong Delta. Operating in close conjunction with riverine forces, HAL-3 was heavily engaged in the anti-infiltration mission.*

causing 18 losses or a loss rate of 1.47 per 100 missiles.

The numbers game up North was similar to the body count situation down South where, in the absence of visible front-lines and terrain to conquer, US forces reported their success based upon the number of enemy bodies located after a battle. These numbers were usually presented at the 'Five O'Clock Follies,' as the MACV briefing for journalists had become known, and were believed by no-one, not even the unfortunate officer giving the briefing. At one point, the US forces claimed to have killed more Viet Cong combatants than could have existed if half the fighting age men in Vietnam were active Communist guerrillas. Not that Hanoi's figures were credible either – Hanoi claimed to have downed 6,000 American aircraft or at least ten times the number actually participating in the fight.

The SAC bomber men who were running a war being fought by non-SAC fighter pilots still wanted to bomb Hanoi back into the stone age – the idea of an aerial campaign against North Vietnam's dikes was being resurrected in Pentagon options papers, as was the notion of an outright carpet-bombing of the cities – while the fighter pilots risking their lives wanted fewer restrictions and simpler rules. The fighter pilots did not understand why 'Thuds' were bombing heavy targets in the North and Stratofortresses were bombing rice paddies in the South. They could not understand why they could fight a MiG in the air but not bomb it on the ground. They wanted to go in and clean out Phuc Yen. They also knew, by now, that they were the first Americans since the revolution to fight an armed conflict without the full support of their own countrymen. It was a situation which could only have seemed incredible and, had it been fiction rather than fact, no-one would have believed it for a moment. To the men in fighter cockpits, at least, there was some relief in sight; to be provided by Colonel Olds and Operation 'Bolo'. But a long slog lay ahead.

On 31 October 1966 US troop strength in South Vietnam had risen to 385,000.

and unity." A fighter pilot wrote to the President to assert that the most important weapons were the 750-lb (340-kg) bombs he was not permitted to drop on the enemy's MiG airfields.

Although the Viet Cong and their North Vietnamese supporters were never able to mount a serious threat against US aircraft carriers operating off the coast, the Navy suffered casualties nonetheless. On 26 October 1966 as two sailors were stowing parachute flares in a storage locker aboard the USS *Oriskany* (CVA-34), a massive fire erupted. Ordnance was touched off by the inferno and flames spread to the hangar deck below and into several living quarters. Flames engulfed the fantail and spread below decks, igniting bombs and ammunition. Through heroic efforts the fire was brought under control, but damage to aircraft and ship was severe. At final count, 44 were dead, 38 injured.

## Navy choppers over the Mekong

The Navy was also active in-country. It had helicopters flying under the most unusual circumstances. Squadron HC-1 operated short-boomed UH-1B Huey helicopter gunships in support of Army and Navy riverine forces in the Mekong Delta. In due course the squadron became the 'Seawolves' of HAL3 with as many as 33 Hueys.

In the now-established tradition of bombing halts, which were supposed to send some kind of signal to Hanoi but only confused everybody, the US declared a Christmas ceasefire over 24-26 December 1966 and repeated the occasion for New Year's, 31 December-2 January. While the Communists were largely ignoring the ceasefire, a Saigon analyst toted up losses for 1966. USAF losses in Southeast Asia came to 379 aircraft, with the 'Thud' again taking the most punishing losses. No fewer than 126 F-105s had been destroyed, of which 111 were over North Vietnam. Four were downed by SAMs, three by MiGs and the remainder by ground AAA fire, which often claimed its victims while they were seeking to elude the other two threats.

Other losses included 56 F-4 Phantoms (42 in combat), 26 F-100s (presumably all in South Vietnam) and 41 A-1 Skyraiders. Similar figures for the Navy were not made available on an annual basis. Always masters of statistics, the Americans concluded that between 1 July 1965 and 31 December 1966, the North Vietnamese had fired 1,219 SAM missiles against US aircraft,

*A doorgunner mans his 7.62-mm M60 machine-gun as a pair of 'Sea Wolves' Hueys head out on patrol over the Mekong Delta. The Viet Cong used sampans on the myriad waterways of the Delta to infiltrate men and equipment from the end of the Ho Chi Minh Trail in Cambodia into the southern provinces of the Republic of Vietnam.*

# Sapper Attacks

It is often forgotten that, unlike in previous wars, Americans in Vietnam fought from bases which were constantly under threat. RF-4C Phantom pilots of the 460th TRW flying from Tan Son Nhut, in the capital of the country they were defending, 'stepped on the gas' to make unusually rapid, high-angle take-offs because of the danger of being hit by Viet Cong mortar or rocket attacks. The enemy was constantly prowling around the perimeters of the airfields. A lesser but persistent danger existed at the Thai airbases, where an insurgency was brewing, although it never reached the scale of the Viet Cong's fighting force.

## Spying on bases

The Americans repeatedly confirmed that the Viet Cong were reconnoitering their bases. An especially vicious attack on Tan Son Nhut took place on 4 December 1966, and the US Air Force Security Police found their own weapons wanting. Sentry dog handlers reported it almost impossible to operate the M16A1 infantry rifle (rapidly becoming the standard ground combat rifle with the Army and Marine Corps but originally developed by the Air Force) while also attempting to handle their guard dogs. It was suggested that the sling be attached to the top rather than the underside of the rifle. This would let the handler sling the weapon from his left shoulder and carry it in a firing position on his right side.

Another criticism was that the M16A1 was too long for easy handling in the airbase defense mission, a problem solved by the manufacturer, Colt, when it

*Viet Cong mortars, rockets, and sappers destroyed more C-130s than did anti-aircraft fire, missiles or MiGs. In this attack on Da Nang, guerrillas inflicted millions of dollars' damage in return for a low-cost, although very courageous, attack.*

produced a modified M16A1 with an 11.5-inch barrel, telescoping stock and sturdier flash hider (a device attached to the muzzle and designed to conceal the muzzle flash). This version eventually evolved into the GAU-5A/A submachine-gun.

## Prisoner intelligence

Prisoners taken after the sapper raid which destroyed several US aircraft told of a two month pre-strike reconnaissance of the base by a seven-man team. It seemed likely that some of the enemy's information about the airbase came from sources on the base itself, a constant problem in a war where the enemy was a part of the population.

The enemy's intelligence was rated as good on the munitions storage area at the base but poor on the runway and aircraft parking aprons. The Viet Cong successfully identified a point to infiltrate Tan Son Nhut's perimeter and cut three wire

*A critic of US support for Saigon swore that the policy could never succeed because the South Vietnamese were not willing to die for their country while the Viet Cong were. It was unfair, perhaps – but these VC showed courage and paid the price.*

*Tan Son Nhut, 13 April 1966. An exhausted airman sleeps as smoke rises from burning fuel tanks hit by Viet Cong mortars. Americans had rarely before been called upon to defend airbases in ground combat – but in Vietnam the war was always close to home.*

*With helmet, M16 rifle and poncho, a member of the 633rd Air Police Squadron stands guard in front of an A-1E Skyraider at Pleiku. Quick reaction forces were kept ready to cope with a full-fledged attack by large numbers of Viet Cong insurgents.*

fences without being detected. They also correctly assessed infiltration cover afforded by excavation work, fixed the positions of aircraft parking areas and traced out routes for undetected access to three munitions bunkers.

Still, the enemy somehow failed to assess correctly the sentry dog units spotted around the base and nine of them were killed by airmen using M16A1 rifles during the attack. The Viet Cong had, however, made a point of which even the most non-combatant of American servicemen were never unaware: although only a small proportion of soldiers regularly saw combat in this war, there were no front lines, no rear areas.

# STAYING THE COURSE

**1967 was to be a year of air-to-air fighting over the North of unprecedented intensity. It was the year of the 'Thud', which continued to carry most of the bombs and would also now perform its share of the MiG killing. The air-to-air fighting was to prove the mettle of the Navy's F-8 Crusader at the very time that it was being supplanted by the F-4B Phantom.**

**A**mong military men who were watching US aircraft losses increase and seeing North Vietnam's defense network grow, a brief success here and there offered little comfort. Brave men were risking their lives and facing death or capture without sharply-defined purpose and with no way of measuring success. On 10 January 1967, CINCPAC Admiral U. S. G. Sharp proposed a stepped-up air campaign which would restore a sense of purpose by assaulting six elements of the North Vietnamese infrastructure: electric power, war industries, transportation, POL facilities, garrison installations and the air defense network.

But despite an occasional success – Operation 'Bolo', when Phantoms from Colonel Robin Olds' 8th TFW 'Wolfpack' shot down seven MiG-21s on 2 January 1967 being one – decision-makers were still not ready for a sensibly orchestrated campaign to take the North out of the war. Sharp was listened to, but not completely. Some new targets were opened up to US air strikes, but

*American credibility is right on the line – and the effectiveness of US bombing strategy being tested to the hilt – as these F-105s taxi out in the third calendar year of the 'Rolling Thunder' campaign against North Vietnam. Already, those who fly the 'One Oh Five' have paid as high a price in battle as any airmen in the history of warfare.*

a 30-mile (48.2-km) 'cordon sanitaire' still existed around Hanoi itself, and the minor changes made in targeting policy were still piecemeal in nature.

In his annual State of the Union speech, also on 10 January 1967, President Johnson continued to assert that the US would prod Hanoi into a settlement by increasing the pressure. "Our pressures must be sustained until North Vietnam realizes that the war it started is costing more than it can ever gain. I know of no strategy more likely to attain that end than the strategy of accumulating slowly, but inexorably, every kind of material resource."

According to Lieutenant General William W. (Spike) Momyer, who had replaced Major General Joseph Moore as the top airman in South Vietnam, by the time of Johnson's address, the 'Rolling Thunder' campaign had three purposes. These were to reduce the flow and increase the cost of infiltration; raise the morale of the South Vietnamese (those on the US side, that is); and convince the North that it must pay a very high price, in its own territory, for its aggression in the South.

It was a familiar litany. Almost nobody believed it any more. An F-105D Thunderchief pilot at Takhli wrote home that morale had slumped to its lowest point. "My pal Jim was shot down the day

# Operation 'Bolo'

## Turning the tables on the NVAF

Life expectancy for American pilots over North Vietnam was falling fast. By 1967, US warplanes had been pounding targets around the Hanoi area for nearly two years. Growing Vietnamese fighter and missile strength was reaping a costly harvest from the American fighter bombers. And the USAF could not strike back at the enemy airfields, forbidden by restrictive rules of engagement dictated in Washington.

Clearly something had to be done, and Colonel Robin Olds was the man to do it. Olds had scored 12 kills flying P-38s and P-51s against the Luftwaffe 20 years before. Now 44, he commanded the 8th Tactical Fighter Wing, the 'Wolfpack', flying F-4C Phantoms out of Ubon in Thailand. Olds was a hard-drinking, seat-of-the pants flyer of the old school. But he was a fine tactician and a superb leader. His task was to draw the North Vietnamese MiGs into battle, and then spring a trap.

But that was more easily said than done. Over the past two years the MiG pilots had generally avoided F-4s, preferring to make hit-and-run attacks on bombers. Even if they missed the F-100s or F-105s, they could force the American pilots to jettison their weapons.

Contrary to details published at the time, Operation 'Bolo' was originally thought up by junior officers at Ubon and not the big deals in Hawaii. Captain John B. Stone was the original guiding light, with considerable input from Colonel Olds. The idea was simple. If the 'Wolfpack' could convince the North Vietnamese that they were bombers rather than fighters, then the MiGs might be lured into combat before they could realize their mistake.

On the morning of 2 January 1967, Olds led his men into the sky. Under his command were Phantoms, 'Wild Weasel' defence suppression F-105s and F-104 Starfighters, a total of nearly 100 aircraft. At least the same number flew in supporting roles. These included EC-121 airborne radar planes, EB-66 electronic warfare platforms, more F-4Cs making diversionary sweeps, and A-1 Skyraiders, F-100s and helicopters on rescue alert.

The Phantoms headed north along Route Package Six, the heavily defended approaches to Hanoi, flying at speeds and heights typical of a large-scale F-105 raid. Each of the F-4Cs was equipped with an ECM pod usually carried by Thunderchiefs, so on the North Vietnamese radar they would look like a bomber.

## The bait is taken

The first wave – three flights of F-4s characteristically led from the front by Olds – wheeled past Phuc Yen, an air base and major petroleum depot south-west of Hanoi. As they headed for the North Vietnamese capital, an EC-121 radar plane over the Gulf of Tonkin warned that MiGs were taking off and others were converging on the Hanoi area. It looked as though the bait had been taken.

The MiG-21s bored in unsuspectingly, and Olds' flight maneuvered to engage. Olds himself fired two Sparrows and a Sidewinder at a silver MiG, but all three missiles missed. However, Lt Ralph Wettrehahn and Captain Walt Radeker, flying Olds 2 and 4 respectively, were more successful, each destroying an enemy.

It was about this time that the North Vietnamese realized what was happening, and immediately began to maneuver defensively. However, by now the 'Wolfpack' was roaring. Olds barrel-rolled around another MiG before shooting it down with a Sidewinder. At the same time Captain Everett T. Raspberry was downing another.

*Col Robin Olds and Capt. John B. Stone were architects of a 2 January 1967 effort codenamed Operation 'Bolo' which shot down seven North Vietnamese MiG-21s. Both men were front-seat F-4C Phantom aircraft commanders in the 8th TFW.*

*F-4C Phantoms of the 8th TFW at Ubon. With careful use of ECM pods, Col Robin Olds' pilots were able to 'disguise' themselves as F-105s – thereby laying a sort of electronic trap for Hanoi's air defense forces. Hanoi's MiGs did no harm to the 'Bolo' force.*

The second Phantom flight, codenamed 'Rambler', now arrived. Diving down on a pair of MiGs Captain John B. Stone in Rambler 1 fired two Sparrows. As one missile hit the target, Stone was attacked from behind by more MiGs. Breaking left and down with Rambler 2, Lt Lawrence Glynn, Stone brought the MiGs into the sights of Major Philip P. Combies in Rambler 4, who shot one of the enemy down. Lieutenant Glynn in Rambler 2 now turned inside the MiGs, loosed off a pair of Sparrows and destroyed a seventh North Vietnamese jet.

The MiGs broke off before any more of the 'Wolfpack' arrived, so there were to be no more successes that day. Olds and his men headed homewards, satisfied in the knowledge that they had downed seven of North Vietnam's best aircraft without loss to themselves.

Colonel Olds had shown the way to beat the MiGs. In the following 12 months, USAF Phantoms were to down another 36 North Vietnamese fighters, with the 'Wolfpack' accounting for 23 of them. Thanks to a politically-motivated bombing halt which lasted until 1972, it was to be another four years before the Air Force achieved similar success.

*By the end of 1966, the once-tiny North Vietnamese air arm was formidable and becoming more so. The MiG-21 was still relatively new, but the Soviet-built fighter was unquestionably a serious threat, one which demanded strong action.*

# Observation Helos

**I** hold my helicopter low, in a light drizzle while my observer in the right seat tells me that the Viet Cong are bunched up in a small gully to our right. This is my job. I'm a Hughes OH-6A Cayuse pilot with the 1st Cav. 'Raise it fifty!' I snap. This tells our artillery guys to adjust their fire.

"'That's it,' my co-pilot/ observer confirms. Rounds impact in the gully, chewing up wet earth and forcing black-garbed VC soldiers back into the trees.

"Just at that instant I spot more Viet Cong. They come running in the open 100 yards to our left. Hunched in my pilot's seat in the Loach – that's what we call the OH-6A – I marvel, as always, at the wrap-around view from the 'egg', our flight crew compartment, which gives us spectacular visibility in all directions with only a tiny blind spot to the rear.

"The new people are shooting at us. I see their red muzzle flashes in the rain. I pull the OH-6 up and out, tracers spending themselves beneath us. This chopper has power! We're okay."

Fred Newman arrived in Vietnam shortly after the 15 February 1967 combat debut of the 'Loach', the soldier's term for the OH-6A, from the term LOH or light observation helicopter.

The US Army in the field had long since found that its Bell OH-13 Sioux and Hiller OH-23 Raven observation helicopters were too old and too difficult to maintain. As an interim measure, the Bell UH-1A and UH-1B Huey were used in the observation role, but by 1966 the Army was beginning to field the purpose-designed Bell OH-58A Kiowa and Hughes OH-6A Cayuse. The latter had been the winner of the 1960 Light Observation Helicopter competition and was highly regarded by Army officers.

"On a typical mission, we spring off with a full load of fuel and go into a hover above friendly troops moving to stake out new positions. If they're attacked, we scuttle up to a good altitude to direct artillery fire against the Cong.

*The 'Loach' drew its nickname from the US Army term LOH, for light observation helicopter. The Hughes OH-6A Cayuse, as it was officially known, was designed to give its crew good visibility while in the air and a strong prospect of surviving if forced down.*

"My hooch mate didn't dance fast enough one day when 'Victor Charlie' bracketed him with a 12.7-mm machine-gun. He took hits which made a horrendous, crunching sound, ripped up some hydraulics, and sent metal fragments whipping around inside the cockpit. He managed to auto-rotate to a 'controlled crash' landing and it was then that we realized the OH-6 is extremely survivable. If you look at the Loach, it's basically an egg with a tailboom. When you crash, the tailboom crumples and the egg just detaches. The crew often can walk out, suck in a deep breath, and continue living."

## Cavalry helicopters

In Newman's period, a typical Air Cavalry troop was equipped with seven to nine OH-6s, an aero rifle platoon with 'slick' transport Hueys and an aero weapons platoon with nine attack helicopters. On an Air Cavalry sortie the OH-6 could be armed with the XM-27 system comprising a 7.62-mm M-134 minigun with 2,000 rounds. Installation of this system meant some sacrifice in performance and degraded the Cayuse's ability to carry from one to three passengers in the space behind the two pilots.

"Our usual tactic in the Air Cavalry was to operate in a White

before yesterday and nobody got a beeper or saw a parachute. Now, there's an empty bunk next to mine. Tomorrow, maybe it will be me. And no-one will tell us why." The writer was killed in combat before the letter reached his parents.

Momyer was deeply concerned about command and control. The question 'who's in charge?' occupied a significant portion of his official writing. The arrangement whereby targets were chosen, almost always requiring decisions in Hawaii and Washington, was so cumbersome that the Viet Cong had time to attack and then escape long before fighter-bombers or B-52s could arrive. After discussions with Westmoreland, in 1967 Momyer obtained greater control over B-52 planning and targeting than he had enjoyed earlier.

## Increasing MiG threat

While General Momyer was trying to run the Air Force's part of the war, the MiG-17 and MiG-21 pilots of North Vietnam's air arm were becoming more numerous, although their actual performance was inconsistent. It appeared that some of the MiG pilots were significantly more capable than others. This could be explained to an extent by the strong suspicion that some Russian and North Korean fighter pilots were participating in the fray but, even then, it remained evident that some North Vietnamese pilots were significantly better than other North Vietnamese pilots. It was not a matter of different units performing differently: those stationed at Kep seemed to be both good and bad, as did those stationed at Phuc Yen. No clear explanation for the disparity emerged, but it did become clear that the better and more aggressive enemy pilots, including the mysterious Colonel Tomb, preferred the MiG-17 to the MiG-21. Though the MiG-17 was older, slower, and usually not armed with IR air-to-air missiles, it was a far more nimble dogfighter and seemed to be far more responsive to a pilot's touch on the controls.

*The Navy's new light-attack aircraft, the A-7 Corsair II, was hurled aloft by a carrier's C13 or C13-1 steam catapult with approximately the kinetic energy of a railroad boxcar being thrown off a cliff. Other carrier jets had this trait but few were as sturdy or as long-legged as the Corsair.*

Team of two Loaches, the 'high guy' keeping watch while the 'low guy' prowled the combat area and trolled for enemy fire. Supporting the movement of our troops on the ground, we used various navigation techniques to keep constant tabs on their whereabouts and to advise them on movements.

"When we hit a sudden, heavy concentration of Viet Cong we called in a Red Team of attack helicopters from the aero weapons platoon to hose down the bad guys, and a Blue Team of Hueys from the aero rifle platoon to insert our troops at a key node where our ground-pounders would be most effective.

"We were scouts and observers, remember, and it was not the Army's intent to pit us head-to-head against highly mobile Viet Cong maneuver units bristling with heavy firepower. Still, there were times when we blasted away at 'Charlie'. And once in a while we could lean out and shoot at him with an M14 or M16 rifle."

**The OH-6A Cayuse introduced a new standard of flexibility to Army helicopter forces. Between 1966 and 1973, 'Loaches' flew more than two million combat hours in roles ranging from armed escort to photo reconnaissance and aerial adjustment of artillery fire.**

On 1 February 1967, command of US Air Force units in the Pacific (PACAF) passed from General Hunter Harris, Jr, to General John D. Ryan, a bomber man who had spent most of his career in SAC. Harris's background was largely in bombers too, but he seemed to have gained the respect of fighter pilots in a way that Ryan was unable to do. Back in Washington, the most famous bomber man in the service's history, General LeMay had long since been replaced as Chief of Staff of the Air Force by General John P. McConnell, a bomber man like LeMay, although his background was more broadly-based. McConnell was widely respected and did not utter unhelpful homilies such as the threat to bomb Hanoi back into the stone age. But it remained true that, in the perception of some at least, SAC-trained bomber generals were running an Air Force which was caught in the midst of a fighter war. Things were 'ass-backwards'. F-105s and other fighters, as has been noted, were assaulting strategic targets in the North while B-52s were unleashing their bombs on rain forest and paddy fields in the South.

No previous ceasefire or bombing halt had produced any result, including the paired bombing halts over Christmas and New Year's period celebrated by Americans and by the Roman Catholic majority of Vietnamese, but a truce and a fifth bombing halt was declared in recognition of the Vietnamese New Year, known as Tet, to last for four days. During the 8-12 February 1967 truce, reconnaissance flights identified more than 1,500 trucks along Route 15 heading south and the evidence that the enemy was using the truce period to supply forces in South Vietnam seemed almost overwhelming.

Halt or no halt, the continuing problems with air-to-air missiles were being subjected to scrutiny and corrective measures. A US Navy instruction dated 8 February and issued to carriers and carrier air wings in the combat theater, pointed out problems in the 'storage, handling and maintenance' of AIM-7 Sparrow and AIM-9 Sidewinders and tasked armament officers to conduct a study to determine whether these problems were related to undocumented but persistent reports of missile failures. No-one had carried out a statistical study to show that the Navy's missiles were not working as well as they should but all pilots believed it. Commander James

*Thumbing their noses at the Americans, the Communists moved their trucks through Mu Gia Pass between North Vietnam and Laos in broad daylight during the Tet truce of 1967 – but not for long. US interdiction forced them to camouflage, subterfuge, and to move by night.*

BETTIE BOOP, *a bombed-up F-100D of the 615th TFS/35th TFW. Following temporary deployments in 1962-64, the Super Sabre arrived in Vietnam to stay in 1965, and eventually equipped four fighter wings, augmented by activated Air National Guard squadrons. Camouflage appeared on 'Huns' in the war-zone from the beginning of 1966 onwards.*

*The three-month Operation 'Junction City' developed into a major battle in the first half of 1967. Involving four ARVN battalions and 22 US battalions from three divisions and two independent brigades, it was supported by several thousand F-100 and F-4 sorties. By June, the Communists had been pushed back into Cambodia with heavy losses.*

McBride, an A-4C Skyhawk pilot aboard USS *Shangri-la*, recalls speculating on whether Crusaders and Phantoms would be able to help him out if needed. "None of us had firm information, but it was clear that there were worries about the reliability and effectiveness of the air-to-air missiles."

The Air Force had similar concerns, which were exacerbated when an F-105 Thunderchief came back to its base with an AIM-7 Sparrow firmly embedded in its burnt, twisted tail section. Had the 'Thud', which survived only by an apparent miracle, been hit by an American missile because of some error in the missile's design? Or was the more likely explanation – pilot error – the cause of a Thunderchief nearly being shot down by a Phantom? In other incidents, US airmen did mistake friendly aircraft for MiGs and zap them with Sparrows or Sidewinders. One American pilot was reputed, perhaps partly in jest, to have shot down as many Phantoms as MiGs! At least one POW in Hanoi came back from imprisonment with persuasive evidence that he had been shot down by a wingman.

Though the radar-guided AIM-7 Sparrow gave US fighters a head-on fighting capability not enjoyed by the MiG, pilots continued to have doubts about its reliability after frequent MiG encounters when the air-to-air missile failed to fire or track properly. Charging Sparrow, a program begun four months earlier in November 1966 and concluded after some delay on 23 February 1967, had required that every F-4C Phantom in inventory launch a Sparrow against an aerial target. Results indicated that only two-thirds of the F-4C force could successfully launch an AIM-7 and that only 80 per cent of the missiles met functional requirements.

On 22 February the 173rd Airborne Brigade started Operation 'Junction City' with the only American parachute assault of the entire war. This was the latest American effort to track down and destroy the enemy's brains and heart, the so-called Central Office for South Vietnam (COSVN). At least one student of Viet Cong activity uttered skepticism that COSVN existed at all, but it scarcely mattered. This huge operation pitted Americans against the Cong and that was what US commanders wanted.

## Operation 'Junction City'

Supported by F-100 Super Sabres and some strikes by naval air, 'Junction City' operations broadened and by early March a major set-piece battle was building. The Army had a fire support base in the Michelin rubber plantation some 20-miles (32-km) north-east of Tay Ninh. On 21 March six enemy battalions (2,500 men) hit the base and the defenders called for air support. An O-1 Bird Dog soon appeared overhead and began directing F-100s from Bien Hoa and F-4s from Camh Ranh Bay in laying Snake and Nape on the VC. Both air bases were but a few miles from the fire support base and the fighter-bombers were quickly on the scene. Soon they were making the round trip, reloading, and returning to the fight. By late morning more than 85 jet fighter-bombers were laying bombs and

# Air Force Rescue

*Courage behind enemy lines*

The first USAF officer to accumulate 6,000 flying hours in a helicopter was Major Kyron V. Hall, a Sikorsky CH-3C Jolly Green pilot of the 20th Helicopter Squadron based at Nha Trang. The record was reached in November.

Another intrepid helicopter pilot was Captain Gerald O. Young. Launched on a rescue mission on 9 November, Captain Young's HH-3E Jolly Green was part of an armada which included another HH-3E, a C-130 Hercules flare ship, and three US Army helicopter gunships. This force was headed toward jungles south-east of Khe Sanh where a US-South Vietnamese reconnaissance team was on the verge of being overwhelmed by NVA troops. The NVA had already shot down two helicopters attempting to rescue the besieged survivors.

Ahead of Captain Young, an HH-3E landed in low cloud and poor visibility and took heavy fire while rescuing three survivors. The lead HH-3E was so badly damaged that it seemed unlikely to return safely to home base at Da Nang.

Young could have escorted his sister ship to safety but chose, instead, to attempt to rescue two Americans and several South Vietnamese who remained in peril on the ground.

## Landing under fire

Young made a perilous landing while under fire from concealed NVA troops, and with the help of his para-rescue jumpers – the fearless 'PJs' – took the friendly ground troops on board. Young applied full power for take-off as the enemy riflemen appeared in the open. They raked the HH-3E with small-arms fire and rifle-launched grenades. Suddenly the right engine sparked and exploded and the blast flipped the HH-3E on its back and sent it cascading down the hill in flames.

Young hung upside-down in the cockpit, his clothing on fire. Frantically he beat out the flames and struggled free, but he had suffered second and third degree burns on one-quarter of his body.

This was only the beginning of an incredible saga. Young snuffed out flames engulfing one of the survivors. A-1E Sandy Skyraiders arrived overhead in the late afternoon and plotted out an effort to mount another rescue attempt at first light the following morning.

At daybreak, when the A-1Es reappeared, Captain Young, after nursing the survivor with burn injuries all night, stuck his head out of hiding and shot a signal flare, trying to warn the Skyraiders that the North Vietnamese would probably use him as bait for a flak trap. But the North Vietnamese seemed to have melted into the jungle. The A-1Es brought in several Army and VNAF helicopters which picked up five survivors and hauled them out.

Suddenly, more North Vietnamese troops appeared. Young hid the wounded man and struck out on his own, trying to lure the NVA away from the survivor.

His scheme worked. The NVA pursued him. Dazed and nearly in shock, he hid frequently to treat his burns. As the day drew on, he found himself leading the NVA in circles through an open region of high elephant grass. He made a decision not to use his beeper radio to communicate with rescue aircraft – still seeking to prevent drawing his comrades into a flak trap. While he continued drawing the NVA away from the original rescue site, helicopters set down there and picked up one survivor and the bodies of those who had been killed.

Seventeen hours after his crash and 6 miles (more than 9 km) from the crash site, Captain Young finally slipped free of his pursuers and was able to signal a friendly helicopter. His ordeal was over.

During 1967 a number of airmen received the Medal of Honor, the highest American award 'for conspicuous gallantry and intrepidity at the risk of life above and beyond the call of duty'. They included Captain Gerald O. Young. Everyone who took part in his rescue operation agreed that the award was thoroughly deserved.

**Above: Though it was rarely done from this high, the HH-3E Jolly Green used its hoist to lower a jungle penetrator – and often a PJ, or para-rescue man with it – to reach a downed pilot and pull him to safety.**

**Below: The air refueling capability of the HC-130 Hercules made it a routine sight whenever a Jolly Green set forth to attempt a rescue. The HC-130 was also a flying headquarters and command and communications post.**

# Navy Rescue

*Plucked to safety from the sea*

In many respects, the US Navy was spared the sort of internecine warfare which went on in the Air Force. The important distinction in the Navy lay not between fighter and bomber men (the Navy's brief attempts to compete with SAC via such outlandish means as the carrier-based P2V-3C Neptune being past history) but lay, instead, between aviators and sailors. Fortunately for the men who flew from carrier decks, virtually everyone in the Navy's chain of command, from the CAG (Carrier Air Wing commander, still abbreviated after the carrier air groups of an earlier era) through task-force commanders right up to to CINCPAC himself, was either an aviator or had personal experience with carrier operations.

The Navy approach differed from the Air Force in a number of ways. With combat rescue, for example, the Air Force relied upon assembling a massive force of tankers, EW aircraft, fighter cover, Sandy strike ships and

helicopters before 'going in' to attempt to extract a survivor. The Navy's view of combat rescue was that speed was everything. Whether or not it could be adequately protected, the

helicopter had to be gotten to the scene of the downed airman as quickly as possible. Initially such rescues were carried out by destroyers operating close in shore, plane-guard helicopters

from the carriers on station in the Gulf of Tonkin, and anti-submarine helicopters operating from various warships of TF.77. Although the Kaman UH-2B Seasprite was considered too

**The UH-2B/C Seasprite became standard on US Navy vessels just as the big build-up in Vietnam gathered momentum. Critics said it needed more armor and range, but it rescued many survivors.**

20-mm cannon fire on the enemy troops.

Like many of the mass troop operations which received American geographical names to obscure their real whereabouts, 'Junction City's' major battle in the plantation, followed by a prolonged series of lesser battles, made important use of close air support. F-100s and F-4s flew more than 5,000 support sorties and in the end both Viet Cong and NVA units were defeated and pushed back into their Cambodian sanctuary. Without air support, the result could have been very different.

On 9 March 1967, Thailand's Prime Minister Thanom Kittikachorn announced what everyone had known for two years – that US aircraft based in Thailand were bombing targets in North Vietnam. On 13 March, he announced something else that everyone knew, namely that the new base at U-Tapao would be used to support B-52 Stratofortress operations. On paper at least, these installations belonged to Kittikachorn's sovereign

government, although the reality was that nearly every man and every aircraft on each airfield was American. Udorn, Ubon and others were called Royal Thai Air Force Bases (RTAFB), although it was difficult to find anyone at a higher level than the cook or shoeshine boy who possessed Thai nationality. U-Tapao, for reasons known to no-one, was called a Royal Thai Naval Base although, despite its proximity to a bay, it was better known for B-52s than for boats.

In March 1967, in another shift of targeting policy, F-105 Thunderchiefs and F-4 Phantoms attacked the Thai Nguyen iron and steel works for the first time. Previously off-limits like many lucrative targets in the North, the Thai Nguyen works were the only ones in Southeast Asia which made bridge sections, barges and POL drums. Several strikes on the steel-works came over a period of a couple of weeks.

## Supersonic at grass-top height

In one of his more daring exploits, MiG killer Colonel Robin Olds led a low-level assault against Thai Nguyen, flying at about 500 knots (800 km/h) at an altitude of 10 feet (3 m) with full bombload. This must surely have been one of the missions General Graham had in mind when he used the word 'suicidal', meaning not that Olds was reckless but that he was a man of almost incomparable courage and leadership. It can be supposed that the workers at Thai Nguyen never knew what hit them. The steel and iron works, however, was never subjected to regular enough and steady enough attack to have a significant effect on its output.

On 10 March 1967, Captain Max C. Brestel of the Takhli-based

*Pilot of a **US Air Force TF-102A** scrutinizes an **F-86D Sabre** (53-0843) of the Thai Air Force's 12th Fighter Wing. Neither Thailand's 'Sabre Dog' interceptors nor Australia's Commonwealth CA-27 Sabres actually saw combat, although they came close on a couple of occasions. In addition to 24 2.75-in air-to-air rockets in a nose tray (not visible), Thailand's F-86Ds had underwing pylons for AIM-9 Sidewinders.*

*The arrival of the SH-3 Sea King gave Navy rescue forces a bigger and longer-ranged rescue asset, enabling helicopter crews like this to penetrate deeper into the heavily-defended areas around Hanoi and Haiphong.*

short-legged and vulnerable for the task, armed examples were to perform combat rescue missions until the American withdrawal from Southeast Asia.

The Sikorsky SH-3A Sea King had much greater range and lifting capacity, and machines from units like Helicopter Anti-Submarine Squadron HS-6 were among the the most effective Navy combat rescue choppers.

In early 1967, squadron HS-2 appeared in the battle zone aboard the USS *Hornet*. It was equipped with 21 anti-submarine SH-3As, and although no serious threat from submarines materialized

during patrols off the North Vietnam coast, one SH-3A was soon lost in an ASW (anti-submarine warfare) exercise. Two further SH-3As were lost shortly afterward in accidents.

A number of the squadron's helicopters had been modified for rescue duties, and the immensely risky missions they were to undertake into hostile airspace were not without cost.

As the year progressed, a rescue attempt on 18 July 1967 was marred when a gunner aboard an SH-3A was killed after intense ground fire from North Vietnamese troops prevented an attempted rescue. A day later, yet another SH-3A was attempting a rescue of the same downed aircrew when it was riddled with gunfire and downed with the loss of all four crew members. It was an incredible and tragic cruise for one of the several Navy helicopter squadrons which contributed significantly to both the ASW and the rescue effort.

# The Last Flying-Boat

The SP-5B variant of the Martin Marlin was the last American flying-boat to serve the US Navy in combat. A distinctive and imposing sight, the SP-5B operated with a detachment from VP-40 based at Sangley Point in the Philippines, forward deployed in the war zone at Cam Ranh Bay.

Marlins were supported by the seaplane tender USS *Cumtuck* (AV-7). The vessel provided food, fuel and supplies to the flying-boat crews while they operated

from Vietnamese waters and flew continuous 8- to 9-hour anti-infiltration patrols. The effort was part of the Navy's larger battle against infiltration known by the program name 'Market Time'.

The SP-5B Marlin served in the war zone intermittently from 1965 to 1967, when the last of these big 'boats' was pulled out of the line. The final operational flight of a Navy seaplane came on 6 November 1967 when an SP-5B from VP-40 flew its last mission after returning to the US.

*Left: An SP-5B Marlin of VP-40 on an Operation 'Market Time' sortie, a marathon flight of up to nine hours. These missions meant long hours of boredom, but could be punctuated by brief moments of surging adrenaline when enemy vessels were found.*

*An SP-5B Marlin of VP-40, the last US Navy squadron to operate flying-boats in combat and the only such unit serving in Southeast Asia, makes a JATO (jet-assisted take-off) at Cam Ranh Bay in April 1967. Soon afterward, the last flying-boat was retired.*

# Navy Strikes

**B**y 1967 it had come to be understood, though it was not necessarily an official part of the ever-present rules of engagement, that while the area around Hanoi belonged to the Air Force (at least most of the time), the area around Haiphong was the Navy's province.

Naval aviators were bedevilled by questions about targeting just as much as their land-based brethren. Even though some of the more restrictive rules had just been relaxed – previously 'no-go' areas such as the military airfields round Hanoi could now be attacked – there was still no consistency.

### A real bombing policy?

President Johnson's tough attitude toward Ho Chi Minh meant that things might change. A change was certainly necessary, with the continuing growth of the North Vietnamese defense systems and the ever-present lure of targets in Haiphong. But lack of decision from on-high caused some Navy captains and admirals to be at loggerheads. One Navy commander wanted to "go in and clean the whole place out". Permission was not yet forthcoming.

Like their Air Force counterparts, particularly those at

Takhli, Navy men made suggestions which were based on solid professional experience – and were ignored. The decisions as to which targets to hit and when to hit them continued to be made in Washington, without regard to the opinions of the experienced men

on the ground – or on the water.

The pilots knew what they had to do to beat the North Vietnamese, but to those aboard ship, as on land, the whole campaign seemed to lack focus, being too arbitrary to convey any clear message to Ho Chi Minh.

*Navy aircraft were involved in supporting ground troops as well as in the war against the North. An F-4B Phantom of VF-154 'Black Knights' unloads on a North Vietnamese artillery site just north of the Demilitarized Zone which had been firing over the border at the 3rd Marine Division.*

---

354th TFS/355th TFW became the first double MiG killer of the war when he shot down two MiG-17s with 20-mm cannon fire. Using the callsign Kangaroo 03, Captain Brestel was flying an F-105D Thunderchief (62-4284). By coincidence the same 'Thud' airframe later received credit for a third MiG-17 kill on 27 October 1967 when flown by Captain Gene I. Basel. Brestel's achievement occurred during a period of exceedingly heavy fighting, a period when courageous F-105 pilots fought against overwhelming odds while, at the same time, remaining hamstrung by restrictions on targets, sanctuaries and stringent rules of engagement.

On the same day that Brestel shot down two MiGs, Captain Merlyn H. Dethlefsen of the 355th TFW went into North Vietnam as number three in a flight of F-105F 'Wild Weasels' on an Iron Hand, or SAM suppression, mission. Using the callsign Lincoln 03,

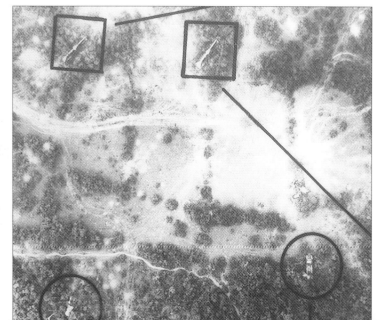

Captain Dethlefsen took his F-105F (63-8354) against SAM sites in the vicinity of Thai Nguyen despite unusually heavy MiG and SAM opposition. Dethlefsen shook off persistent firing passes from MiG-21s without jettisoning his ordnance, and continued to press an unusually courageous attack on SAM sites while under heavy fire.

### Iron Hand Medal of Honor

Dethlefsen became the first airman to receive America's highest award for valor, the Medal of Honor, for action against North Vietnam. Only eight USAF people received the decoration (two for conduct as prisoners of war, along with the Navy's Stockdale) and it was a measure of the intensity of the fighting in March/April 1967 that two fighter pilots earned the Medal of Honor during Iron Hand missions – Major Leo K. Thorsness of the 355th TFW in an F-105F on 19 April and Navy LtCdr Michael J. Estocin of the 'Golden Dragons' of attack squadron VA-192 from USS *Ticonderoga* in an A-4E Skyhawk on 20 and 26 April. Thorsness and Estocin both carried out valiant Strike attacks on SAM sites and Thorsness, whose callsign was Kingfish 01, also shot down a MiG-17. F-105F 'Wild Weasel' pilots at least had their second man in the back seat, the EWO (electronic warfare officer) or Bear, to help search for the Fan Songs used by SAM sites and to assist generally, but the A-4E pilot had to do it all by himself.

Thorsness was shot down a few days later and became a prisoner of war after a series of ghastly mistakes in communication prevented what should have been an easy rescue. With Colonel Jack Broughton and others circling overhead, enemy defenses were effectively suppressed and a helicopter pick-up was possible, but

*"Wild Weasel, wild weasel, they call me by name," began a fighter-jock ballad about attacking North Vietnam's SA-2 'Guideline' SAM sites. "I fly up on Thud Ridge, and play the big game," referring to a ridgeline near Hanoi. "I hide 'neath the mountains and sneak o'er the hills, get up, get down, and go in for the kills." For 'Weasels' stalking the radar sets that guided these pencil-thin SAMs, it was literally kill or be killed.*

**Left:** *Carrier flying was a busy, perilous undertaking, and flight operations went forwards at an intensive rate. This A-4 Skyhawk blasts from the end of the catapult only seconds after one of its squadron mates; visible less than a few hundred yards ahead.*

*A-4 Skyhawks from VA-164 operating from the USS Oriskany pound the Cam Pha railroad/ highway bridge north-east of Haiphong. Lack of a co-ordinated air strategy meant that high-value targets like this could be attacked only sporadically.*

# Tanker Intruders

One success story which won recognition for many naval aviators involved was the KA-6D, the aerial refueling tanker version of the Grumman A-6 Intruder attack aircraft. For reasons which no Pentagon policymaker can enunciate with any assurance of historical accuracy, the Air Force and Navy have always used different refueling systems, the Air Force relying on the flying boom in which a KC-135 'plugs into' its recipient while the Navy employs the British-developed probe and drogue. Today, there is significant interchange between the two systems, but in early 1967 there was not.

The Navy's principal tanker had been the KA-3B Skywarrior but it was quickly becoming clear that the KA-6D Intruder was far less trouble-prone, less expensive to operate, and more flexible for the missions being flown – although it retained one drawback of all Navy tankers in that its crew could not look directly back at the receiver aircraft. The KA-6D had required relatively little modification from the A-6A (and later A-6E) attack aircraft (though tanker and attack missions were not interchangeable in the same air frame). It was also considered a pleasure to fly.

*The 'basket' from a KA-6D Intruder tanker as seen from the right-hand, bombardier-navigator position aboard an A-6A Intruder attack craft. KA-6Ds gave the US Navy greater combat flexibility.*

# 'Thud' Battles

*Air-to-air action in the F-105*

Like traffic at a clogged intersection, A-6A Intruders nudge up against each other hurrying to launch on an Alpha strike, the US Navy's term for an air attack involving different aircraft types and different ordnance directed against a single target. Note bombs under wings.

no-one ordered in the choppers in time. Estocin was first listed as missing, then as KIA (killed in action) following his failure to return from his 26 April mission. His fate, and the agony of his family, typified one of the war's dilemmas: for several years, while considered missing, Estocin was promoted to commander, then captain (men in POW camps also were promoted regularly). Eventually, it was learned that he had, in fact, died on 26 April while a lieutenant commander.

The airbase at Phu Cat became operational on 29 May 1967, providing a home for the F-100D Super Sabres of the 37th Tactical Fighter Wing. Its initial unit was the much-moved 416th TFS, soon joined by the 355th and later the 612th. When a number of Air National Guard (ANG) F-100 units were activated, the 174th TFS of the Iowa ANG joined the wing with its 22 F-100s. At one point this huge wing had between 80 and 110 F-100s, including 15 to 18 F-100F 'Misty FAC' aircraft – two-seat Super Sabres which flew the

The period which began on 10 March 1967 with Brestel's twin MiG kills was a springtime of unusually vicious fighting, especially for the men in F-105 Thunderchiefs operating from Takhli and Korat. While facing greater risks each day, 'Thud' pilots saw their friends killed, captured, or cut down to size by the very nation they served – criticized, denied promotion, and in some cases actually court-martialed for violating rules of engagement so complex that it was almost impossible to memorize them all.

On 26 March, Colonel Robert R. Scott, the commander of the 355th TFW at Takhli, was flying a 'Thud' with the callsign Leech 01 when he tangled with a MiG-17 and shot it down with 20-mm gunfire. A MiG kill was a crowning achievement, but Scott – a virtuoso fighter pilot and respected commander – spent far too much of his time trying to

*An F-105 Thunderchief of the 357th TFS/355th TFW, Takhli. 'Thud' pilots flew some of the most dangerous missions of the war, taking their aircraft into the heart of the most heavily-defended air space in the world. According to one analyst, an F-105 pilot was statistically certain to be shot down by the time of his 68th mission, even though 100 were needed for a ticket home.*

sort out the problems posed by the chain of command and the rules of engagement.

On 19 April, in a furious battle, no fewer than four 'Thud' pilots claimed MiG-17s in air-to-air action. The two-seat 'Wild Weasel' crew of Major Leo K. Thorsness and Captain Harold E. Johnson, flying an F-105F (63-8301), callsign Kingfish 01, claimed a MiG-17 as an incidental part of the already-mentioned sortie against SAM sites which earned Thorsness the Medal of Honor.

Three F-105D pilots from the Takhli-based 355th TFW were also successful. Major Jack W. Hunt, callsign Nitro 01, Captain William E. Eskew, callsign Panda 01, and Major Frederick G.

Flying the F-105 over the North was perilous, but the big bomber was by no means defenseless. Captain Larry D. Wiggins damaged a MiG-17 with this Sidewinder shot on 3 June 1967, closing in to complete the kill with a burst of 20-mm cannon fire.

Tolman each used 20-mm cannon fire to down a MiG-17.

Ironically, Tolman, who also earned high respect from his wingmen as a skilled and courageous fighter pilot, was one of three men later court-martialed for destroying gun camera film of an inadvertent firing upon the Soviet supply vessel *Turkestan* in Haiphong harbor. It had been a fast, furious day in other respects. An attempt to rescue a downed fighter crew went sorely awry when an A-1E Skyraider, attempting to cover a helicopter pick-up, was shot down by a MiG.

## High risk, low gain

Four MiG kills in one day should have been cause for celebration, but the losses were too heavy. In the billets at Takhli and Korat, and aboard carriers at sea, fighter pilots fumed and cursed over the bizarre vagaries of a war which had them taking so much risk for so little gain. A naval aviator aboard USS *Kitty Hawk* (CVA-63) wrote a letter to Secretary of Defense McNamara pleading, courteously, that if they had to risk their lives then they ought to

have the chance to strike more lucrative targets – such as airfields. What the aviator did not know was that McNamara, for the first time in years, was beginning to doubt the effectiveness of continued bombing of an essentially agrarian society. The Navy pilot had the wrong man. So often criticized for not bombing enough, McNamara's thoughts now lay in the direction of not bombing at all. However, the President was now in a tougher frame of mind than McNamara, and decided that a serious gesture of conciliation would have to be made by the North Vietnamese before the bombing could stop. Moreover, Johnson was prepared to 'open up' to US airmen targets they had been previously denied – including airfields.

*F-105 pilot Captain Max Brestel was the first American pilot to shoot down two MiGs in the same mission, achieving the feat on 10 March 1967. He is seen being congratulated by veteran 'Thud' wing commander Colonel Jack Broughton, after Brestel had completed his 100th combat mission over North Vietnam.*

# Republic F-105 Thunderchief

**The F-105 required excessive runway length when operating with heavy loads in the high ambient temperature of Southeast Asia, and performed inadequately at altitude, but pilots swore by it anyway.**

**Camo but no code**
This F-105D (59-1745) wears the T.O. 1-1-4 camouflage which was in use in 1966 but no tailcode. Two-letter codes were in use by mid-1967.

**Sturdy 'Thud'**
Up high it was different, but at low altitude the F-105D was a superb warplane which could survive heavy battle damage and bring its pilot safely home.

**Potent bombload**
This 'Thud' carries the standard load of eight 750-lb (340-kg) bombs, six under the fuselage and two more hanging under the wings – plus external fuel.

forward air controller mission at low level and high speed.

In addition to the 3rd, 35th and 37th wings, the large F-100 Super Sabre force in Southeast Asia (some 490 aircraft) included the 31st TFW at Tuy Hoa from mid-1967 onwards. The 31st Wing included the 308th and 309th TFS and quickly gained the 188th TFS of the New Mexico ANG (the 'Enchilada Air Force') and the 136th TFS of the New York ANG ('Rocky's Raiders'). The Guardsmen operated the F-100C model.

Air traffic was plentiful at an F-100 base which was likely to be very busy. In 1967 Robert R. Rodwell of the British magazine *Flight International*, reporting from Vietnam, called the F-100 base at Bien Hoa the world's busiest airport. Rodwell's numbers showed that an F-100 landed or took off once every 42 seconds.

## Busy Tuy Hoa

Tuy Hoa, on the coast and referred to by writer Dave Anderton as 'The Atlantic City of the South China Sea', was even busier than Bien Hoa for a time. Fuel for the base was piped overland from Vung Ro Bay, some 12 to 15 miles (20 to 25 km). The Viet Cong blew up the pipeline occasionally, and the F-100s dropped bombs on them occasionally. Most F-100 missions continued to be in a 'troops in contact' environment, where the Super Sabre pilots were directly supporting the infantrymen on the ground.

A new ally joined the air war in South Vietnam in April 1967 when the Canberra bombers of No. 2 Squadron, Royal Australian Air Force, were deployed to Phan Rang. The 'Aussie' squadron came under the operational control of Seventh Air Force in Saigon.

As part of the continuing effort to build up South Vietnam's own forces, on 17 April the 18 USAF F-5 Freedom Fighters at Bien Hoa were transferred to the VNAF's 522nd Fighter Squadron. The VNAF was also to receive Cessna A-37 Dragonfly attack aircraft.

On 25 April the familiar C-123 transport reached South Vietnam in a new and improved form when the first of the jet-assisted C-123K Provider assault transports arrived at Tan Son Nhut.

Another new aircraft type in 1967 was the twin-boom Cessna O-2B PSYOPS (psychological operations) aircraft, which was

# First Airfield Attack

Embittered pilots and frustrated field commanders, long denied the chance to attack the MiG airfields, gained their first relief from the long-standing prohibition on 24 April 1967, amid very intense fighting, especially by F-105 squadrons. The main airfield, Phuc Yen, would not be authorized as a target for several months, and Gia Lam (which was also Hanoi's civilian airfield) was spared attack throughout the war because US policymakers decided to permit transport aircraft from China, the Soviet Union and the International Control Commission to have safe access to North Vietnam, even though Gia Lam remained an active MiG base.

But the absolute taboo on attacking airbases was reconsidered not only for political reasons but because the enemy

*Intelligence analysts used the 'product' from various reconnaissance platforms to pinpoint North Vietnam's airfields. They knew where the vital targets were – but only political leaders in Washington could make the decision to launch strikes against them.*

bedded down at Nha Trang. Used for leaflet drops, the O-2Bs were the first examples of the militarized Cessna Skymaster to arrive in the country. The O-2Bs which arrived in May were quickly followed by the O-2A on 2 June 1967, which was intended to replace the familiar single-engined O-1 Bird Dog and make the forward air controller (FAC) job a little safer. The first O-2A aircraft went to Binh Thuy.

The USS *Intrepid* (CVA-11) arrived on the line on 21 June 1967, bringing a new category of aircraft-carrier into the conflict. The ageing World War II veteran, normally a small anti-submarine carrier operating S-2 Tracker and SH-3 Sea King aircraft, had been given three squadrons of A-4C Skyhawks. Squadrons VA-15, VA-34 and VSF-1 (the last-named being an anti-submarine fighter squadron!) were on board. Nicknamed 'Valions', 'Blue Blasters' and 'War Eagles', these Skyhawks flew against targets in North and South Vietnam in just the same manner as did attack aircraft from other carriers.

On 8 July 1967, Secretary of Defense Robert S. McNamara visited South Vietnam for the first time in a full nine months. He received a secret briefing from the Seventh Air Force commander. Momyer's assessment was devoted largely to the war in the South but Momyer could also report a few developments in the campaign north of the 17th Parallel. One was the closely-guarded plan to use

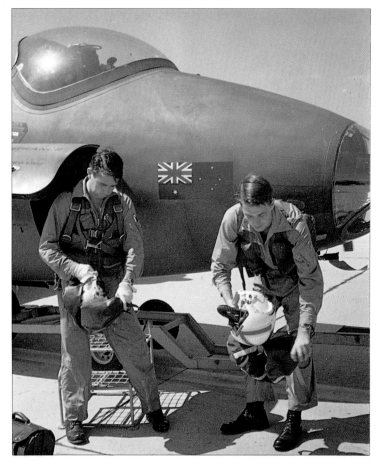

*Australian Canberra crew at Phan Rang. The RAAF's No. 2 Squadron, callsign Magpie, flew 16 Canberras in Vietnam and lost two in combat. Its aircraft were modified to carry two M117 750-lb (340-kg) bombs externally since the Canberra's bomb bay, meant for shorter weapons, could take only four standard US Air Force long-bodied bombs.*

was continuing an ambitious build-up which increased his number of jet-capable airfields from nine to 15. Expansion and improvements were underway at Kep and Phuc Yen while a new Hoa Loc airfield was being completed in the western part of the country.

A rather limp argument for not attacking the airfields, but one that some officers made repeatedly, was that US aircraft losses would exceed the damage inflicted on the enemy. However, since strike forces were already penetrating the areas where the airfields were located, no action by the enemy could make losses greater than they already were over targets in the area.

Relief came when eight F-105Ds attacked Hoa Loc on 24 April and 14 MiGs were reported destroyed on the ground. Throughout the 1965-68 'Rolling Thunder' campaign, authorization for intermittent attacks on airfields would remain the exception rather than the rule. When exceptions were made, neither pilots nor commanders seemed to know why they were permitted to hit a MiG base one day but not another.

*Bombs burst on the main North Vietnamese MiG base at Phuc Yen, one of a number of such facilities around Hanoi. Although some targeting restrictions had been moved, US airmen were not allowed to attack this key airfield for several months.*

# Photo Delivery

**"I**n any typical day, I might fly as much as eight to 10 hours and log five or six missions," recalled Colonel Omni L. Bailes, Jr. Normally an RF-101C Voodoo pilot, Bailes also flew the very different 'Blue Canoe' while at Tan Son Nhut

The twin-engine Cessna 310 had been bought by the USAF for light transport, utility and 'hack' duties. Originally designated L-27 but known as the U-3B since 1962, about a dozen aircraft, in the factory blue/white paint scheme which earned them the nickname, were located at Tan Son Nhut where they were flown by 460th TRW and Seventh Air Force officers.

One little-known role of the Cessna involved getting IPIRs (Intelligence Photo Interpretation Reports, the end result of all photo-reconnaissance missions) to

commanders in the field in the shortest possible time.

"Sometimes it was a real challenge, figuring out how to get through the thunderstorms, find the friendlies instead of the enemy out in the jungle, and sometimes land on strips of mud out in the field. I find flying the RF-101C or the F-4 Phantom much easier in many ways.

"But we did not always have to risk the airplane so much. The U-3B aircraft were modified on the starboard side, in the rear seat area, with an eight-inch pipe and

*The U-3B 'Blue Canoe' (below) began life as a civil aircraft but was found to be an ideal utility craft for military needs. At Tan Son Nhut airfield near Saigon, the blue and white U-3B became a servant of intelligence experts who needed quick transportation for reports and documents. Pilots worked the U-3Bs hard.*

pin. When the pin was pulled, clearing the passage, a container could be dropped through the pipe from an altitude of 50 feet (14 m) to friendly troops on the ground. You simply pulled the pin and ejected the container.

"These contained photos, film and intelligence reports which we could deliver to friendlies without

landing the U-3B."

The Cessna U-3B was also used for various supply and hack duties, often under fire (indeed, as noted earlier, anyone taking off from Tan Son Nhut could come under mortar or rocket fire at any time) and Colonel Bailes logged a total of 133 missions in this little-publicized aircraft type.

*A stray Zuni rocket touched off a fiery inferno aboard USS Forrestal (CVA-59) on 29 July 1967. The ensuing fire cost the lives of 134 sailors. No fewer than 21 aircraft were destroyed. A year later, a second calamity struck the nuclear-powered USS Enterprise (CVAN-65) while en route to the combat zone, this time claiming 28 fatalities.*

Americans were to fly the A-37 while the aircraft was also being readied for the VNAF.

Three days later, on 29 July, sailors operating off the Vietnamese coast experienced the Navy's second major aircraft-carrier fire of the war. The USS *Forrestal* (CVA-59), traditionally assigned to the Atlantic Fleet but now taking her fair turn on a Pacific combat cruise, was *en route* to 'Yankee Station' when tragedy struck.

Aircraft had been spotted on *Forrestal*'s deck, armed and fueled, and were in final preparation to start up for the second launch of the day. As an auxiliary power unit was backed into position to start an F-4 Phantom, its hot exhaust blew directly on the Phantom's Zuni rocket pod. A rocket, ignited by the starter's exhaust heat, streaked across the busy flight deck and slammed into a loaded A-4 Skyhawk, which burst into flames. The fire engulfed the fan-tail and spread quickly below decks, touching off bombs and ammunition.

In a booming barrage of noise, aircraft and ordnance exploded. Men were blown overboard. Some were trapped in searing flames and choking smoke below decks.

## Fighting the inferno

Nearby units came to assist in fighting the fire and caring for the injured. Above deck, the fire was controlled and extinguished within an hour. But in the subterranean depths of the giant carrier, the blaze persisted for 12 hours. There were impressive acts of heroism by ship and air-wing personnel who contained the fire and rescued many potential victims. Bombs and rockets had to be pulled off the loaded and burning aircraft and heaved into the sea. Blisteringly hot 250-lb and 500-lb (113-kg and 227-kg) bombs were carried or rolled to the deck edge to be thrown over the side.

The fire had cost 134 men killed and 62 injured. Twenty-one aircraft were totally destroyed with another 43 damaged. *Forrestal* had to leave the war zone and head home for repairs, estimated at $70 million.

On 8 September the USAF began operating the Sikorsky HH-53B Jolly Green helicopter, an enlarged and farther-reaching outgrowth of the HH-3E Jolly Green Giant. The HH-53 was a big step forward. Air rescue squadrons had previously had to make do with the Kaman HH-43B Huskie, alias 'Pedro', which was a fine machine for local airfield fire-fighting and rescue but which had never been intended for combat rescues under fire, and with the

F-100 Super Sabres as forward air controllers, or 'fast FACs', in the Route Package One area of southern North Vietnam. Commando Sabre, the use of the two-seat F-100F in the Misty FAC role, had commenced a fortnight earlier on 28 June. These aircraft would be concentrated in one squadron at Phu Cat.

The introduction of the F-100F Fast FAC was an important development, introducing a new way of visually finding targets and pinpointing them for strike aircraft. For more than two years to come, Hanoi's intelligence would never succeed in learning the purpose of the F-100Fs which prowled the lower area of the country, nor link them to the precision-guided strikes which followed their appearance.

On 26 July the USAF's 3rd TFW at Bien Hoa AB received its first A-37A Dragonfly aircraft. The attack version was considerably heavier than the T-37B trainer from which it was developed.

# Strategic Reconnaissance

**O**n 27 September 1967, the first operational RC-135M reconnaissance mission, known by the code name 'Combat Apple', was flown by the newly-established 82nd Strategic Reconnaissance Squadron from its base at Kadena on Okinawa.

Strategic reconnaissance, which remained under the jurisdiction of SAC, was a vital part of the war against North Vietnam. The reconnaissance version of the Boeing Stratotanker, although little-publicized, was crucial to these operations, especially since replacing the RB-47 Stratojet in the combat theater at the beginning of the year.

'Combat Apple' consisted of flying 12-hour orbits over the Gulf of Tonkin, and later over Laos, collecting electronic

intelligence with special attention to picking up indications of Fan Song radar signals. If correctly identified, this intelligence made it possible to pinpoint and plan strikes against North Vietnam's ever-growing SAM network. Around 50 'Combat Apple' missions were flown per month at first, a figure which soon settled to a more relaxed 30.

Other strategic reconnaissance operations by variants of the RC-135 and by Mach 3-capable A-12 and SR-71 spyplanes added to the knowledge available to senior commanders who otherwise relied on the more familiar tactical recce flights by RF-101Cs and RF-4Cs. RC-135 aircraft operated by SAC continued to operate through the end of the conflict on various missions which shed light on Hanoi's capabilities and intentions.

*Workhorse of the US Air Force SIGINT (signals intelligence) world was this RC-135M 'Combat Apple' which provided MiG warning, SAM location, and support for search-and-rescue activities. The heavy schedule punished these aircraft and they were covered in patches.*

# Air-to-Air Combat

Throughout the spring and into the summer of 1967, air-to-air action between US and North Vietnamese fighters continued at a heightened pace. This was the mighty Thunderchief's finest hour, with six MiG-17s being claimed by F-105D pilots in only two days. Five more MiG-17 kills by Air Force F-4C Phantoms followed. The next four aerial victories, again all MiG-17s, were achieved by Navy F-8 Crusaders from USS *Bon Homme Richard*.

## Gun for the Phantom

As the fighting went on, more Air Force kills followed. The centerline-mounted SUU-56/A gun pod carrying an M61A1 cannon had been introduced during this period. Although most F-4 kills continued to be made by missiles, the new attachments gave Air Force Phantoms something the MiGs had had all along – the ability to fight with guns in a close-range battle.

At this time, the crew of Lt Col Robert F. Titus and Lt Milan Zimer, flying an F-4C Phantom of the 389th TFS/366th TFW out of Da Nang, managed the unique achievement of racking up three MiG kills, using all three systems available to the Phantom at that time – gun, AIM-7 Sparrow medium-range radar-guided missiles, and AIM-9 Sidewinder short-range heat-seeking missiles.

All three of Titus' kills were MiG-21s, and he had the greatest respect for the Soviet-built fighter, but he also felt that Phantom pilots were developing ways to combat the MiG-21.

## Change of tactics

"Beginning in August 1967," Titus recalls, "fewer MiG-21s directed by better-trained radar controllers achieved greatly improved results through high-speed hit-and-run attacks against trailing or isolated flights. They not only set up for an ideal missile launch position, they also had the speed for an immediate disengagement. If they arrived undetected – which was frequently the case, especially when they had cloud cover – it was difficult, if not impossible, for the CAP [combat air patrol] to accelerate and successfully launch missiles. By early 1968 the enemy controllers were able simultaneously to co-ordinate low and high attacks with mixed forces of MiG-17s and MiG-21s and at greater distances from Hanoi."

"Initially, the F-105 strike formations were flights of four

separated by several minutes from the next succeeding flight, running in at low altitudes and high speeds hoping to achieve surprise. Intense ground fire soon drove us to higher altitudes but ultimately the SAMs forced a compromise to a band of altitudes from roughly 7,000 to 16,000 feet (2133 to 4877 m). As ECM gear became available the advantages of large formations and mass jamming became evident.

"The MiGs helped to drive the character of the formation so that the F-4 escort could provide complete coverage of the force. The F-4s attempted to screen the force from MiG attacks particularly during the dive bomb runs, and also to act as a covering defense during force egress. Eventually the F-4s served in an escort role by joining with the strike aircraft miles short of the target and remaining with them until out of MiG range on the withdrawal.

## Air superiority

"While the term MiGCAP came to be used to denote any role of the F-4s in primary defense of the strike force, it is a misnomer. CAP (Combat Air Patrol) or as the Navy prefers BARCAP, short for barrier CAP, more properly denotes a blocking force separating the target from its fighter defenders. In contrast, Escort implies just that – a protective force that stays with the strike formation. A sweep is another type of counter-air mission, a swing around the enemy air-bases or areas known to be patrolled by enemy fighters. We employed all of these means to maintain air superiority."

Colonel Robin Olds racked up his second, third and eventually

fourth air-to-air kills during this period of intense fighting. At the time, Olds did not receive full credit. The custom at the time, amid the 'Rolling Thunder' campaign, was to award half a credit to each member of a Phantom crew for a MiG defeated in air-to-air action. This made sense in many respects but it was not good for morale, especially for front-seat pilots and most particularly for men with the dedication and fighting spirit of Robin Olds.

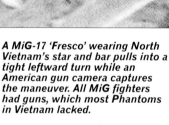
*A MiG-17 'Fresco' wearing North Vietnam's star and bar pulls into a tight leftward turn while an American gun camera captures the maneuver. All MiG fighters had guns, which most Phantoms in Vietnam lacked.*

To turn the equation around, 'Thud' pilot Max Brestel was credited with two kills because his one-man aircraft had shot down two MiGs, while Olds was credited with two kills because his crew (of two) had shot down four. Even this is a simplification, because Olds did not always fly with the same backseater. Anyway, later in the conflict it was decided to award full credit to both men in the Phantom. Many of Olds' wingmen feel that only restrictions and bureaucracy prevented him from attaining the magic fifth kill that would have accorded this superb warrior and fighter leader the unofficial but coveted status as an ace.

*With the arrival of cannon pods in the war zone, US Air Force F-4 Phantom crews had something to celebrate. These F-4C pilots and backseaters of the 366th TFW, soon to be aptly named the 'Gunfighters', pose after using the gun pod to whack a pair of MiGs out of the sky on 14 May 1967. From the left Major James A. Hargrove, his pilot Lt Stephen H. Demuth, together with backseater Captain James T. Craig and his pilot Lt James T. Talley.*

# Ryan's Raiders

### Seizing the dark from Hanoi – and the Navy

The bad weather over North Vietnam, especially in the rainy season at the beginning of the year, was a constant source of frustration. By August 1967, the Air Force was taking steps to be able to operate in the Hanoi-Haiphong region in bad weather and at night. In the same period, debate continued over how targets were being chosen and why some targets were not being bombed. PACAF chief General John D. Ryan was enmeshed in both issues. Whether the civilians who dictated policy allowed his men to attack lucrative targets or not, Ryan wanted a capability to fight in bad weather. It was a source of special embarrassment that, at this time, such a capability was possessed only by the A-6A Intruder being operated by the Navy and Marine Corps.

With new targets under attack for the first time, the MiGs came up. On 10 August, Navy F-4B Phantom crews shot two of them down. Meanwhile, Navy, Marine and Air Force people kept trying to devise new ways to deliver bombs accurately in a region which sometimes went for weeks without a clear day.

Lt Col James McInerney was one of three brothers, the off-spring of the kind of family which quietly and without fanfare sends its young men through the long gray line at West Point and produces a disproportionate share of a nation's warriors, casualties and heroes. One McInerney brother had died in Vietnam. Two others were aloft on 11 August 1967, taking the war to targets which Lyndon Johnson had opened up for the first time.

*A Sidewinder protrudes from the tail of an F-105 which came home with the renegade missile embedded in near-fatal damage.*

Jim McInerney had been associated with the 'Wild Weasel' (anti-SAM) mission since the early days in Super Sabres, back when Captains Pitchford and Trier had been shot down in an F-100F. McInerney commanded the 44th TFS, later 13th TFS, at Korat, a part of the 18th TFW. Four

*From a camouflaged site, an SA-2 'Guideline' surface-to-air missile threatens all American raiders by day and the Navy's A-6s and the USAF's 'Ryan's Raiders' after dark.*

# Attacking the Bridge

The Paul Doumer Bridge was one of the targets which US airmen most wanted to attack. Named for the French Governor-General of Indochina who built the nation's railway system at the end of the 19th century, the bridge was on the outskirts of Hanoi. It was readily visible on most missions in the region and thus seemed to stand out, as if mocking the men who wanted to bomb it but could not. With 19 spans crossing the Red River not far from the industrial area around Gia Lam airfield, the bridge was 5,532-ft (1686-m) long and 38-ft (12-m) wide. Its length became 8,467 ft (2580 m) when approach viaducts were counted. It was by far the longest bridge in North Vietnam and a vital transportation link, although its direct link to the infiltration of the South was questionable.

On 11 August 1967, the first attack on the bridge was mounted by 26 F-105Ds, each carrying one 3,000-lb (1360-kg) bomb, swarming down on the bridge in three waves. Each wave of 'Thuds' was escorted by four F-4C Phantoms in the MiGCAP role, four more for flak suppression, and four F-105F 'Wild Weasels' to suppress SAM sites. The strike force's 'Thuds' climbed from treetop height to 13,000 feet (3965 m), dived at a 45 degree angle, dropped their bombs, lowered air brakes, and pulled out. The use of a single heavy bomb by each 'Thud' might have been more effective if some means of attaining precision accuracy had been attained, but that lay ahead. Still, the number two 'Thud' in the strike force scored a direct hit that dropped one span of the bridge into the water.

A couple of weeks earlier, the F-4D Phantom had been introduced to Route Package Six when 16 F-105Ds from Korat and eight F-4Ds from Ubon made a strike on a railyard near Kep. Captain Thomas G. McInerney, Jim's brother, already a veteran of one tour of duty in Vietnam, had helped to develop ordnance and tactics for the F-4D model at Eglin AFB, Florida, and had come to Ubon with the first F-4Ds. Colonel Robin Olds pulled strings and had the new aircraft assigned to the 555th TFS, the 'Triple Nickel' squadron which was part of his 8th TFW.

Tom McInerney's recollection is that the F-4D Phantom played a critical role in the 11 August 1967 strikes on the Paul Doumer Bridge. Lt Col Jesse Allen, the 'Triple Nickel' skipper, led a mixed force of F-4Cs and F-4Ds which put the finishing touches

*An AGM-12A/B Bullpup missile leaps from a diving F-105 to go flying after a target in North Vietnam. Firing a Bullpup at a bridge was a little like throwing a rock into mud: during the first strikes against the Thanh Hoa span, these missiles infuriated US pilots because even when they hit the target, they bounced off without inflicting any damage.*

months earlier, he and his F-105F aircrews had begun flying night and adverse-weather missions under the most difficult circumstances, performing the same function as the Navy's A-6A.

The new mission had been mandated by General Ryan. McInerney's bad-weather strike function was given the name 'Commando Nail' but his outfit quickly became known as 'Ryan's Raiders'. Their nocturnal sorties were made in F-105Fs equipped with modified radar scopes giving expanded presentation and sharper target definition of enemy radar pulses. Seeking their targets at low-level over enemy territory at night was no easy task, but 'Ryan's Raiders' helped take the pressure off the daytime strikes and considerable success was achieved against North Vietnamese ground installations of all kinds. The literature of the period has created the impression that the 'Raiders' were carrying out the 'Wild Weasel' mission. In fact, while they were the same men and the same aircraft which had been performing the 'Weasel' job during the day, McInerney's crews delivered ordnance against every kind of target and were not

by any means dedicated to the campaign against SAM sites.

On 11 August 1967, in daylight, Lt Col McInerney's men and machines were part of the force that went against the Paul Doumer Bridge. McInerney and his backseater, Captain Fred Shannon, did fly a 'Wild Weasel'

mission on this date. The pair earned the Air Force Cross, the second highest award for valor, for leading a strike that destroyed six SAM sites and damaged four others. One of McInerney's shining achievements was that he never lost a man who flew with him, by day or by night.

*The F-105F Thunderchief had not been designed for nocturnal operations, but it proved to be a handy mount for Lt Col Jim McInerney and the other men who flew with 'Ryan's Raiders'. The back seat provided an extra pair of eyes and ears, and the 'Thud' had room for navigation gear and modified radar scopes.*

on the long highway and rail bridge, completing the job that had been begun by 'Thuds'. The 'dive-toss' mode employed by the F-4D permitted greater accuracy and earlier bomb-release from greater height and was an enormous improvement.

McInerney remembers F-4D Phantom pilots using their automated bomb-release mechanism to drop ordnance at 8,000 feet (2432 m), while F-4C Phantom pilots had to drop their bombs manually at 6,500 feet (1981 m), increasing their exposure to AAA fire. Only one F-4C Phantom is listed as having been lost in combat that day, but McInerney, Allen and others remember that the North Vietnamese AAA fire was furious.

## Quick repairs

At the Paul Doumer Bridge, one railroad and two highway spans were destroyed. The bridge was to be essentially out of service for seven weeks, until it was hit again, but the innovative North Vietnamese quickly found ways to ford the river, getting both vehicles and railcars across via barge. Later strikes temporarily dissuaded the North Vietnamese from their inventive efforts to replace broken spans and, instead,

HANOI RR/HWY BR OV RED RIVER

27 MAY 68

FLOATING CRANE

REPLACED SPANS ←

prodded them to build an adjacent pontoon structure. Unlike the Dragon's Jaw at Thanh Hoa which could not be severed, the Paul Doumer Bridge was temporarily neutralized.

The 11 August 1967 airstrikes took place in a setting where the enemy's MiG opposition remained difficult to measure and evaluate. Many US airmen believed that the North Vietnamese had not

recovered from Operation 'Bolo' eight months earlier, for although the absolute number of MiGs destroyed in that operation (seven) may not have seemed high, it represented an enormous proportion of the MiGs the enemy could get into the air at any one time. It remained true, and unavoidable, that missiles, MiGs and AAA complemented each other and made the

*The Hanoi Railroad and Highway Bridge, better known as the Paul Doumer Bridge was another span which mocked American pilots and refused to go down – until technology provided 'smart' bombs with precision accuracy.*

Americans' job more difficult.

Ensign Francis B. Newman, an F-4B Phantom pilot with the 'Ghostriders' of VF-142 aboard *Constellation*, recalls a different kind of MiG pilot than the kind reported by most Americans during this period – a capable, aggressive, hard-hitting enemy flier in a MiG-21 who began the dogfight on his own terms, stayed in the fight, and refused to give up or back out.

## Bounced by MiG-21s

Newman and his wingman were bounced by a pair of MiG-21s and struggled with them inconclusively for more than five minutes, seemingly an eternity in an air combat situation where fuel is devoured rapidly.

The Americans were unable to add to the total score of 90 MiGs destroyed by this point in the war, and the North Vietnamese were also unable to seize the advantage. It was a hard, evenly fought battle which resulted in no success for either side.

*Major William L. Kirk explains to the crew of a 'College Eye' EC-121 Super Constellation how he used real-time information from the flying radar station to down a MiG. The big four-engined EC-121s, using the callsign Disco, plotted every move by Hanoi's air arm and guided American fighters to the kill.*

HH-3E Jolly Green Giant, which had been very successful rescuing downed airmen but existed only in limited numbers. An earlier variant of the new helicopter, the CH-53A, had been in service with the Marine Corps in South Vietnam. The HH-53B, soon to be joined by the HH-53C, was to become the principal USAF tool of air rescue behind enemy lines, North and South.

The US Navy continued to rely on the Sikorsky SH-3A Sea King, and later the SH-3G variant, operating from the decks of a variety of ships, and the Kaman UH-2A/B Sea Sprite, soon joined by the HH-3H, operating from destroyers in the Gulf of Tonkin. Throughout the war, helicopter pilots and crews who went into harm's way to rescue their buddies rarely received the praise they earned.

The AC-130A Hercules developed under the Gunship II program, and which had been pressed for by General Momyer, was deployed to South Vietnam for an operational test of the concept. The aircraft arrived on 15 September and was soon flying missions into Laos. An entire war was taking place in Laos virtually unnoticed by press, public and congressional critics, even those who found fault with what was going on in South Vietnam.

Also in September, the American preoccupation with numbers reared its ugly head once again when the USAF decided that the one millionth combat sortie was flown in September 1967. The number of Air Force aircraft deployed to Southeast Asia reached 1,500 in October and total aircraft losses passed the 1,000 mark that same month.

The first air-to-air kill for the F-4D Phantom was scored on 24 October 1967. Major William L. Kirk of the 433rd TFS/8th TFW flying with the 'Wolfpack' from Ubon used an externally-mounted 20-mm cannon pod to shoot down a MiG-21. Kirk's backseater, Lt Theodore R. Bongartz, shared credit for the war's 93rd MiG kill.

The air-to-air situation heated up further two days later, when three MiG-17s and one MiG-21 were shot down by Navy and Air Force fliers. Included in the day's tally was the first kill to be scored by the AIM-4D Falcon missile, which had been introduced concurrently with the F-4D. Captain Larry D. Cobb and Captain Alan A. Lavoy of the 555th TFS/8th TFW were the 'Wolfpack' crew who claimed a MiG-17 with the Falcon.

## Air-to-air missile problems

None of the missiles employed by US aircraft had really been designed for fighter-versus-fighter combat but, of the three major types employed, the AIM-4 Falcon proved least suitable. As Thomas McInerney recalls, "the Falcon required all sorts of fancy-setting up and had to be cooled before firing". All infra-red missiles, including the AIM-9 Sidewinder, required cooling before their heat-seeker heads would work, but the arrangement with the Falcon was more cumbersome than most. Most airmen supported Colonel Robin Olds when he trashed the AIM-4 Falcon and ordered AIM-9 Sidewinders installed on the F-4D Phantom, even though the variant had not been designed to accept the Sidewinder.

A 'Thud' pilot and a Navy F-4B crew downed two more MiGs at the end of the month, bringing the war's total to 99.

In October, EC-121 'Warning Star' operations were centralized at Korat to provide better common maintenance and more economical logistical support. The EC-121Ds of the College Eye Task Force relocated to Korat from Udorn to join the sole Rivet Top EC-121K and the newly-assigned EC-121R radio relay aircraft. The latter was simply another of the many means of improving communications throughout Southeast Asia. The EC-121R variant of the Super Constellation, however, lacked the now-familiar 'hump' found on the early-warning aircraft where their radars were located.

## More airfield attacks

The decision at the end of October to permit strikes on Phuc Yen airfield was another of those 'on again, off again' measures which gave conflicting signals to everyone involved. The official line was that the 'Rolling Thunder' campaign was methodically destroying the North Vietnamese supply and transportation network, and the time had come for stronger action against the MiG threat at Phuc Yen. Like all targeting decisions during the period, it was made without any clear reason why it could not have been made earlier or later. A three-day effort against Phuc Yen and Cat Bi resulted in 20 MiGs being damaged or destroyed on the ground but, at the same time, a new threat developed from North Vietnam's SAM installations. Optical tracking devices had been installed at SAM sites, seriously downgrading the effectiveness of the ECM pods which had become so important to the integrity of strike missions.

On 29 October the North Vietnamese Army unleashed two regiments, the 272nd and 273rd, against the isolated town and Special Forces camp at Loc Ninh, north of Saigon near the Cambodian border. The NVA were expected to quickly over-run the camp. But once a battle unfolded, General Westmoreland oversaw the use of Army helicopters to bring reinforcements. A week-long battle ensued, fought at times with artillery, at times in pointblank firefights with rifles. It was here that a young Army lieutenant, under pressure, uttered one of those memorable lines which are remembered long after details are forgotten: "We had to

*Special Forces camps along the Cambodian border were designed to impede the flow of material traveling down the Ho Chi Minh Trail. Even though they were heavily fortified, these isolated sites proved to be magnets for Communist attack, and a great deal of tactical air power had to be assigned to ensure their survival.*

# Enter the A-7A

The A-7A Corsair II, a carrier-based light-attack aircraft intended as an A-4 Skyhawk replacement, entered combat on 4 December 1967. The 'Argonauts' of attack squadron VA-147 under Commander James C. Hill arrived in the combat zone aboard USS *Ranger* (CVA-61), and included a cadre of Air Force officers assigned to test the A-7A in battle in anticipation of their Service purchasing the aircraft.

Hill's squadron flew its first strikes against bridge and highway targets around Vinh. On 17 December, A-4s, A-6s and A-7s

from *Ranger* assaulted the Hai Duong rail and highway bridge complex between Haiphong and Hanoi. Hill evaded a SAM just in time to spot MiGs circling and eyeing him from a distance. Perhaps because the A-7A carried Sidewinders and possessed air-to-air capability, the MiGs did not engage.

Hill and his fellow pilots, including Air Force Major Charles W. McClarren, concluded that the A-7A was a highly-effective attack craft, although it had a nasty tendency to suck up catapult steam and suffer compressor failure. One A-7A went down on

22 December, but it was the only loss on the type's first combat cruise.

The A-7A had made its first flight at Dallas two years earlier on 27 September 1965 with Vought's chief test pilot, John W. Konrad, at the controls. It was thus the first major warplane to take to the skies after the start of the 'Rolling Thunder' campaign. Powered (or, in the view of many, under powered) by a 11,350-lb (5150-kg) thrust non-afterburning Pratt & Whitney TF30-P-6 turbofan, the A-7A could carry a 20,000-lb (9100-kg) bombload and also carried two Sidewinders on the fuselage sides and two Mark 12 internally-mounted 20-mm cannon with 680 rounds. Navy pilots soon found that its considerable combat radius of 715 miles (1150 km) enabled the snub-nosed, swept-wing Corsair II to range over North Vietnam, hounding and harassing the enemy, searching out targets of opportunity and loitering overhead for extended periods when a RESCAP (rescue mission) was necessary.

*They called it the 'SLUF', which stood for 'short little ugly f\*\*ker', but fondness lay beneath this lighthearted scorn of the A-7A Corsair II. In fact, the A-7A's new capability was heartily welcomed.*

*A Corsair II sets forth on a mission. In spite of launching problems, once it was aloft the A-7A could roam anywhere in North Vietnam. It was ugly and under-powered, but it could go farther and carry more than its predecessor, the A-4 Skyhawk. The SLUF gave the US Navy a new standard of ground-attack accuracy and lethality.*

# Walleye Operational

On 24 August 1967, direct hits were observed in the first USAF operational use of the AGM-62A Walleye. The TV-guided missiles were first employed by F-4D Phantoms. A follow-up mission two days later resulted in destruction of a bridge, dropping the two center-spans with the first Walleye used. On this mission, because the first firings were so successful, two F-4D Phantoms returned to base with their ordnance unexpended. A total of 22 of the expensive Walleye weapons was used by USAF aircraft during the year. The Navy employed its own variant of the Walleye with the A-4E Skyhawk.

Like many of the munitions employed in the conflict, Walleye

had been developed earlier and was steadily improved over time by its manufacturer, Martin Marietta. With an 825-lb (374-kg) warhead based on the Mark 84 bomb, the 13-ft 3-in (4.04-m) Walleye II variant was used very successfully by F-4Ds and A-4Es,

and later by Navy A-7 Corsair II aircraft which could launch them at targets from ranges as great as 35 miles (56 km).

*The Walleye was no beauty pageant winner and it was undermined by teething troubles, but the missile had enormous potential. The US Air Force kept up only a limited interest in developing the AGM-62, but the Navy was more patient and brought the missile to maturity.*

# Radar Bombing

Throughout the war, efforts were made to find improved ways of radar bombing from high altitude, a method which would keep US aircraft out of range of most North Vietnamese defensive weapons. Flights of strike aircraft were led to their targets by a pathfinder aircraft, usually an EB-66E Destroyer or an F-4D Phantom equipped with long-range navigation (LORAN) gear.

Using a radar 'fix' on a target established in part by the pathfinder, in part by a Sky Spot or other powerful radar on the ground in the South, the strike aircraft would release their bombs from as high as 30,000 feet (9144 m). However, from that altitude the precision and accuracy of this kind of 'blind' bombing was open to question.

As General Momyer put it: "When we started the radar bombing program, some thought we could sustain the offensive throughout the bad weather months. It was never possible. The nature of the targets was beyond the capability of the radar systems. The magnitude of the enemy defenses made it prohibitive to fly above an overcast. We found from bitter experience that formations above an overcast in a heavy SAM environment [were] not tactically feasible regardless of the effectiveness of the ECM. There

was so much redundancy in the enemy radar system, supplementary data gave accurate position, speed and altitude of the strike force. By the time the pilots saw the missiles coming through the overcast, it was almost too late for evasive action."

On 9 November 1967, Captain Lance P. Sijan was flying one of these high-altitude radar bombing missions. At the controls of an F-4C Phantom (64-781) of the 480th TFS/366th TFW, Captain Sijan was brought down not by enemy gunfire but by a fuse malfunction which caused his bombs to detonate – a malfunction which happened far too often, in all types of aircraft, Air Force and Navy. Although Captain Sijan ejected over Laos, as many airmen did, his story is very much a part of the war against North Vietnam.

## Six weeks on the run

Surrounded by North Vietnamese troops in the hostile Laotian rain forest, Captain Sijan eluded his pursuers for no less than six weeks, surviving on moisture from forest leaves, berries and frogs. During his six-week evasion effort, he suffered severe lacerations, serious injuries to his left leg and right hand, a concussion and horrendous loss of weight. At one point, a C-130 Hercules on a Lamplighter flare-drop mission succeeded in

bringing in an HH-3E helicopter; the HH-3E was within a few feet, lowering its hoist, when Sijan realized that it was about to be bracketed by North Vietnamese guns. Using his survival radio, he ordered the helicopter away. When he was inevitably captured, the weakened Captain Sijan quickly overpowered a guard and escaped. He was recaptured within hours. The North Vietnamese tortured him and kept him confined alone. He was then taken to a village to begin the arduous journey to downtown Hanoi.

Other American POWs observed Captain Sijan's resistance to enemy pressures during the long and punishing truck ride to Hanoi. This ended with Captain Sijan being taken to the Hoa Lo

*An EB-66 Destroyer directs a four-ship flight of 'Thuds' in a high-altitude radar drop. Unlike LORAN-equipped F-4D Phantoms, the F-105 Thunderchief did not have an independent capability for radar bombing. The effectiveness of this type of bombing was rigorously debated.*

prison camp, known to Americans as Vegas. Here, he continued to resist under harsh treatment. His condition was made worse by the inadequate living conditions, poor food and lack of clothing and medical treatment. Shortly after arrival in Hanoi on 18 January 1968, Captain Sijan contracted pneumonia. Because he would have been literally drowned by the fluid in his air passages, he was unable to lie down. For more than

destroy the village in order to save it."

Vertical envelopment – the use of helicopters to position troops – held the town and blocked escape routes. More than two thousand NVA were killed. To quote historian Jim Mesko, "Loc Ninh became a charnel house for the two NVA regiments." Exploiting the mobility afforded by the helicopter, the US field commander had been able to concentrate six US infantry battalions and their supporting artillery within a few days, in a location where no US regular troops existed when the battle began. Loc Ninh was a victory not for the NVA but for the Americans.

An increasingly important part of the war which knew no boundaries was the effort to cut off Communist infiltration into South Vietnam, as well as the movement of North Vietnamese troops into Laos. On 15 November 1967 the US Navy moved nine OP-2E Neptune maritime patrol aircraft up to Nakhon Phanom, Thailand, to take part in 'Mud River', a program to seed the infiltration route – the Ho Chi Minh Trail, Americans called it – with sensors capable of detecting enemy vehicles.

The effort against the Trail also occupied a squadron of EC-121R Constellations at Korat, which relayed signals from the sensors to ground stations and helicopters as well as strike and observation aircraft based at Nakhon Phanom. It quickly became clear that the effort to halt North Vietnamese infiltration was hindered by a number of technical problems with the sensors, delivery systems and support facilities. The program employed modern technology against an enemy using the most ancient of logistics methods – simple manpower.

Although the US Navy's carrier forces received plenty of press and public attention, much of it because of their combat missions over North Vietnam, less publicity accompanied the work of

land-based naval aviation units. From very early in the conflict, patrol squadrons flew out of Cam Ranh Bay, Da Nang and other bases. These flights were aimed at stemming infiltration of personnel and supplies down 1,000 miles (1600 km) of Vietnamese coastline and down innumerable miles of rivers. Patrol aircraft used included P-2 Neptunes, P-5 Marlins, and later P-3 Orions. Each of these aircraft could mount a mission lasting half a day or more. They were well-armed and had the endurance to handle the grueling hours of search punctuated by fast action when the enemy was found.

## 'SLUF' goes into action

On 4 December the Vought A-7A Corsair II light-attack aircraft was introduced into combat by the 'Argonauts' of VA-147 commanded by Commander James Hill. Combat deployment of Hill's squadron had been announced the previous month by Vice-Admiral Thomas F. Connolly, Deputy Chief of Naval Operations (Air). On their first strike, Hill's pilots used 5-inch (127-mm) Zuni rockets to assault bridge and highway targets in the narrow neck of North Vietnam just above the 17th Parallel. In North and South, the A-7 was to be a participant for the remainder of the war.

On 17 December 1967, Captain Doyle D. Baker became the first US Marine Corps officer to receive credit for shooting down a MiG. Baker was serving an exchange tour with the Air Force's 13th TFS/432nd TFW and was at the controls of an F-4D Phantom (667709), nicknamed 'AWOL' (absent without leave), with Lt John D. Ryan, Jr, in the back seat. Baker is said to have 'singed the tail feathers' of a MiG-17 with fire from his cannon pod before employing an AIM-4D Falcon missile for the kill.

Two days later, the crew of an F-105F of the 357th TFS/355th TFW at Takhli, Captain Philip M. Drew and Major William

three days, he struggled to keep his ravaged body in a standing position. He was still resisting when the North Vietnamese took him from his cell. Later, they reported that he had died.

Captain Sijan was the third American POW to be awarded the Medal of Honor while in captivity in North Vietnam. Unlike Jim Stockdale and Bud Day who survived the POW ordeal, Captain Sijan's award was made posthumously.

## Questionable success

Even when the fuses on their bombs worked correctly, men like Sijan were taking enormous risks for something which remained an elusive goal. General Momyer noted that successful high-altitude radar bombing remained "more a requirement than a reality". He did not seem optimistic that radar bombing would become effective under any circumstances: "With tactical targets of the nature one finds in [the North Vietnamese] transportation system, visual conditions are mandatory for target acquisition and attack. We spent many hours trying to develop a radar attack capability organic to the F-105 and F-4. All of these efforts led to the conclusion that we could only work against area targets which had very good radar features. Nevertheless, if we could consider such attacks as harassment, they serve a very decided purpose

*An early mission by standard F-4C Phantoms carrying 750-lb (340-kg) M117 bombs and using an EB-66 Destroyer to navigate. This kind of bombing kept US aircraft away from lower level where the largest concentration of anti-aircraft fire was found.*

of keeping pressure on the enemy. I believe our all-weather capability should be directed to the objective of harassment and not destruction per se.

"[Ours] is not a suitable radar system for a heavily-defended environment such as the one in Route Package Six. In order to get target coverage, it is necessary to employ a formation. Formation flying made us extremely vulnerable to barrage fire from AAA and SAMs. Furthermore, the last part of the bomb run, about 30 miles (48 km) into the target, had to be straight and level. This made the force even more vulnerable to ground fire and MiGs. On 18 November 1967 we lost two F-105D aircraft over Phuc Yen trying to execute a radar bombing attack over a solid overcast. This experience coupled with other missions conclusively demonstrated that our radar bombing was not tactically sound for such a defense environment."

Momyer was later to indicate that despite 'Ryan's Raiders' and despite the radar bombing attempts, there was really no good way for Air Force aircraft to bomb

North Vietnam during the months of bad weather – which meant the early months of the year. If they did not say so, Air Force pilots apparently felt a degree of envy

for the Navy with its A-6A Intruder, the only genuine all-weather system capable of operating inside North Vietnam even during the very worst season.

# Skyhawk Versus MiG

Perhaps the most bizarre MiG kill of the conflict, the 55th, occurred on 1 May 1967. Lt Cdr Theodore R. Schwartz of the 'Spirits' of attack squadron VA-76 launched from the old wooden deck of *Bon Homme Richard* on a fairly standard attack mission. Schwartz joined the heightened air activity taking place around North Vietnamese airfields during this period and, like so many others, found himself in a battle where SAMs, MiGs and Triple-A were lacing the skies all around him.

Intending to make a mess of the end of Kep's runway with ordnance from his A-4C Skyhawk (148609), Schwartz was astounded to see a MiG-17 in the airfield's landing pattern, either unaware of him or under the impression that the small American attack jet was another MiG. Schwartz unleashed a barrage of Zunis – large five-inch caliber rockets intended for air-to-ground work, totally

unguided, and never meant for air combat – and watched their high-explosive warheads blow the MiG to bits.

It must have seemed sweet, sweet revenge, since a VA-76 Skyhawk with Ira Levy on board had been claimed by a MiG a week earlier. Indeed, for months afterward, not merely 148609 but several 'Spirits' Skyhawks would be noted with the red silhouette of a MiG-17 painted on them. Two years later, when the squadron had been transferred to *Independence* and to the Atlantic Fleet, at least two of its Skyhawks (148578, 149645) still carried MiG kill markings to celebrate Schwartz's victory.

*Chances are that no US pilot was ever more surprised at his own achievement than Lt Cdr Theodore R. Schwartz. What began as a traditional air-to-ground sortie by Schwartz ended up giving the US Navy and the A-4 Skyhawk the weirdest MiG kill of the conflict.*

*Even though US air and ground power wreaked fearful havoc on Communist forces, by the end of 1967 troops and equipment continued to flow from the North. Indeed, reinforcements now coming down the Trail indicated that there was likely to be a major escalation early in 1968.*

Wheeler, shot down a MiG-17 with 20-mm fire. The pair were flying the same two-seat 'Wild Weasel' (63-8301) 'Thud' in which Major Leo Thorsness had earlier won the Medal of Honor. On the same day, 19 December, a pair of two-man crews in an F-105F and an F-4D shared credit for a MiG-17 which they had hounded down with 20-mm cannon fire. The 105th air-to-air kill of the war was also the last for the F-105.

At the end of 1967, opposition to the war at home was growing, confidence in President Johnson's policy was at a low, and the 'Rolling Thunder' bombing campaign, now nearly two years old, had failed to disrupt the North Vietnamese transportation network or prevent infiltration of the South. The United States had committed a massive ground force to the fight in South Vietnam, now numbering nearly 400,000 troops and soon to peak above the half-million mark. Few Americans could view the conflict any longer with innocence, fewer still with enthusiasm. It seems

remarkable that brave men fought on, shored up by the support of comrades and by their profession, if not by their nation. An official PACAF history sums up the year in two sentences: "Although the enemy failed to win any major battles in 1967, he demonstrated a willingness to accept the situation and continue to attack, harass and terrorize. He was not beaten, and the war would continue until one side or the other grew tired and opted to quit."

An official wrap-up for 1967 showed that enemy forces launched 16 attacks against airbases in 1967. Eighty-one aircraft were destroyed or damaged in these attacks and nearly 400 casualties inflicted.

## F-105 losses

The venerable 'Thud' remained the principal means employed to carry bombs into North Vietnam. The extent of commitment by the F-105 and the men who flew it was reflected in year-end figures which showed that in 1967 the USAF lost 421 aircraft in Southeast Asia, 334 of them to hostile action and 87 to operational causes.

As in previous years, the F-105 continued to suffer the most, with 113 lost in the year. The increasing use of the F-4 Phantom was reflected by rising losses. In 1967, 95 F-4s (plus 23 RF-4Cs) were lost. Three F-4s and 17 F-105s were claimed by SAMs, while MiGs shot down nine F-4s and 11 F-105s.

On the credit side the number crunchers decided that USAF aircraft flew 878,771 combat sorties in 1967, a 69 per cent increase over 1966. Of the total, B-52s mounted 9,686 'Arc Light' sorties. Munitions expended totaled 681,700 tons, or 87 per cent more than in 1966. It was apparent that the US had now dropped more bombs in Vietnam than it had during the whole of World War II.

Unfortunately some took the numbers to mean that the war was being won. In fact, by the end of 1967 the Viet Cong controlled more territory than they had at any previous time – without having ever won a major battle. Political control of the Viet Cong was now firmly in the hands of the North Vietnamese. To the extent that the insurgency in the South had ever possessed a native character of its own, it now belonged to Hanoi.

*Only by destroying the North's fighter airfields and air defence infrastructure could America hope to affect North Vietnam's ability to wage war. But in spite of pressure from the men on the ground, Washington only occasionally sanctioned such attacks.*

# AC-130 Spectre Gunship

**W**ednesday 27 September 1967 marked the first mission of the C-130 Hercules transport modified to serve as a fixed-wing gunship, a role in which it would eventually be nicknamed Spectre.

Already being used for flare-drop missions in North Vietnam using the callsign Lamplighter, the C-130 was the logical airframe to bring gunship theory to maturity. The gun-armed AC-47 Spooky was the first of the type and had been remarkably successful in hosing down Viet Cong insurgents as they mounted night attacks on installations in the South. Captain Ronald W. Terry, who had done much of the combat flying in the early AC-47, was one of several junior officers who persuaded the Air Force to modify a C-130A transport (54-1626) into a gunship.

### Prototype AC-130

The first machine was converted at Wright-Patterson AFB, Ohio. Although the progenitor of a Spectre force to follow, it did not, itself, receive the 'AC' for 'attack' designation. Terry's C-130A was equipped with four 7.62-mm General Electric GAU-2/A minigun modules and four 20-mm General Electric M61A1 Vulcan cannons. To assist the gunship crew in locating and lining up on its target, the aircraft was also equipped with a night observation device (NOD), or Starlite Scope, an infra-red sensor, a target-tracking computer and a 20-kW searchlight.

Terry and his C-130A made the journey to Southeast Asia and, on their first combat mission, blunted a Viet Cong assault on a firebase. Only weeks later, on 9 November 1967, it was in action over the North, destroying a six-truck convoy in a night mission against the Ho Chi Minh Trail.

### High-tech sensors

The Air Force quickly commissioned E-Systems Inc. of Greenville, Texas, to convert several more airframes to AC-130A standard. These introduced a Texas Instruments AN/AAD-4 forward-looking infra-red (FLIR) sensor, a new fire-control computer and a moving target indicator (MTI) radar. The FLIR package enabled the crew to observe trucks and other targets

*Four 20-mm cannons and four 7.62-mm miniguns made the early gunship version of the C-130 Hercules a formidable weapon. Later armament was to include two 40-mm Bofors cannon and even a 105-mm howitzer.*

*A 16th SOS AC-130A Spectre at Ubon, Thailand. A radome on the port side of the nose housed the ASD-5 'Black Crow' sensor that detected truck ignition motors. The AC-130A also carried ALQ-87 ECM pods which are not visible from this angle.*

on a monitor, effectively removing the benefit of darkness upon which the North Vietnamese supply effort depended. These AC-130A gunships were to join the 16th Special Operations Squadron at Ubon in 1969.

Few of the programs developed during this long and tortured war were as free from growing pains as the AC-130 gunship. Its night combat mission was exceedingly destructive to the enemy at relatively low cost to the US Air Force. It was also about as dangerous as any job that could be undertaken in the air war against North Vietnam. No aircraft used against North Vietnam called for greater ability or courage on the part of its crew. AC-130 pilots and crew members routinely faced every defense the North Vietnamese could muster along the Ho Chi Minh Trail.

*The sinister-appearing AC-130 was by far the most capable gunship developed for Vietnam service. Packed with guns, ECM and sensors, the AC-130A Spectre was right at home in the night war against infiltration routes.*

# THE YEAR OF TET

**1968 was to be the year when domestic events would intrude again and again into American perceptions of the Vietnam War. Few were untouched by a presidential campaign which saw the wounding of Governor George Wallace, the murder of Martin Luther King, and – above all – the death of White House front-runner Robert F. Kennedy in Los Angeles. By mid-summer it was clear that more Americans opposed the war in Vietnam than supported it.**

For a period in January 1968, it appeared that American attention might shift from Southeast Asia to the very different, sub-zero climate of the Korean peninsula, when the seizure of the US spy ship *Pueblo* and a raid on Seoul by North Korean commandos threatened to open a new, major conflict thousands of miles from the war already in progress. The US rapidly reinforced its tactical air units in South Korea at the very time when its men and machines were most needed in Vietnam. But the Korean diversion was brief. By the end of January, attention once more focused on Vietnam where the words Tet, Khe Sanh and Hue became part of the American vocabulary and sharply altered perceptions of the war and its price.

At the beginning of the year, the by-now customary New Year cessation of bombing was supposed to last until 3 January. Once back in action, Navy and Air Force pilots ranging into North Vietnam found little changed in the familiar pattern of threat and counter-threat. There was a severe bombing shortage and some airmen may have flown exceedingly dangerous missions only to deliver very small loads of ordnance. Nothing else was new and as usual the men engaged in the battle sought ways to cope with North Vietnam's defenses. Some men wanted the chance to attack anti-aircraft artillery positions and some wanted to be effective against SAM sites, but throughout the hundreds of pilots flying fighters in Southeast Asia one goal outshone all the others: every man wanted to get a MiG.

*Though Tet was not the victory for the Viet Cong that press reporting made it out to be, Americans at home perceived that Vietnam, far from being a just cause, had become a gateway to fire and doom. This attack by VC guerrillas on the base at Qui Nonh was less successful than it looked, but by 1968 appearances were everything.*

*Largely fabric-covered, the Antonov An-2 'Colt' flew low and slow and was hard to detect on radar. US officers were aware of the fact that the old biplane had the potential to airdrop NVA shock troops into American-held areas, although they were rarely used on such missions.*

On 3 January 1968, Major Bernard J. Bogoslofski of the 'Wolfpack', Ubon's 433rd TFS/8th TFW, was over North Vietnam in an F-4D Phantom with Captain Richard L. Huskey in the back seat. He was carrying a gun-pod beneath the fuselage and when the F-4 became involved in a furious tangle with a MiG-17, Bogoslofski disposed of the North Vietnamese fighter with 20-mm cannon fire. Two weeks later, another Ubon-based Phantom crew despatched another MiG-17 with an AIM-4D Falcon missile.

## Northern air attack

An exceedingly rare attack mission by the North Vietnamese air force occurred on 12 January 1968 when two Antonov An-2 biplanes attacked the government outpost at Phou Pha Thi, Laos. Although Hanoi maintained special forces designed to mount paramilitary operations using the mostly-fabric biplane, the chance to deliver ordnance, drop paratroops or land elite forces was never really exploited. It is not even clear what kind of ordnance was used in the one-of-a-kind Laos attack or why the biplanes were employed on that occasion.

North Vietnam had about 40 of these flying museum pieces, though the number had been reduced by two earlier in the war when, on 20 December 1966, two Navy F-4B Phantom crews happened upon a pair of the slow Antonovs, stalked them with AIM-7E Sparrow missiles and blew them out of the sky. Of the 197 North Vietnamese aircraft shot down during the conflict, these were the only ones with propellers up front.

On 14 January 1968, scarcely half a year after a catastrophic fire aboard the USS *Forrestal*, tragedy struck again while the USS *Enterprise* (CVAN-65) was working up off the coast of Hawaii in preparation for a combat cruise to Southeast Asia. There was an

*The Tet Offensive brought the war into city streets, even in Saigon which had become almost an American enclave. US Army Military Police, or MPs – not always given recognition as combat troops – fought not only from one building to the next, but from room to room. They could not prevent the Viet Cong from assaulting the US embassy itself.*

eerie repeat of an almost impossible circumstance: for the second time, a Zuni rocket ignited by an auxiliary power unit exploded and created a monstrous fire. The conflagration took 28 lives and cost $50 million damage to the nuclear-powered carrier.

As usual, the North Vietnamese had used the respite offered by the New Year truce to increase the flow of military supplies southwards. They were setting up for the siege of the Marine Corps Combat base at Khe Sanh.

North Vietnamese forces equivalent to four divisions closed their snare on the base near the demilitarized zone on 20 January 1968. To many it seemed as if the Communists wanted to turn Khe Sanh into a latter-day Dien Bien Phu, inflicting on the Americans the same kind of dramatic defeat they had handed the French in 1954. The NVA cut the base off from all land transport and communications.

## Siege at Khe Sanh

For four months, only aircraft could support the base and bring in supplies. A brilliantly conceived and directed interservice operation was mounted to supply and eventually relieve the Marine defenders of the tiny bastion, much of the airpower available in Southeast Asia being melded into a radar/computer-controlled pattern of operations known as 'Combat Skyspot'. Crews of C-123s and C-130s made daring landings at Khe Sanh while under fire from mortars and artillery surrounding the base.

But Khe Sanh was soon to be knocked off the headlines back home in America, at least for a time.

*Burned and blasted at its core, the wreckage of a C-47 transport (44-476643) sprawls in front of another C-47 at the 8th Aerial Port ramp at Saigon's Tan Son Nhut airfield following a Viet Cong rocket and mortar attack of 18 February 1968. The Tet Offensive was reported – inaccurately – as a defeat for US forces because of scenes like this.*

# Khe Sanh Air Support

*No repeat of Dien Bien Phu*

*The Viet Cong guerrilla and the North Vietnamese soldier were motivated, trained, experienced, and as courageous as any fighting men. They could never defeat the conscript soldiers of the United States' citizen army in battle, but they persisted, pressed on, and prevailed.*

It had been apparent for months that Viet Cong forces in South Vietnam had secret instructions to prepare for a major offensive. Some Communist guerrillas were told that Ho Chi Minh was in deteriorating health and that an assault had to be mounted to

*The night supposedly belonged to Victor Charlie, but American know-how went some way to counteracting the Communist advantage. C-47s and C-130s dropped flares to light up the night, hindering enemy movement and neutralizing the value of darkness as a weapon.*

General Westmoreland had asked for and gotten a contingency plan, code-named 'Niagara', to provide air support to the Khe Sanh bastion.

The first phase of the operation, 'Niagara I', consisted of building up a comprehensive intelligence picture of the enemy, identifying targets, and earmarking the forces needed to destroy them. 'Niagara II' was the

*Khe Sanh was dug out of the jungle and surrounded by high ground. Fortified outposts like Hill 861 could only be reached by helicopter. As real estate, it was a poor investment, but as a symbol it acquired huge value.*

all-out air campaign implemented on 21 January, as the enemy took the offensive and the siege was at its height.

In the first 24 hours, over 600 tactical air strikes were carried out by Air Force, Navy and Marine squadrons. B-52 Stratofortress strikes devastated those enemy bunkers, trenches and tunnel networks that had been identified in advance. In due course AC-47 gunships joined the fight and kept the pressure on the North Vietnamese. By the end of the Khe Sanh siege in April, 24,000 tactical and 2,700 B-52 strikes had been carried out.

Probably no airmen had more

*A C-130 Hercules at Khe Sanh. A brilliant design, the C-130 landed and took off in short spaces, but even its creators never imagined that it would deliver cargo while taxiing through exploding North Vietnamese artillery shells.*

Above: Marines were under the gun at Khe Sanh, pounded by North Vietnamese artillery firing from the advantage of higher ground. But Hanoi had no counter to US air power, which hammered the NVA day and night and kept the besieged outpost supplied.

Below: Coming into Khe Sanh by air – the only way to reach the hard-pressed combat base – meant running the gauntlet of North Vietnamese fire. This Marine Corps CH-53A heavy-lift helicopter came to grief after a direct hit from a Communist mortar.

courage than those who landed at Khe Sanh to drop off supplies and to pick up wounded. The C-130 Hercules had been designed for LAPES (low-altitude parachute extraction system) which in theory enabled the aircraft to deliver its payload while in flight. But men were bleeding amid the mortar barrages which walked all over the base and the wounded had to be gotten out, which meant the transports had to touch down and come to a halt. Although the runway was pock-marked with shell holes, C-123s and C-130s landed in spite of the mortar and artillery rounds which were still coming in.

In all, 273 landings, 496 parachute drops and 57 LAPES extractions were made by or from C-130 Hercules. C-123 Providers made 179 landings and 105 parachute resupply missions, while eight C-7 Caribou missions were also flown. The cargo aircraft delivered 12,400 tons of materiel to the besieged base. Hill positions around the airfield were supplied by CH-46 Sea Knight helicopters.

Incredibly, despite the bad weather and enemy gunfire, the only tactical aircraft lost were one A-4 Skyhawk, one F-4 Phantom, and 17 Marine helicopters.

Operation 'Pegasus' was the name given to the First Cavalry effort to relieve the Marine garrison at Khe Sanh. By 5 April 1968, a partial reopening of the land route to the Khe Sanh combat base was accomplished when the First Cavalry broke through NVA forces.

# B-52 Missions

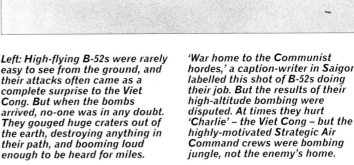

On 1 February 1968, in response to the Tet Offensive, the number of B-52 sorties authorized for Southeast Asia was increased from 800 to 1,200 monthly. On 15 February the figure was increased to 1,800.

B-52F aircraft configured for the strategic nuclear role began these heavy bomber operations. In December 1965 Strategic Air Command had begun the 'Big Belly' modification program to increase the capacity of the B-52D from 27 to 84 500-lb (227-kg) bombs or from 27 to 42 750-lb (384-kg) bombs internally. In addition, the modified B-52D could carry 24 bombs on wing pylons, bringing the number of 500-pounders it could carry up to an astonishing 108 bombs – by far the heaviest combat loads in history. At about this time, crews began referring to their aircraft as the 'Buff', which in its polite version stood for 'Big Ugly Fat Fellow'. The name has stuck.

Although B-52s were used primarily against targets in South Vietnam, they had bombed approaches to the Mu Gia Pass in North Vietnam from April 1966. That month the 'Big Belly' B-52D replaced the B-52F in flying the long, tedious combat missions from Guam. In April 1967 'Buffs' began operating from U-Tapao, Thailand, as well as

*Left: High-flying B-52s were rarely easy to see from the ground, and their attacks often came as a complete surprise to the Viet Cong. But when the bombs arrived, no-one was in any doubt. They gouged huge craters out of the earth, destroying anything in their path, and booming loud enough to be heard for miles.*

'*War home to the Communist hordes,*' a caption-writer in *Saigon* labelled this shot of B-52s doing their job. But the results of their high-altitude bombing were disputed. At times they hurt '*Charlie*' – the Viet Cong – but the highly-motivated **S**trategic Air Command crews were bombing jungle, not the enemy's home.

*Right: American Marines hustle into action during the furious Tet fighting in the ancient imperial capital of Hue. The 1968 battles brought large-scale ground combat to cities which had previously suffered only small raids. Marine Skyhawks, Phantoms and Crusaders supported these troops despite quirky weather and strong enemy fire.*

achieve total victory while Ho still lived.

On 29 January a 36-hour cease-fire for the lunar New Year, known as Tet, began with many South Vietnamese troops going home on leave. On the night of the 30th, Viet Cong and North Vietnamese forces in the South launched an offensive all over South Vietnam. Viet Cong local insurgents and North Vietnamese regulars attacked every important city, provincial capital, and military installation in South Vietnam. In Saigon, Viet Cong blasted holes in the palace and US embassy walls and entered the courtyards.

The six-story chancery building that loomed over much of central Saigon had symbolized the US presence and had not been thought to be vulnerable. Americans felt so secure in the embassy that they had only a few Marines on guard. A sapper squad of 19 Viet Cong, having blasted their way into the courtyards, was all set to storm the building itself. But their leaders had been gunned down by the guards and their assault lost momentum. With Military Police arriving to help the Marines, a six-hour battle ended with bodies everywhere, some American but mostly VC.

The effect on Americans, including those back home who watched the war on their television sets, was stunning. The sudden eruption of massive, close-quarters fighting in the cities was reported by the media as a stunning defeat for Saigon's forces and for the American purpose of securing the independence of the South Vietnam regime. TV viewers watched the fiercest fighting of the war in Pleiku, Nha Trang, Da Nang, Qui Nhon, and especially the ancient imperial city of Hue, which was overwhelmed and over-run.

Tet has been called an attack, a retreat, a victory, a defeat. The

Guam, completing missions from the closer location without in-flight refueling. On 13 September 1967 the 'Big Belly' program was completed with modification of the final B-52D to the 108-bomb configuration.

The 1968 B-52 bombings in support of the siege of Khe Sanh became the largest such campaign so far. Although there was to be a halt in the bombing of North Vietnam later in the year, on 1 November 1968, this did not affect the Buff's 'Arc Light' operations in the South.

*Above: Majesty and folly came together in a B-52 take-off. Spreading its great 185-ft (57.27-m) wings and easing aloft with a full bombload, the Stratofortress exuded power and purpose. But its water-injected J57 turbojet engines expelled gouts of black smoke and its four-piece 'quadricycle' wheels, when coming up, resembled the weird contraptions made famous by cartoonist Rube Goldberg.*

*Right: Thousands of miles from the fighting, ground crews on Guam kept B-52 Stratofortresses airworthy and loaded them with ordnance. It was a new world for men trained to send these bombers into a nuclear conflict with the Soviet Union. Each inboard pylon on the B-52 added up to 16 bombs to the lethal cargo carried in the fuselage bay.*

evidence available shows that the Tet Offensive was a devastating military and political defeat for the North Vietnamese and the Viet Cong. In their attempt to ignite a general uprising against the South Vietnamese government, the Viet Cong, with the assistance of North Vietnamese regulars, had clearly aspired to capture the provincial capitals of South Vietnam.

The best Viet Cong units had led the Tet assault and had been more than decimated: 38,794 men had been killed, 6,991 captured compared with 318 American and 661 South Vietnamese losses. The Communist hope of sparking off a widespread popular uprising

*Marines (below), attired in the flak jacket which became a fixture in the Vietnam conflict, watch a CH-53A Sea Stallion helicopter in action. In the chaos accompanying the Tet Offensive, CH-53A crews flew 4,800 sorties within what one flier called 'spitting distance' of the Viet Cong.*

# Enter the Bronco

*Counter-insurgency specialist*

Another new aircraft type joined the fighting in South Vietnam when the first example of the twin-turboprop OV-10A Bronco arrived and was assembled at the Bien Hoa air base in late July.

The first OV-10As were thrown into the forward air control (FAC) mission, and were assigned to the USAF's 504th Tactical Air Support Group, which had lost four O-1s and four O-2s during the fighting in Hue.

**Left: Dubbed a COIN, or 'counter-insurgency' aircraft, the OV-10A Bronco normally carried pilot and observer in tandem, and was armed with miniguns and rockets to augment its FAC (forward air control) duties. The Bronco was faster than previous FAC aircraft.**

**The US Marine Corps and later the Navy (the latter with its squadron VAL-4 'Black Ponies') operated the OV-10 Bronco for spotting, convoy escort, and other combat duties. To Bronco crews, the enemy was up close and the war was very personal.**

had failed completely and after some initial faltering most of the populace rallied to the Saigon government. Nor did the ARVN collapse – the South Vietnamese Army and Police emerged from Tet more confident and stronger than before. This military action effectively eliminated the Viet Cong as a fighting force and, thereafter, most Viet Cong cadres in the South were really North Vietnamese soldiers posing as southerners.

Unfortunately, in a world where perceptions matter as much as reality, a defeat on the battlefield may have become a victory solely because it was seen as one. Before the dust had settled and the facts were in, the Western press and particularly the American television media, pronounced Tet a devastating defeat for Allied forces. Tet was a triumph for the North Vietnamese precisely and exclusively because it was perceived by American television viewers as a triumph. The fact that Communist forces were soundly defeated in battle did not really matter.

It cannot be emphasized too strongly that during Tet, though they lost the battle, the Communists may have won the war. The harsh truth was that Hanoi was willing to accept 39,000 fatalities while Washington found it difficult to cope with 318 added to the nearly 10,000 already lost in the conflict.

## The television war

Television viewers in their American homes, knowing their husbands and sons were dying, perceived that no progress had been made towards South Vietnam being able to defend itself and, worse, that South Vietnam did not deserve to defend itself or enjoy US support. They resented spending blood and treasure supporting a Saigon regime which could be so easily disrupted. The strongest opponents of what was considered to be Johnson's war, among them Democratic Presidential candidates Eugene McCarthy and Robert Kennedy, found sympathy among countless Americans who just wanted to get the hell out. The few remaining Americans who wanted to stay, fight and win had their views represented by the Republican front-runner, Richard M. Nixon.

According to Harold T. Nelson, a former State Department official who was in South Vietnam at the time, 1968 was the year the Viet Cong was effectively wiped out as a viable fighting force.

"Some of the tactics in 1968, where VC units were sent off to be slaughtered," Nelson explains, "were intentional on the part of the North. The North Vietnamese never wanted the Communists in the South to control the insurgency. The way to do it, of course, was to kill off the southerners who contributed to any differences between the Viet Cong and the North Vietnamese."

The ARVN's own recruiting effort was more successful than it had been. There really were more people who supported the Saigon regime, for all its faults. The South Vietnamese Army was able to form new divisions and increase its size at the very time the Viet Cong were suffering most.

The fiercest fighting of the Tet Offensive took place in the old imperial city of Hue. Viet Cong and North Vietnamese regulars

*A dozen Marine Corps squadrons were to operate the CH-46A Sea Knight after its introduction at Da Nang in 1966. Designed to carry 25 combat-equipped troops or two tons of cargo, it became the main Marine assault transport. At times, when dropping or extracting troops, CH-46A crews were eyeball-to-eyeball with the Cong. During the siege of Khe Sanh, a gunner of HMM-164 reported being so close to the North Vietnamese that "we could see their faces, peering up at us through the treetops".*

# Marine Helos

The US Marine Corps contributed much to the air support of its own people on the ground, and the role of the Marine helicopter has often been overlooked in histories of the Vietnam War. Following the 'Shu Fly' deployment of UH-34D helicopters earlier in the decade, Marines deployed squadron VMO-2 equipped with UH-1E Hueys, all-aluminium versions of the Army's UH-1C. The Hueys were used as both 'slicks' (troop carriers) and gunships. Some were fitted with a TAT 101 twin 7.62-mm gun turret.

UH-1Es of various Marine observation squadrons were used to provide liaison, forward air control, and medical evacuation missions. Finally, there was search and rescue (SAR), which found brave helicopter crews pitting themselves against the enemy on the ground at point-blank range and fighting to save fellow combatants.

## Rescue heroics

SAR missions produced some incredible acts of heroism, and two Marines on such missions – Captain Stephen W. Pless on 19 August 1967 and PFC Raymond M. Clausen on 30 January 1970 received the Medal of Honor for their courage.

Like the Army, the Marines

wanted a helicopter designed from the outset as a gunship – the AH-1G Cobra would not arrive until 1969, the AH-1J Sea Cobra until June 1971. While they were waiting, armed versions of the UH-1E performed the gunship mission.

The twin-rotor Vertol CH-46 was the other important Marine Corps helicopter. Entering service in 1964, it was to become the main Marine sea-borne medium-assault helicopter, although like

*The Marines were slow to adopt the ubiquitous Huey, seeing other helicopters as more suitable for their specialist air-ground mission. But UH-1Es like this tree-skimmer began reaching Marines in Vietnam in 1966.*

most rotary-winged aircraft in Vietnam the Sea Knight was used in a wide variety of roles, from vertical replenishment to medical evacuation. However, its main task was always to take Marines into and out of battle.

*Left: An LZ (landing zone) grew very crowded, very quickly, when a major campaign was under way, like Operation 'Hastings' in 1966 or Operation 'Curtis' in 1968. On top of other challenges, the mundane task of traffic control became vital as CH-46s landed and took off just seconds apart.*

*Below: Operation 'Shu Fly' saw the first Marine HUS-1 helicopters in South Vietnam in 1962. Marines flew into battle every day in a craft the Army saw as too old for this war and even the South Vietnamese used sparingly. The Marine helos were re-designated UH-34D after 1 October 1962.*

*Close-quarters firefights during the Tet Offensive brought to the street weapons like the recoilless rifle (background), the M16A1 rifle carried by this soldier, and the LAW (light anti-tank weapon) on his back. This rubble-strewn urban moonscape is typical of Tet's city battlegrounds.*

fought South Vietnamese troops and American Marines in savage house-to-house combat. The attack began in pre-dawn darkness on 31 January.

At first, American soldiers in the MACV Compound in the New City were able to fight off a battalion-sized NVA assault. In the Old City, however, the elite ARVN Hac Do ('Black Panther') company was overwhelmed. Several battalions of NVA occupied the Old City and took up blocking positions north and south of Hue. Those hold-outs in portions of the old capital not yet under NVA control were cut off from the outside world.

The 1st and 5th US Marines attempted to enter Hue, ran into fierce NVA resistance in bitter house-to-house fighting, and failed. On 1 February a second effort was made to counter-attack the Old City with increased Marine strength. For a time the weather improved slightly, enabling F-8E Crusaders and A-4 Skyhawks to support the men on the ground. West of the city, the 3rd Brigade, First Air Cavalry halted three new NVA regiments moving to reinforce Hue.

## Bloody Hue

It is almost impossible to describe the ferocity of the fighting at Hue. Many years later, film director Stanley Kubrick attempted to recreate it in 'Full Metal Jacket'. The fighting was especially savage for the American Marines – who upheld an honored tradition going back almost to their country's founding. The conventional wisdom has made Khe Sanh the classic battle of the war, but the fighting in

Hue was on a larger scale, at closer quarters.

The Marines' job was made more difficult because of an official hesitance to use heavy weapons (or B-52 bombing) in the ancient capital. Marines made effective use of Ontos, a tracked vehicle mounting batteries of six 106-mm recoilless rifles, and some A-4s and F-8s braved the murky weather to provide support but most of the fighting was with grenades and rifles at point-blank range.

Supporting fire from naval warships was allowed and by 7 February the tide of the battle for Hue had turned against the Communists. The New City was swept clean of NVA by 9 February, but it took until 22 February for Marines and ARVN troops to retake the Old City's ancient Citadel. Air cover played an increasing role as the weather improved. In the fight for Hue, 5,191 naval rounds, 18,091 land artillery rounds and 290,877 lb (131 938 kg) of aerial ordnance were expended.

Brigadier General Foster Lahue, the World War II and Korea veteran who commanded the Marines at Hue, called the fighting "among the worst in our American history".

## VNAF in action

Another aspect of the Tet Offensive and the events which followed was the effect of the fighting on the VNAF. When Tet began, the VNAF had available just 69 A-1 Skyraiders at Bien Hoa, Binh Thuy, Da Nang and Nha Trang, plus F-5 Freedom Fighters at Bien Hoa. These aircraft flew 215 sorties, H-34 helicopters a further 215, reconnaissance aircraft 196 and cargo planes 158 during the hectic final days of January.

During February the number of combat missions increased and the VNAF bombed and strafed Viet Cong forces throughout the country. The helicopter fleet hauled ARVN troops, supplied them, and conducted medical air evacuation missions. The VNAF lost 17

*A-1H 'Spads' of the VNAF 518th Fighter Squadron fly in formation on a sortie from Bien Hoa. This trio is carrying anti-personnel bombs and napalm, a devastating combination when used against ground troops. VNAF aircraft played an important part in the Tet battles, demonstrating that after a shaky beginning the Vietnamese were becoming a force to be reckoned with.*

*Left: Navy Crusaders might have been the elite of the fighter world, but Marine F-8s got 'down and dirty', flying close support to the grunts toiling in the mud. During the vicious fight for the old imperial capital of Hue, Crusaders braved filthy weather to lay bombs, Zuni rockets and cannon fire on enemy positions just a few meters from Marines fighting from house-to-house and room-to-room.*

# RF-4C Versus MiG

**"I** felt a thump. Nothing violent. I looked back and there was a MiG, high and wide and working in on the old man. We were pretty tight together, line abreast about 40-50 yards apart. So I called a break and the Colonel broke right. We had a fire light on the left engine and I said, 'Wayne, I think we've been hit,' and he said, 'Yes, we have...'."

On 13 January 1968, Lt Col Clark Taylor of the 432nd TRW became one of the few recce pilots in the RF-4C Phantom to scrape with a MiG at close range and survive. The war remained very much an individual experience for men in cockpits. Luckily, reconnaissance aircrews did not usually find enemy interceptors to be a hazard over North Vietnam. The greatest danger remained the anti-aircraft system, incorporating radar, observers, SAMs and all calibers of AAA. But Lt Col Taylor's brush with a MiG was too close for comfort.

"We were going to Yen Bai on the Red River. My backseater was Major Wayne Porter and we were flying aircraft 65847. I was flying wingman to the wing commander [Colonel Victor N. Cabas]."

Their speed approaching the notorious MiG airfield at Yen Bai was about 500 knots (820 km/h).

*In 1961 USAF reconnaissance duty was the exclusive province of the RF-101C Voodoo (rear). But as the war expanded they were joined by RF-4C Phantoms and the EB-66 (in the lead), which enhanced the American ability to snoop on the enemy with a range of cameras and electronic sensors.*

They were on the deck. Taylor decided to pop up to about 4,000 feet (1219 m) above the hills, to start their target run.

"We'd been getting some 37-mm and 57-mm AAA and some 85-mm stuff as well. Very black puffs, that 85. It was all radar-controlled and they knew just when to stop firing if the MiGs were coming in. Those gunners on the 85s, if they hit your altitude and got you once ahead and once behind, they'd just walk the stuff up to you and you were finished. They were really great gunners, in fact both optically and by radar."

The two RF-4Cs snapped their target in the midst of the flak barrage and their full attention was focused on the task, leaving the rear unguarded for crucial seconds, which is when Taylor's aircraft was hit.

## Run for safety

With adequate warning, the Phantom had enough power to escape MiG-17s and MiG-21s. Without the warning, the standard technique called for a head-on dash past the interceptor. It was a good alternative and gave the enemy pilot only a split-second to sight and fire. RF-4C pilots were warned, however, never to mix it with MiGs in the hope that they could maneuver out of a spot. It just wouldn't work.

The Phantom went into afterburner and made a dive for the deck, with Major Porter screwing his neck back to watch for the MiG.

"We were about 200 feet off the ground and I was north of the Red and a bit worried about the

MiG and our fuel state. I went on burner with one engine across the Red and then pulled out of the burner when we were well into the green."

It was unlikely the MiG had followed this far – Taylor had probably got away from the interceptor in his rapid dive to the deck.

"But I couldn't put the fire out and I still worried about the MiG. Still, we would have to go up to save fuel. So we climbed to about 12,000 feet, making turns to check our six o'clock."

## No help, no fuel

Taylor got on the radio to see if any fighters in the area could help him. There were none. Worse, there were no tankers.

"But there didn't seem to be any problems so I thought the fire light was just a system malfunction. I homed on the

*Though the RF-4C Phantom was not able to transmit its findings in 'real time', photo analysts had the training and skills to quickly unload its cameras the moment it taxied to a halt. Timely photos of enemy activity were vital to 7th Air Force officers in Saigon.*

Tacan at the Laos border, then we got across and I pulled out my two body-bottles full of water and drank them. It's not until you're safe that you know how thirsty you are. I needed every drop of those two bottles.

"We landed with half flaps at Udorn. We had no brake chute because, as it turned out, the connection had been severed. We had 600 lb of fuel left. That's not even enough for a go-around in the pattern. There was a 3-ft hole in the left inboard trailing-edge flap. We never learned whether the damage had been caused by the flak or the MiG."

# The 'Slow Movers'

*Low-level eye in the sky*

The 'slow movers' forward air controllers in prop-driven Cessna O-1 and O-2 aircraft, were exceedingly active in Route Packages One and Two over the lower regions of North Vietnam. The Cessnas could perform an important role snooping out, identifying and marking targets for the faster jets.

Anywhere farther north than Route Package Two, the defense environment was too sophisticated and too intense. Even in RP One and RP Two, things were bad enough. Men of the 20th TASS from Da Nang faced heavy flak and, as Colonel Robert C. Peck pointed out in a letter to *Air Force* magazine, even had some SAMs

fired at them about 100 nautical miles north of the DMZ.

The Cessna O-1, which had begun life as the L-19, was a simple and straightforward light plane like thousands to be seen at flying clubs all over the world. In Vietnam the O-1F and O-1G variants were powered by 213-hp (159-kW) Continental O-470-11

piston engines, and could fly at just 130 mph (209 km/h). They were rigged to carry small rocket projectiles to mark ground targets for the very fast jet fighters which, without such help, could easily miss even seeing the target.

## Bigger and faster

The larger Cessna O-2 was an 'off-the-shelf' purchase of the push/pull Cessna 337 Super Skymaster, powered by two 210-hp (157-kW) Continentals. With a maximum speed of 200 mph (332 km/h), it was capable of loitering for a respectable period in the target area. A total of 501 O-2As were delivered to the USAF.

A version equipped for psychological warfare entered service as the O-2B, 31 being delivered. On FAC missions, the O-2 had four underwing pylons to carry flares, smoke rockets and light ordnance such as a 7.62-mm (0.3-in) machine-gun pack. It was never really intended that these aircraft would engage North Vietnamese ground installations, so the enterprising FAC who installed an M60 machine-gun in the cabin of his cramped O-1F may have been overdoing things.

It was no easy job, heading across the DMZ and into North

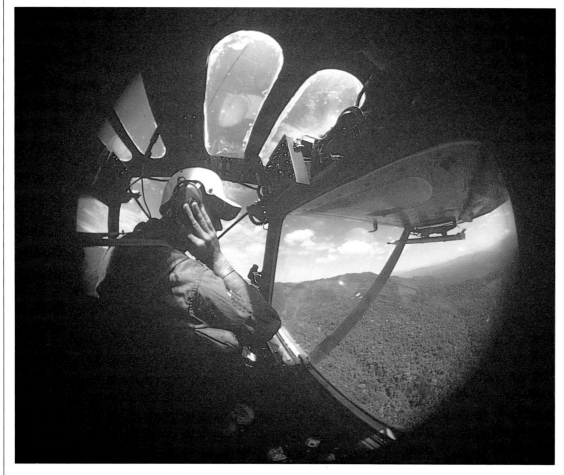

*Thanks to a 'fisheye' lens, this forward air controller's O-1 Bird Dog cockpit looks far larger than it really is. The all-metal O-1, also known to Korean War veterans as the L-19, was a versatile two-man liaison ship, but it did not have too much space. FACs often flew solo, demanding the ability to fly the aircraft while simultaneously spotting and marking targets.*

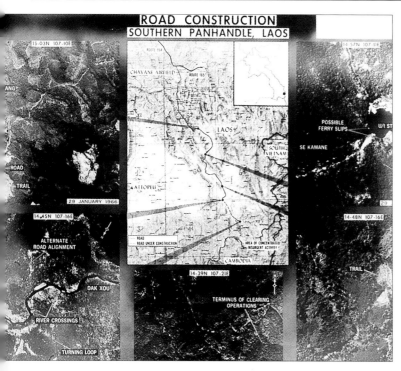

ROAD CONSTRUCTION
SOUTHERN PANHANDLE, LAOS

aircraft; 10 on the ground and seven in the air, the latter figure including five A-1s, one C-47 and one U-17 (a high-wing Cessna 180 derivative).

Although there had been enormous problems getting personnel back to their units during the confusion of Tet, the VNAF had contributed substantially to the fighting during this period. Many believed that the VNAF was now showing maturity as a settled and able fighting force. Others noted that new pilots did not seem to have quite the same courage as some of the older hands. The VNAF seemed to have some men who were excellent and others who were at the other end of the spectrum.

Bombing operations against North Vietnam continued with the principal aim of isolating the harbor at Haiphong from the rest of the country to prevent the distribution within the country of material being imported. This concerted campaign against lines of communication around Haiphong forced the North Vietnamese to adopt extraordinary efforts to maintain a flow of material over existing lines. Distribution problems for Hanoi were further aggravated by the arrival of a near-record number of foreign ships

*As late as mid-1969, a high-ranking Nixon administration figure swore that no Americans were participating in action in Laos. In fact, by the end of 1968, total American sorties over the war-torn country had exceeded 275,000, and at least 200 American airmen had been killed in action, were missing or had been captured there.*

*Left: The O-2 Skymaster was a curious contraption with its push-pull layout. Originally a civil general aviation design, it was pressed urgently into military service with almost no modifications. The O-2 could carry more rockets than the O-1 Bird Dog, loiter over a target longer, and dodge Viet Cong gunfire with more speed and agility.*

*Right: An O-2B of the 9th Special Operations Squadron based at Nha Trang drops propaganda leaflets on a suspected Viet Cong infiltration route near Pleiku in the Central Highlands. O-2s were larger, faster and more versatile than the tiny Bird Dogs which had preceded them, and were used for a variety of missions in addition to forward air control.*

Vietnam. The pilot of the FAC aircraft was very much alone, very much reliant upon his own resources. When he located a target, he was expected to expose .nself to enemy gunfire, partly or the purpose of learning more about the target and of determining the best way that it could be attacked.

No-one really expected the FAC to hit the mark when he fired smoke rockets but, by placing the rockets around a target, he could pass accurate instructions ('about 200 yards uphill from the smoke') to jet fighter pilots.

## Skilled pilots

Most of the FACs were jet fighter pilots themselves, and although some resented being relegated to small, prop-driven flivvers, many exhibited great courage.

It remains unclear whether the Cessna O-2B, used for

psychological operations in the South by the 9th Special Operations Squadron at Nha Trang, ever flew into North Vietnam. The O-2B was equipped to drop propaganda leaflets, a job which was performed over the North on a grander scale by the C-130 Hercules.

Some O-2Bs were fitted with loudspeakers to convey voice messages to enemy troops on the ground. It seems likely that the leaflet mission, if not the loudspeaker work, was performed over the North at some stage.

*A low-flying O-1 Bird Dog passes over the moon-like craters resulting from an earlier Arc Light mission – a B-52 strike. While the USAF used the O-1 for FAC duties, directing fighters in support of ground troops, the US and South Vietnamese armies also relied on the type for artillery spotting, battlefield communication and short-distance liaison duties.*

in Haiphong in January and again in March, when over 40 ships arrived each month for off-loading. The port of Hon Gai was used in February as an off-loading point for a Soviet and a British ship, probably in an effort to reduce the pressure on Haiphong. This port normally served the nearby coal-mining area and did not contribute significantly to the flow of imports into the country.

Expansion of the road transportation net continued as North Vietnam sought to gain greater flexibility by the addition of bypasses and the construction of entirely new road regiments.

## Poor weather affects bombing

This was in spite of the fact that the 'Rolling Thunder' campaign had been seriously hampered by the north-east monsoon. The first three months of the year were normally the time of worst weather and conditions were even worse than predicted. In the northern Route Packages, there was only an average of three days per month on which visual strikes could be carried out. The weather during February was the poorest experienced during any month since the start of the 'Rolling Thunder' campaign. Even so, the strikes were having an effect on the flow of supplies, beyond doubt.

It was because of this effect that military men fumed in private over the 31 March decision by President Johnson to stop all bombing north of the 20th Parallel. In a surprise announcement early in the election year's activities, the President revealed his

decision not to seek re-election. At the same time, he announced a cessation of bombing north of the 20th Parallel, effective 1 April 1968, and this was moved down to the 19th Parallel on 4 April. This, he felt, would resolve the American dilemma in Vietnam by prodding Hanoi towards negotiations. Always shrewd on domestic affairs, Johnson had correctly seen that he was unlikely to win an election campaign, anyway, because of the growing opposition to the war and demands for a total withdrawal of US troops.

Johnson was wrong about the bombing halt, however. He was making a misguided gesture of good faith, the sort of conciliatory step which he frequently employed in domestic politics, at the very time when the cumulative effect of three years of 'Rolling Thunder' air operations was finally beginning to damage the North Vietnamese infrastructure. It was the restraints on the use of airpower which had prevented 'Rolling Thunder' from being a complete success. Removing those restraints and increasing the air strikes might have ended the war on Washington's terms. Johnson was, in short, giving the North Vietnamese a chance to rebuild.

As the air commander on the scene in Saigon, General Momyer had his own views: "I took the position that if the bombing was to be halted to test the sincerity of the North Vietnamese to negotiate, the month of April was the latest it could be done with the least adverse effect on our forces. I further stated that come 1 May, if the North Vietnamese had not reached substantive agreements about a

*An F-105D Thunderchief of the 34th TFS, 388th TFW, launches from Korat, Thailand with the standard warload of two 375-US-gallon fuel tanks, eight 750-lb (340-kg) bombs, and a full load of ammunition for the 20-mm cannon. Although newer aircraft were entering service, the 'Thud' still bore the brunt of the 'Rolling Thunder' campaign against Hanoi.*

*Some Americans dubbed enemy troops 'gomers', a term derived from television comedy figure Gomer Pyle, and lamented the irony of a peasant shooting down a million-dollar aircraft. In truth, North Vietnam had not only thousands of guns but legions of able, experienced men.*

cessation of the war, we should resume the bombing with no restraints on targets. I put 1 May as the date because this was the transition period from the north-east to the south-west monsoon, and operational weather would start to appear with increasing frequency.

"When asked what I thought would happen with a limitation on the bombing I stated the following: the anti-aircraft defenses in the southern Route Packages would increase significantly; more SAMs would be deployed as close to the DMZ as they could get them; MiGs would begin to challenge us as far south as the DMZ; the radar and GCI system would be filled out from Bai Thuong south; airfields at Bai Thuong, Vinh, and possibly Dong Hoi, would become operational; large quantities of supplies would be moved through the lines of communication; supply dumps would shift to the Bai Thuong area since this would shorten the line; marshaling yards, bridges, power plants and other destroyed facilities would be repaired at a feverish pace; finally, I thought the enemy would consider this suspension a sign of weakness and would exploit it by an increased military effort. All of these things happened."

Of course, the bombing limitation did not affect operations in Laos. Until this time, airmen frequently flew missions into Laos one day, and into North Vietnam the next, receiving credit only for the latter.

President Johnson's decision amounted to an end of the three year 'Rolling Thunder' campaign, although the real end would not come until months later (1 October 1968) when the bombline would be brought down to the 17th Parallel and all of North Vietnam would be placed off-limits for US combat aircraft.

Reconnaissance missions verified that North Vietnam was able to repair and improve its supply and transportation network virtually from the moment the bombing stopped north of the 20th Parallel. The roads between Hanoi, Haiphong and Hon Gai were improved

*North Vietnamese missiles bagged their first American warplane in July 1965, and the SAM threat grew as Hanoi expended its air defense network. The missiles claimed plenty of aircraft in their own right, but they also forced Americans to fly at lower altitudes, where they were far more vulnerable to gunfire. Throughout the war, the SA-2 'Guideline' supplied by the Soviet Union was the standard North Vietnamese weapon, supplemented later in the war by the shorter-ranged SA-3 'Goa'.*

One of the more controversial additions to the air effort against North Vietnam came on 17 March 1968 when six General Dynamics F-111A aircraft were introduced to Southeast Asia in Operation 'Combat Lancer'. The F-111 was the product of the TFX, or tactical fighter experimental programme, which Secretary McNamara had originally hoped would prove suitable for both Navy and Air Force use. A swing-wing brute of a long-range strike fighter powered by two 25,100-lb (11 385-kg) thrust Pratt & Whitney TF30 turbofans, the F-111A first flew on 21 December 1964. It had sophisticated low-level terrain-following equipment which seemed to make it ideal for pinpoint navigation on solo missions to sensitive targets around Hanoi. The F-111A reached operational readiness with the 474th Tactical Fighter Wing at Nellis AFB, Nevada under Colonel Frederick C. Blesse, the same fighter commander who had earlier introduced the gun-pod to combat on the Phantom. The initial force of six aircraft was brought over to Southeast Asia by cigar-smoking, tire-kicking Colonel Ivan H. Dethman of the wing's 429th TFS.

## First mission loss

The new aircraft which had been given the unofficial nickname Aardvark because of its drooping nose, quickly ran into serious trouble. In its first combat test, on 25 March, a camouflaged F-111A (66-0022) laden with two ALQ-87 jamming pods and 24 500-lb (227-kg) Mark 82 bombs lifted off from its new home in Takhli.

Heading towards a target in North Vietnam, it was never seen again. A second F-111 was lost five days later, and, following a brief suspension of operations with the type, a third was lost on a solo mission to the North on 22 April.

Eventually, 51 successful combat missions were flown by Colonel Dethman's crews. At the time, the F-111A operations were widely portrayed in the US press as a total failure though, in fact, the aircraft was exceedingly effective in the low-level, solo-strike role. Just how effective was explained by Captain Melvin

Pobre, an F-111A pilot, who recalls a mission to the outskirts of Hanoi where: "We were at an altitude of 250 ft (76.2 m) moving at Mach .87 in a region of odd-shaped peaks and ridges and we were in clouds and haze for the final 14 minutes of our run-in to target – but our bombs landed right where we wanted them..."

## Withdrawn from action

Notwithstanding this enthusiasm, plus the fact that the F-111A provided the all-weather capability so long sought by General Momyer and others, the

*F-111A Aardvarks of the 429th TFS with Col Ivan H. Dethman in the lead, are seen crossing the Pacific on the 'Combat Lancer' deployment to the war zone. The F-111A was largely a creation of Robert S. McNamara, Defense Secretary in the Kennedy and Johnson years: McNamara sought an all-purpose fighter and got a strike aircraft.*

aircraft were soon removed from Southeast Asia and did not return for four years.

Only after the war was over would it become clear that abrupt tailplane failure caused by fatigue at a welding fault threw the F-111A into an uncontrollable dive and that this, not enemy action, had probably caused the first three losses.

Although the F-111A had been a subject of controversy during its development and had had a terrible combat debut, it was to prove in the end an exceedingly well-designed war machine with great potential and a long service life ahead.

*On the ramp at Takhli, the Thai air base which saw US warplanes continuously from 1961 onward, an F-111A prepares for the low-level, high-risk journey to North Vietnam. Critics heaped scorn on the 'One Eleven' long before it became operational. Subsequent troubles in Vietnam in 1968 were caused mostly by trying to do too much, too fast.*

*The F-111A carried every item of ordnance in the US inventory, and carried more of it, farther, and faster than the F-105 or F-4. But in 1968, the 'bugs' had not been worked out of a very complex variable-geometry aircraft, and the 'Combat Lancer' deployment suffered disastrous losses. It would not be until 1972 that the F-111A would redeem itself in combat.*

# Standard Arm Missile

For the continuing campaign against missile sites, the Navy and Air Force needed an anti-radiation missile (ARM) offering a larger warhead and longer range than the Shrike, which was producing indifferent results. The Pomona Division of General Dynamics came up with the Standard ARM, or AGM-78A Mod 0, which was introduced to combat aboard the F-105F 'Wild Weasel' in March 1968. Based on a long-range naval surface-to-air missile it was equipped with the seeker head employed by the Shrike but was soon replaced by the AGM-78B production version with Markson broad-band seeker.

Powered by an Aerojet Mk 27 Mod 4 rocket motor, the AGM-78B was 180-in (4.57-m) long with a body diameter of 13.5 in (343 mm), and a rear fin span of 43 in (1.09 m). At launch, the Standard ARM weighed about 1,400 lb (635 kg).

With its long range the Standard ARM provided greater stand-off capability than the Shrike, enabling a 'Wild Weasel' F-105 to attack SAM sites from safer distances. Like the Shrike, the missile lacked the ability to continue homing on Fan Song

radars after they had been shut down, but shutting down the radars meant that enemy missiles had no guidance and effectively put the SAM installations out of action without actually hitting or destroying them.

Tactics were evolved to make most effective use of the Standard ARM and capability to fire the missile was to be added to A-4E Skyhawk and A-7B Corsair II aircraft. Improved versions of the Standard ARM would remain in service for more than two decades.

*Developed from a long-range naval surface-to-air missile, the AGM-78 Standard ARM was bigger and more versatile than the AGM-45 Shrike, which remained in use. It gave new capability to 'Wild Weasel' crews taking on North Vietnam's air defense radars day after day.*

and maintained. Bridges between Hanoi and Haiphong were repaired and traffic began to flow smoothly during day and night hours. Rolling stock inventories in Hanoi and Haiphong appeared to be on the increase.

Off-loaded cargo at Haiphong was not being stacked but was being loaded directly onto trucks which immediately departed the wharf area. Photographs indicated extensive storage throughout the port area but stockpiles did not remain static, suggesting that cargo flowed unrestricted. The labor supply at the docks was reported adequate and efficient and morale was reported as high.

As General Momyer had predicted, once the presence of US aircraft over the northern portion of the country was stopped, North Vietnam took maximum advantage of the freedom of action

by increasing training activities and all elements of the air defense system. Moves were afoot to locate SAM sites farther south, in the Route Package One area.

## Target limitations

The situation must have been especially frustrating to the kin of pilots and airmen who continued, after 1 April 1968, not merely to fly but to die. Aircraft losses continued unabated while strikes were concentrated in the southern regions of the country. It was some relief not having to fly into Hanoi and Haiphong, but a man could still become a casualty, even while bombing a truck park.

Because of the bad weather and the partial bombing halt, no MiG kills were scored in March and April. On 8 May 1968, a Navy

*Although the North Vietnamese Air Force was a potent threat to American warplanes, it was rarely used in an offensive role. Even the tempting targets presented by the US Navy carrier battle groups operating only a few miles off the coast in the Gulf of Tonkin were rarely troubled by northern attackers. In May and June of 1968 MiGs appeared to be taking a more aggressive stance, but on both occasions the enemy retired when long-range Talos missiles fired from the nuclear-powered cruiser Long Beach destroyed one of the attacking aircraft more than 70 miles from the fleet. This was the first recorded combat use of naval surface-to-air missiles, and US Navy warships were to go on to claim a total of seven aircraft kills during the war.*

# The Last Navy Skyraider

*Veteran seaborne attacker comes ashore*

The US Navy's final combat loss of an A-1H Skyraider had occurred just weeks before President Johnson's speech calling a halt to operations over Hanoi. On 24 February 1968, an A-1H belonging to the 'First of the Fleet', as squadron VA-25 called itself, somehow managed to take enemy fire and go down at sea whilst on a ferry flight from USS *Coral Sea* (CVA-43) to Cubi Point in the Philippines.

The versatility of the Skyraider was legend. So it was a historic moment on 10 April 1968 when another A-1H belonging to VA-25 made an arrested landing on *Coral Sea*, completing the final combat mission by a Navy

Skyraider. It was not the end of the A-1's combat career – the aircraft type would continue to fight in USAF and South Vietnamese colors and serve the navy in support roles. But the Navy's carrier-based attack force would from now on be all-jet.

*EA-1F Skyraiders, carrying radar in a 'guppy' package and packed with electronic black boxes to guard the fleet from submarines, drew the distinction of being the final shipboard 'Spads' of the war.*

*An A-1H Skyraider hangs out its tailhook to catch the wire on a carrier off Vietnam. The 'Spad' gave way to the A-6 Intruder in Navy medium-attack squadrons, but few pilots felt in their hearts that the old warrior could be replaced.*

*An F-4B Phantom of VF-96 'Fighting Falcons' assigned to USS Enterprise (CVAN-65) lands aboard the USS Kitty Hawk (CVA-63) in the Gulf of Tonkin earlier in the war. VF-96 was caught up in the heavy fighting which accompanied the final months of the 'Rolling Thunder' campaign in 1968, with one of the squadron's F-4Bs making a MiG-kill in May.*

F-4B Phantom with an Air Force exchange officer in the front seat scored a probable kill of a MiG-17, apparently in a very southerly location. Major John P. Hofferman was flying with the 'Fighting Falcons' of VF-96, operating from the deck of the nuclear-powered USS *Enterprise* (CVAN-65). His aircraft was an F-4B Phantom using the squadron's radio callsign Showtime, and his weapon was the AIM-7E Sparrow missile. LtJg Frank A. Schumaker was the radar intercept officer in the Phantom's back seat.

With the bombline now moved down to the 19th Parallel, air strikes were being flown only in Route Packages One and Two, and a southerly portion of Route Package Three. North Vietnam's jet fighter force was thus provided with sanctuary. There were no jet-capable airfields within reach of Air Force and Navy strike aircraft which were actually being used by the North Vietnamese. The MiGs could sit in their revetments, safe from assault.

*A USAF C-130A Hercules runs up numbers two and three engines preparing to taxi out on a ramp of AM-2 aluminum planking. Fuel tanks outboard of the numbers one and four engines were an identifying feature of the A model 'Herc': the C-130B had no external tanks. On later versions, tanks were between inner and outer engines. In Vietnam, all C-130s had AN/APN-59 radar in a 'Pinocchio' nose.*

Communist efforts to move the MiG force farther south were half-hearted and until the end of 'Rolling Thunder' the North Vietnamese never succeeded in their goal of shooting down a B-52. On 23 May 1968, a force of MiGs did venture down into Route Package Two and the off-shore area nearby. One MiG-21 was downed by a Talos surface-to-air missile fired from a US Navy vessel in the Gulf of Tonkin. Later in the year, Navy Crusaders would add to their laurels with new MiG kills, but the presidential bombing halt had effectively ended the air-to-air war.

The troops in Vietnam read about peace talks in their Stars and Stripes, but few expected the negotiations to have much effect on their lives. After a 34-day impasse over location, preliminary peace talks opened in Paris on 10 May 1968. The Communist side almost immediately made a tactical mistake by allowing itself to be seen quibbling over the size and shape of the negotiating table instead of showing interest in working towards peace.

## Eclipse of the Viet Cong

At the Paris peace talks the Viet Cong, or the National Liberation Front as they called themselves, were represented separately from the North Vietnamese. Their political arm was now called the PRG, the Peoples Revolutionary Government. The irony was supreme. For many years, while the US had insisted that the Viet Cong was a powerless puppet of the North, the Communist insurgency in the South had actually been led by southerners. At the very time that the separateness of the Viet Cong was being recognized in Paris, it had ceased to exist thanks to the bloody Tet battles. The American view of the situation had become self-fulfilling: now the Viet Cong were completely controlled by Hanoi.

In May attention shifted to the Special Forces camp at Kham Duc, which became increasingly difficult to hold under pressure from the Viet Cong and was not, in any event, of much value. From 12 to 14 May C-130 Hercules extracted personnel from

Kham Duc, including ARVN troops and the 2nd Battalion of the US 1st Infantry.

Robert McNamara, who was forever to be linked to the enormous build-up of American forces, was replaced as Secretary of Defense on 1 April by Clark M. Clifford. After having shaped Vietnam policy for two presidents, Robert S. McNamara was visibly discouraged and disillusioned. McNamara was particularly concerned that the 'Rolling Thunder' campaign had failed to sever North Vietnam's supply and transportation network. According to reporter Stanley Karnow, McNamara was on the verge of a nervous breakdown.

Clifford was an old-time Washington lawyer and savvy insider who had worked quietly for several administrations. But he was better known as a lobbyist than as a military expert; he certainly was not an authority on the use of airpower. Many key positions remained unchanged. General Joseph McConnell remained as Air

*Though the West seemed to ignore it, North Vietnamese fighters like this MiG-21PFM 'Fishbed F' of the 927th Fighter Regiment drew blood repeatedly. Hanoi's jets had accounted for only five per cent of USAF aircraft downed in 1965 but the figure leaped to 17 per cent by March 1968.*

# More Corsair Squadrons

### *Replacing the Skyhawk*

Two new squadrons employing the A-7A Corsair II attack aircraft arrived in Southeast Asia aboard the USS *America* (CVA-66), an Atlantic Fleet carrier taking its turn in the combat zone. The 'Marauders' of VA-82 under Commander John E. Jones and the 'Sidewinders' of VA-86 under Commander Jack E. Russ began flying missions at the end of May, targeted against a barracks complex, a supply depot and truck parks.

## Combat loss

The newly-arrived squadrons suffered their first casualty when Lt Ken W. Fields' aircraft was hit by ground fire just north of the DMZ. Ejecting, Fields parachuted into thickly-vegetated terrain swarming with North Vietnamese regular troops. The Navy flier had the use of his survival radio and was able to talk to other Corsair pilots overhead as he scrambled away from the enemy troops. An HH-3E Jolly Green helicopter piloted by Major Lewis Yuhas succeeded in locating Fields and plucked him out after a marathon 39 hours on the ground. During the same mission, another A-7A suffered fuel starvation and its pilot ejected safely near the carrier.

A typical bombload consisted of 12 500-lb (227-kg) Mark 81 bombs fitted on multiple ejector racks. Lieutenant Benjamin Short was carrying this payload when he located a concrete bridge on Route One, about 300- to 400-ft (90- to 120-m) long. Being somewhat new to the low-level attack business, Short decided to dump his entire bombload on the bridge. He made his run-in and cut across the bridge at a slight angle, putting eight or nine of the bombs on the bridge. As he

pulled off, he rolled up on a wingtip after getting his nose well above the horizon to observe the hits. There was a lot of smoke and fire but after the smoke blew away Short was astonished to see no sign of damage to the bridge!

## Target of opportunity

On another occasion, Short spotted a small brush fire on the ground near a canal. Anything north of the bombline belonged to the enemy, so he decided to drop a couple of bombs on the fire. His hit was long, but he got a secondary explosion and got another fire going. He dropped the rest of his ordnance on the fire and saw more secondary explosions. In jest, Short told himself that some North Vietnamese barge driver let his rice-cooking fire get away from him, and Short's A-7A came along and spoiled the whole

evening. The fire was still burning when the next flight of Corsairs crossed the beach an hour and a half later. The next flight dropped its ordnance on the fire as well.

Men like Ben Short were discovering that the A-7A, with its low gaping nose air intake, had a way of ingesting steam from the carrier's catapults and then stalling out. Steam-induced compressor stalls were the cause of several

*Among the last squadrons to fly the A-7A variant of the Corsair II was VA-93 'Ravens', decked on USS Midway (CVA-41). By 1968, the Navy was receiving the A-7B model, with minor changes. The improved A-7E still lay ahead.*

A-7A losses, and the design of the new attack aircraft was not really perfected until much later when the A-7E variant, with the much more efficient TF41 turbofan engine entered service.

*Above: The A-7 Corsair II looked like a 'scrunched-up' F-8 Crusader, as one pilot described it, but was more docile and handled better when coming aboard the ship. Here, the tailhook is down and a deck landing only seconds away.*

*Right: VA-192 'Golden Dragons' and VA-195 'Dam Busters' share a deck. Two VA-192 Corsairs are being shepherded out of temporary parking spots and are taxiing toward the bow where a catapult will slam them skyward.*

# Enter the F-4J

Also aboard *America* with Ben Short's Corsairs were two fighter squadrons employing the new F-4J variant of the Phantom. The F-4J had made its first flight two years earlier on 27 May 1966 and had been designed with higher gross landing weight and lower approach speed to permit for more flexible carrier operations.

The 'Tarsiers' of VF-33 and the 'Diamondbacks' of VF-102, although both traditionally east-coast Atlantic Fleet-based squadrons, had been chosen to

*The F-4J Phantom was readily identified by its bullet-shaped radome, which lacked the 'chin' sensor housing of the F-4B. The J model combined the AWG-10 missile control system, AJB-7 bombing system, and AN/APG-59 radar. It also made use of the larger (30 x 11.5-in, or 77 x 29-cm) main landing gear tires which had first been put on the Phantom by the US Air Force.*

Force Chief of Staff, General John D. Ryan as commander, PACAF, and Admiral U. S. G. Sharp as CINCPAC. General Westmoreland remained in Saigon, for the moment, as did the Seventh Air Force commander, General Momyer. Changes would come over the next few months, but by then many Americans would regard the flagging Johnson administration as a lame duck government.

## More troops

There were widespread rumors that General Westmoreland wanted 200,000 more American troops in addition to the half million already committed. In fact, General Earl Wheeler, chairman of the JCS, and Westmoreland wanted only about half that number but the ceaseless demand for more troops, like the body counts from which enemy casualty figures were derived, were no longer credible. Critics were referring to the Saigon commander as 'General Waste More Men', and Westmoreland was constantly a target of abuse in the rhetoric of the anti-war movement.

Soon thereafter, General Creighton W. Abrams was named to replace Westmoreland as Commander, MACV and took over as the US field commander in Saigon on 10 June 1968. Westmoreland was to become Army Chief of Staff. Abrams was a tough former armor officer who was widely respected inside the Army. Clifford and Abrams were heirs to a situation they had had no part in creating. Both were well aware that it was election year again and that the war was issue number one to the voters.

After the lavish expenditure of munitions and supplies in support of the besieged Marines, the combat base at Khe Sanh was dismantled and abandoned on 23 June. President Johnson had hailed the defence of the base as a decisive victory, but the success

*Vice-President Hubert Humphrey, Gen. William C. Westmoreland and Marine Lt Gen. Robert E. Cushman, Jr (at rear) visit Chu Lai. Humphrey campaigned against Richard Nixon for the US Presidency in 1968, but although personally opposed to the war he was unable to overcome domestic perceptions to the contrary. Rightly or not, like Gen. 'Waste More Men', as critics dubbed Westmoreland, Humphrey was tarnished with the brush of the increasingly unpopular war.*

*With its data-link capability for improved performance in the pattern around the carrier and more extensive electronics fit, the F-4J was costlier to operate than the F-4B it replaced in the fleet. This example flies with VF-103, an Atlantic Fleet squadron called the 'Sluggers' which did not reach the combat theater until 1972 aboard USS Saratoga (CVA-60).*

take the new machine into battle.

In the F-4J the Navy had not elected to add an internal gun, even though the Air Force was doing exactly this with its upcoming F-4E. The F-4J was equipped with APG-59 radar with a 32-in (81-cm) dish and AWG-10 pulse-doppler fire control system, permitting the detection and tracking of low- and high-altitude targets. The F-4J also incorporated space provisions for the AN/ASW-25A datalink landing system originally introduced on the Navy F-4G. The J model also had improved

TACAN and an upgraded AN/AJB-7 bombing system as well as APR32 radar homing and early-warning system (RHAWS).

The new variant was powered by two 17,900-lb (8120-kg) thrust General Electric J79-GE-19 engines with afterburners.

Approach speed was reduced from 137 to 125 knots (253 km/h to 231 km/h) with the installation of drooped flaps.

# Smart Bombs

The 'smart' bomb, one of the most dramatic technical advances of the entire conflict, arrived just when the bombing halt deprived it of the chance to inflict more than token punishment.

The 'Pave' family of target-illumination devices, developed and controlled by the USAF's Systems Command, were sent to Vietnam for prolonged evaluation. They began with the bulky Pave Sword laser designator carried in a long cylindrical tube under the F-4D fuselage, an arrangement which caused serious drag, weight and balance problems. The next generation of

*An F-4D Phantom with LORAN (a long-distance navigation system) drops one of the early Paveway bombs on a pioneering mission. 'Smart' bombs reached Vietnam in 1968 and before long were transforming ground-attack missions against key targets.*

laser designators, Pave Knife, was in a drooped wing pod in the F-4D and was followed by the smaller, more effective Pave Spike pod which could be accommodated in the Sparrow bay of a Phantom.

The 8th TFW at Ubon under Colonel Robert V. Spencer made the first use of a Paveway laser-guided bomb (LGB) in combat near the end of May 1968. Only five LGBs were employed by the 'Wolfpack' in May, but the results were excellent. The F-4D Phantom, unlike the earlier F-4C, was equipped from the start to carry the new precision-guided ordnance while modified F-4Ds equipped with laser illuminators were used to designate targets for the strikes.

In practice, laser designator F-4Ds created a 'basket' or inverted cone of space over a target: if laser-bomber Phantoms dropped their LGBs within this 'basket',

the bombs were almost certain to detect the laser 'splash' from the target and would steer to and detonate within inches of the aiming point.

A second campaign against North Vietnam, still four years in the future, would be vastly more successful than 'Rolling Thunder' largely because of LGBs.

*F-4 Phantoms of the 8th TFW 'Wolfpack', made famous by ace Col Robin Olds, began flying with precision-guided munitions (PGMs) in September 1967, soon after Olds had been succeeded by Col Robert Spencer. Using the same squadrons for both air-to-air and air-to-ground work was an unwise practice which was later to be discontinued during the campaigns of 1972.*

# Canberras Prowl the Mekong

The Martin RB-57E Canberras of the 'Patricia Lynn' reconnaissance programme, which had been in South Vietnam since May 1963, suffered their second casualty on 25 October 1968 when aircraft 55-4264 was hit by ground fire in the left engine. Captain J. J. Johnson and Major Phil Walker ejected safely. The dull black Canberra, sinister in its appearance, augered down and exploded in the jungle. In due course a replacement was assigned to keep the complement of RB-57Es at five.

With their callsign changed to Moon River, the RB-57Es began gathering intelligence with a system called Compass Eagle. The RB-57E was equipped with an infra-red scanner and an in-flight display screen which showed, in real-time, what was happening in the darkness below. The RB-57E could prowl the Saigon River at night, detect sampans being used by the enemy to move supplies, and call in artillery fire, gunships or PBR patrol boats to despatch the enemy. Throughout the war there were difficulties in communication between those who gathered intelligence and those who used it, but this sidelight to the RB-57E story was apparently a successful one.

*A cousin to the 'Patricia Lynn' aircraft, this B-57G (53-3906) is testing a weapon system called PAVE GAT, a gimbal-mounted, downward-firing M61A1 20-mm cannon, at Eglin AFB, Florida. Another high-tech program, TROPIC MOON II, evaluated a B-57 with a belly gun.*

was overshadowed by the pessimism generated by the Tet Offensive. The base had outlived its usefulness and there was no reason to keep it any longer.

The candidate opposed to the US role in Vietnam with the greatest chance of winning the US Presidential election was snuffed out on 5 June 1968 in Los Angeles when a gunman shot and killed Robert F. Kennedy. It now appeared that Vice-President Hubert Humphrey would be nominated to run against a former holder of the same office, Richard M. Nixon. Humphrey was in favor of a US withdrawal, but was slow in distancing himself from the policies of the administration where he still served.

Two Navy F-8H Crusader pilots had shot down MiGs in June and July and now it was time for the new F-4J Phantom to score its first MiG kill. Lt Roy Cash, Jr, of the 'Tarsiers' was aloft on 10 July 1968 in an F-4J Phantom with Lt Joseph E. Kain, Jr, in the back seat. Using the callsign Rootbeer, the two-man F-4J crew became engaged in a fight with a MiG-21. They picked it off with an AIM-9 Sidewinder, scoring the first kill for the F-4J and the 115th of the war. Unfortunately, two more F-4J Phantoms were lost on America's first combat cruise with the new type, both victims of conventional anti-aircraft fire.

## Crusader's swan song

The Crusader was doing better than the Phantom but its time was approaching an end. It would be years before Navy Phantoms, denied good targets because of the Johnson bombing halt, were to be given a rematch against the MiG.

On 23 July 1968, Major General Robert F. Worley, who had replaced Major General Gordon M. Graham in Saigon as deputy commander of Seventh Air Force, was killed. Worley was flying an RF-4C Phantom of the 460th TRW at Tan Son Nhut and his backseater, Major Robert F. Brodman also perished after the aircraft took ground fire near the DMZ and was lost in a landing attempt. At the time, Worley's loss provoked a storm of criticism about generals flying combat aircraft, but in retrospect there seems to have been no other way to lead men in battle.

Graham, who has also flown repeated combat missions in the RF-4C, puts it this way: "When Bob Worley came over as my replacement, I had two weeks overlap. I flew with him several times to thoroughly indoctrinate him in what needed to be done, and

*The best way to load up an F-8 Crusader on a thronged carrier deck is... well, gingerly. Few Crusaders were configured for air-to-ground work but the F-8E model, here being loaded with rocket projectiles, was an exception. During the Tet Offensive, everything with wings became an air-to-ground weapon, even the Crusader, which proponents viewed as the purest of dogfighting machines. Rocket-laden F-8s sneaked under dismal cloud cover at Hue to shoot up North Vietnamese gun positions.*

# 'Igloo White'

### Striking at Hanoi's busy supply line

On 31 May 1968 a little-known programme called 'Muscle Shoals' was re-named 'Igloo White'. This was to become an ambitious effort to plant mines along the Ho Chi Minh Trail infiltration network – mines equipped with sensors which could detect the presence of men and machines moving south. With North Vietnam mostly off-limits, some of the 'Igloo White' effort was directed towards supply trails running through Laos on their snake-line excursion into South Vietnam.

## Scenting the enemy

Some of the sensors, dropped by tactical aircraft like the F-4 and F-105, could 'smell' human beings moving down the trail; others detected sound and movement. Spikebuoy sensors dropped and planted by A-1E Skyraiders automatically radioed signals triggered by the vibrations of passing traffic. Air Delivered Seismic Intruder Devices (ASID), dropped by US Navy OP-2E and SP-2H Neptunes, also transmitted

*Right: Hanoi's bag of tricks seemed to be inexhaustible. It was inevitable that the supply route would be guarded with AAA guns and that the North Vietnamese would remember to camouflage the guns carefully. Every US warplane interdicting the route was engaged by these guns.*

signals from traffic vibrations.

The job of relaying sensor signals to a ground command post (which could then order strikes against the infiltrators) fell to the large and vulnerable EC-121R Super Constellations known as 'Batcats', which operated from Nakhom Phanom, alias 'Naked Fanny'. Later, in March 1969, the relay job was attempted with five Beechcraft YQU-22As, designed for operation either piloted or as unmanned drones. These were unsuccessful and not much improvement was offered with the five QU-22B aircraft which came later, in June 1970. As it turned out, the EC-121R served in this role until the end of the conflict.

There were, of course, other ways of keeping tabs on North

PM8R

Vietnam. The US made no secret of the fact that reconnaissance flights were continuing and would continue. In addition, drones were employed. The Teledyne-Ryan AQM-34L remotely-piloted vehicle (RPV) carried a 2,000-exposure camera and a TV system which

*Neptune may have been the king of the deep, but when it came to zapping the Ho Chi Minh Trail, the OP-2E Neptune was a very formidable land-based weapon.*

transmitted real-time reconnaissance pictures to an airborne receiving station. These could be relayed at ranges up to 150 miles (240 km).

Photographic runs over the target were made at 1,500 ft (450 m); the RPV climbed to above 50,000 ft (15 250 m) for the flight home. Control was by pre-programmed on-board navigation system or by remote control from an airborne or ground-control station. C-130 Hercules aircraft were sometimes employed to carry the AQM-34L drones on their missions.

*An F-4D rigged to carry sensors and mines prowls the infiltration route. 'Igloo White' seeded the supply line day and night, but its effectiveness was debated.*

*Left: An OP-2E Neptune of VO-67 dispenses electronic sensing devices on the Ho Chi Minh Trail, part of the massive, well-orchestrated effort aimed at hampering the flow of men and equipment from North to South.*

*Below: This Beech YQU-22A was one of five civil light planes converted for drone operation, which were deployed to Nakhon Phanom in 1968. They were intended to relay signals from 'Igloo White' sensors.*

**Two-position wing**
The F-8's high wing could be raised above the fuselage line to increase angle of attack, thus improving slow-speed performance during take-off and when landing on the carrier.

**Classic design**
The Crusader was what traditionalist jocks insisted it should be – a single-seater with guns, nimble and agile. In short, it was all the F-4 Phantom was not. Pilots sang its praises – often to the point of over-rating it.

## Crusader

**This typical Crusader is an F-8E (bureau no. 149158) of VF-53 'Iron Angels', part of Carrier Air Wing Five aboard USS *Hancock* (CVA-19) on a Gulf of Tonkin cruise of January-July 1967. Burn marks around the cannon ports say it all: this F-8E was in a fight and came home with ammunition expended.**

**Flying blowtorch**
The Crusader was powered by the proven Pratt & Whitney J57-P-20 turbojet which offered 10,700-lb (4853-kg) thrust, a figure which rose to 18,000 lb (8164 kg) when the afterburner was blasting away. This was plenty of power for a jet which weighed 34,100 lb (15467 kg) when sent aloft.

To Commander Lowell R. (Moose) Meyers, skipper of VF-51 on 'Bonnie Dick', the Crusader was the warplane in which he had logged more than 1,000 hours whilst awaiting the chance for the ultimate test. It came on 26 June 1968 when Meyers was on a MiGCAP mission in an F-8H. Meyers was returning from North Vietnam when he got into a scrape with MiG-21s and shot one of them down, using an AIM-9 Sidewinder missile. Meyer's 'Screaming Eagles' had been in the conflict since the Gulf of Tonkin air strikes; the squadron's one-time skipper Jim Stockdale was a POW in Hanoi and the victory over the MiG, the 113th of the war, was welcomed by all of VF-51's people.

On 9 July 1968, Lieutenant commander John B. Nichols III from VF-191 on the *Hancock* was flying escort for a reconnaissance flight, a circumstance which permitted him to be north of the 19th Parallel bombline. Nichols' fighter with the callsign Feedbag

101 had become tangled in a protracted fight with a MiG-17, a battle in which Nichols' adversary stubbornly refused to go down. Nichols scored a hit with an AIM-9 Sidewinder, drawing clots of smoke. The MiG continued to try to turn inside him, sputtering but fighting tenaciously. Nichols maneuvered into position to unleash 20-mm cannon fire, saw his shells impacting against the MiG, and still could not bring it down. He closed in and fired again from pointblank range. Finally, the MiG-17 disintegrated and fell in flames.

The war's next MiG kill in chronological order was the first aerial victory for the F-4J Phantom on 10 July 1968. All carriers larger than the 'Essex' class

*VF-111 'Sundowners' was one of only two squadrons to fly the F-8D version of the Crusader in combat. Shark's teeth poised, this F-8D is preparing to move up to the catapult on USS Midway (CVA-41). The steam rising around deck crewmen is from the ship's previous launch.*

*Although Navy fighter jocks took pride in the Crusader's cannon, all but one of the MiGs shot down by F-8s fell prey to the lethal AIM-9 Sidewinder heat-seeking missile (at left). In fact, the AIM-9 racked up more kills than any other weapon of the conflict.*

were now Phantom-equipped, but the F-4J interlude was the only break in a consistent series of Crusader achievements.

On 24 July 1968, Commander Guy Cane of VF-53 flying an F-8E Crusader from *Bon Homme* *Richard* shot down a MiG-17 with an AIM-9 Sidewinder. A week later, the penultimate MiG kill of 'Rolling Thunder' was also credited to a Crusader. It happened on 1 August 1968. Lt Norman K. McCoy, another

'Screaming Eagle' from VF-51 on 'Bonnie Dick', was flying an F-8H Crusader when he, too, employed a Sidewinder to prevail over an opponent, this time a MiG-21. Cane and McCoy were also very experienced Crusader pilots who had waited over the full years of a career for the chance to claim an enemy aircraft.

As the presidential campaign narrowed to a contest between Hubert Humphrey and Richard M. Nixon, a Crusader pilot scored the final kill of 1968, the final kill of the 'Rolling Thunder' campaign, and the last until 1970.

These distinctions went to Lt Anthony J. Nargi on 19 September 1968. It was the 118th MiG kill of the war and the last

credited to a Crusader. Nargi was detached from VF-111 aboard the anti-submarine carrier *Intrepid*. He and his wingman were informed of MiGs aloft within the vicinity of the vessel and were catapulted upward to intercept. The MiG-21 pilots apparently sighted the Crusaders and took evasive action. Nargi went into a tight turn and wracked his F-8C behind one of the enemy. The AIM-9 he launched went off its rail cleanly, tracked perfectly, went up the MiG's tailpipe, and blew the North Vietnamese fighter to pieces. The MiG pilot ejected and a characteristic red-orange North Vietnamese parachute furled back into the slipstream.

The remaining MiG-21 pilot, undaunted, proved exceedingly aggressive in dueling with the two Crusaders. Nargi and his wingman maneuvered with the MiG and fired missiles at it but without result.

For the moment, the air-to-air war was over.

# Crusader Climax
## *Curtain call for a superstar*

The final months of 'Rolling Thunder' also brought the finest hour for the Crusader. From the beginning of 1968 through the total bombing halt which finally clamped down on 30 October 1968, no fewer than four of the small 'Essex'-class carriers were working in the Gulf of Tonkin. USS *Bon Homme Richard*, *Hancock*, *Oriskany* and *Ticonderoga* each had two Crusader squadrons on board. In addition, the anti-submarine carrier *Intrepid* carried a small detachment of Crusaders to provide fighter protection. Further, most of the large-deck carriers like the USS *America* had a detachment of recce Crusaders.

The pilots who flew pre-strike and post-strike photo missions in the RF-8G Crusader continued to face high risk and were not necessarily bound by President

*VMF(AW)-235 'Death Angels' had the most patriotic, as well as the most colorful, markings of any Marine Corps squadron in Southeast Asia. These Marine F-8E Crusaders typically carried Zuni rockets as well as bombs and cannon for support work.*

Johnson's edict, which between April and October limited strike missions to the lower part of North Vietnam. Two RF-8Gs from detachments of squadron VFP-63 were lost during the final months of 'Rolling Thunder', one from *Ticonderoga* on 28 March (while over Laos) and one from *Bonnie Dick* on 22 May. Navy RF-8G pilots were among the privileged few who could still fly over Hanoi and Haiphong, and it happened more than once that a recce Crusader sped out of Route Package Six with a MiG on its tail. There is no record of a

MiG ever shooting down a Crusader photo ship, however, and only 10 RF-8As and seven RF-8Gs were lost in combat over the entire war.

Losses for Crusader fighters were also comfortingly low. Marine Corps pilots who operated the type with the 'Red Devils' of VMF-232 and the 'Lancers' of VMF-235 at Da Nang had a particularly good record with the aircraft. The

Marines flew into the southerly Route Packages fairly frequently, but in the entire war lost only two Crusaders in North Vietnam. Their excellent combat record could not prevent the occasional accident, however.

For the Navy, the end of 'Rolling Thunder' brought low losses of 'fighter' Crusaders and some very satisfying MiG kills. The 'Sundowners' of VF-111 on *Oriskany* lost an F-8C on 2 January, VF-194 on *Ticonderoga* lost an F-8E on 14 February, and an F-8H from *Hancock* went down on 17 September 1968. None of these was claimed by a MiG and a total of only four combat losses over a prolonged period of sustained operations was a respectable figure indeed.

*"When you're out of F-8s, you're out of fighters." That quote, a not-so-subtle jab at the F-4 Phantom, began with Navy pilots but found its way to a Vought brochure. On the catapult or in the sky, pilots saw the F-8 as the ultimate air combat machine.*

*The F-102A Delta Dagger interceptor and the two-seat, combat-capable TF-102A (above), were deployed to Vietnam to counter Hanoi's Il-28 'Beagle' bombers. For the F-102, the wrap-up score was nothing to one: no F-102A ever bagged a North Vietnamese aircraft – the Il-28s were never used – but one Dagger was shot down by a MiG.*

what to expect to encounter, and what needed to be done as well. He did everything right until the last mission he flew. He and I were the only Air Force General officers who flew combat missions in fighters. Momyer knew of it and forbade it. In fact, he threatened to court-martial me if I didn't stop. I did it and Bob did it because we believed that someone in the upper levels of command needed to know the straight story. Intelligence officers, wing commanders and buck pilots were fine to listen to, but much of the time were either biased, self-serving, plain wrong or misguided. When Bob was killed all hell broke loose and a witch hunt of gigantic proportions occurred. Momyer handled it rather well, but no Air Force General officer ever flew a fighter mission again."

On 31 July, General John D. Ryan departed the PACAF commander's slot in Honolulu, to be replaced by General Joseph J. Nazzaro. Ryan later became Air Force Vice-Chief of Staff. Nazzaro, like Ryan, was a 'SAC weenie', a Curtis LeMay protégé who had made his career in bombers while the Vietnam war was being fought with fighters. And on 31 July, General William W. Momyer was about to depart his posting in Saigon as commander of Seventh Air Force, to be replaced by General George Brown.

Presidents Johnson and Thieu met in Honolulu for two days, 19 and 20 July 1968, to discuss the war. Johnson called rumors of a major US policy change "absolute tommyrot and fiction", an almost certain sign that the rumors were true. The presidential meeting had been preceded by the visit to Saigon in early July of Defense Secretary Clark Clifford, who also denied that anything new was impending. By now the race for the White House was boiling down to a contest between Humphrey and Richard M. Nixon.

*"Accordingly, I shall not seek, nor will I accept..." With his shocking decision not to campaign for re-election in 1968, Lyndon Johnson – who had once hoped to focus on domestic politics and build a 'Great Society' at home – acknowledged being defeated by a growing war on foreign soil. Johnson's detractors claim that John F. Kennedy, had he not been assassinated in 1963, would never have agreed to a massive build-up of US forces in Southeast Asia. There is no proof either way.*

Nixon, not in public office and with no visible power base, continued in March 1968 to make slow but relentless progress toward attaining the nomination of the opposition Republican Party. Traditionally more conservative than the more numerous Democrats, the Republicans were not yet moved by those in their ranks who opposed the US role in Southeast Asia. They were, however, exceedingly interested in foreign policy and Nixon's credentials were impressive. He had even been photographed pointing a finger in challenge at the Soviet leader, Khruschev.

## Delta Daggers finally depart

The longstanding, on-again, off-again deployment of a detachment of F-102A interceptors to Bien Hoa ended on 25 September and the delta-winged fighters were removed from South Vietnam for the last time.

The bombing of most of North Vietnam, halted on 1 October 1968, was replaced on 1 November by a prohibition against US combat sorties anywhere in the North. Reconnaissance missions continued and revealed that the enemy was moving rapidly to repair bridges and roads, strengthen anti-aircraft defenses, and improve airfields. Truck movements of supplies to the South increased four-fold.

President Johnson had suffered the humiliation of having to abandon any thought of re-election in 1968. Now his party had to suffer a devastating loss. In a country rapidly being torn asunder by violence in the streets, much of it directed against US participation in the war, Nixon defeated Humphrey in the 5 November 1968 presidential election. Nixon had gotten into office in part by announcing that he had a plan to end the war, but he had not said what the plan was.

As the year drew to a close, in a deployment called 'Combat Hornet', the first of the newly modified AC-119G gunships arrived at Nha Trang on 22 December. Deployment of the AC-119G had been delayed due to the overweight condition of the airframes after modification. In yet another deployment, dubbed 'Combat Cougar', EC-47Q Sentinel Eagle aircraft arrived in South Vietnam

# 'Rolling Thunder' Results

'Rolling Thunder' must go down in the history of aerial warfare as the most ambitious, wasteful and ineffective campaign ever mounted. And President Johnson may receive history's judgment as one of the most indecisive and paralyzed war leaders to ever exist. While damage was done to many targets in the North, no lasting objective was achieved, even the limited goals earlier mentioned. Hanoi emerged as the winner of 'Rolling Thunder'.

Many Air Force, Navy and Marine officers and pilots, who felt that their hands were tied behind their backs, summed up the prolonged air campaign as a violation of the basic principle of combat: when you fight a war, you must fight to win. Men in 'Thuds' and Crusaders, Skyhawks and Phantoms believed that they had been sent against formidable defenses, to attack questionable targets, under too many restrictions, with no realistic chance of waging the war in a manner that would make it possible to win. At the very time when anti-war opponents back home criticized them for bombing raids which the uninformed regarded as atrocious, military men felt impotent.

Despite all the restrictions, the on-again, off-again mood of the campaign, and the general confusion, these pilots had, in fact, done more damage to North Vietnam than is generally recognized. In the years since the conflict, a few North Vietnamese officials, speaking with uncharacteristic candor, have acknowledged that at various points in 1967 and 1968 the bombing was hurting badly. The diversion of resources to repair, maintain and expand bridges, roads and railways – to say nothing of infiltration routes – was a drain on an already

*The purpose of the 'Rolling Thunder' campaign was to persuade the North Vietnamese to give up the fight. However, because the aerial campaign was not pressed home to the full, its prime effect was to make North Vietnam one of the most heavily-defended countries on Earth.*

overburdened society. Prior to the Tet Offensive, when Hanoi did not fully control the Viet Cong anyway, a more vigorous bombing campaign might have caused North Vietnam's leaders to sue for a settlement. But each time that North Vietnam started to hurt, the US relaxed the pressure.

By the end of 'Rolling Thunder' on 30 October 1968, preliminary peace talks were taking shape in Paris. The talks had not progressed beyond such

issues as the shape of the table to be used at meetings. The Saigon authorities refused to talk to any representative from Hanoi. The North Vietnamese wanted to talk directly with the US and were not prepared to negotiate with the South Vietnamese. The weak start of the talks seemed to have no relation to the air battles that had been fought in Route Package Six. The talks were going nowhere.

With the benefit of hindsight, it is clear that 'Rolling Thunder' could have been successful only if the civilian leaders in Washington had made a policy decision to use military power effectively. Most professional airmen believed then, and still believe now, that North Vietnam could have been taken out of the war in a matter of

*American explosives transformed large parts of Southeast Asia, particularly areas adjacent to the Ho Chi Minh Trail, into a cratered, pock-marked wasteland. But in spite of the awesome tonnage of bombs dropped, Communist supplies still got through.*

*In this bizarre war, bombers (i.e. B-52s) pounded the jungle while fighters (like this 'Thud') hauled bombs to the enemy's homeland. 'Rolling Thunder' was to cost the F-105 dearly, with hundreds being lost over the North.*

weeks with the men and machines already located in Southeast Asia, and with no additional resources. What was missing was a plan, a policy, a coherent decision to use airmen and aircraft as they were intended to be used. Because men in mufti were seeking to turn warplanes into weapons of policy rather than to employ them correctly as weapons of war, 'Rolling Thunder' failed.

Although the Communist side never won a major victory in battle, not on land, sea or air, the massive 'Rolling Thunder' effort failed because the policymakers in Washington gave the war away by default. It happened just as Lt Col Edward Hillding's F-4Es were working up to participate in a conflict which now seemed to have come to an end.

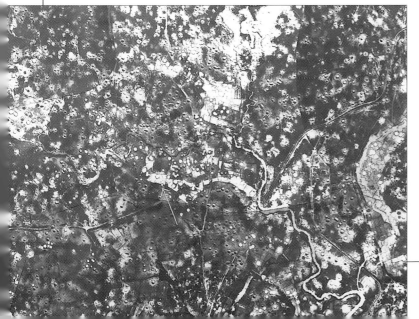

# Enter the F-4E

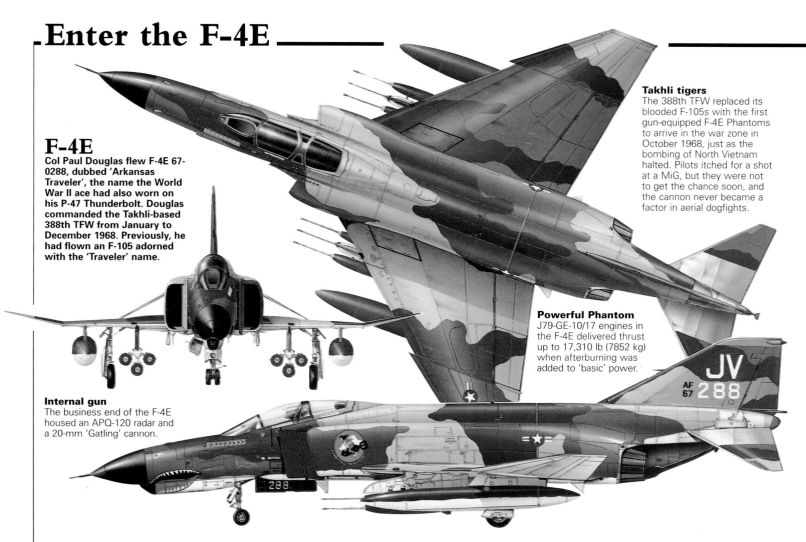

## F-4E
Col Paul Douglas flew F-4E 67-0288, dubbed 'Arkansas Traveler', the name the World War II ace had also worn on his P-47 Thunderbolt. Douglas commanded the Takhli-based 388th TFW from January to December 1968. Previously, he had flown an F-105 adorned with the 'Traveler' name.

### Internal gun
The business end of the F-4E housed an APQ-120 radar and a 20-mm 'Gatling' cannon.

### Takhli tigers
The 388th TFW replaced its blooded F-105s with the first gun-equipped F-4E Phantoms to arrive in the war zone in October 1968, just as the bombing of North Vietnam halted. Pilots itched for a shot at a MiG, but they were not to get the chance soon, and the cannon never became a factor in aerial dogfights.

### Powerful Phantom
J79-GE-10/17 engines in the F-4E delivered thrust up to 17,310 lb (7852 kg) when afterburning was added to 'basic' power.

The F-4E was a very different Phantom. It was longer, heavier, with different fuel capacity, different radar. "Everybody wanted to jump into one and go shoot down a MiG," recalled Lieutenant Colonel Edward Hillding, commander of the first unit to take the type into battle. Based on Vietnam experience and first flown on 30 June the previous year, 1967, the F-4E carried an internally-mounted General Electric M61A1 Vulcan six-barrel rotary cannon with provision for 640 rounds while retaining full Sidewinder and Sparrow capability. The F-4E also had an additional (seventh) fuel cell in the fuselage which counter-balanced the weight of the gun. Installed in the redesigned nose was a Westinghouse APQ-120 solid-state radar fire control system with a reduced, elliptical dish. Power was provided by two 17,900-lb (8120-kg) thrust General Electric J79-GE-17 afterburning engines.

Captain Thomas McInerney, who had been one of the first pilots to take the F-4D into battle,

# Shark's Teeth

During the working up of the F-4E at Eglin, Captain Steve Stephens designed a colorful patch for the 40th TFS and painted shark's teeth on the Phantoms. General Momyer, now Tactical Air Command chief following his stint in Saigon, did not want shark's teeth – throughout the Vietnam conflict, leaders failed to grasp the morale-building benefit of such insignia – but was persuaded to remember those which had been painted on his own P-40 Warhawk in World War II.

While pausing en route at Hickam AFB, Hawaii, Hillding's F-4E squadron attracted some unwanted attention from a 'PACAF weenie' who objected strongly to the teeth painted on the aircraft and, in weeks ahead,

would complain about it. The instant the tires screeched on Korat's runway, Hillding's squadron became the 469th TFS – formerly, and proudly, one of the 'Thud' elements of P.P. Douglas' 388th TFW.

Colonel Paul Douglas was one of the best fighter wing commanders in the business. In World War II, Douglas had had a P-47D Thunderbolt named 'Arkansas Traveler'. During 'Rolling Thunder', he'd applied the same nickname to a 'Thud'. He would eventually turn one of Hillding's F-4Es into yet another

*Tanked-off and ready, F-4E Phantoms of the 34th TFS form up temporarily on a KC-135 from which they have just taken fuel. The shark's teeth violated a rule and annoyed a general, but they stayed on the Phantoms anyway.*

'Arkansas Traveler'.

The squadron commander stepped out of his aircraft to find numerous people, including a couple of generals, welcoming the arrival of the F-4E. There was much good cheer, camaraderie and talk about carrying the war to the enemy. There was also a message from Hickam, drafted by the 'PACAF weenie', commanding Hillding to remove the teeth from his aircraft. Hillding, a man with an easy grasp for priorities, was more concerned with the morale of his men than the message. He devised an excuse to delay removing the unique marking which gave the 469th TFS its identity, its spirit, its aggressiveness. The teeth stayed.

*Navigation lights winking, an F-4E of the 469th TFS/388th TFW prowls the sky on a sortie from Thailand's very busy Takhli airbase. Because President Lyndon Johnson halted bombing up North, most missions were flown over South Vietnam or next door in Laos.*

now joined Hillding's squadron to do the same with the F-4E.

'Working up' in the F-4E at Eglin was an exciting time for the men who believed that the bombing halt would not last long. Many were seasoned combat veterans. Tom McInerney had the job of Weapons Officer and was tasked to bring the squadron up to par with the new Phantom's cannon and its other systems, including the very unpopular Bullpup-B missile. Captain Jack Isham was given the job of preparing the men for ground survival, in advance of the usual survival exercises carried out in the Philippines *en route* to the battle zone.

Hillding, Stephens, McInerney, Isham and the other men of the F-4E squadron at Eglin spent more than a year 'working up'. They had everything: the tactics,

the cannon, the aggressive fighter pilot spirit which, in the end, matters most. Some of them were going to become aces – a feat even the exalted Robin Olds had been unable to achieve. When they learned that they were going to Southeast Asia in November, and that combat missions over North Vietnam had halted at the end of October, some of the men were impossible to be around.

## Combat debut

The first combat missions in the F-4E Phantom were flown on 26 November 1968, 19 days after the 40th FS had deployed as a unit to Korat and became the 469th TFS. By this time, there were no missions over North Vietnam. Hillding's men went into Laos.

Soon afterwards, Hillding, McInerney and others discovered that the Air Force was planning to

*The JV tailcode went to the 469th TFS/388th TFW, the very first outfit to reach the combat theater with the cannon-armed F-4E. An artist and fighter jock with the unlikely name Capt. Steven Steven painted the shark teeth on these bomb-laden Phantoms.*

put a new breed of animal in the back seat. Until now, Air Force Phantoms had been flown by two pilots. Now the 469th TFS was to receive a new animal called a weapons systems officer (WSO), a term no-one ever used. The term actually employed was, simply, navigator.

Not long after the first combat missions of the E model in November 1968, Chaplain Joe blessed the first missions in which the backseater was not a pilot.

It appears that the first F-4E lost in combat was 67-286 of Hillding's 469th TFS/388th TFS, downed over Laos on 1 January 1969.

In Saigon, following Momyer as chief of Seventh Air Force, General George Brown settled

*Before being shot down and put in the brig with other POWs, 34th TFS/388th TFW backseater Don Logan snapped this portrait of a gun-equipped F-4E Phantom just after its arrival in Southeast Asia.*

into the job and the war. Brown, too, had spent much of his career in SAC. He felt overburdened with a war in Laos which was not publicly acknowledged, and for which his men received no credit, and he was not pleased with the decision to cease bombing North Vietnam.

General Brown wanted to get the next squadron of F-4Es, and the next, into the fight. Losses of 'Thuds' had been so heavy that the F-105 could no longer be the primary strike aircraft. It was now the time of the Phantom.

in December 1968. Essentially an electronic snooper version of the venerable 'Gooney Bird', the EC-47Q carried radio and electronics receiver gear and a crew of specialists.

Fighting over Laos was a continuing challenge for American airmen. On 15 November 1968, a series of interdiction campaigns known as 'Commando Hunt' began in Laotian airspace. That same week saw the arrival of the F-4E Phantom, and, on 19 November, the departure of the F-111A detachment, which pulled out of Southeast Asia to return to Nellis AFB, Nevada. It could not have been foreseen that the F-111A would return to fight over North Vietnamese skies again.

At the end of 1968, the number of US combat troops in South Vietnam had reached 536,100, a figure very close to the final peak of about 550,000 which would be reached before the Nixon administration began slow and phased withdrawals. In the ground war in South Vietnam, the Communist side continued to exhibit an almost limitless capacity for absorbing casualties, enduring suffering and pressing the fight. On the home-front, the opposition to the war continued to gather strength, making Americans less willing to sacrifice than their enemy.

New problems were becoming firmly rooted among the US forces: racial conflict, in an army where the number of blacks was double the black share of the US population; narcotics problems in a combat zone where hash, morphine, opium and heroin were regularly available. Thus, at the height of its commitment to the war, the US had stopped bombing North Vietnam and was

*Drones were used extensively over Southeast Asia from 1964 through to 1975, gathering an enormous amount of photographic and electronic intelligence. This AQM-34M, seen being pre-programmed with its mission course, is a low-level tactical reconnaissance platform, the bulges on top of the fuselage housing the film magazines for the drone's two main reconnaissance cameras.*

# Changing the Kill to Loss Ratio

## Air action and the Ault Report

From August 1964 to October 1968, air-to-air combat resulted in 118 MiGs shot down, a figure which, thanks to steady re-supply, was higher than the total number of MiGs in the North Vietnamese air force at any given time. During the same period, 56 US aircraft were lost in air-to-air action. The 2:1 kill ratio marked the poorest performance by American fighters in any conflict and was a sharp contrast to the Korean War where the kill ratio, even if never reaching the claimed 15:1, was still a highly respectable 7:1.

Pilot experience did not seem to be a factor. Most US pilots during 'Rolling Thunder' were highly experienced. The Red Baron study conducted by the Air Force after the war showed that before 1966 more than half of all fighter pilots had 2,000 flying hours, and the average pilot had logged 510 hours in the aircraft type he flew in combat; at this juncture the kill ratio was a slightly more favorable 3:1. By the end of 'Rolling Thunder' in October 1968, the average fighter pilot had only 240 hours in his aircraft type and the score had fallen to less than 1:1. The study showed that total flying hours had no direct correlation to a pilot's chances of being shot down by a MiG. On the other hand – witness the case of Colonel Robin Olds – a seasoned pilot with more flight time in his logbook stood the best chance of shooting down a MiG.

### Combat training

The Navy felt that training in air combat maneuvering (ACM) was the key to improving the air-to-air combat skills of its pilots. An analysis of air-to-air combat over North Vietnam was completed in 1968 by Captain Frank W. Ault, and this led to the Navy instituting an ACM program with three goals: to improve air combat capabilities among all US Navy fighter squadrons, to improve the reliability of air-to-air missiles, and to create an elite cadre of high-capability combat instructors. It was almost as if Ault and others were prescient, as if they knew another day might come to fight over North Vietnam.

Ault was right, of course, and in retrospect the Navy's decision not to mount an internal cannon on its F-4 Phantoms proved to be less significant than it seemed at the time. The US Navy

*A North Vietnamese MiG-17 'Fresco' caught in the reticle as an F-105 bores in for a kill. The nimble, heavily-armed MiG-17 was often the shooter rather than the victim, prompting a Pentagon study to learn why US fighter pilots were being outclassed in the sky near Hanoi.*

watching its own forces move in the direction of disarray while the Communist enemy – who, to be sure, had problems of his own – fought on.

Losses of US Navy and Marine Corps aircraft in 1968 had continued at about the same rate as the previous year, even though bad weather at the beginning of the year and a bombing halt at the end reduced the total number of sorties. Despite its much-envied all-weather capability, the advanced A-6A Intruder was not entirely bug-free, and for the moment the new bomber remained somewhat loss-prone and very controversial.

The number-keepers concluded at the end of 1968 that 392 USAF aircraft had been lost in Southeast Asia, no fewer than 257 of these to ground fire. Of the total, 304 were combat losses, 88 operational. The cost of the aircraft lost was $441 million. Ground attacks on air bases in South Vietnam had resulted in 35 aircraft being destroyed. Up North, surface-to-air missiles (SAMs) and MiG fighters had claimed only 12 USAF aircraft as compared with 40 the

*F-111A Aardvarks arrive in Thailand, making a flyover with their variable-geometry wings swept back unnecessarily, just for show. The showboating ended when the 1968 deployment of these warplanes proved to be a disaster. They returned to the United States to lick their wounds. The F-111 resumed fighting with better results in 1972.*

Postgraduate Course in Fighter Weapons, Tactics and Doctrine, soon to be re-named Top Gun, was launched by squadron VF-121 at NAS Miramar, California. The program involved three weeks and about 35 flight hours of realistic, if simulated, air combat against actual adversaries flying 'dissimilar' aircraft, these being A-4F Skyhawks and T-38A Talons, the latter being an excellent stand-in for the MiG-21.

## Top Gun

Top Gun created superb Phantom pilots like Ronald (Mugs) McKeown and Randall (Duke) Cunningham, who would be very well prepared if, indeed, a second round of fighting did erupt over North Vietnam. In fact, because of Top Gun and the similar 'Aggressor' ACM training introduced by the Air Force later, the findings about flying experience would be reversed and the greatest successes in the future would be achieved by younger pilots with fewer flight hours but with realistic combat training under their belts. The Air Force, which in 1968 still had not acquired its own ACM syllabus, was still talking about the gun-armed Phantom as the means of attaining a better kill ratio and had sent Lt Col Edward Hillding to Eglin AFB, Florida to 'work up' the 40th TFS, the squadron that would take the cannon-armed F-4E into combat.

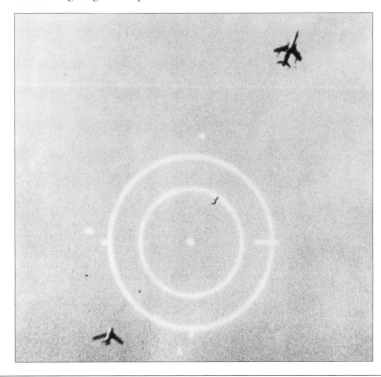

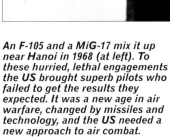

*An F-105 and a MiG-17 mix it up near Hanoi in 1968 (at left). To these hurried, lethal engagements the US brought superb pilots who failed to get the results they expected. It was a new age in air warfare, changed by missiles and technology, and the US needed a new approach to air combat.*

*Robin Olds' hard-charging style pointed the way to dominate the skies the previous year, but under less inspiring leadership American pilots did not do as well as his 8th TFW. In 1968, MiGs were still a major threat, and it was clear to some that USAF and USN training methods needed revision.*

*An A-1E Skyraider on the mat at Nakhon Phanom, Thailand with a fuel air explosive (FAE) bomb, designed to create a monster explosion and wipe out troop concentrations. The bomb was little-used, with disputed results.*

*Tightly packed into an airfield ramp with too little space or shelter, these A-1H Skyraiders (at right) are vulnerable to attack by Viet Cong sappers when not facing traditional risks on low-level combat missions.*

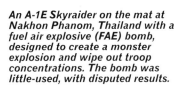

*'Thuds' up North. With the end of the on-again, off-again 'Rolling Thunder' campaign in October 1968, these F-105 Thunderchiefs no longer had to face Hanoi's missiles, MiGs and triple-A (anti-aircraft artillery). The bombing failed in its goal – to make Ho Chi Minh re-think the situation and bring a halt to North Vietnam's efforts to undermine the South.*

previous year, which reflected the halt in bombing of North Vietnam. Again, the F-105 Thunderchief bore a heavy share of the losses, with the F-4 Phantom close behind. But the day of the 'Thud' was ending.

More numbers: Air Force air munitions expended in 1968 totaled 1,092,200 tons, a 60 per cent increase over 1967 expenditures. The USAF flew 1,034,839 combat sorties, 20,568 of which were B-52 'Arc Light' strikes.

But, except for the occasional reconnaissance flight, not a single American aircraft now flew in the skies over North Vietnam.

*Vietnam saw many radical new solutions to old problems. The use of helicopters in blade-snapping jungle vegetation had been a problem to the British in Malaya in the 1950s, the potential value of rotary-winged craft always being hampered by the need to find suitable landing sites. In Vietnam, American ingenuity came up with a solution to the problem. Drop a five- or seven-tonne bomb from a C-130 or a CH-54 flying crane, and hey-presto, you have an instant helicopter landing zone, ready with minimal clearing for almost immediate use.*

# AC-119 'Shadow'

On 22 December 1968, the first of the newly-arrived AC-119G gunships went into service at Nha Trang AB. Other terms, including Gunship III and Combat Hornet, were used to describe this gunship derived from the ageing C-119G Flying Boxcar transport, but as AC-47 was known as 'Spooky' and the AC-130 became 'Spectre', the AC-119G quickly acquired the name 'Shadow'. A later variant, the jet-assisted AC-119K became known as the 'Stinger'.

General George Brown, the commander of Seventh Air Force in Saigon who had replaced Momyer, was especially enthusiastic about the big, twin-boomed craft, which was painted an ominous black. The Air Force had selected the 'One Nineteen' as its third gunship type, in addition to the AC-47 and AC-

*Pilots often describe their aircraft as 'stable' in flight. The AC-119, which drew upon the twin-boom Flying Boxcar transport, was more than steady – one pilot said that while in a pylon turn his bulky mount was "as stable as an anvil".*

*An AC-119K 'Stinger', readily distinguished from the AC-119G 'Shadow' by the jet engines under its wing, heads off on a support mission over Vietnam. This second-generation gunship augmented the pioneering AC-47 'Spooky' gunship.*

130, because of the availability of airframes, sturdiness and long loiter times. The 'Shadow' was to become an important weapons system in South Vietnam and an incidental part of the fighting in Laos and 'up North'.

## Heavy armament

Like other gunships, the AC-119G was a sort of flying tank. Equipment specified for the aircraft included Southeast Asia communications gear, the GAU-2B/A six-barrel 7.62-mm machine-gun, no fewer than 50,000 rounds of ammunition for day flights and 35,000 rounds plus 60 flares for night missions. The later AC-119K had 20-mm cannons added.

The AC-119G had been late arriving in South Vietnam because of program delays and equipment problems. A function as simple as venting gun smoke from the fuselage interior required weeks or months of evaluations, changes and further tests before acceptance.

Eventually, 26 airframes were converted by the Fairchild-Hiller plant in St Augustine, Florida. The aircraft were assigned to the 71st Special Operations Squadron of the 14th Special Operations (formerly Air Commando) Wing at Nha Trang. Some were later assigned to Phan Rang AB and Tan Son Nhut AB. 'Shadow' joined the bigger 'Spectre' in the continuing conflict but, in late 1969, was not supposed to be flown into North Vietnam.

*Below: When a gunship settled into a pylon turn and began blazing away as seen here near Saigon, the result made a spectacular time-lapse photo.*

*Above: One of the first AC-119 gun ships wears the dark, night-optimized battle paint which was standard for all of these aged warriors in Vietnam.*

# YEAR OF TRANSITION

Although the war was still pretty hot in the South and over Laos, 1 January 1969 began a year in which no Americans other than the intrepid fliers of reconnaissance aircraft were to fly combat missions into North Vietnam. American prisoners, of course, remained in the North, scattered in a half-dozen camps where treatment varied from poor to execrable.

*On 14 January 1969, a Zuni rocket overheated and exploded aboard **USS Enterprise (CVAN-65)** while the ship exercised off Hawaii en route to the war zone. The conflagration was grim evidence of the burden on sailors at sea: the fire killed 27, injured 344, and burned up 15 aircraft. Still, the crew repaired **Enterprise** and had it in combat by 31 March.*

The total bombing halt which had gone into effect on 1 November 1968 could not have been more awkwardly timed from the standpoint of military men. The F-4E Phantom, the new model armed with an internal 20-mm cannon, had arrived in Thailand, piloted by men who were psyched up for missions against MiGs. The General Dynamics F-111A variable-geometry wing fighter-bomber had arrived in Thailand as well, making a temporary deployment which was widely regarded as

unsuccessful, although it would return. Even the battleship *New Jersey* (BB-62) was refurbished and put to sea on a Vietnam combat cruise, to employ its mighty guns against targets well inland from the shoreline. F-4E, F-111A, and *New Jersey* were armed to the teeth for a vigorous war against North Vietnam – but it was not happening.

Peace talks progressed at a snail's pace in Paris. A US Congress Armed Services Committee report stated that since the 31 October 1968 bombing halt, the increase in North Vietnamese movement toward Laos and the DMZ were of such volume that it appeared that North Vietnam was establishing a massive logistics system as a foundation for future expanded operations. The report concluded with the obvious: if peace talks failed, the bombing halt would have

# Reconnaissance

The only airmen who continued to brave North Vietnam's defenses with any regularity during the bombing halt were the reconnaissance pilots. In Pentagon discussions, Secretary Laird and others pondered what to do if Hanoi's SAMs or AAA shot down a recce aircraft. Should a combat mission be mounted to attempt a rescue? Would that violate the terms of the bombing halt? Should warplanes be despatched with full loads of ordnance, solely to engage AAA batteries that were firing on recce aircraft? In a curious twist of reasoning, Laird and others said that Hanoi would be guilty of aggression if it fired at American jets flying over its own territory!

*A trio of SR-71s flying from Kadena Field racked up 'Habu' mission marks (named for a snake unique to Okinawa) for sorties over North Vietnam.*

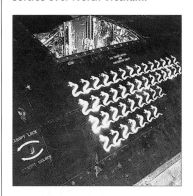

*The marvelous SR-71 Blackbird took over strategic 'recon' from its forebear, the CIA's A-12 'Oxcart'. Strategic Air Command SR-71s went into high gear over North Vietnam in 1969 following a first sortie on 21 March 1968.*

The role of the recce pilot and his crew has been remarked upon frequently in this narrative. By 1969 some RF-4C Phantoms were carrying a weapon systems officer (WSO) in the back seat instead of a pilot and were introducing new types of ECM pods and other accoutrements. Flying the RF-4C remained a risky, unforgiving challenge. Bombing halt or no bombing halt, Paris peace talks or no Paris peace talks, Hanoi's gunners did not hesitate to shoot. Many an RF-4C returned with battle damage. Early in the year, when the weather was excruciatingly poor, every step of a mission was fraught with peril. Once hit by AAA fire, with navigation systems damaged, a pilot faced a difficult job relocating a KC-135 tanker or coaxing his craft to its home base.

North Vietnam, of course, continued to hold that reconnaissance missions were 'provocative' and 'warlike'.

*Conceived as an atomic bomber, the North American RA-5C Vigilante became a superb reconnaissance ship in Vietnam. The RA-5C was the heaviest and fastest warplane ever to fly routinely from carrier decks.*

*The McDonnell RF-101C Voodoo first appeared in Vietnam in 1960 and equipped three squadrons by the mid-1960s. Though difficult to fly, the Voodoo was superb as a high-speed gatherer of intelligence.*

*An SA-2 missile explodes near a 432nd TRW RF-4C Phantom over North Vietnam. SAMs posed a frightful risk to 'recce' crews from July 1965 onward. Losses mounted in part because tacticians were slow to shift the war to treetop altitudes.*

provided Hanoi with a new lease on life, and the war would drag on much longer.

Richard M. Nixon took office as president on 20 January 1969, in part because he had promised a way out of the deepening quagmire in Vietnam. An early step by Nixon was to name Henry Cabot Lodge – his vice-presidential running mate in 1960 and a former ambassador to Saigon – as senior American negotiator at the Paris peace talks. Henry Kissinger was named as the new national security advisor.

It seems clear that Nixon was uncomfortable with the absence of American aircraft in North Vietnam's skies and concerned that Hanoi was recovering and rebuilding. Nixon knew that any solution to the war would require a stronger South Vietnam, serious action against Hanoi's infiltration routes, and a withdrawal of at least some American troops as a visible sign of progress. But the pressure to withdraw American troops brought with it pressure to show that the enemy was being harmed. To bring the boys home, Nixon might have to go North again.

Before he revealed his plan to end the Vietnam war, Nixon asked for a review of the South Vietnamese forces – telegraphing his intent to shift much of the burden of the war to Saigon's own troops.

## Operations over Laos

The little-publicized air campaign over Laos was continuing in fits and starts, with the authorities increasing the number of missions while denying that they were going on. Much of that campaign, known as 'Commando Hunt', was directed against the segments of the Ho Chi Minh Trail which circled through Laos *en route* to South Vietnam. Virtually all the aircraft which had been flying from Thailand against North Vietnam prior to the bombing halt up North were now directed towards Laos. This meant no increase in the number of warplanes available for the war in South Vietnam.

There were fewer examples of the ageing, chugging A-1 Skyraider in the skies, being replaced for many tasks by jets like the F-5 and A-37, but the venerable 'Spad' continued to be important – not just with the VNAF but with American units as well. In South Vietnam, as it had done up North before the bombing halt, the A-1 continued to be best known as the warplane which covered the scene when a friendly pilot was down.

A 15 February 1969 combat rescue mission involving Skyraiders was notable for the unusual weapons employed. It began when an F-4 Phantom was hit by gunfire and went down in the

# Maritime Patrol

*Land-based naval air power in action*

Land-based naval aircraft continued to fly unpublicized missions which often crossed borders as they sought to block the north-south flow of weapons and supplies. The US Navy's use of the Lockheed P-2 Neptune patrol bomber was not limited to any single geographical sector.

VO-67, the only 'observation' squadron in the Navy in two decades, had operated the OP-2E variant of the Neptune against the Ho Chi Minh Trail, flying from Nakon Phanom, Thailand, in unique jungle-green camouflage during 1967-68. Anti-submarine sensors were removed and provisions were made for window-mounted machine-gun stations. A camera installation was positioned in a bulge beneath the fuselage under the tail. The Navy's contribution to the

*An AP-2H Neptune of VAH-21 at NAF Cam Ranh Bay in about 1969. These gunship Neptunes carried sensors for night interdiction and engine exhaust silencers to reduce detectibility during their low-level missions.*

NVA-dominated A Shau Valley near the Laotian border. North Vietnamese gunners shot down and killed the rescue commander in his A-1 Skyraider. There appeared to be no way that a new rescue commander could authorize helicopters to move in when NVA gunfire was so heavy. The entire mission might have to be abandoned, leaving the Phantom crew to their fate.

*Often overlooked for its dynamic role in Southeast Asia was the ageing but formidable Neptune in its traditional guise as a maritime patrol ship. This Lockheed SP-2H of Patrol Squadron One (VP-1, alias the 'Fleet's Finest') is stalking North Vietnamese infiltration vessels during a 'Market Time' patrol over the South China Sea. With both piston and turbojet power, Neptune crews took a perverse pride in the gruelling length of 10- to 12-hour sorties with "two turnin' and two burnin'".*

already-described 'Igloo White' program, the OP-2E was used to drop Spikebuoy and Adsid acoustical sensors along the North Vietnamese infiltration routes. This was to prove a vain attempt to build an electronic 'shroud'

*The interior of the Neptune was roomy (though with no place on board where a man could stand erect). The glazed nose offered a high-visibility perch from which to snoop and direct an aerial attack.*

around North Vietnam.

VAH-21, a heavy attack squadron at Cam Ranh Bay, flew heavily instrumented AP-2H Neptunes with the TRIM (Trails and Roads Interdiction, Multi-Sensor) electro-optical system in bombing missions against the Trail in 1968/69. Equipped with cannons, grenade launchers, forward-looking infra-red (FLIR) and low-light level television (LLLTV), the AP-2H Neptune

was in essence the Navy's version of the fixed-wing gunship. These aircraft were painted in a new multi-shade, mottled gray paint scheme with reduced-size national insignia. The LLLTV unit was mounted in the chin beneath the nose and required extra windows in that area.

More traditional patrol squadrons such as VP-1 operated SP-2H Neptunes in 'Market Time' operations. These were an

all embracing air and sea campaign against enemy coastal and river traffic. The aim was simple: to interdict supplies intended for the Viet Cong from coming to South Vietnam by sea.

*In 1969, US warplanes were not bombing North Vietnam. However, the US Navy pressured infiltration routes with VAH-21's four, mottled-gray TRIM-equipped (Trails and Roads Interdiction, Multi-sensor) AP-2H Neptunes.*

A decision was made to attempt a rescue using riot control munitions. Skyraiders from the 8th Special Operations Squadron at Pleiku were loaded up with CBU-19 tear gas ordnance and proceeded to the scene. Running a gauntlet of 37-mm and 57-mm anti-aircraft fire, the Skyraiders flew straight and level at less than 100 meters for almost two kilometers, dispensing the bombs on NVA anti-aircraft gun positions. An HH-3E Jolly Green helicopter, its crew wearing gas masks, was ready and moved in while North Vietnamese gun crews retched, coughed, and choked. The helicopter pick-up brought the F-4 pilot out of harm's way.

Beginning in April, Project 'Misty Bronco' was a test to evaluate the effectiveness of armed OV-10A Broncos providing an immediate Air Force strike presence just as readily available to ground troops as their own artillery. This meant arming Broncos with rockets and gun-pods, and enhancing communication between air and ground. The concept of using the OV-10A as a kind of flying artillery piece was deemed successful and the arming of all OV-10As was authorized on 10 June 1969.

## Small wars

With the war itself readjusting to a new administration in Washington and the entire breadth of North Vietnam off-limits to US warplanes, 1969 was apparently the year of the "little guy in the little airplane", to quote Captain Verne Saxon – as thousands of men struggled to keep the fight going amidst confusion of purpose and flagging morale.

Saxon, with the 19th Tactical Air Support Squadron and flying his O-1 from a detachment near Pleiku, never hesitated in his determination to do his job and get his part of the war taken care of. When a proposal was lofted to rename the forward air controller (FAC) and make him a forward air guide, Saxon and his buddies shouted up a storm in protest over the acronym likely to result from the change. They continued, however, to fly their fragile O-1 Bird Dogs in harm's way.

Perhaps the littlest guy of all was the PJ, or para-rescue jumper, who flew as a crew member on a rescue helicopter and mastered a variety of special operations skills to save downed airmen.

*The Cessna O-2 Skymaster made a snappy entry into combat, eyeballing a North Vietnamese battalion on its first sortie as a FAC (forward air controller). The 'off-the-shelf' O-2, based on a general aviation design, joined Cessna's O-1 Bird Dog. The O-2B version drew duty in 'psychological operations' with leaflets and loudspeakers.*

On 18 February 1969 Sergeant Michael E. Fish, a PJ from Detachment 11, 38th Aerospace Rescue and Recovery Squadron, responded to the crash of a US Army UH-1 Huey in a hostile area approximately 25-miles (40-km) south-west of Tuy Hoa. Five men were reported trapped inside the Huey wreckage.

A Kaman HH-43 Huskie, or 'Pedro', helicopter reached the scene and lowered Fish and a firefighter to the ground. Despite sporadic enemy fire, three of the trapped survivors were quickly freed and hoisted aboard the HH-43. Another survivor and a deceased soldier were extracted by another Army Huey. Still, one

# Phantoms to the Fore

The F-4 Phantom, already well established for its role in the out-country fighting, was becoming increasingly important within South Vietnam and was soon to be almost as visible as the ubiquitous F-100 Super Sabre. It had become the dominant tactical aircraft in the battle zone, the Navy and Marine Corps operating the F-4B and F-4J, the Air Force flying the F-4C, RF-4C, F-4D and F-4E. News releases from the period showed Phantoms carrying heavy bombloads on missions 'in Southeast Asia' – the closest anyone came to publicly admitting that, in addition to the continuing struggle in South Vietnam, American fliers were operating in Laos.

On a close-support mission the F-4 could carry eight 340-kg bombs or napalm tanks, or a variety of rockets and rocket projectiles. The extra crewman in the back seat gave the Phantom pilot an extra pair of eyes and ears, an extra opinion, and sometimes the edge over the battlefield which enabled the pilot to overcome the disadvantages of a fast jet and achieve accuracy while bombing. Working with a forward air controller, a flight of four F-4

*Hauling an air-to-air missile load on a MiGCAP (MiG combat air patrol), a USAF F-4 Phantom snuggles up to a KC-135 tanker to refuel. Phantoms overcame maintenance headaches to excel at a variety of combat missions.*

Phantoms could bring a truly devastating amount of ordnance into the fray.

But the Phantom was also expensive, sophisticated and difficult to maintain. It did not like the wet gloom which often hung over Vietnam at low level, or the red dust which seemed to get everywhere in the dry season. Its afterburning J-79 engines infuriated crews with their long, black exhaust plumes which made an inviting target for Viet Cong gunners. Even so, men who flew the Phantom respected the aircraft and consciously sought to avoid mistakes.

The Marines, who were always asked to do more with less, were flying some of the oldest F-4B Phantoms at the time the Navy

*Rolling in, this Phantom displays the broad, bent wings and the 'double ugly' look of a twin-jet with unprecedented, brute power. When hit by gunfire, the sturdy Phantom often got home safely.*

had already introduced, and was rapidly shifting to, the improved F-4J model. Neither had a gun. Marine pilots bolted on cannon

pods and used the Phantom to strafe the enemy, wondering why such a superb aircraft had been built without guns.

*Marines hunker down and get help from a brace of Phantoms. 'Fast movers' were seldom as accurate as prop-driven aircraft like the A-1 Skyraider, but in the right hands the Phantom could be potent when summoned to support 'troops in contact'.*

*F-4D Phantom of the 366th Tactical Fighter Wing from Da Nang, the 'Gunfighters'. This proud outfit introduced a cannon pod in an aircraft that had been designed for missile armament only. There were no MiG kills in 1969 but more were to come.*

injured man remained trapped inside the downed helicopter.

As night fell, Fish's own helicopter was forced to depart. Enemy forces attempted to infiltrate the position but Fish and friendly troops fought them off. Early on the morning of 19 February, still under sporadic fire, the rescue HH-43 returned. Fish freed the trapped survivor and finally all were evacuated from the area. "The hardest part of it all for me," said Fish, "was appearing later on the TV program *This Is Your Life* and being treated like a celebrity."

In March 1969, PACAF's first F-4C 'Wild Weasel' aircraft arrived at Yokota AB and was assigned to the 347th TFW. Thirty-six F-4Cs were modified for the electronic-warfare role, giving them the ability to carry Shrike missiles for action against SAM sites. They could be distinguished externally by a small antenna 'bump' on the fuselage side above the wing root. It was not yet their time, but the Phantom 'Wild Weasels' of the Kadena-based 67th TFS/18th TFW would eventually fly anti-missile missions over

North Vietnam, replacing the F-100F, F-105F and F-105G.

The 37th TFW at Phu Cat AB was deactivated on 31 March 1969, while the 12th TFW wing designation was moved from Cam Ranh Bay to Phu Cat, as the latter airfield replaced F-100D Super Sabres with F-4D Phantoms.

The AGM-12E Bullpup, a modified version of the earlier AGM-12B with a cluster warhead, was introduced into Southeast Asia combat, almost certainly in action in Laos, in April. The new missile was employed by the F-4 Phantom wings at Da Nang and Udorn.

## The first step backwards

Saigon's President Thieu visited Korea from 27 May to 3 June, his first trip to an ally which had put two divisions totalling nearly 50,000 troops on the ground in South Vietnam. Presidents Nixon and Thieu met at Midway Island on 8 June. General Abrams was present. The withdrawal of 25,000 US servicemen from Vietnam

**The Phantom**
With its two 17,000-lb (7711-kg) thrust General Electric J79-GE-15 afterburning turbojets, the bent-wing, two-seat F-4C Phantom was capable of 910 km/h (1464 km/h, or Mach 1.19) at low level. Building this magnificent, multi-role fighter without a gun was a mistake, but few other flaws marred its stellar performance.

**Destructive cargo**
Designed to carry up to 16,000 lb (7257 kg) of bombs and missiles on five wing and fuselage pylons, the F-4C could carry 18 750-lb (340-kg) bombs, though a more realistic load on a long mission was eight. Other loads: 11 150-US-gal napalm tanks, four AGM-12 Bullpup ASMs, or four pods each containing 19 2.75-in (96-cm) rocket projectiles.

**Colorless killer**
US Air Force Phantoms initially wore – and went to Vietnam with – the same gray/white paint scheme which adorned Navy combat aircraft throughout the conflict. Camouflage, not widely used since early-World War II, was introduced as the American buildup progressed in 1965. Two-letter tailcodes to identify squadrons began to appear in 1966. In 1972, tailcodes were allocated to Air Force combat wings rather than individual squadrons, a practice still in widespread use today.

## Doomed warrior

**Although more advanced versions of the Phantom were now entering service, many of the aircraft holding the line in Vietnam were older F-4Cs. Peeling paint and air-to-air missile load augmented by a centerline gun-pod were typical of the era. This aircraft, its tailcode indicating the 558th TFS/12th TFW at Cam Ranh Bay, had been shot down by a North Vietnamese SAM in December 1966, Captain Kenneth W. Cordier and backseater 1st Lt Bob Lane becoming POWs.**

was ordered, the first really significant attempt to wind down the war and turn it over to the South Vietnamese. The US actually withdrew the 25,000 men by late August, a remarkable reversal of the established trend of increase after increase.

For all his talk of ending the war President Nixon had not officially committed himself to a total withdrawal. He felt that the pace at which South Vietnam could take over the bulk of its defense was dependent upon balancing domestic opinion against both Communist activity and South Vietnamese capabilities. Nixon had inherited the Paris peace talks and, with them, had also acquired their frustrating lack of concrete negotiation and progress.

Nevertheless, the mere talk of 'getting out' had a devastating effect on the morale of American soldiers in South Vietnam. Many were draftees. Most had been willing enough to take risks and fight as long as they saw a purpose, but the news of withdrawal seemed to undermine any sense of purpose. Sagging morale led to the first

reports of men using drugs, of racial tensions, and of 'fragging' – killing your own officers with weapons intended for use on the enemy. Perhaps the worst indication came in September, when US Army Lieutenant William Calley was charged with war crimes in the previous year's My Lai massacre.

The collapse of morale probably had the smallest impact on pilots and aircrew, who were more likely to be volunteers and professionals. Still, even among Air Force and Navy support people, evidence of low spirits was everywhere. The rate of AWOLs (absences without leave) went up 20.3 per cent from 1967 to 1969. A few Americans simply deserted – some of them proceeding to Sweden for refuge.

Unburdened with morale problems, the Viet Cong launched country-wide attacks on installations and population centers in mid-May. Meanwhile, the National Liberation Front offered a 10-point peace proposal at the stagnated talks in Paris. The offer came on 8 May

1969, virtually a year after the talks had opened on 10 May 1968.

On 5 June 1969, North Vietnamese AAA batteries hit an RF-4C Phantom from the 11th TRS/432nd TRW at Udorn. The reconnaissance aircraft limped out of North Vietnam and crashed at sea. In retaliation, the Nixon administration ordered the first air strikes into North Vietnam since the end of 'Rolling Thunder' eight months earlier. A limited number of strikes by Air Force and Navy aircraft were carried out against AAA, SAM and radar sites associated with the shootdown. Later, Defense Secretary Melvin Laird would give them a name by coining one of the unforgettable terms of the war – the "limited duration, protective reaction air strike".

Carrier-based Navy aircraft continued to handle a major part of the reconnaissance commitment over North Vietnam; the production line for the RA-5C Vigilante was reopened and a number of RF-8A Crusaders were brought up to RF-8G standard. But the Air Force's ageing and corrosion-prone RF-101C Voodoo remained the principal tactical recce asset 'up North', only gradually being replaced by the RF-4C Phantom. Strategic reconnaissance by RC-135s, SR-71s and other platforms continued at a reduced level, the aircraft following flight paths tailored to avoid any accusation of provocation by Hanoi.

## B-52 raids reduced

On 15 July, as another token step in winding down the war and just a week before Korean War veteran Neil Armstrong made his 'one giant leap for mankind' on the moon, the number of authorized B-52 sorties was reduced by 200 to a rate of 1,600 per month. They were further reduced to 1,400 in October.

One of the most important pronouncements of the war came from President Nixon on 25 July 1969 during a visit to Guam. Known at first as the Guam Doctrine and later as the Nixon Doctrine, it said that the Asian allies would provide the bulk of the manpower in their own defense and the US would support them with outside aid.

Translated into plain English, it meant that Nixon was going to withdraw Americans from South Vietnam in response to domestic opposition, and that Saigon was going to have to defend itself, with US-supplied weapons. In short, US servicemen would not be

*An RA-5C Vigilante comes aboard USS Enterprise (CVAN-65). Operating from the decks of larger carriers throughout the Southeast Asia fray, eight Vigilante squadrons suffered grievous losses, with 27 RA-5Cs succumbing to enemy gunfire or to mishaps.*

**I**mportant to the war on the ground in South Vietnam – described by American soldier Sid Reeder as a "stinking, lousy, gut-wrenching point-blank slugfest" – was the progress being made with the USAF's fixed-wing gunships. The employment of sideways-firing guns on an aircraft making a pylon turn at low level over 'Charlie' and the NVA – begun dramatically with the AC-47 'Gooney Bird' – had now extended to an entire family of gunships.

Eerie names from the spirit world identified these aeroplanes: 'Spooky' was the twin-engined AC-47, also known as 'Puff the Magic Dragon', now used regularly to relieve besieged friendly outposts, especially at night. 'Spectre' was the name assigned to the AC-130 gunship – bigger, heavier, with four engines, long range, and greater loiter time and now being refined and enhanced under an improvement program known as 'Surprise Package'.

'Shadow' was the AC-119G Flying Boxcar and 'Stinger' the AC-119K version, equipped with two General Electric turbojets which increased its ability to evade enemy gunfire. In due course it was planned that AC-47 and AC-119 gunships would be flown not merely by the USAF

*Gunships were among the few weapons which could seize control of the night from the Viet Cong. Orbiting unseen high in the sky, they could deliver an awesome amount of fire.*

but by the VNAF as well.

Flying in a gunship was not exactly like airline travel. At low altitude, the aircraft could buck and tremble in turbulence, to which was added the confusing and disorientating effect of flares and muzzle flashes.

The early AC-130A Spectre, a sinister black, armed version of the ubiquitous Hercules transport, was operating primarily in the out-country war, flying night missions to attack men, vehicles and supplies moving south over the infiltration route known as the Ho Chi Minh Trail. The Trail was a spiderweb-like network of supply routes which began in North Vietnam and reached the South either by directly crossing the DMZ (demilitarized zone) or by swinging around to the west, poking through Laos, and then stabbing into South Vietnam to terminate in the A Shau Valley or

*Gunships like the AC-130 'Spectre' wreaked havoc and terror on their targets, usually at night. On the morning after, the scene resembled a moonscape ripped asunder, devoid of life.*

*Fire-control operators aboard the AC-130 gunship – the US Air Force's term for men earlier known as gunners – lived in a dark cavern of hi-tech, coping with the stress of pylon-turn maneuvers and stalking the VC.*

*The AC-119G 'Shadow' (above) and the jet-boosted AC-119K 'Stinger' spearheaded a second generation of gunships, between the AC-47 and AC-130. The 'Dollar Nineteen' was not easy to fly but was a potent foe in battle.*

farther south around Kontum.

By 1969, supplies were coming down the Ho Chi Minh Trail in trucks and their numbers were going up exponentially. "It gets bumper-to-bumper like the Los Angeles freeway," said one of the early AC-130 pilots. Even then, at night, over hostile terrain, cutting off the supplies was no easy task.

The 'Surprise Package' improvements to the AC-130A 'Spectre' were intended to give the gunship greater stand-off range to improve its capacity for survival and better night-targeting equipment. Two of the AC-130A's four 20-mm Gatling-type guns were to be replaced with 40-mm Bofors cannon. A variety of improved sensors were to be installed, including FLIR, low-light-level television, a Black Crow direction-finding radar, and a digital fire-control computer. 'Surprise Package' aircraft reached Southeast Asia by year's end.

The AC-130 gunship worked effectively as part of a 'hunter killer' team when operating in conjunction with F-4D Phantoms or B-26K Invaders. "We just loved working over the Trail with the B-26Ks from Naked Fanny," said Hercules pilot Curt Messex.

"They moved at about the same speed as us, carried an inexhaustible amount of ordnance, and could roam over the Trail with us all night long. They were professionals, every one of them, and they were always ready to take on the other guys in a fight." The B-26Ks were eventually withdrawn from action later in 1969, worn out from accumulating too many airframe hours.

## Laser designation

When working with Phantoms, the gunships detected and used lasers to illuminate targets for F-4Ds carrying precision-guided munitions (PGM), or 'smart' bombs. AC-130s attacking North Vietnamese truck convoys were often engaged by anti-aircraft or SAM batteries which, in turn, came under attack from the escorting F-4Ds.

The AC-119G Shadow was more important within South Vietnam. It had four GAU-2B/A 7.62-mm machine-guns, 50,000 rounds of ammunition for day operations (35,000 rounds and 60 flares for night), and ceramic armor protection for a crew of six to eight. The 'Shadow' began

operational sorties and its combat evaluation in January 1969 and the USAF's 71st Special Operations Squadron under Lieutenant Colonel James E. Pyle was up to strength by 11 March.

As part of the deployment codenamed 'Coronet Hornet', the first six examples of the jet-augmented AC-119K 'Stinger', belonging to the 18th Special Operations Squadron under Lieutenant Colonel Ernest E. Johnson, arrived at Phan Rang. With two AC-119 squadrons in South Vietnam, the USAF deactivated its two AC-47 squadrons and scattered their machines among Laotian and South Vietnamese units.

A typical ground-support

mission by the gunship occurred on 7 June 1969 when enemy forces tried to over-run Fire Base Crook, a 25th Infantry Division outpost in Tay Ninh Province. Fighters and both AC-47 and AC-119G gunships were called in to help the fire base's defenders. While fighters delivered high-explosive and napalm, the gunships roved over the area using flares and miniguns. In a characteristic example of the oft-used and oft-deceiving body count, friendly forces later found 323 enemy dead. Prisoners told of being awed by the gunships.

*The 'executive office' of a gunship offered few comforts, guaranteed motion sickness, and some prospect of being zapped.*

# The Little Guy's War

*Forward air controllers*

The Cessna A-37 'Dragonfly' was powerful, robust, and heavier than the T-37 'Tweet' primary trainer on which it was based. It was ideal for the Vietnamese Air Force (VNAF) but Americans flew it too: this one was in the USAF 604th Special Operations Squadron at Bien Hoa.

expected to do the bleeding and dying in Asian wars. To most people the new policy meant something called 'Vietnamization'. The war would be 'Vietnamized'. Critics argued that this was exactly what the Viet Cong had been trying to do all along.

On 15 August Defense Secretary Melvin Laird issued a statement formalizing the Nixon Doctrine by assigning new missions to US troops – in effect, reducing their combat role and turning more of the ground fighting over to Saigon's troops.

## Starting to withdraw

The initial increment of the American withdrawal, known as Operation 'Keystone Eagle', was completed on 29 August. President Nixon was now able to show the American public that 25,000 young men had been pulled out and brought home. This was only a token to anti-war protesters and really satisfied no-one, but the policy was continued. On 16 September Nixon ordered the second round of withdrawals, involving 35,000 troops by mid-December. The second round was known as 'Operation Keystone Cardinal'. On 15 December the President announced the withdrawal of 50,000 more troops from Southeast Asia by 15 April 1970.

As part of Vietnamization, the newly designated and activated VNAF 8th and 90th Attack Squadrons at Bien Hoa were fully equipped with the improved A-37B by the end of December, adding to the strength of VNAF fighter squadrons already described. Earlier models of the A-37 in Vietnam were also slated for replacement by A-37Bs. Plans existed to increase the size of the VNAF by no fewer than 1,100 additional aircraft.

Looking at its achievements in 1969, the USAF's history for the period pointed out: "The improvement and modernization program for the VNAF, formalized in 1968, was greatly expanded and stepped up in 1969. Seventh Air Force was directed to place as much emphasis on training the VNAF as on conducting combat operations. The VNAF was to be doubled in size by 1972, with more modern and effective aircraft. The ultimate goal was for the VNAF to be self-sufficient in all areas and capable of handling the combined VC/NVA threat."

While an argument raged as to whether the war was being won – whether, indeed, the Saigon government was winning the 'hearts and minds' of its people – on 4 September 1969 North Vietnam announced the death of Ho Chi Minh at age 79. The charismatic Hanoi leader who had devoted a lifetime to ridding his land of foreign occupiers left the reins of leadership in the hands of party head Le Duan and Prime Minister Pham Van Dong. In name only, there was still a separate Viet Cong leadership in the South but in fact, 'Victor Charlie' was a spent force, no longer independent, who

On a typical mission, forward air controller Captain Verne Saxon would slip a flak vest over his flight coveralls, stash the nearly useless parachute in the back seat, and take the O-1 off for a mission lasting between one and three hours, pinpointing enemy troops and guiding in fighter-bombers.

"At one point I got into a personal disagreement with some Viet Cong in black pajamas who had laid siege to an ARVN fire base and would neither attack nor go away. When fighters were not immediately available, I went down in my O-1 and zapped some smoke rockets at them, hoping somehow that the small, lightweight projectiles would do 'Victor Charlie' some harm. I got some muzzle flashes – in daylight,

it's usually hard to see them shooting at you – and I actually saw one of my rockets scatter some of them!"

They were shooting at Saxon and he had nothing with which to shoot back. After some time, he was given a flight of F-100s and was able to direct them to accurate bombing passes on the enemy, which solved his and the ARVN problem.

A FAC's most rewarding experience was often his direct communication with Army troops on the ground. These men might be mere specks to the pilot of a fast-moving jet fighter, but in an O-1 Bird Dog they became very personal.

"I never forgot that we were helping out the footsoldier on the ground. No matter what the politicians might think the war was for, we always got satisfaction out of knowing we were helping our own guys."

The US Army created the O-1 Bird Dog (known in the Korean War as the L-19) but by the time Vietnam boiled over, this high-visibility pilot's perch was the 'front office' for US and Vietnamese Army and Air Force FACs, or forward air controllers.

# Corsair Recollections

The aircraft-carrier remained a high-tension, high-risk place to work, while the carrier-based pilot continued to plunge ahead with perhaps the most dangerous occupation of all. Apart from the undeclared and unadmitted war in Laos, the bombing of North Vietnam remained off-limits, so naval air power was used to a greater extent in the South.

Lieutenant Ben Short communicated some of the flavor of Corsair missions in a personal log. "We lost one pilot during the first line period by USS *Independence* (CVA-62), Randy Ford. He was out on an early

Vought A-7 Corsair ready to be slammed aloft by a carrier's steam catapult. By 1969, the 'Sluf' was replacing A-4 Skyhawks in light-attack units.

*The sheer enormity of the forward air controller's job is being confronted by this O-1 Bird Dog jock in the Central Highlands. He must control his finicky, lightweight aircraft, keep up steady communication, find the Viet Cong, call in the 'fast movers', and avoid gunfire – all on a mission he usually flies solo with an empty back seat.*

*An O-1G Bird Dog (51-11976), nicknamed Little Puff, was one of two modified to test the effectiveness of a .30-caliber (7.62-mm) M60A1 machine-gun rigged in the back seat, and examined here by Captain Roger Krell. This experiment proved impractical but O-1 pilots often fired M16 rifles or pistols from their cockpits.*

*A-7 Corsairs of VA-93 'Ravens', a squadron on USS Midway (CVA-41) haul bombs into harm's way. A-7s replaced A-4 Skyhawks in light-attack squadrons. Now, pilots had the fuel to rove anywhere in North Vietnam and strike at will.*

the other A-7s was so badly holed he ran out of gas over the gulf heading for Da Nang. Only the third A-7 survived. We picked up the skipper [who had ejected safely] the next morning and also got the pilot out of the Gulf. The two F-4 [crew members] were captured."

*This A-7 Corsair pilot, if typical, is pumping more adrenaline on approach to the carrier than he did confronting North Vietnamese flak. The A-7 had a fine safety record at sea and a good chance of survival if it hit while aloft.*

morning flight and suddenly ejected. While on the ground he never said [over his beeper radio] what happened. We surmise he was captured just about sun-up. I launched just before dawn, and talked to him a couple of times. We learned many years later that he died, shortly after he was taken prisoner."

There was the continuing problem with bomb fuses, which caused bombs to explode the instant the pilot pressed the pickle button. "The skipper [of squadron VA-86] was out on a night mission in South Vietnam with an Air Force F-4 leading on a LORAN drop [a high-altitude, instrumented bomb release]. The skipper used electrical and mechanical fusing for a straight and level drop from 16,000 ft [4877 m] and one of the electric fuses went off at the end of safe separation time. It blew the skipper's aircraft and the F-4 out of the sky almost instantly. One of

now took his marching orders from Ho's northerners.

Because it was such a difficult war to evaluate, symbols were important, and Saigon's Thieu and Ky were never able to muster the popular appeal that Ho had enjoyed. The struggle for the will of the people was serious – the Americans even had department of State officers humping around in the boondocks, lugging M-16 rifles and preaching civic action – but in the absence of visible military success it was hard to claim that moral success was being achieved. It was not true, as a Green Beret lieutenant asserted, that "if you grab 'em by the balls, their hearts and minds will follow".

On 20 September 1969 an F-4D Phantom of the 366th Tactical Fighter Wing at Da Nang collided in mid-air with an Air Vietnam DC-4 approximately two miles north of the air base. The DC-4 crashed, killing 75 people on board and two on the ground. The Phantom landed safely only after its backseater ejected.

On 8 October 1969, Souvanna Phouma, the neutralist premier of Laos, requested increased American aid to meet pressure from North Vietnamese forces operating in his country. The request drew almost no public notice, like the continued bombing missions being flown in that country.

### Canberras leave – for the moment

Also in October 1969, the Canberra bomber was finally withdrawn. The 8th TBS was inactivated and its B-57s ferried to the continental US for storage. The B-57 had been among the first US aircraft to deploy to Vietnam and the departure of these airframes left no American Canberras in the war zone, although Tropic Moon B-57G aircraft would return a year later on 15 September 1970.

In another October move, the 44th TFS moved from Korat to Takhli, thus ending the presence of the F-105 at the former base and concentrating all Southeast Asia Thunderchiefs at the latter.

The 41st TEWS at Udorn was made inactive on 31 October 1969 and its EB-66 aircraft were redistributed to other units or returned to the US. During November, detachments of F-102A Delta Dagger aircraft at Udorn and Da Nang – never really significant participants in the conflict – were withdrawn. The 609th SOS operating the B-26K Invader at Nakhon Phanom was also deactivated in November and its aircraft returned to the US the following month. Finally, the US presence at Nha Trang AB, where the 'Green Hornet' Huey helicopters of the 20th SOS had operated, was ended entirely – another step towards Vietnamization, as the airfield was now occupied solely by South Vietnamese units.

The hard-working Vietnamese Air Force (VNAF) was now becoming a jet force. This was not necessarily a good thing: earlier attempts to provide the Vietnamese with advanced warplanes had foundered on the rock of providing adequately trained service and technical support.

Nevertheless, the Cessna A-37

As a measure of the low level of operations directed against the North during the long bombing halt, figures showed that during 1969 only 779 out of 966,949 combat sorties in Southeast Asia were flown over North Vietnam by USAF aircraft. By contrast, B-52s flew 19,498 Arc Light strikes in Laos and South Vietnam.

The numbers count for 1969 held that Air Force aircraft losses for the year were 294, or 97 fewer than in 1968. The total number of USAF aircraft lost in Southeast Asia was put at 1,783, valued at $2,254,948,000.

One number really meant something. For the first time, figures proved that the war, at least on the American side, was winding down. By 31 December 1969, the number of US troops in South Vietnam had been reduced to 474,000. During the final six months of the year, USAF strength in Southeast Asia was reduced from 96,372 to 92,086.

*A Douglas A-26A (B-26K) Invader of the 609th Special Operations Squadron at Nakhon Phanom air base, Thailand prepares to launch on the type's final combat mission. These veterans of World War II and Korea using the callsign Nimrod, struck repeatedly at the Ho Chi Minh Trail and in Laos and North Vietnam.*

Dragonfly, derived from the T-37 basic trainer, was very effective in Vietnamese hands, perhaps in part due to its simplicity.

## Squadron service

By early 1969 no fewer than 54 A-37s were in action with three VNAF squadrons. An ambitious program was under way in the US to train Vietnamese pilots on this aircraft.

The A-37 really was simple, but it was also a tough, potent fighting machine. The pilot sat

*Ready to draw blood is an A-37B Dragonfly of the Vietnamese Air Force's 514th Fighter Squadron at Bien Hoa. By the time the A-37 reached them, VNAF pilots had thousands of combat sorties and transitioned easily to the jet.*

beneath a high round clamshell cockpit. Although the aircraft had been conceived as a two-seater, it was almost always flown by one man. This had some disadvantages. It was hard to roll in on a target from the right, for example, for visibility was less effective on the side located away from the pilot. But the six-tonne A-37 could carry a formidable load of napalm or HE (high explosive) bombs and was fast enough to be relatively immune to Viet Cong ground fire. It was no Phantom, but it was just what the Vietnamese needed.

First deliveries were of the A-37A model, which was a rebuild of the T-37 trainer. Soon afterwards came the sturdier A-37B, a new-build aircraft.

A young and energetic officer, Nguyen Cao Nguyen, had the thankless job of being the Vietnamese Air Force's chief of maintenance. Nguyen began work with the 83rd Special Group, Premier Nguyen Cao Ky's outfit, equipped with A-1H Skyraiders and C-47 transports. The C-47s were used to drop special operations troops – often, it was widely rumored, inside North Vietnam.

"Maintenance never received the resources it needed," says Nguyen.

Nguyen remembers an occasion when Ky visited a base under fire from the Viet Cong. Ky's wife Mai was present. "A very average pilot" was how Nguyen described the dashing prime minister. "He climbs in, he doesn't know where the starter is." But Ky was also a man of unquestioned bravery. When the mortar rounds started to come in, "he refused to hide from the incoming fire".

According to Nguyen, the VNAF had considerable difficulty keeping the Cessna A-37 and Northrop F-5s in the air. These

types had been chosen precisely because they were simple and easily maintained, and America had gone to some length to set up an effective supply line for needed parts and equipment. "Somehow we always had everything but what we wanted."

There were some leadership problems, says Nguyen, because Ky appointed officers who were better known for their loyalties than their strengths. "The A-37 may have been cost-effective, but was not an improvement over the Skyraider."

The hand-over of 20 A-37A

*Turning wrenches on the 'Spad' was no easy task. A-1s had generations of wiring in wings and fuselage. Some was still functional, but there were some wires for which no-one could remember the original purpose. VNAF ground crews did well, learning as they went along.*

Dragonflies to the VNAF's 524th Fighter Squadron at Nha Trang was accomplished with considerable ceremony on 19 April 1969. Major Dang Duy Lac, squadron commander, praised the aircraft. Less fanfare attended the equipping of the 526th and 528th Squadrons with the same aircraft.

Another VNAF 'first' occurred with the conversion to turbo-powered Bell UH-1H Huey helicopters in mid-1969. Three VNAF squadrons had converted from H-34s to UH-1Hs by the end of the year.

"We were receiving equipment very rapidly," says Nguyen. "Some of us worked very hard to integrate it into our forces. We were not always sure we succeeded."

*The Northrop F-5 Freedom Fighter was trumpeted as a low-cost, no-frills warplane for a Third World budget. The VNAF had skilled, dedicated pilots and maintenance men but little jet experience and did not take immediately to the F-5A/B/C of 1969, nor to the later F-5E of the early 1970s. 'Out of commission' rates were high.*

*The A-37 was an 'off-the-shelf' item deemed ideal for the VNAF. Following a combat evaluation, the Dragonfly began to reach Vietnamese units in November 1968. Ultimately, 12 squadrons of the VNAF operated the type. Operating costs were reasonable, and the few A-37As and many A-37Bs were effective as air-to-ground warriors.*

# HOLDING THE LINE

**Americans drew some encouragement from the public commitment of the Nixon administration to end the US role in Southeast Asia by 'Vietnamization'. But growing numbers were still not satisfied. They wanted out immediately, even if it meant leaving South Vietnam in the lurch.**

The objective of the 'Vietnamization' program was progressively to transfer to Saigon's forces responsibility for all aspects of the war. Since the South Vietnamese armed forces had grown to nearly one million men, out of a population of only 17 million, an enormous strain was placed on the technical and administrative skills of the country's civilian and military leaders.

The effort included enhancing the VNAF's capabilities. Vietnamization efforts focused on in-country improvements to maintenance and logistical capabilities, and improved equipment. By the end of the year the VNAF was able to fly approximately 50 per cent of the in-country combat sorties and was successfully planning and conducting complex operations, including interdiction, close air support, and troop lift missions.

As yet another symbol of the 'drawing down' of the US presence, three US fighter squadrons at Cam Ranh Bay were deactivated on 31 March 1970, and the 12th Tactical Fighter Wing was moved to Phu Cat; the change released three squadrons of F-4C Phantoms which returned to the USA.

In spite of considerable growth, some plans to bolster Saigon's air arm did not work out successfully. The VNAF's brief experience with the B-57 Canberra bomber had been a failure, apparently because the B-57 was too sophisticated for the people charged with maintaining and flying it. The VNAF apparently acquired some C-7A Caribou transports, but no record exists of their being employed operationally, for reasons not clear.

*The most familiar sight of the war – a Huey at an LZ. Landing zones were sometimes hacked out of the jungle with sweat, toil and sharp machete blades. With a fuselage stretch of 3 ft 5 in (1.07 m), the UH-1H model replaced the UH-1B as the US Army's standard in Vietnam. Bell turned out 5,435 UH-1Hs and nearly half were lost in the conflict.*

# VNAF F-5s

*Pesky but troubled jet lightweights*

The Vietnamese Air Force continued to grow, probably at a greater rate than its personnel could handle. VNAF pilots flying the Northrop F-5 were getting better and better with their lightweight, nimble fighter-bomber. The F-5 was effective in close support operations, including many flown in support of the Cambodian episode. The twin-engined configuration of the Northrop fighter greatly improved its prospects for survival when hit, while its supersonic speed reduced the chances of getting hit in the first place.

The F-5A and virtually identical F-5C used by the VNAF were extremely reliable but there were occasional problems. As had sometimes happened with the wing tanks of the F-4 Phantom, it was found that 750-lb (340-kg) napalm tanks sometimes failed to separate cleanly from the F-5's ordnance pylons. At their worst, the napalm tanks bucked and hit the underside of the wing. The F-5 was also prone to trouble when its guns caused the windshield to cloud up during a firing run.

The integration of the F-5A/C into the VNAF was perhaps only slightly more troublesome than

that of the A-37, yet for more than five years the 522nd remained the only F-5 squadron.

USAF Lieutenant George Swannman went for a flight in one of the few two-seat F-5B Freedom Fighters assigned to the VNAF, an aircraft which in performance was identical to the F-5A/C. Not solely a trainer, the combat-capable F-5B was carrying two 750-lb (340-kg) HE bombs. It was one of four F-5s

being scrambled to attempt contact with Viet Cong troops spotted in the field not far from Bien Hoa, to which the VNAF F-5 squadron had moved from Tan Son Nhut in January 1968.

## Tiger in an F-5

"My pilot was a young lieutenant who had been through the F-5 training syllabus in the US," said Swannman. "He was a spindly guy with glasses but inside that F-5, he became a tiger. Have you ever heard of a fighter pilot getting motion sickness? I almost did, in the back seat with that guy. The F-5 can handle something like six Gs fairly easily, and he wasn't reluctant to fling it around the sky."

Swannman was impressed that the flight of four F-5s pilots went

*A study in contrasts. The A-1 (background) was old, heavy, and difficult to maintain. The F-5 was new, light, carried less, went half as far – and was equally a headache to keep airworthy.*

*F-5A/C Freedom Fighters from a squadron of the VNAF 23rd Tactical Wing on a combat sortie from Bien Hoa in 1970. The F-5 required more maintenance and logistical support than expected.*

to the trouble to make their firing passes from different directions. All too often in the past, American and Vietnamese pilots alike had made it too easy for enemy gunners on the ground. "These guys had it all orchestrated. To the observer, it must have looked as if F-5s were heading in all directions with no plan. In fact, they got back together very smoothly – just like a stunt team at an air show."

Swannman's impression was that most of the VNAF pilots were capable fliers and were willing to take risks. But for a period of time the VNAF had more F-5s than it had F-5 pilots. Later in the war, when additional squadrons of F-5As and later F-5Es came into being, this imbalance became even worse.

In the realm of the fixed-wing gunship, the 817th Attack Squadron at Nha Trang equipped with AC-47s was noticeably busy and useful. The 819th and 821st Attack Squadrons at Tan Son Nhut, equipped with the AC-119G 'Shadow' and AC-119K 'Stinger' respectively, never made a mark on the war and today there are no surviving photographs or documents from either unit.

An F-105G Thunderchief (63-8329) of the 44th TFS/355th TFW at Takhli was on a 'protective reaction' mission into North Vietnam when it was shot down on 28 January 1969. An HH-53C helicopter orbiting over Laos and awaiting clearance to enter North Vietnam to pick up the downed crew suddenly came to quick and unexpected grief. In the first encounter with a MiG since the bombing halt and perhaps the first MiG incursion into Laos, a MiG-21 shot down the HH-53C with an air-to-air missile. This is

*The backseater in the two-man F-105F and F-105G Thunderchief was a 'Bear', or EWO (electronic warfare officer) itching to take on North Vietnamese missile sites. The F-105G introduced ALQ-105 and ALT-24 jammers in fuselage pods and carried the AGM-78B Standard ARM anti-radiation missile along with the proven AGM-45 Shrike and 20-mm gun.*

The CH-47 Chinook became the 'Shithook' in the insolent jargon of the American ground soldier. The twin-tandem heavy hauler from Vertol (later Boeing) became a boon to US Army divisions which needed rapid supply by a helicopter able to accommodate a substantial load. An armed gunship version of the Chinook was less successful than the transport.

believed to be the only instance of a helicopter being downed by a fighter in this manner.

On 1 February 1970, it was noted that a more fortunate F-105D, 611-0159 of the 354th TFS/355th TFW at Takhli, had more than 4,000 airframe hours and 600 combat missions to its credit – more than any other 'Thud'. It was nicknamed 'Have Gun Will Travel', the name appearing on the fuselage below the cockpit, and was credited with a MiG kill.

On 18 March 1970, Cambodia's Prince Norodom Sihanouk was ousted by his premier, General Lon Nol. The Department of

During the 1970 sweep into Cambodia, as in other actions, US troops seized vast numbers of Soviet-bloc weapons. One was this Degtyarev 12.7-mm (.50-cal) DShK-38 gas-operated anti-aircraft cannon. The optical sight may appear crude, but the North Vietnamese were adroit at using primitive-looking equipment to achieve world-class results.

Diplomats were ordered to speak of 'force reduction' rather than a 'withdrawal' but by the end of 1970 US troop strength was down to 335,800 (from nearly twice that figure), including this helicopter door gunner with an M60 machine-gun and .30-cal (7.62-mm) ammunition.

Defense revealed that prior to March 1970, the USAF had secretly carried out 3,630 B-52 strikes in Cambodia. Sihanouk's ouster apparently did little to reduce North Vietnamese influence in Cambodia. Behind the scenes, Nixon administration officials debated the idea of a move into Cambodia to 'clean out' Hanoi's sanctuaries in that country.

The first MiG kill in nearly two years occurred when USS Constellation (CVA-64) launched another round of 'protective reaction' strikes into North Vietnam on 28 March 1970. Lt Jerome E. Beaulier of the 'Ghostriders', squadron VF-142, was at the controls of an F-4J Phantom with Lt Stephen J. Barkley in the back seat. Beaulier used an AIM-9 Sidewinder missile to despatch a MiG-21.

The 12th TFW at Phu Cat AB in South Vietnam was now fully operational in the F-4D Phantom and was eventually to have the peculiar distinction of operating over all four countries of Indochina – South Vietnam, North Vietnam, Laos and Cambodia. Like the other Phantom units scattered around the region and on board carriers at sea, its pilots kept hoping that something would change to give them a crack at a MiG. It did not, during 1970, but the 12th TFW became especially effective in the air-to-ground 'mud-moving' part of the war.

## Protest marches in Washington

On 4 April, 50,000 people gathered in Washington to protest President Nixon's conduct of the war. Their numbers would have been higher had they known what was coming next. On 21 April 1970 President Nixon announced that 150,000 more American troops were to be withdrawn from Vietnam. But if Nixon wanted to please opponents of the US role in the war, any chance he might have had disappeared with the decision that came next.

In the bland manner of official histories, a document from the period notes that "joint US and South Vietnamese operations into Cambodia were launched after Prince Sihanouk was ousted as chief of state by General Lon Nol.

"For five years," the document continued, "sanctuaries in Cambodia had afforded the enemy a safe haven and a massive supply storehouse, all secure from US air attack." The Cambodian 'incursion' (the administration's word) was designed to eliminate enemy forces and supplies in those safe havens.

US and ARVN forces launched massive ground operations into Cambodia on 30 April. The talk of 'flushing out' North Vietnamese

# 'Understanding' on Reconnaissance

*War 'up North' during the bombing halt*

**W**ith the cessation of bombing, there was supposed to be an understanding that the US would continue unarmed photo reconnaissance – primarily with tactical aircraft like the RF-101C rather than strategic platforms like the SR-71 – to observe efforts by the North Vietnamese to move men and materiel into the South.

Once recon planes started falling victim to North Vietnam's formidable defences, directives were issued to escort the photo planes with armed fighter-bombers. Colonel Ed Hillding's 469th TFS at Korat with its shark-teethed F-4E Phantoms drew this job more than once. US Navy F-4J Phantoms heavily laden with ordnance also appeared in the company of photo planes. Normally, there

***One purpose of reconnaissance flights was to pinpoint Hanoi's SA-2 Guideline SAMs. Under the 'understanding' missiles would not be fired at them. But North Vietnam did not always comply.***

were two to four fighter-bomber escorts for the recce plane, depending on the threat, the environment and anticipated hostile action.

The rules of engagement, or the specific instructions prescribing the conditions under which the fighter-bombers were authorized to attack enemy targets, prohibited counteraction except when they, or the reconnaissance aircraft being escorted, were fired upon.

The escort aircraft were required to have evidence that they or the reconnaissance aircraft they were escorting had been fired upon before they could attack the missile or anti-aircraft sites. This authority came to be known as 'protective reaction', a term which the press attributed to Defense Secretary Laird.

Over an extended period of time it was necessary continually to update and modify the rules depending upon the situation at a given time. For example, when the North Vietnamese attempted

to move their MiG force farther south and position fighters at jet-capable fields near the DMZ the terms under which MiGs could be engaged were 'loosened'. In addition to the escort aircraft protecting the recce plane from ground fire, it now became necessary to provide high-altitude MiGCAP cover as well. Likewise, the rules of engagement had to be revised when Hanoi introduced improved weaponry, such as a co-ordinated net of SAM and AAA sites centrally controlled from long range by a sophisticated version of the already familiar Fan Song radar. Thus, even during the bombing 'interlude', it was necessary to employ a stand-off anti-radiation missile such as the

***The North Vietnamese were furious about the SR-71 Blackbird. They complained but could do nothing. The spy plane whisked over their heads at 70,000 ft (2167 m) or higher, flying at three times the speed of sound. Their guns never touched it.***

Shrike or Standard ARM – carried by the F-105G, which had replaced the F-105F in the 'Wild Weasel' role. The rules were changed to permit attacking the Fan Song radar/missile sites when they were 'activated against' the reconnaissance or escort aircraft. The US might not have been bombing the North, but all that changed the moment the North Vietnamese began tracking its aircraft on radar!

***While escorting a reconnaissance mission in 1969, an F-4D Phantom of the 366th TFW, seen here as a shadow, uses its gun-pod to strafe enemy troops gathered in the I Corps region.***

***An RA-5C Vigilante (bureau no. 149284) ignites full afterburner to lift off from USS Enterprise (CVAN-65) during the bombing halt. The 'Viggie' was vital to reconnaissance work 'up North'.***

# RF-4C Mission

It was never easy being a reconnaissance pilot. Major Kent Harbaugh arrived at Tan Son Nhut in early 1970 to join the 460th Wing, flying the RF-4C Phantom. He and his fellow pilots lived in two-story concrete block billets which, except for those belonging to MACV, were the only air-conditioned buildings available. Harbaugh and his fellow pilots were flying visual daylight reconnaissance and night missions with photo-flash cartridges over South Vietnam, Laos and Cambodia.

For a daylight mission, an RF-4C pilot would go to the squadron four hours before scheduled take-off. The squadron's own truck would transport him from his billet to the ready room.

Each pilot had a small but distinctive scarf, not the flamboyant World War I type but only 1½ inches wide, used by the truck driver to identify the squadron; the scarf was removed before flight.

At the old French colonial two-story concrete Operations Building, the pilot picked up the frag order giving groupings of targets and reconnaissance parameters wanted (scale, heading, etc.) and was assigned to an individual RF-4C. After a weather briefing, pilot and backseater 'attacked the maps'. The navigator did pre-mission paperwork while the pilot determined the IP (initial point) for his photo run.

## Crew briefing

Still preparing for the mission, the crew briefed together on emergency procedures, escape and evasion possibilities, radio frequencies, and other details related to survival. The crew then proceeded to the life support room, across the ramp closer to the aircraft, to suit up with G-suit, harness, and vest and arm themselves with a Smith & Wesson .38. Their survival radio ("a kind of big Walkman") was

*An RF-4C photo-Phantom of the 11th TRS/432nd TRW, one of a few equipped with LORAN navigation gear (the 'towel rack' atop its fuselage), gets a cartridge start at Udorn in Thailand.*

bastions in Cambodia initially involved 12,000 South Vietnamese troops and their American advisors attacking at the region known as the Parrot's Beak.

By 1 May 1970, the 'incursion' had become a full-scale invasion, with large American involvement. The heaviest military operations were carried out by ARVN troops in the Parrot's Beak and by the First Cavalry Division in the Fishhook, both being protuberances on the map of the Cambodian frontier. US Army helicopter gunships were sent against formations of Viet Cong and NVA. Fighter-bombers, B-52s and fixed-wing gunships supported ARVN and American ground troops. On 2 May, the USAF lost its first aircraft in Cambodia, an F-4D Phantom of the 480th TFS/12th TFW at Phu Cat.

Like Tet, this was another campaign where perception was more important than reality. The Cambodian incursion was a success in that it led to the capture of enemy food and supplies and millions of rounds of ammunition. The ability of the enemy to hide in his Cambodian sanctuary was snatched away from him. But in another way the Cambodian incursion was a colossal failure.

It was the last straw for an American public increasingly convinced that the US effort in Vietnam was misguided, if not

*A UH-1 Huey, the best-known aircraft in the world during the Vietnam years, waits to snatch up South Vietnamese troopers during the Cambodian incursion. The US and its ally in Saigon pulled off a successful campaign in Cambodia but stirred the fires of revolution on America's streets: back home, Cambodia proved to be a catastrophe.*

hand-operated and gave two-way communication or could be used as a beacon for a rescue helicopter in the 'transmit only' mode. This was the same 'beeper' used by most crews in Southeast Asia.

The RF-4Cs were in hangarettes. The navigator checked cameras, started up the inertial nav. system. The pilot did the usual pre-flight checks.

On a typical mission the RF-4C's panoramic camera took pictures horizon-to-horizon. This was one Phantom whose pilot did not have to worry about seeing over his aeroplane's long nose: at medium altitude, the viewfinder showed what was obscured by the nose and told the pilot if it was being recorded on film.

It was hard to say which was worse, day take-offs ("lots of planes queued up to take off and had to be cleared by the tower on to the runway, knowing they could be targets for VC mortars the whole time") or night landings ("you come back and don't know who owns the runway; we know

*In some ways less versatile than the RF-101C Voodoo it replaced, the RF-4C Phantom nevertheless quickly established a position as the USAF's standard tactical reconnaissance craft for its era.*

there can be VC in the area outside the runway; you can have a look with your landing lights but that also makes you a target").

downright wrong. In the US, a horrible blunder by inexperienced Ohio National Guardsmen resulted in the fatal shooting of protesting college students at Kent State University. The slaughter of citizens doing nothing more than exercising their right of speech triggered off a new round of demonstrations – some of them fully fledged riots – against the war, against the move into Cambodia, and against Nixon. To Americans who knew nothing of Asia, the word Vietnam became a symbol of divisions on their own domestic scene and which were wrenching their country apart.

## Congress takes steps

The US Congress had a Democratic majority and was anything but a rubber stamp for the White House. Reflecting domestic opposition to the war, Congress passed the Cooper-Church Amendment, making it illegal to insert American troops into Laos or Cambodia after 30 June. In due course there would be additional legislative constraints against the use of American troops in South Vietnam itself.

In later years the North Vietnamese would willingly admit that they had done everything in their power to encourage domestic dissent by Americans back home. But the truth was, they had almost no influence. No Communist conspiracy lay behind the waving of signs, the chanting, the singing, the unfurling of protest banners in the streets. Opposition to the war was a genuine popular sentiment, growing now to the point where most Americans opposed the war. Those who still supported the commitment, and who sneered at the demonstrators, had forgotten that their own society was rooted in majority rule.

While protests went on about Cambodia, the US armed forces were being weakened by racial disputes and drug problems. The Army which had beaten the North Vietnamese regulars in 1965 was described in 1970 as being incapable of fighting its way out of a paper bag. This was an exaggeration, for many dedicated warriors remained.

It was not uncommon for black and white soldiers to reinforce the very segregation that many had fought against earlier in the 1960s, gathering at segregated places of amusement in off-duty hours. In the tacky, tinsel boom towns which grew up around

*At the peak of US involvement in the war, 200 Americans a week were coming home in body bags. When National Guardsmen shot students at Kent State University, the war was suddenly closer to home. By 1970, polls showed more Americans opposing the war than supporting it.*

American bases, blacks and whites each had their own bars, their own beer halls, their own women. One fighter wing commander at Da Nang was more concerned about racial tensions among his enlisted troops – there were several incidents of knife fights, and one death – than about the very real prospect of the Viet Cong mortaring his F-4 Phantoms.

In Saigon or any populated Vietnamese location, marijuana and heroin were readily available to anyone who wanted them. Dope

# Enter the A-7E

*A more powerful, more potent Corsair II*

The A-7E variant of the Navy's Corsair II attack aircraft, powered by a 14,250-lb (6465-kg) thrust TF41-A-2 turbofan, equipped with improved throttles and armed with an M61A1 Vulcan 20-mm cannon, offered something no other aircraft had yet been able to provide: the pilot knew his exact longitude and latitude on Earth, precisely to the foot. The navigation and weapons delivery system (NWDS) on the A-7E was the most advanced of its time, and 'E' also seemed to be a Corsair with enough power, free of the steam-ingestion problems encountered by the underpowered A-7A and A-7B variants.

The first squadrons to employ the A-7E variant on an operational basis were the 'Blue Diamonds' of VA-146 and the 'Argonauts' of VA-147. They took the new aircraft aboard USS *America* (CVA-66), an Atlantic Fleet carrier which was about to handle its share of the burden in the combat theater.

*America* transited the Panama Canal and made the Pacific crossing to Dixie Station, off the coast of South Vietnam. On 26 May 1970, LtJg Dave Lichtermann of VA-146 was catapulted from *America*'s deck in the first A-7E to be launched in combat. The 'Diamonds'' skipper followed and led a strafing attack against a Viet Cong emplacement. An hour later, Commander Livingston and LtCdr Gravely of the 'Argonauts' rolled in on an enemy supply route to deliver the first bombs dropped in anger by the A-7E. There would be no action 'up North' for these squadrons at this juncture but the A-7E would eventually have its day over North Vietnam, too.

"The A-7E model resolved any doubts we had about sufficient power in the aircraft," said LtJg Fredric Neuman, who flew the E in combat with another squadron. In fact, some felt that the only flaw of the long-ranged, accurate Corsair II was that it never had quite enough power, even in the final version.

*A VA-147 'Argonauts' A-7E is hurled past the hull number on the bow of USS Constellation (CVA-64) by the carrier's powerful SC-11 steam catapult. Next stop: a target in Vietnam.*

*By 1970, the proven Corsair II was becoming standard issue in the US Navy's light-attack units aboard big-deck carriers. The A-7E smoothed out 'kinks' in the aircraft design and gave naval aviators the world's most accurate bombing capability.*

*C-123 Providers spray herbicide in Vietnam. The aerial bombardment of rain forest canopy with Agent Orange and other chemicals did not at first arouse much comment. But when it became clear that defoliants were harmful to people as well as plants, Agent Orange became a symbol for protesters opposed to the war. Its use was halted in 1970.*

smoking became so common and so widespread, particularly among ground combat soldiers, that commanders sometimes had no choice but to look the other way. The local heroin in particular was extremely powerful and, of course, addictive. The Army instituted urine tests, but these helped only to identify some careless offenders.

There were still men of incomparable courage in American uniform, and in general the Air Force and Navy were less affected by these problems than the Army and Marine Corps, but things were falling apart. Everyone knew the war was winding down and nobody wanted to be the last American to die in Vietnam.

## Chemical defoliation comes to an end

A controversial program came to an end when herbicide operations by C-123 Provider aircraft of the 12th Special Operations Squadron at Bien Hoa ended on 14 May 1970. Stocks of herbicide White were exhausted and restrictions on the use of herbicide Orange prevented further use. Spraying of Agent White, itself not controversial, was resumed at a later date but Agent Orange was to be known, hereafter, only to those veterans whose health was harmed by the chemical.

The US pulled out of four air bases during 1970. Binh Thuy in the Delta area was turned over to the VNAF in March. Pleiku was handed over in June and Tuy Hoa in December. In July Air Force flying units were moved out of Vung Tau. During the year no fewer than six USAF combat wings were made inactive or transferred out of country. The Nixon administration periodically put out statements reminding the public that a withdrawal was under way.

# High Stress

T he naval air war involved a considerable degree of struggle and sacrifice. Carriers put forth to sea for cruises of up to six months' duration.

Once in the battle zone, a carrier would spend weeks 'on the line' in the South China Sea or the Gulf of Tonkin, gaining brief respite by retiring to Subic Bay in the Philippines, before returning to the 'line' again for further weeks.

The men who maintained and flew carrier-based warplanes lived in cramped, noisy, hot conditions with 'round-the-clock' work schedules and almost no free time except for sleep, of which there was never enough. Men in billets near the bow of the carrier were likely to be driven from their

*US Navy statistics showed that nearly two F-4 Phantoms were lost in mishaps for every one shot down in combat. Anything could go wrong on a carrier deck, especially at night, and sailors were ever mindful of the risks.*

bunks by the noise and heat of steam catapults slamming aircraft into the sky round the clock.

For pilots, studies showed that landing an aircraft on a carrier, especially at night, produced greater stress and tension than 'rolling in' on a heavily-defended target in Route Package Six.

*Navy fliers went into high-risk carrier operations with superb training. This F-4B Phantom (bureau no. 148385) belongs to training squadron VF-101 'Grim Reapers', which prepped crews before they went into battle.*

*LtJg William E. Belden of VA-152 'Wild Aces' ejects from his A-4E Skyhawk as it dips over the port side of USS Shangri-la (CVS-38) after a brake failure. The pilot survived this dramatic mishap. The A-4E, restrained by a catwalk, never got wet and, in fact, flew again.*

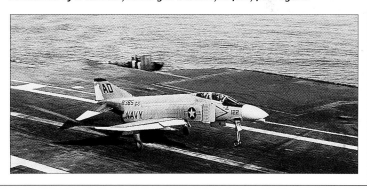

The introduction of a notable new aircraft type to the conflict occurred when the Military Airlift Command's first mission with the Lockheed C-5A Galaxy to Vietnam occurred on a 5 June 1970 trip to Cam Ranh Bay. A C-5 Air Transportable Loading Dock was placed in operation at Cam Ranh Bay on 10 August.

On 15 June 1970, the final 'Blind Bat' flaredrop mission by a C-130A Hercules was flown in Laos. The C-130A aircraft assigned to this mission were transferred to Naha AB, Okinawa, ending another of the many roles performed by the Hercules during the conflict.

## Cambodian withdrawal

On 29 June 1970, US ground troops were withdrawn from Cambodia, the Nixon administration insisting that the men's job was finished and that it was not bowing to protest. Operations over Cambodia by Air Force and Navy aircraft would continue. On that same date, almost unnoticed with Cambodia on the front-pages of newspapers, the Joint Chiefs of Staff put in writing a summary of the rules of engagement which indicated when, and whether, US aircraft could attack targets in North Vietnam. Secretary Laird's 'limited duration, protective reaction' air strikes could be carried out only if reconnaissance flights were engaged or were about to be engaged by SAM sites.

The first trans-Pacific helicopter flight was completed by two

HH-53s of the 37th Aerospace Rescue and Recovery Squadron on 24 August 1970. The two aircraft were ferried from Eglin AFB, Florida, to Da Nang. Two HC-130N Hercules tankers accompanied the helicopters, providing 13 aerial refuelings during the 8,000-mile flight.

General Lucius D. Clay, Jr, took over Seventh Air Force on 1 September 1970. It was still a four-star job, but it was receiving less attention than it had a couple of years earlier. Clay's predecessor, General George S. Brown, had completed a tour of duty without

*A CH-47 Chinook helicopter is unloaded from a Military Airlift Command C-5A Galaxy at Cam Ranh Bay in 1970. Though plagued by problems in the development stage, the 81 C-5As produced over 1966-70 gave airlift crews the capability to carry cargos weighing up to 250,000 lb (113400 kg). The C-5's giant wing spanned 222 ft 8.5 in (67.88 m).*

making any mark on the conduct of the war.

As the combat cruise of USS *America* (CVA-66) continued in mid-1970, pilots gained experience with the A-6C Intruder, a new variant of the all-weather attack craft which had already proven so successful. The A-6C incorporated the TRIM feature (Trails, Roads, Interdiction Multi-Sensor) with large wing-mounted pods containing electro-optical sensors. A video display available to the second crewman on the A-6C, the bombardier-navigator (B/N), assisted in the detection and identification of targets along infiltration routes. Also on board *America* was the KA-6D Intruder tanker aircraft, one of the war's unsung heroes.

The USAF's 13th TBD returned to Southeast Asia on 15 September 1970 with Tropic Moon B-57Gs for night and all-weather interdiction. The squadron was based at Ubon and immediately began flying against North Vietnamese supply routes.

### 'Wild Weasel' 'Thuds'

The earlier consolidation of F-105 assets at Takhli was undone when Detachment 1, 12th TFS moved to Korat from Takhli with six F-105G 'Wild Weasel' aircraft. The unit was given a new provisional designation as the 6,010th 'Wild Weasel' Squadron two months later on 1 November. In December, six EB-66 aircraft deployed to Korat to augment the 42nd TEWS/388th TFW and more F-105Gs were added to the squadron, giving the 6,010th WWS a total of 12 two-seat 'Thuds'. An official history makes it clear that the additional EB-66 and F-105G assets were needed to support B-52 Arc Light operations in Cambodia. Flying and fighting over Cambodia would continue – indeed, it would continue beyond the end of the war against North Vietnam – but little was said about it publicly. In the meanwhile, all F-4C Phantom 'Wild Weasel' aircraft were temporarily consolidated in the 80th TFW at Yokota AB, Japan.

In yet another shift of the 'Thud' population, on 10 December 1970, the 355th TFW and its associated units deactivated at Takhli. The wing's squadrons had played an important part in the war, but now it had come to an end with a 12 aircraft fly-past, with most of the wing's airframes being sent back to McConnell AFB, Kansas. The only 'Thuds' remaining in the combat zone were the 'Wild Weasels' of the 6,010th at Korat.

One other notable departure: the 45th Tactical Reconnaissance Squadron ('Polka Dots'), which had first deployed its RF-101C Voodoos over Vietnam in 1961, departed Tan Son Nhut on 16 November 1970, ending the Voodoo chapter in Southeast Asia. The powerful RF-101C had been one of the first American

*An A-6C Intruder of VA-165 'Boomers' sports a detachable and rather obscene TRIM (Trails, Roads, Interdiction Multi-sensor) package during one of 675 A-6C combat sorties between 26 May and 7 November 1970. TRIM, also used on the AP-2H Neptune, was a hi-tech tool to detect infiltrators 'coming down the pike' on the Ho Chi Minh Trail.*

warplanes in combat. It had flown the fastest combat missions ever carried out by any tactical aircraft in any war – routinely carrying out its reconnaissance sorties at speeds up around 2,240 km/h or Mach 2.0, which was much faster than the 'Thud' or Phantom flew under actual fighting conditions. At one point a Voodoo squadron had more planes than pilots, yet had kept up a daily schedule of two combat missions per aircraft daily. Most of these missions were up North and a disproportionate number of RF-101C pilots were languishing in the Hanoi Hilton while fruitless peace talks foundered.

Once again at year's end, numbers were put together – and again they looked impressive. Air Force combat sorties flown in Southeast Asia in 1970 totaled 711,400, which represented a 27 per cent reduction from the previous year. Nearly 30,000 sorties were flown in Cambodia. B-52s flew 15,103 'Arc Light' sorties, of which 1,292 were in Cambodia. More than 774,000 tons of air munitions were expended. Although the total number of sorties was less than in the previous year, PACAF had been reduced by 19 tactical squadrons

*A difficult aircraft to fly and maintain but impossible not to love, the RF-101C carried a variety of sensors and flew the fastest combat missions ever undertaken (save those of the unique SR-71). But by 1970, the Voodoo was cantankerous and senile. For a new decade, 7th Air Force headquarters decreed replacement by the RF-4C Phantom.*

# B-52 Operations

Although the number and frequency of B-52 Stratofortress missions had been drastically reduced with the slow-down of the war, the big bombers continued to operate from U-Tapao, Thailand, as well as distant Anderson AFB on Guam. Stratofortresses were also being used for bombing operations in Cambodia which were supposed to be secret. The Cambodian incursion brought them out into the open.

## Non-combat losses

No B-52 had ever fallen to enemy fire – in South Vietnam, none ever did – but there were tragic instances when men and machines were lost. At U-Tapao a B-52 mishap occurred because of confusion between one pilot's airspeed indication and the other's. At near-rotation speed near the middle of the runway's length, the pilot aborted and the B-52 hydroplaned into the grass with a full bombload.

Although the crew evacuated the Stratofortress safely, there was a communications mix-up which caused the pilot of a Kaman HH-43 rescue helicopter to understand that the gunner was still trapped inside the B-52. Passing over the burning bomber to drop fire-retardant, the HH-43 was engulfed by the final explosion and both men aboard the helicopter were killed.

Operation 'Good Luck',

launched in 1970, kept B-52s busy bombing targets on Laos, while the number of their missions over South Vietnam remained low. Occasionally, friendly forces would move in to try to confirm that the big bombers had inflicted damage on the enemy. Most of the time any assessment of bomb damage relied on intelligence – and when the enemy moved silently and swiftly through the jungle, intelligence was never easy to acquire.

*The B-52D tail gunner was separated from the rest of the crew by most of the 160-ft 11-in (56.39-m) fuselage. In a crisis, he could blow away the tailcone and bail out on his own.*

*Connected to the pilot with a headset and microphone, a crew chief performs a visual safety check and signals the B-52D to taxi out. As of 1970, no B-52D had ever been hit by enemy fire.*

# Hercules Happenings

The little-known and wholly unpublicized men who flew C-130 Hercules airborne command posts underwent a minor change on 16 September 1970, as the USAF moved to consolidate its C-130 forces as a part of the draw-down of American troops.

The 11 HC-130P Hercules aircraft belonging to the 39th Aerospace Rescue and Recovery Squadron were moved on that date from Tuy Hoa to Cam Ranh Bay. This was a move of only 70-miles (113-km) down the coast,

but it was the only major move of a USAF unit inside Vietnam in 1970.

The change had little effect on the ability of the HC-130P fleet to serve as airborne command and control centers (ABCCCs) or to refuel other aircraft on combat rescue missions. The squadron continued to keep one aircraft on airborne alert and two more ready to be scrambled on short notice.

The 'vanilla' or basic C-130 Hercules was now the backbone of the tactical airlift effort inside

South Vietnam. Although it could not land at as many airfields as the C-7 Caribou or C-123 Provider, the Hercules nonetheless took its crews into tight spots. In one incident, knowing their aircraft would be destroyed if left overnight for engine repairs, a crew was forced to make a three-engine emergency take-off from Song Be at dusk, under small-arms fire from enemy troops less

*The HC-130P had numerous capabilities but was employed in 1970 as a kind of flying headquarters to co-ordinate air-ground actions in South Vietnam.*

*The Hercules could make an assault landing on unpaved ground in just 3,000 ft (928 m). The absence of wing tanks marks this 'slick' as a C-130B model.*

than 300 yards away.

All the while, the heavily burdened C-130 crews carried the ammunition, gasoline, supplies, animals and people knowing that. In June, there were 296 men available as C-130 crews for the three tactical airlift wings – which under normal manning levels had a minimum requirement for 400 men.

# POWs

For prisoners of war who had been held in North Vietnam for years and had gone more than two years without hearing American warplanes overhead, the Son Tay raid was not the glimmer of hope its planners expected. "We learned about it months later," said Major Ken Cordier, held in a Hanoi prison. "It seemed a sign of desperation. If they would go to such lengths to try to get us out, it meant there was no hope of getting out any other way."

These men were sorely mistreated, tortured, isolated, and

*Prisoners like this US Air Force officer (here, being escorted by North Vietnamese army troops) were tortured, denied medical treatment, and badgered to sign untrue 'confessions' of criminal wrong-doing. Hanoi saw the POWs as a pawn in negotiations over the outcome of the war.*

denied medical treatment. In four groups, a total of 12 were released early by the North Vietnamese, all but one of these without permission of the POW commander, Colonel John Flynn. The premature releases were apparently intended to generate propaganda for Hanoi; instead, they drew attention to how badly the men were being treated. The 11 unauthorized releases are viewed with contempt by those who stayed – many of whom were prisoners for five, six, seven

years – but the remaining 555 military and eight civilian prisoners resisted the North Vietnamese to the end. Many died in captivity, some from gross mistreatment, some when attempting to escape. Three men were awarded the Medal of Honor for their conduct as prisoners – Air Force F-100 'Misty FAC' pilot Colonel George (Bud) Day, Air Force F-4D Phantom pilot Captain Lance Sijan, and Navy A-4 Skyhawk pilot Captain James Bond Stockdale. Sijan's award was posthumous, for the young captain never came home from imprisonment by the North Vietnamese.

If they never managed to ask the right questions to get intelligence data, the North

*POWs jeeringly referred to Hoa Loa prison as the 'Hanoi Hilton', and the nickname soon was used to refer to all camps in North Vietnam. Accommodations were sparse, food was ghastly, treatment was grim, and armed guards lurked everywhere.*

Vietnamese were masters of the propaganda side of the POW situation. While prisoners were tortured, visiting American peace activists were treated like royalty.

The POWs were to become increasingly important to any understanding of the war in the south, for Hanoi hoped – with some reason – that the US could be wearied down to the point where it would agree to a settlement with no condition other than the return of its prisoners.

with over 500 aircraft and 32,000 personnel, so the remaining units were heavily tasked.

The numbers-keepers reported that in 1970, 171 USAF aircraft were lost in Southeast Asia, 127 in combat and 44 to operational causes. The total number of aircraft lost in Southeast Asia was now put at 1,950, representing a cost of $2,500 million.

US Navy carrier-based aircraft logged a total of 86,000 missions during the calendar year 1970, the overwhelming majority of which were in South Vietnam. Figures were not kept for land-based US Marine aircraft at Da Nang, Chu Lai and elsewhere, but the Marines continued to play an important role in the overall conflict. Marine A-4E Skyhawks, A-6A Intruders and F-4B Phantoms, soon to be replaced by the F-4J, were maintained and operated under some of the most difficult conditions in Southeast Asia, yet their loss figures were no higher than those of the other services. The Marines lost only four Phantoms in combat during the year, one of

*An A-4F Skyhawk of VA-55 'Warhorses' passes muster after a smooth final approach and, with tailhook extended, prepares to take the wire on the busy deck of USS Hancock (CVA-19). Though being supplanted by the A-7 Corsair II, the A-4, or 'Scooter', was never fully replaced during the conflict. VA-55 alone completed eight A-4 combat cruises.*

which collided with a Vietnamese air force O-1 Bird Dog. Significant progress had been made in 1970 towards getting the South Vietnamese air force to handle more of the burden of the fighting in the South. A total of 1,512 aircraft of all types had been delivered to the Vietnamese air force since the beginning of US aid, 415 of which had been lost to combat or operational causes. By 31 December 1970, the VNAF had 728 aircraft in 30 squadrons. They flew a total of 292,523 sorties in 1970. But Saigon's air arm would never be able to operate against the high-density defenses of the North, however, and the feeling was growing that another round of fighting awaited in the North. "You have this year to do as you like," ran a line from Hemingway. "But the year after that, or the year after that, they will fight."

The number on most Americans' minds, as always, was the size of the commitment. At year's end, just as Congress repealed the Gulf of Tonkin Resolution which had once given Lyndon Johnson broad powers, American military strength in South Vietnam was 335,800.

# Son Tay Raid

### A remarkable feat of daring

Just before midnight, 20 November 1970, American airmen and special forces troops clambered aboard two C-130E Combat Talon transports, five HH-53C and one HH-3E on the ramp at Udorn. Taking off, they flew through heavy darkness on a course for the Son Tay prison 28-miles (40-km) northwest of Hanoi, where intelligence had reported US POWs were held. The most daring rescue attempt of the war was under way.

The Son Tay raiders were not stationed in Southeast Asia; the force had been assembled in secret in the US and came to bases in Thailand only at the last minute to mount the raid. It was a massive operation, supported by KC-135s and other Hercules, escorted by Skyraiders, Phantoms and 'Thuds', and helped out by a finely-orchestrated and wholly diversionary Alpha Strike by Navy Skyhawks, Intruders and Phantoms on targets around Haiphong.

Reconnaissance coverage of the Son Tay camp, including SR-71 photography, had indicated continuing activity. No-one could know that because of flooding which had ruined the camp's water supply and as part of a relocation effort ironically aimed at improving prisoner treatment, North Vietnam had in fact closed down the Son Tay camp four months previously.

One of the HH-53C Super Jolly Green helicopters went slightly off course when pilot Major Frederick M. Donohue made a courageous decision to ignore a warning light telling him (inaccurately, as he gambled) of a transmission failure. Donohue's gunners opened up on guard towers when he discovered that he had overshot the camp and was approaching the adjacent North Vietnamese sapper school. The sole HH-3E – intended to crash-land in the center of the POW camp while the HH-53Cs

*An HH-3E like this one went to Son Tay on a planned one-way trip. The attackers put the helicopter into the center of the camp, hoping to achieve surprise and to quickly wipe away resistance while moving to free American prisoners.*

surrounded it on the outside – began by landing in the wrong place. The HH-3E lifted up again but another HH-53C set down and disgorged some assault troops in the wrong place. The result was a fire fight at the sapper school which, according to some participants, killed Russian advisors as well as North Vietnamese troops.

Finally, the attack force got to the right place. Donohue flew his HH-53C across the camp raking its guard towers with his 7.62-mm GAU-2A/B miniguns. The HH-3E dropped into the camp's center courtyard, wrecked beyond repair as had been expected. Assault troops fanned from the HH-3E to seize the initial advantage inside the camp. An officer used a bullhorn to shout, "Keep down! We're Americans!" No POWs were present to hear him.

While the fire fight was unfolding – the only time American troops fought on the

ground deep inside North Vietnam – the Navy diversions were wreaking havoc with Hanoi's defense net.

Inside the prison, two-man assault teams systematically cleared each cell block, breaking in on the camp commander and killing him in his bed. Less than a half hour from the beginning of the raid, the assault troops blew up what remained of the HH-3E and withdrew in the HH-53C helicopters. Belatedly, SAMs flew through the night around the covering force. Two 'Thuds' took near misses from SAM explosions. One limped out of the combat zone and recovered at Udorn. The other F-105G from the Korat-based 12th TFS/388th TFW could not make it back. The crew ejected over Laos.

A MiG-21 stalked the HH-53C piloted by Lt Col Royal H. Brown, firing a heat-seeking Atoll missile at the helicopter but

*As with every phase of the hush-hush mission deep behind enemy lines, the air refueling of the Son Tay raiders was accomplished with great precision. The high-pressure Son Tay assault set new standards for planning and executing 'special operations'.*

missing. Brown's and another HH-53C were delayed on the way home by a complex and ultimately successful effort to recover the crew of the F-105G.

It is widely written that when American POWs learned of the Son Tay raid, they were heartened and their morale shot up. This does not seem to be true. Major Kenneth W. Cordier, already a prisoner for nearly four years, was thrown into the depths of despair. Cordier viewed the Son Tay raid as evidence of American desperation. "The raid convinced me that there was no hope we would ever get out of North Vietnam. They would only attempt such a rescue mission if there was no other way – and, of course, it wouldn't work twice." Cordier and his fellow POWs continued to suffer. No such ambitious attempt was mounted again.

*Major Don Kilgus, who snapped this high-flying self portrait after the raid, was the only pilot shot down on the Son Tay mission. Kilgus and his backseater ejected from their F-105G 'Wild Weasel' and were rescued intact.*

# WINDING DOWN

**For all the blood spilled by both sides, it was by no means certain that the future of South Vietnam would now be decided in battle. Any conclusion to the fighting would have to honor the appearance, at least, that South Vietnam was able to survive on its own – but Hanoi understood correctly that the USA had few bargaining chips.**

*31 July 1971 marked the end of the story for the F-100 Super Sabre in Southeast Asia. In eight years of combat, Super Sabres flew 360,283 combat sorties. The USAF lost 186 F-100s to anti-aircraft fire, seven during Viet Cong assaults on air bases, and 45 in accidents.*

Still, the skies above the 17th Parallel were devoid of US warplanes except for the reconnaissance aircraft which continued to tweak Hanoi's defenses; still, the American prisoners of war in North Vietnam waited, many of them now in despair that their seemingly interminable captivity would ever end; still, the publicly-acknowledged negotiations in Paris were producing no visible result.

South Vietnam's embattled leaders, particularly President Thieu, could not help but fear that their interests would be abandoned by their American allies. Earlier in the year the American leadership had seemed determined to stay the course. Even now, leaders from President Nixon on down repeatedly said that they would never abandon Saigon. Such statements were becoming less and less credible.

A brief campaign, apparently in response to SAM sites tracking a US recce aircraft, took place in the Ban Korai Pass area in February

1971 and was given the evocative name 'Louisville Slugger'. This brief venture into North Vietnam involved Air Force aircraft only, and totalled 67 sorties. A number of SAM transporters were reported destroyed.

With a single exception, there was no major military operation in 1971 capable of influencing the course of the war. It was a war of dirty, small-unit actions. A vast number of American troops – and some South Vietnamese – were REMFs (a derogatory term for rear-area troopers), but the men at the sharp end were in constant action. In previous wars men fought for a day or a week, then went for a week or a month without being in action. In Vietnam combat soldiers were on the front line – except that there was no front line – every minute of every day and night. Often the logistics provided by cargo planes, the airmobility offered by helicopters and the cover provided by fighter-bombers made the difference to these soldiers. But few of their combat actions made the headlines.

The exception: Saigon's President Thieu announced on 8 February 1971 that South Vietnamese troops, supported by US aircraft and artillery, had crossed the border into Laos to cut the Ho Chi Minh Trail and interdict the flow of supplies from the North. Three ARVN divisions were involved in Operation 'Lam Son 719'.

# Caribou Pilot

*Tough transport work in Vietnam's hinterlands*

**6 6** To navigate, you'd be looking at a map, and you'd find a road and river intersection. 'Well,' you'd say to the co-pilot, 'if that's this road and this river, then our destination is up ahead. On the other hand, if that's this road, we have the side of the mountain coming up at us.'"

Lieutenant Larry Nilssen arrived at Cam Ranh Bay in March 1971, when everyone was aware that the war was winding down. His task was to begin flying the C-7A Caribou on short, risky, in-country airlift missions.

Most of the pilots were young, highly motivated new airmen who wanted to fly the F-4 or the B-52. But their more mundane-appearing job was just as important, and possibly even more perilous. It was no easy thing, flying strange cargos over the Central Highlands in bad weather. "It was a part of the job," recalled Nilssen. "There was not much fear of death."

## Ammo resupply

On alert at Cam Ranh with another C-7A driver named 'Combat' Kelly, Nilssen got word that Pleiku was under attack. Nilssen and Kelly with their crews and two C-7As flew ammunition into a besieged outpost near Pleiku with the enemy shooting at them.

The C-7A typically carried a payload of around 6,000 lb (2722 kg), although it wouldn't take that much very far – "that's with no gas" – or 17 combat-equipped troops. But although short-ranged, it could go where other airlifters could not. As a rule of thumb, pilots were told that the Caribou could land in 1,000 ft (305 m), the C-123 Provider in

*In the operations shack used by one C-7 Caribou squadron in Vietnam, a fanciful poster announced to the world that this was the home of 'Go Anywhere, Do Anything Airlines'. It was an exaggeration, but not by much, witness this view of a C-7 descending over a remote village.*

2,000 ft (606 m), the C-130 Hercules in 3,000 ft (908 m). Nilssen often hauled people and supplies into Ha Than, where the runway was just 870-ft (265-m) long. On one end of the runway was a stream and on the other a cliff, so there was no way to increase runway length. There were also trips up to montagnard redoubts in the Central Highlands – places like Dak To, which had been a scene of heavy fighting in the past – where runways were dust or mud, depending on the season.

## Teamwork

The crew of pilot, co-pilot, and flight engineer/loadmaster often worked together to get out of a 'hot spot' as quickly as possible. "The airplane obviously becomes a target once it lands. If they can hit it with a mortar, we lose an airplane. If they can hit while on the runway, they also tie up a runway." The aircraft had rollers to unload cargo through its rear door and Nilssen often carried

*The balmy clime of Cam Ranh Bay is home for these camouflaged, KC-coded C-7A/B Caribous of the USAF's 458th Tactical Airlift Squadron, part of the 483rd Tactical Airlift Wing. The 'Bou' was a resilient and versatile intra-theater transport.*

out what he called a speed offload. He untied the cargo, reversed propellers to start the aircraft going backwards, then when up to about 5 mph (8 km/h), he kicked the propellers forward. The untied cargo then rolled smartly and smoothly out the back. "It works like a champ." Nilssen had a flight engineer/loadmaster, Tom Agee, who stood on the cargo while it rolled out. Paradrops and LAPES (low-altitude parachute extraction) were too exotic for the mission being carried out and were never used.

Even with the war petering out, there were still American

soldiers at farflung outposts and the most popular cargo was mail or beer. C-7A Caribous did a lot of relocating people. They carried live animals like pigs and cows as well as artillery shells.

Because things were winding down, Nilssen was at one time or another a member of various squadrons, including the 436th and 535th Tactical Airlift Squadrons. He and his companions were told that they would turn over 100 Caribous to the VNAF. At one time Nilssen was assigned a Vietnamese co-pilot. But the turnover never happened and many C-7As were later relocated stateside.

*The C-7 Caribou offered STOL (Short Take-Off and Landing) capability which made it the ideal craft to supply small outposts where runways were short and unpaved. Pilots were pleased that the Caribou handled well on such tricky missions.*

# Cobras

*'Snakes' carry on the gunship war*

The AH-1G Cobra gunship, employed with considerable success by the Army and Marine Corps, was neither as easy to maintain nor as amenable to rough airfields as earlier helicopters, but the Cobra was an effective weapons system and its contribution was undeniable.

Although the G model had been conceived for the Army, Marine Corps AH-1Gs had been in combat since early April 1969 when the first few joined squadron VMO-2 at Marble Mountain. After a three-month evaluation period, which solved some of the problems of bringing a new type into service, AH-1Gs began to replace UH-1E Huey gunships. The Cobra proved far superior to the UH-1E in the delivery of accurate, close-in fire support during helicopter assault operations. Furthermore, the gunships were able to free the Marines' hard-pressed UH-1E gunships to perform the light helicopter missions for which they had originally been intended.

In the American withdrawal from South Vietnam, the Marines, who had arrived in large numbers first, were also the first to leave. Although Marine units began their pull-out from Vietnam as early as August 1969, the leathernecks'

*Left: AH-1G HueyCobra gunships on the prowl. The Cobra was a new concept to US Army soldiers, but one that evolved naturally from the proven Huey. In time, soldiers remedied mechanical problems with the AH-1G that were prolonged and exasperating.*

*Below: The Army set up a Cobra Transition School at Vung Tau, South Vietnam. Here, pilots, gunners and maintainers were taken through an exhaustive introduction to flight characteristics and weapons. Tactics were still evolving.*

The ARVN forces around which the attack was planned were the 1st Infantry Division, the 1st Airborne Division, the Marine Division, the 1st Armored Brigade, and three Ranger battalions. Extensive US air support prevented the operation from turning into a disaster when ARVN forces found themselves over-extended and out-numbered, and were forced to conduct a fighting withdrawal from Laos. Again the public in the US became riled at the idea that the war was being expanded.

Marine Corps AH-1G Cobra gunships and US Army helicopters played a major role in supporting 'Lam Son 719'. Army AH-1G Cobras were far more numerous and proved to be extremely rugged, capable of absorbing damage and inflicting it. The Boeing Vertol CH-47 Chinook was a solid workhorse, while the UH-1H Huey did its usual invaluable job, although its relative vulnerability to ground fire meant that large numbers were lost.

Most analysts now believe that in spite of the difficulties and the individual tragedies, 'Lam Son 719' was a successful operation which dealt a serious setback to the North Vietnamese. A Nixon administration official opined that the success of the operation would make it possible to speed up the Vietnamization process and to withdraw US troops from South Vietnam even more rapidly. Much of the American public had by now lost interest in whether the North Vietnamese were set back. To many Americans, the only objectives to be achieved were to get out, and to secure the release of prisoners of war. To their credit, even the staunchest anti-war critics insisted that the POWs would have to come home in any settlement.

## Hard-working Skycranes

Not often mentioned in accounts of the air war in Vietnam, the Sikorsky CH-54 Tarhe, or Skycrane, performed herculean cargo-moving tasks during 'Lam Son 719', often shifting heavy items of equipment such as tractors and bulldozers. Designed round the concept that its cargo could be detachable and thereby easily loaded and unloaded; the CH-54 had more load-lifting capacity than most of the heavy helicopters. It had been in action since the arrival of the First Cavalry Division in 1965.

One of the more unusual weapons of the war was the CH-54 equipped with a 10,000-lb (4535-kg) bomb. The purpose was not bombardment, but rather the clearing of jungle foliage to create helicopter LZs (landing zones). A similar operation was carried out by the Air Force dropping a bomb of the same size from a C-130 Hercules. The technique was not widely used and its cost effectiveness is debatable.

More mundane problems continued to plague air war planners. In March 1971, two QU-22B Beech drone aircraft crashed, bringing the total number of these aircraft lost to four. It had already been determined that these drones, known under the program

*An AH-1G Cobra stands ready to go into action, with gun pods and 2.75-in rocket canisters hanging from its weapon stations. The Cobra introduced the now-standard gunship layout; the pilot sat in the rear of the tandem, two-seat cockpit while the gunner aimed his weapons from a handy centerline perch and enjoyed a wide field of vision in front.*

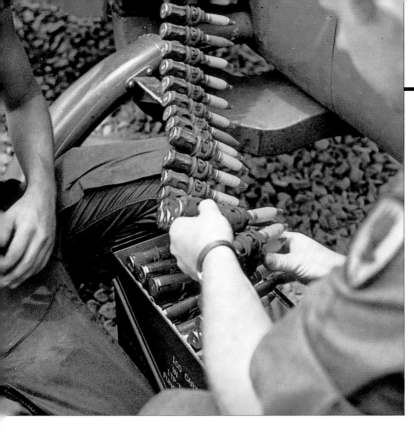

*Ground crewmen of the 334th Aviation Company at Bien Hoa load cannon rounds into a Cobra. AH-1Gs could carry the six-barrel XM35 Vulcan 20-mm cannon under the left stub wing, or a lighter three-barrel M197 cannon in the nose turret.*

AH-1G Cobras remained in service until well into 1971 and, indeed, served during Operation 'Lam Son 719', the incursion into Laos early that year. On 26 May 1971 the Marine Corps' last squadron flying the G model Cobra, HML-167, ended its participation in combat and began

its return to stateside duty.

A considerable amount of work was going on to improve the Cobra for both the Army and the Marine Corps. Included in these efforts was the development of the TOW (tube-launched, optically sighted, wire-guided) missile, intended primarily for anti-armor operations against the hordes of Soviet tanks poised on Europe's Central Front.

In 1971 there didn't seem to be much need for an anti-tank weapon in Vietnam, but it would not be long before the North Vietnamese would change all that.

### Combat-tested Cobra

One of the few aircraft actually to reach the war zone after actual combat experience from Vietnam went into its design, the AH-1G was developed as the AAFSS (Advanced Aerial Fire Support System) after a design competition which began in August 1965.

## Bell AH-1G Huey Cobra

This remarkable aircraft with its rotary-wing performance and fighter-like appearance began as a private venture. As the specialized gunship version of the famous Huey, the AH-1G built up an impressive combat record and helped reduce transport helicopter losses by providing effective fire suppression during airmobile operations. Resplendent in tigermouth markings, this HueyCobra gunship is armed with a 40-mm grenade launcher and a 7.62-mm Minigun in the nose turret, and 52 rockets in four pods beneath the stub wings. Nicknames and caricatures were almost lost against the olive-drab Army paint but they reflected the fighting spirit of individual soldiers.

### 'Huey' parts
Incredibly, in spite of having little outward resemblance to the UH-1 Huey, being in many ways a new aircraft, the HueyCobra used 64 per cent of mechanical components from the earlier helicopter, including the rotor design and rotor drive train.

### Combat capability
The AH-1G began life with a single 7.62-mm gun in a TAT-102A chin turret but this was changed early in the production run to two machine-guns, two 40-mm grenade launchers, or one of each plus up to 76 2.75-in rockets in pods.

### Cobra power
The AH-1G was the first production version, put into production on 13 April 1966. Powered by a 1,400-shp T53-L-13 engine downrated to 1,100 shp, the slim-bodied Cobra was faster than the earlier Huey.

UNITED STATES ARMY

# Carrier War

There had been some reduction in the number and duration of aircraft-carrier line periods to put the sea-going Navy in sync with everybody else, but carrier action was continuing. Indeed, carrier aircraft helped to facilitate the withdrawal from land bases.

AO2 Richard Leach was an aviation ordnanceman aboard the carrier USS *Shangri-la* (CVA-38). She was an ageing, wooden flight-decked ship which dated to World War II and was one of a number of carriers which repeatedly pulled combat cruises in the war zone. Leach worked in an ordnance shop with 20 men. Putting bullets, bombs and rockets aboard the Navy's warplanes was gruelling work. It was hard manual labor – "everything was loaded by hand," he recalled.

Life aboard a carrier was a constant reminder of danger. Leach watched an A-4 skid wildly while attempting to land, miss the arresting wire, and come to a halt only after hitting a helicopter hard enough to send it careering off the flight deck and into the drink. On another occasion a malfunction on one of Leach's A-4 Skyhawks caused it to fire a cannon round into another

---

name 'Pave Eagle', would not be able to replace the EC-121R Super Constellation as a relay aircraft for signals from 'Igloo White' sensors. Now it was realized that the fallback plan of 'keeping on' the EC-121R was not going to work either. As an alternative made necessary by the severe ageing of the EC-121Rs, the sensor gear from a QU-22B was installed aboard a C-130 Hercules airborne battlefield command and control center (ABCCC) for testing. The success of this project led to the conversion of additional ABCCC Hercules airframes to perform relay functions and allowed the number of ECRs to be reduced to six.

Another round of 'protective reaction' airstrikes occurred on 21-22 March 1971, apparently in retaliation for attempted action against a US reconnaissance aircraft. Known as 'Operation Fracture Cross Alpha', the strikes involved both Air Force and Navy aircraft. Twenty armed reconnaissance strikes were accompanied by 234 attack missions.

The first US aircraft lost to a SAM over Laos was an O-2A Skymaster of the Nakhon Phantom-based 56th SOW, shot down on 26 April 1971. The aircraft had been flying north-west of the Ban Karai Pass.

## Low-level reconnaissance

The US Army continued to make effective use of one fixed-wing aircraft the Air Force had not succeeded in taking away. The Grumman OV-1 Mohawk was employed to collect intelligence on the enemy's whereabouts and movements. Since the machine could virtually slide over the grass and look over the enemy's shoulder, the information was invaluable in planning B-52 strikes against the Ho Chi Minh Trail, naval artillery missions against coastal targets, and fighter-bomber missions.

Designed with a kindly view towards the wrench jockey who had to keep it flying, the Mohawk was relatively easy to maintain and repair, even when it operated from rough forward airfields. The US Army holds that the Mohawk had the highest sustained operational readiness rate of any Army aircraft that served in Vietnam, often producing an availability rate of better than 95 per cent.

President Nixon announced on 7 April 1971 that he intended to withdraw 100,000 more US troops from South Vietnam by 1 December. These incremental announcements were the President's way of making it clear that his administration had a plan, although

*The EC-121R was a Super Constellation like the flying radar stations that orbited in the Gulf of Tonkin, but was packed with electronic gear instead of the radar systems of the AWACS models. It was still in service in 1971, relaying signals from 'Igloo White' sensors along the Ho Chi Minh Trail.*

aircraft further along the deck.

Turning around an A-4 Skyhawk to enable the light-attack aircraft to fly a new sortie in less than 90 minutes was a finely orchestrated event. "Everybody moved and moved fast."

There was an awkward cavity called the 'hell hole' inside the A-4 where 20-mm cartridges had to be inserted. To arm the guns pneumatically, you had to push an air compressor around the deck with a 100-ft (30-m) line.

As one of the last steps before a Skyhawk was catapulted off the ship, "you always made damn sure that people knew how to pull safety pins from the bomb fuses. You'd pull the pins and hold them high in the air to show the pilot so he'd know."

Deck personnel on carriers could be distinguished by the colors they wore. Red denoted ordnance men like Leach, green signified avionics personnel, and brown the squadron line crew, including the plane captain. All these men belonged to the squadrons embarked on the ship. Purple indicated aviation bosun's mates and yellow signified aircraft directors, both members not of the squadrons but of the ship's company.

Fewer than 200 men among the 3,800 to 5,000 aboard a carrier like *Shangri-la* ever strapped into a fast jet and flew off to bomb the enemy. The vital contribution made by the others is difficult to quantify and easy to ignore. A few were lost at sea. They should not be forgotten.

**Above: The guided missile destroyer USS Parsons escorts the veteran USS Bon Homme Richard as the old carrier leaves Yankee Station for the last time. By 1971 such small-deck carriers were being withdrawn from service, being replaced on the line by much larger vessels with more powerful aircraft.**

**Right: From the bombardier-navigator's seat in an A-6A, the deck of even a relatively large carrier like USS Midway looked small, narrow, and unstable. Flying from carriers was a unique and perilous undertaking that demanded immense skill and courage, even without the added danger of combat.**

further details of the planning process were not revealed. Nixon's first concern was the American soldier on the ground and he had not yet decided that all American airpower could be withdrawn from the war zone.

As often happened during this period of low intensity conflict, what happened at home was more important than what transpired on the battlefield. On 13 June 1971 the *New York Times* began releasing the 'Pentagon Papers', a top-secret study of US involvement in the Vietnam war which had been originally prepared for Defence Secretary McNamara and was leaked to the press by Daniel Ellsberg. The 'Papers' contained dozens of previously highly classified documents which seemed to show that American officials had lied publicly about the 'how' and 'why' of US escalation of the war.

## Changes of command

1 August 1971 saw Air Force command changes which did not attract much attention at the time but would later. General Lucius D. Clay, Jr, who had held the post as chief of the Seventh Air Force in Saigon, moved to Hawaii to assume duties as PACAF commander in chief, replacing General Joseph J. Nazzaro. It was the first time that the man in charge was not a 'SAC weenie', a sign of changes that were taking place within an Air Force no longer dominated solely by bomber men – although Chief of Staff General John Ryan obviously was just such a SAC veteran.

To replace Clay in Saigon, General John D. Lavelle, formerly PACAF vice-commander in chief, received a fourth star and was assigned to head Seventh Air Force. Lavelle's was an honored name in the Air Force, but he would be remembered almost exclusively because of charges that he permitted unauthorized air strikes into North Vietnam.

In August 1971 the USAF withdrew the last Martin RB-57E

Canberra operating with the 'Patricia Lynn' reconnaissance program. The RB-57E was widely viewed as the most cost-efficient reconnaissance aircraft in the conflict. According to Canberra pilot Robert C. Mikesh, the RB-57E excelled in stability, maneuverability, versatility of equipment, long duration over target, and – not to be overlooked – crew ability.

While flying from Tan Son Nhut on missions in Laos, the small 'Patricia Lynn' detachment – never more than five aircraft – had been commended by MACV for providing 94 per cent of all battlefield intelligence. Apparently the few Canberras acquired more targets, day and night, than the two RF-4C Phantom and one

**At Chu Lai, pilot Warrant Officer Jerry Egroth oversees refueling of his OV-1 Mohawk. The US Army was not supposed to operate fixed-wing combat aircraft, but the service managed to keep its Mohawks after giving up its C-7 Caribou fleet to the US Air Force.**

*The B-57G Canberra was the ultimate USAF night intruder in Vietnam. Crews wore a patch with a caricature of a three-headed dragon, inspired by the B-57G's three systems for tracking ground targets. These Canberras finally departed the war zone on 12 April 1972.*

RF-101C Voodoo squadrons of the 460th Tactical Reconnaissance Wing. It was said that with only four more RB-57Es, the 'Patricia Lynn' outfit could handle all day and night reconnaissance in-country for the entire war.

In September it was announced that US troop strength in South Vietnam would be down to 177,000 by December. With a real withdrawal undeniably taking place, the numbers of men in the country became more important to TV audiences back home than the body counts and casualty totals which had so far been the center of attention. What was more important, massive amounts of equipment were being withdrawn or transferred.

On 8 September 1971 the final AC-119G 'Shadow' gunship was transferred to the Vietnamese. The VNAF's 819th Attack Squadron at Tan Son Nhut did not distinguish itself with these aircraft, nor did the 821st at a later time when it received the jet-augmented AC-119K 'Stinger'.

Another 'protective reaction' move on 21 September 1971 saw USAF and US Navy aircraft striking the Dong Hoi POL storage facilities and destroying 350,000 gallons of fuel.

## Phantoms start to leave

The Phu Cat-based 12th TFW with its F-4D Phantoms reached a turning point when the F-4Ds from the 389th TFS – reassigned without personnel to the United States – were flown to the US for IRAN (inspect and repair as necessary) on 8 October 1971. In November, Phu Cat's other squadron, the inactivated 480th TFS, was flown to Taiwan for IRAN prior to assignment to RAF Lakenheath, England. In their move to a European clime, the F-4Ds would again replace F-100s. The move left Phu Cat without Phantoms.

The USAF's AC-130A 'Spectre' and the improved AC-130 'Surprise Package' gunships gave way to still further improvements of this highly successful design. A program to convert C-130E Hercules aircraft to the 'Surprise Package' configuration was well under way. In addition, tactics were being improved. In 1971 Air Force Secretary Robert Seamans approved a program which would

# 'Lam Son 719'
## Striking at Hanoi's forces in Laos

**N**orth Vietnamese forces continued to build up in the panhandle where the country was divided. A major move, perhaps even more significant than the Cambodian incursion of the previous year, seemed necessary to blunt the enemy's operations in Laos. Jointly planned in Washington and Saigon, the new operation was nicknamed 'Lam Son 719', commemorating a Vietnamese victory over the Chinese in the fifteenth century.

On 8 February 1971, South Vietnam's President Nguyen Van Thieu made the announcement of 'Lam Son 719', stating that South Vietnamese troops supported by US aircraft and artillery had crossed the border into Laos to cut off the Ho Chi Minh Trail and interdict the flow of supplies from the North.

*'Down and dirty,' right in the middle of the action, US Army helicopter crews had a very personal role in the Laotian incursion. Good communication was not always achieved between US aircraft and South Vietnamese troops on the ground.*

### Massive attack

Some 16,000 South Vietnamese troops from three infantry divisions, aided not merely by US tactical airpower but also by massive heli-lifts, found themselves in conflict with North Vietnamese forces at least twice as numerous as they. It quickly became apparent that the South Vietnamese forces were over extended and the amount of US air support needed to prevent a disaster became far more than originally anticipated.

The American portion of the operation, nicknamed 'Dewey Canyon II', quickly proved essential. 'Lam Son 719' eventually would involve 8,000 US tactical air strikes and the loss of six USAF, one Navy and one Marine aircraft as well as no fewer than 107 US Army helicopters. Communications

*The ground sweep into Laos was supported by air power, including naval aviation. These A-4 Skyhawks are representative of warplanes which flew unusually long sorties from their carriers to provide support to ground troops in 'Lam Son 719'.*

foul-ups were common as South Vietnamese army, US Army, US Air Force and US Navy people discovered that their methods of talking with each other were not always compatible. On one instance, faulty information from a forward air controller (FAC) caused a flight of USAF Phantoms to release their ordnance on friendly forces.

### Mixed results

'Lam Son 719' was filled with images which were confusing and contradictory. On 6 March 1971, B-52 Stratofortresses began to bomb the Tchepone area where North Vietnamese troops were concentrated; while military damage was unquestionably inflicted, the US news media focused on reports of civilians killed in the bombing.

Pictures of seemingly panicked South Vietnamese troops hanging from helicopter skids contributed to the perception that the operation was a fiasco. Poor co-ordination between FACs, Army helicopters and Hancock's A-4F Skyhawks has been documented –

one confusing incident resulting in downed helicopter crews being captured while faulty communication forced a flight of Skyhawks to ditch its ordnance.

Most analysts now believe that in spite of the difficulties and the individual tragedies, 'Lam Son 719' was a successful operation which dealt a serious setback to the North

*Below: The Viet Cong and North Vietnamese forces using Laos as a sanctuary were highly mobile and managed to move out quickly, but they left plenty of equipment behind – including one of the first PT-76 tanks seen in the Vietnam conflict.*

Vietnamese. A Nixon administration official opined that the success of the operation would make it possible to speed up the Vietnamization process and to withdraw US troops from South Vietnam even more rapidly. Much of the American public had by now lost interest in whether the North Vietnamese were set back. To many Americans, the only objectives to be achieved were to get out, and to secure the release of

prisoners of war. To their credit, even the staunchest anti-war critics insisted that the POWs would have to come home in any settlement.

*A US Army CH-54 Tarhe, better known as the Skycrane, delivers an M114 155-mm Howitzer to a South Vietnamese firebase in Laos. The ability to move such heavy firepower at aviation speeds gave the ARVN a major advantage in large-scale offensive operations like these.*

*The Vietnamese penetration into Laos was to a large extent made possible by massive US helicopter support. The help by supposedly non-combatant Americans was not without cost: more than 100 Army helicopters were lost in the action.*

put 11 of the latest-model AC-130A aircraft, all modified to the 'Surprise Package' configuration, into Southeast Asia by 1 October 1971. In addition, six further improved AC-130E 'Spectres' would be in the area by 1 January 1972 and eventual procurement would total 12 AC-130Es. The E model, under the Pave Aegis project, would include a 105-mm howitzer in place of one of the two 40-mm Bofors cannon.

The truck-killing record of fighters escorting the AC-130 had improved dramatically with the introduction of laser-guided bombs and the Pave Sword laser seeker pod employed by F-4 Phantoms. In the first combat test of this 'smart' weapon on 3 February 1971, F-4 Phantoms accompanying an AC-130 A Spectre destroyed a 37-mm gun position with a laser-guided bomb. The technology became fairly widespread as 1971 continued.

On 10 December 1971 President Nixon warned that North Vietnam would be bombed if it increased the level of fighting while US troops were being withdrawn from the South. Here again political forces were sometimes more important than military: Hanoi knew full well that Nixon wanted to find a way out of the war that could be seen as honorable and would probably accept any reasonable way out which included the return of the POWs. Nixon knew full well – his intelligence advisors frequently reminded him – that Hanoi had the potential to mount a combat offensive if it chose to do so. Nixon's 'warning' could be viewed as taking credit for the low level of conflict Hanoi had maintained for more than two years.

## Vietnamization of bases

The US presence ended at two more air bases during the year, Bien Hoa and Phu Cat being transferred to the VNAF in August and December respectively. To some extent these turnovers were symbolic. A few American aircraft continued to operate from both.

On 7-8 November 1971, yet another major foray into North Vietnam caused critics of the war to ask if, perhaps, the US was doing a little more than merely 'reacting'. Apparently in reaction to another 'lock-on' by a SAM site against a recce aircraft, Air Force and Navy fighter-bombers struck airfields at Dong Hoi, Vinh and Quang Lang. The very new, MiG-capable strip at Quang Lang was to remain a principal cause of concern. Farther south than other North Vietnamese airfields, Quang Lang existed solely because Hanoi wanted to shoot down one of the B-52 Stratofortresses

*Combat evaluation of an improved AC-130 called 'Surprise Package' uncovered a few minor snags in 1969-70, but was generally successful and the more powerful armament and sensors became standard. Then, in 1971, AC-130As like the ship above were supplanted by the improved AC-130E which carried a modified Army 105-mm howitzer. This AC-130A is assigned to the 16th Special Operations Squadron, part of the 8th Tactical Fighter Wing, at Ubon, Thailand.*

operating in South Vietnam, Laos and Cambodia.

Although no-one knew it yet, this was the period when Seventh Air Force commander, General John D. Lavelle, allegedly made false reports about North Vietnamese reaction to US recce flights, precisely for the purpose of being able to retaliate.

Christmas Day turned out to be the eve of the largest 'protective reaction' campaign yet. Over 26-30 December 1971, in response to a North Vietnamese build-up, and in particular an increase in the number of SAM sites in the lower part of the country, Air Force and Navy aircraft flew 1,025 sorties. All of this action took place south of the 20th Parallel. The campaign was given the name 'Proud Deep Alpha', and represented the most extensive air operations up North since the November 1968 bombing halt. The North Vietnamese could be forgiven for wondering if the new year would hold further problems for them. It would.

## A powerful air force – on paper

Progress with the South Vietnamese Air Force was one measure of Nixon's Vietnamization effort: by the end of 1971, Saigon's air arm had 1,202 aircraft and, according to the numbers experts, had flown a total of 524,152 sorties, 59,805 of which were combat sorties. And what were all the others? And did anyone know that the correct figure was not 524,151 or 524,153? One accurate number: 57 South Vietnamese air force aircraft were lost to combat and operational causes in 1971.

Although many Americans had been withdrawn by year's end, those who kept the numbers were not among them. USAF aircraft flew a total of 450,031 combat sorties and expended 642,900 tons of munitions in Southeast Asia operations with a loss of 87 aircraft. Sorties included 87,052 attack sorties and 12,554 B-52 missions. KC-135 Stratotankers performed over 62,500 refuelings. Tactical airlift operations within South Vietnam moved 2,282,883 passengers and 283,556 tons of cargo. Eighty-seven USAF aircraft were lost during the year, 70 to combat causes.

# Departures

In June 1971, the last O-1 Bird Dog in USAF service was transferred to the South Vietnamese air force. Those who wallow in numbers would have it that during their Southeast Asia service the O-1s had flown 471,186 combat sorties and had suffered 119 losses. It has already been noted that the 'slow movers' occasionally flew in the lower reaches of North Vietnam during the period when combat operations were conducted up North.

## The last 'Hun'

The last F-100 Super Sabre wing in Southeast Asia, the 35th TFW at Phan Rang AB, ceased operations on 26 June 1971. The last of the F100s departed South Vietnam for the continental US on 30 July 1971, ending a combat deployment which, according to the keepers of the numbers, had encompassed 360,283 combat sorties and the loss of 243 aircraft.

Though it had never been a significant player north of the 17th Parallel, the F-100 or 'Hun' was a bona fide veteran of the fight against Hanoi and even more of the in-country war. Even if its replacement, the Phantom, was a far more capable aircraft, the 'Hun' would be much-missed.

## C-47 soldiers on

Bird Dog and Super Sabre were thus 'outlasted' by the oldest airframe in US Air Force inventory, the venerable C-47 Gooney Bird, which carried out a variety of missions throughout the conflict. Flown on rare instance north of the 17th Parallel, the Gooney Bird was also an important asset in gathering intelligence on enemy operations. The EC-47P airframes of the 361st TEWS at Phu Cat frequently ventured into Laos and apparently Cambodia as well, their crews taking enormous risk.

All AGM-12 Bullpup air-to-ground missiles which had not been used in combat by August 1971 were shipped back to the United States for disposition.

An official history, remarking upon the missile, concludes: "This action reduced the USAF's AGM-12 capability to zero."

There were those who felt the capability had been zero all along, especially when recalling how during 'Rolling Thunder', Bullpup missiles had been accurate enough, but generally bounced off North Vietnamese bridges without causing any great damage to the structures.

*This F-100C Super Sabre of the 120th TFS at Phan Rang was gone by mid-1969 when the Colorado Air National Guard squadron went home. Other units at Phan Rang remained until the 35th TFW ceased operations on 26 June 1971 after six years of continuous fighting.*

*Two-seat F-100Fs (foreground) and single-seat F-100Ds (behind) receive attention in their revetments. Individual bays for aircraft were common as Viet Cong sapper activity soared to epidemic level. The base is Phan Rang where the 35th TFW operated until mid-1971.*

*Left: Not regarded as successful, the much-produced AGM-12A/B Bullpup air-to-surface missile finally reached the end of the road in 1971. This example is being launched by a US Navy P-3 Orion, a relative newcomer. The Bullpup was accurate but its warhead was often ineffective.*

*In 1971, the last US Air Force FAC O-1 was withdrawn after nearly a decade of combat service in Southeast Asia, and more than 20 years after the type's first flight in US military colors. However, a few examples were still being used by the US Army 'in-country', and these continued to fly.*

# NEW WAR

**It was another election year in the United States. In South Vietnam the ground war appeared at a low ebb, both sides avoiding any full-scale test of strength. But the relative quiet was about to be shattered by a full-scale northern invasion.**

Negotiations were under way – secret talks between Henry Kissinger and Le Duc Tho were to be the most important sessions of the year – and the stakes were little changed from the preceding two years. The American decision to withdraw was irreversible. The survival of the Saigon regime did not seem to be assured. It was widely understood that the Americans were going to seek little more than the return of their prisoners of war. Perhaps, said some, there was no reason for Hanoi to fight. The talks would end it.

USAF personnel in South Vietnam were in the contradictory position of simultaneously conducting a fully fledged air campaign and carrying out reductions in force. The reductions were consistent with what the American public and its leaders wanted. At the same time, Hanoi must have seen the reductions as an invitation to achieve the final victory and overwhelm South Vietnam. For

*Upon completion of combat mission no. 100 by its crew, Captain Steve Mosier taxies in Caroline, an F-4D Phantom (66-7767) of the 433rd Tactical Fighter Squadron, amid clouds of celebratory red smoke. The location is the 8th TFW ramp at Ubon, Thailand.*

# Cunningham's First Kill

On 19 January 1972, a break in the monsoon murk enabled the USS *Constellation* to launch a reconnaissance RA-5C Vigilante against the airfield at Quang Lang, where the North Vietnamese were suspected of basing MiG-21s. It was escorted by Intruders, Corsairs and Phantoms. Lieutenant Randall H. (Duke) Cunningham of the 'Fighting Falcons' of VF-96 flew an F-4J with RIO LtJg William P. Driscoll in the back seat. The Viggie and its companions made an end run to position themselves for an eastward run-in over Quang Lang, cutting across South Vietnam near Hue, backtracking over Laos, and descending towards the North Vietnamese airfield.

## Under fire

The RA-5C was fired on by AAA and SAMS, which were in turn attacked by the Intruders and Corsairs. Cunningham's section, which included the Phantom flown by Lieutenants Brian Grant and Jerry Sullivan, positioned themselves between Quang Lang and the MiG field at Bai Thiong, so as to intercept any MiGs coming down from the latter base to threaten the strike group.

Cunningham dodged two missiles, plunging downward from 15,000 feet (4570 m) in the process. He spotted what he first thought to be a pair of A-7E Corsairs following their own shadows north-east over the jungle treetops. Cunningham spotted twin plumes of flame as the two aircraft went into afterburner – and the Corsair doesn't have an afterburner.

Reversing, he closed on what turned out to be two Bai Thiong-based MiG-21s. Driscoll shouted at him from the back seat to engage from a distance with Sparrows but the pilot distrusted the radar-guided missile and wanted to get close enough for heat-seeking Sidewinders.

## Sidewinder strike

Once close enough, Cunningham selected Sidewinder, got a good tone in his earphones, and fired. As the AIM-9 went off its launch rail, the MiG-21 broke hard into the attacking Phantom, throwing off the missile. Cunningham maneuvered furiously, taking advantage of the 'Top Gun' training that had exposed him to more than 150 realistic ACM engagements. He caught sight of the second MiG which, to his relief, was high-tailing it to the north-east. Able to concentrate fully on the first MiG, Cunningham pulled his Phantom's nose toward the adversary.

The other pilot seemed to lose sight of the Phantom. Now, the MiG-21 reversed its flight path directly in front of the VF-96 fighter. Cunningham fired a second Sidewinder which tracked straight and exploded in a blinding flash, tearing off the MiGs empennage and sending it augering to the ground. Cunningham was ready for more, action, but the second MiG had

*Above: The F-4J Phantom in the background (bureau no. 157267) was flown by Cunningham and Driscoll when they got their first kill. The F-4J is seen after its subsequent transfer from Cunningham's squadron, VF-96 'Fighting Falcons' to VF-114 'Aardvarks'.*

quit the fray entirely and fled.

Cunningham and Driscoll were close to bingo fuel and now turned back toward Laos for the long journey back to the *Constellation*. The photo mission, which had cost no US losses, was a complete success. The MiG kill was the 122nd of the war and the first in nearly two years. And Cunningham and Driscoll would be heard from again.

*The US supposedly had an 'understanding' that reconnaissance aircraft like this RA-5C Vigilante would not be fired upon. Hanoi never acknowledged that it was party to any such arrangement. In January 1972 a Vigilante was engaged by AAA batteries, which enabled the ace team of Cunningham and Driscoll to open their combat account.*

# Tank Killing

Once Quang Tri had fallen, it appeared that the North Vietnamese were in an excellent position to drive on to Hue, the old imperial capital which had been the scene of heavy fighting during the 1968 Tet Offensive. The weather continued to be generally bad but some aircraft were able to get into the fight against an enemy who had suddenly become capable of fielding tanks and missiles. An Air Force report quotes an OV-10 Bronco forward air controller, Lieutenant Colonel Ray Stratton, who described the new conflict between tanks and 'smart' bombs.

## Engaging tanks

"I found two tanks just north of (a force of South Vietnamese) on the My Chanh River. It was at twilight. There was a PT-76 and a T-54. The PT-76 was trying to pull the T-54 out of a dry stream bed. They were just about a mile to the east of [the road] and about a mile and a half north of the town. I called for ordnance and there was none available. I waited and finally 'Schlitz' and 'Raccoon', two F-4s out of Ubon, showed up. They were equipped with a laser-illuminated bomb system known as Paveway One.

Raccoon was the illuminator, that is, he carried the laser gun used to direct the laser energy on to the target. Schlitz carried laser-guided bombs, or LGBs.

"They checked in with two or three minutes of fuel left. I briefed them on the way in to save time. I put the smoke down marking the target. By this time, the illuminator was in orbit. He asked me which tank we wanted to hit first. I suggested the one that was not stuck. Within about 30 seconds he said, 'I've started the music,' meaning the laser beam was on the target. Schlitz was already in position for the drop, and the LGB hit right on that PT-76, blew the turret off and flipped the tank over. The blast covered the second tank with mud, so I put another smoke rocket down. Raccoon 'started the music' again. Schlitz meanwhile had pulled right back up on the porch for another run. The whole operation was

*A hard-sweating armorer loads 2.75-in Hydra air-to-ground rocket projectiles into an AH-1G Cobra. The appearance of tanks during North Vietnam's 1972 offensive – even lightweights like the Soviet-built PT-76 – posed a new challenge for US Army gunship crews.*

*Above: B-52D Stratofortresses flying from Guam drop bombs on a Viet Cong position from high altitude. The North Vietnamese pumped vast resources into a network of visual and radar warning outposts to give themselves warning of a coming B-52 mission. Soviet trawlers in the Pacific tracked B-52 take-offs and landings and Moscow shared this information with Hanoi. The Americans helped their adversary by using unimaginative tactics and scheduling missions on a predictable basis.*

months, intelligence reports had hinted at a North Vietnamese plan for a dramatic final effort, perhaps around Easter.

Obvious and ominous build-ups in North Vietnamese infiltration and logistic stockpiling were countered by an increase in air sorties, and a surge of B-52 Stratofortress activity at the start of 1972 rendered more difficult Hanoi's prospects for a coming offensive, but reductions in the number of warplanes available, coupled with vastly improved enemy defenses, restricted these efforts and preparations for the offensive continued unabated.

The previous year's 'Proud Deep Alpha' strikes had proven that whenever there were obvious and threatening build-ups in the North, the US was prepared to fly interdiction strikes, but the reduced number of aircraft available to cope with vastly improved North Vietnamese air defenses meant that each new trip above the

*Below: An OV-10 Bronco on a forward air control mission. By 1972, OV-10s of the 23rd Tactical Air Support Squadron at Nakhon Phanom, Thailand, were equipped with the Pave Nail installation – an electronic package that enabled the Bronco to operate at night and to stalk North Vietnamese infiltrators on the Ho Chi Minh Trail.*

**Left:** *PT-76 tanks under fire from AH-1G Cobras. In the 1972 Easter Offensive, Hanoi sent everything pouring southward. US fliers destroyed some PT-76s by killing crews with 'near miss' blasts of air-to-ground rocket projectiles.*

**Above:** *To the invading North Vietnamese, the AH-1G Cobra was a formidable adversary. Jets were too fast to be accurate but the Cobra could work its way inside a fight, stay there, and shoot it out with great success.*

over in three minutes. Two bombs – two tanks destroyed. I logged them in at 6.18 and off at 6.21. That must be a record of some kind."

Although the new laser-guided bombs were the most efficient air-delivered munition against armor, most tanks were destroyed by 500-lb (227-kg) bombs of the older, 'dumb' variety. Many were released from VNAF A-1s and A-37s – more accurate than F-4s with the same bombs but not as accurate as F-4s with LGBs.

Surprisingly, the North Vietnamese tanks were also being out-gunned by ARVN M48 main battle tanks, which were far from new and were fitted with a smaller-caliber gun.

For US Army AH-1G Cobras, battling the newly fielded enemy tanks was a tougher proposition. CW2 Neal Thompson was at the controls of a Cobra when he came upon a PT-76 tank in the Que Son Valley, not far from Da Nang. Thompson attacked with 2.7-in folding-fin aircraft rockets (FFAR). Although these projectiles lacked the power and explosive force to penetrate the tank's armor, the hammering on the PT-76 hull killed the crew and halted the vehicle.

17th Parallel was fraught with peril.

A USAF squadron which had been in South Vietnam longer than any other finally departed the country on 15 January 1972. The 19th TASS had been in the war so long that few could remember when Defence Secretary McNamara had said it would be withdrawn at the end of the war – in 1964! After nearly a decade with the O-1 Bird Dog and a few months with the OV-10 Bronco, the 19th TASS finally left Phan Rang and was relocated to Korea.

On 30 March 1972 North Vietnam invaded the South. After more than two years of low-level activity by both sides, the 'Spring Offensive' – or 'Easter Invasion' – was the all-out assault which had been predicted by analysts, making use of forces Hanoi had long held in reserve.

The architect of the 1972 'Spring Offensive', as far as US intelligence could tell, was General Vo Nguyen Giap of North Vietnam. Giap had been an early associate of Ho Chi Minh and had laid siege to the French at Dien Bien Phu. Unlike previous episodes, he now had the use of well-organized regular Army forces including tanks.

*The 388th Tactical Fighter Wing at Korat had started receiving cannon-armed F-4E Phantoms immediately after the 1968 bombing halt imposed by President Johnson and did not have a chance to take them into North Vietnam until 1972. This example is flying a mission during the 1972 'Linebacker' campaign when fighting 'up North' was hot and heavy.*

*Above: An AGM-62 Walleye air-to-surface missile is taken into battle by an A-7A Corsair II of VA-37 'Bulls', flying from the deck of USS Saratoga (CVA-60) during the 'Linebacker' campaign of 1972. Walleye proved most effective when used by two-plane 'hunter/killer' teams.*

In fact, the invasion was backed up by a staggering array of weaponry which the Communists had previously used not at all or only in limited numbers – T-34, T-54, and PT-76 tanks, SA-2 and SA-1 surface-to-air missiles (SAMs), 130-mm howitzers, and the AT-3 'Sagger' wire-guided anti-armor missile. About all the Communists lacked was air cover. Their MiGs never joined the fray in the South, although the recent growth of enemy air power up North was a complicating factor.

The weather seemed to favor Hanoi. In the first days of the invasion, low ceilings, thick overcasts, and intermittent rain hampered efforts to provide air support.

*As the pace of fighting picked up after the Communist invasion, warplanes were deployed on TDY (temporary duty) to reinforce the combat zone. This F-4D Phantom (66-8704) of the 523rd Tactical Fighter Squadron, Clark Field, Philippines, has come to Udorn, Thailand to be part of the mounting pressure against North Vietnam.*

The invasion was really three separate but well-co-ordinated actions – straight across the DMZ, south then east toward Kontum in the central highlands, and farther south across the Cambodian border towards the border provinces immediately north and north-west of Saigon.

In Saigon, General Lavelle committed virtually all of Seventh Air Force's assets to responding to the invasion and made it known that he would need reinforcement from outside. Because of the continuous withdrawals since the advent of the Nixon administration, the US fighter-bomber force in South Vietnam was but a shadow of its former size and strength. The US had only three F-4 Phantom and one A-37 Dragonfly squadrons in the country, just 76 aircraft in all.

## Rapid reinforcement

The invasion caused an instantaneous reaction aimed at bolstering tactical airpower in the war zone. Plans were immediately carried out to reinforce US air strength in South Vietnam. Perhaps the quickest action based on these plans occurred on 31 March when F-4D Phantoms of the 3rd Tactical Fighter Wing in Korea deployed to Da Nang and Ubon to augment existing fighter forces. On 3 April the USS *Kitty Hawk* (CVA-63) was the first of four additional carriers to join the two already on station off Vietnam.

On 2 April 1972, the invading North Vietnamese forces captured the provincial capital of Quang Tri. 6 April 1972 marked a major White House decision to return to North Vietnam – the beginning of an air campaign known as 'Freedom Train'. The old restraints of the Johnson years were off and targets were opened up – this was not going to be a repetition of 'Rolling Thunder'. With US warplanes going North again on a sustained basis for the first time in nearly four years, it was a new war...

Close on the heels of the F-4D deployment from Korea, the USAF rapidly deployed a number of tactical squadrons under the nickname 'Constant Guard', to augment the depleted residual air units remaining in Southeast Asia after the withdrawals of the previous years.

'Constant Guard' movements were to become... well, constant. 'Constant Guard I' was the move of F-105G Thunderchiefs and F-4E Phantoms from stateside bases to Korat and Ubon in Thailand. On 5 April these USAF fighter-bombers began reinforcing units in

# Combat Rescue

*"That others might live"*

Reconnaissance missions into 'Route Package One', the panhandle of North Vietnam, had become risky as the enemy was thought to be installing SAM sites. The prospect of the SAM and MiG threat moving closer to aircraft operating in the South and in Laos was on everyone's mind. An RF-4C Phantom reconnaissance crew from Udorn's 14th TRS/432nd TRW received two Distinguished Flying Crosses for the 'hairy' job of trying to ferret out those SAMs. When RF-4C Phantom 68-598 embarked on the same mission on 20 April 1972, it was hit by AAA fire and shot down near Vinh. NVA troops almost immediately overwhelmed and captured the pilot, Major Edward Elias – subsequently one of the third trio of prisoners of war to be released early by Hanoi.

## Epic effort

The backseater of the aircraft, Captain Ernest (Woody) Clark became the subject of an unusually prolonged rescue effort.

Clark was luckier than the pilot, if a man could be called lucky when his parachute was ripped to shreds by tree branches and he struck the ground hard enough to break several ribs. He heard North Vietnamese troops moving toward him from the next valley, a scant 600 meters away.

Jolted and hurt, Woody Clark retained the use of his AN/ARC-64 survival radio which gave him beeper and voice contact with friendly aircraft overhead. One of those friendlies was another RF-4C Phantom piloted by squadron mate Captain Donald S. Pickard.

World opinion had forced Hanoi to treat the POWs somewhat better than in earlier days, but this was little comfort to Woody Clark. An airman shot down in North Vietnam could still expect mistreatment, denial of medical treatment, even torture.

## Jungle survival

While Clark clawed and fought his way through jungle, up hillsides, across streams – sleeping infrequently and once coming within a few meters of a North Vietnamese soldier – RF-4C pilots Pickard and Greg Bailey criss-crossed the area, getting D/F fixes on Woody's hand-held radio. Captain Pickard even devised an elaborate scheme to drop Woody an RF-4C wingtank filled with food and medical supplies, though the plan was not carried out. Dozens of airmen, including 'Sandy' Skyraiders were looking for Clark.

In the end, he was one of the lucky ones. After two days and nights, an HH-53C Super Jolly Green settled down and a para-rescueman lifted him aboard. Clark had successfully evaded capture for what was, so far, the longest period of all – although Major Bob Lodge's backseater, Captain Roger Locher, would eventually surpass his 50-hour record a dozen times over.

*Above: Authorities in Hanoi released this graphic photo, possibly doctored to enhance its dramatic effect, showing an American aircraft plummeting out of the sky in flames. When it happened in North Vietnam, prospects for rescue were thin.*

*Below: Flown by courageous crews, the HH-53B/C Super Jolly Green plucked many airmen to safety after shootdowns, among them Phantom backseaters Woody Clark and Roger Locher who were on the ground in North Vietnam for extended periods.*

*An EB-66 Destroyer launches on a 'Linebacker' sortie. Designed as a bomber, the EB-66 served throughout the Southeast Asia campaign as an electronic warfare aircraft, jamming North Vietnamese radar and communications and flying as a pathfinder on radar-bombing missions.*

Thailand. Also included in 'Constant Guard I' were several EB-66 electronic warfare aircraft.

On 6 April Marine aircraft began landing at Da Nang. The Chairman of the Joint Chiefs of Staff, Admiral Thomas W. Moorer, announced a resumption of aerial attack and naval bombardment against North Vietnam. This was a limited undertaking but Moorer and other advisors to President Nixon were talking seriously about renewing a prolonged campaign.

To go along with the 'Constant Guard' movements of tactical jets from the US to Southeast Asia, Strategic Air Command began to deploy B-52D and B-52G Stratofortresses to Andersen AFB, Guam – in addition to those already on station – under the program

names 'Bullet Shot I' through 'V'. Some bombers were flying missions within 72 hours of receiving deployment alert at their stateside bases. Early 'Bullet Shot' deployments were made by the 306th Bomb Wing at McCoy AFB, Florida, and the 96th Bomb Wing at Dyess AFB, Texas.

The abrupt build-up of the B-52 force in the Western Pacific for a conventional bombing role posed a mighty challenge to SAC General John C. Meyer and the men on the scene. At this juncture the B-52 remained a key part of the strategic triad of bombers, ICBMs and sub-launched missiles, and it was no easy task to maintain readiness for nuclear war while freeing up more than one third of all B-52s for Vietnam.

## Build-up on 'The Rock'

On 'The Rock', as B-52 crews called Guam – actually, the top of a 35,000-ft (10670-m) mountain rising from the bottom of the ocean with its roots in the deepest part of the Marianas Trench – normal operations had to continue while the force of B-52s in residence grew in number. Included were 'Olympic Torch' U-2 missions, 'Combat Apple' RC-135 intelligence-gathering flights, and 'Giant Scale' SR-71 missions, some of them flown over Vietnamese soil. B-52s began to use parking slots, fuel and facilities hitherto reserved for other types. At the height of 'Bullet Shot' movements, Andersen AFB abruptly had 12,000 more men than it had billets for. Tent cities were a partial solution in an era of improvisation.

The B-52 had had a key role in striking enemy forces in South Vietnam all along. Bombing strikes against targets in North Vietnam by B-52s were resumed on 9 April. On the 11th the first strikes against the interior of the country were launched against Vinh. On the 15th major POL storage areas near Haiphong were hit.

General Lavelle was officially relieved of 7th Air Force command on 11 April and replaced by General John W. Vogt, Jr. Lavelle was charged with falsifying reports of unauthorized air strikes against North Vietnam. A full report on the Lavelle case would fill a book, but it should be noted that the general was charged with ordering about two dozen unauthorized bombings of military targets in

*Below: The B-52 force builds up. In 1972, in addition to these wings operating from crowded Anderson AFB on Guam, Buffs were flying from Kadena AB, Okinawa, and U-Tapao airfield in Thailand. And for the first time, the strategic bomber commitment to the conflict in Southeast Asia undermined US readiness for nuclear war.*

# Mining Haiphong

*Economic warfare bites deep*

It was inevitable that the 'Easter Invasion' would draw a response. On 8 May 1972 President Nixon announced the mining of North Vietnamese ports and the bombing of rail lines to "keep the weapons of war out of the hands of the international outlaws" in Hanoi.

## Using mines

He also stated that the US would stop all acts of force if the enemy would agree to return all American prisoners of war and consent to an internationally supervised ceasefire.

The use of aerial mines in warfare had been a rare event since 1945 but one for which US forces had maintained a capability. The dropping of barrel-shaped anti-shipping mines in and around Haiphong was carried out by A-6 Intruders and A-7 Corsairs.

Commander David Moss, skipper of the 'Mighty Shrikes' of VA-94 aboard the USS *Coral Sea* (CVA-43), led one of the first mining strikes and was surprised that the North Vietnamese did not mount even token resistance.

## Without a fight

No shore batteries, no SAMs, no MiGs. Rafael Iungerich, an intelligence officer with Seventh Air Force headquarters in Saigon, scrutinized the action reports of the mining missions and prepared a report for General Vogt, saying that the job had been carried out with incredible efficiency. "We zipped up that port tight," says

*A-6A Intruders of VA-96 'Main Battery' head for trouble with payloads of Mark 82 bombs. In 1972, A-6s were used to deliver bombs modified with pressure, acoustic and magnetic fuses to enable them to function as mines. The aim was to interdict and cut off North Vietnam's primary maritime supply route into the port of Haiphong.*

Iungerich. "After the first few sorties, there wasn't going to be any merchant ship going in or out of the harbor, no matter what."

North Vietnam between 7 November 1971 and 9 March 1972. On the latter date, the Inspector General of the Air Force went to Vietnam to look into allegations and on 23 March 1972, the inspector reported to Chief of Staff General John D. Ryan. Three days later, Lavelle was summoned to Washington, relieved of his assignment, and permitted to retire.

The whole time that Lavelle had ordered 'protective reaction' strikes in violation of the rules given him, the US had been bombing Cambodia in secret. The difference, of course, was that the latter bombing had been authorized by the President. Lavelle's error was not in attacking a few AAA and SAM sites but rather usurping civilian authority.

## Siege of An Loc

The battle for the town of An Loc in South Vietnam began in earnest on 13 April 1972, and two strong northern thrusts were repulsed with the aid of continued air strikes. On the 15th the town was besieged by NVA forces, and a massive airlift to supply the defenders was conducted in co-ordination with close air support.

The airlift effort at An Loc was superhuman. From 15 April until ground supply routes were reopened on 23 July, a total of 763 sorties air-dropped 10,081 tons of supplies. Several cargo aircraft were lost during the An Loc operations. Heavy B-52 support contributed greatly to the defeat of the NVA forces. As happened all too frequently, the town was destroyed in order to save it. An

*Below: In a tight spot like An Loc, South Vietnamese troops would have been quickly overwhelmed had they not been supported by tactical airlifters like this C-130 Hercules. This 'slick-winged' C-130B lacked the external fuel tanks carried under the wings of other C-130 variants and was about 15-mph (23-km/h) faster than all other versions.*

# 'Linebacker'

Nixon's decision to send US warplanes back to North Vietnam in force evoked memories of the 1965-68 'Rolling Thunder' air campaign over the North. That had not been a success, since it had not reduced the southward flow of supplies or forced Hanoi to make concessions at the conference table. This time, said the men who planned the bombing of the North, it was going to be different.

'Linebacker' was the name given to the new air campaign. It was aimed at the entire North Vietnamese transportation system, and was a continuing effort involving USAF and Navy tactical airpower and naval gunfire support. One of the differences was that 'smart' precision-guided munitions were being used. Aerial bombardment had always been an imprecise weapon, but now for the first time in history it had the means for real accuracy.

As the Intruder mining missions bottled up no fewer than 27 merchant vessels in Haiphong – and virtually sealed off North Vietnam's supply of AAA shells and SAM missiles – the Udorn-based crowd in the 432nd TRW was also in the air for 'Linebacker's' first day. A MiG-17 kill scored by Major Barton P. Crews and backseater Captain Keith W. Jones, Jr, using a Sparrow, proved to be the third of the war for F-4D Phantom airframe 66-7463 which had previously drawn blood at the hands of Kittinger and Olmsted. 463 would probably become the best-known Phantom of the war, but it was another F-4D aircraft (65-784) which was taken into battle on 8 May 1972 by the war's best pilot, Major Robert A.

Lodge. Lodge and backseater Roger C. Locher, who had been promoted to captain since their previous kill on 21 February, engaged a MiG-21.

Major Lodge was leading Oyster flight, a four-ship of F-4Ds charged with providing MiGCAP for Air Force and Navy strike aircraft carrying out missions in the Hanoi area. Oyster one and three had improved radar sets that enabled them to detect MiGs at extended range. The Navy's radar picket ship, known by its callsign Red Crown, was also available to provide early warning protection.

## MiG hunting

When Lodge put himself on a due-north heading, his intention was to go to the aid of Crews and Jones who, as it turned out, did not need it. Red Crown advised Lodge that he was about to be bounced by MiGs. Lodge brought his flight into a hard right turn to an easterly heading.

Captain Locher picked up the MiGs on the Phantom's radar at a distance of 40 miles (64 km).

*Left: A B-52D Stratofortress (56-0684) on a combat mission in 1972. The B-52 force worked for the brass in Saigon but remained under the Strategic Air Command which never turned its aircraft over to theater commanders.*

Loc was reduced to rubble.

In spite of the dramatic escalation of the war, the United States held to its decision to withdraw. On 26 April 1972, in the midst of the North Vietnamese invasion, President Nixon announced plans to reduce 20,000 more personnel so that American strength in South Vietnam would fall to 49,000 by July.

## Further reinforcement

'Constant Guard II', the next stage in the cycling of stateside tactical fighters back into Southeast Asia to cope with the invasion and its aftermath, commenced on 26 April. In this stage, squadrons of F-4E Phantoms from two US locations were moved to Udorn, Thailand. The base already occupied by Lodge, Locher, Curtis, Ritchie, Olmsted, Feinstein, Bailey, Clark and Pickard was becoming very, very crowded.

A week later an entire wing, the 48th Tactical Fighter Wing from Holloman AFB, New Mexico, consisting of four squadrons of F-4D Phantoms, was moved to Takhli, also in Thailand. This 'Constant Guard III' movement was accompanied by the airlift of over 8 million tons of cargo, and combat operations began within 24 hours of the arrival of the Phantoms. 'Constant Guard IV' came next, the movement of two squadrons of C-130E Hercules from the US to nearby Taiwan.

The sudden intensity of the new war was highlighted on 16 April 1972 when three MiG-21s were shot down in one day by Phantom crews of the Udorn-based 432nd TRW. One pilot, Captain

*Left: An F-4D Phantom of the 435th TFS, part of the fabled 8th TFW 'Wolfpack' flying from Ubon, Thailand, is seen taking on fuel during a 1972 'Linebacker' strike. Like so many of the surviving portraits of combat aircraft en route to North Vietnam, this image was captured by a Phantom crew while loitering at 'anchor' waiting to refuel from the tanker. KC-135 Stratotanker crews also did their share of photography during refueling operations.*

*Above: VA-165 'Boomers' flew A-6A Intruders from USS Constellation. By 1972, teething troubles with the Intruder's navigation and bombing systems were history and the A-6A had proven itself an accurate and hard-hitting warplane.*

Lodge maneuvered aggressively to get within missile range but the MiGs, apparently under ground control, turned away. To be certain that he did not fire on a friendly aircraft, Lodge went into afterburner and drew close enough to make visual confirmation of a brace of MiG-21s. He closed to within about a mile (1.6 km) and unleashed a Sparrow. The MiG went down. It was the second kill for Lodge and Locher who celebrated by

painting a second red star on the splitter vane of 65-784. Nobody at Udorn had the slightest doubt who the first ace of the war was going to be.

They were wrong. On 10 May 1972 the 'Linebacker' campaign brought the biggest day of air combat of the war, when strikes were carried out against bridges, marshaling yards, and other targets, nine MiGs were shot down, and a Navy F-4J Phantom crew became the war's first aces.

*Right: The F-4 Phantom in the foreground and the A-4E Skyhawk were mainstays of Marine Corps ground attack aviation capability. During the 'Linebacker' era, the Marines kept up the pressure with a record number of sorties.*

Frederick S. Olmsted, Jr, achieved the distinction of getting his own second MiG kill while also chalking up the second kill for the airframe he was flying, F-4D Phantom 66-7463 which had previously scored with Kittinger at the controls. Another Udorn crew credited with a MiG-21 on that day was Major Edward D. Cherry and Captain Jeffrey S. Feinstein. Major Robert A. Lodge did not score on that day but like Lodge, Feinstein was not yet finished with his war...

On 28 April Dong Ha fell. On 1 May Quang Tri city fell to the North Vietnamese. The ARVN troops who mounted a defence fought valiantly, but the 40,000 NVA in the area outnumbered the friendlies at least three to one. The weather continued to make air support virtually impossible.

## Three Navy kills

6 May 1972 also brought no fewer than three MiG kills as the 'Screaming Eagles' of VF-51 on *Coral Sea* and the 'Aardvarks' of VF-114 on *Kitty Hawk* pitted their Phantoms against the North Vietnamese air force, reportedly led by the infamous Colonel Tomb. A VF-51 F-4B Phantom bagged a MiG-17, while two VF-114 F-4Js shot down a pair of MiG-21s.

'Freedom Train' was not a total solution to the Northern problem. An even wider air war up North was now being planned.

The new campaign had been under consideration for some time. Kissinger had advised Nixon that it might force North Vietnam to negotiate seriously, but that it could also threaten a summit meeting

*Right: F-4 Phantom backseater Captain Jeffrey S. Feinstein of the 13th Tactical Fighter Squadron became the third US Air Force air ace of the Vietnam war. Feinstein, a member of the 13th TRS/432nd TRW at Udorn, racked up his fifth aerial victory on 13 October 1972. Like many pilots and weapons systems officers, Feinstein credited his success on hard-working ground crews, including crew chief SSgt Salvador Herrera who handled the Phantom flown by Lt Col Griff Bailey and Feinstein.*

with Soviet President Brezhnev, now in the final planning stages. The JCS had recommended that the best way to deliver a telling blow to North Vietnam was to mine Haiphong harbor. Nixon ignored the risk to US-Soviet relations, accepted the howl of protest that would come from the anti-war protest lobby, and ordered the go-ahead. 'Freedom Train' was replaced by the harder-hitting operation 'Linebacker'.

On 8 May 1972, A-6A Intruders from the three carriers now at Yankee Station seeded Haiphong harbor and surrounding areas with airdropped anti-shipping mines. A-7E Corsairs supported the mining operation. Commander David Moss, skipper of the A-7E-equipped 'Mighty Shrikes' of VA-94 on *Coral Sea*, survived being hit by a SAM. Parachuting into waters just off Haiphong, he was rescued while under fire from shore batteries. F-4B and F-4J Phantoms flew top cover for the mine-scattering mission and in the process VF-96's Randy Cunningham and his backseater Willie Driscoll racked up their second MiG kill. At about the same time, a Navy surface ship downed a MiG with a Talos surface-to-air missile – one of the few times when one of North Vietnam's fighters threatened the Fleet.

## Large-scale air battles

The furious level of fighting on 10 May 1972 was many things to many people: in the US, it sparked new protests about a perceived escalation in the conflict. In Hanoi, it was a stunning blow – perhaps the first time the North Vietnamese had experienced the potential of unfettered American air power. The loss of 11 MiGs in air-to-air combat, even when measured against the loss of a valued combat leader like Major Bob Lodge, had to be a serious blow to the North Vietnamese air force. The bottling-up of Haiphong harbor and the severing of the country's major bridge spans – none of which had been accomplished during the 1965-68 'Rolling Thunder' effort – was felt in Hanoi. Captured documents showed that key officials in the Communist government felt that their invasion of the South had bogged down and that the infrastructure of their own nation in the North was being ripped asunder. No-one knew it at the time, least of all the anti-war demonstrators back home, but a remarkable thing was happening. The United States

*Above: Aboard USS Constellation in the Gulf of Tonkin, Air Wing Nine Phantoms, Corsairs, and Vigilantes are being prepared for strikes against the Haiphong area. It is 9 May 1972, and the strikes the next day will lead to the biggest air fight of the war. F-4J Phantoms from MiG-killing squadrons VF-92 and VF-96 are at the stern of the ship.*

*Below: A MiG-21 'Fishbed' of the North Vietnamese air arm. Some of Hanoi's aces reportedly preferred the MiG-17 because, although older, it was the more nimble of the two widely-used fighters. But the MiG-21, with its infra-red missiles, was a serious threat, and the air-to-air results achieved by the MiG-21 fleet were far from negligible.*

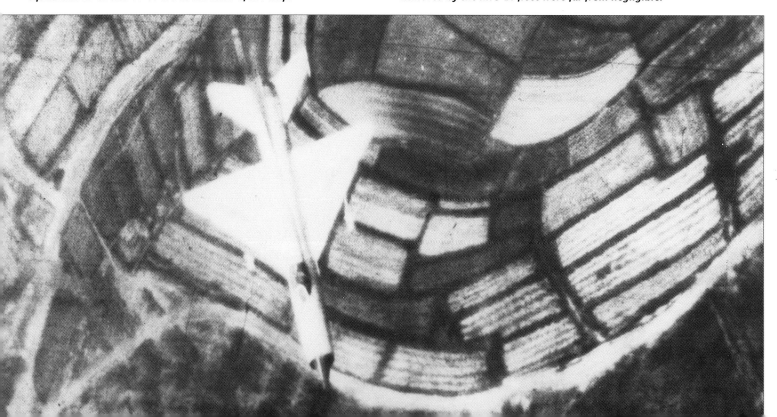

# Tenth of May: the Battle Begins

*The biggest air-to-air duel of the war*

May 1972 was the third day of 'Linebacker', notable for the largest air-to-air score of the war, 11 MiGs shot down. It was the day LtJG Curtis R. Dose of the 'Silver Kings' of VF-92 redeemed a family's investment over two generations by joining the ranks of MiG killers; the day the Navy's Cunningham and Driscoll became aces; and the day Major Robert A. Lodge collided with destiny. To many, including Hanoi's Colonel Tomb, it was the biggest day of the war...

Curt Dose was the son of Bob Dose, skipper of a World War II fighter squadron, later commanding officer of *Midway*, and a renowned test pilot of the 1950s. Curt had gone through the Naval Academy at Annapolis and ACM training at 'Top Gun'; he was a seasoned veteran of a previous cruise with VF-92, with 160 missions under his belt.

## Hornet's nest

At 08.30 hours, Dose and Lieutenant Austin Hawkins launched in a two-aircraft F-4J Phantom division from USS *Constellation* (CVA-64). In the back seat of Dose's F-4J (157269) was radar intercept officer Lcdr James McDevitt. En route to the busy tend threatening airfield at Kep, already alerted that MiG-21s were preparing to launch, Dose was about to stir up a hornet's nest.

Curt Dose and Austin

Hawkins' pair of Connie F-4Js from VF-92 stirred up enemy defenses first and almost certainly provoked MiG action against the later strikes of the day. The two Phantom pilots went in at low level and 'beat up' Kep airfield, obtaining a spectacular view of two MiG-21s running up their engines in clouds of dust at runway's end. Dose was pondering a shot at them when his backseater reported that they were rolling. Dose and Hawkins abruptly found themselves engaging two MiG-21s at perilously low level in the Kep pattern.

## Close combat

The North Vietnamese pilots were fully aware of the Phantoms; they pickled off their centerline tanks and went into some fancy maneuvering to try to improve their situation. Dose did some fancier maneuvering. At 09.05 hours, the VF-92 pilot unleashed a pair of AIM-9 Sidewinders in quick succession at one of the MiGs. It was possibly the first time a Navy aviator had fired Sidewinders while at supersonic speed and treetop level. Another Sidewinder from Hawkins, like Dose's two, missed. Dose got off his third Sidewinder and watched it rush up the MiGs tailpipe and explode.

Air Force strikes were being mounted by Colonel Carl S. Miller's 8th TFW, the Ubon-based 'Wolfpack', and by Colonel

Charles Gabriel's 432nd TRW at Udorn. The latter also put up a two aircraft RF-4C recce mission from the 14th TRS/432nd TRW, which went aloft at 08.30 hours. Major Sidney S. Rogers and Captain Donald S. Pickard took their RF-4Cs up toward the Yen Bai airfield complex and the Paul Doumer Bridge. Pickard was about to have his day ruined by his Phantom's wingtanks.

Also from Udorn, four F-4D Phantoms under experienced fighter leader Major Robert A. Lodge, again using the callsign Oyster flight, headed up towards Hanoi on another MiGCAP.

The fiery, aggressive Lodge

*A Phantom is tied to the bridle on one of the steam catapults aboard Constellation. The carrier's Air Wing Nine and its F-4Js were to achieve stunning success in the unprecedented 10 May fight.*

pushed his men hard, himself harder. When another F-4D flight was delayed in approaching the Hanoi-Haiphong area, Lodge took the assigned areas of both flights for himself.

*Below: Late in the day on 10 May, Lt Matthew Connelly of VF-96 uses classic fighter-jock language to describe a difference of opinion with one of two MiG-17s that he downed that day. Thomas J. Blonski, his RIO, looks on.*

# Tenth of May: Navy Aces

Above: The slab-cheeked B-57G Canberras of the 13th Bomb Squadron, were packed with high-tech sensors for the night attack mission. The B-57G was the last light bomber to serve in the USA, and the type came to the end of their meritorious combat odyssey in 1972, after almost 50 thousand sorties over Southeast Asia.

was actually winning the war against the Communists.

Along with his hawk's claws, President Nixon had also extended an olive branch: in public statements connected with the heavy fighting on 10 May 1972, Nixon said that the US would stop all acts of force if the enemy agreed to return all American POWs and an internationally supervised ceasefire were agreed upon. The POWs remained all-important. Not exactly stated in explicit terms but clearly implied was that the Nixon administration would settle for a simple end to the fighting: "Give us our POWs, leave South Vietnam in existence, and we'll go home."

## Talking tough

Nixon's people were talking and fighting tough, but were willing to accept a settlement on reasonable terms. Indeed, the withdrawal of US forces and the Vietnamization of the war continued. During May, the Tropic Moon B-57G Canberras of the 13th TBS were returned to the United States. The combat career of the B-57 had finally ended. The venerable 'Thud' was also finally phased out of the Pacific region with the sole exception of the F-105G 'Wild Weasel' aircraft of the 17th WWS operating at Korat.

Addition of the Grumman E-2A Hawkeye AWACS aircraft to the Fleet off the North Vietnamese coast greatly enhanced the potential of carrier-based squadrons to inflict harm on Hanoi's homeland. Operating in unison with Disco and Red Crown, the Hawkeye did more than merely guard Yankee Station's carrier forces from attack. The early-warning aircraft provided radar and electronic information about SAM and MiG operations, giving American crews a distinct edge. The improved E-2B variant soon followed and was in action with squadron VAW-116 on Coral Sea during the hectic fighting of May and June 1972.

On 31 May 1972, USAF fighters claimed two MiG-21s in air battles. Captain Steve Ritchie got one of these while flying an F-4D Phantom of the 555th TFS/432nd TRW, his backseater being Captain Lawrence H. Pettit. While the two men of a Navy crew always flew together, Air Force crews did not. This was Ritchie's

**D**ose's 'Silver Kites' had a sister squadron on *Constellation*, the 'Fighting Falcons' of VF-96. While Dose and Hawkins worked over Kep, VF-96 fliers Randy Cunningham and Willie Driscoll were still 'mounting up'. The pair's two previous MiG kills had been achieved in the same F-4J Phantom (157267) but today they were flying another, the squadron's CAG aircraft (155800). Cunningham and Driscoll were part of the Navy's second strike of the day, an Alpha Strike of 27 Phantoms, Intruders and Corsairs from 'Connie' heading to attack the marshaling yards at Hai Duong, a crucial supply bottleneck between Hanoi and Haiphong.

## Ground attack

Randy Cunningham and his usual wingman Lt Brian Grant began their mission by hurtling downward through 37-mm and 57-mm AAA at Hai Duong to deliver Rockeye cluster bombs. Then Cunningham heard warnings that MiGs were in the air approaching the strike group.

Cunningham was first to spot the incoming enemy. He called, "MiG-17! MiG-17! Brian, he's on my tail. I'm dragging him! Get him, baby!" This high-risk attempt to set up a kill for Grant, a measure of Cunningham's value as a team player, proved unsuccessful. Moments later, reversing and turning into the MiG, Cunningham fired a Sidewinder. The missile accelerated off the rail and tracked straight towards the enemy, causing a quick, brittle blast that blew the MiG to bits.

Cunningham's squadron mate Lieutenant Michael J. Connelly, flying a VF-96 Phantom (155769) with RIO Lt Thomas J. J. Blonski in the back seat, shot down two MiG-17s in quick succession. Yet another Phantom crew from the same squadron, Lt Stephen C. Shoemaker and LtJg Keith V. Crenshaw, dispatched another MiG-17 with an AIM-9.

## Second kill

Cunningham and Driscoll rescued a wingman by using another Sidewinder to bag a MiG-17 – their second kill of the day and fourth of the war. But they were not finished yet...

Randy Cunningham saw another hostile aircraft rushing at him. Positioning his F-4J to pass the MiG close aboard as he had done so often during 'Top Gun' training, Cunningham almost forgot that these guys had 23-mm and 37-mm nose cannons. The MiG pilot fired quick careful bursts at him while Cunningham pulled abruptly into a vertical climb. He looked back to see that the MiG was in the climb with him – a difficult maneuver that could have been accomplished only by one of the most aggressive and experienced of

*Below: A battle-stricken MiG-17 trails smoke – possibly not enough to be fatal – after being hit near Hanoi. In 1972, US naval aviators with improved training under their belts more than matched these agile foes.*

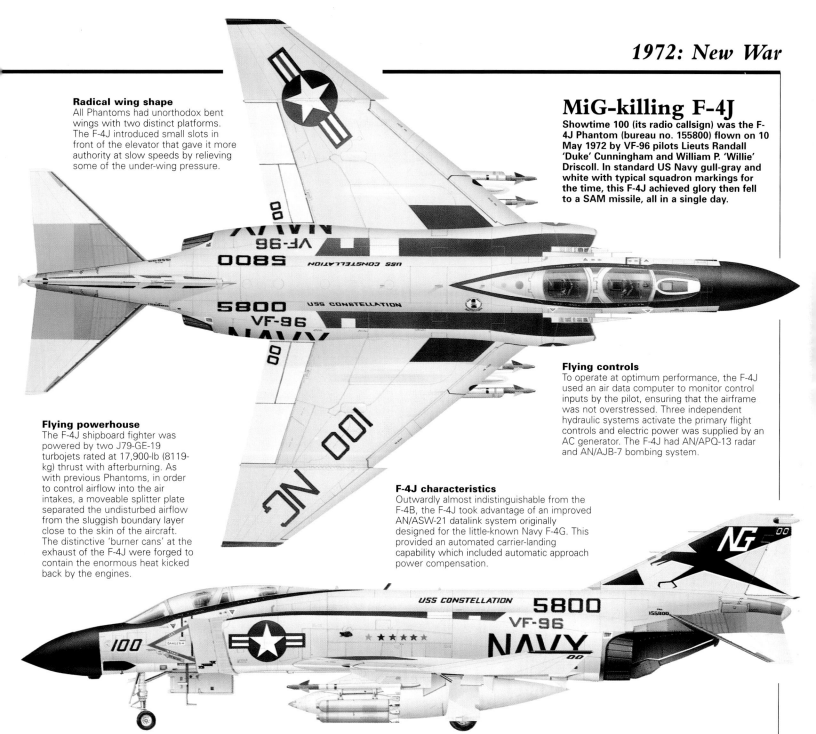

**Radical wing shape**
All Phantoms had unorthodox bent wings with two distinct platforms. The F-4J introduced small slots in front of the elevator that gave it more authority at slow speeds by relieving some of the under-wing pressure.

## MiG-killing F-4J

Showtime 100 (its radio callsign) was the F-4J Phantom (bureau no. 155800) flown on 10 May 1972 by VF-96 pilots Lieuts Randall 'Duke' Cunningham and William P. 'Willie' Driscoll. In standard US Navy gull-gray and white with typical squadron markings for the time, this F-4J achieved glory then fell to a SAM missile, all in a single day.

**Flying powerhouse**
The F-4J shipboard fighter was powered by two J79-GE-19 turbojets rated at 17,900-lb (8119-kg) thrust with afterburning. As with previous Phantoms, in order to control airflow into the air intakes, a moveable splitter plate separated the undisturbed airflow from the sluggish boundary layer close to the skin of the aircraft. The distinctive 'burner cans' at the exhaust of the F-4J were forged to contain the enormous heat kicked back by the engines.

**Flying controls**
To operate at optimum performance, the F-4J used an air data computer to monitor control inputs by the pilot, ensuring that the airframe was not overstressed. Three independent hydraulic systems activate the primary flight controls and electric power was supplied by an AC generator. The F-4J had AN/APQ-13 radar and AN/AJB-7 bombing system.

**F-4J characteristics**
Outwardly almost indistinguishable from the F-4B, the F-4J took advantage of an improved AN/ASW-21 datalink system originally designed for the little-known Navy F-4G. This provided an automated carrier-landing capability which included automatic approach power compensation.

North Vietnamese pilots. The MiG-17 was believed to have been flown by the infamous Colonel Tomb.

There ensued a furious dogfight in which each pilot tested the other's skills to the limit. After some minutes of dueling with the MiG and keeping watch on his fuel state, Cunningham went into a vertical climb again. Again, the MiG-17 stayed with him.

### Slowing down

This time, Cunningham did the unexpected. He retarded both throttles to idle and put out the speed brakes. In the same motion, while heading straight up, he applied hard rudder to force the Phantom into a shuddering movement which brought the F-4J beneath the belly of the MiG.

The MiG, just on the edge of

slow-speed control, pitched back toward the ground and attempted to escape straight down. But the Phantom was now in perfect position. An AIM-9 missile went straight at the MiG. Long seconds ticked past and Cunningham and Driscoll were certain they had missed. Then, a flash of flame and black smoke erupted from the MiG-17, which flew into the ground. There was no parachute.

Cunningham was heading seawards when he heard a SAM warning, and a missile detonated within feet of the F-4. It quickly became evident to Cunningham

*Duke Cunningham and Willie Driscoll strike a pose on an F-4J. 'Hero' pictures of crews routinely hung in a squadron's ready room were also called 'go to hell' pictures, but this one could be displayed with good reason.*

that he was losing hydraulics and lateral control and he had to battle to reach the coast. Using a combination of manual rudder, afterburner and downright imagination, Cunningham somehow got over water. He and

Driscoll ejected and were scooped out of the drink. They had achieved their third, fourth and fifth MiG kills, had apparently taken out North Vietnam's best pilot, and had become aces – the first of the long and difficult war.

# Tenth of May: Busting the Bridge

**"T**hey got a little place down south of the ridge. Name of the place is the Doumer Bridge..." began a fighter pilot's song about the 5,532-ft (1686-m) Paul Doumer Bridge, the 19-span rail and highway trestle at Hanoi. It had shrugged off everything the Americans had thrown at it in previous years. Today the Air Force's 'Wolfpack', the 8th TFW, arrived over the bridge carrying laser-guided and electro-optical guided bombs. Captain Thomas P. Messett was one of the pilots in the initial strike force.

## Formation attack

Messett's Phantoms drew within sight of the long bridge basking beneath clear sky – the pilots'

*Below: F-4D Phantoms of the 433rd and 435th TFSs, 8th TFW, set off on a mission armed with Paveway LGBs (laser-guided bombs). The combination ultimately severed key bridge spans deep in North Vietnam.*

view broken only by bursting AAA shells. Messett and his wingmen had to maintain rigid flight discipline while rolling in on

the bridge so that their 1,000-lb (454-kg) Mark 84 bombs could enter the laser 'basket' – a cone of airspace, created by the Paveway

*Above: Bridges are probably the most under-estimated targets in all of aerial warfare. The North Vietnamese stood up to hundreds of attacks. But by 1972, 'smart' bombs gave the attackers a good chance of success.*

laser designator carried by their flight leader, within which the bombs would guide. These 'smart' bombs had not been used up North before and they were going to change everything.

Criss-crossing tracers joined bursting 57-mm and 85-mm shells over the bridge as Messett's force went in, but the AAA threat was less serious than previously: with the F-4D's automated bombing system, it was possible to release ordnance at 14,000 ft (4270 m), well out of range of the smaller-caliber AAA.

Pulling off, Messett was certain

second MiG victory, but with a different GIB (guy in back) than on the first.

The internally-mounted cannon on the F-4E finally claimed a MiG on 2 June 1972, when Major Philip W. Handley and Lt John J. Smallwood claimed a MiG-19. Their unit, the 58th TFS/432nd TRW, was one of a number of squadrons that had been brought into Southeast Asia as reinforcements.

The SA-7 man-portable, shoulder-launched SAM was introduced to South Vietnam in April with the invasion. Designed to home in on its target with an infra-red heat-seeker, the SA-7 became at once a serious threat to all aircraft, especially to helicopters and slow-flying machines such as the A-1 Skyraider and AC-130 'Spectre' gunship.

Tactics had not really been developed to cope with a SAM that could be carried by a single infantry soldier and the first response – which was simply to fly missions at higher altitude – almost proved disastrous when pilots belatedly learned that the SA-7 was effective

*Left: At Nakon Phanom, Thailand in April 1972, these proven A-1E Skyraiders are soon to face a new weapon of war – the shoulder-mounted, man-portable missile in the form of the Soviet-designed SA-7 'Strela', often known by its NATO codename of 'Grail'. North Vietnamese forces began using the SA-7 during their 1972 'Easter Invasion'.*

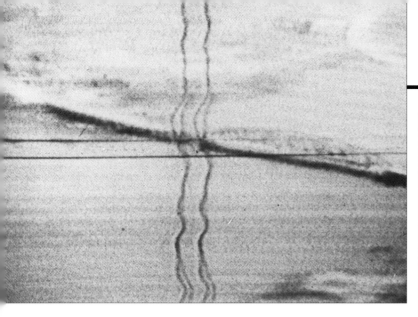

that some of his Mark 84s broke the trestle's span.

Recce pilots were not having an easy day. In their RF-4C Phantoms, Sid Rogers and Don Pickard headed deep into Route Package Six to position themselves for immediate poststrike photography, to see how well Messett and mates had done against the Doumer Bridge. For a sustained time of struggle and discomfort, they eluded SAMs and MiGs that seemed to be everywhere around them, and Pickard later brought home a grainy photograph of a MiG-17 stalking him from below and behind.

### Self-inflicted damage

Rogers and Pickard both made their photo run successfully. Moments later, Pickard's Phantom (68-606) was severely damaged, not by North Vietnam's ground-to-air arsenal but by his own starboard wingtank: as soon as he jettisoned his tanks, one of them damaged the wing, causing a fuel leak.

This happened at about 12.15 hours and marked the beginning

*Photos relayed from the guidance camera of a Walleye missile show the precision with which advanced munitions could strike. But all too often the damage was temporary. Only one thing was more resilient than bridges, and that was the North Vietnamese capacity for finding alternatives, detouring, rebuilding, and getting their traffic back on the move.*

of a long and difficult fight for survival. Unable to team up with a tanker, Pickard coaxed and prodded his way home, at one point steering towards the Marine airstrip at Nam Phong when Udorn's pattern was cluttered with battle-damaged aircraft.

Pickard egressed, crossed Laos near Vientiane, and in the end decided to land at Udorn after all. Flying on one engine, hardly approved procedure in the Phantom, Captain Pickard was limping on a straight-in approach when a malfunction of the cockpit de-fog system filled the inside of his canopy with ice. 'Blind', Pickard was talked-in by his wingman. He set down at Udorn with barely enough fuel to taxi off the runway.

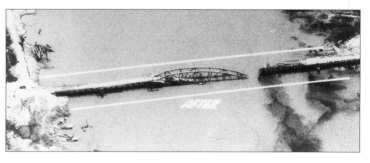

up to 5,000 ft (1524 m). During April and May several A-1 Skyraiders, O-1 Bird Dogs and O-2 Skymasters fell victim, partly because they were too slow, partly because pilots had never been trained to evade the tiny lethal missile.

The first AC-130 'Spectre' ever be shot down in South Vietnam fell to the SA-7 on 18 June. The gunship was flying south-west of Hue – next after Quang Tri as a likely target of the Communist assault – its crew believing that it was high enough to escape harm from the missile. Sergeant William B. Patterson was the lookout for the aircraft, which had the callsign Spectre II. Patterson lay on the aft cargo door, actually hanging out into the airstream so that he could spot the tell-tale flash of light when a missile was fired.

Everything worked the way it was supposed to. Patterson gave the warning when an SA-7 was fired and came rushing up at the AC-130, its rocket motor burning with an eerie blue-white light – boring straight at the gunship rather than porpoising back and forth the way SA-7s usually did. The pilot fired a decoy flare and began

*Right: The abrupt appearance of the SA-7 shoulder-mounted missile was not a total surprise to US and South Vietnamese officers. Even so, few pilots had adequate training in how to avoid the heat-seeking weapon. But the authorities in Saigon worked hard to get the word out, and training sessions were improvised to cope with the new threat.*

*Left: Having gotten into this struggle when the concept of 'limited war' was fashionable, Americans and their South Vietnamese allies now found themselves in a setting rife with the ferocity of all-out conflict. An Loc during the 1972 invasion was a charnel house of slain enemy troopers and wrecked light tanks and trucks – all wrought by air power.*

an evasive turn but the SA-7 reached Spectre II anyway, colliding with the number three engine.

The violent, booming explosion shook the aircraft. The AC-130 bucked, threw its nose up, and settled again as the right inboard engine separated from the wing. There was a confusion of voices on the intercom as crew members reported the AC-130 heading downward and beginning to disintegrate.

Sergeant Patterson rolled back into the aircraft, unhooked the restraining strap which kept him from falling out, and reached for his chest-pack parachute. At about that time the right wing came off and the aircraft started into a cartwheeling roll. Patterson managed to hook only one side of his parachute to his body harness, in his haste attaching it backwards, when new explosions sent him hurtling into the black void outside. Only three men survived this mid-air encounter. Patterson was one of them.

## Assault at Kontum

In general, ARVN troops were holding well against North Vietnamese might – including the tanks. The friendlies could not, however, prevent a Communist attack in force on Kontum in the Central Highlands on 25 May 1972. As the enemy probed the outskirts of the city with massed infantry and tanks, all available air and gunship support was put aloft to help the defenders.

As the battle progressed and the North Vietnamese continued to attack and fight with their big guns, it was time for the first combat use of a small force of US Army helicopters equipped with TOW (tube-launched, optically-tracked, wire-guided) anti-tank missiles. Three UH-1B Huey helicopters and crews along with mechanics and hardware for the TOW system had arrived in late April 1972, traveling via the much-used MAC C-141 StarLifter. The

*Below: After years of guerrilla insurgency and 'peoples' conflict', the North Vietnamese were now confronting their opponents with a conventional – and very potent – all-out military assault. This Soviet-designed T-54 main battle-tank belonging to Hanoi's forces was captured and is being displayed by ARVN troops in Saigon.*

# Tenth of May: Fight for An Loc

The 1972 invasion saw powerful conventional forces launched against the South. American air power was needed to help the ARVN and VNAF throw back the assault.

The siege of An Loc came to a climax on 10 May, as seven Communist regiments launched an assault to try to overwhelm the 4,000 defenders of the city – a quarter of whom were wounded. The siege had started on 5 April when the NVA offensive against III Corps started with a three-division drive south into Binh Long Province from Cambodia. Highway 13 from Saigon was cut, and the ARVN 5th Division was surrounded in An Loc.

Between 7 and 11 April the garrison was reinforced by two Ranger and two infantry battalions, moved in by helicopter. On 9 April, the ARVN began shifting units north from IV Corps to relieve An Loc, and over the next few days B-52s were committed to aid the city's defenders. In spite of these measures a Communist spearhead of four tank companies and a reinforced regiment penetrated An Loc's perimeter on 13 April. By the next day, the ARVN 1st Airborne Brigade had reached a position adjacent to An Loc by helicopter and effectively increased its perimeter.

## Supply from the air

For more than two months, supplies could only be brought in by air. At first helicopters and VNAF C-123s were used, but losses were prohibitive, and by the middle of April An Loc relied completely upon US C-130 parachute drops for survival.

Air Force Captain Thomas Hammons flew his O-2A observation plane daily over the city, chatting calmly over the radio with a US advisor sweating out the North Vietnamese attacks below. Hammons' job was to act as an intermediary between those in need below and the swarm of Phantoms, Corsairs, A-37s, AC-130s and Cobra gunships which he could call up and direct. Hammons learned nothing about the man, not even his name. Talk was confined to business – but there was plenty of that, as was reported in a *Time* magazine interview.

"'I'd like napalm south of town, napalm and CBUs (cluster bomb units) in town and hard bombs seven klicks north-west of town,' the adviser on the ground would order in a typical conversation. Or occasionally, after a bombing run, 'Babe, that was too close for us. Keep your stuff at least 600 meters to the east, O.K.?'"

"During one attack on NVA positions around An Loc, a Cobra pilot complained when F-4 Phantoms running short of fuel were assigned his target. The man on the ground blew up. 'We ain't playing no goddam game, boy. If you can't take it, you get your ass back to base until you cool off. You hear me, babe?' Hammons gauges a day over An Loc hopeful or hairy by the voice of his unseen colleague. 'When he's calm, he stutters a little bit. When things are hot, he shoots those words out without a pause.'"

## Steady resistance

The 10th of May attacks were met by stout ARVN resistence, bolstered by massive B-52 and tactical air strikes. Relieving forces pressed north on Highway 13, and got to within two miles of An Loc by 19 May. On 9 June part of the relief force broke through to the city but the Communists resealed the gap and continued the siege. Smashed from the air and the ground, the exhausted North Vietnamese finally broke off the siege on 11 July and retired to Cambodia.

*Forward air controllers in O-2s played a crucial part in the defense of An Loc. Air support, was provided by a wide range of combat warplanes, ranging from attack helicopters and fighters to AC-130 gunships (top).*

*The presence of Communist armor in significant numbers made the 1972 invasion more dangerous than anything which had gone before. But it also provided American fliers with much better targets than the jungle guerrillas they had faced up to now, and many Northern tanks like this T-54 at An Loc were destroyed.*

# Keeping the Bombers Flying

*The tanker force's all-out effort*

**B**y June the number of B-52 Stratofortresses based in the western Pacific totalled 206 aircraft, the largest Strategic Air Command (SAC) bomber force ever assembled in the region. And 172 KC-135 Stratotankers were assembled to support the bombers.

It is almost impossible to exaggerate the importance of the KC-135 tankers, which faced an ever-growing workload. Besides being essential to the movement of newly arriving aircraft across the Pacific, they had to serve aircraft flying combat missions in a war zone which now encompassed four countries – Cambodia, Laos, North and South Vietnam. Until the enemy offensive, most B-52 missions had been flown from U-Tapao, the Thai air base from which any target could be reached without mid-air refueling.

Now, B-52s from Guam had to fly thousands of miles to reach their targets. This required en route refueling, and a force of KC-135 tankers took position at Kadena for this purpose. With augmentations of US airpower under the 'Constant Guard' deployments, air refueling requirements rose from a stabilized commitment of 36 per day to a peak of 130 daily. SAC also positioned 46 tankers at U-Tapao and several other bases.

**Above: The KC-135 had a crew of five comprising two pilots, navigator, flight engineer and boom operator. The enlisted 'boomer' is earning his keep here as a Stratotanker performs the laborious job of pumping JP-4 jet fuel into a ravenous eight-engined B-52G Stratofortress.**

**Below: In 1965, KC-135s flew 9,282 sorties, and replenished 31,250 aircraft. By 1972, intense operations meant that the tankers flew 34,728 sorties and refueled a total of 67,655 aircraft. Over the course of the war, the busy Stratotanker performed a remarkable 813,878 refuelings.**

wire-guided missiles were released at close range and packed a substantial warhead.

At first light on the second day of the fight for Kontum, TOW engaged the enemy's tanks. Among the first 101 firings of the missile only 12 were evaluated as misses. Through 12 June the Army claimed 26 tank kills by the helicopter-borne TOWs, including no fewer than 11 formidable T-54s in the Kontum area.

USS *Saratoga* (CV-60), an eastcoast/Atlantic Fleet carrier, arrived at Yankee Station. She was the first Navy carrier to drop the CVA (attack carrier) in favor of the CV (carrier), a decision which resulted from Sara carrying her own ASW (anti-submarine warfare) elements. The carrier had not originally been scheduled for a WestPac cruise, but the sudden intensity of fighting occasioned by the 'Easter Invasion' and the 'Linebacker' campaign meant that the ship was needed urgently. Commander Lewis Dunton, an A-7A Corsair pilot, recalls the ship being literally uprooted on 'hours' notice for her very first-ever combat deployment.

Several more MiGs fell in air action in June, without the Communists achieving significant success in return. On 21 June 1972, it was *Saratoga*'s turn. Cdr Samuel C. Flynn, Jr, executive officer of VF-31, launched from Sara at the controls of an F-4J Phantom with Lt William H. John in the back seat. Flynn and John, using the callsign Bandwagon, were given vectors to lead a division towards a flight of MiG-21s. A relatively close-quarters battle ensued and Flynn employed a heat-seeking Sidewinder to bring down his quarry.

Operations by *Saratoga*'s air wing, especially her Corsairs, along with Air Force missions were important in breaking the siege of An Loc and thus bring to an end any prospect that Hanoi's invasion would achieve its intended purpose. The obvious bears repeating: Hanoi had intended that the invasion would achieve the final victory over the South. It did not.

On 29 June 1972, General Frederick C. Weyand replaced General Creighton Abrams as the American field commander in Saigon. Weyand had earlier commanded the 25th Infantry Division in Vietnam and had been military advisor to the Paris peace talks in 1968-70.

## Attrition tactics

It seems unique to the American character to behave like a loser while winning, and vice-versa. Since the mining of Haiphong, North Vietnam was having the greatest difficulty merely surviving, let alone fighting, and the relentless 'Linebacker' effort was wearing the enemy down. Yet Washington was willing to accept terms which made it seem the US was losing instead of winning. It was another election year. The incumbent Nixon was in many respects at the peak of his popularity. There had been a break-in at Democratic party headquarters in the Watergate Hotel in Washington, and the Democrats were about to nominate a staunch anti-war campaigner (and former B-24 Liberator pilot), Senator George McGovern, to stand against Nixon. Nixon's supporters were playing dirty tricks with the Democrats when they were so far ahead, they did not need to; the Washington policy makers were willing to make concessions to Hanoi when they were winning by

# Alpha Strikes

With 'Connie's' successes receiving so much attention, it might have gone unnoticed that *Coral Sea* and *Kitty Hawk* also had Phantom squadrons in the air. An F-4B Phantom flown by Lieutenant Kenneth L. Cannon of the 'Screaming Eagles' of VF-51, with Lt Roy A. Morris, Jr, in the back seat, scored the 11th and final MiG kill of the day, shooting down a MiG-17 near Hanoi.

Perhaps even less noticed were the courageous actions of men who flew Intruders, Corsairs and other types in the massive air battles. *Coral Sea* sent Commander David Moss and other A-7E Corsair pilots of the 'Mighty Shrikes' of VA-94 to suppress SAM installations around the Haiphong region. *Kitty Hawk* mounted several strikes by its A-7E Corsair squadrons, the 'Golden Dragons' of VA-192 under Commander D. R. Taylor and the 'Dam Busters' of VA-19s under Commander Mason L. Gilfry.

## A serious business

One of the 'Dam Busters', Lieutenant Michael A. Ruth, began that day the way most combat pilots did.

"You feel a concern. It's not fear, because the people who experience fear can't do this. But you're concerned and you're very quiet. You know that you'll talk wildly when it's all over, but beforehand you're just quiet and serious."

The Paul Doumer was not the only important bridge in North Vietnam. Ruth was part of a 37-ship Intruder and Corsair strike force from *Kitty Hawk* aimed at the strategic rail and highway span at Hai Duong.

A document put out by Vice-Admiral William P. Mack, commander of the Seventh Fleet, said that "...the destruction of this vital bridge (will) cut the east-west flow of military supplies and limit the enemy's freedom of logistical movement in support of their (sic) forces in the South."

## Iron Hand

A massive Alpha Strike swarmed down on the area around the Hai Duong Bridge. Executive officer of the 'Dam Busters', LtCdr Norman D. Campbell led an Iron Hand flight, his A-7E carrying four AGM-45 Shrike anti-radiation missiles. To attack the bridge's center span came VA-195's Lt Charlie Brewer and Lt Mike Ruth. Their two Corsairs were carrying Mark 83 1,000-lb (454-kg) and Mark 84 2,000-lb (908-kg) bombs configured to combine minimal drag with heavy punch.

SAMs and AAA fire were everywhere as Mike Ruth lined up behind Brewer and began his run-in. Tracers criss-crossed the air in front of him but, because of the earlier efforts by Phantom crews, there was no threat from MiGs. This was small comfort. Ruth was under exceedingly heavy fire.

## Medal mission

His citation for the Distinguished Service Cross says that he "continually maintained close section integrity... despite intense enemy opposition. Positioning his aircraft at an optimum roll-in point, Lt Ruth commenced a devastating attack and despite a wall of intensive anti-aircraft artillery fire placed all ordnance directly on target."

*Above: VF-102 'Diamondbacks', an eastcoast squadron, made their first combat cruise in F-4J Phantoms aboard USS America (CVA-66) from 10 April to 6 December 1968. The increased tempo of operations in 1972 saw more Atlantic Fleet squadrons returning on America's decks to play their part in the fight.*

*With a **USAF F-4D Phantom** from the 8th TFW as pathfinder, a 'joint package' puts bombs on the target. This strike force includes A-6A Intruders from VA-75 'Sunday Punchers' and F-4J Phantoms from the Marines' VMFA-232 'Red Devils'. The date is August 1972, the location North Vietnam.*

# Phantom Supreme

On 11 May 1972, an analysis presented to General Vogt at Seventh Air Force in Saigon and also made available to Admiral Mack at Seventh Fleet seemed to confirm the general impression that the new campaign was having an impact on Hanoi. The air operations seemed to be stopping the flow of supplies entering North Vietnam by land and were disrupting the enemy's entire transportation system. It was noted that the use of precision guided weapons, 'smart' bombs, was a significant factor in the campaign's effectiveness.

Deprived of Colonel Tomb's leadership, the North Vietnamese MiG force continued to suffer losses. On 11 May, a MiG-21 was downed in a fray with F-4D Phantoms but the action was so furious and confusing that no credit was awarded to any individual crew for the kill. On 12 May 1972, Lt Col Wayne T. Frye and Lt Col James P. Cooney of the 'Triple Nickel' 555th TFS/432nd TRW at Udorn, the pilot and backseater of an F-4D Phantom (66-8756) shot down a MiG-19 using a radar-guided Sparrow. Frye and Cooney believed that they deserved "a world's record for the total age of a Phantom aircrew for a MiG kill". Between the two, they had lived 85 years on this planet. They were also the first and only pair of lieutenant colonels in the same aircraft to get a MiG.

### F-4s in command

Phantom crews at this juncture commanded the skies. Tactics had now incorporated earlier Vietnam lessons, and had finally reached the point where they worked. The emphasis on speed which had been so important in fighter combat in previous wars was almost forgotten, for both the Phantom and MiG-21 could fly much faster than they could fight.

American pilots used a 'fluid

*Of three million Americans who served in Southeast Asia between 22 December 1961 and 7 May 1975 (the US Congress' official dates for the Vietnam war for the purpose of determining veterans' benefits), only about 60,000 saw actual combat. Most had non-combat roles, but many like these tower operators nevertheless performed essential duties.*

*Below: F-4Ds and F-4Es of the 432nd TRW and 33rd TFW head for Hanoi. By 1972, the Phantom had been in service for more than a decade and, while it had some irritating flaws, the F-4 reigned supreme as the fighter against which every competitor in the world had to be measured.*

so much, they had no need to concede anything at all.

There were now six American carriers operating off the enemy coast, virtually half of the carrier force available to the entire US Navy – *America*, *Hancock*, *Kitty Hawk*, *Midway*, *Oriskany* and *Saratoga*. Every mission being flown up North, from bombing to reconnaissance, was impeded by the poor weather conditions. For the crew of *Oriskany*, things were made worse when the ageing World War II carrier bumped up against an ammunition ship in a collision which wrecked one of its aircraft elevators. The carrier completed its cruise, but with severe difficulty.

As of 12 August 1972, all US combat troops had departed South Vietnam. Some 43,500 Americans remained in the country in advisory and administrative roles. It was announced on 29 August that 12,000 more troops would be withdrawn by 1 December, leaving authorized strength at 27,000.

The fighting up North was fast and furious. Among participants were the US Marine fliers of the 'Red Devils' of VMFA-232, fighting from the dust-strewn Rose Garden at Nam Phong. On 26 August 1972, a Marine F-4J Phantom was lost in air-to-air combat

for the first time in the war. Notwithstanding greatly improved training, there were bound to be times when this sort of thing happened. In this instance, the loss of a Phantom in air-to-air combat was attributed to poor airmanship on the part of the section lead. On other occasions, simple failure in communication was often a problem.

Intelligence reports make it clear that Hanoi really was 'hurting' under the burden of the 'Linebacker' campaign and that leaders of the Communist regime were having second thoughts, for the first time in more than a generation, about their prospects of taking over South Vietnam. 'Linebacker' still imposed some restrictions on US aircrews, and a few inviting targets still escaped American attention, but there was no doubt that Washington's strategy, for once, was

*The AU-23A Peacemaker, an American adaptation of the Swiss PC-6 Turbo-Porter utility aircraft, was designed to provide the USAF with a STOL (short take-off/landing) capability for COIN (counter-insurgency) operations in Southeast Asia. The USAF acquired 36 in 1972, and turned 33 of them over to the Thai air force and Thai police.*

*Above: When the F-4E arrived in Southeast Asia in the late 1960s it remedied what had long been seen as a fault in the Phantom, being equipped with a fast-firing internal Vulcan 20-mm cannon. However, the first aerial victories for F-4E had to wait until 1972, and were achieved with missiles.*

*Above: Flight decks sailors worked hard but very cautiously. Getting in the way of an F-4 being launched was not a good idea: at a combat weight of around 20 tons, a Phantom being hurled aloft by an aircraft carrier's steam catapults had the kinetic energy of a railroad boxcar being heaved off a cliff.*

four' formation which enabled each set of two aircraft in a four-ship flight to be ready to move when MiGs were spotted. Barrel roll and vertical scissors attacks, trading speed for position, were used effectively against the MiGs despite the latter's advantage in maneuverability over the Phantom. All reference to 'up' and 'down' was discarded as air combat became a matter of energy maneuvering, irrespective of an

aircraft's location relative to the ground.

Two MiGs fell to Navy crews on 18 May 1972, one of these being the first use of the more advanced AIM-9G variant of the Sidewinder missile. Air Force and Navy crews claimed no fewer than four MiGs on 23 May 1972, one of these being the first downed by an F-4E Phantom, although the internal 20-mm cannon with which E model was fitted was not used for the kill.

*In what was to become a familiar scene in 1972, Lt Oran Brown and his pilot Lt Bart Bartholomy are joined by Lt Patrick Arwood and his RIO Lt Michael Bell as the four naval aviators from VF-161 celebrate aboard Midway. The two Phantom crews had just downed two MiGs north-east of Hanoi.*

working. Not that protest against the US role in the war slackened, but some Americans felt that they could finally see the end in sight – an end with South Vietnam intact.

On 1 September 1972, Admiral Noel Gayler became CINCPAC. The new chief of US forces in the Pacific was a representative of a new generation of naval officer, partly a fighter, partly a technocrat. Gayler left considerable authority in the hands of the Seventh Fleet and Task Force 77 commanders, as well as the skippers and CAGs aboard his carriers.

On 9 September 1972, the team of Captain John A. Madden, Jr, and Captain Charles B. DeBellevue, aboard an F-4D Phantom of the 555th TFS/432nd TRW, shot down two MiG-19s in a single fight. For DeBellevue, the kills were his fifth and sixth, making him

*Right: Capt Lawrence H. Pettit belonged to what its members called the 'fightin'est' squadron of the war, the 555th TFS 'Triple Nickel'. Pettit, who with his pilot Captain John A. Madden was to down a MiG by maneuver in October 1972, is comparing notes with a crew chief who kept his very busy 432nd TRW F-4D Phantom in the air.*

Above: The F-111A 'Aardvark' returned with a vengeance for the new round of fighting in 1972, far readier for battle than it had been during its disastrous first deployment four years earlier. Here, an F-111A paves the way for a brace of F-4 Phantoms. The F-111A was much larger than the F-4 and carried heavier bombloads over greater distances.

the ranking American ace of the war. Madden would eventually claim three MiGs and would have a claim for a fourth denied by the Seventh Air Force Enemy Aircraft Claims Evaluation Board because of 'insufficient evidence'.

There were, of course, continuing losses and an increasing population of 'new guy' POWs. Men who had been in captivity for as much as eight years considered the 'new guy' captives to be junior to them in every respect.

Below: With variable geometry wings swept forward for improved low-speed performance in the airfield pattern, an F-111A 'Aardvark' from the 474th Tactical Fighter Wing touches down at a base in Thailand. F-111As fought throughout the 1972 'Linebacker' campaigns and continued bombing Cambodia after the 27 January 1973 ceasefire in Vietnam.

At the time, of course, none knew if they would ever get out of North Vietnam, but the state of despondency they had felt earlier had been replaced by simple joy at the knowledge that American warplanes were operating in Hanoi's skies again. On 10 September an A-7B pilot of VA-82 from USS *America* (CVA-66) became the latest POW, and the Communists went to unusual lengths to photograph the remains of his Corsair in a pond.

On 16 September an operation by South Vietnamese troops recaptured Quang Tri city, but most of Quang Tri province remained in Communist hands.

The next step in the continuing movement of US aircraft into Southeast Asia was 'Constant Guard V' on 28 September, when two F-111A squadrons from Nellis AFB, Nevada, arrived at Takhli. They relieved the F-4D Phantom squadrons of the 49th TFW which had deployed under 'Constant Guard III' in May. The return of the F-111A to Southeast Asia was long overdue and most important. Although the earlier deployment in 1968 had been star-crossed, the 'Aardvark' now proved itself to be a well-designed and thoroughly able fighting machine. Its superb navigation system and all-weather capability, coupled with ordnance-carrying capacity, made it the only Air Force craft capable of the kind of 'lone wolf' night/bad-weather operation which had been routine for the Navy's A-6A Intruder.

## Air Force A-7s

Beginning on 10 October in 'Constant Guard VI', two squadrons of Vought A-7D aircraft (not given the Corsair nickname assigned to Navy versions) deployed to Korat to replace the F-4E Phantoms of 'Constant Guard II'. This was the first appearance in the combat zone of the USAF version of the A-7. Combat missions by Air Force A-7s began on 16 October 1972, and plans were finalized to use the A-7D as a replacement for the A-1 Skyraider in the Sandy role as the escort for combat rescues.

Early in October, with very little notice, the 186th MiG kill of the war had been achieved by an F-4D Phantom of the 13th TFS/432nd TRW with Lt Col Curtis D. Westphal in the front seat and Captain Jeffrey S. Feinstein in the back. The crew had used a Sparrow to blast a MiG-21 out of the sky. Feinstein, who flew more often in the company of Lt Col Carl G. (Griff) Baily, rarely did

# Enter the Prowler

*Electronic warrior takes to Vietnamese skies*

July 1972 saw the introduction to battle of the Grumman EA-6B Prowler, a modified electronic warfare version of the A-6 Intruder with a 40-in (103-cm) extension of its fuselage to make room for its third and fourth crew members, and with a variety of 'black box' devices designed to make life difficult for the enemy's sensors. The EA-6B had made its maiden flight on 25 May 1968, powered by two Pratt & Whitney J52 engines. The Prowler was configured to carry jamming pods which covered eight frequency bands. Possibly ahead of its time, the Prowler was the premier electronic warfare aircraft in the world when it was introduced to combat.

First operations were flown by a crew of VAQ-132 from the USS *America* (CVA-66), another eastcoast/Atlantic Fleet carrier which had returned to the conflict. *America's* cruise was also of interest for another reason. Its air wing included the F-4J Phantoms of VMFA-333

'Shamrocks', one of the very few Marine units to fly against North Vietnam from aboard ship.

*Above: The black cross on the radome is to make certain a landing signal officer does not mistake it for an A-6A Intruder. This EA-6B Prowler was relatively slow and short-legged, but it introduced much needed electronic warfare technology to carriers at a critical time.*

*Above: Crowded skies. F-4D and F-4E Phantoms from the 432nd TRW and 388th TFW form on a KC-135 tanker to pay yet another visit to Ho Chi Minh's successors. The bombs on the F-4E in the foreground carry extended 'daisy cutter' fuses designed to detonate the weapons bombs above the ground level, so scattering the explosive effect more widely.*

anything to call attention to himself but he had just achieved a kind of immortality. Feinstein was the fifth and last American ace of the war and the second man to attain this status who sat in the back seat of a Phantom and who was not a pilot.

Were Feinstein and his mates winning the war? By October 1972, the skies over North Vietnam were much as they had been over Nazi Germany in 1945: American warplanes roamed at will, unchallenged, uncontested. The North Vietnamese had virtually no AAA ammunition or SAMs left. They had squandered their principal national force of 12 army divisions (leaving only one division in reserve at home) on an invasion that had failed. By every possible measure, North Vietnam in October 1972 had lost its war against the United States. As one official put it, perhaps with a premonition: "The only thing we haven't done is to fly B-52s over their heads around the clock."

*Above: Mark 80 series Snakeye retarded bombs dangle from the wing pylons of this A-7 Corsair. In 1972, the Navy was flying A-7A, A-7C and A-7E models from carrier decks on Yankee Station in the Gulf of Tonkin. Each successive version of the Corsair II introduced a more powerful engine, an attempt each time to give more thrust to an otherwise fine warplane which remained woefully underpowered.*

Incredibly, at the very point when it had won the war, the US backed off. Henry Kissinger announced that, as a result of his talks with Le, "Peace is at hand". On 23 October 1972, 'Linebacker' operations against North Vietnam were halted and all bombing north of the 20th Parallel was curtailed. Once again, the skies over Hanoi and Haiphong were free of US warplanes. An official history says simply: "Termination of 'Linebacker' was the result of perceived progress in the ongoing peace negotiations. Unfortunately, the desired effect was not realized."

## Another bombing halt

Why was the 'Linebacker' campaign ended and bombing north of the 20th Parallel brought to a halt? Those are questions not for airmen but for policy makers. In a week's time, the American people were going to re-elect Richard Nixon as President, Watergate or no Watergate, and everybody knew it. Nixon, then, needed no face-saving gesture toward opponents of the war. He appears to have halted the bombing because he genuinely believed that Hanoi was now ready to settle the conflict at last.

He was almost right. Some in Hanoi were ready. Some were going to need more persuasion.

"Peace is at hand," Kissinger said. This, too, was a mistake. The United States embarked on Project 'Enhance Plus', designed to build up the VNAF to a level adequate to conduct operations after a ceasefire or withdrawal by US forces. Between September and November in a rush effort, no fewer than 288 additional aircraft had been transferred to the VNAF (116 F-5A/Bs, 90 A-37s, 28 A-1s, 22 AC-119Gs and 32 C-130As). There could no longer be any doubt that the VNAF, now the world's third largest air force, had far more aircraft than it could possibly use. Some of the F-5s delivered to Saigon's air arm had been aircraft originally slated for Taiwan and South Korea.

Overstocking the VNAF was a conscious decision. Although neither side had tabled the proposed text of an agreement to end the war, US leaders felt that any such armistice might include a prohibition against introducing new combat aircraft into Vietnam.

*Above: An A-37B Dragonfly unleashes fin-retarded Mark 84 Snakeye 1,000-lb (907-kg) bombs on the Viet Cong. Although based on the T-37 primary trainer, the A-37B was actually a larger and more powerful aircraft. It remained relatively simple to maintain, which made it a suitable candidate when Saigon's air arm converted from props to jets.*

*Lt Colonel Carl G. 'Griff' Baily and Captain Jeffrey S. Feinstein of the 13th TFS make a final check of their flight charts before boarding their F-4E in August 1972. Bailey was the pilot for two of Feinstein's five aerial victories, against MiG-21s in July 1972.*

The Navy had an ace. The Air Force had none. But on 8 July 1972, for the first time, it began to look like the USAF might catch up. Captain Steve Ritchie went aloft from Udorn in an F-4E Phantom with Captain Charles B. DeBellevue in the back seat.

Ritchie's Paula flight was assigned the MiGCAP role for a 'Linebacker' strike, flying at low altitude west of Phu Tho and south of Yen Bai – the latter a 'sore thumb' that the Americans yearned to cut off. Disco and Red Crown advised Ritchie of

*MiG killers of the 432nd TRW at Udorn, Thailand on 11 August 1972. Front row: Capts Charles Debellevue (6 MiGs) and Richard S. (Steve) Ritchie (5 MiGs). Back row: Lt Col Griff Baily (2 MiGs) and Capt. Jeffrey Feinstein (5 MiGs).*

MiG-21s about 40-miles (62-km) south-east of his position. Ritchie took Paula flight toward the hostile aircraft in patrol formation and crossed the Black River on a southerly course. Red Crown informed him that his own radar image had just merged with that of the MiGs.

Ritchie turned north. He spotted two MiG-21s at his 10 o'clock position. He ordered the flight to punch off its external fuel tanks and executed a hard left turn as the MiGs swung to the right. Ritchie was able to get off a radar-guided Sparrow

*Left: Flown by Joe Kittinger, Fred Olmstead and Steve Ritchie, F-4D Phantom 66-7463 became the most successful fighter of the war, and showed its six kills proudly in this post-Vietnam portrait (in 1980s camouflage). No other jet downed more than three MiGs.*

*Below: Captain Charles B. DeBellevue flew back seat for Steve Ritchie in four of his air combat victories, beginning with a kill in the great battles of 10 May. He added two more with Captain John A. Madden to become the highest-scoring American ace.*

missile which struck a MiG dead-center causing it to explode and disintegrate in mid-flight.

Ritchie then turned hard right, rebuilding lost energy, and pursued the lead MiG-21, which was now in a rear-quarter attack on one of his wingmen. Again, he was able to 'acquire' the target for the radar-guided Sparrow. He fired one Sparrow which hit the MiG-21 and caused a brilliant yellow fireball. The aircraft went into the ground. Steve Ritchie had now matched Robin Olds' feat of achieving four air-to-air victories over North Vietnam and his backseater, Chuck DeBellevue, had credit for three.

## More MiG kills

The next two Udorn MiG kills were scored by the team of Lt Col Carl G. Baily and Captain Jeffrey S. Feinstein. This left Feinstein with three MiG kills, Baily with two. 'Ace fever' was rampant at Udorn. Somebody, it seemed, was going to match Cunningham and Driscoll of the Navy by downing five North Vietnamese aircraft.

It was inevitable. As the fighting continued, the Air Force finally achieved what the Navy had accomplished already. As an official history puts it, "Captain Richard S. Ritchie, 555th TFS, Udorn, shot down his fifth MiG-21 over NVN on 28 August 1972 to become the first USAF ace of the conflict."

Ritchie's backseater, Captain Charles B. DeBellevue, who was not yet an ace himself but would be, was an honest advocate for the aircraft they were flying:

*Right: Steve Ritchie looked like a recruiting poster or a Hollywood hero, but he was the real thing – the ace pilot with a rare touch on stick, rudder, and Sparrow missile. The captain scored two kills in F-4Es and three in F-4D 66-7463, in which four different pilots claimed a total of six MiGs.*

"Well, not having flown anything but an F-4 and, of course, the various models each handle a little differently, I'd say the F-4 is very honest. It talks to you. If you're doing something it doesn't want to do, it will let you know.

## Going too far

Now, you can press the issue and keep going with it – in which case the airplane will pretty much take over, go out of control or whatever. But before you lose control, it will talk to you. The wings will start rocking or, in the D model, which is what we flew in SEA, once you reach a regime approaching the limits of maximum performance, you can't see the instrument

panel because the airplane is vibrating and shuddering so much. It's talking to you. If you know how to fly it, you'll ease off a little bit – no big deal." DeBellevue later became a front-seat pilot in the Phantom.

Ritchie performed a victory roll when he returned to Udorn. Upon landing, he was met by fire engines, high-pressure water and champagne. Some say Ritchie was steered to his fifth

kill, set up for it, as part of a team effort. In fact, Ritchie was in a somewhat unfavorable position relative to the MiG-21, fired two Sparrow missiles to get himself into better shape, and finally fired two more Sparrows to achieve the MiG kill. It was the crowning success of Steve Ritchie's second combat tour in Southeast Asia, and he fully deserved credit for a major achievement.

*Above: Pulling out the stops as the first, prolonged 'Linebacker' effort went on, US warplanes attacked many of the plum targets that had been off-limits for much of the war. Here, a US Navy Alpha Strike has paid a visit to a vital POL (petroleum, oil, lubricant) storage area in Haiphong, North Vietnam's most important port city.*

*Above: During the 'Linebacker' campaigns, aircraft 'bed-down' space was at a premium as temporary-duty units kept arriving to bolster the US air power inventory. This aerial view of Thailand's Takhli airfield in September 1972 shows F-4 Phantoms of the 388th TFW and other combat units snuggled chock-a-block with no shelter against attack.*

(Such a prohibition was part of the 1953 Korean ceasefire and was abrogated in 1958 not by the Communist side but by the US.) Even if they were not bound by such an agreement, Nixon administration leaders knew very well that the US Congress might prevent them from supplying military equipment to Saigon's armed forces in any future conflict – and, indeed, they were correct in their interpretation of Congress's intent.

Americans who re-elected Nixon that first week in November genuinely believed, as did Kissinger, that peace was coming. But these hopes were abruptly dashed. Once the bombing stopped the Communists simply followed past form and began rebuilding. As a kind of symbolic display of their real intentions, on 22 November 1972 the North Vietnamese succeeded at last – after seven years of trying – in shooting down a B-52. A B-52D Stratofortress of the 307th Strategic Wing from U-Tapao, itself operating south of the 20th Parallel in keeping with Nixon's show of restraint, was hit by a SAM. The Stratofortress made it to Thailand where the crew ejected and were recovered. In finally claiming a Buff, Hanoi may have committed a serious error: this juncture in history was not the right moment to get people thinking about B-52s. Nor did the North Vietnamese assist matters by stomping out of the peace talks on 13 December.

# A-7D 'Sluf'

**J**ust as 'Linebacker' was coming to an end, the 354th TFW of Myrtle Beach AFB, South Carolina, deployed to Korat in Thailand. Colonel Thomas M. Knoles III led three squadrons of a new addition to the USAF combat inventory. Although technically not given the name Corsair II, the A-7D was virtually identical to the Navy A-7E which had already been flying in combat from carrier decks for two years. Knoles's wing was soon joined by a locally-activated PACAF squadron, the 3rd TFS, under Lt Col Edward R. (Moose) Skowron, also operating the A-7D. The SLUF ('short little ugly fella') was more popular with pilots than many realized and the aircraft acquitted itself well during bombing missions in the final week of 'Linebacker'.

## Sandy replacement

As part of the Vietnamization effort, A-1 Skyraiders were desperately needed for turnover to the South Vietnamese air force. The air force chose the A-7D to relieve the Skyraiders in the 'Sandy' role, escorting armed helicopters into enemy territory on combat rescue missions. Tactics had to be changed, for the A-7 could not fly slowly enough to keep pace with an HH-53C Super Jolly Green helicopter. Instead of directly escorting the chopper, A-7D pilots flew slow lazy circles while leading rescue forces to the scene where downed airmen needed help.

## Rescue mission

In November 1972, a two-man F-105G 'Wild Weasel' was shot down south of the 20th Parallel in the heavily-defended Vinh region. Captain Colin A. (Arnie) Clarke of the Korat-based 354th TFW spent nearly 12 hours in his A-7D cockpit, with four refuelings from KC-135 tankers, fighting poor weather, faulty communications and heavy ground fire to guide HH-53Cs to the rescue. Clarke was hit by a 57-mm shell in a running battle with AAA batteries, repeatedly risking getting below fuel minimums while taking damage. Clarke's was a marathon effort which resulted in the rescue of the crew of the last F-105 shot down in Southeast Asia. For his perseverance, Clarke was decorated with the second highest American award for valor, the Air Force Cross.

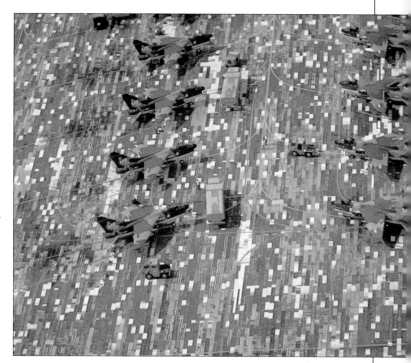

*Above: A-7Ds merge into the camouflaged ramp at Korat in 1972. The 354th TFW brought the 'D' model to Asia with its 353rd, 355th and 356th Tactical Fighter Squadrons. The A-7D made a superb bomber and a fine escort for rescue aircraft.*

*Below: Technically, the US Navy's Corsair II name did not apply to US Air Force A-7Ds. The ship in the foreground (71-304) belongs to the 354th TFW and, together with others in a formation, is being observed from inside a KC-135 tanker.*

*Right: An uncommonly pleasing portrait of the rescue forces' busy Super Jolly Green captured by the camera of USAF SSgt Norman Taylor. This HH-53C (68-10360) belongs to the 37th Aerospace Rescue and Recovery Squadron at Da Nang, but is seen visiting Phu Cat. The basic design of this powerful helicopter had been created at the urging of the US Marine Corps – for decades, a pioneer among the US services in helicopter development – which had needed a versatile, heavy-lift craft to support ground combat troops. To the US Air Force, it was a logical improvement upon the HH-3E Jolly Green which performed many of the early combat rescues in Vietnam.*

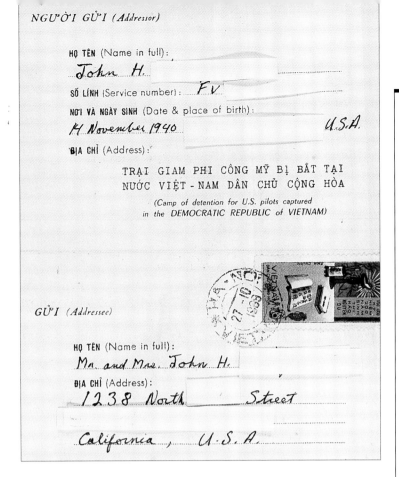

*Possibly for the first time in Vietnam, America was fighting for clearly defined goals. Every one of the very few heavily censored letters home which made it out of North Vietnamese prison camps underlined the fact that thousands of American fighting men were prisoners or missing, and a major aim of the 'Linebacker' campaigns was to win their release.*

The peace Kissinger had predicted was elusive. On 18 December 1972 the third and final campaign over North Vietnam was launched. 'Linebacker II' was directed against military targets in the Hanoi/Haiphong area. The message to field commanders minced no words: "You are directed to commence... a maximum effort, repeat maximum effort, of B-52/Tacair strikes in the Hanoi/Haiphong areas..."

The largest number of B-52s ever assembled – now between one-third and one-half of SAC's worldwide force – was to carry the brunt of 'Linebacker II' strikes against the North Vietnamese heartland. For once the restrictions which hamstrung American airmen over the North were removed. 'Linebacker II' was to be an all-out effort.

To those who supported the campaign it was the 'Eleven-Day War'. To those who opposed it, including folk singer Joan Baez who was on the ground in Hanoi, it was the Christmas bombing – although the campaign was briefly halted on 25 December.

It is generally understood that 'Linebacker II' inflicted such a painful blow to Hanoi that Le Duc Tho was finally forced to ink an agreement with Henry Kissinger. In the South, the campaign heartened Saigon's leaders who were delighted to see a massive show of force.

## Coming to a close

US Air Force people in Saigon who kept the numbers decided that tactical forces in PACAF flew 254,895 combat sorties and expended just under 900,000 tons of munitions in Southeast Asia during the year, suffering the loss of 194 aircraft. These figures include 115,298 attack sorties and 28,383 B-52 Arc Light sorties. KC-135 Stratotankers accomplished 111,770 aerial refuelings. A summary of the 'Eleven-Day War' from 18 to 29 December over North Vietnam shows 714 B-52 sorties, 830 USAF tactical sorties, and 386 US Navy/Marine sorties. Nineteen aircraft were lost to enemy action during 'Linebacker II' – 15 B-52s, two F-4 Phantoms, and two F-111As. The North Vietnamese launched a total of 1,293 SAMs during the operation.

On 31 December 1972 there were only 7,600 USAF personnel remaining in South Vietnam.

# 'Linebacker II'

There was, in the end, no choice for the American President. Richard Nixon was determined not to give the mixed signals or the indications of weakness which had been transmitted by his predecessor. Secure in his election victory, convinced that force would end the war, Nixon prepared for the first time to authorize a maximum, round-the-clock bombing effort against the urban centers of Hanoi and Haiphong. Steps were taken to strip the Strategic Air Command's force of about 450 B-52 Stratofortresses around the world and to commit fully one-half of that force to the new bombing effort.

Folk singer Joan Baez, visiting Hanoi, would call it the 'Christmas bombing' (although, in truth, a respite would come on that holiday). SAC people would call it the 'Eleven-Day War'. But the official name was inevitable. The final campaign of the American war against North Vietnam was to be known as 'Linebacker II'.

## Eleven days

The final campaign was fought over the 11-day stretch from 18 to 29 December 1972. It brought the population at Andersen AFB, Guam, up to some 12,000, or nearly three times the number of people the base was intended to accommodate – meaning that B-52 people ate, slept and moved around the base in improvised fashion. Even the base gymnasium was pressed into service to accommodate the overflow, this quickly taking on the appearance of a huge dormitory which provided little privacy or respite from the demands of a 72-hour work week. The 'Linebacker II'

*Below: The B-52 looked like a dark, brooding giant even when sitting idle on the ramp. But idle B-52s were not very common during the 'Eleven Day War'. Andersen Air Force Base on Guam was in constant turmoil as the huge bombers left, returned, and left again, day after day.*

campaign was to cost no fewer than 15 B-52s shot down by Hanoi's surface-to-air missiles, although none were lost to MiGs, despite enemy claims. It was to demand an unusual measure of commitment from everyone involved.

On 18 December 1972 – the first day of the campaign, and also the day when F-4D pilot Captain John Madden claimed a MiG kill which was disallowed – waves of B-52 Stratofortresses swarmed over the Hanoi/Haiphong region. SSgt Samuel O. Turner, the fire control operator or tail-gunner of an U-Tapao-based B-52D Stratofortress flying in a three-ship cell called Brown flight, became the first enlisted man and the first gunner to shoot down a MiG-21. Another B-52 tail-gunner claimed a MiG kill that night which was disallowed for lack of sufficient evidence.

There has been much debate about the B-52 tactics. The bomber crews had for years requested changes in their tactics, pointing out that straight-line approaches were adequate in the South but that jinking and dodging techniques were needed up North. Dana K. Drenkowski, a B-52 pilot, argues that SAC crews indoctrinated for lone-wolf nuclear missions simply never had the training for mass formation flying and were in constant danger of repeating the tragic collision that had marred the first Arc Light mission back in 1965.

## Dangerous habits

Careless actions, like the turning on and testing of ECM a certain number of minutes prior to bomb release and the repeated use of the same approach to a target, increased the chance that a B-52 would be shot down before it could inflict any harm on North Vietnam. Against the thousands of SAMs in the Hanoi/Haiphong region (most brought in after the 23 October cessation of bombing in that very region), masses of B-52 Stratofortresses flew in a straight line, taking no evasive

**Right:** *This B-52D carries a heavier bombload than a tactical fighter on its left inboard pylon alone, and its total load of 108 bombs is the heaviest ever carried into battle by a warplane. Since the B-52D carried more bombs than the newer B-52G, crew members in the latter version of the 'Buff' were very much aware that they flew the same distance, took the same risks, and suffered the same casualties, to inflict less damage to North Vietnam's heavily-defended targets.*

**Below:** *During 'Linebacker II', a considerable portion of the flying was done at night, and air refueling after dark always added to the level of stress – already high – because B-52 crews had disturbingly accurate information about the size and scope of Hanoi's air defense effort. No longer was a B-52 sortie an easy or routine proposition it had been in the Arc Light days.*

action, the intervals between three-ship cells of B-52s being known and anticipated by North Vietnamese gunners.

The simple fact that crews kept flying while exhausted made their job difficult. Morale was lowest at U-Tapao, where weary men flew at least one mission per day, while crews from Guam, coming longer distances, flew only once every second or third day. Drenkowski and others faulted the Air Force

for piecemeal attacks, lack of surprise, lack of flexibility, a poor sense of priorities and a lack of internal communication – so that the men flying the missions were often the last to know what was happening.

Of course, B-52s were not the only aircraft in North Vietnam's skies. Air Force F-4s, F-105Gs, A-7Ds and F-111As carried bombs against carefully-picked targets while Navy carrier-based F-4s,

A-6s and A-7s carried their share of the load, but 'Linebacker II' will always be remembered as a B-52 operation, and perhaps it can be understood better from the viewpoint of the crew of one participant.

## Multiple missiles

Approaching Hanoi on the night of 27 December 1972 as pilot of a B-52D from the 307th Strategic Wing at U-Tapao, Captain John D. Mize looked out to see five or six SAMs hurtling through the sky in front of him. Mize's tail-gunner, TSgt Peter E. Whalen, peered from his lonely perch in the rear of the B-52D. Whalen later described it. "When the SAMs come up, you see a bright glow as the rocket fire reflects on the cloud. The clouds magnify the light and make the SAM look bigger than it really is. When the sky is clear, you can see the initial flash when the SAM is launched." Captain Mize had learned that the SAM you could see coming wasn't the one that would kill you.

By this ninth day of the battle, North Vietnam's defenses were badly battered and SAMs were 'unguided missiles', being fired in salvoes as if sheer numbers alone would do the job. As his B-52D approached its target (one of the SAM sites ringing Hanoi), John Mize now saw 15 SAMs airborne at once. Ten seconds after

releasing its load of 84 500-lb bombs, the Buff was shaken by a tremendous concussion on its left side. Shrapnel from the exploding SAM wounded Mize in the left thigh and lower left leg. His right hand, still on the control column, was gashed by flying steel.

Tail-gunner Whalen was hit by shrapnel. Radar navigator Captain Bill North, with no windows, knew the aircraft was hit when his lights and electrical systems went out. Navigator Lt Bill Robinson, in the same location, felt shards of metal tear into his leg.

The big bomber lurched left, then right. Mize was hurled forward against his harness. Engine fire warning lights flashed in front of his face. The abrupt loss of three of its eight engines sent the bomber plummeting several thousand feet.

Hurt, Mize struggled to regain control. With sheer physical effort, he brought the B-52 into level flight. He called each man in the crew of six to determine how badly they were injured and to check damage. Navigator Robinson gave Mize a heading to leave the target area. Mize felt there was a remote chance of reaching Nakhon Phanom, the nearest Thai airbase, but his first concern was to reach a safer place to eject. Busy with these emergency reactions, he also struggled with a fourth engine on

*continued over page*

# 'Linebacker II'

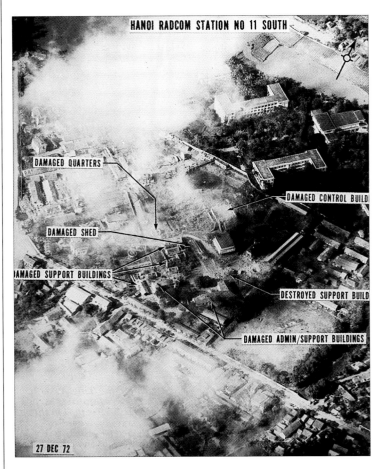

HANOI RADCOM STATION NO 11 SOUTH

DAMAGED QUARTERS

DAMAGED CONTROL BUILD

DAMAGED SHED

DAMAGED SUPPORT BUILDINGS

DESTROYED SUPPORT BUILD

DAMAGED ADMIN/SUPPORT BUILDINGS

27 DEC 72

*Above: US air power was far more accurate in 1972 than earlier, and reconnaissance was better, too. Thus, the Pentagon could release images like this, emphasizing that military targets, and not civilians, were being attacked.*

the left side of the aircraft.

Later, the B-52D pilot would make his struggle for life sound almost routine. "I'm not the first guy to fly a B-52 on four engines," Captain Mize later told a group at his home unit, the 7th Bombardment Squadron at

Ellsworth AFB, SD. "I had not previously done 'flying by the seat of your pants,' but the B-52 can be flown that way."

In fact, the situation was critical. All four lost engines were on the port side, giving Mize power on starboard only. The B-52 was burning and shaking. It could become a torch any time.

## Crippled Buff

With all of his automatic navigation equipment gone or shut down, Robinson used airspeed and distance traveled in minutes along with estimated headings to try to get the burning Stratofortress to Thailand. His difficulty was compounded by the airspeed indicator being unreliable because of damage.

Rescue forces were alerted. A rescue HC-130 Hercules command ship joined Mize near the border of North Vietnam and Laos, just as his crew made a last-minute check of their ejection seats. They were at 12,000 feet over mountainous terrain with sheer cliffsides. Robinson's calculations were that by going another 30 miles they could have

*Although the B-52 made a very large target, it had a sting in the tail to deter enemy fighters. The B-52D was the last operational American bomber to have a manned tail turret, and two B-52 gunners downed MiGs over Hanoi.*

HANOI TANK TRUCK CONVERSION FACILITY

29 DEC 72

much safer flat terrain.

Altitude was of critical importance, with only half the engines working and only enough electrical system for cockpit lights and a radio. Mize flew the aircraft with a brute-force method which consisted of descending about 1,500 feet to pick up airspeed, then climbing 1,000 feet. More than an hour after 'bombs away' on Hanoi, he finally reached more hospitable terrain in Thailand.

## From bad to worse

The situation rapidly deteriorated. The bomb bay doors fell open, one landing gear started cycling maddeningly up and down, and other electrical systems went amuck. Mize knew, now, that there was no hope of coaxing the B-52D to a crash landing at Nakhon Phanom. When he could hold it no longer and feared loss of the intercom, he ordered the crew to bail out.

Four men blew themselves out into the night sky, including co-pilot Captain Terrance Gauthers. The navigator pulled his eject handle and nothing happened. Bill Robinson's downward ejection seat would not function.

"Climb out!" Mize barked. He wanted Robinson to jump through the hole opened up where Bill North had ejected. Robinson got up to do this and the two men could no longer communicate. Still, Mize delayed his own ejection, wanting to be satisfied that the navigator had gotten out.

By now, the only lighting in the B-52D was in the forward cabin. Flames were spreading from the wing. Captain Mize continued

*The 'Linebacker II' raids had a simple aim – to smash Hanoi's military, transport and industrial infrastructure in one massive series of raids. The Hanoi factory used to convert the trucks carrying fuel to the fighters in the South was almost obliterated.*

to struggle with the controls but the bomber was falling now, relentlessly. Wait, he thought, mentally going through his own ejection procedure but worried about Robinson.

Though Mize had no way to know, Robinson jumped successfully. Captain Mize did not know either that rescue forces had set up a string of covering aircraft and helicopters which followed the crippled B-52's path, setting up the largest mass pickup of the war.

Time ran out. The electrical system died. Mize ejected.

In the night and the cold in the Thai jungle, helicopters homed in on the URC-64 beeper radios carried by each crewman and all six from the bomber were rescued within 15 minutes of Captain Mize's bailout. Though Mize himself soft-pedals it, it was only a superhuman effort by the Stratofortress pilot which enabled the B-52D to reach a location

HANOI/BAC MAI AIRFIELD

6 DESTROYED SUPPORT BUILDINGS

6 DESTROYED SUPPORT BUILDINGS

RUNWAY INTERDICTED

18 DESTROYED

*Hanoi's Bac Mai airfield was another of the targets left untouched for most of the war which was hit hard by the B-52 raids in December 1972.*

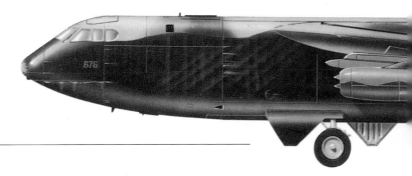

60596

676

where rescue was possible. The final moments in the life of the big plane fully justified Mize's award of the Air Force Cross, the second highest American decoration for valor. The medal was presented by General John C. Meyer, commander in chief of the Strategic Air Command, Mize being the only SAC member to win this honor in the conflict.

Over the 11-day period of 'Linebacker II', 714 B-52 Stratofortress sorties, 830 USAF tactical sorties and 386 US Navy/US Marine Corps tactical sorties were flown. The North Vietnamese fired no fewer than 1,293 SAMs during the battle. Two F-4 Phantoms and two F-111As were among other US casualties.

A second B-52D tail-gunner, AIC Albert E. Moore, was also credited with a MiG kill.

There was an uproar in the US; Joan Baez wrote a song about it; people protested; not a few supported Nixon; and while all the debate raged, North Vietnam was devastated. After many years of conflict, it had taken only 11 days to prove what airpower could do. For all practical purposes, North Vietnam had been taken out of the conflict.

*Above: During the 'Linebacker II' effort, B-52D Stratofortresses (shown) and B-52Gs flew in three-ship cells, creating what had previously been a very rare opportunity to observe 'Buffs' going to war in formation.*

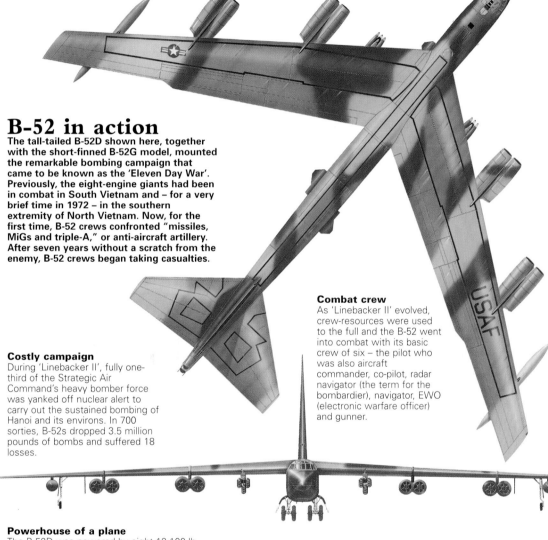

# B-52 in action

The tall-tailed B-52D shown here, together with the short-finned B-52G model, mounted the remarkable bombing campaign that came to be known as the 'Eleven Day War'. Previously, the eight-engine giants had been in combat in South Vietnam and – for a very brief time in 1972 – in the southern extremity of North Vietnam. Now, for the first time, B-52 crews confronted "missiles, MiGs and triple-A," or anti-aircraft artillery. After seven years without a scratch from the enemy, B-52 crews began taking casualties.

### Combat crew
As 'Linebacker II' evolved, crew-resources were used to the full and the B-52 went into combat with its basic crew of six – the pilot who was also aircraft commander, co-pilot, radar navigator (the term for the bombardier), navigator, EWO (electronic warfare officer) and gunner.

### Wide-reaching wing
The B-52's 185-ft (56.39-m) wing drooped almost low enough to touch the ground when the bomber was fully loaded. In flight at lighter weights the wing tips flexed through an arc of 17 ft (5.13 m) until the outer sections were pointed upward. Wing area was 4,000 sq ft (371.6 sq m).

### Costly campaign
During 'Linebacker II', fully one-third of the Strategic Air Command's heavy bomber force was yanked off nuclear alert to carry out the sustained bombing of Hanoi and its environs. In 700 sorties, B-52s dropped 3.5 million pounds of bombs and suffered 18 losses.

### Powerhouse of a plane
The B-52D was powered by eight 12,100-lb (5490-kg) thrust Pratt & Whitney J57-P-29WA turbojet engines with water injection that created enormous clouds of black smoke on take-off. B-52Ds with the 'Big Belly' modification carried 108 conventional 500-lb (227-kg) bombs as well as tail armament of four .50-caliber machine-guns.

### Cluttered interior
Although the B-52 was one of the largest operational warplanes in the world, with a 156-ft 7-in (47.73-m) fuselage and gross weight of 450,000 lb (204 120 kg), its crew had to be shoe-horned in; apart from a narrow aisleway it had not a square inch of unused volume in the interior of the aircraft.

# AMERICAN WITHDRAWAL

*VF-21 'Freelancers' were on a combat cruise aboard **USS** Ranger (CVA-61) when the 1973 ceasefire took effect. Their F-4J Phantoms usually carried Sparrow missiles below the fuselage rather than under the wing as shown. Either way, VF-21 stayed on to guard the truce.*

**Combat operations in South Vietnam resumed on 1 January 1973 after a 24-hour New Year's break. Air strikes against North Vietnam resumed the following day.**

Another bombing halt to commemorate a holiday, this time a 24-hour cessation to 2 January 1973, was followed by resumption of strikes into North Vietnam. During the first two weeks of the new year, B-52 Stratofortress operations continued at a reduced pace. By the time operations halted, the Stratofortresses had flown a further 535 sorties, while Phantoms and other tactical aircraft flew an additional 716 sorties against North Vietnam.

The 197th and last MiG kill of the war took place on 12 January 1973 when Lt Victor T. Kovaleski of the 'Chargers' of VF-165 operating from USS *Midway* (CVA-41) used a Sidewinder to take down a MiG-17. Kovaleski's backseat RIO on this mission was LtJg James A. Wise. It should be noted that the carrier *Midway* scored the first and last MiG kills of the war and that Lt Kovaleski also had the peculiar distinction of piloting the last aircraft to be shot down over North Vietnam, a Phantom downed two days later on 14 January 1973. He and his RIO were rescued.

It was only when peace negotiations genuinely began to make progress for the first time that all air strikes against North Vietnam were halted, on 15 January 1973. Reconnaissance flights over the North continued until the halt of all United States combat operations in North and South Vietnam on 27 January 1973, the final day of the war, although fighting in Laos and Cambodia would continue.

On 20 January 1973 Richard M. Nixon was inaugurated for the second time in a low-key ceremony. Nixon had swept the election the previous November with little serious challenge from South Dakota's Senator George S. McGovern – despite the Senator's appeal to anti-war sentiment. Curiously, McGovern never made it well known that his distaste for war was based on experience: in World War II Nixon was a naval officer in an administrative slot and was best remembered for his shrewdness at poker; McGovern was the highly decorated pilot of a B-17 Flying Fortress in Europe.

If never popular or well liked, Nixon had always been respected for his command of foreign policy and he was appreciated for opening a new American initiative towards China while the Vietnam situation worked itself out. Were it not for growing domestic scandal, Nixon might by now have carte blanche from almost every portion of the electorate.

## Nixon's 'dirty' victory

Whether Nixon had any role in it or not, his victory at the polls had been accompanied by a slew of supporters' 'dirty tricks', loosely known as Watergate. Within months South Carolina's feisty Senator Sam Ervin would be holding televised hearings on the Watergate scandal and cover-up, drawing attention away from other matters, including the President's success in ending the American role in the war.

# Missing in Action

In addition to agreeing to release American prisoners, Hanoi had taken on an obligation to account for all missing Americans about whom it possessed knowledge. Many Americans whose names did not appear on the roster of POWs were officially listed as missing in action (MIA), yet the Communist side had knowledge of them – and in the opinion of some, even held some against their will.

A classic case was an F-100 Super Sabre pilot who had gone down in the Mekong Delta region on a routine close-support mission years earlier. His wingmen knew that he had ejected safely and reached the ground alive. He was never listed as a prisoner. No remains were ever found. Yet a casual conversation with a North Vietnamese after the war made it absolutely clear that Hanoi knew exactly what had happened to the man. He had died in a crossfire between NVA troops pursuing him. Because Hanoi never revealed what it knew – until much later, when it happened more or less by accident – his family spent years wondering what had happened.

## Fate of the missing

Hanoi was to give conflicting signals on the issue of accounting for the missing in action. Yet there was never any doubt that the North Vietnamese knew far more than they were saying. RF-101C Voodoo pilot Captain Vincent J. Connolly was another of the missing, shot down in his reconnaissance aircraft on 4 November 1966 and listed as MIA. The community of men who flew the sleek, powerful

*Right: When a combat aircraft suffered mortal damage and fell, others in the air often had difficulty observing the fate of the crew. Many Americans listed as missing actually perished when they were shot down.*

RF-101C was small – and its losses high – and all the men wanted to know what had happened to Vince. Surely with the war ending, the North Vietnamese would tell what they knew?

They did not. Connolly's widow, Honey, went through years of suffering and uncertainty, never able to find out whether her man was dead or alive. When he was not listed among the POWs and was presumed dead, Honey Connolly kept searching for someone who could tell her, at least, how Vince had died. RF-101C Voodoos often flew alone. There were no American witnesses. No-one knew.

## Not telling the truth

Yet a short time after the end of the conflict, an individual named Trung H. Huynh published a letter in a western magazine claiming that Connolly had become disconcerted when he discovered that he was flying into a narrow valley being flooded – in a unique defensive measure – by NVA weather balloons. According to Huynh, no sooner had Connolly found a way to avoid the balloons than he was felled by anti-aircraft fire.

The North Vietnamese possessed this kind of information in almost excruciating detail, yet Honey Connolly could learn nothing of what had happened to Vince. During the period after his death, while the North

Vietnamese knew that he was dead, Connolly was listed as MIA and promoted to major, then to lieutenant colonel. It was only in 1984 that Hanoi finally announced it was holding Connolly's remains and facilitated his return to the US and burial at

Arlington National Cemetery. As late as 1990 Hanoi still possessed information about other MIA which it did not share. In this and many other respects, the North Vietnamese side simply violated the ceasefire agreement from the outset.

*Ensign James W. Laing ejects from an F-4B Phantom piloted by Lt Charles E. (Ev) Southwick just after shooting down a MiG-17 on 24 April 1967. Many airmen bailing out from crippled fighters were to become prisoners, but all too often their fate was to become one of the 'Missing in Action'.*

# 1973: American Withdrawal

Air action over South Vietnam continued until 27 January 1973, the agreed date for the end of the American role in the conflict. The last B-52 'Arc Light' strikes against targets in South Vietnam, which had been continuous since 1965, recorded a TOT (time over target) of 06.28 a.m. on 28 January.

On 28 January the Kissinger-Tho accord, called 'The Agreement of Ending the War and Restoring the Peace in South Vietnam', was formally signed in Paris. Signatories of this ceasefire agreement were the US, North Vietnam, South Vietnam, and the Provisional Revolutionary Government (PRG) – the Viet Cong. Within 60 days from the signature date, all US and allied personnel, except those authorized under the peace accords, were to be withdrawn from South Vietnam.

With the signing of the ceasefire, all US air operations over North and South Vietnam ended. Virtually all US tactical aircraft were out of South Vietnam anyway, but the milestone had little meaning for US Air Force and Marine Corps fighter pilots at bases in Thailand, or for Navy men on carriers at sea. Although public support was largely lacking, American aircraft were to continue bombing in Laos until 22 February and Cambodia until 15 August.

The 15 August cut-off date was determined by Congress's Cooper-Church Amendment, which in effect stripped the President of authority to commit forces into Vietnam, Laos and Cambodia. This included a congressional ban on use of aerial weapons in Southeast Asia – a fact not appreciated by most observers over the next two years. Further, now that US troops were out of South Vietnam, Congress voted to stop all spending on military activities in or over Southeast Asia.

## No more involvement in Asia

The law passed by Congress simply reaffirmed what public sentiment had already decided. Opposition to the war in the US now made it exceedingly unlikely that South Vietnam would receive the financial and other aid necessary to guarantee the peace.

More important, the Cooper-Church Amendment and the sentiment which created it eliminated a major means of leverage to deter North Vietnam from launching a major offensive. The US was making it very clear that it would not fight.

When the air-to-air statistics were tallied and ready for study, it appeared that the US had ended up with about a two-to-one advantage over the North Vietnamese MiG – not nearly as well as American pilots had done in previous wars and not nearly good enough. One of the most significant results of the air-to-air conflict over the North was the creation of the US Navy's 'Top Gun' and the USAF's 'Aggressors' – the mock enemies which gave truly realistic air-to-air combat training.

With the benefit of dissimilar air combat (DAC) maneuvering as a part of their development syllabus, American pilots should never again have to be challenged by anyone like Colonel Tomb.

Depending upon point of view, either the North Vietnamese or the Americans finally had what they wanted – although it was not clear that South Vietnam had anything at all. Officially, Saigon's diplomats had a full role in negotiations, as did the Viet Cong. In fact, both were pretty much ignored by Kissinger and Tho.

Hanoi would now confront the South without Americans standing in the way. Washington would get its POWs back and domestic opposition to the war, hopefully, would be silenced. In Saigon, as one ARVN officer put it, it was time "to suck in our breath, hold it, and wonder what happens to us". American CIA official Frank Snepp charged that the US was doing nothing more than assuring a 'decent interval' between its departure and the gobbling up of South Vietnam by the North.

The NVA had suffered terrible losses in Hanoi's 1972 'Easter Invasion' and the North's supply of manpower was far from inexhaustible. After the invasion failed, the North Vietnamese then suffered the devastation wreaked by the 'Linebacker II' bombings. Skeptics were always able to find something wrong with this

# Prisoners
*Misery, mistreatment, and – finally – freedom*

Under the terms of the ceasefire, American prisoners were to be released and the last 23,700 American troops withdrawn from South Vietnam within 60 days. Pulling out American troops was something the USAF was getting very good at – more than a decade earlier, the practice of sending American soldiers overseas by ship had ended – but the new situation meant that Military Airlift Command would have to fly some unique missions.

Lieutenant Colonel Philip J. Riede, commander of the 345th Tactical Airlift Squadron, drew the precedent-setting job of taking two C-130s to Hanoi to pick up the Communist delegations to the joint military commission, a newly formed group intended to police the agreement. Piloting the second C-130 into Hanoi was Captain Theodore C. Appelbaum. As the USAF describes their mission:

"The two C-130s took off from Tan Son Nhut on the morning of 29 January. Upon reaching Da Nang, both crews circled for nearly an hour awaiting clearance to enter Communist territory. The planned flight route was mostly over water, but new instructions called for westward flight to a point well inland, then northward to Hanoi.

"With strong reservations, the C-130 crews set forth on the new routing. Back in Saigon, General Vogt monitored the progress of the historic mission. Fifteen minutes before reaching Hanoi the crews established radio contact with Gia Lam airport and obtained landing instructions. Colonel Riede flew the arranged approach and broke out from the clouds at about 3,000 feet. Before landing, the C-130 crewmen were able to look over bomb damage to the bridges around Hanoi. They landed on a patched surface, of which a runway length of about 6,000 feet was usable.

## Evidence of bombing

"On the ground at Hanoi's principal airport, buildings were in shambles from the recent American bombings. Hundreds of civilians came to look at the Americans and their C-130s, but kept a respectful distance at the end of the ramp. Conversations were cordial and an English-speaking official invited the crewmen to a small building for tea. Carrying the delegations, both planes took off shortly after noon, landing at Tan Son Nhut three hours later.

"The only hitch came midway in the flight when the Americans

*Left: They called it the Hanoi Hilton. It was a place where men were tested to the limit. Most POW's never lost their courage.*

*Above: A US Army officer briefs freed prisoners of war. The POWs finally began their journey home on release in March 1973.*

asked the Communists to fill out visa forms. After landing at Tan Son Nhut, the Communists remained on the C-130s for more than 24 hours while a dispute about visas was thrashed out. There was a principle involved: applying for a visa would mean recognizing South Vietnam as a sovereign state, something the Communists would not do."

## Shuttle to Hanoi

The C-130 mission was the beginning of numerous MAC flights into Communist North Vietnam, a new experience for those involved.

One American who visited Hanoi's Gia Lam airport where the prisoner release took place, Colonel William Hubbell, recalls that Gia Lam was European in character, as it was built by the French: "a normal, small airport with no shops or anything like that, very bland". Few people were seen doing routine business at the airport, although Hubbell did see "plenty of the Russian version of the Boeing 727" – actually the Tupolev Tu-154.

Between the city and the airport was a rickety bridge, crossed by a few vehicles and countless people on bicycles. The bridge was closed when the prisoners were sent to the airfield.

On the first C-141A bringing the men out from Hanoi, Colonel John Flynn, the courageous commander of the men in captivity – the Fourth Allied POW Wing, they called themselves, their slogan, 'Return with honor' – pulled rank on Commander Everett Alvarez, the longest-held prisoner, and so Flynn became the first released POW to step out of the C-141A at Clark Field in the Philippines. When Alvarez did step out, he expressed thoughts which sounded simple but were deepfelt for this man of conviction who had been a captive for nearly eight years: "God bless the President and God bless you, Mr and Mrs America, you did not forget us."

The releases were to continue into March. March was also the first month since July 1963 that no combat losses were recorded by US forces.

*Right: The US withdrawal in 1973 had an orderly quality about it that was to be sorely lacking two years later. Here, UH-1 Huey helicopters are loaded aboard ship to be returned to the United States. American forces took hundreds of aircraft out of Vietnam but left many behind.*

employment of American airpower, but captured documents proved that Stratofortresses, Phantoms, and F-111s had a damaging impact on NVA morale and materiel. Hanoi had been battered by a 'double whammy' and was in no immediate position to exploit its gains from the Kissinger-Tho accord.

## Northern aims not yet met

Hanoi was punished, too, by the inexorable impact of time. Although Ho Chi Minh's followers had been struggling for more than a generation to take over South Vietnam, in 1972 they were no closer to achieving this goal than in 1965. So Kissinger got less than he should have asked for – a bad deal, critics said. Kissinger got the POWs plus an easy way out, they argued. With tougher negotiations, or a prolonging of the 'Eleven-Day War', or both, Kissinger might have gotten much, much more...

President Thieu, as if on a different planet, called for an invasion of North Vietnam. Thieu was making other utterances as well, some of them more realistic in recognizing the plight of his regime and his country, but only a few arch-conservative US leaders were listening and they lacked the clout to drum up support for military aid. Of his proposed invasion, Thieu said, "Had we bombed North Vietnam continuously, had we landed in North Vietnam, the war would be over by now." More than a few people believed Thieu was right, but he was at least 10 years too late.

The 30-year civil war in Laos officially ended on 21 February. US air strikes were halted. A coalition government embracing all three warring factions was to be formed a year later.

Inside South Vietnam there was a lull. Both sides were vying for advantage with troop movements, but actual fighting was at a standstill. North Vietnam's continuing expansion of its air force had only an indirect effect on the South, but Saigon's planners knew that MiGs or Ilyushins could appear in their skies at any time. South Vietnam's expansion of its air arm had gone as far as it could. There were a few improvements that could be made, but the basic composition and structure of the VNAF was to remain unchanged for the next two years.

The problem that faced the VNAF and its American supporters was simple enough to understand: while the ink was still drying on the ceasefire agreement, Ho Chi Minh's successors were planning to take over the South. The failure of their 1972 'Easter Invasion' had been a major setback, but with the Americans leaving, conquest of the South seemed a realistic goal after – to re-use Snepp's term – "a decent interval".

No longer worried about defending their own airspace from B-52s or anything else, the North Vietnamese could now move anti-aircraft defenses and missiles farther south, to help them in any future thrust towards Saigon. Jet-capable airfields were being paved in the southern portion of North Vietnam to counter the VNAF. Khe Sanh, where American Marines had made a stand, now belonged to Hanoi's forces and was being enlarged so that its runway would have limited accommodation for jet aircraft.

For the departing Americans, the major event of 1973 – after the ceasefire itself – was the homecoming of the POWs. The release of American prisoners of war began when the first group of 116 were freed by Hanoi on 12 February 1973.

The last American troops left South Vietnam on 29 March 1973. Military Assistance Command Vietnam (MACV) was disestablished on 29 March 1973, and Headquarters Seventh Air Force ceased to exist. Henceforth the only men in uniform would be those assigned to the embassy in Saigon.

The Defense Attache Office (DAO), located in the former MACV building at Tan Son Nhut airport, was perhaps the strangest in any American embassy in the world. In almost any other country, the DAO was a small office inside the embassy chancery, preoccupied with protocol matters and the gathering of intelligence. In Saigon, however, the DAO existed to manage

*Left: This Marine is crew chief of a 'Whitehat' airline CH-46 Sea Knight operating over the Mekong Delta in late 1972 and early 1973 – based at Cubi Point, Philippines and temporarily stationed at Saigon's Tan Son Nhut airport.*

# Mine Clearing

As part of the agreement between the Americans and North Vietnamese – the other two signatories, South Vietnam and the Viet Cong, were not really full partners in the accord – the US agreed to clear North Vietnamese ports of the mines sown by Navy A-6 Intruder and A-7 Corsair aircraft the previous year. Called Operation 'End Sweep', the mine-clearing operation was carried out by RH-53D helicopters of US Task Force 78. The helicopter carried an electronic mine-detector, designed to trail behind it in the water.

RH-53D pilots had been trained to fly their mine-clearing mission under combat conditions. But even with no-one shooting at them, the chore of cleaning up the deadly munitions was far from easy. "We had to operate without an infrastructure in place to support us," says Commander George Timil. During the period beginning at the end of January, the USS *America* (CVA-66), *Constellation* (CVA-64), *Coral Sea* (CVA-43), *Enterprise* (CVAN-65) and *Ranger* (CVA-61) provided logistic support for 'End Sweep' and provided air cover for the operations. But conditions for the RH-53D helicopters remained difficult.

The helicopters, along with CH-53s specially configured for the mine-clearing mission, came from Navy squadron HM-12 and Marine squadrons HMH-463 and HMM-165 which operated from the decks of two amphibious assault ships, USS *Inchon*

*Above: On a typical mission, the RH-53D trolled for mines pulling a sled which was too large to be carried inside the helicopter. Endurance of a sortie was usually about two hours.*

(LPH-12) and *New Orleans* (LPH-11). Mine-clearing operations ended on 27 July 1973 after CH-53 and RH-53D helicopter pilots had devoted more than 1,100 flying hours to the operation.

*Above – The minesweeping sled was attached to a cable from the open rear ramp of the RH-53D Although probably less effective than seaborne minesweepers, the helicopters worked much faster.*

*Below: An RH-53D of Task Force 77 flies above deceptively serene karst outcroppings along the North Vietnamese coast. The North Vietnamese benefited greatly from the mine-clearing operation.*

succeeding. VNAF problems were especially vexing. In Saigon's air arm, training was inadequate, operational readiness was almost a joke, and airlift performance – particularly the C-130A Hercules – was dismal.

The VNAF still lacked high-performance aircraft that would be able to cope with the North's MiGs if a direct challenge should come. Saigon's air arm was also without sophisticated ECM equipment and precision-guided munitions ('smart' bombs) needed for operations in high-threat areas and to interdict enemy supply lines along the Ho Chi Minh Trail. These deficiencies apparently had not been given much thought, but they were to make life easier for the North Vietnamese as they planned a recovery from their losses in the 1972 invasion and a new effort to take over the entire country.

## War Powers Resolution

On 7 November 1973 the US Congress over-rode President Nixon's veto and passed the War Powers Resolution, making it illegal to commit US forces for more than 60 days without congressional approval. Coupled with the earlier ban on bombing, these limitations assured the North Vietnamese that the US was practically powerless to intervene in Vietnam any longer. In Saigon leaders knew that Congress had a strong anti-war sentiment and that the President was increasingly tied up with domestic reactions to the Watergate scandal.

Despite the ceasefire, some combat activity continued in South Vietnam as both sides sought advantages. The VNAF, with only limited US advice and assistance, possessed a total of 2,075 aircraft by year's end and flew 458,468 sorties during the year. VNAF aircraft losses reached 185, including 91 UH-1 Huey helicopters, 265 O-1 Bird Dogs and 22 A-37Bs.

In October the North Vietnamese Central Committee's 21st Plenum adopted a resolution stating that the path of revolution in the South left no alternative but to conduct a revolutionary war and liberate the South. Ironically, events of the past decade had given Hanoi complete control of the Viet Cong apparatus in the South which, in the earliest days of US involvement, had begun as an indigenous insurgency. The North Vietnamese began a series of raids against selected targets during the first week of November.

## The cost of the war

For the American services, 1973 was the year to tot up what the war in Vietnam had meant and what it had cost.

The US Navy had employed 17 attack carriers, 10 from the Pacific Fleet and seven from the Atlantic: indeed, every carrier in its inventory with the sole exception of the USS *John F. Kennedy* (CVA-67). These capital ships had spent 8,248 days on the line during 73 combat cruises between August 1964 and August 1973.

In its loss column, the Navy could list 530 fixed-wing aircraft (most of them carrier-based) and 13 helicopters downed by the enemy. A total of 317 Navy aircrews lost their lives.

During its long years of combat operations in Southeast Asia – including operations in South Vietnam from October 1961 to March 1973 – the US Air Force had suffered 2,118 deaths, 3,460 wounded and 599 missing. 2,257 aircraft had been lost in combat or to operational causes in 5,226,701 sorties, representing a loss rate of 0.04 per cent (compared with 2.0 per cent in Korea and 9.7 per cent in World War II).

Were the Air Force's number-crunchers certain that the number of sorties in a seemingly endless war was not 5,226,700 or 5,226,702? Apparently so. Losses included 445 F-4 Phantoms, 397 F-105 Thunderchiefs, 243 F-100 Super Sabres and 30 B-52s. The value of aircraft lost was estimated at $3,129,948,000.

continuing resupply, local maintenance and contractor support for South Vietnam's armed forces. The DAO was initially authorized no fewer than 50 military and 1,200 US civilian personnel slots. When Vietnamese employees were added, the DAO became an organization of 4,750 individuals. Its first boss was Major General John E. Murray.

Murray was in a 'no win' situation. If South Vietnam found some way to achieve stability, he would go unnoticed. If Saigon fell, he would be the goat. An army officer in a slot many felt should go to an airman, Murray had a realistic view of events around him, and they were not encouraging.

On 30 September 1973 in a periodic report, General Murray set forth a grave warning that the North Vietnamese were gathering strength. He reported that the Vietnamization program was not

# Still on Yankee Station

## 1973: American Withdrawal

*Staying on guard for trouble*

"It was no holiday pushing around 250-lb (113-kg) bombs on a cart," ordnanceman Gary Wright recalled. "It was a bitch. Everything had to be done by hand."

American ground troops had finally left South Vietnam, but the Navy was still on station. Wright was aboard the USS *Oriskany* (CVA-34) on the last cruise made by that ship, from June 1972 to May 1973. Things were tense enough on the carrier when the war was still on and the ship was on station a surprisingly scant 18-miles (29-km) south-west of Haiphong – a 5-minute flight by F-8 Crusader or A-7 Corsair. But the fact that the old 'Essex'-class carrier was not as well equipped with support equipment as the newer vessels added to the tension.

The HLU-196 loading device hooked up to the pylon of an A-7 with preloaded MERs (multiple ejector racks) and TERs (triple ejector racks), but the actual loading of the bombs had to be done "by sweat and muscle". You also had to be exceedingly careful. Apart from the fact that *Oriskany* had already suffered one major fire during its years in Southeast Asia, "The gunner [ordnance chief] just doesn't like it when bombs roll across the deck."

Carrier sailors like Wright had a compact living space just over 3-ft wide. Bunks stacked three high, with a locker under the bottom bunk. There was a small reading light, but no room to sit. At the end of each bunk was the OBA (oxygen breathing apparatus) for use if a fire should again fill the interior of the ship with smoke. Like many of his crewmates, Wright obtained canvas and safety wire from the ship's parachute riggers and used it to fashion a privacy curtain. He was never comfortable: others slept when he was awake and vice-versa.

*Oriskany* flew missions until the end. There have been numerous conflicting claims to have flown the last mission in Vietnam, and the carrier had some of the claimants – but no certain holder of this dubious honor has ever been identified. With the end of bombing over both North and South Vietnam, a mood of celebration was noticeable on the ship, but not for long. Although combat had ended, pilots and crews on the carrier continued to stand alert, fly defensive missions, and maintain readiness.

Before the ceasefire, there were the inevitable mishaps at sea. Wright was standing in the arm, de-arm area between catapults one night just after the ceasefire when an F-8 Crusader of VF-194 veered off course and passed within a few feet. The F-8 went over the side and its pilot was killed.

A few days afterwards Wright was on his way forward carrying a MER when the carrier's Air

*The Oriskany was one of the last of the modified 'Essex'-class carriers to serve on the front line. The ship made eight deployments to Vietnamese waters between 1965 and 1974.*

Boss shouted "Heads up!" on the loudspeaker. The right landing strut of an incoming VF-191 Crusader broke. The jet fighter ripped its tailhook from the cable and came careering straight at Gary:

"I dropped that MER. A lot of guys ran to starboard. I ran towards the numbers [the large 34 for the carrier's hull number, painted on the forward deck]. I'm gonna jump, gonna jump, I told myself, ready to heave myself over the side as the Crusader came at me.

"There was a big explosion. Everything stopped. The blast knocked me over and there was a rip across the front of my flight deck vest. A piece of the ship's antenna went sailing over my head. I knew I wasn't dead and as everything started again, I wondered why I had been saved.

Another guy leaped into the port net (on the side of the carrier) and the Crusader went right over top of him, missing by inches. The port strut of the Crusader had caught in the port catwalk and hit a fire main. There was water spewing up, a geyser. The Crusader went into the drink."

Wright did not see it but the pilot ejected safely.

*Like the Oriskany, the USS Hancock (CVA-19) made a great contribution to the war. It was one of the first US Navy carriers in the Vietnam conflict and was also one of the last. The carrier was on station when America's fighting came to an end in 1973.*

# BEFORE THE STORM

Returning Vietnam veterans did not receive the thanks of the nation. Major Don Kilgus, who had flown F-100s and F-105s in the conflict, was spat on while walking in uniform in a West Coast city. Another much-decorated fighter-bomber pilot was upbraided by a neighbor who called him a 'baby killer', furthering the fiction that Americans had bombed indiscriminately.

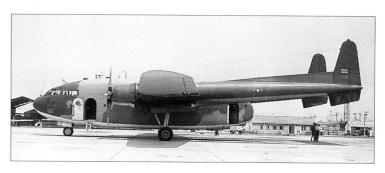

*Above: C-119G Flying Boxcars carted supplies around Vietnam from March 1968 onward. It became a standard Vietnamese airlifter, operated by the VNAF's 413th Transport Squadron at Tan Son Nhut.*

**M**en who left the armed forces to return to civilian life found that mentioning Vietnam combat service did not enhance a resume. Those who went to the Veterans Administration for benefits, such as help with educational costs, found that unlike survivors of previous wars they had few benefits to collect. Men who remained in uniform found the services being wrenched apart by racial conflict.

The war to defend South Vietnam killed the citizen army which had defended American interests since 1940. By 1974 the wheels were in motion to end it forever. The following year the armed forces would become 'all volunteer' – ending forever the role of the draft in American life.

1974 was the year of preoccupation with Watergate. President

Nixon might have fulfilled his promise to end American involvement in the war – he had also opened the door to China and achieved detente with the Soviet Union – but his administration's cover-up of the irregularities of the 1972 election was the only issue on the public's mind. Nixon was heading for a fall.

It was still possible to arrive at Tan Son Nhut airport outside Saigon, see tourist billboards praising the joys of travel to sunny Vietnam, and perhaps observe the occasional A-37B or F-5E taking off with a bombload. Small-scale fighting was taking place regularly

*A VNAF pilot makes a landing in an A-1E Skyraider (bureau no. 135047) of the 518th Fighter Squadron. With US forces withdrawn and North Vietnam still threatening, Saigon's air arm was now attempting to go it alone.*

# VNAF Grounded

**F**inancial assistance to Saigon was so far below what had been anticipated or planned for that the Vietnamese had no choice but to continue to store aircraft which the VNAF lacked the means to operate. In 1974 over 200 aircraft were retired to flyable storage, including nearly all A-1 Skyraiders, O-1 Bird Dog observation craft, and C-7, C-47 and C-119 transports. In addition, a significant number of helicopters were taken out of use and set aside. The capacity of the Vietnamese armed forces to carry out helicopter missions was cut back by no less than 70 per cent.

To make matters worse, the 32 C-130A Hercules of the VNAF were suffering from fuel leaks, wing cracks, parts shortages and cutbacks in flying time. Only four to eight C-130As were flyable at any given time.

The storage of aircraft which could not be used tied up some 500 people who had to inspect and maintain them. Still, the result was greater efficiency in the employment of the aircraft

that remained. In 1974 the VNAF had 1,484 aircraft in service, having lost 299 to combat, operational causes, or transfers. The VNAF had 62,585 personnel on duty.

At some point in 1974 – the record is unclear when – the VNAF took some of its prop-driven A-1 Skyraiders out of mothballs and began using them again in limited skirmishes against the NVA. Virtually all battles were with NVA regular troops now that the Viet Cong had been swallowed up by its supporter in the North. Apparently someone had decided that the Skyraider was more

*Above: This 'Gooney Bird' is a venerable C-47 Skytrain used for VIP transportation by the 413th Transport Squadron of the VNAF. This craft was detached to Pleiku and assigned to the II Corps commander. The bottom-wing insigne on this VNAF C-47 was mistakenly painted backwards.*

effective for some missions than the F-5E and A-37B jets which had entered inventory more recently.

*Left: VNAF forward air controllers flying the O-1 Bird Dog were no longer safe from heavy ground fire following the ceasefire. With shoulder-mounted SAMs now in Communist hands, they flew some missions at altitudes of 10,000 ft (3096 m).*

*Below: An F-5C Freedom Fighter (65-10558). VNAF pilots liked the agile handling characteristics of the agile F-5, four squadrons of which eventually equipped the South Vietnamese air arm – all in the 23rd Tactical Wing, flying from Bien Hoa airfield.*

*The AU-24 Stallion was a V/STOL aircraft able to get in and out of a tight spot, and it became a favorite for clandestine CIA missions – both before and after US troops were out of the combat zone. This aircraft is seen in Thailand prior to being transferred to the Khmer Air Force.*

in the north-west portion of South Vietnam, and a battle occasionally broke out elsewhere while both sides pretended that it was not a shooting war – at least for the moment.

Although the mood in the US remained strongly against providing assistance to Saigon, eight more F-5E fighters were delivered to the VNAF in March 1974. This final delivery was a holdover, arranged before Congress cracked down. It was increasingly clear to leaders in Saigon that they were not going to get much from their American allies, especially since Washington was preoccupied with Watergate and the Arab oil embargo.

US aid to South Vietnam, limited to $1 billion by Congress for fiscal year 1975, was reduced when stricter accounting procedures under a single Department of Defense audit agency were adopted on 1 July 1974. Audits disclosed that amounts some $296.3 million in excess of the limit had been scheduled.

The amount of aid to be received by South Vietnam was further reduced following President Nixon's resignation in August, to a ceiling of $700 million. In August 1974 Gerald Ford inherited the job of President with virtually no options left that would permit aid to the Saigon government.

Facing a solid wall of resistance to providing aid to the Saigon government, US officials in South Vietnam urged conservation measures on the VNAF. Eleven squadrons were grounded, flying hours and bombing missions were reduced, and other stringent measures taken to conserve funds. As USAF leaders saw it,

"Congress seemed intent on making [South Vietnam] a military invalid" even though "further cuts in military aid to South Vietnam could be equated with real estate lost to North Vietnam". Aid cuts took effect just at the time that North Vietnam launched a series of strategic raids.

But by 1974 there was probably nothing anyone could do to save South Vietnam. In all likelihood, additional aid or equipment would only have prolonged the end. North Vietnam had 13 divisions already in South Vietnam and seven in reserve. Partly thanks to aid from the Soviet Union, Hanoi possessed the supplies for a 15- to 20-month campaign.

## North Vietnam's plans

By the end of the year, although actual combat was scattered and sporadic, it was clear that North Vietnam's forces – strengthened and rebuilt since Hanoi's reverses in 1972 – were getting ready for something. With SA-2 surface-to-air missiles located farther south than ever before (although still in North Vietnam), and with ground troops carrying SA-7 missiles around on their shoulders, the effectiveness of the VNAF was markedly reduced without a shot being fired. South Vietnamese intelligence remained good and many in Saigon were warning that trouble was coming.

The NVA began making trouble at the airstrip at Song Be, a scant 100-miles (160-km) north of Saigon, the critical point of entry for men and supplies in Phuoc Long Province. The NVA heavily shelled and then seized an adjacent hilltop, set up mortars on the peak, and forced the ARVN and VNAF to evacuate the much-needed airfield.

President Thieu visited Da Nang in late 1974 to confer with military advisors about how to handle increasing NVA military action. A few leaders, including VNAF commander Lieutenant General Tran Van Minh, were courageous enough to tell Thieu bad news. Several recommended that a future withdrawal from the Central Highlands would be essential to any defense of the remainder of South Vietnam. This idea of giving up some territory to preserve the rest was utterly wrongheaded, but no-one could see so at the time.

The officers argued that shortening their supply lines would ease the task of logistic supply. Defending a smaller area of turf would also help to conserve men and machinery, supplies and ammunition. Given the uncertainty of future US aid, this kind of conservation had to be a part of South Vietnamese planning.

In December 1974 an intelligence report noted that the North Vietnamese were probing around Phuoc Binh. This was to become the first provincial capital in more than two years faced with possible enemy seizure. This was the first move in what was to become the final push by Hanoi's forces.

*In 1961, with the war small and adventurous, Saigon was the 'Paris of the Orient'. Here, Americans found bistros along the boulevard, haute cuisine in restaurants, and sensual delight in the back alleys. In 1974, it was all fading to a memory. Saigon was soon to change – forever.*

# Preparing for the Worst

As late as the end of 1974, remnants of American airpower were still located next door in Thailand – B-52 bombers and KC-135 tankers at U-Tapao, A-7s, AC-130s, F-4s and F-111As at Korat. In Saigon the well-informed citizen might be forgiven if he deduced that the warplanes next door had a purpose. Given the mood of the American public, there was no possibility of American ground soldiers ever again fighting in Vietnam. But while no-one had ever actually said so, American leaders had strongly hinted that American airpower was available in case of trouble. Likewise, US Navy aircraft-carriers remained on station near South Vietnam, fully able to return and help South Vietnam's armed forces if the need arose.

In a sense, the Vietnamese people were misled. While it was important for the United States to show its intention to stand fast and not betray its South Vietnamese ally, public sentiment was against providing that help. A more accurate measure of American intentions was the secret preparations being made for a complete withdrawal.

Every US embassy and consulate abroad was required to have an 'E & E' (emergency and evacuation) plan to cover the withdrawal of private American citizens and government civilians in the event of earthquake, flood, or (as in Saigon) war. In 1974 an evacuation plan named 'Talon Vise' set forth details of how the American embassy and consulates in South Vietnam would be evacuated – with combat support, if necessary, from the forces stationed in Thailand.

The escape plan called for close contact between the embassy and airlines serving Saigon. By 1974 the various airline companies which flew into the Vietnamese capital – Northwest, Pan American, World, were virtually an extension of the US military, most of their payloads being the limited numbers of parts and equipment that could still be supplied to the South Vietnamese. To be ready for an evacuation, embassy consular officers conferred with airline officials and made contingency plans.

By the time it became necessary to implement 'Talon Vise', it was to be renamed 'Frequent Wind'. But in 1974 evacuation was still a prospect covered only in files and file folders. The planners of both 'Talon Vise' and 'Frequent Wind' had given much attention to saving American civilians and almost no attention to the thousands of South Vietnamese who had been directly employed by the US.

*Above: This F-4 Phantom setting off on a 1974 patrol in the South China Sea symbolized the role of the aircraft carrier in guarding the truce settlement. But the battle was in Washington, not Vietnam, and by 1974 the US Congress was no longer prepared to support a defense of Saigon.*

*Below: South Vietnam needed American weapons and ammunition as well as air support and large-scale economic aid. Unfortunately, the politicians in Washington felt that the Vietnamese should be able to defend themselves – but would not give them the means to do so.*

*Above: The 388th TFW was still flying out of Korat, Thailand. But 1974 was the year Richard Nixon became the first US president to resign in disgrace. There was no political will to use US Air Force fighter-bombers to react to Hanoi's truce violations.*

*Right: Hercules transports like this C-130A were vital to South Vietnam. But the time was coming when their only use would be to evacuate a small minority of the men, women, and children who had been portrayed as staunch allies entitled to US support.*

# FALL OF THE SOUTH

**North Vietnamese forces launched an offensive in the South on 28 February 1975. Hanoi's troops were attacking with everything they had – as they had done without success in 1972 – but this time resistance was uneven, and to those in the know it seemed the beginning of the end.**

On 6 January 1975 Phuoc Binh, the capital of South Vietnam's Phuoc Long Province, had fallen to North Vietnamese troops after a week of heavy fighting. President Ford asked Congress for an additional $300 million for aid to South Vietnam. On Capitol Hill the mood was strongly against any such spending. The funds were not forthcoming.

Once the offensive was launched, Northern progress was rapid. On 14 March the NVA captured Ban Me Thuot. The seizure of this vital city turned over another airfield and a number of aircraft to the Communists. President Thieu made the tactical decision which had been recommended to him by some subordinates the previous December to withdraw some of his forces from the highlands. The idea had been a mistake, and proved disastrous. It precipitated a rout.

The city of Hue had to be abandoned on 26 March, the retreating South Vietnamese troops leaving more than $1 billion worth of US supplied arms. On 31 March a C-130 Hercules evacuated the nuclear fuel from the atomic reactor at Da Lat, in Tuyen Duc Province, to keep it from falling to the North Vietnamese.

After Saigon, Da Nang was perhaps the best known Vietnamese city, port, and airfield, and by 25 March 1975 it was clear that North Vietnamese forces were massing to over-run the city. On that date Al Francis, the American consul general, ordered the evacuation of all American citizens in the area, plus a few South Vietnamese who had worked for the US and warranted assistance. Ed Daly, head of World Airways, which did a considerable amount of military contract flying for the US, was even more certain than Francis that Da Nang was about to fall – and after Da Nang, all of South Vietnam. Without any assurance that anyone would

*Below: **Once the evacuation got under way, aircraft fleeing South Vietnam arrived so rapidly that carrier decks became desperately overcrowded. The painful choice had to be made to heave them overboard. This UH-1 Huey helicopter had been part of a relatively new batch and had few flying hours when pushed into Davey Jones' Locker.***

# Evacuation Plans

*Operation 'Frequent Wind' gets going*

*Left: In Operation 'New Life', South Vietnamese civilian employees who worked for the US are crammed into a C-130 in the Philippines, en route to new lives. The US took in 140,000 Vietnamese refugees in 1975, seven times the annual maximum prescribed by immigration law.*

*Above: 30 April 1975 was the last day in Saigon. Chaos reigned in the capital as thousands besieged the US chancery, hoping to be chosen for evacuation. Operation 'Frequent Wind' saved an incredible number, but many with close ties to the US had to be left behind.*

**B**rigadier General Leroy Swenson, who arrived to replace General Baughn as Deputy Defense Attache, watched the 'Eagle Pull' evacuation from Cambodia to get ideas for the much larger 'Frequent Wind' pull-out from Saigon. Swenson was now urging retired American military personnel and civil contract Americans to get out of South Vietnam without delay.

Although many were able to leave South Vietnam by sea up until the final days, the period 20–28 April 1975 (culminating with the Communist seizure of Tan Son Nhut airfield) saw the largest fixed-wing evacuation ever undertaken. During this period, Ed Daly of World Airways made a Douglas DC-8 available to some evacuees without proper authorization, an act which made him an instant hero. At one point 20 C-141s were moving out at 30-minute intervals. A similar number of C-130s brought people out daily. Although Ambassador Martin still denied that it was happening, Operation 'Frequent Wind' was under way and the long American presence was nearing its end.

*Below: With a busy H-46 Sea Knight in background, civilian evacuees arrive on the 7th Fleet's command ship USS Blue Ridge (LCC-19) on 29 April 1975. Some Americans who had worked in 'Nam' for years came out with only one suitcase.*

# 'Frequent Wind'

*Above: On 29 April 1975, Nguyen Cao Ky, former South Vietnamese premier and head of the VNAF, was flown to the carrier USS Midway (CVA-41) by Air America. Ky later settled in southern California.*

reimburse him for it, Daly decided to increase the number of World Airways airliners assisting in the evacuations.

On the evening of 26 March one of Daly's Boeing 727s landed at Da Nang to bring out American citizens and, possibly, a few Vietnamese. Suddenly panic was let loose. While evacuees scheduled to fly on the 727 climbed aboard, a nervous crowd surrounded the aircraft. Some Vietnamese seeking to delay its departure blocked the Boeing's path with vehicles, then tried to force their way aboard. While the World Airways flight crew looked on with disbelief, many people who were not manifested began forcing their way aboard. The unauthorized passengers filled the aisles, the galleys, even the toilets.

## Overloaded airliners

By some miracle, this Boeing 727 and others on 27 March were able to get out of Da Nang in spite of the overcrowding. In one tragic incident a Vietnamese citizen seeking escape from the coming Communist onslaught hid inside the landing gear well of an airliner – and fell to his death shortly after take-off. A mass air and sea exodus emptied Da Nang by 28 March, allowing the NVA to come in and take over the city with only sporadic fighting.

Just as South Vietnam seemed to be "going down the tubes", as one US airman put it, Cambodia went first. President Lon Nol left Cambodia on 1 April. On the 12th Operation 'Eagle Pull' brought out the remaining American embassy staff and some private American citizens by helicopter. The principal means of getting the job done was the Sikorsky CH-53A Sea Stallion, the same craft which had served so many other purposes during the conflict. 'Eagle Pull' was, unfortunately, not the last helicopter evacuation to occur in Southeast Asia.

It was as clear to VNAF pilots as anyone else that the sky was falling in. Some pondered how to escape their home country with their families. One remarkable flier eventually got out of South Vietnam in an A-1 Skyraider with five people aboard!

A few changed sides. On 8 April a VNAF Northrop F-5E dropped two 500-lb (227-kg) bombs on the presidential palace, apparently hastening President Thieu's decision to hit the road. On the evening of 28 April – when everyone except US Ambassador Graham Martin could see that the end was near – a tower operator at Tan Son Nhut airfield queried three approaching Cessna A-37 Dragonflies as to their identity and purpose. The approaching A-37

No-one was yet acknowledging in public that the end was near, but by 1 April 1975 the largest fixed-wing evacuation in history was under way. Contract airliners and military transports hauled people out of Saigon. An embassy planning group struggled mightily to figure out who was entitled to evacuation. What about a Vietnamese who had worked for the embassy? A Vietnamese whose brother was an American citizen? The Vietnamese wife of an American soldier? Later there was to be much criticism of this process, but in general it was handled efficiently.

Brigadier General Richard M. Baughn, who served under Major General Smith in the thankless position of Deputy Defense Attache, ordered provision to be made to evacuate 100 employees per day, then 200. This figure covered most Americans who needed to get out, but failed to help the immediate families of many Americans. A number of

*Below: In the final weeks, panic moved southward at a faster rate than the North Vietnamese army. Here, pandemonium has set in at Nha Trang three weeks before the end in Saigon. As happened so often, a few are saved while many stay behind.*

career diplomats who had served earlier in Saigon now returned in their own time, at their own expense, to locate people who had worked with them, as well as Vietnamese relatives. Some virtually forced the Air Force to carry out the people they wanted to save. In later years these men were to be commended for acting on their own.

On 4 April schedulers at Tan Son Nhut noted that a C-5A Galaxy was coming in with a shipment of 105-mm howitzers for beleaguered South Vietnamese forces. Some 37 civilian employees of the Defense Attache office were rounded up to escort 250 Vietnamese infants who would be taken out in Operation 'Baby Lift'. In later years this aspect of the evacuation would draw fire because the infants, billed as Vietnamese orphans heading to the US for adoption, were for the most part not orphans at all. In the meanwhile, however, it seemed a sterling humanitarian deed. TV and news crews assembled to record the departure of the giant C-5A for the US.

On 4 April 1975 the fully loaded C-5A Galaxy (aircraft 68-0218) took off from Tan Son Nhut. The C-5A had just begun this very first flight in Operation

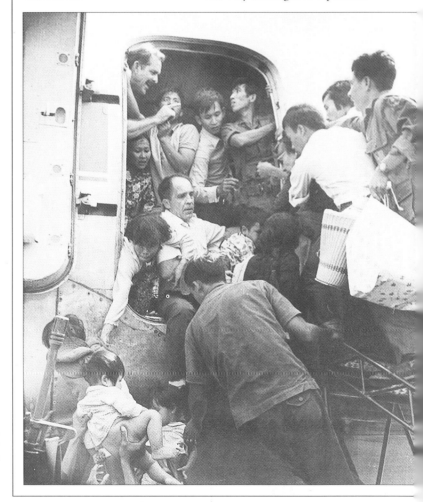

*Left: A C-5A Galaxy participating in Operation 'Baby Lift' crashed while evacuating adults and children from South Vietnam. Other C-5As made the most of their heavy-lift capabilities in the final weeks, bringing out thousands of people and tons of equipment.*

*Below: In a vivid image which can only be painful to those who fought so long to prevent this from happening, North Vietnamese regulars seize the VNAF transport area at Tan Son Nhut on 30 April 1975. Hanoi later used the C-7s and C-47s.*

'Baby Lift' with its crew convinced they were leaving a country now rapidly falling apart. Pilot Captain Dennis Traylor leveled off at 23,000 ft (7010 m) some 10 miles (16 km) off the Vietnamese coast when the giant aircraft – at the time, the largest aircraft type in the world – underwent a massive structural failure in the rear cargo door area.

Captain Traylor exerted considerable airmanship but could not get the Galaxy back to Tan Son Nhut. The C-5A grazed the earth east of the Saigon River, bounced, and came to rest a half-mile away on the west side. One hundred and seventy five survivors and the crew were able to get out. Two hundred and six people, including most of the infants and their escorts, were killed.

The C-5A Galaxy was the biggest aircraft loss, with the greatest loss of life, of the Vietnam war. In later years some people, including other C-5A pilots, have suspected that the catastrophe was set off by an SA-7 shoulder-launched missile or even that the C-5A may have been hit by small-arms fire.

The loss of the 'Baby Lift' C-5A cast a pall over evacuation plans. Those seeking to be ready for a final pull-out also faced obstacles because of Ambassador Graham Martin's firm refusal to acknowledge that anything was wrong. Despite problems, workers began identifying locations where UH-1 Huey, CH-46 Sea Knight and CH-53 Sea Stallion helicopters would be able to land if they were needed.

Above: Only minutes before the final surrender, this O-1 Bird Dog was shot down and crashed in Saigon's thronged Cholon district. Many VNAF pilots and air crews, even after they fully understood that defeat was upon them, continued to fight valiantly to the very end.

It had started for America in the days of President Kennedy's Camelot, as a small, quixotic war in some out of the way place. It came to an end with an ignominious, heli-borne retreat from a war that could not be won.

flight leader gave a vague reply, stating that his was an "American-built aircraft".

No other information was needed when the A-37s began releasing bombs on the airfield. Their approach had been calculated to enable them to strafe Tan Son Nhut's flight line, then turn north. Six bombs exploded on the ramp, damaging several C-47s and AC-119s. Shells flew around the scene of devastation.

F-5 fighters scrambled to intercept the A-37s but were unable to catch them. The A-37 attack was unique: it was the first and only time that airpower was used against the South Vietnamese. Whether the A-37 pilots were turncoats or North Vietnamese using captured machines scarcely seemed to matter. The attack had a devastating effect on the morale of the few South Vietnamese who where still willing to fight.

For the Americans who increasingly felt themselves under siege in their classy new embassy building in Saigon, and in the defense attache's office at Tan Son Nhut, it was apparent that North Vietnamese troops were coming down the pike and that South Vietnam's forces were not going to stop them. US Information Agency chief Alan Carter began telling Ambassador Martin that it was time to make practical plans for an evacuation. Martin kept telling Thieu that the United States would not evacuate, would not abandon its ally. Martin, who clearly believed it himself, kept saying that the US would stand fast, even after the Communists had over-run Da Nang. No-one else believed it. A few brave Foreign Service and military officers began plotting to evacuate those South Vietnamese citizens who had worked most closely with Americans. On the morning of 28 April, junior diplomat Peter Orr glanced out of the window of the embassy to see Marine guards cutting down trees with chainsaws. He leaned out, "What are you guys doing?"

"Sir, we're creating landing zones for helicopters."

At about that time the last flights left Tan Son Nhut, NVA troops stormed the airfield, and fixed-wing aircraft were no longer an option for anyone wanting to leave.

On 21 April President Thieu resigned, charging that the US was an untrustworthy ally. The end came just over a week later. On 29 April Operation 'Frequent Wind' evacuated 395 US citizens and 5,205 foreign nationals from Saigon by helicopter. Three aircraft were lost and two US Marines killed during the evacuation. The Saigon government finally surrendered on 30 April 1975, and the long war was over.

## Massive evacuation, more left behind

Beginning in April 1975, Americans assisted in the evacuation of up to 160,000 Vietnamese refugees. Some were 'boat people' who washed ashore in Singapore, Malaysia, the Philippines and Hong Kong. Some were picked up by American vessels and taken to Guam. In early May 1975 one of the authors of this volume, along with State Department officer Andrew F. Antippas, and Immigration Service boss General Leonard F. Chapman sat around a table and hurriedly created the guidelines under which tens of thousands of these refugees were permitted to enter the United States. Refugee processing camps were set up at Eglin AFB, Florida, Indiantown Gap, Pennsylvania, Fort Chaffee, Arkansas, and Camp Pendelton, California.

It has been argued that the Vietnamese who escaped with American help were not always those who deserved it the most, while many other Vietnamese who labored on the anti-Communist side were left behind. Once North Vietnamese troops seized Saigon on 30 April 1975, one of their first steps was to assign thousands of former South Vietnamese officials to 're-education' camps in the North. This turned out to be the first of many cruelties the new regime embarked upon.

The Vietnamese Air Force, which had fought so valiantly for so many years, was swallowed up by its North Vietnamese enemy. Vietnam now became one nation (the Socialist Republic of Vietnam) and its new Communist rulers operated a few of the F-5s, C-130s, and other American aircraft types seized from the VNAF – without a lot of success and without a flow of spare parts. In later years the new Vietnam's Soviet ally would fly 'Bear' reconnaissance aircraft and MiG-23 fighters from the magnificent airfield built by the Americans at Cam Ranh Bay.

Left: The most potent warplanes left behind by fleeing South Vietnamese were their F-5 Freedom Fighters. This weary-looking F-5B is seen with the markings of the new Socialist Republic of Vietnam inside its US-built shelter. Once having captured these aircraft, Hanoi's airmen had difficulty keeping them maintained well enough to stay airworthy.

# Air Support

he US Air Force in Thailand and the US Navy at sea off the Vietnamese coast flew support for the evacuation of Saigon. A few of these missions were flown by a new aircraft type, the Grumman F-14A Tomcat, which was making one of its first operational cruises aboard the USS *Enterprise* (CVAN-65). US aircraft met no aerial opposition.

## Heroic escapes

The tales of harrowing escapes from Saigon would fill a book. An O-1E Bird Dog pilot got out with several people aboard his two-seat ship and landed safely aboard the USS *Midway* (CVA-41). Some helicopters filled with escapees landed aboard American carriers at sea and had to be dumped overboard to make space for more. A VNAF pilot flew a C-130 to Thailand and found he had to park in a sea of A-37Bs and A-1 Skyraiders, which had escaped earlier.

On the last day for the city of Saigon – the wonderful capital which had been the Paris of the Orient and which was now to slide into a long dark night under its new name, Ho Chi Minh city – a few men made the decision to fight to the end. As a final gesture, a VNAF AC-119G gunship flanked by two A-1H Skyraiders took off from Tan Son Nhut as Communist troops were coming through the wire on the airfield perimeter. Weaving through gunfire and

*When US forces returned to Vietnam for the evacuation, they brought with them a new aircraft that had been designed using experience from the war. The Tomcat's appearance was brief and involved no combat.*

criss-crossing SA-7 missiles, the gunship and the two Skyraiders made a last-ditch stand within view of much of the population of Saigon.

Repeatedly the VNAF warplanes flew into enemy fire in order to unleash their own shells and ordnance and slow down the NVA advance. Finally, the gunship and one A-1H were blown out of the sky by missiles. The remaining A-1H Skyraider – the last aircraft seen to fly in combat in South Vietnam – was last observed trailing smoke up the Saigon River, in the direction of more enemy. There are those who say that the Skyraider is still flying and fighting out there in some eternal combat zone in the sky, destined to continue flying so long as men believe it worth the price to lay their lives on the line in defense of freedom.

For everybody else, the long air war in South Vietnam had finally ended.

*The USS Enterprise (CVAN-65) carries a full load of CH-53 helicopters to help in the final evacuation of Saigon. It also carries two squadrons of Grumman F-14 Tomcats, the advanced new Navy fighter which was entering a combat zone for the first time.*

*A Soviet-built T-54 smashes through the gates of the Presidential Palace in Saigon, the overwhelming North Vietnamese triumph bringing to an end more than 40 years of conflict.*

# Major air bases in Vietnam

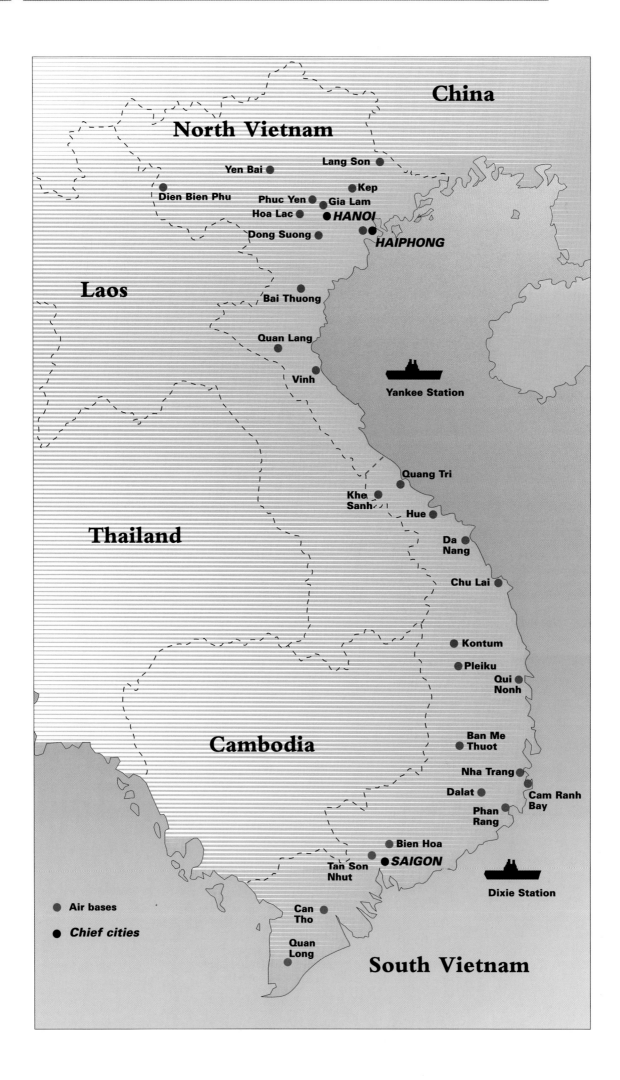

China

North Vietnam

Yen Bai

Lang Son

Dien Bien Phu

Kep

Phuc Yen  Gia Lam

Hoa Lac

**HANOI**

Dong Suong

**HAIPHONG**

Laos

Bai Thuong

Quan Lang

Vinh

Yankee Station

Quang Tri

Khe Sanh

Hue

Thailand

Da Nang

Chu Lai

Kontum

Pleiku

Qui Nonh

Ban Me Thuot

Cambodia

Nha Trang

Dalat

Cam Ranh Bay

Phan Rang

Bien Hoa

Tan Son Nhut

**SAIGON**

Dixie Station

Air bases

Chief cities

Can Tho

Quan Long

**South Vietnam**

# Major air bases in Thailand

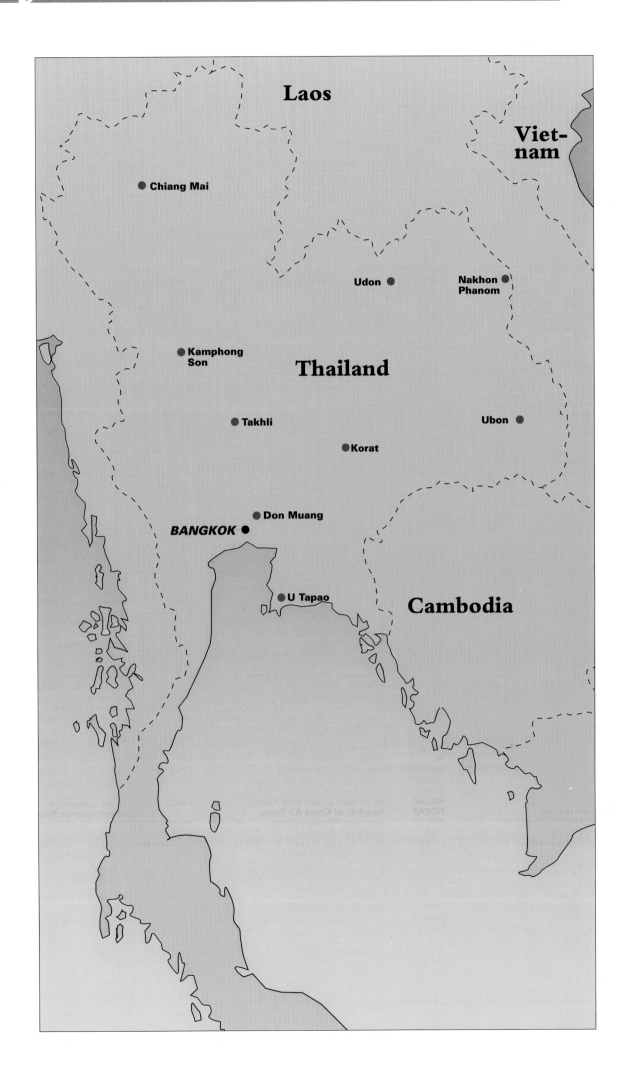

# Abbreviations

| | |
|---|---|
| AAA | Anti-Aircraft Artillery |
| AAAGV | Australian Army Assistance Group, Vietnam |
| AAFSS | Advanced Aerial Fire Support System |
| AAFV | Australian Army Force, Vietnam |
| AATTV | Australian Army Training Team, Vietnam |
| AB | Air Base |
| ABCCC | Airborne Battlefield Command and Control Centers |
| ACS | Air Commando Squadron |
| ACV | Air Cushion Vehicle |
| AEW | Airborne Early Warning |
| AFB | Air Force Base |
| ALARS | Air-Launched Acoustical Reconnaissance Sensor |
| ANZAC | Australian-New Zealand Army Corps |
| APOE | Aerial Port of Embarkation |
| ARRSq | Aerospace Rescue and Recovery Squadron |
| ARefS | Air Refueling Squadron |
| ARVN | Army of the Republic of Vietnam |
| ASW | Anti-Submarine Warfare |
| AWADS | Adverse Weather Aerial Delivery Systems |
| BARCAP | Barrier Combat Air Patrol |
| CBI | China-Burma-India Theater of Operations |
| CBU | Cluster Bomb Units |
| CCTS | Combat Crew Training Squadron |
| CDS | Container Delivery System |
| CEFEO | Corps Expeditionnaire Francais d'Extreme Orient |
| CIA | Central Intelligence Agency |
| CNAF | Chinese Nationalist Air Force |
| COD | Carrier Onboard Delivery |
| COMINT | Communications Intelligence |
| CONUS | Continental United States |
| CTF | Carrier Task Force |
| CVA | Attack Carrier |
| CVS | Anti-submarine Support Aircraft Carrier |
| CVSG | Anti-submarine Carrier Air Group |
| CVW | Carrier Air Wing |
| CW | Continuous Wave |
| DIC | Division d'Infanterie Coloniale |
| DMZ | Demilitarized Zone |
| DOD | Department of Defense |
| ECM | Electronic Countermeasures |
| ELINT | Electronic Intelligence |
| EMEO | Escadrille de Marche d'Extreme Orient |
| EOGB | Electro-Optical Guided Bomb |
| EROM | Escadrille de Reconnaissance d'Outre Mer |
| ERP | Escadrille de Reconnaissance Photographique |
| ESM | Electronic Support Measures |
| FAC | Forward Air Controller |
| FAC(A) | Forward Air Controller (Airborne) |
| FCO | Fire Control Operator |
| FIS | Fighter Interceptor Squadron |
| FMF | Fleet Marine Force |
| FORCECAP | Task Force Combat Air Patrol |
| GAOA | Groupe d'Aviation d'Observation d'Artillerie |
| GB | Groupe de Bombardement |
| GC | Groupe de Chasse |
| GCI | Ground-Controlled Intercept |
| GM | Groupe de Marche |
| GMTEO | Groupe de Marche de Transport d'Extreme Orient |
| GPES | Ground Proximity Extraction System |
| GT | Groupe de Transport |
| HC | Helicopter Combat Support Squadron |
| HE | High Explosive |
| HMA | Marine Helicopter Attack Squadron |

| | |
|---|---|
| HMH | Marine Heavy Helicopter Squadron |
| HML | Marine Light Helicopter Squadron |
| HMM | Marine Medium Helicopter Squadron |
| H&MS | Marine HQ & Maintenance Squadron |
| HU | Helicopter Utility Squadron |
| IFF | Identification, Friend or Foe |
| JATO | Jet-Assisted Take Off |
| KIA | Killed in Action |
| LAPES | Low-Altitude Parachute Extraction System |
| LGB | Laser-Guided Bomb |
| LLLTV | Low-Light-Level Television |
| LOC | Line of Communication |
| LORAN | Long-Range Navigation |
| LS | Landing Site |
| LZ | Landing Zone |
| MAAG | Military Assistance Advisory Group |
| MACV | Military Assistance Command Vietnam |
| MAC | Military Airlift Command |
| MAD | Mortar Air Delivery |
| MAG | Marine Aircraft Group |
| MARS | Mid-Air Retrieval System |
| MATS | Military Air Transport Service |
| MAW | Marine Aircraft Wing |
| MCAS | Marine Corps Air Station |
| MEB | Marine Expeditionary Brigade |
| MEF | Marine Expeditionary Force |
| MIA | Missing in Action |
| MIGCAP | Combat Air Patrol against MiG aircraft |
| NAF | Naval Air Facility |
| NAS | Naval Air Station |
| NATO | North Atlantic Treaty Organization |
| NATRACOM | Naval Air Training Command |
| NMCB | Naval Mobile Construction Battalion |
| NVA | North Vietnamese Army |
| NVNAF | North Vietnamese Air Force |
| OSS | Office of Strategic Services |
| PACAF | Pacific Air Forces |
| PBR | Patrol Boat, River |
| PCI | Indochinese Communist Party |
| PJ | Parajumper |
| POL | Petroleum, Oil, and Lubricants |
| POW | Prisoner of War |
| PRC | People's Republic of China |
| QOR | Qualified Operational Requirement |
| RAAF | Royal Australian Air Force |
| RC | Route Coloniale |
| RESCAP | Rescue Combat Air Patrol |
| RHAW | Radar Homing and Warning |
| RLAF | Royal Lao Air Force |
| RNZAF | Royal New Zealand Air Force |
| ROKAF | Republic of Korea Air Force |
| RPV | Remotely Piloted Vehicle |
| R&R | Rest and Relaxation |
| RTAB | Royal Thai Air Base |
| RTAF | Royal Thai Air Force |
| RTAFB | Royal Thai Air Force Base |
| RTNAF | Royal Thai Naval Air Facility |
| RVAH | Heavy Reconnaissance Attack Squadron |
| RVN | Republic of Vietnam |
| RVNAF | Republic of Vietnam Armed Forces |
| SAC | Strategic Air Command |
| SACADVON | SAC Advanced Echelon |
| SAGFTA | Societe Auxiliaire de Gerance et de Transports Aeriens |
| SAL | Sections Aerienne de Liaison |
| SAM | Surface-to-Air Missile |
| SAR | Sea Air Rescue |
| SAS | Special Air Service |

| | |
|---|---|
| SATS | Short Airfield for Tactical Support |
| SEATO | South East Asia Defense Treaty Organization |
| SIGINT | Signals Intelligence |
| SLF | Special Landing Forces |
| SOG | Special Operations Group |
| SOS | Special Operations Squadron |
| SRS | Strategic Reconnaissance Squadron |
| SRW | Strategic Reconnaissance Wing |
| STOL | Short Take-Off and Landing |
| SW | Strategic Wing |
| TAC | Tactical Air Command |
| TAC(A) | Tactical Air Controller (Airborne) |
| TACAN | Tactical Air Navigation |
| TACOS | Tanker and Countermeasures Strike Support |
| TAFDS | Tactical Airfield Fuel Dispensing System |
| TARCAP | Target Combat Air Patrol |
| TAS | Tactical Airlift Squadron |
| TASS | Tactical Air Support Squadron |
| TAW | Tactical Airlift Wing |
| TBS | Tactical Bombardment Squadron |
| TCS | Troop Carrier Squadron |
| TCW | Troop Carrier Wing |
| TDY | Temporary Duty |
| TF | Task Force |
| TFA | Task Force Alpha |
| TFS | Tactical Fighter Squadron |
| TFW | Tactical Fighter Wing |
| TK | Temporary Kit |
| TOW | Tube launched, Optical tracked, Wire guided |
| TRIM | Trail and Road Interdiction Multisensor |
| TRS | Tactical Reconnaissance Squadron |
| TRW | Tactical Reconnaissance Wing |
| TUOC | Tactical Unit Operations Center |
| USA | United States Army |
| USAAF | United States Army Air Force(s) |
| USAF | United States Air Force |
| USAFE | United States Air Forces in Europe |
| USAID | United States Agency for International Development |
| USIA | United States Information Agency |
| USS | United States Ship |
| VA | Attack Squadron |
| VAH | Heavy Attack Squadron |
| VAL | Light Attack Squadron |
| VAP | Heavy Photographic Reconnaissance Squadron |
| VAQ | Carrier Tactical Electronics Warfare Squadron |
| VAW | Carrier Air Early Warning Squadron |
| VC | Viet Cong |
| VF | Fighter Squadron |
| VFP | Light Photographic Squadron |
| VMA | Marine Attack Squadron |
| VMA(AW) | Marine All-Weather Attack Squadron |
| VMCJ | Marine Composite Reconnaissance Squadron |
| VMFA | Marine Fighter Attack Squadron |
| VMF(AW) | Marine All-Weather Fighter Squadron |
| VMGR | Marine Aerial Refueler Transport Squadron |
| VMO | Marine Observation Squadron |
| VNAF | Vietnamese Air Force |
| VO | Observation Squadron |
| VP | Patrol Squadron |
| VQ | Fleet Air Reconnaissance Squadron |
| VR | Fleet Logistics Support Squadron |
| VRC | Fleet Tactical Support Squadron |
| VSF | Anti-submarine Fighter Squadron |
| VW | Fleet Early Warning Squadron |
| WSO | Weapons Systems Officer |

# Code Names

**Able Mable**
Reconnaissance operations over Laos by RF-101s deployed to Don Muang Airport, Thailand, beginning in the fall of 1961.

**Arc Light**
Tactical support B-52 bombing operations primarily in South Vietnam.

**Banish Beach**
C-130 operations during which fuel drums were dropped to start fires in an effort to deprive forest sanctuaries to the Viet Cong.

**Barrel Roll**
Armed reconnaissance sorties flown over Laos beginning in December 1964.

**Belfry Express**
RPV reconnaissance operations from the USS *Ranger* beginning in November 1969.

**Bell Tone I & II**
Deployment of F-100s and F-102s to Don Muang Air Port, Thailand, in 1960/61.

**Big Eye**
USAF EC-121 airborne early-warning operations from April 1965 until March 1967.

**Blue Chip**
Callsign for 7 AF command center.

**Blue Springs**
RPV reconnaissance operations initiated in August 1974.

**Bolo**
Anti-MiG fighter sweep on 2 February 1967.

**Brave Bull**
C-97 fitted with infra-red equipment for reconnaissance in Southeast Asia during 1963.

**Brown Cradle**
EB-66C equipped with ECM equipment for jamming enemy fire control radars.

**Bullet Shot**
Build-up of SAC B-52 forces in the Western Pacific beginning in February 1972.

**Candlestick**
Flaredropping operations.

**Candy Machine**
Intermittent deployments of F-102s to South Vietnam for air defence duty from Tan Son Nhut and Da Nang.

**Cheesebrick**
US codename for North Vietnamese passive tracking network.

**College Eye**
USAF EC-121 airborne early-warning operations (formerly Big Eye).

**Combat Apple**
Electronic reconnaissance, MiG warning, and sea-air rescue support missions flown by RC-135Ms beginning in the fall of 1967.

**Combat Dawn**
Electronic data collection by RPVs operating from South Korea.

**Combat Lightning**
KC-135 radio relay missions to extend the range of ground communications in Southeast Asia.

**Combat Proof**
All-weather sorties controlled by ground-based MSQ-77 radars. Codename later changed to Combat Skyspot.

**Combat Skyspot**
New codename for all-weather sorties previously known as Combat Proof.

**Combat Talon**
Support missions flown by C-130s during sea-air rescue operations in the North.

**Commando Hunt**
Interdiction campaign against enemy infiltration routes in Laos.

**Commando Sabre**
High-speed FAC sorties flown by F-100Fs beginning in June 1967.

**Commando Scarf**
Munition drop missions flown by C-130s in southern Laos.

**Commando Vault**
C-130 missions during which super-heavy M121 and BLU-82 bombs were dropped to blast out helicopter landing zones in the jungle.

**Constant Guard**
Build-up of tactical aircraft forces in Southeast Asia starting in early 1972.

**Credible Chase**
Concept and plan to use STOL (Short Take-Off and Landing) Fairchild AU-23s and Helio AU-24s as mini-gunships.

**Dragon Lady**
Clandestine U-2 reconnaissance operations begun from Bien Hoa in December 1963.

**Eagle Pull**
Final evacuation of US personnel and Cambodian VIPs from Phnom Penh in April 1975.

**Endsweep**
Mine-sweeping operations in North Vietnam undertaken by the US over a six-month period in 1973 in accordance with the Paris Agreement.

**Enhance Plus**
Massive delivery of aircraft to the VNAF prior to the signing of the Paris Agreement.

**Fan Song**
Soviet-built fire-control radar for the SA-2 'Guideline' surface-to-air missile system.

**Farm Gate**
Detachment of USAF air commandos deployed to South Vietnam in November 1961.

**Field Goal**
RT-33 reconnaissance sorties over Laos in April-May 1961.

**Flaming Dart**
Initial air operations over North Vietnam in February 1965.

**Flycatcher**
Supply of aircraft to the Khmer Air Force in 1974.

**Fogbound**
ECM/ESM missions over North Vietnam by Marine EF-10Bs.

**Freedom Porch**
Initial B-52 operations over the Red River Valley in April 1972.

**Freedom Train**
Operations against North Vietnam, below the 20th parallel, in April 1972.

**Frequent Wind**
Final evacuation of US personnel and some South Vietnamese VIPs from Saigon in April 1975.

**Game Warden**
Navy riverine operations in the Mekong Delta.

**Gunboat**
Modification of a C-130A to serve as prototype of a more advanced 'Gunship II'.

**Hawk Eye**
EC-47s fitted with radio direction-finding equipment to locate Viet Cong radio transmissions.

**High Drink**
Refueling of hovering rescue helicopters by US Navy vessels in the Gulf of Tonkin.

**Hilo Hattie**
C-54 fitted with infra-red reconnaissance equipment which operated in South Vietnam from March 1962 until February 1963.

**Homecoming**
Repatriation of POWs from North Vietnam in early 1973.

**Igloo White**
Surveillance system used on Ho Chi Minh Trail consisting of hand-implanted and air-delivered sensors, relay aircraft, reporting to an infiltration surveillance center. Previously known as Muscle Shoals.

**Iron Hand**
US Navy SAM suppression sorties.

**Junction City**
Large ground operation in South Vietnam's Tay Ninh Province, from 28 February 1967 to 14 May 1967.

**Lam Song 719/Dewey Canyon II**
Large-scale offensive operations against Communist lines of communications in Laos from 30 January 1971 to 6 April 1971.

**Lima Site**
Primitive airstrips in Laos used for US covert operations and by rescue helicopters.

**Linebacker I**
Air operations over North Vietnam from April through October 1972.

**Linebacker II**
'Eleven-day war' against Hanoi/Haiphong region in December 1972.

**Litterbug**
RPV operations during which propaganda leaflets were dropped over North Vietnam.

**Little Brother**
Projected use of Cessna O-2s fitted with side-firing miniguns.

**Market Time**
Coastal and ASW operations by Navy Patrol Squadrons and fast patrol craft.

**Mud River/Muscle Shoals**
Initial codename for the Igloo White surveillance system along the Ho Chi Minh Trail.

**Mule Train**
Initial deployments of C-123 tactical transports to South Vietnam in January 1962.

**Niagara**
Air operations during the siege of Khe Sanh in early 1968.

**OPLAN 34-A**
Operation Plan for covert operations in North Vietnam in 1964.

**Patricia Lynn**
RB-57Es fitted with ReconofaxVI infra-red sensors intended to detect camouflaged Viet Cong targets.

**Pave Eagle**
Unmanned Beech QU-22s used as relay platforms for data collected by the Igloo White surveillance system.

**Pave Nail**
Night observation system fitted to some USAF OV-10As.

**Pave Spot**
Laser designator fitted to some USAF OV-10As.

**Pink Rose**
Three B-52 missions in 1967 designed to set the jungle afire by massive use of incendiary bombs.

**Pipe Stem**
Temporary deployment of RF-101Cs to Tan Son Nhut in the fall of 1961.

**Pocket Money**
Aerial mining campaign against North Vietnam beginning in May 1972.

**Prize Crew**
Operational evaluation of the Lockheed QT-2PC quiet observation aircraft.

**Proud Deep**
US Navy protective reaction strikes flown against North Vietnam in December 1971.

**Ranch Hand**
C-123 detachment to South Vietnam for defoliation operations beginning in January 1962.

**Red Crown**
A radar-warning and aircraft control ship of the US Navy stationed in the Gulf of Tonkin on a rotational basis.

**Red Horse**
Air Force construction units.

**Rivet Top**
EC-121M early-warning aircraft fitted with improved airborne radar.

**Rolling Thunder**
Air offensive against North Vietnam from February 1965 until November 1968.

**Shu Fly**
Initial deployment of Marine helicopters and supporting fixed-wing aircraft to South Vietnam, beginning in April 1962.

**Skoshi Tiger**
Operational evaluation of the Northrop F-5A light fighter.

**Steel Tiger**
Strike operations in southern Laos first undertaken in April 1965.

**Surprise Package**
Improved armament and systems first tested in a modified AC-130A.

**Tally Ho**
Marine strikes in the North Vietnamese panhandle beginning in July 1966.

**Task Force Alpha**
Infiltration surveillance center, first located at Tan Son Nhut AB and then moved to Nakhon Phanom RTAFB, destination for Igloo White data.

**Tiger Hound**
Steel Tiger operations in Laos undertaken south of the 17th parallel under FAC control.

**Top Gun**
US Navy training programme to improve air combat skills of fighter pilots.

**Tropic Moon**
A-1Es (Tropic Moon I), B-57Bs (Tropic Moon II) and B-57Gs (Tropic Moon III) fitted with LLLTV and other systems for night attacks along the Ho Chi Minh Trail.

**Water Glass**
F-102 and AD-5Q air defence operations in South Vietnam from March 1962 until May 1963.

**Water Pump**
Training of Laotian T-28 crews by 1st ACW in the spring of 1964.

**Wild Weasel**
Tactical aircraft (F-100F, F-105F, F-105G, F-4C) fitted with RHAW and anti-radiation missiles for operations against North Vietnamese air defence sites.

## MAJOR USAF UNITS IN SOUTHEAST ASIA 1964-1973

| Unit | Initial Aircraft Type | Service Dates | Base |
|---|---|---|---|
| **Tactical Fighter Wings:** | | | |
| 3rd TFW | F-100 | 7/65-3/70 | Bien Hoa (1) |
| 4th TFW | F-4 | 4/72-10/72 | Udorn, Thai (2) |
| 8th TFW | F-4 | 17/65-1/73 | Ubon, Thai |
| 12th TFW | F-4 | 11/65-3/70 | Cam Ranh Bay |
| | | 4/70-11/71 | Phu Cat |
| 31st TFW | F-100 | 1/67-10/70 | Tuy Hoa |
| 35th TFW | F-4 | 7/65-9/66 | Da Nang (3) |
| | | 10/66-6/71 | Phan Rang |
| 37th TFW | F-100 | 3/67-3/70 | Phu Cat |
| 49th TFW | F-4 | 5/72-10/72 | Takhli, Thai (2) |
| 355th TFW | F-105 | 11/65-11/70 | Takhli, Thai |
| 366th TFW | F-4 | 4/66-9/66 | Phan Rang |
| | | 10/66-6/72 | Da Nang |
| | | 7/72-10/72 | Takhli, Thai |
| 388th TFW | F-105 | 4/65-3/73 | Korat, Thai (4) |
| **Tactical Reconnaissance Wings:** | | | |
| 432nd TRW | RF-4 | 4/66-post-war | Udorn, Thai |
| 460th TRW | RF-4 | 2/66-8/71 | Tan Son Nhut |
| 553rd TRW | RF-4 | 11/67-12/70 | Korat, Thai |
| **Special Operations Wings** ('Air Commando Wings' until 8/68): | | | |
| 14th SOW | AC-47/119 | 3/66-9/69 | Nha Trang |
| | | 10/69-9/71 | Phan Rang |
| 56th SOW | AC-119 | 4/67-6/74 | Nakhon Phanom, Thai |
| 315th SOW | C-123 | 3/66-6/67 | Tan Son Nhut (5) |
| | | 7/67-3/72 | Phan Rang |
| 633rd SOW | AC-119 | 7/68-3/70 | Nakhon Phanom, Thai |
| **Tactical Airlift Wings** ('Troop Carrier Wings' until 8/67): | | | |
| 314th TAW | C-130 | pre-3/66 | Clark, Philippines |
| | | 4/66-6/71 | C.C.K., Taiwan (6) |
| 374th TAW | C-130 | 8/66-5/71 | Naha, Okinawa (7) |
| | | 6/71-post-war | C.C.K. |
| 463rd TAW | C-130 | 12/65-12/71 | Clark, Philippines |
| 483rd TAW | C-7 | 1/66-4/72 | Cam Ranh Bay (8) |

| Unit | Initial Aircraft Type | Service Dates | Base |
|---|---|---|---|
| Rotational squadrons from the US were attached to the following: | | | |
| 315 Air Div. | C-130 | 2/68-4/69 | Tachikawa, Japan (9) |
| 834 Air Div. | C-130 | 11/66-11/70 | Tan Son Nhut (9) |
| **Strategic Air Command** ('Bombardment' or 'Strategic' Wings): | | | |
| 307th SW | B-52 | 6/66-post-war | U-Tapao, Thai (10) |
| 4,133rd BW (11) | B-52 | 2/66-6/70 | Andersen, Guam |
| 4,252nd SW | B-52 | 1/65-3/70 | Kadena, Okinawa |

**Notes:**
1. Designated 6,251st TFW until 11/65.
2. Emergency reinforcement during NVA Spring 1972 Offensive.
3. Designated 6,252nd TFW until 4/66.
4. Designated 6,234th TFW until 4/66.
5. The 315th SOW, used for defoliant spray operations, was redesignated as 315th Tactical Airlift Wing on 1/1/70.
6. 'C.C.K.' is Ching Chuan Kang in Taiwan.
7. Since early 1965, 3 x independent squadrons were at Naha.
8. Formed from six US Army aviation companies which had arrived in Vietnam between 7/63 and 1/66.
9. These Air Divisions had C-130s in wing strength during the periods noted.
10. Designated 4,258th SW until 4/70. Under command of 17th Air Division (Provisional) from 6/72.
11. Conducted operations under 3rd Air Division until that formation was inactivated 31/3/70. Thereafter, bombing operations from Guam were controlled by 8th Air Force, which replaced 3rd Air Division. During the NVA Spring 1972 Offensive, 57th Air Division (Provisional) was formed to handle increased bombing operations (6/72).

**General Notes:**
A. Several smaller units also operated in Vietnam during the period, including: 3rd Aero Rescue & Recovery Group, 504th Tactical Air Support Group, and 505th Tactical Control Group.
B. Operations in South Vietnam were controlled by 2nd Air Division (formed 10/62) until that formation was replaced by Seventh Air Force (4/66). Thirteenth Air Force, located at Clark Air Base in the Philippines, controlled other elements, while a subsidiary command, 7th/13th Air Force, operated from Thailand.

## B-52 EFFORT IN SOUTHEAST ASIA

| Representative Date | Sortie Rate (Monthly) |
|---|---|
| Jul '65 | 300 |
| Nov '66 | 600 |
| Feb '67 | 800 |
| Feb '68 | 1,200 |
| Apr '68 | 1,800 |
| Jul '69 | 1,600 |
| Oct '69 | 1,400 |
| Jun '71 | 1,000 |
| Feb '72 | 1,200 |
| Mar '72 | 1,500 |
| Apr '72 | 1,800 |
| Jun '72 | 3,150 |

**Notes:**
The B-52 effort, which utilized over 200 aircraft at its peak, ultimately delivered 5,898,000,000 pounds of bombs in 124,532 sorties, only 6% of which were conducted against North Vietnam itself.
Over half (55%) of all B-52 missions were flown in support of operations within South Vietnam, while the balance of the combat sorties carried out by the big strategic bomber formed an important part of the interdiction campaigns in Laos (27%) and Cambodia (12%).

## SOUTH VIETNAMESE AIR FORCE ORDER OF BATTLE – 1975

**1st AIR DIVISION (Da Nang, Hue, Quang Ngai)**
2 x F-5E fighter squadrons
4 x A-37B ground-attack squadrons
1 x A-1H ground-attack squadron
2 x O-1, O-2, U-17 spotter squadrons
5 x UH-1 assault helicopter squadrons
1 x CH-47 transport helicopter squadron

**2nd AIR DIVISION (Nha Trang, Phan Rang)**
2 x A-37 ground-attack squadrons
1 x O-1, O-2, U-17 spotter squadron
1 x UH-1 assault helicopter squadron
1 x T-37 training squadron
1 x T-41 training squadron

**3rd AIR DIVISION (Bien Hoa)**
4 x F-5A fighter squadrons
2 x A-37B ground-attack squadrons
1 x O-1, O-2, U-17 spotter squadron
5 x UH-1 assault helicopter squadrons
1 x CH-47 transport helicopter squadron

**4th AIR DIVISION (Binh Thuy, Soc Trang)**
3 x A-37B ground-attack squadrons

2 x O-1, O-2, U-17 spotter squadrons
5 x UH-1 assault helicopter squadrons
1 x CH-47 transport helicopter squadron

**5th AIR DIVISION (Tan Son Nhut)**
2 x AC-119 gunship squadrons
1 x EC-47 electronic recon squadron
1 x RC-119 photo recon squadron 1
1 x VC-17/UH-1 special mission squadron
1 x C-47 transport squadron
3 x C-7 transport squadrons
1 x C-119 transport squadron
2 x C-123 transport squadrons
2 x C-130 transport squadrons
1 x UH-1 assault helicopter squadron

**6th AIR DIVISION (Pleiku, Phu Cat)**
1 x F-5E fighter squadron
1 x A-1H ground-attack squadron
1 x AC-119 gunship squadron
1 x O-1, O-2, U-17 spotter squadron
3 x UH-1 assault helicopter squadrons
1 x CH-47 transport helicopter squadron

# TASK FORCE 77 MAY 1964 TO MAY 1975

## MODIFIED 'ESSEX' CLASS

| | |
|---|---|
| Completion Dates | 1943-1950 |
| Full Load Displacement | 41,000 tons |
| Flight Deck | 899 ft x 172-195 ft; 2 x catapults |
| Complement | 3,200 |
| Air wing | 70-80 aircraft |

### Intrepid (CVS 11)

| | |
|---|---|
| 1/5/66-30/10/66 | CVW 10 |
| 9/6/67-9/12/67 | CVW 10 |
| 6/7/68-16/1/69 | CVW 10 |

Note:
Anti-submarine carrier, employed in a limited attack role.
First deployment was to Dixie Station.

### Ticonderoga (CVA 14)

| | |
|---|---|
| 11/5/64-10/12/64 | CVW 5 |
| 25/10/65-7/5/66 | CVW 5 |
| 27/10/66-22/5/67 | CVW 19 |
| 13/1/68-9/8/68 | CVW 19 |
| 18/2/69-10/9/69 | CVW 16 |

### Hancock (CVA 19)

| | |
|---|---|
| 16/11/64-11/5/65 | CVW 21 |
| 6/12/65-24/7/66 | CVW 21 |
| 20/1/67-14/7/67 | CVW 5 |
| 6/8/68-23/2/69 | CVW 21 |
| 21/8/69-6/4/70 | CVW 21 |
| 7/11/70-19/5/71 | CVW 21 |
| 28/1/72-25/9/72 | CVW 21 |
| 19/5/73-24/12/73 | CVW 21 |
| 6/4/75-31/5/75 | CVW 21 |

### Bon Homme Richard (CVA 31)

| | |
|---|---|
| 24/2/64-20/11/64 | CVW 19 |
| 12/5/65-4/1/66 | CVW 19 |
| 10/2/67-17/8/67 | CVW 21 |
| 9/2/68-29/9/68 | CVW 5 |
| 6/4/69-19/10/69 | CVW 5 |
| 21/4/70-3/11/70 | CVW 5 |

### Oriskany (CVA 34)

| | |
|---|---|
| 27/4/65-6/12/65 | CVW 16 |
| 11/6/66-8/11/66 | CVW 16 |
| 26/6/67-23/1/68 | CVW 16 |
| 5/5/69-10/11/69 | CVW 19 |
| 1/6/70-29/11/70 | CVW 19 |
| 4/6/71-8/12/71 | CVW 19 |
| 21/6/72-20/3/73 | CVW 19 |
| 30/10/73-17/5/74 | CVW 19 |

Note:
Major fire on board during second deployment.

### Shangri-La (CVS 38)

| | |
|---|---|
| 30/3/70-24/11/70 | CVW 8 |

## 'MIDWAY' CLASS

| | |
|---|---|
| Completion Dates | 1945-1947 |
| Full Load Displacement | 64,000 tons |
| Flight Deck | 979 ft x 238 ft; 2 x catapults (3 on Coral Sea) |
| Complement | 4,500 |
| Air Wing | 75 aircraft |

### Midway (CVA 41)

| | |
|---|---|
| 22/3/65-14/11/65 | CVW 2 |
| 7/5/71-24/10/71 | CVW 5 |
| 21/4/72-23/2/73 | CVW 5 |
| 2/10/73-27/2/74 | CVW 5 |
| 25/10/74-1/5/75 | CVW 5 |

### Franklin D. Roosevelt (CVA 42)

| | |
|---|---|
| 25/7/66-29/1/67 | CVW 1 |

### Coral Sea (CVA 43)

| | |
|---|---|
| 23/1/65-23/10/65 | CVW 15 |
| 11/8/66-16/2/67 | CVW 2 |
| 10/8/67-29/3/68 | CVW 15 |
| 23/9/68-11/4/69 | CVW 15 |
| 14/10/69-18/6/70 | CVW 15 |
| 8/12/71-11/7/72 | CVW 15 |
| 20/3/73-30/10/73 | CVW 15 |
| 29/12/74-24/S/75 | CVW 15 |

## 'FORRESTAL' CLASS

| | |
|---|---|
| Completion Dates | 1955-1959 |
| Full Load Displacement | 76,000 to 79,000 tons |
| Flight Deck | 1,063 to 1,086 ft x 252 ft; 4 x catapults |
| Complement | 5,000 |
| Air Wing | 90-100 aircraft (70 for CVA 59) |

### Forrestal (CVA 59)

| | |
|---|---|
| 8/7/67-22/8/67 | CVW 17 |

Note:
Catastrophic fire curtailed deployment.

### Saratoga (CVA 60)

| | |
|---|---|
| 8/5/72-16/1/73 | CVW 3 |

### Ranger (CVA 61)

| | |
|---|---|
| 17/8/64-24/4/65 | CVW 9 |
| 3/1/66-18/8/66 | CVW 14 |
| 20/11/67-18/5/68 | CVW 2 |
| 12/11/68-10/5/69 | CVW 2 |
| 4/11/69-23/5/70 | CVW 2 |
| 11/11/70-9/6/71 | CVW 2 |
| 28/11/72-14/6/73 | CVW 2 |
| 24/5/74-27/9/74 | CVW 2 |

Note:
Embarked first A-7 attack jets on third deployment.

### Independence (CVA 62)

| | |
|---|---|
| 5/6/65-21/11/65 | CVW 7 |

Note:
Deployed first A-6 all-weather bombers.

## 'KITTY HAWK' CLASS

| | |
|---|---|
| Completion Dates | 1961-1965 |
| Full Load Displacement | 79,000-81,000 tons |
| Flight Deck | 1,047 ft x 252 ft; 4 x catapults |
| Complement | 5,000 |
| Air Wing | 85 aircraft |

### Kitty Hawk (CVA 63)

| | |
|---|---|
| 15/11/65-6/6/66 | CVW 11 |
| 17/11/66-12/6/67 | CVW 11 |
| 6/12/67-20/6/68 | CVW 11 |
| 15/1/69-27/8/69 | CVW 11 |
| 27/11/70-6/7/71 | CVW 11 |
| 1/3/72-17/11/72 | CVW 11 |
| 1/1/74-19/6/74 | CVW 11 |

### Constellation (CVA 64)

| | |
|---|---|
| 11/6/64-14/1/65 | CVW 14 |
| 29/5/66-24/11/66 | CVW 15 |
| 15/5/67-26/11/67 | CVW 14 |
| 14/6/68-23/1/69 | CVW 14 |
| 1/9/69-29/4/70 | CVW 14 |
| 27/10/71-24/6/72 | CVW 9 |
| 16/1/73-2/10/73 | CVW 9 |
| 11/7/74-29/10/74 | CVW 15 |

### America (CVA 66)

| | |
|---|---|
| 12/5/68-20/11/68 | CVW 6 |
| 12/5/70-23/11/70 | CVW 9 |
| 1/7/72-4/3/73 | CVW 8 |

## 'ENTERPRISE' CLASS

| | |
|---|---|
| Completion Date | 1961 |
| Full Load Displacement | 90,000 tons |
| Flight Deck | 1,102 ft x 252 ft; 4 x catapults |
| Complement | 5,500 |
| Air Wing | 85+ aircraft |

### Enterprise (CVAN 65)

| | |
|---|---|
| 21/11/65-14/6/66 | CVW 9 |
| 3/12/66-30/6/67 | CVW 9 |
| 14/1/68-12/7/68 | CVW 9 |
| 15/3/69-26/6/69 | CVW 9 |
| 27/6/71-2/2/72 | CVW 14 |
| 19/9/72-3/6/73 | CVW 14 |
| 16/10/74-24/12/74 | CVW 14 |
| 26/2/75-4/5/75 | CVW 14 |

Note:
First nuclear-powered ship in combat. Major fire while working up for fourth deployment.

# MiG Killers

| | Date | Weapon | Aircraft | Serial | Crew | Unit | Tailcode | Base | Callsign | Opponent |
|---|---|---|---|---|---|---|---|---|---|---|
| 1. | 9 Apr '65 | AIM-7 | F-4B | 151403 | LTJG Terence M. Murphy/ENS Ronald J. Fegan | VF-96/CVW-9 | NG-602 | CVA-61 | SHOWTIME | MiG-17 |
| 2. | 17 Jun '65 | AIM-7 | F-4B | 151488 | CDR Louis Page/LT John C. Smith. Jr | VF-21/CVW-2 | NE-101 | CVA-41 | SUNDOWN | MiG-17 |
| 3. | 17 Jun '65 | AIM-7 | F-4B | 152219 | LT Jack E. D. Batson, Jr/LCDR Robert B. Doremus | VF-21/CVW-2 | NE-102 | CVA-41 | SUNDOWN | MiG-17 |
| 4. | 20 Jun '65 | 20 mm | A-1H | 137523 | LT Charlie Hartman | VA-25/CVW-2 | NE-573 | CVA-41 | CANASTA | MiG-17 |
| | | 20 mm | A-1H | 139768 | LT Clinton B. Johnson | VA-25/CVW-2 | NE-577 | CVA-41 | CANASTA | |
| 5. | 10 Jul '65 | AIM-9 | F-4C | | Capt. Kenneth E. Holcombe/Capt. Arthur C. Clark | 45 TFS/2AD | None | Ubon | | MiG-17 |
| 6. | 10 Jul '65 | AIM-9 | F-4C | | Capt. Thomas S. Roberts/Capt. Ronald C. Anderson | 45 TFS/2AD | None | Ubon | | MiG-17 |
| 7. | 23 Apr '66 | AIM-9 | F-4C | | Capt. Max F. Cameron/1Lt Robert E. Evans | 555 TFS/8 TFW | None | Ubon | | MiG-17 |
| 8. | 23 Apr '66 | AIM-7 | F-4C | 64-699 | Capt. Robert E. Blake/1Lt S. W. George | 555 TFS/8 TFW | None | Ubon | | MiG-17 |
| 9. | 26 Apr '66 | AIM-9 | F-4C | 64-752 | Major Paul J. Gilmore/1Lt William T. Smith | 480 TFS/35 TFW | None | Da Nang | | MiG-21 |
| 10. | 29 Apr '66 | Maneuver | F-4C | | Capt. Larry R. Keith/1Lt Robert A. Bleakley | 555 TFS/8 TFW | | Ubon | | MiG-17 |
| 11. | 29 Apr '66 | AIM-9 | F-4C | | Capt. William B. Dowell/1Lt Halbert E. Gossard | 555 TFS/8 TFW | None | Ubon | | MiG-17 |
| 12. | 30 Apr '66 | AIM-9 | F-4C | | Capt. Lawrence H. Golberg/1Lt Gerald D. Hardgrave | 555 TFS/8 TFW | None | Ubon | | MiG-17 |
| 13. | 12 May '66 | AIM-9 | F-4C | 64-660 | Major Wilbur R. Dudley/1Lt Imants Kringelis | 390 TFS/35 TFW | None | Da Nang | | MiG-17 |
| 14. | 12 Jun '66 | AIM-9D | F-8E | 150924 | CDR Harold L. Marr | VF-211/CVW-21 | NP | CVA-19 | NICKEL | MiG-17 |
| 15. | 21 Jun '66 | AIM-9D | F-8E | 150924 | LTJG Phillip V. Vampatella | VF-211/CVW-21 | NP-104 | CVA-19 | NICKEL | MiG-17 |
| 16. | 21 Jun '66 | AIM-9D | F-8E | 150867 | LT Eugene J. Chancy | VF-211/CVW-21 | NP-101 | CVA-19 | NICKEL | MiG-17 |
| 17. | 29 Jun '66 | 20 mm | F-105D | | Major Fred L. Tracy | 44 TFS/388 TFW | | Korat | | MiG-17 |
| 18. | 13 Jul '66 | AIM-9D | F-4B | 151500 | LT William M. McGuigan | VF-161/CVW-15 | NL-216 | CVA-64 | ROCK RIVER | MiG-17 |
| 19. | 14 Jul '66 | AIM-9 | F-4C | | 1Lt Ronald G. Martin/1Lt Richard N. Krieps | 480 TFS/35 TFW | None | Da Nang | | MiG-21 |
| 20. | 14 Jul '66 | AIM-9 | F-4C | 63-7489 | Capt. William J. Swendner/1Lt Duane A. Buttell, Jr | 480 TFS/35 TFW | None | Da Nang | | MiG-21 |
| 21. | 18 Aug '66 | 20 mm | F-105D | | Major Kenneth T. Blank | 34 TFS/388 TFW | None | Korat | HONDA 02 | MiG-17 |
| 22. | 16 Sep '66 | AIM-9 | F-4C | 63-7650 | 1Lt Jerry W. Jameson/1Lt Douglas B. Rose | 555 TFS/8 TFW | None | Ubon | | MiG-17 |
| 23. | 21 Sep '66 | 20 mm | F-105D | | 1Lt Fred A. Wilson, Jr | 333 TFS/355 TFW | None | Takhli | VEGAS 02 | MiG-17 |
| 24. | 21 Sep '66 | 20 mm | F-105D | 59-1766 | 1Lt Karl W. Richter | 421 TFS/388 TFW | None | Korat | FORD 03 | MiG-17 |
| 25. | 09 Oct '66 | AIM-9 | F-8E | 149159 | CDR Richard M. Bellinger | VF-162/CVW-16 | AH-210 | CVA-34 | SUPERHEAT | MiG-21 |
| 26. | 09 Oct '66 | 20 mm | A-1H | 137543 | LTJG William T. Patton | VA-176/CVW-10 | AK-409 | CVS-11 | PAPOOSE 409 | MiG-17 |
| 27. | 05 Nov '66 | AIM-9 | F-4C | 63-7535 | 1Lt Wilbur J. Latham, Jr/1Lt Klaus J. Klause | 480 TFS/366 TFW | None | Da Nang | OPAL 02 | MiG-21 |
| 28. | 05 Nov '66 | AIM-7 | F-4C | 63-7541 | Major James E. Tuck/1Lt John J. Rabeni, Jr | 480 TFS/366 TFW | None | Da Nang | OPAL 01 | MiG-21 |
| 29. | 04 Dec '66 | 20 mm | F-105D | 60-451 | Major Roy S. Dickey | 469 TFS/388 TFW | None | Korat | ELGIN 04 | MiG-17 |
| 30. | 20 Dec '66 | AIM-7E | F-4B | 153022 | LT H. Dennis Wisely/LTJG David L. Jordan | VF-114/CVW-II | NH-215 | CVA-63 | LINFIELD | An-2 |
| 31. | 20 Dec '66 | AIM-7E | F-4B | 153019 | LT David McCrea/ENS David Nichols | VF-213/CVW-II | NH-110 | CVA-63 | BLACK LION | An-2 |
| 32. | 2 Jan '67 | AIM-7 | F-4C | 63-7589 | 1Lt Ralph F. Wetterhahn/1Lt Jerry K. Sharp | 555 TFS/8 TFW | FY | Ubon | OLDS 02 | MiG-21 |
| 33. | 2 Jan '67 | AIM-9 | F-4C | 63-7680 | Colonel Robin Olds/1Lt Charles C. Clifton | 555 TFS/8 TFW | FY | Ubon | OLDS 01 | MiG-21 |
| 34. | 2 Jan '67 | AIM-9 | F-4C | 63-7683 | Capt. Walter S. Radeker III/1Lt James E. Murray III | 555 TFS/8 TFW | FY | Ubon | OLDS 04 | MiG-21 |
| 35. | 2 Jan '67 | AIM-9 | F-4C | 63-7710 | Capt. Everett T. Raspberry, Jr/1Lt Robert W. Western | 555 TFS/8 TFW | FY | Ubon | FORD 02 | MiG-21 |
| 36 | 2 Jan '67 | AIM-7 | F-4C | 64-692 | 1Lt Lawrence J. Glynn, Jr/1Lt Lawrence E. Cary | 433 TFS/8 TFW | FG | Ubon | RAMBLER 02 | MiG-21 |
| 37. | 2 Jan '67 | AIM-7 | F-4C | 64-720 | Capt. John B. Stone/1Lt Clifton P. Dunnegan, Jr | 433 TFS/8 TFW | FG | Ubon | RAMBLER 01 | MiG-21 |
| 38. | 2 Jan '67 | AIM-7 | F-4C | 64-838 | Major Philip P. Combies/1Lt Lee R. Dutton | 433 TFS/8 TFW | FG | Ubon | RAMBLER 04 | MiG-21 |
| 39. | 6 Jan '67 | AIM-7 | F-4C | | Major Thomas M. Hirsch/1Lt Roger J. Strasswimmeh | 555 TFS/8 TFW | FY | Ubon | CRAB 02 | MiG-21 |
| 40. | 6 Jan '67 | AIM-7 | F-4C | 64-839 | Capt. Richard M. Pascoe/1Lt Norman E. Wells | 555 TFS/8 TFW | FP | Ubon | CRAB 01 | MiG-21 |
| 41. | 10 Mar '67 | 20 mm | F-105D | 62-4284 | Capt. Max C. Brestel | 354 TFS/355 TFW | None | Takhli | KANGAROO 03 | MiG-17 |
| 42. | 10 Mar '67 | 20 mm | F-105D | 62-4284 | Capt. Max C. Brestel | 354 TFS/355 TFW | None | Takhli | KANGAROO 03 | MiG-17 |
| 43. | 26 Mar '67 | 20 mm | F-105D | | Colonel Robert R. Scott | 333 TFS/355 TFW | None | Takhli | LEECH 01 | MiG-17 |
| 44. | 19 Apr '67 | 20 mm | F-105D | | Major Frederick G. Tolman | 354 TFS/355 TFW | None | Takhli | NITRO 03 | MiG-17 |
| 45. | 19 Apr '67 | 20 mm | F-105D | | Capt. William E. Eskew | 354 TFS/355 TFW | None | Takhli | PANDA 01 | MiG-17 |
| 46. | 19 Apr '67 | 20 mm | F-105D | 58-1168 | Major Jack W. Hunt | 354 TFS/355 TFW | None | Takhli | NITRO 01 | MiG-17 |
| 47. | 19 Apr '67 | 20 mm | F-105F | 63-8301 | Major Leo K. Thorsness/Capt. Harold E. Johnson | 357 TFS/355 TFW | None | Takhli | KINGFISH 01 | MiG-17 |
| 48. | 23 Apr '67 | AIM-7 | F-4C | 64-776 | Major Robert D. Anderson/Capt. Fred D. Kjer | 389 TFS/366 TFW | AK | Da Nang | CHICAGO 03 | MiG-21 |
| 49. | 24 Apr '67 | AIM-9B | F-4B | 153000 | LT Charles E. Southwick/ENS James W. Laing | VF-114/CVW-11 | NH-210 | CVA-63 | LINFIELD | MiG-17 |
| 50. | 24 Apr '67 | AIM-9D | F-4B | 153037 | LT H. Dennis Wisely/LTJG Gareth L. Anderson | VF-114/CVW-11 | NH | CVA-63 | LINFIELD | MiG-17 |
| 51. | 26 Apr '67 | AIM-7 | F-4C | 64-797 | Major Rolland W. Moore, Jr/1Lt James F. Sears | 389 TFS/366 TFW | A | Da Nang | CACTUS 01 | MiG-21 |
| 52. | 28 Apr '67 | 20 mm | F-105D | | Major Harry E. Higgins | 357 TFS/355 TFW | None | Takhli | SPITFIRE 01 | MiG-17 |
| 53. | 28 Apr '67 | 20 mm | F-105D | | Lt Col Arthur E. Dennis | 357 TFS/355 TFW | None | Takhli | ATLANTA 01 | MiG-17 |
| 54. | 30 Apr '67 | 20 mm | F-105D | | Capt. Thomas C. Lesan | 333 TFS/355 TFW | None | Takhli | RATTLER 01 | MiG-17 |
| 55. | 1 May '67 | Maneuver | F-4C | 63-7577 | Major Robert G. Dilger/1Lt Mack Theis | 390 TFS/366 TFW | B | Da Nang | STINGER 01 | MiG-17 |
| 56. | 1 May '67 | Zuni | A-4C | 148609 | LCDR Theodore R. Swartz | VA-76/CVW-21 | NP-685 | CVA-31 | SUN GLASS | MiG-17 |
| 57. | 1 May '67 | AIM-9D | F-8E | 150303 | LCDR Marshall O. Wright | VF-211/CVW-21 | NP-104 | CVA-31 | NICKEL | MiG-17 |
| 58. | 4 May '67 | AIM-9 | F-4C | 63-7668 | Colonel Robin Olds/1Lt William D. Lafever | 555 TFS/8 TFW | FP | Ubon | FLAMINGO 01 | MiG-21 |
| 59. | 12 May '67 | 20 mm | F-105D | | Capt. Jacques A. Suzanne | 333 TFS/355 TFW | None | Takhli | CROSSBOW 01 | MiG-17 |
| 60. | 13 May '67 | 20 mm | F-105D | | Lt Col Philip C. Gast | 354 TFS/355 TFW | None | Takhli | CHEVROLET 01 | MiG-17 |
| 61. | 13 May '67 | 20 mm | F-105D | | Capt. Charles W. Couch | 354 TFS/355 TFW | None | Takhli | CHEVROLET 03 | MiG-17 |
| 62. | 13 May '67 | AIM-9 | F-105D | | Major Robert G. Rilling | 333 TFS/355 TFW | None | Takhli | RANDOM 01 | MiG-17 |
| 63. | 13 May '67 | AIM-9 | F-105D | | Major Carl D. Osborne | 333 TFS/355 TFW | None | Takhli | RANDOM 03 | MiG-17 |
| 64. | 13 May '67 | 20 mm | F-105D | | Major Maurice E. Seaver, Jr | 44 TFS/388 TFW | None | Korat | KIMONA 02 | MiG-17 |
| 65. | 13 May '67 | AIM-7 | F-4C | 64-680 | Lt Col Fred A. Haeffner/1Lt Michael R. Bever | 433 TFS/8 TFW | FG | Ubon | HARPOON 03 | MiG-17 |
| 66. | 13 May '67 | AIM-9 | F-4C | 64-739 | Major William L. Kirk/1Lt Stephen A. Wayne | 433 TFS/8 TFW | FG | Ubon | HARPOON 01 | MiG-17 |
| 67. | 14 May '67 | 20 mm | F-4C | 64-660 | Major James A. Hargrove, Jr/1Lt Stephen H. Demuth | 480 TFS/366 TFW | C | Da Nang | SPEEDO 01 | MiG-17 |
| 68. | 14 May '67 | 20 mm | F-4C | 63-7704 | Capt. James T. Craig, Jr/1Lt James T. Talley | 480 TFS/366 TFW | C | Da Nang | SPEEDO 03 | MiG-17 |
| 69. | 14 May '67 | AIM-7 | F-4C | 63-7699 | Major Samuel O. Bakkel/Capt. Robert W. Lambery | 480 TFS/366 TFW | CE | Da Nang | ELGIN 01 | MiG-17 |
| 70. | 19 May '67 | AIM-9D | F-8E | 150348 | CDR Paul H. Speer | VF-211/CVW-21 | NP-101 | CVA-31 | NICKEL | MiG-17 |
| 71. | 19 May '67 | AIM-9D | F-8E | 150661 | LTJG Joseph M. Shea | VF-211/CVW-21 | NP | CVA-31 | NICKEL | MiG-17 |
| 72. | 19 May '67 | AIM-9D | F-8C | 146981 | LCDR Bobby C. Lee | VF-24/CVW-21 | NP | CVA-31 | PAGE BOY | MiG-17 |
| 73. | 19 May '67 | AIM-9D | F-8C | 147029 | LT Phillip R. Wood | VF-24/CVW-21 | NP-405 | CVA-31 | PAGE BOY | MiG-17 |
| 74. | 20 May '67 | AIM-9 | F-4C | 63-7623 | Major John R. Pardo/1Lt Stephen H. Wayne | 433 TFS/8 TFW | FG | Ubon | TAMPA 03 | MiG-17 |
| 75. | 20 May '67 | AIM-9 | F-4C | 64-673 | Major Philip R. Combies/1Lt Daniel L. Lafferty | 433 TFS/8 TFW | FG | Ubon | BALLOT 01 | MiG-17 |
| 76. | 20 May '67 | AIM-9 | F-4C | 64-748 | Major Robert D. Janca/1Lt William E. Roberts, jr | 389 TFS/366 TFW | A | Da Nang | ELGIN 01 | MiG-21 |
| 77. | 20 May '67 | AIM-7 | F-4C | 64-777 | Lt Col Robert F. Titus/1Lt Milan Zimer | 389 TFS/366 TFW | A | Da Nang | ELGIN 03 | MiG-21 |
| 78. | 20 May '67 | AIM-7 | F-4C | 64-829 | Colonel Robin Olds/1Lt Stephen B. Croker | 433 TFS/8 TFW | FG | Ubon | TAMPA 01 | MiG-17 |
| 79. | 20 May '67 | AIM-9 | F-4C | 64-829 | Colonel Robin Olds/1Lt Stephen B. Croker | 433 TFS/8 TFW | FG | Ubon | TAMPA 01 | MiG-17 |
| 80. | 22 May '67 | AIM-9 | F-4C | 64-776 | Lt Col Robert F. Titus/1Lt Milan Zimer | 389 TFS/366 TFW | AK | Da Nang | WANDER 01 | MiG-21 |
| 81. | 22 May '67 | 20 mm | F-4C | 64-776 | Lt Col Robert F. Titus/1Lt Milan Zimer | 389 TFS/366 TFW | AK | Da Nang | WANDER 01 | MiG-21 |
| 82. | 3 Jun '67 | 20 mm | F-105D | | Major Ralph L. Kuster, Jr | 13 TFS/388 TFW | None | Korat | HAMBONE 02 | MiG-17 |
| 83. | 3 Jun '67 | AIM-9/20 mm | F-105D | 61-69 | Capt. Larry D. Wiggins | 469 TFS/388 TFW | None | Korat | HAMBONE 03 | MiG-17 |
| 84. | 5 Jun '67 | AIM-7 | F-4D | 66-249 | Major Everett T. Raspberry, Jr/Capt. Francis M. Gullick | 555 TFS/8 TFW | FY | Ubon | DRILL 01 | MiG-17 |
| 85. | 5 Jun '67 | AIM-9 | F-4C | 63-7647 | Major Richard M. Pascoe/Capt. Norman E. Wells | 555 TFS/8 TFW | FP | Ubon | CHICAGO 02 | MiG-17 |
| 86. | 5 Jun '67 | 20 mm | F-4C | 64-660 | Major Durwood K. Priester/Capt. John E. Pankhurst | 480 TFS/366 TFW | C | Da Nang | OAKLAND 01 | MiG-17 |
| 87. | 21 Jul '67 | AIM-9D | F-8C | 147018 | LCDR Marion H. Isaacks | VF-24/CVW-21 | NP-442 | CVA-31 | PAGE BOY | MiG-17 |
| 88. | 21 Jul '67 | AIM-9/20 mm | F-8C | 146992 | LCDR Robert L. Kirkwood | VF-24/CVW-21 | NP | CVA-31 | PAGE BOY | MiG-17 |
| 89. | 21 Jul '67 | 20 mm/Zuni | F-8E | 150859 | LCDR Ray G. Hubbard | VF-211/CVW-21 | NP | CVA-31 | NICKEL | MiG-17 |
| 90. | 10 Aug '67 | AIM-9 | F-4B | 152247 | LT Guy H. Freeborn/LTJG Robert J. Elliot | VF-142/CVW-14 | NK-202 | CVA-64 | DAKOTA | MiG-21 |
| 91. | 10 Aug '67 | AIM-9 | F-4B | 150431 | LCDR Robert C. Davis/LCDR Gayle O. Elie | VF-142/CVW-14 | NK | CVA-64 | DAKOTA | MiG-21 |
| 92. | 23 Aug '67 | 20 mm | F-105D | 61-132 | 1Lt David B. Waldrop, III | 34 TFS/388 TFW | JJ | Korat | CROSSBOW 03 | MiG-17 |
| 93. | 18 Oct '67 | 20 mm | F-105D | | Major Donald M. Russell | 333 TFS/355 TFW | RK | Takhli | WILDCAT 04 | MiG-17 |
| 94. | 24 Oct '67 | 20 mm | F-4D | | Major William L. Kirk/1Lt Theodore R. Bongartz | 433 TFS/8 TFW | FG | Ubon | BUICK 01 | MiG-21 |
| 95. | 26 Oct '67 | AIM-7 | F-4B | 149411 | LTJG Robert P. Hickey, Jr/LTJG Jeremy G. Morris | VF-143/CVW-14 | NK | CVA-64 | TAPROOM | MiG-21 |
| 96. | 26 Oct '67 | AIM-7 | F-4D | | Capt. William S. Gordon, III/1Lt James H. Monsees | 555 TFS/8 TFW | FY | Ubon | FORD 03 | MiG-17 |
| 97. | 26 Oct '67 | AIM-4 | F-4D | | Capt. Larry D. Cobb/Capt. Alan A. Lavoy | 555 TFS/8 TFW | FY | Ubon | FORD 04 | MiG-17 |
| 98. | 26 Oct '67 | AIM-7 | F-4D | 66-8793 | Capt. John D. Logeman, Jr/1Lt Frederick E. McCoy, II | 555 TFS/8 TFW | FY | Ubon | FORD 01 | MiG-17 |
| 99. | 27 Oct '67 | 20 mm | F-105D | 62-4284 | Capt. Gene I. Basel | 354 TFS/355 TFW | RM | Takhli | BISON 01 | MiG-17 |
| 100. | 30 Oct '67 | AIM-7E | F-4B | 150629 | LCDR Eugene P. Lund/LTJG James R. Borst | VF-142/CVW-14 | NK-203 | CVA-64 | DAKOTA | MiG-17 |
| 101. | 6 Nov '67 | 20 mm | F-4D | 66-7554 | Capt. Darrell D. Simmonds/1Lt George H. McKinney, Jr | 435 TFS/8 TFW | FP | Ubon | SAPPHIRE 01 | MiG-17 |
| 102. | 6 Nov '67 | 20 mm | F-4D | 66-7554 | Capt. Darrell D. Simmonds/1Lt George H. McKinney, Jr | 435 TFS/8 TFW | FP | Ubon | SAPPHIRE 01 | MiG-17 |

| | Date | Weapon | Aircraft | Serial | Crew | Unit | Tailcode | Base | Callsign | Opponent |
|---|---|---|---|---|---|---|---|---|---|---|
| 103. | 14 Dec '67 | AIM-9D | F-8E | 150879 | LT Richard E. Wyman | VF-162/CVW-16 | AH-204 | CVA-34 | SUPERHEAT | MiG-17 |
| 104 | 17 Dec '67 | AIM-4 | F-4D | 66-7709 | Capt. Doyle D. Baker USMC/1Lt John D. Ryan, Jr | 13 TFS/432 TRW | OC | Ubon | GAMBIT 03 | MiG-17 |
| 105. | 19 Dec '67 | 20 mm | F-105F | 63-8301 | Capt. Philip M. Drew/Major William H. Wheeler | 357 TFS/355 TFW | RU | Takhli | OTTER 03 | MiG-17 |
| 106. | 19 Dec '67 | 20 mm | F-105F | 63-8320 | Major William M. Dalton/Major James L. Graham | 333 TFS/355 TFW | RK | Takhli | OTTER 02 | MiG-17 |
| | 19 Dec '67 | 20 mm | F-4D | 66-7601 | Major Joseph D. Moore/1Lt George H. McKinney, Jr | 435 TFS/8 TFW | FO | Ubon | NASH 01 | |
| 107. | 3 Jan '68 | AIM-4 | F-4D | 66-7594 | Lt Col Clayton K. Squier/1Lt Michael D. Muldoon | 435 TFS/8 TFW | FO | Ubon | OLDS 01 | MiG-17 |
| 108. | 3 Jan '68 | 20 mm | F-4D | 66-7748 | Major Bernard J. Bogoslofski/Capt. Richard L. Huskey | 433 TFS/8 TFW | FG | Ubon | TAMPA 01 | MiG-17 |
| 109. | 18 Jan '68 | AIM-4 | F-4D | | Major Kenneth A. Simonet/1Lt Wayne O. Smith | 435 TFS/8 TFW | FO | Ubon | OTTER 01 | MiG-17 |
| 110. | 5 Feb '68 | AIM-4 | F-4D | 66-8714 | Capt. Robert G. Hill/1Lt Bruce V. Huneke | 13 TFS/432 TRW | OC | Udorn | GAMBIT 03 | MiG-21 |
| 111. | 6 Feb '68 | AIM-7 | F-4D | 66-8688 | Capt. Robert H. Boles/1Lt Robert B. Battista | 433 TFS/8 TFW | FG | Ubon | BUICK 04 | MiG-21 |
| 112. | 12 Feb '68 | AIM-7 | F-4D | | Lt Col Alfred E. Lang, Jr/1Lt Randy P. Moss | 435 TFS/8 TFW | FO | Ubon | BUICK 01 | MiG-21 |
| 113. | 14 Feb '68 | AIM-7 | F-4D | | Colonel David O. Williams, Jr/1Lt James P. Feighny, Jr | 435 TFS/8 TFW | FO | Ubon | KILLER 01 | MiG-17 |
| 114. | 14 Feb '68 | 20 mm | F-4D | | Major Rex D. Howerton/1Lt Ted L. Voight, II | 555 TFS/8 TFW | FY | Ubon | NASH 03 | MiG-17 |
| 115. | 26 Jun '68 | AIM-9 | F-8H | 148710 | CDR Lowell R (Moose) Meyers | VF-51/CVW-15 | NL-116 | CVA-31 | SCREAMING EAGLE | MiG-21 |
| 116. | 9 Jul '68 | AIM-9/20 mm | F-8E | 150926 | LCDR John B. Nichols, III | VF-191/CVW-19 | NM-107 | CVA-31 | FEED BAG | MiG-17 |
| 117. | 10 Jul '68 | AIM-9 | F-4J | 155553 | LT Roy Cash, Jr/LT Joseph E. Kain, Jr | VF-33/CVW-6 | AG-212 | CVA-66 | ROOTBEER | MiG-21 |
| 118. | 29 Jul '68 | AIM-9 | F-8E | 150349 | CDR Guy Cane | VF-53/CVW-5 | NF-203 | CVA-31 | FIREFIGHTER | MiG-17 |
| 119. | 1 Aug '68 | AIM-9 | F-8H | 147916 | LT Norman K. McCoy | VF-51/CVW-5 | NF-102 | CVA-31 | SCREAMING EAGLE | MiG-21 |
| 120. | 28 Mar '70 | AIM-9 | F-4J | 155875 | LT Jerome E. Beaulier/LT Steven J. Barkley | VF-142/CVW-14 | NK-201 | CVA-64 | DAKOTA | MiG-21 |
| 121. | 19 Jan '72 | AIM-9 | F-4J | 157267 | LT Randall H. Cunningham/LT William P. Driscoll | VF-96/CVW-9 | NG-112 | CVA-64 | SHOWTIME | MiG-21 |
| 122. | 21 Feb '72 | AIM-7 | F-4D | 65-784 | Major Robert A. Lodge/1Lt Roger C. Locher | 555 TFS/432 TRW | OY | Udorn | FALCON 62 | MiG-21 |
| 123. | 1 Mar '72 | AIM-9 | F-4D | 66-7463 | Lt Col Joseph W. Kittinger, Jr/1Lt Leigh A. Hodgdon | 555 TFS/432 TRW | OY | Udorn | FALCON 54 | MiG-21 |
| 124. | 6 Mar '72 | AIM-9 | F-4B | 153019 | LT Garry L. Weigand/LTJG William C. Freckleton | VF-111/CVW-15 | NL-201 | CVA-43 | OLD NICK | MiG-17 |
| 125. | 30 Mar '72 | AIM-7 | F-4D | 66-230 | Capt. Frederick S. Olmsted, Jr/Capt. Gerald R. Volloy | 13 TFS/432 TRW | OY | Udorn | PAPA 01 | MiG-21 |
| 126. | 16 Apr '72 | AIM-7 | F-4D | 66-280 | Capt. James C. Null/Capt. Michael D. Vahue | 523 TFS/432 TRW | OY | Udorn | PAPA 03 | MiG-21 |
| 127. | 16 Apr '72 | AIM-7 | F-4D | 66-7550 | Major Edward D. Cherry/Capt. Jeffrey S. Feinstein | 13 TFS/432 TRW | PN | Udorn | BASCO 03 | MiG-21 |
| 128. | 16 Apr '72 | AIM-7 | F-4D | 66-7463 | Capt. Frederick S. Olmsted, Jr/Capt. Stuart W. Mass | 13 TFS/432 TRW | OY | Udorn | BASCO 01 | MiG-21 |
| 129. | 6 May '72 | AIM-9 | F-4B | 150456 | LCDR Jerry B. Houston/LT Kevin T. Moore | VF-51/CVW-15 | NL-100 | CVA-43 | SCREAMING EAGLE | MiG-17 |
| 130. | 6 May '72 | AIM-9 | F-4J | 157249 | LT Robert G. Hughes/LTJG Adolph J. (Joe) Cruz | VF-114/CVW-11 | NH-206 | CVA-63 | LINFIELD | MiG-21 |
| 131. | 6 May '72 | AIM-9 | F-4J | 157245 | LCDR Kenneth W. Pettigrew/LTJG Michael J. McCabe | VF-114/CVW-11 | NH-201 | CVA-63 | LINFIELD | MiG-21 |
| 132. | 8 May '72 | AIM-9 | F-4J | 157267 | LT Randall H. Cunningham/LT William P. Driscoll | VF-96/CVW-9 | NG-112 | CVA-64 | SHOWTIME | MiG-17 |
| 133. | 8 May '72 | AIM-7 | F-4D | 65-784 | Major Robert A. Lodge/Capt. Roger C. Locher | 555 TFS/432 TRW | OY | Udorn | OYSTER 01 | MiG-21 |
| 134. | 8 May '72 | AIM-7 | F-4D | 66-7463 | Major Barton P. Crews/Capt. Keith W. Jones, Jr | 13 TFS/432 TRW | OY | Udorn | GALORE 03 | MiG-17 |
| 135. | 10 May '72 | AIM-9 | F-4J | 157269 | LT Curt Dose/LT James McDevitt | VF-92/CVW-9 | NG-211 | CVA-64 | SILVER KITE | MiG-21 |
| 136. | 10 May '72 | AIM-9 | F-4J | 155769 | LT Michael J (Matt) Connelly/LT Thomas J. J. Blonski | VF-96/CVW-9 | NG-106 | CVA-64 | SHOWTIME | MiG-17 |
| 137. | 10 May '72 | AIM-9 | F-4J | 155769 | LT Michael J (Matt) Connelly/LT Thomas J. J. Blonski | VF-96/CVW-9 | NG-106 | CVA-64 | SHOWTIME | MiG-17 |
| 138. | 10 May '72 | AIM-9 | F-4B | 151398 | LT Kenneth L. Cannon/LT Roy A. (Bud) Morris, Jr | VF-51/CVW-15 | NL-111 | CVA-43 | SCREAMING EAGLE | MiG-17 |
| 139. | 10 May '72 | AIM-9 | F-4J | 155749 | LT Steven C. Shoemaker/LTJG Keith V. Crenshaw | VF-96/CVW-9 | NG-111 | CVA-64 | SHOWTIME | MiG-17 |
| 140. | 10 May '72 | AIM-9 | F-4J | 155800 | LT Randall H. Cunningham/LT William P. Driscoll | VF-96/CVW-9 | NG-100 | CVA-64 | SHOWTIME | MiG-17 |
| 141. | 10 May '72 | AIM-9 | F-4J | 155800 | LT Randall H. Cunningham/LT William P. Driscoll | VF-96/CVW-9 | NG-100 | CVA-64 | SHOWTIME | MiG-17 |
| 142. | 10 May '72 | AIM-9 | F-4J | 155800 | LT Randall H. Cunningham/LT William P. Driscoll | VF-96/CVW-9 | NG-100 | CVA-64 | SHOWTIME | MiG-17 |
| 143. | 10 May '72 | AIM-7 | F-4D | 65-784 | Major Robert A. Lodge/Capt. Roger C. Locher | 555 TFS/432 TRW | OY | Udorn | OYSTER 01 | MiG-21 |
| 144. | 10 May '72 | AIM-7 | F-4D | 66-7463 | Capt. Richard S. Ritchie/Capt. Charles B. DeBellevue | 555 TFS/432 TRW | OY | Udorn | OYSTER 03 | MiG-21 |
| 145. | 10 May '72 | AIM-7 | F-4D | 66-8734 | 1Lt John D. Markle/Capt. Stephen D. Eaves | 555 TFS/432 TRW | OY | Udorn | OYSTER 02 | MiG-21 |
| 146. | 11 May '72 | | F-4D | | | | | | | MiG-21 |
| 147. | 12 May '72 | AIM-7 | F-4D | 66-8756 | Lt Col Wayne T. Frye/Lt Col James P. Cooney | 555 TFS/432 TRW | OY | Udorn | HARLOW 02 | MiG-17 |
| 148. | 18 May '72 | AIM-9 | F-4 | 153068 | LT Henry A. Bartholomay/LT Oran R. Brown | VF-161/CVW-5 | NF-110 | CVA-41 | ROCK RIVER | MiG-17 |
| 149. | 18 May '72 | AIM-9G | F-4B | 153915 | LT Patrick E (Pat) Arwood/LT James M. Bell | VF-161/CVW-5 | NF-105 | CVA-41 | ROCK RIVER | MiG-17 |
| 150. | 23 May '72 | AIM-7 | F-4E | | Lt Col Lyle E. Beckers/Capt. John F. Huwe | 35 TFS/366 TFW | | Da Nang | BALTER 01 | MiG-17 |
| 151. | 23 May '72 | 20 mm | F-4E | | Capt. James M. Beatty, Jr/1Lt James M. Sumner | 35 TFS/366 TFW | | Da Nang | BALTER 03 | MiG-21 |
| 152. | 23 May '72 | AIM-9 | F-4B | 153020 | LCDR Ronald E. McKeown/LT John C. Ensch | VF-161/CVW-5 | NF-100 | CVA-41 | ROCK RIVER | MiG-17 |
| 153. | 23 May '72 | AIM-9 | F-4B | 153020 | LCDR Ronald E. McKeown/LT John C. Ensch | VF-161/CVW-5 | NF-100 | CVA-41 | ROCK RIVER | MiG-17 |
| 154. | 31 May '72 | AIM-7 | F-4D | 65-801 | Capt. Richard S. Ritchie/Capt. Lawrence H. Pettit | 555 TFS/432 TRW | OC | Udorn | ICEBAG 01 | MiG-21 |
| 155. | 31 May '72 | AIM-9 | F-4E | 68-338 | Capt. Bruce G. Leonard, Jr/Capt. Jeffrey S. Feinstein | 13 TFS/432 TRW | | Udorn | GOPHER 03 | MiG-21 |
| 156. | 2 Jun '72 | 20 mm | F-4E | 67-210 | Major Philip W. Handley/1Lt John J. Smallwood | 58 TFS/432 TRW | ZF | | BRENDA 01 | MiG-17 |
| 157. | 11 Jun '72 | AIM-9 | F-4B | 149473 | CDR Foster S. Teague/LT Ralph M. Howell | VF-51/CVW-15 | NL-114 | CVA-43 | SCREAMING EAGLE | MiG-17 |
| 158. | 11 Jun '72 | AIM-9 | F-4B | 149457 | LT Winston W. Copeland/LT Donald R. Bouchoux | VF-51/CVW-15 | NL-113 | CVA-43 | SCREAMING EAGLE | MiG-17 |
| 159. | 21 Jun '72 | AIM-9 | F-4J | 157293 | CDR Samuel C. Flynn, Jr/LT William H. John | VF-31/CVW-3 | AC-101 | CVA-60 | BANDWAGON | MiG-21 |
| 160. | 21 Jun '72 | AIM-9 | F-4E | 67-296 | Lt Col Von R. Christianson/Major Kaye M. Harden | 469 TFS/388 TFW | JV | Korat | ICEMAN 03 | MiG-21 |
| 161. | 8 Jul '72 | AIM-7 | F-4E | 67-270 | Capt. Richard F. Hardy/Capt. Paul T. Lewinski | 4 TFS/366 TFW | LA | Da Nang | BRENDA 03 | MiG-21 |
| 162. | 8 Jul '72 | AIM-7 | F-4E | 67-362 | Capt. Richard S. Ritchie/Capt. Charles B. DeBellevue | 555 TFS/432 TRW | ED | Udorn | PAULA 01 | MiG-21 |
| 163. | 8 Jul '72 | AIM-7 | F-4E | 67-362 | Capt. Richard S. Ritchie/Capt. Charles B. DeBellevue | 555 TFS/432 TRW | ED | Udorn | PAULA 01 | MiG-21 |
| 164. | 18 Jul '72 | AIM-9 | F-4D | 66-271 | Lt Col Carl G. Baily/Capt. Jeffrey S. Feinstein | 13 TFS/432 TRW | OC | Udorn | SNUG 01 | MiG-21 |
| 165. | 29 Jul '72 | AIM-7 | F-4D | 66-271 | Lt Col Carl G. Baily/Capt. Jeffrey S. Feinstein | 13 TFS/432 TRW | OC | Udorn | CADILLAC 01 | MiG-21 |
| 166. | 29 Jul '72 | AIM-7 | F-4E | 67-270 | Lt Col Gene E. Taft/Capt. Stanley M. Imaye | 4 TFS/366 TFW | LA | | PISTOL 01 | MiG-21 |
| 167. | 10 Aug '72 | AIM-7E | F-4J | 157299 | LCDR Robert E. Tucker, Jr/LTJG Stanley B. Edens | VF-103/CVW-3 | AC-296 | CVA-60 | CLUBLEAF | MiG-21 |
| 168. | 12 Aug '72 | AIM-7 | F-4E | 67-239 | Capt. Lawrence G. Richard USMC/ LCDR Michael J. Ettel USN | 58 TFS/432 TRW | ZF | Udorn | DODGE 01 | MiG-21 |
| 169. | 15 Aug '72 | AIM-7 | F-4E | 69-7235 | Capt. Fred W. Sheffler/Capt. Mark A. Massen | 336 TFS/8 TFS | SC | Ubon | DATE 04 | MiG-21 |
| 170. | 19 Aug '72 | AIM-7 | F-4E | 69-291 | Capt. Sammy C. White/Capt. Frank J. Bettine | 4 TFS/366 TFW | LA | Da Nang | PISTOL 03 | MiG-21 |
| 171. | 28 Aug '72 | AIM-7 | F-4D | 66-7463 | Capt. Richard S. Ritchie/Capt. Charles B. DeBellevue | 555 TFS/432 TRW | OY | Udorn | BUICK 01 | MiG-21 |
| 172. | 2 Sep '72 | AIM-7 | F-4E | 67-392 | Major John I. Lucas/1Lt Douglas G. Malloy | 34 TFS/388 TFW | JV | Korat | EAGLE 03 | MiG-17 |
| 173. | 9 Sep '72 | AIM-9 | F-4D | 66-267 | Capt. John A. Madden, Jr/Capt. Charles B. DeBellevue | 555 TFS/432 TRW | OY | Udorn | OLDS 01 | MiG-17 |
| 174. | 9 Sep '72 | AIM-9 | F-4D | 66-267 | Capt. John A. Madden, Jr/Capt. Charles B. DeBellevue | 555 TFS/432 TRW | OY | Udorn | OLDS 01 | MiG-17 |
| 175. | 9 Sep '72 | 20 mm | F-4E | 67-327 | Capt. Calvin B. Tibbett/1Lt William S. Hargrove | 555 TFS/432 TRW | ZF | Udorn | OLDS 03 | MiG-21 |
| 176. | 11 Sep '72 | AIM-9G | F-4J | 155526 | Maj. Lee T. (Bear) Lasseter/Capt. John D. Cummings | VMFA-333/CVW-8 | AJ-201 | CVA-66 | SHAMROCK | MiG-21 |
| 177. | 12 Sep '72 | AIM-9 | F-4 | | Capt. Michael J. Mahaffey/1Lt George I. Shields | 469 TFS/388 TFW | | Korat | ROBIN 02 | MiG-21 |
| 178. | 12 Sep '72 | AIM-9/20 mm | F-4E | 67-275 | Lt Col Lyle L. Beickers/1Lt Thomas M. Griffin | 35 TFS/388 TFW | JJ | Korat | FINCH 01 | MiG-21 |
| 179. | 12 Sep '72 | 20 mm | F-4E | 68-468 | Major Gary L. Retterbush/1Lt Daniel L. Autrey | 35 TFS/388 TFW | | Korat | FINCH 03 | MiG-21 |
| 180. | 16 Sep '72 | AIM-9 | F-4E | 67-338 | Capt. Calvin B. Tibbett/1Lt William S. Hargrove | 555 TFS/432 TRW | ED | Udorn | CHEVY 03 | MiG-21 |
| 181. | 5 Oct '72 | AIM-7 | F-4E | 68-493 | Capt. Richard E. Coe/1Lt Omri K. Webb | 34 TFS/388 TFW | JJ | Udorn | ROBIN 01 | MiG-21 |
| 182. | 6 Oct '72 | Maneuver | F-4E | 66-313 | Major Gordon L. Clouser/1Lt Cecil H. Brunson | 34 TFS/388 TFW | JJ | Korat | EAGLE 03 | MiG-17 |
| | 6 Oct '72 | Maneuver | F-4E | 67-392 | Capt. Charles D. Barton/1Lt George D. Watson | 34 TFS/388 TFW | JV | Korat | EAGLE 04 | |
| 183. | 12 Oct '72 | 20 mm | F-4E | | Maj. Gary L. Retterbush/Capt. Robert H. Jasperson | 35 TFS/388 TFW | | Korat | LARK 01 | MiG-21 |
| 184. | 12 Oct '72 | Maneuver | F-4D | 66-268 | Capt. John A. Madden, Jr/Capt. Lawrence H. Pettit | 555 TFS/432 TRW | OY | Udorn | VEGA 03 | MiG-21 |
| 185. | 13 Oct '72 | AIM-7 | F-4D | 66-7501 | Lt Col Curtis D Westphal/Capt. Jeffrey S. Feinstein | 13 TFS/432 TRW | OC | Udorn | OLDS 01 | MiG-21 |
| 186. | 15 Oct '72 | AIM-9 | F-4D | 66-7463 | Capt. Ivy J. McCoy, Jr/Major Frederick W. Brown | 523 TFS/432 TRW | OY | Udorn | CHEVY 01 | MiG-21 |
| 187. | 15 Oct '72 | 20 mm | F-4E | 67-232 | Capt. Gary M. Rubus/Capt. James L Hendrickson | 307 TFS/432 TRW | ZF | Udorn | BUICK 03 | MiG-21 |
| 188. | 15 Oct '72 | AIM-9 | F-4E | 57-301 | Major Robert L. Holtz/1Lt William C. Diehl | 34 TFS/388 TFW | JJ | Korat | PARROT 03 | MiG-21 |
| 189. | 18 Dec '72 | .50-cal | B-52D | 56-676 | SSGT Samuel O. Turner | 307 SW | None | U-Tapao | BROWN 03 | MiG-21 |
| 190. | 21 Dec '72 | Maneuver | F-4D | 66-240 | Capt. Gary L. Sholders/1Lt Eldon D. Binkley | 555 TFS/432 TRW | OY | Udorn | BUCKET 01 | MiG-21 |
| 191. | 22 Dec '72 | AIM-7 | F-4D | 66-269 | Lt Col James E. Brunson/Major Ralph S. Pickett | 555 TFS/432 TRW | OY | Udorn | BUICK 01 | MiG-21 |
| 192. | 24 Dec '72 | .50-cal | B-52D | 55-83 | AIC Albert E. Moore | 307 SW | None | U-Tapao | RUBY III | MiG-21 |
| 193. | 28 Dec '72 | AIM-7 | F-4D | 66-7468 | Major Harry L. McKee, Jr/Capt. John E. Dubler | 555 TFS/432 TRW | OY | Udorn | LIST 01 | MiG-21 |
| 194. | 28 Dec '72 | AIM-9 | F-4J | 155846 | LTJG Scott H. Davis/LTJG Geoffrey H. Ulrich | VF-142/CVW-14 | NK-214 | CVN-65 | DAKOTA | MiG-21 |
| 195. | 8 Jan '73 | AIM-7 | F-4D | 65-796 | Capt. Paul D. Howman/1Lt Lawrence W. Kullman | 4 TFS/432 TRW | | Udorn | CRAFTY 01 | MiG-21 |
| 196. | 12 Jan '73 | AIM-9 | F-4B | 153045 | LT Victor T. Kovaleski/LTJG James A. Wise | VF-161/CVW-5 | NF-102 | CVA-41 | ROCK RIVER | MiG-17 |

*Built in France as the AAC.1 Toucan, the long-serving Junkers Ju 52 was a mainstay of the French transport effort in Indochina.*

## AAC.1 TOUCAN
Following the end of World War II, manufacture of the German-designed Junkers Ju 52/3M g7e continued in France and, as the AAC.1 Toucan, the type was selected to re-equip some of the post-war French transport units. The aircraft's rugged construction and minimal field requirements led to its large-scale employment by units of the Armée de l'Air operating in Indochina. The aircraft was used as a transport and as a makeshift bomber until supplanted by more modern types.

**Specification**
**Type:** 18-seat military transport
**Powerplant:** three 830-hp (619-kW) BMW132A radial piston engines
**Performance:** maximum speed 165 mph (266 km/h) at sea level; service ceiling 18,000 ft (5486 m); combat range 800 miles (1285 km)
**Weights:** empty 14,325 lb (6498 kg); loaded 24,200 lb (10977 kg)
**Dimensions:** span 95 ft 10 in (29.21 m); length 62 ft (18.90 m); height 14 ft 10 in (4.52 m); wing area 1,184 sq ft (110 m²)
**Armament:** could carry up to 2,205 lb (1000 kg) of bombs when used as a bomber.

## AERO COMMANDER 520
This American-built twin-engined light transport saw limited service with the VNAF and the Royal Lao Air Force during the 1950s and early-1960s.

**Specification**
**Type:** five/seven-seat light transport
**Powerplant:** two 260-hp (194-kW) Lycoming GO 435 C2 six-cylinder horizontally opposed air-cooled engines
**Performance:** maximum speed 211 mph (340 km/h) at sea level; climb rate 1,800 ft/min (550 m/min); service ceiling 24,400 ft (7440 m); range 850 miles (1368 km)
**Weights:** empty 3,970 lb (1801 kg); loaded 6,000 lb (2722 kg)
**Dimensions:** span 44 ft (13.41 m); length 36 ft (10.97 m); height 14 ft (4.27 m); wing area 242 sq ft (22.5 m²)
**Armament:** none.

## AICHI E13A1A JAKE
Eight of these Japanese single-engined floatplanes, which had been left in Indochina by the defeated Imperial Japanese Navy, were used by Escadrille 8S of the Aéronautique Navale between the end of 1945 and the summer of 1947.

**Specification**
**Type:** twin-float reconnaissance seaplane
**Powerplant:** one 1,060-hp (790-kW) Mitsubishi Kinsei 43 radial piston engine
**Performance:** maximum speed 234 mph (377 km/h) at 7,155 ft (2180 m); climb rate 9,845 ft (3000 m) in 6 min 5 sec, service ceiling 28,640 ft (8730 m); combat range 1,300 miles (2090 km)
**Weights:** empty 5,825 lb (2642 kg); loaded 8,025 lb (3640 kg)
**Dimensions:** span 47 ft 7 in (14.50 m); length 37 ft 1 in (11.30 m); height 24 ft 3.5 in (7.40 m); wing area 387.5 sq ft (36 m²)
**Armament:** one 0 303-in (7.7-mm) cockpit machine-gun, plus 550-lb (250-kg) bombload.

## ANTONOV AN-2 COLT
Rugged and possessing good STOL characteristics, this large Soviet single-engined biplane proved well suited to operations in the less-developed areas of North Vietnam and neighboring countries. As such, it was used by the NVNAF for the resupply of isolated outposts and Pathet Lao forces. One of these aircraft gained the doubtful distinction of becoming the first confirmed 'kill' by helicopters. The Royal Khmer Air Force also received a handful of An-2s.

*Left over from the Japanese occupation during World War II, the Aichi E13 was briefly pressed into service by the French.*

**Specification**
**Type:** 14-troop transport biplane
**Powerplant:** one 1,000-hp (746-kW) Shvetsov ASh-62M radial piston engine
**Performance:** maximum speed 157 mph (253 km/h) at 5,740 ft (1750 m); climb rate 550 ft/min (168 m/min); service ceiling 14,270 ft (4350 m); range 560 miles (900 km)
**Weights:** loaded 12,125 lb (5500 kg)
**Dimensions:** span 59 ft 7.7 in (18.18 m); length 41 ft 9.6 in (12.74 m); height 13 ft 1.5 in (4.00 m); wing area total 770.7 sq ft (71.60 m²)
**Armament:** none.

## BEECH C-45G EXPEDITER
Among the aircraft rushed to Indochina by the United States to help the French at the time of the Dien Bien Phu battle were 10 C-45Gs, based on Beech's classic light twin transport. Taken over by the VNAF in 1955, these aircraft were used briefly for communications and staff transport. The Marines also flew a few UC-45Js in Vietnam.

**Specification**
**Type:** 7-passenger light transport
**Powerplant:** two 450-hp (336-kW) Pratt & Whitney R985-AN-1 radial piston engines
**Performance:** maximum speed 215 mph (346 km/h) at 5,000 ft (1525 m); climb rate 10,000 ft (3050 m) in 8.6 min; service ceiling 20,000 ft (6095 m); range 700 miles (1127 km)
**Weights:** empty 5,890 lb (2672 kg); loaded 7,850 lb (3560 kg)
**Dimensions:** span 47 ft 8 in (14.53 m); length 34 ft 3 in (10.44 m); height 9 ft 8 in (2.95 m); wing area 349 sq ft (32.42 m²)
**Armament:** none.

## BEECH U-8 SEMINOLE
Military equivalent of the Beech Twin Bonanza executive aircraft, the U-8 was operated in Southeast Asia by the US Army for staff transport and general liaison work. The larger U-8F was a military version of the Queen Air 65, and was the forerunner of the U-21/C-12 family.

**Specification (U-8F)**
**Type:** 6-seat staff transport
**Powerplant:** two 340-hp (254-kW) Lycoming IGSO-480 A1A6 air-cooled piston engines
**Performance:** maximum speed 240 mph (386 km/h); climb rate 1,300 ft/min (396 m/min); service ceiling 27,000 ft (8230 m); range 1,370 miles (2205 km)
**Weights:** empty 4,996 lb (2266 kg); loaded 7,700 lb (3493 kg)
**Dimensions:** span 45 ft 10.5 in (13.98 m); length 33 ft 4 in (10.16 m); height 14 ft 2 in (4.32 m); wing area 277 sq ft (25.73 m²)
**Armament:** none.

## BEECH U-21
The Beech U-21 was the US Army's standard liaison aircraft for much of the war, supplementing its U-8 staff transports. It also had a combat role, specially fitted versions of this light twin-turboprop aircraft being used for battlefield reconnaissance and electronic/communications surveillance duties.

**Specification (RU-21C)**
**Type:** special reconnaissance transport
**Powerplant:** two 550-shp (410-kW) Pratt & Whitney T74-CP-700 turboprops
**Performance:** maximum speed 249 mph (401 km/h) at 11,000 ft (3350 m); climb rate 2,000 ft/min (610 m/min): service ceiling 25,500 ft (7775 m); range 1,170 miles (1885 km)
**Weights:** empty 5,464 lb (2478 kg); loaded 9,650 lb (4377 kg)
**Dimensions:** span 45 ft 10.5 in (13.98 m); length 35 ft 6 in (10.82 m); height 14 ft 2.5 in (4.33 m); wing area 279.7 sq ft (25.98 m²)
**Armament:** none.

## BEECH QU-22
Derived from the popular Beech Bonanza private aircraft, the QU-22B was an electronic intelligence-gathering drone which could be flown manned or unmanned. It was used by the USAF in high-threat areas of the Ho Chi Minh Trail to relay data collected by 'Igloo White' sensors.

**Specification (QU-22B)**
**Type:** electronic intelligence-gathering drone
**Powerplant:** one 285-hp (213-kW) Continental 10-520-B air-cooled piston engine
**Performance:** maximum speed 204 mph (328 km/h)
**Weight:** loaded 3,600 lb (1633 kg)
**Dimensions:** span 32 ft 10 in (10.01 m); length 26 ft 4 in (8.03 m)
**Armament:** none.

## BELL AH-1 HUEYCOBRA
Principal helicopter gunship of the war, the AH-1 could carry a variety of weapons, including rockets, grenade-launchers and guns. Designed by Bell Helicopters as a

*The Beech U-21 was an unpressurized military version of the turboprop-powered Beech Model 90 King Air executive twin.*

private venture, the HueyCobra proved an outstanding success. During the war AH-1Gs were used in large numbers by US Army units while the Marine Corps operated both single-engined AH-1Gs and twin-engined AH-1Js.

**Specification (AH-1G)**
**Type:** two-seat attack helicopter
**Powerplant:** one 1,400-shp (1044-kW) Lycoming T53-L-13 turboshaft
**Performance:** maximum speed 219 mph (352 km/h) at sea level; climb rate 1,580 ft/min (482 m/min); service ceiling 10,000 ft (3050 m); combat range 257 miles (414 km)
**Weights:** empty 6,096 lb (2765 kg); loaded 9,500 lb (4310 kg)
**Dimensions:** rotor diameter 44 ft (13.41 m), fuselage length 44 ft 5 in (13.54 m), height 13 ft 5.4 in (4.10 m)
**Armament:** four underwing hardpoints for gun or rocket pods; nose turret with 40-mm grenade launcher or 7.62-mm Minigun.

### BELL UH-1 IROQUOIS
Perhaps the most representative and certainly one of the most identifiable aircraft of the Vietnam War, the UH-1 or 'Huey' made its appearance in the theater in 1962 with the US Army's 57th Medical Detachment. Numerically the most important helicopter in Southeast Asia, it was used in short fuselage (UH-1A, UH-1B, UH-1C, UH-1E and UH-1P) and long fuselage (UH-1D, UH-1F, UH-1H and UH-1N) versions. Hueys were used for a great variety of missions, including troop transport, observation, medical evacuation, search and rescue, fire support, riverine patrol, staff transport, psyops and cargo transport. UH-1s were operated by the US Army, the Air Force, the Navy and the Marine Corps, as well as by the air forces of the Republic of Vietnam, Australia and Cambodia.

**Specification (UH-1H)**
**Type:** 12/15-seat utility helicopter
**Powerplant:** one 1,400-shp (1044-kW) Lycoming T53-L-13A turboshaft
**Performance:** maximum speed 127 mph (204 km/h) at sea level; climb rate 1,680 ft/min (512 m/min); service ceiling 19,700 ft (6005 m); combat range 345 miles (555 km)
**Weights:** empty 5,082 lb (2305 kg); loaded 9,500 lb (4309 kg)
**Dimensions:** rotor diameter 48 ft (14.63 m); fuselage length 41 ft 6 in (12.65 m); height 14 ft 6 in (4.42 m)
**Armament:** varied, but typically two door-mounted 0.30-in (7.62-mm) M60 machine-guns.

### BELL OH-13 SIOUX
One of the earliest practical helicopters, the Bell Model 47 pioneered many duties including observation, medical evacuation and liaison. When the US Army began fighting in Vietnam, Model 47s – US Army designation OH-13 – were used for observation duties. This obsolete type, however, was soon replaced by more modern machines, notably the Bell OH-58 and Hughes OH-6.

**Specification (OH-13S)**
**Type:** 3-seat utility and observation helicopter
**Powerplant:** one 260-hp (194-kW) Lycoming TVO-435 A1A air-cooled piston engine
**Performance:** maximum speed 105 mph (169 km/h) at sea level; climb rate 1,190 ft/min (363 m/min); service ceiling 13,200 ft (4025 m); range 325 miles (525 km)
**Weights:** empty 1,936 lb (877 kg): loaded 2,850 lb (1295 kg)
**Dimensions:** rotor diameter 37 ft 1.5 in (11.31 m); fuselage length 32 ft 6 in (9.91 m); height 9 ft 3 in (2.82 m)
**Armament:** none.

### BELL OH-58 KIOWA
Co-winner of the 1960 Army competition for Light Observation Helicopters, this five-seat turboshaft-powered observation helicopter was not originally ordered by the military. But when the OH-6 proved expensive, the Kiowa was taken into service, and made its combat debut in 1970. Based on the best-selling civil JetRanger, good speed and agility have led to a successful career as a military scout.

**Specification (OH-58A)**
**Type:** five-seat utility and observation helicopter
**Powerplant:** one 400-shp (298-kW) Allison T63-A-700 turboshaft
**Performance:** maximum speed 138 mph (222 km/h) at sea level; climb rate 1,780 ft/min (543 m/min); service ceiling 19,000 ft (5790 m); range 355 miles (570 km)
**Weights:** empty 1,583 lb (718 kg); loaded 3,000 lb (1360 kg)
**Dimensions:** rotor diameter 35 ft 4 in (10.77 m); fuselage length 31 ft 2 in (9.50 m); height 9 ft 6.5 in (2.91 m)
**Armament:** one XM-27 kit with a 0.30-in (7.62-mm) Minigun.

### BELL P-63 KINGCOBRA
Three-hundred P-63Cs were received by France to help equip the Armée de l'Air at the end of World War II. The type was obsolete for use in Europe, but its heavy armament and metal construction appeared to suit it for operations in Indochina. In this theater, however, the Kingcobra's reliance on well-prepared airfields limited its usefulness.

*Developed from the Bell UH-1, the potent AH-1 HueyCobra was the first of the modern helicopter gunships to enter service.*

*The UH-1 was the classic helicopter of the war. This Air America UH-1B is landing on a carrier during the final American evacuation of Saigon.*

**Specification (P-63C)**
**Type:** single-seat fighter-bomber
**Powerplant:** one 1,425-hp (1063-kW) Allison V-1710-109 inline liquid-cooled piston engine
**Performance:** maximum speed 410 mph (660 km/h) at 25,000 ft (7620 m); climb rate 28,000 ft (8535 m) in 8.6 min; service ceiling 38,600 ft (11765 m); combat range 320 miles (515 km)
**Weights:** empty 6,800 lb (3084 kg); loaded 9,300 lb (4218 kg)
**Dimensions:** span 38 ft 4 in (11.68 m); length 32 ft 8 in (9.96 m); height 12 ft 7 in (3.84 m); wing area 248 sq ft (23.04 m²)
**Armament:** one 37-mm cannon and four 0.50-in (12.7-mm) machine-guns, plus three 500-lb (226-kg) bombs.

### BOEING RB-47H STRATOJET
One of Strategic Air Command's primary intelligence gatherers during the early years of the Cold War, the Boeing RB-47H was being phased out from the SAC inventory when the United States went to war in Southeast Asia. Until replaced by the RC-135 it was operated by the 55th Strategic Reconnaissance Wing to relay electronic signals gathered over North Vietnam by Ryan 147D and 147E drones.

**Specification**
**Type:** 6-seat electronic reconnaissance aircraft
**Powerplant:** six 7,200-lb (3266-kg) thrust General Electric J47-GE-25 turbojets
**Performance:** maximum speed 594 mph (956 km/h) at 15,000 ft (4570 m); climb rate 3,700 ft/min (1128 m/min); service ceiling 31,500 ft (9600 m); combat range 3,040 miles (4890 km)
**Weights:** empty 89,230 lb (40474 kg); loaded 191,135 lb (86697 kg)
**Dimensions:** span 116 ft 4 in (35.46 m); length 108 ft 8.4 in (33.13 m); height 28 ft (8.53 m); wing area 1,428 sq ft (132.67 m²)
**Armament:** none.

### BOEING KB-50J
When American aircraft made their first long-range tactical strikes into Laos in June 1964, the only tankers available to support the F-100s and RF-101s were the jet-augmented KB-50Js of the 421st ARefS. These obsolete aircraft did sterling work for another seven months before the inactivation of PACAF's only Air Refueling Squadron and the assignment of SAC tankers to Southeast Asia.

**Specification**
**Type:** inflight-refueling tanker
**Powerplant:** four 3,500-hp (2610-kW) Pratt & Whitney R-4360-35 radial piston engines and two 5,620-lb (2549-kg) thrust General Electric J47 GE-23 turbojets
**Performance:** maximum speed 444 mph (714 km/h) at 17,000 ft (5180 m); climb rate 3,260 ft/min (994 m/min); service ceiling 39,700 ft (12100 m); combat range 2,300 miles (3700 km)
**Weights:** empty 93,200 lb (42275 kg); loaded 179,500 lb (81420 kg)
**Dimensions:** span 141 ft 3 in (43.05 m); length 105 ft 1 in (32.03 m); height 33 ft 7 in (10.24 m); wing area 1,720 sq ft (159.79 m²)
**Armament:** none.

### BOEING B-52 STRATOFORTRESS
The Boeing B-52 provided the backbone of the American bombing campaign in

*Boeing's RB-47 was Strategic Air Command's primary electronic intelligence-gathering platform during the early years in Vietnam.*

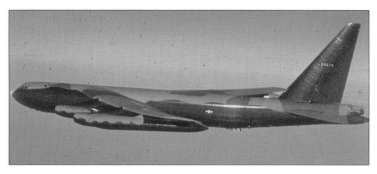

*Flying from Guam and Thailand, 'Big Belly' Boeing B-52Ds bore the brunt of America's bombing campaigns in Southeast Asia.*

Southeast Asia. They were used for most of the war in saturation raids against suspected enemy camps and concentrations in South Vietnam, Laos and Cambodia, and for the interdiction campaign along the Ho Chi Minh Trail in Laos and the North Vietnamese panhandle. If their effectiveness in these roles is somewhat questionable, there is no doubt that B-52s proved highly effective during 'Linebacker II' when they dropped nearly three-fourths of the bombs in this 11-day attack. The B-52Fs initially used in Southeast Asia had bomb bays optimized for carrying nuclear stores and were soon supplanted by 'Big Belly' B-52Ds modified to carry an increased load of conventional bombs internally and externally. B-52Gs were added to the force in time for the 'Linebacker II' offensive.

**Specification (B-52D)**
**Type:** strategic bomber
**Powerplant:** eight 12,100-lb (5488-kg) thrust Pratt & Whitney J57-P-19W turbojets
**Performance:** maximum speed 628 mph (1010 km/h); climb rate 2,460 ft/min (750 m/min); service ceiling 38,050 ft (11600 m); combat range 7,290 miles (11730 km)
**Weights:** empty 165,110 lb (74893 kg); loaded 450,000 lb (204117 kg)
**Dimensions:** span 185 ft (56.39 m); length 156 ft 7.25 in (47.73 m); height 48 ft 4 in (14.73 m); wing area 4,000 sq ft (371.60 m²)
**Armament:** four 0.50-in (12.7-mm) machine-guns in tail turret and up to 60,000 lb (27215 kg) of bombs; 'Big Belly' aircraft could carry 81,000 lb (36740 kg).

## BOEING C-97
The transport version of the Boeing B-29 Superfortress first flew in 1944, and entered service with both civil and military operators in the late-1940s. Although obsolete by the time of the war in Vietnam, C-97s operated by Air National Guard units were used on the air bridge from the USA to Southeast Asia. Although the majority of the bulbous freighters had been converted to KC-97 tanker configuration by this time, they were used purely as transports.

**Specification**
**Type:** tanker/transport
**Powerplant:** four 3,500-hp (2610-kW) Pratt & Whitney R-4360-59 radial piston engines
**Performance:** maximum speed 375 mph (604 km/h) cruising speed 300 mph (483 km/h); range 4,300 miles (6920 km)
**Weights:** empty 82,500 lb (37421 kg); loaded 175,000 lb (79379 kg)
**Dimensions:** span 141 ft 3 in (43.05 m); length 110 ft 4 in (33.63 m); height 38 ft 3 in (11.66 m); wing area 1,720 sq ft (159.79 m²)
**Armament:** none.

## BOEING KC-135 STRATOTANKER
The KC-135A tanker was one of the most important aircraft of the war. It allowed heavily-laden tactical aircraft to fly long missions, and supported B-52 bombers operating from Andersen AFB on distant Guam. Its greatest value, however, was its direct contribution to saving aircrews and aircraft which were running out of fuel either due to operational problems or battle damage. The specially configured KC-135Q also provided air refueling for SR-71s. Other missions undertaken during the war by specialized versions of the Stratotanker included Combat Lightning radio relay sorties by KC-135As and EC-135Ls, and Combat Apple electronic intelligence-gathering sorties by RC-135Cs, RC-135Ds and RC-135Ms.

**Specification (KC-135A)**
**Type:** inflight-refueling tanker
**Powerplant:** four 13,750-lb (6237-kg) thrust Pratt & Whitney J57-P-59W turbojets
**Performance:** maximum speed 585 mph (941 km/h) at 30,000 ft (9145 m); climb rate

*The Boeing KC-135 Stratotanker was tasked primarily with supporting bombers and strike aircraft on raids against North Vietnam.*

2,000 ft/min (610 m/min); service ceiling 50,000 ft (15240 m); range 1,150 miles (1850 km) carrying 120,000 lb (54430 kg) of transfer fuel
**Weights:** empty 98,446 lb (44654 kg); loaded 297,000 lb (134717 kg)
**Dimensions:** span 130 ft 10 in (39.88 m); length 136 ft 3 in (41.53 m); height 38 ft 4 in (11.68 m); wing area 2,433 sq ft (226.03 m²)
**Armament:** none.

## BOEING-VERTOL CH-46 SEA KNIGHT
Marine assault missions were largely handled by the twin-rotor CH-46 Sea Knight. Navy CH-46s were used for the vertical replenishment of vessels at sea. After suffering more than their fair share of teething problems, the Marine machines became very effective medium-transport vehicles, a role which they continued to perform into the 1990s. Their last employment in Southeast Asia was during 'Frequent Wind', the final evacuation of Saigon in April 1975.

**Specification (CH-46A)**
**Type:** 17-man assault/medium-transport helicopter
**Powerplant:** two 1,250-shp (932-kW) General Electric T58-GE-8B turboshafts
**Performance:** maximum speed 160 mph (257 km/h) at sea level; climb rate 1,540 ft/min (469 m/min); service ceiling 12,800 ft (3900 m); combat range 245 miles (395 km)
**Weights:** empty 11,708 lb (5311 kg); loaded 18,700 lb (8482 kg)
**Dimensions:** rotor diameter (each) 50 ft (15.24 m); fuselage length 44 ft 10 in (13.66 m); height 16 ft 8.5 in (5.09 m)
**Armament:** none, though in the assault role M2 0.50-in (12.7-mm) or M60 0.30-in (7.62-mm) door guns were generally fitted.

## BOEING-VERTOL CH-47 CHINOOK
Resembling a scaled-up CH-46, the Chinook was the main Army medium-transport helicopter, also operated by the VNAF. An immensely powerful machine, it was used to transport heavy loads of fuel and freight, and equipment such as artillery. Chinooks were also used as assault transports, one helicopter being able to do the job of four or five UH-1s. A version of the CH-47 was tested as a very heavily-armed helicopter gunship.

**Specification (CH-47C)**
**Type:** 44-man medium/heavy-transport helicopter
**Powerplant:** two 3,750-shp (2796-kW) Lycoming T55-L-11 turboshafts
**Performance:** maximum speed 190 mph (306 km/h) at sea level; climb rate 2,880 ft/min (878 m/min); service ceiling 15,000 ft (4570 m); combat range 230 miles (370 km)
**Weights:** empty 20,378 lb (9243 kg); loaded 46,000 lb (20865 kg)
**Dimensions:** rotor diameter (each) 60 ft (18.29 m); fuselage length 51 ft (15.54 m); height 18 ft 7 in (5.66 m)
**Armament:** one door-mounted 0.30-in (7.62-mm) flexible machine-gun.

## CESSNA A-37 DRAGONFLY
Following the successful combat evaluation of the A-37A, an armed version of the T-37 trainer, the more powerful A-37B was extensively used by the USAF in South Vietnam for close support and convoy escort. As a result of the 'Vietnamization' Programme, A-37Bs became the most numerous combat aircraft in the VNAF inventory; a few were also delivered to the Khmer Air Force.

**Specification (A-37B)**
**Type:** light-strike aircraft
**Powerplant:** two 2,850-lb (1293-kg) thrust General Electric J85-GE-17A turbojets
**Performance:** maximum speed 507 mph (816 km/h) at 16,000 ft (4875 m); climb rate 6,990 ft/min (2130 m/min); service ceiling 41,765 ft (12730 m); combat range 460 miles (740 km)
**Weights:** empty 6,210 lb (2817 kg); loaded 14,000 lb (6350 kg)
**Dimensions:** span 35 ft 10.5 in (10.93 m); length 29 ft 3 in (8.92 m); height 8 ft 10.5 in (2.70 m); wing area 184 sq ft (17.10 m²)
**Armament:** one 0.30-in (7.62-mm) Minigun and up to 5,680 lb (2576 kg) of stores.

## CESSNA O-1 BIRD DOG
Upon reaching full independence, the Republic of Vietnam took over from the French inventory 20 of the high-wing Cessna L-19s which had been supplied by the United States at the time of the Dien Bien Phu emergency. Redesignated O-1 in 1962, this fragile observation aircraft went on to see extensive service. It was deployed in large numbers not only with the VNAF, but also with the USAF, the US Army, the Marines, and the Royal Khmer Aviation/Khmer Air Force.

**Specification (O-1E)**
**Type:** two-seat observation and forward air control aircraft
**Powerplant:** one 213-hp (159-kW) Continental 0-470-11 air-cooled piston engine
**Performance:** maximum speed 115 mph (185 km/h) at sea level; climb rate 1,150

*The CH-47 Chinook was widely used by the US Army for the transport of heavy items such as artillery and fuel as well as for moving troops.*

ft/min (351 m/min); service ceiling 18,500 ft (5640 m); range 530 miles (850 km)
**Weights:** empty 1,614 lb (732 kg); loaded 2,400 lb (1088 kg)
**Dimensions:** span 36 ft (10.97 m); length 25 ft 10 in (7.87 m); height 7 ft 4 in (2.23 m); wing area 174 sq ft (16.16 m²)
**Armament:** four target-marking rockets.

## CESSNA O-2

To supplement its O-1s in the FAC role the USAF began acquiring the larger twin-engined O-2A in 1967. Based on the twin-boomed push-pull Cessna Model 337 Skymaster, the O-2 was much more heavily armed than its predecessor, and were used as light-strike/counter-insurgency aircraft as well as for forward air control. Thirty one of the generally similar O-2B were also deployed in Southeast Asia. These were psychological warfare aircraft fitted with air to-ground broadcasting equipment and a leaflet dispenser.

**Specification (O-2A)**
**Type:** two-seat observation and forward air control aircraft
**Powerplant:** two 210-hp (157-kW) Continental 10-360C/D air-cooled piston engines
**Performance:** maximum speed 199 mph (320 km/h) at sea level; climb rate 1,100 ft/min (335 m/min); service ceiling 18,000 ft (5490 m); range 1,060 miles (1705 km)
**Weights:** empty 2,848 lb (1291 kg); loaded 4,630 lb (2100 kg)
**Dimensions:** span 38 ft 2 in (11.63 m) length 29 ft 9 in (9.07 m); height 9 ft 4 in (2.84 m); wing area 202.5 sq ft (18.81 m²)
**Armament:** four underwing hard points for target-marking rockets or 0.30-in (7-62 mm) Minigun pods.

## CESSNA T-37

The Cessna T-37 was the USAF's basic jet trainer in the 1960s. In addition to being extensively used in the United States for training American and Vietnamese aircrews, this light twinjet was operated by the 920th Training Squadron of the VNAF at Nha Trang. Strengthened and modified, it also formed the basis for the A-37 light-attack jet.

**Specification (T-37C)**
**Type:** two-seat basic trainer
**Powerplant:** two 1,025-lb (465-kg) thrust Continental T69-T-25 turbojets
**Performance:** maximum speed 425 mph (684 km/h) at 20,000 ft (6100 m); climb rate 3,370 ft/min (1027 m/min); service ceiling 39,200 ft (11950 m); range 930 miles (1495 km)
**Weights:** empty 4,480 lb (2032 kg); loaded 8,007 lb (3632 kg)
**Dimensions:** span 33 ft 9.25 in (10.29 m); length 29 ft 3.5 in (8.93 m); height 9 ft 2 in (2.79 m); wing area 183.9 sq ft (17.08 m²)
**Armament:** two underwing hard points for gun pods.

## CESSNA T-41A MESCALERO

Good stability and forgiving flying qualities made the military version of the Cessna 172 light aircraft an ideal basic-training aircraft. The type was operated by the USAF Air Training Command in its Undergraduate Pilot Training Program, by the VNAF's 912th Training Squadron, and by the Khmer Air Force.

**Specification**
**Type:** two-seat primary trainer
**Powerplant:** one 150-hp (112-kW) Lycoming 0-320-E2D air-cooled piston engine
**Performance:** maximum speed 153 mph (246 km/h) at sea level; climb rate 880 ft/min (268 m/min); service ceiling 17,000 ft (5180 m); range 1,010 miles (1625 km)
**Weights:** empty 1,405 lb (637 kg); loaded 2,550 lb (1156 kg)
**Dimensions:** span 35 ft 10 in (10.92 m); length 26 ft 11 in (8.20 m); height 8 ft 9.5 in (2.68 m); wing area 174 sq ft (16.16 m²)
**Armament:** none.

## CESSNA U-3 'BLUE CANOE'

Deriving its nickname from its colorful paint scheme, the 'Blue Canoe' was a staff transport developed from the Cessna 310 twin-engined executive aircraft, which was also used to deliver intelligence data from headquarters into the field. In Southeast Asia the USAF flew both U-3As with conventional vertical tail surfaces and U-3Bs with swept fin and rudder.

**Specification (U-3A)**
**Type:** five-seat staff transport
**Powerplant:** two 240-hp (179-kW) Continental O-470-M air-cooled piston engines
**Performance:** maximum speed 231 mph (372 km/h) at sea level; climb rate 1,640 ft/min (500 m/min); service ceiling 28,100 ft (8565 m); range 1,400 miles (2250 km)
**Weights:** empty 2,965 lb (1345 kg); loaded 4,830 lb (2190 kg)
**Dimensions:** span 36 ft 1 in (11.0 m); length 27 ft 1 in (8.25 m); height 10 ft 5 in (3.17 m); wing area 175 sq ft (16.26 m²)
**Armament:** none.

*Cessna's high-wing Bird Dog saw extensive use with many of the air forces involved in the struggle for Southeast Asia.*

## CESSNA U-17 SKYWAGON

For light utility work and flight training the VNAF and the Royal Lao Air Force received some U-17s (military equivalent of the civil Cessna 185). A small number of the Vietnamese aircraft were fitted out for psychological warfare with air-to-ground broadcasting equipment and leaflet dispensers.

**Specification (U-17A)**
**Type:** six-seat utility aircraft
**Powerplant:** one 300-hp (224-kW) Continental 10-520-D air-cooled piston engine
**Performance:** maximum speed 178 mph (286 km/h) at sea level; climb rate 1,010 ft/min (308 m/min); service ceiling 17,150 ft (5230 m); range 1,075 miles (1730 km)
**Weights:** empty 1,585 lb (719 kg); loaded 3,350 lb (1519 kg)
**Dimensions:** span 35 ft 10 in (10.92 m); length 25 ft 9 in (7.85 m); height 7 ft 9 in (2.36 m); wing area 174 sq ft (16.16 m²)
**Armament:** none.

## CHANCE VOUGHT AU-1 CORSAIR

Trained on the F4U-7, the final version of the famous World War II Corsair carrier fighter, Flottille 14F of the French Navy was sent to Indochina without aircraft during the fight for Dien Bien Phu. There the unit flew another version of the Corsair, the ground-attack AU-1. Twenty-five examples had been loaned by the United States in the closing year of the war. Corsairs flew exclusively from land bases in Indochina.

**Specification**
**Type:** carrier-based fighter-bomber
**Powerplant:** one 2,300-hp (1715-kW) Pratt & Whitney R-2800-83W radial piston engine
**Performance:** maximum speed 438 mph (705 km/h) at 9,500 ft (2895 m); climb rate 2,920 ft/min (890 m/min); service ceiling 39,500 ft (12040 m); combat range 485 miles (780 km)
**Weights:** empty 9,835 lb (4461 kg); loaded 19,400 lb (8800 kg)
**Dimensions:** span 41 ft (12.50 m); length 34 ft 1 in (10.39 m); height 14 ft 10 in (4.52 m); wing area 314 sq ft (29.17 m²)
**Armament:** four 20-mm cannon and 4,000 lb (1814 kg) of external stores.

## CONSOLIDATED PBY-5A CATALINA

In 1945 these old and slow amphibians were the first aircraft taken to Indochina by France's Aéronautique Navale. There they served in their intended maritime patrol role and also performed bombing and medical evacuation missions until phased out in 1950.

**Specification**
**Type:** maritime patrol amphibian
**Powerplant:** two 1,200-hp (895-kW) Pratt & Whitney R-1830-92 radial piston engines
**Performance:** maximum speed 196 mph (315 km/h) at 7,000 ft (2135 m); climb rate 620 ft/min (189 m/min); service ceiling 13,000 ft (3960 m); range 2,350 miles (3780 km)
**Weights:** empty 20,910 lb (9485 kg); loaded 35,420 lb (16066 kg)
**Dimensions:** span 104 ft (31.70 m); length 63 ft 10 in (19.46 m); height 20 ft 2 in (6.15 m); wing area 1,400 sq ft (130.06 m²)
**Armament:** three 0.30-in (7.62-mm) and two 0.50-in (12.7-mm) machine-guns, plus 4,000 lb (1814 kg) of bombs.

## CONSOLIDATED PB4Y PRIVATEER

Replacing the lumbering Catalina, the Privateer was a much-modified version of the

*Widely used by the VNAF, the A-37 flew most forms of light-strike mission, including rescue escort, counter-insurgency, and fast FAC.*

*Larger and heavier than the Bird Dog, the Cessna O-2 was an altogether more capable, if much more noisy, forward air control machine.*

*Deployed to South Vietnam to counter North Vietnamese Il-28 bombers, the Convair F-102 was never called upon in its air defence role.*

wartime Liberator heavy bomber. The largest aircraft flown by French forces in Indochina, the PB4Y-2S land-based maritime patrol aircraft were operated by Flottille 8F/28F and introduced a much greater bombing capacity from the last part of 1950 until the French withdrawal from their former colony.

**Specification (PB4Y-2S)**
**Type:** four-engined bomber
**Powerplant:** four 1,350-hp (1007-kW) Pratt & Whitney R-1830-94 radial piston engines
**Performance:** maximum speed 237 mph (381 km/h) at 13,750 ft (4190 m); climb rate 1,090 ft/min (332 m/min); service ceiling 20,700 ft (6310 m); combat range 2,800 miles (4505 km)
**Weights:** empty 37,485 lb (17003 kg); loaded 65,000 lb (29484 kg)
**Dimensions:** span 110 ft (33.53 m); length 74 ft 7 in (22.73 m); height 30 ft 1 in (9.17 m); wing area 1,048 sq ft (97.36 m²)
**Armament:** 12 0.50-in (12.7-mm) machine-guns in one nose, two dorsal, two waist, and one tail turret, plus up to 12,800 lb (5805 kg) of bombs.

## CONVAIR F-102 DELTA DAGGER
The first operational supersonic delta-winged fighter was the standard American interceptor of the late-1950s and early-1960s. Initially deployed to South Vietnam to serve in the air defence role, F-102s also flew escort for B-52s flying against targets in the North Vietnamese panhandle. F-102s never shot down any enemy fighters, but an F-102A of the 509th FIS was brought down on 3 February 1968 by an 'Atoll' air-to-air missile fired by a MiG-21.

**Specification (F-102A)**
**Type:** single-seat interceptor fighter
**Powerplant:** one 11,700-lb (5307-kg) dry thrust and 17,200-lb (7802-kg) afterburning thrust Pratt & Whitney J57-P-23 turbojet
**Performance:** maximum speed 825 mph (1328 km/h) at 40,000 ft (12190 m); climb rate 13,000 ft/min (3962 m/min); service ceiling 54,000 ft (16460 m), combat range 670 miles (1080 km)
**Weights:** empty 19,350 lb (8777 kg); loaded 31,276 lb (14187 kg)
**Dimensions:** span 38 ft 1.5 in (11.62 m); length 68 ft 4.5 in (20.84 m); height 21 ft 2.5 in (6.46 m); wing area 661.5 sq ft (61.45 m²)
**Armament:** six AIM-4 Falcon air-to-air missiles.

## CURTISS SB2C-5 HELLDIVER
After widespread service in the Pacific during the later years of World War II, the Helldiver continued flying combat missions from French carrier decks over Southeast Asia. Standard carrier-borne bomber of the Aéronautique Navale, the SB2C-5 operated from the decks of the *Arromanches*, *La Fayette*, and *Bois Belleau*, as well as from shore bases in Indochina.

**Specification**
**Type:** two-seat carrier-based dive bomber
**Powerplant:** one 1,900-hp (1417-kW) Wright R-2600-20 radial piston engine
**Performance:** maximum speed 290 mph (467 km/h) at 16,500 ft (5030 m); climb rate

*The Curtiss SB2C was a World War II US carrier-bomber which was used extensively by the French navy against the Viet Minh.*

1,850 ft/min (564 m/min); service ceiling 27,600 ft (8410 m); combat range 1,165 miles (1875 km)
**Weights:** empty 10,589 lb (4803 kg); loaded 14,415 lb (6539 kg)
**Dimensions:** span 49 ft 9 in (15.16 m); length 36 ft 8 in (11.18 m); height 13 ft 2 in (4.01 m); wing area 422 sq ft (39.20 m²)
**Armament:** two wing-mounted 20-mm cannon and two 0.30-in (7.62-mm) flexible machine-guns plus up to 2000 lb (907 kg) of bombs.

## DASSAULT FLAMANT
As one of the first post-World War II aircraft of French design to enter service with the Armée de l'Air, the Flamant was too late to see much use in Indochina. Primarily a staff and liaison transport, it could also be used for medevac missions. In the mid-1950s five MD 315s were delivered to the Royal Khmer Aviation and a few MD 312s were briefly operated by the VNAF before being returned to France.

**Specification**
**Type:** six-seat liaison aircraft
**Powerplant:** two 580-hp (433-kW) SNECMA-Renault 12S 02-201 inline liquid-cooled piston engines
**Performance:** maximum speed 236 mph (380 km/h); climb rate 984 ft/min (300 m/min); service ceiling 26,245 ft (8000 m); range 746 miles (1200 km)
**Weights:** empty 9,347 lb (4240 kg); loaded 12,754 lb (5785 kg)
**Dimensions:** span 67 ft 9 in (20.65 m); length 41 ft (12.50 m); height 14 ft 9.2 in (4.50 m): wing area 508 sq ft (47.20 m²)
**Armament:** none.

## DE HAVILLAND MOSQUITO
Aware of the good results obtained with Mosquitoes by the RAF in Burma during World War II and later in Malaya, the Armée de l'Air entertained high hopes for the Mosquitoes of G.C.1/3 'Corse'. Heavily armed and possessing suitable range for operations in Indochina, the British-built twin-engined aircraft appeared to be an excellent choice. Unfortunately, a combination of problems with the aircraft's wooden structures compounded by the humid tropical climate, and the age of its airframe led to serious maintenance difficulties, forcing the French Mosquito out of operation after only six months in Indochina.

**Specification (Mosquito FB.Mk VI)**
**Type:** two-seat fighter bomber
**Powerplant:** two 1,635-hp (1219-kW) Rolls-Royce Merlin 25 inline liquid-cooled piston engines
**Performance:** maximum speed 378 mph (608 km/h); climb rate 2,850 ft/min (869 m/min); service ceiling 33,000 ft (10060 m); combat range 1,205 miles (1940 km)
**Weights:** empty 14,344 lb (6506 kg); loaded 22,258 lb (10096 kg)
**Dimensions:** span 54 ft 2 in (16.51 m); length 40 ft 6 in (12.34 m); height 12 ft 6 in (3.81 m); wing area 454 sq ft (42.18 m²)
**Armament:** four 0.303-in (7.7-mm) machine-guns, four 20-mm cannon, plus eight 60-lb (27.2-kg) rockets.

## DE HAVILLAND CANADA C-7 CARIBOU
Initially operated in Southeast Asia by Army Aviation Companies, the Caribous were taken over by the USAF in January 1967. The 'Boos', which the USAF had considered less capable than its C-123s, soon proved themselves in Air Force service. Possessed of excellent short- and rough-field capability, the Caribou was primarily used to supply outlying outposts and special forces camps too small to accept larger transports. Caribous were also operated by the VNAF and the Royal Australian Air Force.

**Specification (C-7A)**
**Type:** tactical transport (32 troops or 8,740 lb/3965 kg of cargo)
**Powerplant:** two 1,450-hp (1081-kW) Pratt & Whitney R-2000-7M2 radial piston engines
**Performance:** maximum speed 216 mph (347 km/h) at 6,500 ft (1980 m); climb rate 1,355 ft/min (413 m/min); service ceiling 24,800 ft (7560 m); range with maximum payload 242 miles (390 km)
**Weights:** empty 18,260 lb (8283 kg); loaded 28,500 lb (12928 kg)
**Dimensions:** span 95 ft 7.5 in (29.15 m); length 72 ft 7 in (22.12 m); height 31 ft 9 in (9.68 m); wing area 912 sq ft (84.72 m²)
**Armament:** none.

## DE HAVILLAND CANADA U-1A OTTER
Nearly one half of the Canadian production of this large single-engined STOL aircraft was absorbed by the US military. Most of them were operated by the US Army, for light transport, but a number of RU-1s were used by Radio Research Companies to track down NVA communications. More than 20 Otters were lost in Vietnam as a result of hostile actions or operational accidents between 1963 and 1970.

*Canadian-built C-7 Caribous were tough, capable short-take-off transports used to supply remote jungle and highland outposts.*

**Specification**
**Type:** nine-passenger utility transport
**Powerplant:** one 600-hp (447-kW) Pratt & Whitney R-1340-S1H1-G radial piston engine
**Performance:** maximum speed 160 mph (257 km/h) at 5,000 ft (1525 m); climb rate 735 ft/min (224 m/min); service ceiling 18,800 ft (5730 m); range 960 miles (1545 km)
**Weights:** empty 4,168 lb (1891 kg); loaded 8,000 lb (3629 kg)
**Dimensions:** span 58 ft (17.68 m); length 41 ft 10 in (12.75 m); height 12 ft 7 in (3.84 m); wing area 375 sq ft (34.84 m²)
**Armament:** none.

### DE HAVILLAND CANADA U-6A BEAVER

One of the all-time classic designs, the Beaver was designed to operate in Canada's remote northern wilderness, but proved equally adept at handling the rough mountainous terrain of Vietnam. First acquired by US military forces during the Korean War under the L-20 designation, a few were transferred to France in 1954 for use in Indochina. Later, the STOL characteristics of this aircraft (redesignated U-6 in 1962) were put to good use in Vietnam by the USA and the VNAF, with the latter also using the type for psychological warfare.

**Specification**
**Type:** seven-passenger utility aircraft
**Powerplant:** one 450-hp (336-kW) Pratt & Whitney R-985-AN-1 radial piston engine
**Performance:** maximum speed 163 mph (262 km/h) at 5,000 ft (1525 m); climb rate 1,020 ft/min (311 m/min); service ceiling 18,000 ft (5485 m); range 455 miles (730 km)
**Weights:** empty 2,850 lb (1293 kg); loaded 5,100 lb (2313 kg)
**Dimensions:** span 48 ft (14.63 m); length 30 ft 3 in (9.22 m); height 9 ft (2.74 m); wing area 250 sq ft (23.23 m²)
**Armament:** none.

### DOUGLAS A-1 SKYRAIDER

Designed as a torpedo/attack bomber at the end of World War II, the Skyraider still equipped numerous Navy attack squadrons at the time of the Gulf of Tonkin Incident in 1964. A-1Hs and A-1Js played an active role during the early offensive against the North until progressively replaced by jets. Detachments of four-seat EA-1Fs provided ECM support for CTF 77, with the last of these detachments leaving the Gulf of Tonkin in January 1969 aboard the USS *Intrepid*. On land, the Skyraider had been adopted in 1964 to equip Air Commando Squadrons, single-seat and two-seat versions seeing considerable USAF service providing close support, interdicting the Ho Chi Minh Trail, and escorting rescue helicopters. Rescue A-1s continued to fly operations until the end of 1972. The VNAF received its first AD-6s (A-1Hs) in 1960 and operated both single-seat and two-seat versions of the Skyraider until 1975. At about the same time France transferred 15 AD-4NAs (A-1Ds) to the Khmer Air Force in spite of US Government opposition.

**Specification (A-1H)**
**Type:** single-seat attack aircraft
**Powerplant:** one 2,700-hp (2013-kW) Wright R-3350-26WA radial piston engine
**Performance:** maximum speed 322 mph (518 km/h) at 18,000 ft (5485 m); climb rate 2,850 ft/min (869 m/min); service ceiling 28,500 ft (8685 m); combat range 1,315 miles (2115 km)
**Weights:** empty 11,968 lb (5429 kg); loaded 18,106 lb (8213 kg)
**Dimensions:** span 50 ft 0.25 in (15.25 m); length 38 ft 10 in (11.84 m); height 15 ft 8.25 in (4.78 m); wing area 400.33 sq ft (37.19 m²)
**Armament:** four wing-mounted 20-mm cannon, plus up to 8,000 lb (3630 kg) of external stores.

### DOUGLAS A-3 SKYWARRIOR

Although designed as the largest bomber ever to fly from carrier decks, the A-3B Skywarrior only flew a limited number of bombing missions over North and South Vietnam in 1965 and 1966. The type was to contribute much more to the war as the KA-3B aerial tanker, the dual-role EKA-3B tanker and electronic support aircraft, the RA-3B reconnaissance platform and the EA-3B ECM and electronic intelligence aircraft.

**Specification (KA-3B)**
**Type:** three-seat carrier-based tanker
**Powerplant:** two 10,500-lb (4763-kg) dry thrust and 12,400-lb (5625-kg) thrust with water injection Pratt & Whitney J57-P-10 turbojets
**Performance:** maximum speed 620 mph (998 km/h) at sea level; service ceiling 41,100 ft (12525 m); climb rate 5,620 ft/min (1713 m/min); combat range 2,100 miles (3380 km)
**Weights:** empty 37,329 lb (16932 kg); loaded 70,000 lb (31751 kg)
**Dimensions:** span 72 ft 6 in (22.10 m); length 76 ft 4 in (23.27 m); height 22 ft 9.5 in

*Designed for bush operations in the far north of Canada, the U-6A Beaver proved equally adept in the challenging terrain of Southeast Asia.*

(6.95 m); wing area 812 sq ft (75.44 m²)
**Armament:** none.

### DOUGLAS A-4 SKYHAWK

Single-seat versions of the Skyhawk, a carrier-based light-attack aircraft powered by a Wright J65 turbojet (A-4B and A-4C) or Pratt & Whitney J52 (A-4E and A-4F), bore the brunt of the Navy offensive against the North until from the Gulf of Tonkin reprisal raids of 1964 until 1968. Although replaced aboard big-deck carriers by the A-7, Skyhawks continued in operation aboard the older carriers until the US withdrawal. As a result of their long and active combat life, more A-4s were lost during the Southeast Asia War than any other types of carrier-based aircraft and accounted for nearly 37 per cent of Navy combat losses (compared with just above 10 per cent for the A-7s). Likewise, 36 per cent of the Marine combat losses were accounted for by single-seat A-4s and two-seat TA-4Fs, the latter being flown in the TAC(A) role.

**SPECIFICATION (A-4E)**
**Type:** single-seat carrier-based attack aircraft
**Powerplant:** one 8,500-lb (3856-kg) thrust Pratt & Whitney J52-P-6A turbojet
**Performance:** maximum speed 673 mph (1083 km/h) at sea level; climb rate 5,750 ft/min (1753 m/min); service ceiling 42,700 ft (13015 m); combat range 1,160 miles (1865 km)
**Weights:** empty 9,853 lb (4469 kg); loaded 16,216 lb (7355 kg)
**Dimensions:** span 27 ft 6 in (8.38 m); length 40 ft 1.5 in (12.23 m); height 15 ft 2 in (4.62 m); wing area 260 sq ft (24.15 m²)
**Armament:** two 20-mm cannon plus up to 8,200 lb (3719 kg) of external stores.

### DOUGLAS B-26 (A-26) INVADER

Possibly the ultimate in World War II attack bombers, the B-26 Invader was fast, long-legged, rugged and heavily armed with up to 14 forward-firing 0.50-in machine-guns in its 'solid nose' B-26B version, plus two tonnes of bombs, napalm canisters or rockets. It was undoubtedly the most effective combat aircraft operated by the Armée de l'Air in Indochina, and its fighting qualities led to its use by the American Farm Gate detachment beginning in 1961. Fatigue-induced structural failures led to the type being withdrawn from use in 1964. The A-26A (initially designated B-26K) was a modernized version with strengthened structure which was used by the USAF for interdiction missions over the Ho Chi Minh Trail between 1966 and 1969.

**Specification (A-26A)**
**Type:** twin-engined counter-insurgency attack aircraft
**Powerplant:** two 2,500-hp (1864-kW) Pratt & Whitney R-2800-52W radial piston engines
**Performance:** maximum speed 327 mph (526 km/h) at 15,000 ft (4570 m); climb rate 2,050 ft/min (625 m/min); service ceiling 30,500 ft (9295 m); combat range 1,480 miles (2380 km)
**Weights:** empty 25,130 lb (11399 kg); loaded 37,000 lb (16783 kg)
**Dimensions:** span 71 ft 6 in (21.79 m); length 51 ft 7.3 in (15.73 m); height 19 ft (5.79 m); wing area 541 sq ft (50.26 m²)
**Armament:** eight 0.50-in (12.7-mm) forward-firing machine-guns, plus 8,000 lb (3629 kg) of internal and external stores.

### DOUGLAS B-66 DESTROYER

Developed for the USAF from the Navy A-3 Skywarrior as a medium-range

*One of the great workhorses of the war, the Douglas A-1 Skyraider saw service in Vietnam from 1960 to the final days of the conflict.*

*'Heinemann's Hotrod', the Douglas A-4 Skyhawk, was for much of the war the standard attack bomber for the US Navy and the USMC.*

*Designed as a nuclear bomber, massive A-3 Skywarrior was used for a wide variety of carrier-based support missions.*

*Developed from the Navy's Skywarrior, the USAF's B-66 Destroyer was used primarily as an electronic warfare platform in Vietnam.*

tactical/nuclear reconnaissance bomber, the B-66 series saw only limited service in its original role with the USAF. However, its EB-66C version was the only type of ESM/ECM aircraft in the Air Force inventory when operations over North Vietnam resulted in an urgent need for electronic countermeasures aircraft. Accordingly, the EB-66Cs were soon supplemented in Southeast Asia by EB-66Bs and EB-66Es obtained by modifying B-/RB66Bs for ECM warfare.

**Specification (EB-66C)**
**Type:** seven-seat electronic warfare aircraft
**Powerplant:** two 10,200-lb (4627-kg) thrust Allison J71-A-13 turbojets
**Performance:** maximum speed 641 mph (1032 km/h) at 3,000 ft (915 m); climb rate 3,950 ft/min (1204 m/min); service ceiling 35,700 ft (10880 m); combat range 2,035 miles (3275 km)
**Weights:** empty 44,771 lb (20308 kg); loaded 76,967 lb (34912 kg)
**Dimensions:** span 74 ft 7 in (22.73 m); length 75 ft 2 in (22.91 m); height 23 ft 7 in (7.19 m); wing area 781 sq ft (72.55 m²)
**Armament:** none.

## DOUGLAS C-9A NIGHTINGALE
Specially acquired by the Air Force for aeromedical evacuation, the C-9A was a military version of the DC-9-32CF jetliner. Beginning in 1972, C-9As were flown in their intended role in Southeast Asia and within CONUS where they provided an efficient link between specialized military hospitals.

**Specification**
**Type:** aeromedical evacuation transport
**Powerplant:** two 14,500-lb (6577-kg) thrust Pratt & Whitney JT8D-9 turbofans
**Performance:** maximum speed 575 mph (925 km/h); range 1,245 miles (2005 km)
**Weight:** loaded 108,000 lb (48988 kg)
**Dimensions:** span 93 ft 5 in (28.47 m); length 119 ft 4 in (36.37 m); height 27 ft 6 in (8.38 m); wing area 1,000.7 sq ft (92.97 m²)
**Armament:** none.

## DOUGLAS C-47
Used to transport the first French troops to return to Indochina in 1945, the ubiquitous C-47 was to be a common sight for the entire three decades of fighting in Indochina. It was operated by all combatants – the NVNAF, the Royal Khmer Air Force, and the Royal Lao Air Force flew a small number of Lisunov Li-2 transports, a Soviet-built version of the original DC-3 airliner. In addition to the C-47s and C-117s used as transports, this famous Douglas aircraft was used as a makeshift bomber by the French and South Vietnamese, for psychological warfare and for conventional and reconnaissance duties (SC-47D, EC-47P, EC-47Q and EC-47N) by the USAF and the VNAF. The AC-47 was the first of the fixed-wing gunships, and saw combat with the USAF, and VNAF, the Khmer Air Force and the RLAF.

**Specification (C-117D)**
**Type:** twin-engined personnel (33 troops) or cargo transport
**Powerplant:** two 1,475-hp (1100-kW) Wright R-1820-80 radial piston engines
**Performance:** maximum speed 270 mph (435 km/h) at 5,900 ft (1800 m); climb rate 1,300 ft/min (396 m/min); range 1,750 miles (2815 km)
**Weights:** empty 19,537 lb (8862 kg); loaded 31,000 lb (14061 kg)
**Dimensions:** span 90 ft (27.43 m); length 67 ft 9 in (20.65 m); height 18 ft 3 in (5.56

*Playing a major role in Southeast Asia for more than three decades, the classic Douglas C-47 saw service with many air forces.*

m); wing area 969 sq ft (90.02 m²)
**Armament:** none.

## DOUGLAS C-54 SKYMASTER
Until 1955, France utilized Douglas DC-4 commercial transports and their C-54 military variants for logistic support between Metropolitan France and Indochina. By the time America became involved the big airliner was obsolete, and use was limited to Navy reserve crews and Marine H&MS squadrons flying C-54s in the transport role, while the USAF briefly flew specially fitted versions as air rescue command posts (SC-54D) and infra-red reconnaissance platforms known as Hilo Hattie.

**Specification (C-54G)**
**Type:** military personnel (50 troops) or cargo (max payload of 32,000 lb (14515 kg) transport
**Powerplant:** four 1,450-hp (1081-kW) Pratt & Whitney R-2000-9 radial piston engines
**Performance:** maximum speed 275 mph (442 km/h) at 17,500 ft (5335 m); climb rate 10,000 ft (3048 m) in 11 min; service ceiling 26,000 ft (7925 m); range 3,500 miles (5630 km) with payload of 10,000 lb (4535 kg)
**Weights:** empty 38,930 lb (17659 kg); loaded 62,000 lb (28123 kg)
**Dimensions:** span 117 ft 6 in (35.81 m); length 93 ft 10 in (28.60 m); height 27 ft 6 in (8.38 m); wing area 1,460 sq ft (135.63 m²)
**Armament:** none.

## DOUGLAS C-118 LIFTMASTER
A natural enlargement of the DC-4/C-54, the C-118 was a military version of the DC-6 airliner. In the early years of America's involvement in Southeast Asia the ageing C-118A was used for staff transport, but its primary mission was aeromedical evacuation.

**Specification (C-118A)**
**Type:** military personnel (74 troops) or cargo (maximum payload of 27,000 lb/12247 kg) transport
**Powerplant:** four 2,500-hp (1864-kW) Pratt & Whitney R-2800-52W radial piston engines
**Performance:** maximum speed 315 mph (507 km/h); climb rate 1,120 ft/min; range 3,005 miles (4835 km) with payload of 24,565 lb (11142 kg)
**Weights:** empty 55,357 lb (25110 kg); loaded 107,000 lb (48534 kg)
**Dimensions:** span 117 ft 6 in (35.81 m); length 106 ft 10 in (32.56 m); height 28 ft 8 in (8.74 m); wing area 1,463 sq ft (135.92 m²)
**Armament:** none.

## DOUGLAS C-124 GLOBEMASTER II
USAF Globemaster IIs flew logistics missions between France and Indochina to rush troops and equipment to the hard-pressed French forces during 1954-55. Although it was slow and obsolete when the United States became fully involved in the Vietnamese conflict the capacious Globemaster II proved invaluable; until the Lockheed C-5A entered service it was the only USAF transport capable of carrying large combat vehicles and bulky pieces of construction equipment.

**Specification (C-124C)**
**Type:** military cargo transport (maximum payload of 74,000 lb/33565 kg) or

*A Douglas C-9 Nightingale taxis out from the ramp at Ubon on the last aeromedical evacuation flight of the conflict.*

personnel transport (200 troops or 168 patients and 15 medical attendants)
**Powerplant:** four 3,800-hp (2834-kW) Pratt & Whitney R-4360-63A radial piston engines
**Performance:** maximum speed 304 mph (489 km/h) at 20,800 ft (6340 m); climb rate 760 ft/min (232 m/min); service ceiling 21,800 ft (6645 m); range 4,030 miles (6585 km) with a payload of 26,375 lb (11963 kg)
**Weights:** empty 101,165 lb (45888 kg); loaded 185,000 lb (83915 kg)
**Dimensions:** span 174 ft 1.5 in (53.07 m); length 130 ft 5 in (39.75 m); height 48 ft 35 in (14.72 m); wing area 2,506 sq ft (232.82 m²)
**Armament:** none.

## DOUGLAS C-133 CARGOMASTER
Plagued by engine unreliability and fatigue problems, the turboprop-powered C-133 was nevertheless much needed for logistic support of operations in Southeast Asia. It had a capacious fuselage and was much faster than the C-124. The type was withdrawn from use in 1971 after the entry into service of the Lockheed C-5A.

**Specification** (C-133B)
**Type:** military cargo transport
**Powerplant:** four 7,500-eshp (5593-ekW) Pratt & Whitney T34-P-9W turboprops
**Performance:** maximum speed 359 mph (578 km/h) at 8,700 ft (2650 m); climb rate 1,280 ft/min (390 m/min); service ceiling 29,950 ft (9130 m); range 4,000 miles (6435 km) with payload of 52,000 lb (23587 kg)
**Weights:** empty 120,263 lb (54550 kg); loaded 275,000 lb (124738 kg)
**Dimensions:** span 179 ft 8 in (54.76 m); length 157 ft 6 in (48.01 m); height 48 ft 3 in (14.71 m); wing area 2,673 sq ft (248.33 m²)
**Armament:** none.

## DOUGLAS EF-10B SKYKNIGHT
Although by the early-1960s the US Navy's first jet night-fighter was no longer suitable for combat operations, its EF-10B electronic warfare version became much needed a few years later. At the beginning of the Vietnam War the Skyknight was the only jet-powered ECM aircraft in naval aviation service. In this role, the type was operated over North and South Vietnam by Marine squadron VMCJ-1 from 1965 until 1969.

**Specification**
**Type:** two-seat electronic warfare aircraft
**Powerplant:** two 3,400-lb (1542-kg) thrust Westinghouse J34-WE 36 turbojets
**Performance:** maximum speed 565 mph (909 km/h) at 20,000 ft (6095 m); climb rate 4000 ft/min (1219 m/min); service ceiling 38,300 ft (11675 m); maximum range 1,540 miles (2480 km)
**Weights:** empty 18,160 lb (8237 kg); loaded 23,575 lb (10693 kg)
**Dimensions:** span 50 ft (15.24 m); length 45 ft 6 in (1387 m); height 16 ft 1 in (4.90 m); wing area 400 sq ft (37.16 m²)
**Armament:** four 20-mm cannon in the nose.

## DOUGLAS SBD-5 DAUNTLESS
Although the famous Dauntless had sunk more Japanese shipping during World War II than any other aircraft type, it was already obsolete when the Aéronautique Navale received its first SBD-5s after the liberation in 1944. Nevertheless, Dauntlesses made three deployments to Indochina in 1947-48 aboard the escort carrier *Dixemude* and the light fleet carrier *Arromanches*.

**Specification**
**Type:** two-seat carrier-based dive bomber
**Powerplant:** one 1,200-hp (895-kW) Wright R-1820-60 radial piston engine
**Performance:** maximum speed 255 mph (410 km/h) at 14,000 ft (4265 m); climb rate 1,700 ft/min (518 m/min); service ceiling 25,530 ft (7780 m); combat range 1,115 miles (1795 km)
**Weights:** empty 6,404 lb (2905 kg); loaded 9,359 lb (4245 kg)
**Dimensions:** span 41 ft 6.4 in (12.66 m); length 33 ft 1.25 in (10.09 m); height 13 ft 7 in (4.14 m); wing area 325 sq ft (30.19 m²)
**Armament:** two 0.50-in (12.7-mm) forward-firing machine-guns and two 0.30-in (7.62-mm) flexible machine-guns, plus a maximum bombload of 2,250 lb (1020 kg).

## ENGLISH ELECTRIC CANBERRA B.MK 20
(see Martin B-57.)

## FAIRCHILD C-119 FLYING BOXCAR
To help make up shortages in the military transport system in Indochina, the United States temporarily lent France a number of C-119Cs in 1954. These aircraft were returned to the USAF in 1955 and the type was not again used in Vietnam until January 1969, when heavily-armed AC-119G 'Shadow' gunships were deployed by the USAF. Later in the same year, they were joined by jet augmented AC-119K 'Stingers'. Subsequently the VNAF were supplied with C-119G/L transports and AC-

*C-119s were used as transports by the French and the South Vietnamese. The USAF only flew the AC-119 gunship in Southeast Asia.*

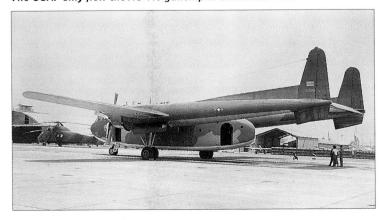

*The remarkable C-124 Globemaster was used on the Pacific air bridge, ferrying outsize items between the USA and Southeast Asia.*

119G/K gunships. On 30 April 1975 an AC-119K became the last VNAF aircraft to be lost in combat.

**Specification** (AC-119K)
**Type:** fixed-wing gunship
**Powerplant:** two 3,700-hp (2759-kW) Wright R-3350 89B radial piston engines and two 2,850-lb (1293-kg) thrust General Electric J85-GE-17 turbojets
**Performance:** maximum speed 243 mph (391 km/h) at 10,000 ft (3050 m); combat range 990 miles (1595 km)
**Weights:** empty 44,747 lb (20300 kg); loaded 77,000 lb (34925 kg)
**Dimensions:** span 109 ft 3 in (33.29 m); length 86 ft 6 in (26.36 m); height 26 ft 6 in (8.08 m); wing area 1,447 sq ft (134.43 m²)
**Armament:** four 0.30-in (7.62-mm) Miniguns and two Vulcan 20-mm six-barrel cannon.

## FAIRCHILD C-123 PROVIDER
For 10¹/₂ years beginning in January 1962, USAF C-123Bs and C-123Ks (the latter being a jet-augmented version which arrived in Vietnam in May 1967) contributed a substantial share of in-country airlift and resupply operations. Provider transports were also operated in Southeast Asia by the CIA (Air America), the VNAF, the Khmer Air Force, the Royal Lao Air Force and the Royal Thai Air Force. But although a key transport, the type was best known as the chemical spraying UC-123 of the Ranch Hand defoliation programme.

**Specification** (C-123K)
**Type:** tactical assault transport (60 troops or 15,000 lb/6800 kg of cargo)
**Powerplant:** two 2,500-hp (1864-kW) Pratt & Whitney R-2800-99W radial piston engines and two 2,850-lb (1293-kg) thrust General Electric J85-GE-17 turbojets
**Performance:** maximum speed 228 mph (367 km/h) at 10,000 ft (3050 m); climb rate 1,220 ft/min (372 m/min); service ceiling 21,100 ft (6430 m); combat range 1,470 miles (2365 km)
**Weights:** empty 35,366 lb (16042 kg); loaded 60,000 lb (27215 kg)
**Dimensions:** span 110 ft (33.53 m); length 76 ft 3 in (23.24 m); height 34 ft 1 in (10.39 m); wing area 1,223 sq ft (113.62 m²)
**Armament:** none.

## FAIRCHILD AU-23A PEACEMAKER
As part of the *Credible Chase* project the Air Force evaluated both the AU-23A and the Helio AU-24A as mini gunships. Neither was retained for service with the USAF but a few AU-23As (the gunship version of the Swiss-designed Pilatus Turbo-Porter built under licence by Fairchild Industries) were delivered to the Khmer Air Force in 1974 as part of *Project Flycatcher*. Fairchild-built Turbo-Porters were also used by Air America, the CIA airline, as STOL transports and for covert insertion missions.

**Specification**
**Type:** mini-gunship
**Powerplant:** one 576-eshp (430-ekW) AiResearch TPE 331-1-101 turboprop
**Performance:** maximum speed 164 mph (264 km/h) at 10,000 ft (3050 m); climb rate 1,607 ft/min (490 m/min); service ceiling 27,875 ft (8500 m); combat range 683 miles (1100 km)
**Weights:** empty 2,612 lb (1185 kg); loaded 4,850 lb (2200 kg)
**Dimensions:** span 49 ft 8 in (15.13 m); length 35 ft 9 in (10.90 m); height 10 ft 6 in

*For more than a decade, the Fairchild C-123 Provider was one of the workhorses of the in-country transport effort.*

*Developed from the Swiss-designed Pilatus Turbo Porter STOL transport, the Fairchild AU-23 was an experimental 'mini-gunship.'*

*After a catastrophic introduction to combat in 1968, the F-111 was to go on to become one of the most effective bombers of the war.*

(3.20 m); wing area 310 sq ft (28.80 m²)
**Armament:** one 20-mm XM-197 cannon in aft cabin, plus up to 2,000 lb (907 kg) of external stores.

### FLETCHER FD-25 DEFENDER
Designed in the United States as a light ground-support aircraft for use by small or undeveloped air forces, the Defender was built under licence by Toyo Aircraft Company. Japanese-built Defenders (FD-25A two-seaters and FD-25B single-seaters) were among the first aircraft acquired by the Royal Khmer Aviation.

**Specification (FD-25B)**
**Type:** light counter-insurgency aircraft
**Powerplant:** one 225-hp (168-kW) Continental E-225-8 air-cooled piston engine
**Performance:** maximum speed 187 mph (301 km/h); climb rate 1,725 ft/min (526 m/min); range 630 miles (1015 km)
**Weights:** empty 1,428 lb (648 kg); loaded 2,700 lb (1225 kg)
**Dimensions:** span 30 ft (9.14 m); length 20 ft 11 in (6.38 m); height 6 ft 3 in (1.91 m); wing area 150 sq ft (13.94 m²)
**Armament:** two 0.30-in (7.62-mm) machine-guns and an external load of up to 500 lb (227 kg).

### GENERAL DYNAMICS F-111A
It was the most advanced warplane in the world when it arrived in Vietnam in 1968, but following the loss of three aircraft, the initial Combat Lancer deployment of F-111As to Southeast Asia was terminated abruptly. F-111As were not to fly above North Vietnam for four years, but by 1972, teething troubles solved, the F-111 was a much better warplane. It performed with great success during the 'Linebacker' campaigns, its sophisticated terrain-following and blind-bombing radar enabling solo aircraft to hit difficult targets accurately even under appalling weather conditions.

**Specification**
**Type:** two-seat tactical strike fighter
**Powerplant:** two 12,000-lb (5443-kg) dry thrust and 18,500-lb (8391-kg) afterburning thrust Pratt & Whitney TF30-P-3 turbojets
**Performance:** maximum speed 1,650 mph (2655 km/h) at 40,000 ft (12190 m); combat range 1,500 miles (2415 km) with maximum weapons load
**Weights:** empty 42,500 lb (19278 kg); loaded 92,500 lb (41957 kg)
**Dimensions:** span unswept 63 ft (19.20 m) span swept 31 ft 11.4 in (9.74 m); length 73 ft 6 in (22.40 m); height 17 ft 1.5 in (5.22 m); wing area 525 sq ft (48.77 m²)
**Armament:** one 20-mm M61 Vulcan six-barrel cannon and up to 30,000 lb (13608 kg) of internal and external stores.

### GRUMMAN A-6 INTRUDER
One of the first warplanes capable of all-weather precision strike, the A-6A began combat operations in July 1965 from the USS *Independence*. The Intruder proved to be an outstanding aircraft, and quickly became the standard carrier-based medium-attack aircraft of the US Navy and US Marine Corps. Specialized attack variants included the A-6B, equipped to fire Standard ARMs (anti-radiation missiles), and the A-6C, with sensors for detecting and attacking truck convoys. The KA-6D, a tanker version, saw extensive service with carrier-based units. The two-seat EA-6A

*Possessed of one of the most advanced avionics suites in the world, the Grumman A-6 was the Navy's premier all-weather strike bomber.*

operated by the Marines and the four-seat EA-6B Prowler flown by Navy squadrons were sophisticated electronic countermeasure aircraft.

**Specification (A-6A)**
**Type:** carrier-based all-weather attack aircraft
**Powerplant:** two 9,300-lb (4218-kg) thrust Pratt & Whitney J52-P-8A turbojets
**Performance:** maximum speed 685 mph (1102 km/h) at sea level; climb rate 6,950 ft/min (2118 m/min); service ceiling 41,660 ft (12700 m); combat range 1,920 miles (3090 km)
**Weights:** empty 25,684 lb (11650 kg); loaded 60,280 lb (27343 kg)
**Dimensions:** span 53 ft (16.15 m); length 54 ft 7 in (16.64 m); height 15 ft 7 in (4.75 m); wing area 529 sq ft (49.15 m²)
**Armament:** up to 15,000 lb (6804 kg) of external stores.

### GRUMMAN C-1 TRADER/E-1B TRACER
The Grumman C-1 Trader COD (carrier onboard delivery) plane was a modified version of the S-2 Tracker ASW aircraft. It was used to ferry cargo and personnel between shore bases and carriers in the Gulf of Tonkin. Based on the Trader airframe, the Tracer was one of the first 'all-in-one' flying radar stations. Immediately identifiable by the massive dorsal radome, it was used to provide airborne early warning over the Gulf of Tonkin. It was replaced in big-deck carriers by the much more capable turboprop-powered E-2 Hawkeye, though it served on smaller carriers to the end of the American involvement.

**Specification**
**Type:** carrier-based airborne early-warning aircraft
**Powerplant:** two 1,525-hp (1137-kW) Wright R-1820-82 radial piston engines
**Performance:** maximum speed 228 mph (367 km/h) at 5,000 ft (1525 m); climb rate 1,120 ft/min (341 m/min); service ceiling 15,800 ft (4815 m); combat range 875 miles (1410 km)
**Weights:** empty 20,638 lb (9361 kg); loaded 26,600 lb (12065 kg)
**Dimensions:** span 72 ft 4.75 in (22.07 m); length 45 ft 3.5 in (13.80 m); height 16 ft 10 in (5.13 m); wing area 506 sq ft (47.01 m²)
**Armament:** none.

### GRUMMAN E-2 HAWKEYE/C-2A GREYHOUND
Carrying a powerful radar scanner in a rotating housing or 'rotodome', the Hawkeye marked a significant upgrade in US Navy airborne early-warning capability. E-2As were first deployed to the Gulf of Tonkin aboard the USS *Kitty Hawk* at the end of 1965, and this and later versions progressively replaced the older Tracers aboard the larger carriers. A transport derivative, the C-2A Greyhound, supplemented the C-1A Trader in the important COD mission.

**Specification (E-2A)**
**Type:** carrier-based airborne early-warning aircraft
**Powerplant:** two 4,050-eshp (3020-ekW) Allison T56-A-8A turboprops
**Performance:** maximum speed 370 mph (595 km/h); service ceiling 31,700 ft (9660 m); combat range 1400 miles (2250 km)
**Weights:** empty 36,063 lb (16358 kg); loaded 49,638 lb (22515 kg)
**Dimensions:** span 80 ft 7 in (24.56 m); length 56 ft 4 in (17.17 m); height 18 ft 4 in

*The Grumman E-1 Tracer was based on the C-1 Trader, modified with twin fins and a dorsal radome housing the APS-82 early-warning radar.*

(5.59 m); wing area 700 sq ft (65.03 m²)
**Armament:** none.

## GRUMMAN F6F-5 HELLCAT
Between November 1950 and January 1953, after the United States began supplying military aircraft for use by French forces in Indochina, ex-US-Navy Hellcats were operated by three *Groupes de Chasse* of the Armée de l'Air. Beginning in September 1951, Hellcats of the Aéronautique Navale were also deployed to Indochina aboard the carriers *Arromanches* and *La Fayette*.

### Specification
**Type:** carrier-based fighter
**Powerplant:** one 2,000-hp (1491-kW) Pratt & Whitney R-2800-10W radial piston engine
**Performance:** maximum speed 380 mph (611 km/h) at 23,400 ft (7130 m); climb rate 2,980 ft/min (908 m/min); service ceiling 37,300 ft (11370 m); combat range 945 miles (1520 km)
**Weights:** empty 9,238 lb (4190 kg); loaded 15,413 lb (6991 kg)
**Dimensions:** span 42 ft 10 in (13.06 m); length 33 ft 7 in (10.24 m); height 13 ft 1 in (3.99 m); wing area 334 sq ft (31.03 m²)
**Armament:** six wing-mounted 0.50-in (12.7-mm) machine-guns and 1,000 lb (454 kg) of bombs or rockets.

## GRUMMAN F8F BEARCAT
The origins of the Bearcat date back to a 1943 US Navy requirement for a carrier-based interceptor. However, it was as a land-based fighter-bomber with G.C. 3/6 'Roussillon' that the Bearcat made its combat debut in March 1951. The type went on to become the Armée de l'Air's most numerous and important fighter in Indochina and served with distinction during the battle for Dien Bien Phu. The Bearcat was also the first VNAF fighter, and 28 Bearcats served in Vietnamese colors until August 1959.

### Specification (F8F-1B)
**Type:** carrier-based fighter
**Powerplant:** one 2,100-hp (1566-kW) Pratt & Whitney R-2800-34W radial piston engine
**Performance:** maximum speed 421 mph (677 km/h) at 19,700 ft (6005 m); climb rate 4,570 ft/min (1392 m/min); service ceiling 38,700 ft (11795 m); combat range 1,105 miles (1780 km)
**Weights:** empty 7,070 lb (3207 kg); loaded 12,947 lb (5873 kg)
**Dimensions:** span 35 ft 10 in (10.92 m); length 28 ft 3 in (8.61 m); height 13 ft 10 in (4.22 m); wing area 244 sq ft (22.67 m²)
**Armament:** four wing-mounted 20-mm cannon plus 1,000 lb (454 kg) of bombs or rockets.

## GRUMMAN TF-9J COUGAR
Having become the standard Navy advanced trainer during the late-1950s, the F9F-8T (TF-9J after 1962) helped most naval pilots to hone their skills prior to joining operational squadrons and deploying to the Gulf of Tonkin. The type saw limited combat service with the USMC, which used the TF-9J in the TAC(A) role beginning in 1966.

### Specification
**Type:** two-seat advanced jet trainer and forward air control aircraft
**Powerplant:** one 7,200-lb (3266-kg) thrust Pratt & Whitney J48-P-8A turbojet
**Performance:** maximum speed 705 mph (1135 km/h) at sea level; climb rate 40,000 ft (12192 m) in 8.5 min; service ceiling 50,000 ft (15240 m); combat range 600 miles (965 km)
**Weight:** loaded 20,600 lb (9344 kg)
**Dimensions:** span 34 ft 6 in (10.52 m); length 44 ft 5 in (13.54 m); height 12 ft 3 in (3.73 m); wing area 337 sq ft (31.31 m²)
**Armament:** two 20-mm cannon and 2,000 lb (907 kg) of external stores.

## GRUMMAN F-14A TOMCAT
Tomcats, which arrived too late to be used while the US Navy was operating against North Vietnam, made a brief appearance in the theater during the closing days of Operation 'Frequent Wind'. Navy fighter squadrons VF-1 and VF-2, operating from the USS *Enterprise* provided air cover during the final American evacuation of Saigon in April 1975.

### Specification
**Type:** two-seat carrier-based fighter
**Powerplant:** two 20,600-lb (9344-kg) afterburning thrust Pratt & Whitney TF30-P-412 turbofans
**Performance:** maximum speed 1,564 mph (2517 km/h) at 40,000 ft (12190 m); climb

*Seen on the grass airstrip at Dien Bien Phu, the Grumman F8F Bearcat was the most potent fighter-bomber used by France in Indochina.*

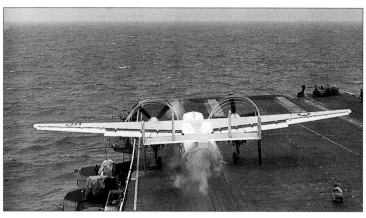

*Far more capable than the piston-engined Trader it replaced, the turboprop Grumman C-2 Greyhound was based on the E-2 Hawkeye.*

rate 30,000 ft/min (9144 m/min); service ceiling 60,000 ft (18290 m); combat range 2,000 miles (3220 km)
**Weights:** empty 37,500 lb (17010 kg); loaded 57,300 lb (25990 kg)
**Dimensions:** unswept span 64 ft 1.5 in (19.55 m); swept span 38 ft 2 in (11.63 m); length 62 ft 8 in (19.10 m); height 16 ft (4.87 m); wing area 565 sq ft (52.49 m²)
**Armament:** one 20-mm M61 six-barrel cannon plus four AIM-7 Sparrow and four AIM-9 Sidewinder air-to-air missiles; or cannon and six AIM-54 Phoenix air-to-air missiles.

## GRUMMAN JRF-5 GOOSE
Beginning in February 1952, 12 JRF-5 light twin-engined flying-boats were operated in Indochina by Escadrille 8S for maritime surveillance. Some of these aircraft were fitted with twin side-firing machine-guns in their left fuselage door, thus in a primitive fashion becoming the first fixed-wing gunships to be used in Southeast Asia.

### Specification
**Type:** utility transport (4-7 passengers) amphibian
**Powerplant:** two 450-hp (336-kW) Pratt & Whitney R-985-AN-6 radial piston engines
**Performance:** maximum speed 201 mph (323 km/h) at 5,000 ft (1525 m); climb rate 1,100 ft/min (335 m/min); service ceiling 21,300 ft (6490 m); range 640 miles (1030 km)
**Weights:** empty 5,425 lb (2461 kg); loaded 8,000 lb (3629 kg)
**Dimensions:** span 49 ft (14.94 m); length 38 ft 6 in (11.73 m); height 16 ft 2 in (4.93 m); wing area 375 sq ft (34.84 m²)
**Armament:** (French Navy modification) twin 0.50-in (12.7-mm) machine-guns firing sideways.

## GRUMMAN S-2 TRACKER
Developed in the 1950s as the US Navy's primary carrier-borne anti-submarine platform, the S-2 was deployed during the early phases of US operations in the Gulf of Tonkin, when possible intervention by Chinese submarines was feared. Trackers based aboard CVS (anti-submarine) carriers provided ASW cover for the attack carriers of CTF-77. Utility versions (US-2A, US-2B and US-2C) of the Tracker were used in support of the Fleet and Marine activities, while the specialized C-1A Trader was the main COD aircraft shuttling personnel, mail and urgently needed parts from shore bases to carriers.

### Specification (S-2E)
**Type:** carrier-based anti-submarine aircraft
**Powerplant:** two 1,525-hp (1137-kW) Wright R-1820-82WA radial piston engines
**Performance:** maximum speed 265 mph (426 km/h) at sea level; climb rate 1,390 ft/min (424 m/min); service ceiling 21,000 ft (6400 m); combat range 1,150 miles (1850 km)
**Weights:** empty 18,750 lb (8505 kg); loaded 26,867 lb (12187 kg)
**Dimensions:** span 72 ft 7 in (22.12 m); length 43 ft 6 in (13.26 m); height 16 ft 7.5 in (5.06 m); wing area 496 sq ft (46.08 m²)
**Armament:** up to 4,810 lb (2182 kg) of depth charges, torpedoes, mines or rockets.

## GRUMMAN HU-16B ALBATROSS
Last and biggest of a long line of Grumman flying-boats and amphibians, the

*Although generally relegated to non-combatant roles, the Grumman TF-9 Cougar was used by the Marines as a forward air control aircraft.*

*Hiller helicopters were used by the French in Indochina, primarily for medical evacuation. US forces also used them briefly.*

*The long-serving Grumman Hu-16 Albatross amphibian was used for combat rescue in the early years of America's involvement in Vietnam.*

Albatross was used for sea-air rescue by the USAF, US Navy and US Coast Guard. It provided early combat rescue coverage for the USAF in Southeast Asia, serving from June 1964 until September 1967, when its duties were taken over by the air-refuelable HH-3 helicopter.

**Specification**
**Type:** 22-passenger sea-air rescue amphibian
**Powerplant:** two 1,425-hp (1063-kW) Wright R-1820-76B radial piston engines
**Performance:** maximum speed 236 mph (379 km/h) at sea level; climb rate 1,450 ft/min (442 m/min); service ceiling 21,500 ft (6550 m); range 2,850 miles (4585 km)
**Weights:** empty 22,883 lb (10380 kg); loaded 30,353 lb (13768 kg)
**Dimensions:** span 96 ft 8 in (29.46 m); length 62 ft 10 in (19.15 m); height 25 ft 10 in (7.87 m); wing area 1,035 sq ft (96.15 m²)
**Armament:** none.

## GRUMMAN OV-1 MOHAWK
The high-performance Mohawk observation aircraft saw extensive service in Vietnam, where it was first deployed by the US Army during the summer of 1962. The basic OV-1A version was complemented by the OV-1B with underfuselage SLAR (side-looking airborne radar), the OV-1C with infra-red sensors, and the OV-1D with either SLAR or infra-red sensors. Some Mohawks were fitted to carry external stores but this practice was not standardized.

**Specification (OV-10A)**
**Type:** two-seat STOL observation aircraft
**Powerplant:** two 1,150-eshp (858-kW) Lycoming T53-L-7 turboprops
**Performance:** maximum speed 308 mph (496 km/h) at 5,000 ft (1525 m); climb rate 2,950 ft/min (899 m/min); service ceiling 30,300 ft (9235 m); range 1,230 miles (1980 m)
**Weights:** empty 9,937 lb (4507 kg); loaded 12,672 lb (5748 kg)
**Dimensions:** span 42 ft (12.80 m); length 41 ft (12.50 m); height 12 ft 8 in (3.86 m); wing area 330 sq ft (30.65 m²)
**Armament:** none.

## HANDLEY PAGE HASTINGS C.3
Until replaced in the late-1960s by the Lockheed C-130H, three examples of this British-built transport, which had been acquired by the Royal New Zealand Air Force in 1951, were used by its No. 41 Squadron for logistic flights between New Zealand and South Vietnam.

**Specification**
**Type:** 50-troop military transport aircraft
**Powerplant:** four 1,675-hp (1249-kW) Bristol Hercules 737 radial piston engines
**Performance:** maximum speed 350 mph (564 km/h); climb rate 890 ft/min (271 m/min); service ceiling 26,500 ft (8075 m); range with maximum payload 1,690 miles (2720 km)
**Weights:** empty 48,600 lb (22045 kg); loaded 80,000 lb (36287 kg)
**Dimensions:** span 113 ft (34.44 m); length 82 ft 8 in (25.20 m); height 22 ft 6 in (6.86 m); wing area 1,408 sq ft (130.80 m²)
**Armament:** none.

*Standard British troop carrier of the 1950s, the Handley Page Hastings flew regular supply missions between New Zealand and Vietnam.*

## HELIO U-10 AND AU-24
U-10A STOL utility aircraft were among the types sent in late-1962 to boost the strength of the Farm Gate detachment. Later on, Air Commando Squadrons flew U-10As and U-10Ds primarily to resupply Lima Sites in Laos. Fifteen AU-24A, which differed from U-10s in being powered by a Pratt & Whitney PT6 turboprop and armed with a side-firing XM197 20-mm gun, were evaluated as part of the Credible Chase mini-gunship project.

**Specification (U-10A)**
**Type:** five-seat utility aircraft
**Powerplant:** one 295-hp (220-kW) Lycoming GO-480-G1D6 air-cooled piston engine
**Performance:** maximum speed 176 mph (283 km/h) at 8,200 ft (2500 m); climb rate 1,350 ft/min (411 m/min); range 670 miles (1080 km)
**Weights:** empty 2,037 lb (924 kg); loaded 3,920 lb (1778 kg)
**Dimensions:** span 39 ft (11.89 m), length 30 ft 9 in (9.37 m); height 8 ft 10 in (2.69 m); wing area 231 sq ft (21.46 m²)
**Armament:** none.

## HILLER OH-23 RAVEN
The first helicopters to be operated for war-related activities in Indochina were a pair of civil Hiller 360s acquired by the Service de Sante d'Indochine and used for medical evacuation. They were soon joined by a small number of H-23As and H-23Bs (military versions of the Hiller 360) which were supplied to the Armée de l'Air by the United States. Later on, the US Army in Vietnam made limited use of more modern versions of this light helicopter.

**Specification (OH-23G)**
**Type:** three-seat utility and observation helicopter
**Powerplant:** one 305-hp (227-kW) Lycoming VO-540-A1B air-cooled piston engine
**Performance:** maximum speed 96 mph (154 km/h) at sea level; climb rate 1,290 ft/min (393 m/min); service ceiling 15,200 ft (4635 m); range 250 miles (400 km)
**Weights:** empty 1,755 lb (796 kg); loaded 2,800 lb (1270 kg)
**Dimensions:** rotor diameter 35 ft 5 in (10.79 m); fuselage length 28 ft 6 in (8.69 m); height 10 ft 1.5 in (3.09 m)
**Armament:** none.

## HUGHES OH-6 CAYUSE
The Cayuse was nicknamed 'loach' in service from the LOH or light-observation helicopter designation. Winner of the LOH competition of the 1960s, it often operated as a team with the Bell AH-1 HueyCobra, with the OH-6 finding targets for the Cobra to destroy. Although it was only used by the US Army the OH-6 was, next to the ubiquitous Huey, numerically the most important helicopter in Southeast Asia. The observation mission was dangerous: OH-6s destroyed in combat and operationally accounted for 22 per cent of all US helicopter losses.

**Specification (OH-6A)**
**Type:** six-seat utility and observation helicopter
**Powerplant:** one 317-shp (236-kW) Allison T63-A-5A turboshaft
**Performance:** maximum speed 150 mph (241 km/h) at sea level; climb rate 1,700

*Helio U-10s were sent to Vietnam in 1962 as part of the Farm Gate detachment. The AU-24 was a turbo-powered mini-gunship variant.*

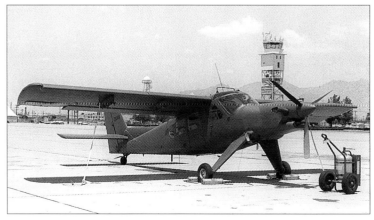

ft/min (518 m/min); service ceiling 15,800 ft (4815 m); range 380 miles (610 km)
**Weights:** empty 1,146 lb (520 kg); loaded 2,400 lb (1090 kg)
**Dimensions:** rotor diameter 26 ft 4 in (8.03 m); fuselage length 23 ft (7.01 m); height 8 ft 1.5 in (2.48 m)
**Armament:** one XM-27 kit with one 0.30-in (7.62-mm) Minigun.

## ILYUSHIN IL-12 'COACH' AND IL-14 'CRATE'

Standard post-World War II Soviet transports, the Il-12 'Coach' and its modernized and slightly enlarged Il-14 'Crate' derivative were intended as replacements for the long-serving DC-3 family, which as the Li-2 had been built in large numbers in Russia. Widely exported by the Soviet Union to allies and client states, these Ilyushin transports were operated by the NVNAF and the Royal Khmer Air Force.

**Specification (Il-14M 'Crate')**
**Type:** twin-engined transport
**Powerplant:** two 1,900-hp (1417-kW) Shvetsov ASh-82T radial piston engines
**Performance:** maximum speed 261 mph (420 km/h); climb rate 1,230 ft/min (375 m/min); service ceiling 21,980 ft (6700 m); range 1,555 miles (2500 km)
**Weights:** empty 27,778 lb (12600 kg); loaded 39,683 lb (18000 kg)
**Dimensions:** span 104 ft (31.70 m); length 73 ft 2 in (22.30 m); height 25 ft 11 in (7.90 m); wing area 1,076.4 sq ft (100 m²)
**Armament:** none.

## ILYUSHIN IL-28 'BEAGLE'

One of the first jet bombers to enter service, the Il-28 was roughly comparable to the Canberra, with a fair weapons load though lacking the agility and ceiling of the British jet. It was considered by American forces to be a potential threat to the ships of CTF 77 in the Gulf of Tonkin and to installations in South Vietnam and Thailand. In fact, the few jet bombers of this type possessed by the NVNAF were never thrown into the battle; indeed, they spent most of their time at Chinese bases to avoid American raids.

**Specification**
**Type:** three-seat tactical jet bomber
**Powerplant:** two 5,952-lb (2700-kg) thrust Klimov VK-1 turbojets
**Performance:** maximum speed 559 mph (900 km/h) at 14,765 ft (4500 m); climb rate 2,955 ft/min (900 m/min); service ceiling 40,355 ft (12300 m); combat range 1,365 miles (2200 km)
**Weights:** empty 28,417 lb (12890 kg); loaded 40,565 lb (18400 kg)
**Dimensions:** span 70 ft 45 in (21.45 m); length 57 ft 10.9 in (17.65 m); wing area 654.47 sq ft (60.80 m²)
**Armament:** two fixed forward-firing 23-mm NR-23 cannon and two 23-mm NR 23 cannon in the tail turret, plus a bombload of 6,614 lb (3000 kg).

## KAMAN HH-43 HUSKIE

Although initially deployed to Southeast Asia to provide crash rescue at various air bases, the distinctive Huskie, known by its callsign 'Pedro' had the scope of its activities enlarged to include combat rescue of downed crews. For this task, the unarmed HH-43Bs were supplemented by armed and armored HH-43Fs. Never more than an interim combat rescue type, the HH-43 was replaced in the role by larger and much more capable HH-3 Jolly Greens. However, both Huskie models were retained for base rescue and fire-fighting operations until the US withdrawal.

**Specification (HH-43F)**
**Type:** search-and-rescue helicopter
**Powerplant:** one 825-shp (615-kW) Lycoming T53-L-11A turboshaft
**Performance:** maximum speed 120 mph (193 km/h); climb rate 1,800 ft/min (549 m/min); service ceiling 23,000 ft (7010 m); combat range 500 miles (810 km)
**Weights:** empty 4,619 lb (2095 kg); loaded 6,504 lb (2950 kg)
**Dimensions:** rotor diameter 47 ft (14.33 m); length 25 ft 2 in (7.67 m); height 15 ft 6.5 in (4.73 m)
**Armament:** one 0.30-in (7.62-mm) flexible machine-gun.

## KAMAN UH-2 SEASPRITE

Designed as a shipboard light anti-submarine and utility helicopter, the Seasprite was the standard 'plane guard' helicopter of the US Navy from the mid-1960s. Single-engined UH-2As and UH-2Bs, and later twin-engined UH-2Cs, served aboard most carriers in the Gulf of Tonkin until replaced by larger and more capable SH-3s. Armed and armored HH-2Cs based on destroyers and frigates operating close to the shore were used for combat rescue.

**Specification (UH-2A)**
**Type:** shipborne utility helicopter
**Powerplant:** one 1,250-shp (932-kW) General Electric T58-GE-8B turboshaft
**Performance:** maximum speed 162 mph (261 km/h) at sea level; climb rate 1,740

*With a conventional rotor in place of the usual Kaman twin intermeshing arrangement, the UH-2 Seasprite was used in a variety of roles.*

*Early combat rescue missions in Vietnam were carried out by the distinctive Kaman HH-43 Huskie, known by its callsign 'Pedro'.*

ft/min (530 m/min); service ceiling 17,400 ft (5305 m); combat range 670 miles
**Weights:** empty 6,100 lb (2767 kg); loaded 10,200 lb (4627 kg)
**Dimensions:** rotor diameter 44 ft (13.41 m); length 52 ft 2 in (15.90 m); height 13 ft 6 in (4.11 m)
**Armament:** none.

## LISUNOV LI-2 'CAB'
(see Douglas C-47.)

## LOCKHEED C-5A GALAXY

The mighty Galaxy was the world's largest aircraft for nearly two decades from its first flight in the mid-1960s. Placed in trans-Pacific service shortly after its squadron debut in 1970, the C-5A provided the USAF with its first jet transport capable of carrying bulky and heavy military combat vehicles. This capability became particularly useful in the last half of 1972 when large quantities of aircraft and tanks were rushed to the ARVN prior to the signing of the Paris Agreement.

**Specification**
**Type:** heavy-lift (maximum payload of 265,000 lb/120200 kg) strategic freighter
**Powerplant:** four 41,100-lb (18643-kg) thrust General Electric TF39-GE-1 turbofans
**Performance:** maximum speed 564 mph (907 km/h) at 25,000 ft (7620 m); climb rate 5,840 ft/min (1780 m/min); service ceiling 47,700 ft (14540 m); range 1,875 miles (3015 km) with maximum payload
**Weights:** empty 321,000 lb (145603 kg); loaded 769,000 lb (348812 kg)
**Dimensions:** span 222 ft 8.5 in (67.88 m); length 247 ft 9.5 in (75.53 m); height 65 ft 1.25 in (19.84 m); wing area 6,200 sq ft (576 m²)
**Armament:** none.

## LOCKHEED EC-121 WARNING STAR

Derived from the pioneering long-range airliner, the primary mission of the military Super Constellation in Vietnam was the airborne early warning provided by Air Force EC-121Ds, Navy EC-121Ks and the EC-121Ms used by both services. But Constellations were versatile, and performed many different tasks, including television relay and broadcasting for American forces in Vietnam by Navy aircraft; aeromedical evacuation (C-121C and C-121G), electronic reconnaissance/countermeasures (EC-121S) by the Air National Guard, and relay of data from the 'Igloo White' detection network by the Air Force EC-121Rs.

**Specification (EC-121D)**
**Type:** airborne early-warning aircraft
**Powerplant:** four 3,400-hp (2535-kW) Wright R-3350-34 radial piston engines
**Performance:** maximum speed 321 mph (516 km/h) at 20,000 ft (6095 m); climb rate 845 ft/min (258 m/min); service ceiling 20,600 ft (6280 m); combat range 4,600 miles (7400 km)
**Weights:** empty 80,611 lb (36565 kg); loaded 143,600 lb (65136 kg)
**Dimensions:** span 123 ft 5 in (37.62 m) length 116 ft 2 in (35.41 m); height 27 ft (8.23 m), wing area 1,654 sq ft (153.66 m²)
**Armament:** none.

*Lockheed EC-121s patrolling over Thailand and the Gulf of Tonkin provided airborne early warning to US aircraft attacking the North.*

*One of the great aircraft in history, the Lockheed C-130 was used in many roles in Vietnam. This is a DC-130 drone launcher and controller.*

*When it entered service in 1965, the Lockheed C-141 revolutionized trans-Pacific transport and logistics with its jet-powered performance.*

## LOCKHEED C-130 HERCULES

First flown in 1954, the Lockheed C-130 Hercules is one of the greatest aircraft of all time. The airlift versions of the Hercules (C-130A/B/E/H) were the most important military transport aircraft during the war in Southeast Asia, and were used both for intra-theater logistics by the USAF and the VNAF, and for strategic airlift by the USAF, the RAAF and the RNZAF. But Hercules were far more than simple transports. Air Force C-130s were used for tasks as varied as ABCCC, or airborne battlefield command and control centers, dropping super-heavy bombs for clearing helicopter landing sites in the jungle, and electronic warfare. The Marines used their KC-130Fs for transport and for refueling tactical aircraft. Specialized versions were developed for drone-launching and monitoring (DC-130A and DC-130E), for air rescue work (HC-130H) and for refueling helicopters (HC-130P). Heavily-armed AC-130As and AC-130Es were the ultimate expression of the sideways-firing gunship, and proved lethal to Communist supplies moving down the Ho Chi Minh Trail.

**Specification (C-130A)**
**Type:** military 92-troop or 45,000-lb (20410-kg) cargo transport
**Powerplant:** four 3,750-eshp (2796-kW) Allison T56-A-9 turboprops
**Performance:** maximum speed 383 mph (616 km/h) at 20,400 ft (6220 m); climb rate 2,570 ft/min (783 m/min); service ceiling 41,300 ft (12590 m); range 2,090 miles (3365 km) with payload of 35,000 lb (15875 kg)
**Weights:** empty 59,328 lb (26911 kg); loaded 108,000 lb (48988 kg)
**Dimensions:** span 132 ft 7 in (40.41 m); length 97 ft 9 in (29.79 m); height 38 ft 6 in (11.73 m); wing area 1,745.5 sq ft (162.16 m²)
**Armament:** none.

## LOCKHEED C-141A STARLIFTER

The US Air Force's first specialized cargo jet transport flew in prototype form in December 1963, and began operations with Military Airlift Command in April 1965. StarLifters were active on trans-Pacific logistic flights from August of that year, and were to be a major part of the air bridge over the next decade, right up to the 'Frequent Wind' evacuation of Saigon. StarLifters steadily gained in importance, carrying cargo and personnel on westbound flights and performing aeromedical evacuation on the return trip.

**Specification**
**Type:** long-range 123-troop or 62,717-lb (28448-kg) cargo transport
**Powerplant:** four 21,000-lb (9525-kg) thrust Pratt & Whitney TF33-P-7 turbofans
**Performance:** maximum speed 565 mph (909 km/h) at 24,400 ft (7440 m); climb rate 7,925 ft/min (2416 m/min); service ceiling 51,700 ft (15760 m); range 4,155 miles (6685 km) with payload of 62,717 lb (28448 kg)
**Weights:** empty 136,900 lb (62097 kg); loaded 323,100 lb (146556 kg)
**Dimensions:** span 160 ft (48.77 m); length 145 ft (44.20 m); height 39 ft 4 in (11.99 m); wing area 3,228.1 sq ft (299.90 m²)
**Armament:** none.

## LOCKHEED F-104 STARFIGHTER

Although one of the first fighters capable of near-Mach 2 speeds, the Starfighter was never really a success in US service. Briefly deployed to Vietnam, the F-104C and its two-seat F-104D version did no better there than in any other theater. They carried too few air-to-surface weapons for the in-country war, and in spite of the

*The Lockheed F-104 Starfighter lacked the range to operate effectively over north Vietnam and the ground-attack ability to fight in the South.*

addition of a fixed refueling probe they lacked the range for operations over the North. Eight F-104s were lost in combat and six were destroyed in operational accidents without obtaining compensating results.

**Specification (F-104C)**
**Type:** single-seat tactical fighter
**Powerplant:** one 10,000-lb (4536-kg) dry thrust and 15,800-lb (7167-kg) afterburning thrust General Electric J79-GE 7 turbojet
**Performance:** maximum speed 1,150 mph (1850 km/h) at 50,000 ft (15240 m); climb rate 54,000 ft/min (16459 m/min); service ceiling 58,000 ft (17680 m); combat range 850 miles (1370 km)
**Weights:** empty 12,760 lb (5788 kg); loaded 19,470 lb (8831 kg)
**Dimensions:** span 21 ft 9 in (6.63 m); length 54 ft 8 in (16.66 m); height 13 ft 5 in (4.09 m); wing area 196.1 sq ft (18.22 m²)
**Armament:** one 20-mm M61 six-barrel cannon, plus external stores up to 4,000 lb (1814 kg).

## LOCKHEED QT-2PC AND YO-3

One of the most unique ideas to be tried during the war involved the use of low-performance but extremely quiet aircraft in the covert detection of enemy activities in South Vietnam. The concept was validated in 1968 when two QT-2PCs, based on a modified Schweitzer sailplane structure, made a successful test deployment. This led to the 1970 deployment of the 13 YO-3As of the 1st Army Security Agency Company. Featuring a more conventional fuselage allied to a sailplane wing, the YO-3A had a slow turning propeller and was fitted with a large muffler.

**Specification (YO-3A)**
**Type:** two-seat clandestine observation aircraft
**Powerplant:** one 210-hp (157-kW) Continental IO-360D air-cooled piston engine
**Performance:** maximum speed 138 mph (222 km/h) at sea level; climb rate 615 ft/min (187 m/min); service ceiling 14,000 ft (4265 m); endurance 4.4 hours
**Weights:** empty 3,129 lb (1419 kg); loaded 3,519 lb (1596 kg)
**Dimensions:** span 57 ft 9 in (17.37 m); length 29 ft 4 in (8.94 m); height 9 ft 1 in (2.77 m); wing area 205 sq ft (19.04 m²)
**Armament:** none.

## LOCKHEED P-2 NEPTUNE

First proposed at the end of World War II as a long-range maritime patrol bomber, the P-2 Neptune was used extensively by the US Navy over Southeast Asia. Standard maritime patrol SP-2Hs were initially used for 'Market Time' flights, deterring Communist supply and infiltration by junk. The OP-2E version of the Neptune was used to seed ALARS sensors along the Ho Chi Minh Trail, while heavily-armed AP-2Hs flew night interdiction sorties over the Mekong Delta. The Army's 1st Radio Research Company employed AP-2Es for airborne radio relays and for COMINT.

**Specification (SP-2H)**
**Type:** maritime patrol aircraft
**Powerplant:** two 3,500-hp (2610-kW) Wright R-3350-32W radial piston engines and two 3,400-lb (1540-kg) thrust Westinghouse J34-WE-36 turbojets
**Performance:** maximum speed 403 mph (648 km/h) at 14,000 ft (4625 m); climb rate 1,760 ft/min (536 m/min); service ceiling 22,000 ft (6705 m); combat range 2,200 miles (3540 km)
**Weights:** empty 49,935 lb (22650 kg); loaded 73,139 lb (33175 kg)
**Dimensions:** span 103 ft 10 in (31.65 m); length 91 ft 8 in (27.94 m); height 29 ft 4 in

*An early experiment in low-observability, the Lockheed QT-2 was a modified sailplane designed to fly almost silently to avoid detection.*

(8.94 m); wing area 1,000 sq ft (92.90 m²)
**Armament:** up to 8,000 lb (3629 kg) of bombs, torpedoes, mines, depth charges or rockets.

## LOCKHEED P-3 ORION

Developed from the technically successful but relatively poor-selling Lockheed Electra airliner, the P-3 first entered service in 1962, and quickly replaced the P-2 Neptune as the US Navy's standard long-range patroller. As more of these very capable maritime aircraft became operational through the 1960s, Orions gradually took over the 'Market Time' maritime surveillance role from Neptunes.

**Specification (P-3B)**
**Type:** maritime patrol aircraft
**Powerplant:** four 4,910-eshp (3661-ekW) Allison T56-A-14 turboprops
**Performance:** maximum speed 473 mph (761 km/h) at 15,000 ft (4570 m); climb rate 1,950 ft/min (594 m/min); service ceiling 28,300 ft (8625 m); mission radius with 3 hr on station 1,550 miles (2495 km)
**Weights:** empty 61,491 lb (27892 kg); loaded 135,000 lb (61235 kg)
**Dimensions:** span 99 ft 8 in (30.38 m); length 116 ft 10 in (35.61 m); height 33 ft 8.5 in (10.27 m); wing area 1,300 sq ft (120.77 m²)
**Armament:** up to 19,250 lb (8732 kg) of bombs, torpedoes, mines, depth charges or rockets.

## LOCKHEED SR-71A 'BLACKBIRD'

Developed in great secrecy by Lockheed's 'Skunk Works', the amazing Lockheed SR-71 was for its entire 30-year career the world's fastest and highest-flying jet. Developed as an Air Force version of the CIA's A-12 spyplane, the impressive speed and ceiling of the 'Blackbird' made it immune from interception. During the Vietnam conflict SR-71s, and possibly A-12s, were ideal vehicles for sensitive reconnaissance operations over the southern coast of the Peoples Republic of China and along the China-Vietnam border.

**Specification**
**Type:** strategic reconnaissance aircraft
**Powerplant:** two 32,500-lb (14742-kg) afterburning thrust Pratt & Whitney J58-P-20 turbojets
**Performance:** maximum speed 2,250 mph (3620 km/h); service ceiling 100,000 ft (30480 m); combat range 3,000 miles (4830 km)
**Weight:** loaded 170,000 lb (77111 kg)
**Dimensions:** span 55 ft 7 in (16.94 m); length 107 ft 5 in (32.74 m); height 18 ft 6 in (5.64 m)
**Armament:** none.

## LOCKHEED RT-33A

Easily passing in the eyes of the uninitiated for its less pugnacious advanced jet trainer progenitor, the RT-33A tactical reconnaissance aircraft was selected by the Air Force to undertake covert Field Goal sorties over Laos in 1961. Within a year they were supplanted by RF-101 Voodoos as the need for more intelligence mandated the use of increasingly capable systems.

**Specification**
**Type:** tactical reconnaissance aircraft
**Powerplant:** one 5,200-lb (2359-kg) thrust Allison J33-A-35 turbojet
**Performance:** maximum speed 600 mph (965 km/h) at sea level; climb rate 4,870 ft/min (1484 m/min); service ceiling 48,000 ft (14630 m); combat range 1,025 miles (1650 km)
**Weights:** empty 8,365 lb (3794 kg); loaded 12,071 lb (5475 kg)
**Dimensions:** span 38 ft 105 in (11.85 m); length 37 ft 9 in (11.51 m); height 11 ft 8 in (3.55 m); wing area 234.8 sq ft (21.81 m²)
**Armament:** none.

## LOCKHEED U-2

Developed for the CIA in the 1950s, the U-2 was designed to fly high above enemy air defences. Notwithstanding the large-scale use of reconnaissance drones and tactical reconnaissance aircraft, U-2s were also needed for operations over North Vietnam and across the PRC border as their high-altitude capability and effective passive defence systems enabled them to fly at will over the most difficult targets. U-2 missions over Southeast Asia started in December 1963, and continued until well after the official ending of US operations over the North.

**Specification (U-2C)**
**Type:** high-altitude reconnaissance aircraft
**Powerplant:** one 17,000-lb (7711-kg) thrust Pratt & Whitney J75-P-13B turbojet
**Performance:** cruising speed 460 mph (740 km/h) at 65,000 ft (19810 m); combat ceiling 75,100 ft (22890 m); range 4,750 miles (7645 km)
**Weights:** empty 13,870 lb (6291 kg); loaded 23,970 lb (10873 kg)
**Dimensions:** span 80 ft 2 in (24.43 m); length 49 ft 8.5 in (15.15 m); height 15 ft (4.57 m); wing area 600 sq ft (55.74 m²)
**Armament:** none.

*High-flying partner to the SR-71, the Lockheed U-2 originally flew its missions from Bien Hoa, moving to U-Tapao in 1970.*

*Lockheed's amazing SR-71 flew so high and so fast that it was immune to interception. It was not immune to landing accidents, however.*

## LOIRE 130M

Brought to Indochina by France's Aéronautique Navale prior to World War II, Loire 130 observation flying-boats fought against the Thais in 1940 and against the Japanese in 1944. Two survivors were operated by Escadrille 8S during the early phase of the Indochina War.

**Specification**
**Type:** three-seat observation flying-boat
**Powerplant:** one 720-hp (537-kW) Hispano-Suiza 12Xirsl liquid-cooled piston engine
**Performance:** maximum speed 137 mph (220 km/h) at 6,890 ft (2100 m); climb to 9,840 ft (3000 m) in 12 min; service ceiling 19,685 ft (6000 m); endurance 7.5 hours
**Weights:** empty 4,519 lb (2050 kg); loaded 7,716 lb (3500 kg)
**Dimensions:** span 52 ft 5.9 in (16.00 m); length 37 ft 0.9 in (11.30 m); height 12 ft 7.5 in (3.85 m); wing area 411.19 sq ft (38.20 m²)
**Armament:** two 0.295-in (7.5-mm) machine-guns, one each in bow and dorsal positions, plus 165 lb (75 kg) of bombs.

## MARTIN B-57 CANBERRA

An American-built and modified English Electric Canberra twin-jet bomber, the Martin B-57B and B-57C tactical bombers flew the USAF's first in-country offensive sorties on 18 February 1965. B-57Bs, -Cs and -Es were also used in the interdiction campaign along the Trail, but it was the B-57G version of the Martin bomber which was better suited to this task as it had been fitted with a variety of night sensors. Longer lived than either the standard B-57 tactical bomber or the B-57G night interdiction aircraft, the sensor-packed RB-57Es codenamed 'Patricia Lynn' were among the most effective US aircraft for locating hidden enemy bases and depots. B-57s on loan from the USAF were operated for a few months by the VNAF. Australian-built Canberras were operated in Vietnam between 1967 and 1971 by the Royal Australian Air Force.

**Specification (B-57B)**
**Type:** two-seat tactical bomber
**Powerplant:** two 7,200-lb (3266-kg) thrust Wright J65-W-5 turbojets
**Performance:** maximum speed 582 mph (936 km/h) at 40,000 ft (12190 m); climb rate 3,500 ft/min (1067 m/min); service ceiling 48,000 ft (14630 m); combat range 2,300 miles (3700 km)
**Weights:** empty 28,793 lb (13060 kg); loaded 56,965 lb (25839 kg)
**Dimensions:** span 64 ft (19.51 m); length 65 ft 6 in (19.96 m); height 15 ft 7 in (4.75 m); wing area 960 sq ft (89.18 m²)
**Armament:** eight wing-mounted 0.50-in (12.7-mm) machine-guns plus 6,000 lb (2722 kg) of internal and external stores.

## MARTIN P-5 MARLIN

The heyday of the flying-boat in most of the world's navies had long gone by the time America became embroiled in the Southeast Asian struggle. Martin Marlins, the last operational US Navy combat flying-boats, flew 'Market Time' patrols from seaplane tenders in the South China Sea until May 1967.

*Night-interdiction versions of the long-serving B-57 Canberra were operational in Vietnam through the early 1970s.*

*Last of the US Navy's big flying-boats, the Martin Marlin was an anti-submarine platform used for coastal patrol and search and rescue.*

**Specification** (P-5B)
**Type:** maritime patrol flying-boat
**Powerplant:** two 3,450-hp (2573-kW) Wright R-3350-32WA radial piston engines
**Performance:** maximum speed 251 mph (404 km/h) at sea level; climb rate 1,200 ft/min (366 m/min); service ceiling 24,000 ft (7315 m); combat range 2,050 miles (3300 km)
**Weights:** empty 50,485 lb (22900 kg); loaded 85,000 lb (38555 kg)
**Dimensions:** span 118 ft 2 in (36.02 m) length 100 ft 7 in (30.66 m); height 32 ft 8.5 in (9.97 m); wing area 1,406 sq ft (130.62 m²)
**Armament:** up to 8,000 lb (3629 kg) of bombs, torpedoes, depth charges, mines or rockets.

## MCDONNELL F-4 PHANTOM II
The Phantom was the greatest fighter of the post-war years, and was used in larger numbers than any other western high-performance warplane. In air combat against MiGs, F-4s obtained 145.5 kills and achieved a kill-to-loss ratio of 3.73 to 1. Navy F-4Bs first flew combat sorties from the USS *Constellation* in 1964 during the Gulf of Tonkin incident, and F-4Js were first deployed in 1968 aboard the USS *America*; the rare naval F-4G was deployed aboard the USS *Kitty Hawk* in 1965-66. Marine F-4Bs and F-4Js were primarily employed from Chu Lai and Da Nang, but also flew from Laos and from the USS *America*. The Marines also flew RF-4Bs in Vietnam beginning in October 1966. The first Air Force Phantom IIs in Southeast Asia were the F-4Cs of the 45th TFS which were sent to Ubon in April 1965. This initial fighter version was joined by F-4Ds in May 1967 and gun-armed F-4Es in November 1968. RF-4C reconnaissance aircraft were first used in October 1967 by the 16th TRS and, by November 1970, had fully replaced the RF-101C. The extensive use of the Phantom is reflected in the fact that more F-4 fighters and RF-4 reconnaissance aircraft were lost in Southeast Asia than any other type of aircraft, accounting for 20.1 per cent of total fixed-wing combat and operational losses.

**Specification** (F-4B)
**Type:** two-seat carrier-based fighter
**Powerplant:** two 10,900-lb (4944-kg) dry thrust and 17,000-lb (7711-kg) afterburning thrust General Electric J79-GE-8 turbojets
**Performance:** maximum speed 1,485 mph (2390 km/h) at 48,000 ft (14630 m); climb rate 28,000 ft/min (8534 m/min); service ceiling 62,000 ft (18900 m); combat range 800 miles (1285 km)
**Weights:** empty 28,000 lb (12701 kg); loaded 44,600 lb (20230 kg)
**Dimensions:** span 38 ft 4.9 in (11.71 m); length 58 ft 3.75 in (17.77 m); height 16 ft 3 in (4.95 m); wing area 530 sq ft (49.24 m²)
**Armament:** four AIM-7 Sparrow and four AIM-9 Sidewinder air-to-air missiles; up to 16,000 lb (7257 kg) of external stores.

## MCDONNELL RF-101 VOODOO
Designed originally as a long-range escort fighter adapted to nuclear-strike roles, the Voodoo was used in Vietnam as a very-high-speed reconnaissance platform. RF-101Cs first flew reconnaissance sorties in Southeast Asia in 1961 when the USAF sent the 'Pipe Stem' and 'Able Mable' detachments to South Vietnam and Thailand

*Entering service with the US Navy in 1961, the McDonnell Douglas F-4 Phantom became the most important tactical aircraft in Southeast Asia.*

*Though most Phantoms were fighters or fighter-bombers, a significant number of RF-4C reconnaissance aircraft saw service in Vietnam.*

respectively. Often operating alone, RF-101s brought back much intelligence from North Vietnam in the first years of the war. Gradually superseded by reconnaissance Phantoms, the last Voodoo was withdrawn from Tan Son Nhut in November 1970.

**Specification** (RF-101C)
**Type:** single-seat tactical reconnaissance aircraft
**Powerplant:** two 10,200-lb (4627-kg) dry thrust and 15,000-lb (6804-kg) afterburning thrust Pratt & Whitney J57-P-13 turbojets
**Performance:** maximum speed 1,012 mph (1629 km/h) at 35,000 ft (10670 m); climb rate 45,550 ft/min (13885 m/min); service ceiling 55,300 ft (16855 m); combat range 2,045 miles (3290 km)
**Weights:** empty 26,136 lb (11855 kg); loaded 48,133 lb (21832 kg)
**Dimensions:** span 39 ft 8 in (12.09 m); length 69 ft 4 in (21.13 m); height 18 ft (5.49 m); wing area 368 sq ft (34.19 m²)
**Armament:** none.

## MIKOYAN-GUREVICH MIG-15 'FAGOT'
Already obsolete when the United States began air operations against North Vietnam, this famous Soviet fighter was used by the NVNAF only for advanced training (primarily at Chinese air bases), with the single-seat MiG-15bis 'Fagot' operating alongside the two-seat MiG-15UTI 'Midget'. A few MiG-15bis were also operated briefly by the Royal Khmer Air Force during the mid-1960s.

**Specification** (MiG-15UTI)
**Type:** two-seat jet trainer
**Powerplant:** one 5,952-lb (2700-kg) thrust Klimov VK-1 turbojet
**Performance:** maximum speed 630 mph (1015 km/h) at sea level, climb rate 10,235 ft/min (3120 m/min); service ceiling 47,980 ft (14625 m); range 590 miles (950 km)
**Weights:** empty 8,818 lb (4000 kg); loaded 10,692 lb (4850 kg)
**Dimensions:** span 33 ft 0.9 in (10.08 m); length 32 ft 11.3 in (10.04 m); height 12 ft 1.7 in (3.70 m); wing area 221.74 sq ft (20.6 m²)
**Armament:** one 23-mm NS-23 cannon.

## MIKOYAN-GUREVICH MIG-17 'FRESCO'
Even though the subsonic MiG-17 had less than half the speed of American F-4s and F-8s, the Soviet-built fighter was one of the most maneuverable jet aircraft ever built and carried a heavy cannon armament. It proved a formidable foe for US strike aircraft and their escorting fighters. From 1965 onward the NVNAF primarily operated MiG-17F clear-weather interceptors (as well as some Chinese-built Shenyang F-4s), although it also received some MiG-17PF limited all-weather fighters and MiG-17PFUs in which the cannon armament was replaced by a pair of AA-1 'Alkali' radar-homing air-to-air missiles. In 1964-65, a few MiG-17Fs were also supplied by the USSR to the Royal Khmer Air Force.

**Specification**
**Type:** single-seat clear-weather interceptor
**Powerplant:** one 5,732-lb (2600-kg) dry thrust and 7,452-lb (3380 kg) afterburning thrust Klimov VK-1F turbojet

*Although relatively slow, the agile and powerfully-armed Mikoyan-Gurevich MiG-17 'Fresco' was a potent foe to faster US fighters.*

**Performance:** maximum speed 711 mph (1145 km/h) at 9,840 ft (3000 m); climb rate 12,485 ft/min (3805 m/min); service ceiling 54,460 ft (16600 m); combat range 915 miles (1470 km)
**Weights:** empty 9,855 lb (4470 kg); loaded 13,382 lb (6070 kg)
**Dimensions:** span 31 ft 7.1 in (9.63 m); length 36 ft 4.6 in (11.09 m); height 12 ft 5.6 in (3.80 m); wing area 243.27 sq ft (22.6 m²)
**Armament:** one 37-mm N-37 and two 23-mm NR-23 cannon.

## MIKOYAN-GUREVICH MIG-19 'FARMER'

Most of the aircraft of this type, which served with the NVNAF in relatively small numbers from about 1970, appear to have been Chinese-built Shenyang F-6s. Nevertheless, it can be safely assumed that the NVNAF also received examples of the Soviet-built MiG-19S (the pattern version for the F-6), as well as some MiG-19PMs in which the cannon armament was replaced by four AA-1 'Alkali' radar-homing air-to-air missiles.

**Specification** (MiG-19S 'Farmer-A')
**Type:** single-seat clear-weather interceptor
**Powerplant:** two 5,732-lb (2600-kg) dry thrust and 7,165-lb (3250-kg) afterburning thrust Tumansky RD-9B turbojets
**Performance:** maximum speed 901 mph (1450 km/h) at 32,810 ft (10000 m); climb rate 22,640 ft/min (6900 m/min); service ceiling 54,135 ft (16500 m); combat range 870 miles (1400 km)
**Weights:** empty 12,699 lb (5760 kg); loaded 16,755 lb (7600 kg)
**Dimensions:** span 29 ft 6.3 in (9.00 m); length 42 ft 11.75 in (13.10 m); height 13 ft 23 in (4.02 m); wing area 269.1 sq ft (25.00 m²)
**Armament:** three 30-mm NR-30 cannon.

## MIKOYAN-GUREVICH MIG-21 'FISHBED'

This classic warplane, built in larger numbers than any other post-war supersonic fighter, became the sharp-end of North Vietnam's defences. First encountered in small numbers in April 1966, the MiG-21 progressively became the most important interceptor in NVNAF service. Lighter and nimbler than contemporary American fighters, the type was highly respected by US airmen and proved to be a formidable foe. Principal versions used in Vietnam were the MiG-21F 'Fishbed C' clear-weather interceptor, the MiG-21PF 'Fishbed-D' and MiG-21PFS 'Fishbed-E' limited all-weather interceptors, and the MiG-21PFMA 'Fishbed-J' which incorporated numerous improvements and featured a heavier missile armament.

**Specification** (MiG-21PFS 'Fishbed E')
**Type:** single-seat limited all-weather interceptor
**Powerplant:** one 8,598-lb (3900-kg) dry thrust and 13,669-lb (6200-kg) afterburning thrust Tumansky R-11-F2S-300 turbojet
**Performance:** maximum speed 1,386 mph (2230 km/h) at 36,090 ft (11000 m); climb rate 24,605 ft/min (7500 m/min); service ceiling 59,055 ft (18000 m); combat range 930 miles (1500 km)
**Weights:** empty 11,464 lb (5200 kg); loaded 18,740 lb (8500 kg)
**Dimensions:** span 23 ft 5.5 in (7.15 m); length 46 ft 11 in (14.30 m); height 14 ft 9 in (4.50 m); wing area 247.57 sq ft (23.0 m²)
**Armament:** twin-barrel 23-mm GSh-23 cannon and two K-13A 'Atoll' infra-red homing air-to-air missiles.

## MORANE-SAULNIER M.S.500 CRIQUET

As part of their scheme during World War II to make use of aircraft production facilities in occupied Europe, the Germans had ordered Morane-Saulnier to undertake the manufacture of Fieseler Fi 156 Storch observation aircraft. After the liberation of France, the type remained in production as the M.S.500 powered by an Argus As 41 OC engine, the M.S.501 with a Renault 6Q, and the M.S.502 with a Salmson 9AB. In addition to being extensively used for observation, liaison and artillery spotting by the Armée de l'Air in Indochina, Criquets were the first aircraft delivered in 1951 to the newly-organized Vietnamese Air Training Center at Nha Trang.

**Specification** (M.S.502)
**Type:** three-seat artillery spotting and observation aircraft
**Powerplant:** one 230-hp (172-kW) Salmson 9AB radial piston engine
**Performance:** maximum speed 106 mph (170 km/h) at sea level; climb rate 3,280 ft (1000 m) in 5.5 min; service ceiling 14,110 ft (4300 m); combat range 435 miles (700 km)
**Weights:** empty 2,094 lb (950 kg); loaded 3,142 lb (1425 kg)
**Dimensions:** span 46 ft 9 in (14.25 m); length 31 ft 8 in (9.65 m); height 10 ft 2 in (3.10 m); wing area 279.9 sq ft (26.0 m²)
**Armament:** none.

*Fastest of the North Vietnamese fighters, the Mach 2 MiG-21 'Fishbed' was an extremely potent warplane in skilled hands.*

## MORANE-SAULNIER M.S.733 ALCYON

Developed as a basic trainer, the Alcyon saw limited service in Indochina. In 1955 France gave seven Alcyons (four fitted with light armament for gunnery training and police duties) to Cambodia, as a gift to the newly-formed Aviation Royale Khmer.

**Specification**
**Type:** two/three-seat basic trainer
**Powerplant:** one 240-hp (179-kW) Potez 6D-30 air-cooled inline piston engine
**Performance:** maximum speed 162 mph (260 km/h) at sea level; climb rate 820 ft/min (250 m/min); service ceiling 15,750 ft (4800 m); endurance 4 hours
**Weights:** empty 2,778 lb (1260 kg); loaded 3,682 lb (1670 kg)
**Dimensions:** span 37 ft 0.9 in (11.30 m); length 30 ft 6.1 in (9.30 m); height 8 ft (2.44 m); wing area 235.7 sq ft (21.90 m²)
**Armament:** four 3-in (76.2-mm) unguided rockets.

## NAKAJIMA A6M-2N 'RUFE'

One of the floatplane fighters, which the Japanese had left in Indochina, was impressed into service with the Aéronautique Navale immediately after the war, but crashed almost immediately after being overhauled.

**Specification**
**Type:** single-seat floatplane fighter
**Powerplant:** one 940-hp (701-kW) Nakajima NK1C Sakae 12 radial piston engine
**Performance:** maximum speed 270 mph (435 km/h) at 16,405 ft (5000 m); climb rate 16,405 ft (5000 m) in 6 min 43 sec; service ceiling 32,810 ft (10000 m); combat range 715 miles (1150 km)
**Weights:** empty 4,215 lb (1912 kg); loaded 5,423 lb (2460 kg)
**Dimensions:** span 39 ft 4.4 in (120 m); length 33 ft 1.6 in (10.10 m); height 14 ft 1.3 in (4.30 m); wing area 241.5 sq ft (22.44 m²)
**Armament:** two fuselage-mounted 0.303-in (7.7-mm) machine-guns and two wing-mounted 20-mm cannon plus two 132-lb (60-kg) bombs.

## NAKAJIMA KI-43 'OSCAR'

Pending arrival of new Spitfires, the Armée de l'Air tried with little success to put back in operation a dozen war-weary Japanese Ki-43-IIs and Ki-43-IIIs. Taken on charge in December 1945 by G.C. 1/7 'Provence', the impossibility of obtaining spares meant that these aircraft were not used in combat.

**Specification** (Ki-43-IIb)
**Type:** single-seat fighter
**Powerplant:** one 1,150-hp (856-kW) Nakajima Ha-115 radial piston engine
**Performance:** maximum speed 329 mph (1530 km/h) at 13,125 ft (4000 m); climb rate 16,405 ft (5000 m) in 5 min 49 sec; service ceiling 36,750 ft (11200 m); combat range 1,095 miles (1760 km)
**Weights:** empty 4,211 lb (1910 kg); loaded 5,710 lb (2590 kg)
**Dimensions:** span 35 ft 6.8 in (10.84 m); length 29 ft 3.2 in (8.92 m); height 10 ft 8.7 in (3.27 m); wing area 230.3 sq ft (21.4 m²)
**Armament:** two fuselage-mounted 0.5-in (12.7-mm) machine-guns plus two 66-lb (30-kg) bombs.

*Supplied to the Royal Khmer Air Force as a basic trainer, the Morane-Saulnier Alcyon was also used as a light-attack aircraft.*

*One of the first operational supersonic jets, the MiG-19 or its Chinese-built copy served in small numbers with the North Vietnamese.*

*The twin-boom Nord Noratlas, one of the products of the resurgent post-war French aviation industry, served in small numbers in Indochina.*

*Designed as a nuclear bomber, the advanced RA-5 Vigilante was the US Navy's most important reconnaissance aircraft.*

### NORD 1001 AND 1002 PINGOUIN

These four-seat liaison aircraft are further examples of German aircraft of World War II, in this instance the Messerschmitt Bf 108, which remained in production after the Liberation for use by the French military. French versions had their Argus engines replaced by Renault 6Q-I0 (Nord 1001) or 6Q-11 (Nord 1002) powerplants. A small number of both models were operated in Indochina.

**Specification** (Nord 1002)
**Type:** four-seat liaison aircraft
**Powerplant:** one 240-hp (179-kW) Renault 6Q-11 inline piston engine
**Performance:** maximum speed 190 mph (305 km/h); service ceiling 20,340 ft (6200 m); range 620 miles (1000 km)
**Weights:** empty 1,775 lb (805 kg); loaded 2,976 lb (1350 kg)
**Dimensions:** span 34 ft 5.4 in (10.50 m); length 27 ft 2.8 in (8.30 m); height 7 ft 6.6 in (2.30 m); wing area 172.2 sq ft (16.0 m²)
**Armament:** none.

### NORD 2501 NORATLAS

Similar in layout to the twin-boom Fairchild C-119, but smaller and lighter than the American aircraft, the Nord 2501 military transport made its appearance in Indochina during the last phase of French air operations. The type was mainly used to relocate non-Communist Vietnamese from the North to the South.

**Specification**
**Type:** 45-troop or 13,227-lb/6000-kg cargo transport
**Powerplant:** two 2,090-hp (1559-kW) SNECMA-built Bristol Hercules 738 radial piston engines
**Performance:** maximum speed 252 mph (405 km/h) at 9,845 ft (3000 m); climb rate 1,180 ft/min (360 m/min); service ceiling 23,295 ft (7100 m); range 1,710 miles (2750 km) with 14,990-lb/6800-kg payload
**Weights:** empty 29,321 lb (13300 kg); loaded 48,502 lb (22000 kg)
**Dimensions:** span 106 ft 7.5 in (32.50 m); length 72 ft 0.2 in (21.95 m); height 19 ft 8.2 in (6.00 m); wing area 1,087.2 sq ft (101.0 m²)
**Armament:** none.

### NORD CENTRE N.C. 701 MARTINET

Martinets were French-built versions of German wartime communications aircraft. The N.C. 701 was originally the Siebel Si 204D with unstepped glazed nose, and the N.C.702 was the Si 204A with a conventional stepped nose. Both were powered by French Renault engines instead of the original German Argus As 410s.

**Specification**
**Type:** eight-passenger liaison aircraft
**Powerplant:** two 590-hp (440-kW) Renault 12S-00 inline piston engines
**Performance:** maximum speed 226 mph (364 km/h) at 9,845 ft (3000 m); climb rate 3,280 ft (1000 m) in 3.3 min; service ceiling 24,605 ft (7500 m); range 1,120 miles (1800 km)
**Weights:** empty 8,708 lb (3950 kg); loaded 12,346 lb (5600 kg)
**Dimensions:** span 69 ft 11.8 in (21.33 m); length 39 ft 2.5 in (11.95 m); height 13 ft 11.3 in (4.25 m); wing area 49.5 sq ft (46.0 m²)
**Armament:** none.

*The Nord Martinet light transport, originally the Siebel Si 204, was another wartime German design built in France after the war.*

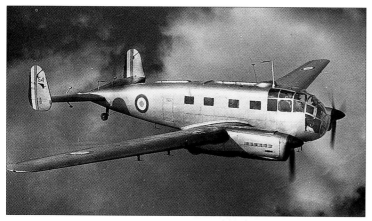

### NORTH AMERICAN RA-5C VIGILANTE

The world's first supersonic carrier-borne nuclear bomber and one of the largest aircraft ever to operate from carrier decks, the elegant Vigilante had all but given up the strategic mission by the time America became embroiled in Vietnam. Exchanging nuclear weapons for cameras, however, it was to make its mark on the war as the US Navy's most important reconnaissance platform. Along with the RF-8 and the RA-3B, RA-5Cs from RVAH squadrons provided reconnaissance for CTF-77 throughout the duration of US involvement in Southeast Asia.

**Specification**
**Type:** two-seat carrier-based reconnaissance aircraft
**Powerplant:** two 11,870-lb (5384-kg) dry thrust and 17,860-lb (8101-kg) afterburning thrust General Electric J79-GE-10 turbojets
**Performance:** maximum speed 1,385 mph (2230 km/h) at 40,000 ft (12190 m); service ceiling 64,000 ft (19505 m); combat range 2,650 miles (4265 km)
**Weight:** loaded 66,818 lb (30308 kg)
**Dimensions:** span 53 ft (16.15 m); length 75 ft 10 in (23.11 m); height 19 ft 5 in (5.92 m); wing area 769 sq ft (71.44 m²)
**Armament:** none.

### NORTH AMERICAN F-100 SUPER SABRE

Developed as America's first supersonic interceptor, the Super Sabre became, on 9 June 1964, the first jet warplane to drop ordnance in Southeast Asia. Backbone of USAF strength in the first years of conflict, the type grew in importance until by 1967 F-100Ds were the most numerous fighters in South Vietnam. In addition to their all-important role in the in-country war, both single-seat F-100Ds and two-seat F-100Fs were also active in Laos and, to a lesser extent, in Cambodia and over the North Vietnamese panhandle. It provided the platform for the first 'Wild Weasel' defence suppression fighters when Detachment 1 of the Tactical Warfare Center deployed its specially-configured F-100Fs to Korat in November 1965. The last Super Sabres in Southeast Asia were those of the 35th TFW which ceased operations at Phan Rang AB in June 1971.

**Specification** (F-100D)
**Type:** single-seat tactical fighter
**Powerplant:** one 11,700-lb (5307-kg) dry thrust and 16,950-lb (7688-kg) afterburning thrust Pratt & Whitney J57-P-21A turbojet
**Performance:** maximum speed 864 mph (1390 km/h) at 35,000 ft (10670 m); climb rate 16,000 ft/min (4875 m/min); service ceiling 45,000 ft (13720 m); combat range 1,500 miles (2415 km)
**Weights:** empty 21,000 lb (9525 kg); loaded 29,762 lb (13500 kg)
**Dimensions:** span 38 ft 9 in (11.81 m); length 49 ft 6 in (15.09 m); height 16 ft 2.9 in (4.95 m); wing area 385.2 sq ft (35.79 m²)
**Armament:** four 20-mm M39 cannon and up to 7,500 lb (3402 kg) of external stores.

### NORTH AMERICAN OV-10 BRONCO

Developed to meet tri-service requirements for a counter-insurgency aircraft (with secondary light transport/aeromedical evacuation capabilities), the Bronco was a very agile aircraft flown in Southeast Asia by Air Force, Navy and Marine units. The Bronco's main mission was forward air control, for which the large

*One of the few aircraft designed as a counter-insurgency weapon, the North American OV-10 served with Navy, Air Force and Marine units.*

cockpit gave an excellent view. It could carry quite a heavy weapons load, however, and the Navy used OV-10As as light-attack aircraft in support of riverine operations.

**Specification (OV-10A)**
**Type:** two-seat counter-insurgency aircraft
**Powerplant:** two 715-eshp (533-ekW) AiResearch T76-G-10 turboprops
**Performance:** maximum speed 281 mph (452 km/h) at 10,000 ft (3050 m); climb rate 2,800 ft/min (853 m/min); service ceiling 29,000 ft (8840 m); combat range 380 miles (610 km)
**Weights:** empty 7,190 lb (3261 kg); loaded 12,500 lb (5670 kg)
**Dimensions:** span 40 ft (12.19 m); length 39 ft 9 in (12.12 m); height 15 ft 1 in (4.60 m); wing area 291 sq ft (27.03 m²)
**Armament:** four 0.30-in (7.62-mm) machine-guns and 3,600 lb (1633 kg) of external stores.

## NORTH AMERICAN T-6G TEXAN
The classic World War II trainer was used all over the world in the decades following the allied victory in 1945. Fifty-five T-6Gs were delivered to the VNAF when the United States took over responsibility for the training of Vietnamese aircrews in 1955. Their usefulness was limited as most Vietnamese pilots soon received their advanced training at American facilities in CONUS.

**Specification**
**Type:** two-seat basic trainer
**Powerplant:** one 550-hp (410-kW) Pratt & Whitney R-1340-AN-1 radial piston engine
**Performance:** maximum speed 212 mph (341 km/h) at 5,000 ft (1525 m); climb rate 1,640 ft/min (500 m/min); service ceiling 24,750 ft (7540 m); range 870 miles (1400 km)
**Weights:** empty 4,271 lb (1937 kg); loaded 5,617 lb (2548 kg)
**Dimensions:** span 42 ft (12.80 m); length 29 ft 6 in (8.99 m); height 11 ft 8.25 in (3 56 m); wing area 253.7 sq ft (23.57 m²)
**Armament:** none.

## NORTH AMERICAN T-28 TROJAN
The USAF's standard advanced trainer until displaced by jet designs, the Trojan proved easily adaptable to the counter-insurgency role. Both ex-USAF T-28As and ex-Navy T-28Bs were used in this capacity by the VNAF (including some RT-28Bs for reconnaissance), the Royal Khmer Aviation, and the USAF's Farm Gate detachment. After these early versions were grounded due to structural failures, T-28Ds, with more powerful engines, heavier armament and beefed-up structure, were also operated by the Khmer Air Force and the Royal Lao Air Force.

**Specification (T-28D)**
**Type:** two-seat counter-insurgency aircraft
**Powerplant:** one 1,300-hp (969-kW) Wright R-1820-56S radial piston engine
**Performance:** maximum speed 352 mph (566 km/h) at 18,000 ft (5485 m); climb rate 5,130 ft/min (1564 m/min); service ceiling 37,000 ft (11280 m); combat range 1,200 miles (1930 km)
**Weights:** empty 6,512 lb (2954 kg); loaded 8,118 lb (3682 kg)
**Dimensions:** span 40 ft 7 in (12.37 m); length 32 ft 10 in (10.00 m); height 12 ft 8 in (3.86 m); wing area 271.2 sq ft (25.19 m²)
**Armament:** up to 4,000 lb (1814 kg) of external stores, including gun pods.

## NORTHROP F-5 FREEDOM FIGHTER AND TIGER II
Procured for MAP delivery to allied air forces in developing countries, the single-seat F-5A and two-seat F-5B fighters were intended to see only limited USAF service in training foreign pilots. Prior to proceeding with a plan to procure additional aircraft (the projected F-5C and F-5D versions) for Air Force use in Southeast Asia, F-5As and F-5Bs were sent to South Vietnam to undergo the Skoshi Tiger combat evaluation. This six-month project in 1965-66 was followed by 15 months of regular operations. Even though the type proved quite effective, it was considered to lack sufficient range and offensive load-carrying capability for continued Air Force use. It was nevertheless selected as the first jet fighter aircraft for the VNAF. Obtaining 17 F-5As and F-5Bs in June 1967, the VNAF received 126 Freedom Fighters (including the RF-5A reconnaissance version) during Enhance Plus. Beginning in May 1974, more capable F-5E and F-5F Tiger IIs replaced some of the earlier models.

**Specification (F-5A)**
**Type:** single-seat tactical fighter
**Powerplant:** two 2,720-lb (1233-kg) dry thrust and 4,080-lb (1850-kg) afterburning thrust General Electric J85-GE-13 turbojets
**Performance:** maximum speed 977 mph (1572 km/h); at 36,000 ft (10975 m); climb rate 33,000 ft/min (10060 m/min); service ceiling 50,300 ft (15330 m); combat range

*Built in huge numbers during World War II, the T-6 Texan was used as a trainer by the VNAF as well as by the Khmers and the Thais.*

*North America's big piston-powered trainer proved very suitable for counter-insurgency use by Third World air forces.*

1150 miles (1850 km)
**Weights:** empty 10380 lb (4708 kg); loaded 14,150 lb (6418 kg)
**Dimensions:** span 25 ft 3 in (7.70 m); length 47 ft 2 in (14.38 m); height 13 ft 2 in (4.01 m); wing area 170 sq ft (15.79 m²)
**Armament:** two 20-mm M39 cannon and 6,200 lb (2812 kg) of external stores.

## PIASECKI CH-21 WORKHORSE
The obsolescent twin-rotor Workhorse was one of the first American aircraft to deploy to Southeast Asia. Flown from December 1961 by Army Transportation Companies in Vietnam, it remained on active service for two years.

**Specification (CH-21C)**
**Type:** 14-troop military transport helicopter
**Powerplant:** one 1,425-hp (1063-kW) Wright R-1820-103 radial piston engine
**Performance:** maximum speed 131 mph (211 km/h) at sea level; climb rate 1,080 ft/min (329 m/min); service ceiling 9,450 ft (2880 m)
**Weights:** empty 8,665 lb (3926 kg); loaded 15,000 lb (6804 kg)
**Dimensions:** rotor diameter (each) 44 ft (13.41 m); fuselage length 52 ft 6 in (16.00 m); height 15 ft 5 in (4.70 m)
**Armament:** none.

## PIPER L-4B GRASSHOPPER
Built in huge numbers during and after World War II, military versions of the Piper Cub served all over the world. A small number of L-4Bs were used in 1945-46 for artillery spotting and observation by the French Army's 9ème Division d'Infanterie Coloniale.

**Specification**
**Type:** two-seat artillery spotting and observation aircraft
**Powerplant:** one 65-hp (48-kW) Continental 0-170-3 air-cooled piston engine
**Performance:** maximum speed 83 mph (134 km/h) at sea level; climb rate 5,000 ft (1525 m) in 14.4 min; service ceiling 9,300 ft (2835 m); range 190 miles (305 km)
**Weights:** empty 730 lb (331 kg); loaded 1,220 lb (553 kg)
**Dimensions:** span 35 ft 3 in (10.74 m); length 22 ft 5 in (6.83 m); height 6 ft 8 in (2.03 m); wing area 179 sq ft (16.63 m²)
**Armament:** none.

## REPUBLIC F-105 THUNDERCHIEF
Designed as a nuclear-strike fighter with internal stowage for a special weapon, the Thunderchief or 'Thud' was one of the biggest and fastest single-seat tactical aircraft of its time. But it was considered to be lacking in multi-mission capability, and production was terminated in favor of the more flexible F-4 Phantom. Nevertheless, single-seat F-105Ds and two-seat F-105Fs, modified for external carriage of large loads of conventional stores, became the USAF's primary strike aircraft against the North from 1965 until 1970, delivering a huge tonnage of bombs onto North Vietnamese targets, and achieving some air-to-air success against NVNAF fighters in the process. In addition to their conventional missions, F-105D/Fs were used extensively for Iron Hand defense suppression missions. F-105Fs and specially-configured F-105Gs took over the 'Wild Weasel' mission from the Super Sabre, continuing in this role until the US withdrawal. Blind-bombing sorties were flown by 30 T-Stick IIs (F-105Ds with additional electronic equipment in a bulged

*The Republic F-105 Thunderchief suffered heavy losses in Vietnam, a reflection of the huge numbers of missions it flew against the North.*

*Of the many versions of the Sikorsky H-3 used in Vietnam, none were more important than the CH/HH-3 combat rescue machines.*

dorsal spine). Although the F-105 was an extremely potent warplane, intensive use on the most dangerous missions of the war was costly. All told, 397 Thunderchiefs were destroyed in combat or operationally in Southeast Asia, or nearly one in five of all USAF fixed-wing losses.

**Specification (F-105D)**
**Type:** single-seat tactical fighter
**Powerplant:** one 17,200-lb (7802-kg) dry thrust and 24,500-lb (11113-kg) afterburning thrust Pratt & Whitney J75-P-19W turbojet
**Performance:** maximum speed 1,390 mph (2237 km/h) at 36,000 ft (10975 m); climb rate 34,500 ft/min (10515 m/min); service ceiling 52,000 ft (15850 m), combat range 1,850 miles (2975 km)
**Weights:** empty 27,500 lb (12474 kg); loaded 38,034 lb (17252 kg)
**Dimensions:** span 34 ft 11.25 in (10.65 m); length 64 ft 3 in (19.58 m); height 19 ft 8 in (5.99 m) wing area 385 sq ft (35.76 m²)
**Armament:** one 20-mm M61 cannon and up to 14,000 lb (6350 kg) of external and internal stores.

### SIKORSKY CH-3, HH-3 JOLLY GREEN, AND SH-3 SEA KING
Serving in far fewer number than the UH-1s, OH-6s, CH-46s and CH-47s, the military versions of the Sikorsky S-61 and S-61R provided a useful adjunct to the American helicopter inventory in Southeast Asia. The principal Air Force versions were the CH-3A and CH-3E with a rear vehicle-loading ramp, which were used for logistic support and drone-recovery, and the HH-3E with armor, armament and retractable flight-refueling probe, which flew daring combat rescue-and-recovery missions deep into enemy-held territory. The main Navy versions were the SH-3A, SH-3D and SH-3G, which were deployed aboard carriers for 'plane guard' and anti-submarine operations, and the HH-3A which was used for combat rescue and recovery.

**Specification (HH-3E)**
**Type:** search-and-rescue helicopter
**Powerplant:** two 1,400-shp (1044-kW) General Electric T58-GE-10 turboshafts
**Performance:** maximum speed 162 mph (261 km/h) at sea level; climb rate 1,310 ft/min (399 m/min); service ceiling 12,000 ft (3660 m); combat range 625 miles (1005 km)
**Weights:** empty 13,255 lb (6012 kg); loaded 18,000 lb (8165 kg)
**Dimensions:** rotor diameter 62 ft (18.90 m); fuselage length 57 ft 3 in (17.45 m); height 18 ft 1 in (5.51 m)
**Armament:** two 0.30-in (7.62-mm) M60 machine-guns or six-barrel miniguns.

### SIKORSKY UH-19 CHICKASAW
One of the first truly successful transport helicopters, the Sikorsky S-55 was flown by the French on transport and assault missions. The first French aircraft were British license-built Westland examples, but the Armée de l'Air subsequently received military Sikorsky H-19s from the United States, The French-purchased S-55s were retained by the Armée de l'Air, but 10 of the US-supplied H-19s were transferred to the VNAF in 1955.

*Principal US Marine Corps assault helicopter in the early years of the war, the Sikorsky UH-34 was replaced by the UH-1 and the CH-46.*

**Specification (H-19B)**
**Type:** 10-troop transport helicopter
**Powerplant:** one 800-hp (597-kW) Wright R-1300-3 radial piston engine
**Performance:** maximum speed 112 mph (180 km/h) at sea level; climb rate 1,020 ft/min (311 m/min); service ceiling 10,500 ft (3200 m); range 360 miles (580 km)
**Weights:** empty 5,250 lb (2381 kg); loaded 7,900 lb (3583 kg)
**Dimensions:** rotor diameter 53 ft (16.15 m); fuselage length 42 ft 3 in (12.88 m); height 13 ft 4 in (4.06 m)
**Armament:** none.

### SIKORSKY UH-34 CHOCTAW
The Sikorsky S-58 was similar in layout to the preceding H-19, but larger, more powerful, and with a revised rear fuselage. Known to the military as the H-34 or UH-34 Choctaw, it was used in greater number than any other type of piston-powered helicopter. Choctaws were the main assault transport helicopters of the USMC and VNAF until fully replaced by UH-1s in the late-1960s. Prior to the 1968 phase-out of their Choctaws, the Marines lost more H-34s than UH-1s.

**Specification (UH-34D)**
**Type:** 18-troop transport helicopter
**Powerplant:** one 1,525-hp (1137-kW) Wright R-1820-84 radial piston engine
**Performance:** maximum speed 123 mph (198 km/h) at sea level; climb rate 1,100 ft/min (335 m/min); service ceiling 9,500 ft (2895 m); range 185 miles (300 km)
**Weights:** empty 7,900 lb (3583 kg); loaded 14,000 lb (6350 kg)
**Dimensions:** rotor diameter 56 ft (17.07 m); fuselage length 46 ft 9 in (14.25 m); height 14 ft 3.5 in (4.36 m)
**Armament:** TK-1 kit consisting of two 0.30-in (7.62-mm) M60 forward-firing machine-guns and two pods with 18 2.75-in (70-mm) rockets.

### SIKORSKY CH-37 MOJAVE
Until the advent of twin turboshaft helicopters, the CH-37 was the only type of helicopter in service with the US military capable of airlifting damaged aircraft. However, although powerful, the Mojave was not very reliable and saw only limited use with the US Army and the US Marine Corps.

**Specification (CH-37C)**
**Type:** 20-troop or 6,675-lb/3028-kg heavy-transport helicopter
**Powerplant:** two 2,100-hp (1566-kW) Pratt & Whitney R-2800-54 radial piston engines
**Performance:** maximum speed 121 mph (195 km/h) at sea level; climb rate 1,280 ft/min (390 m/min); service ceiling 13,800 ft (4205 m); range 335 miles (540 km)
**Weights:** empty 21,502 lb (9753 kg); loaded 31,000 lb (14061 kg)
**Dimensions:** rotor diameter 72 ft (21.95 m); fuselage length 58 ft 5 in (17.81 m); height 16 ft 8 in (5.08 m)
**Armament:** none.

### SIKORSKY CH-53 SEA STALLION AND HH-53 SUPER JOLLY GREEN
The CH-53A was a large assault helicopter specially developed for the Marine Corps and was first deployed to Vietnam in January 1967. The most powerful assault helicopter of its time, it was followed into Marine service by the uprated CH-53D. The same basic airframe was adopted by the US Navy as the RH-53A mine-sweeping and countermeasures helicopter, and by the USAF as the HH-53B and HH-53C Super Jolly combat rescue-and-recovery machines. The big helicopter had greater speed and range, better armor and more armament than its predecessors, and greatly enhanced combat rescue capability in Southeast Asia.

**Specification (CH-53D)**
**Type:** 38-troop heavy-assault helicopter
**Powerplant:** two 3,925-shp (2927-kW) General Electric T64-GE-13 turboshafts
**Performance:** maximum speed 172 mph (277 km/h) at sea level; climb rate 2,180 ft/min (664 m/min); service ceiling 17,500 ft (5335 m); range 885 miles (1425 km)
**Weights:** empty 23,628 lb (10717 kg); loaded 36,695 lb (16645 kg)
**Dimensions:** rotor diameter 72 ft 2.7 in (22.01 m); fuselage length 67 ft 2 in (20.47 m); height 24 ft 11 in (7.60 m)
**Armament:** none.

### SIKORSKY CH-54 TARHE
CH-54 flying cranes were the most powerful rotary-wing aircraft deployed to Southeast Asia – the gearbox could absorb 7,900 hp (5891 kW) from the two T37 turboshafts powering the CH-54B version. Tarhes were used to transport a wide variety of loads, from construction equipment and light armored vehicles to cargo

*With its unique flying crane configuration, the CH-54 could airlift a wide variety of loads weighing up to nine tons.*

pods and super-heavy bombs. Above all, the Tarhe was used to recover downed aircraft, and was credited with salvaging more than 380 aircraft valued at over $210 million.

**Specification (CH-54B)**
**Type:** heavy flying-crane helicopter
**Powerplant:** two 4,800-shp (3579-kW) Pratt & Whitney T37-P-700 turboshafts
**Performance:** maximum speed 127 mph (204 km/h) at sea level; climb rate 1,700 ft/min (518 m/min); range 255 miles (410 km)
**Weights:** empty 19,234 lb (8724 kg); loaded 42,000 lb (19050 kg)
**Dimensions:** rotor diameter 72 ft (21.95 m); fuselage length 70 ft 3 in (21.41 m); height 25 ft 5 in (7.75 m)
**Armament:** none.

## SUPERMARINE SEAFIRE AND SPITFIRE
Unable at first to send the American fighters equipping its European Squadrons out to the Far East, the Armée de l'Air elected to equip its *Groupes de Chasse* in Indochina with British-made Spitfire Mk IXs and Mk XVIs. In 1945-46, pending arrival of these aircraft from France, G.C. 11/7 operated a number of Mk VIIIs on loan from the RAF. The Mk IXs and Mk XVIs remained in Indochina until November 1950. Two Griffon-powered Seafire Mk XVs saw limited use from the carrier *Arromanches* in 1948 and 1949.

**Specification (Spitfire LF IXE)**
**Type:** single-seat fighter
**Powerplant:** one 1,720-hp (1283-kW) Rolls-Royce Merlin 66 liquid-cooled piston engine
**Performance:** maximum speed 404 mph (650 km/h) at 21,000 ft (6400 m); climb rate 20,000 ft (6096 m) in 6.4 min; service ceiling 42,500 ft (12955 m); combat range 430 miles (690 km)
**Weights:** empty 5,610 lb (2545 kg); loaded 7,500 lb (3402 kg)
**Dimensions:** span 32 ft 7 in (9.93 m); length 31 ft 4.5 in (9.56 m); height 12 ft 7.75 in (3.85 m); wing area 230 sq ft (21.37 m²)
**Armament:** two 0.50-in (12.7-mm) machine-guns and two 20-mm cannon plus two 250-lb (113-kg) bombs.

## SUPERMARINE SEA OTTER
Derived from the pre-war Walrus, the Sea Otter single-engined biplane flying-boat was used by France for coastal patrol in Indochina. Sea Otters, including six originally acquired by the Customs Administration, were in service from 1947 until 1952 by Escadrilles 8S and 9S of the French Navy.

**Specification**
**Type:** four-seat utility flying-boat
**Powerplant:** one 965-hp (720-kW) Bristol Mercury XXX radial piston engine
**Performance:** maximum speed 163 mph (262 km/h) at 4,500 ft (1370 m); climb rate 870 ft/min (265 m/min) service ceiling 17,000 ft (5180 m); range 690 miles (1110 km)
**Weights:** empty 6,805 lb (3087 kg); loaded 10,000 lb (4536 kg)
**Dimensions:** span 46 ft (14.02 m); length 39 ft 10.75 in (12.16 m); height 15 ft 1.5 in (4.61 m); wing area 610 sq ft (56.67 m²)
**Armament:** none normally fitted to French aircraft.

## VOUGHT A-7 CORSAIR II
The intended successor of the Skyhawk light-attack aircraft was first deployed to the Gulf of Tonkin in December 1967. Thereafter rapidly increasing numbers of US Navy attack squadrons converted from A-4s, first to TF30-powered A-7As, A-7Bs and A-7Cs, and then to TF41-powered A-7Es, so that by 1972 only three VA Squadrons aboard the small-deck carrier *Hancock* still flew A-4Fs. The Air Force adopted the Corsair II as a limited all-weather tactical fighter, and the first A-7Ds were deployed to Thailand in October 1972. Air Force A-7Ds and Navy A-7Es were among the last US aircraft to fly combat sorties in Southeast Asia when in the spring of 1975, they supported the 'Mayaguez' rescue and the 'Eagle Pull' and 'Frequent Wind' evacuations.

**Specification (A-7D)**
**Type:** tactical fighter/fighter-bomber
**Powerplant:** one 14,250-lb (6464-kg) thrust Allison TF41-A-1 turbofan
**Performance:** maximum speed 698 mph (1123 km/h) at sea level; climb rate 8,000 ft/min (2438 m/min); service ceiling 37,000 ft (11280 m); combat range 1,430 miles (2300 km)
**Weights:** empty 19,490 lb (8841 kg); loaded 42,000 lb (19051 kg)
**Dimensions:** span 38 ft 8.25 in (11.79 m); length 46 ft 1.25 in (14.05 m); height 16 ft (4.88 m); wing area 375 sq ft (34.84 m²)
**Armament:** one 20-mm M61 cannon and up to 15,000 lb (6804 kg) of external stores.

*Originally designed as a carrier attack plane, the Vought A-7 was adopted by the US Air Force as a replacement for the A-1 Skyraider.*

*Designed by the same man who created the Spitfire, the Sea Otter was a pre-war British flying-boat design used by France between 1947 and 1952.*

## VOUGHT F-8 CRUSADER
When the Navy went to war in Southeast Asia, the gun-and-missile Crusader had already been replaced in the fighter squadrons aboard larger carriers by the missile-armed Phantom II. However, the smaller carriers of the World War II 'Essex' class could not handle the Phantom, no matter how much they were modernized, which ensured a continued role for the F-8s. Popular with its pilots, thanks in part to the fact that it still carried a gun, the Crusader played a significant part in the early air battles over the North. In Marine service, Crusader fighters and RF-8A reconnaissance planes operated from Da Nang between 1965 and 1967, with some also detached to serve aboard ship. As the war progressed, F-8C, F-8D and F-8E Crusaders withdrawn from land-based Marine squadrons were rebuilt and updated respectively to F-8K, F-8H and F-8J standards for service aboard the small-deck carriers. Similarly, the RF-8As operated by detachments of VFP-63 aboard many of the CTF-77 carriers were brought up to the RF-8G standards.

**Specification (F-8J)**
**Type:** single-seat carrier-based fighter
**Powerplant:** one 10,700-lb (4856-kg) dry thrust and 18,000 lb (8165-kg) afterburning thrust Pratt & Whitney J57-P 20A turbojet
**Performance:** maximum speed 1,120 mph (1802 km/h) at 40,000 ft (12190 m); climb rate 57,000 ft (17375 m) in 6.5 min; service ceiling 58,000 ft (17680 m); combat range 1,200 miles (1930 km)
**Weight:** loaded 27,500 lb (12474 kg)
**Dimensions:** span 35 ft 8 in (10.87 m); length 54 ft 6 in (16.61 m); height 15 ft 9 in (4.80 m); wing area 375 sq ft (34.84 m²)
**Armament:** four 20-mm MK-12 cannon and four AIM-9 Sidewinder infra-red guided air-to-air missiles.

## WESTLAND S-51
Four Westland-built Sikorsky S-51s ordered in 1952 by the Armée de l'Air were the first helicopters intended for operations in Indochina. An additional batch was procured later for use by the 65ème Escadre d'helicopteres alongside Westland-built S-55s and Sikorsky H-19s.

**Specification (S-51 Mk IA)**
**Type:** four-seat utility helicopter
**Powerplant:** one 540-hp (403-kW) Alvis Leonides 521 radial piston engine
**Performance:** maximum speed 95 mph (153 km/h); climb rate 1,000 ft/min (305 m/min); service ceiling 13,200 ft (4025 m); range 300 miles (485 km)
**Weights:** empty 4,366 lb (1980 kg); loaded 5,700 lb (2585 kg)
**Dimensions:** rotor diameter 49 ft (14.94 m); fuselage length 41 ft 1.75 in (12.54 m); height 12 ft 11.5 in (3.95 m)
**Armament:** none.

*Standard US Navy carrier fighter before the arrival of the Phantom, the Vought F-8 Corsair was used from small-deck carriers off Vietnam.*

# Index